Hydraulic Modeling

Scrivener Publishing
100 Cummings Center, Suite 541J
Beverly, MA 01915-6106

Publishers at Scrivener
Martin Scrivener(martin@scrivenerpublishing.com)
Phillip Carmical (pcarmical@scrivenerpublishing.com)

Hydraulic Modeling

Victor M. Lyatkher
Alexander M. Proudovsky

Scrivener Publishing

WILEY

Co-published by John Wiley & Sons, Inc. Hoboken, New Jersey, and Scrivener Publishing LLC, Salem, Massachusetts.
Published simultaneously in Canada.

For general information on our other products and services or for technical support, please contact our Customer Care Department within the United States at (800) 762-2974, outside the United States at (317) 572-3993 or fax (317) 572-4002.

Wiley also publishes its books in a variety of electronic formats. Some content that appears in print may not be available in electronic formats. For more information about Wiley products, visit our web site at www.wiley.com.

For more information about Scrivener products please visit www.scrivenerpublishing.com.

Cover design by Kris Hackerott

Library of Congress Cataloging-in-Publication Data:

ISBN 978-1-118-94619-0

Printed in the United States of America

10 9 8 7 6 5 4 3 2 1

"I appreciate the ability of creating analogies, which, if they are spirited and rational, take us beyond the limits of what the nature wished to open for us, allowing us to anticipate facts before we see them."

J. L. D'Alembert, "Encyclopedia", (1751)

Contents

Introduction

Hydraulic problems, put forward by practice, are very complicated, varied and numerous. This is because there are hydraulic phenomena in a wide range of processes, being typical for all sectors of public activity. Engineering hydraulics acts as the basis of not only water supply, navigation and hydroenergetics – but the sciences, for which water movement is the main subject of study. And for heat and nuclear power energetics, hydraulic problems, associated with energy transformation, are no less important than problems of thermodynamics and nuclear physics.

The oldest branch of energetics - wind energetics - operates with the laws of aerodynamics at air speeds much lesser than the sound velocity, when these laws are similar to the laws of hydraulics. The scales of modern energetics are so, that its interaction with the environment has not only local, but also global character. When assessing the impact of energetics on the environment by discovering restrictive measures for limitation of both negative and positive consequences of this impact, it is necessary to provide the forecast of different hydraulic phenomena. The complexity of hydraulic energy problems is determined by the fact that these problems have borderlines with many other sciences: dynamics of structures, thermodynamics, soil mechanics, meteorology, ecology, etc.

Hydraulics is going through a special period of its long history associated with the widespread introduction of numerical methods based on the use of modern computers. The use of computers has greatly expanded the range of hydraulic problems that can be solved by calculating without conduction of laboratory research, which has created the opportunity to solve complicated problems (especially lying on the borders with other sciences), which until recently were beyond the technical capabilities of hydraulics. However, increased implementation of numerical methods (numerical modeling) has not led to a decrease of significance in laboratory tests (physical modeling). This situation is connected with the incompleteness of mathematical models of hydraulic phenomena in many practically important cases. There are some technical reasons due to which the physical modeling has some advantages over the numerical modeling in solving concrete problems. Optimal hydraulic research combines both numerical and physical modeling. Hydraulic (physical) modeling, the wide use of which began many decades ago, continues to improve, as does its connection with the development of numerical modeling. Computers in the structure of physical experiments are used to improve techniques of laboratory research and for the purposes of control over them. Complication of hydraulic problems leads to the necessity of solving fundamental issues of modeling, which are not sufficiently developed. These issues include the problem of approximate hydraulic similarity. Ideas of similarity of natural phenomena, which are based, in particular, on physical modeling, go back to the days of Leonardo da Vinci. Galileo, Newton and Fourier. However, the present doctrine of similarity has been formed in the second half of the 19th and early 20th centuries. Among scientists, whose works have formed the basis of the similarity theory and the theory of dimensions (Bertrand, Buckingham, Federman), the most significant place is occupied by Russian specialists - T.A. Afanasieva-Erenfest and V.L. Kirpichev. Some general questions of the similarity theory have been developed by the USSR scientists - M.V. Kirpichev [63], L. I. Sedov [138] A. A. Guhman [45] and others. First works on hydraulic and related thermodynamic modeling have appeared in literature in the 30-ies of the 20th century. Along with the famous work of F. Eisner "Experimental hydraulic structures and open channels", translated into Russian with additions of S. A. Egorov and B. A. Fidman, the original works of Soviet authors - S.V. Izbash [55], A.P. Zegzhda [52], P.K. Konakov [66], I. I. Levi [76] have been published.

Interest in hydraulic modeling has resulted in the appearance of a great number of works in this field [177, 179, 182, 204, 216, 218, 226, 227] during the last 40 years. In 1971, the authors published a book [91], which outlines the results related to general issues of hydraulic modeling. However, their practical application was associated mainly with new specialized types of hydraulic models - pressure models of open channels. In 1984, the authors published the more complete work, which is now available in English, with some modifications and additions.

Along with general problems of the physical modeling theory set out in ch.1, close attention is paid throughout the book to the approximate similarity of modern hydrodynamics tendencies with physical modeling [28, 64, 91, 193, 205]. The book shows that conditions of the approximate similarity are significantly associated with the accepted mathematical description of modeled phenomenon, and that makes it necessary to address mathematical models of fluid flows (Chapter 2), precessing presentation of the approximate similarity theory (Chapter 3). Chapters 4 - 8 contain proposals for hydraulic modeling at the decision of specific problems for determination of the currents in natural and artificial channels parameters, study of the dam spillways, estimation of deformations of channels and processes in hydraulic tanks, hydraulic transport and slag-disposal systems, assessment of efficiency of heat exchangers and water-coolers of thermal and nuclear power plants, identification of consequences of the discharge of warm waters into natural water reservoirs and streams, and many other problems. Chapter 9, focused on the dynamic loads and structures reaction, has not been published in the edition of 1984.

Along with practical recommendations on modeling, the illustrations of general methods and approximate similarity methods are given in the book. Among the hydraulic modeling objects, those selected were from authors with the most experience.

For the most part, the materials used in the 1984 version of the book have accumulated from many years of work by two authors in the Scientific research sector of the "Hydroproject" Institute, which is named after S.Y. Zhuk. Formation of the book material is distributed among them as follows:

V.M. Lyatkher – Chapters 2, 4, 9, Sections 5.4, 6.1, 6.2; 8.2 and 8.3;

A.M. Proudovsky – Chapters 1, 3, 7, Sections 6.3, 6.4, 8.1, 8.4 and 8.5;

Chapter 5, except Section 5.4, was co-written by the authors.

The book was translated into English by V.M. Lyatkher due to the untimely death of A.M. Proudovsky. Additional references on literature in the given publication are executed as a separate list with the index A.

1

Fundamentals of Modeling

1.1 Modeling as the Method of Cognition

Modeling is one of the most important ways of cognition. When using this method the object of cognition (the original, nature, prototype) is realized through studying of its substitute, which is called the model. If the nature of N is characterized by a number of $X_N \in N$, values, then when modeling such an object M is created, the characteristics $X_M \in M$ of which are determined according to the nature values:

$$X_M \rightarrow X_N$$

The term "model" in the theory of knowledge is rather ambiguous, making classifying models complicated. For our purposes it is important to divide models as substantive and symbolic. The first of them are material objects, whose characteristics are somehow corresponding to the characteristics of the nature. The second represent notation symbols (diagrams, graphs, drawings, formulas, words, and so on). The most important type of symbolic models are the mathematical (logical-mathematical) models, realized by the means of mathematical language and logic.

Mathematical models of fluid flows include continuity equations, conservation of momentum equations, energy conservation and condition equations in one or another form. For multiphase fluids the equations are written for each phase with the inclusion of terms that characterize the interaction of phases. The equations contain some schematization of hydraulic phenomena. The quality of mathematical models depends on how successful the schematization is: some models can be better than others, but they all have some degree of uncertainty and inaccuracies, as they are based on a hypothesis. Quality assessment of a mathematical model (relevancy of underlying hypotheses) is the comparison of values, corresponding to the hypothesis used, with the measured characteristics of the real phenomena to which they relate. Of course, there are new challenges associated with the estimation of accuracy of measurement results, which usually cannot be executed without using the model of the phenomenon. Thus, the problem of estimation of the model is very complicated in principle.

Formulation of the mathematical model does not exhaust the modeling process. To predict the phenomenon it is necessary to establish a correspondence between the values X''_N, characterizing the problem specification and values of X'_N, forming its solution. Such a correspondence is set up by a certain operator O:

$$X'_N = 0(X''_N) \tag{1.1}$$

The operation O is executed using different computational tools. The way of realization of the operator is the main characteristic for classification of modeling in engineering. On this basis it is possible to allocate the first two large classes.

Modeling of the first class combines the cases in which the operator is represented in the form of an assistant operators function:

$$0 = \Phi(0_1, 0_2, \ldots, 0_n) \tag{1.2}$$

The solution is resulted from consecutive impact of operators from the set $\{O_i\}$ on basic values and the intermediate results according to plan, designed in accordance with the type of the Φ function. In this case we speak of a computational process. The order of operations, providing representation of the source data in the solution of this problem is called the algorithm of its solution. Modeling, using computational process can be called numerical modeling.

The principal place among computing devices, used in modeling and belonging to this class, is occupied by digital electronic computing machines (computers). It is easy to notice that the operations carried out by a computer at "manual" solving of the physical problem, are a particular case of numerical modeling.

The second class modeling uses methods and tools, implying the direct, carried out in one time representation of quantities included in the problem specification, its solution. These means include analog devices, and each of them represents a physical model of a particular class of mathematical problems. This model allows carrying out direct measurement of the considered characteristics, corresponding to these or that basic values. Modeling using analog means is called analog modeling.

The process of analog modeling of a phenomenon can be described by the following scheme:

phenomenon (nature) ->mathematical model (system of mathematical equations) ->
physical model (analog medium) -> - nature

The physical model included in this scheme is commonly called the phenomenon model. It is clear that this phenomenon model corresponds to the studied phenomenon so its mathematical model is accurate.

Thus, in case of analog modeling, the physical model and nature are related through formally similar mathematical model. Here phenomena in kind and on the model may have different physical nature in general case. The fact that various phenomena have the same mathematical description is not associated with the random formal analogy of the mathematical apparatus. It is concerned with the unity of regularities of processes of different kinds of material motion.

The models representing the phenomenon of the same kind show characteristics which you want to predict, and constitute the special type of analog means. With the understanding that further such analog devices shall be called physical models, unlike the analogs in those cases, the nature and the model represent heterogeneous phenomena.

The main difference of the physical model and the analogous is that the physical model's natural characteristics correspond to the homogeneous (one-nominal) characteristics (speed - the speed, pressure-pressure, etc.), and the analog portion of them (or all) can comply with heterogeneous characteristics. In this sense, the flow of fluid may be physical model (routine hydraulic and aerodynamic modeling) and analog (gas hydraulic, gravity-elastic analogy).

A physical model of the hydraulic phenomenon is usually called a hydraulic model and the modeling with the use of such models – hydraulic modeling. This definition is inaccurate, as any hydraulic modeling phenomena refers to hydraulics and can be called hydraulic. Here, however, the author decided not to break the tradition and, moreover, this term in the title of the book.

1.2 Hydraulic and Numerical Modeling

Hydraulic and numerical modeling of hydraulic phenomena shall be compared now. If hydraulic modeling is a traditional method of hydraulic engineering, successfully used in the last century, numerical modeling with the use of computers - is the latest achievement. The range of problems solved by means of numerical modeling is constantly expanding. It opens new perspectives in solving complex hydraulic problems. Optimal for the development of applied hydromechanics is to use the advantages of hydraulic and numerical modeling in combination.

Between hydraulic and numerical modeling has a great community, namely, that, first, they are based on a mathematical model of the phenomenon, reflecting the most significant side of the studied object, and, secondly, when modeling the object significantly schematized. Differences in hydraulic and numerical modeling can be caused by the following circumstances. Hydraulic model is a highly specialized tool, while computers can be a solution for the most diverse problems. The only condition is the possibility of receiving the decision, in their algorithmic solvability of a problem on the selected set of operators $\{O_i\}$. Modern computers have successful from this point of view, the set of elementary operators.

The main advantage of hydraulic models is that with their help it is possible to find the solution of problems even in cases where the mathematical model of the phenomenon are not complete and take advantage of the numerical modeling impossible. As is known, up to now there is not a closed system of equations describing the averaged velocity field and pressure turbulent flow. However, if we assume that these equations have the same form for nature and models, it is possible to determine the conditions of conversion of measurement results on models in nature (see Section 1.3).

Another advantage of hydraulic models is the relative simplicity of the complex conditions of the solution uniqueness. Uniqueness conditions (first of all the geometric shape of the boundaries) for natural flows are especially complicated. To set the channel form on a computer, you need to put into it a lot of figures characterizing at least from the bottom to the length and width of the stream. In addition, you need to enter the operation of the "smoothing" of these data. On hydraulic model channel form a relatively simple set when building the model.

The choice of method of modeling in each case is determined by many circumstances, among which are the paramount principle limits the possibilities of its use. For hydraulic modeling the main of such restrictions is the incompatibility of the defining criteria of similarity (see Section 3.1), and for the numerical modeling is not a closed system of equations that constitute a mathematical model of the phenomenon. Along with the principal constraints exist practical ones. In the case of hydraulic modeling these include limited laboratory resources (size of experimental facilities, pumping capacity, availability of materials and so on), which does not allow fulfillment of the similarity conditions. And in the case of numerical modeling constraints include characteristics of computing machinery (storage capacity, processing speed) that are inadequate to the problem set. These factors should be taken into account such requirements as specified accuracy of the research, the simplicity of its implementation, the required time and cost, visualization of results, the possibility of refining the methodology, taking into consideration the field data, etc.

Account of these circumstances provides an opportunity to highlight areas of pre-emptive use of modeling techniques, what made, for example, in [181]. The share of numerical modeling, at present, it is advisable to refer mainly to the solution of one-dimensional and two-dimensional problems, with relatively simple boundary conditions and the great length of the studied objects, and also problems of filtration in a porous material. Primary areas of using hydraulic modeling are local spatial problems and problems related to relatively poorly studied hydraulic phenomena.

But within the studied object, you can select different areas to explore appropriate to apply different methods of modeling. In some cases, complex real-world phenomenon can be split into simpler phenomena, modeling, which is advisable to be implemented separately in the appropriate way. Therefore, when solving part of the problems, it is rational to implement both numerical and hydraulic modeling simultaneously, and that is used in the idea of "hybrid" models.

In fact, hybrid modeling includes all the cases of implementation of different methods of modeling in one study. However, it can be realized in another way. Segmentation of large areas of currents on extensive areas, suitable for one-dimensional or two-dimensional schematization and relatively small areas of complex spatial flows (areas of facilities location, water discharge and intakes and so on) has become routine in practice of recent years. The first of them are studied using numerical modeling, the second of them - on hydraulic model. The models relation is realized through conditions on the boundaries of an area. This research was conducted in the time scale of a hydraulic model, and computers also provide the hydraulic model control (setting of conditions on its boundaries), collection and processing of experimental data.

Great achievements of recent years in the field of numerical modeling, success in increasing the capabilities of computer technology and the reduction of its cost, it would seem, should have led to the displacement of the subject modeling of the process of research. However, the current practice of hydraulic research indicates that in our days the physical modeling has not lost its significance. The international community of technicians in the hydraulics sphere clearly formed opinion about the need for complex problems using both these methods of modeling within one study [19a and 90a].

The earliest proposal on the concurrent implementation of physical and numerical modeling in hydraulics was the proposal to divide the considered object (flow) on areas, in studying of which different modeling techniques are used [99a]. Here the broader area is investigated using numerical modeling, and an area, directly containing the relatively complex phenomenon, forecasting of which can be difficult in case of numerical modeling, is reproduced on the physical model. Conditions of uniqueness for the physical model are determined by numerical modeling. Such organization of studies was named the "hybrid modeling."

In our practice successful use of numerical modeling for determination of boundary conditions of the physical model with an abrupt limitation of possibility of appointment of the dimensions of this model refers to the study of the water intake conditions to the HPP water inlets from a deep reservoir. The results of this study are shown in Figure 1.1. Characterization of the flow on the major part of the considered area of the reservoir was executed by the means of numerical modeling. However used, the numerical model is no assessment of funnel development ahead of the HPP underground water intakes. This problem is solved on the physical model.

Figure 1.2 represents an example the research scheme of distribution of thermal pollution from the NPP, located on the coastal area in the presence of tidal and wind currents [195], in which the described above technique is used.

The separate implementation of hydraulic and numerical modeling, where the whole process of research should be related to hybrid modeling, is also possible. Such a case occurs when using a numerical model are determined boundary conditions that are then played on a hydraulic model of steady flow. Non-simultaneous use of numerical and hydraulic modeling occurs when due numerical modeling adjustments are made to the results of hydraulic modeling, which is not reproduced certain effects

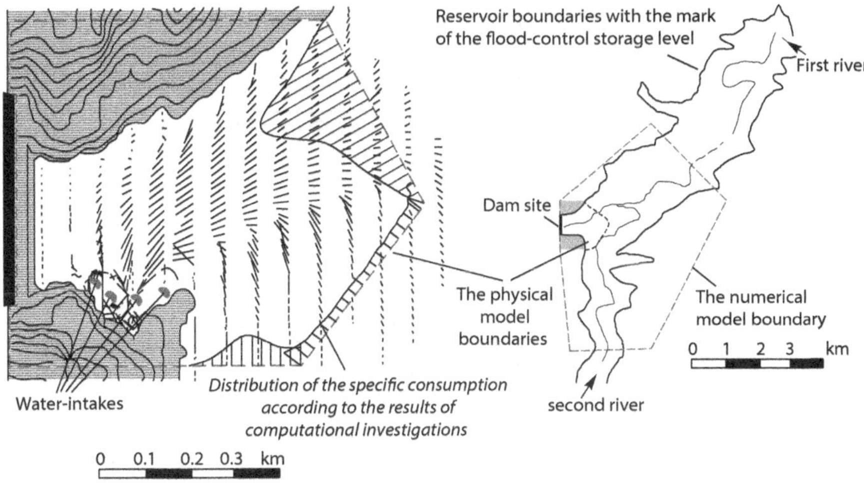

Figure 1.1 Conditions of water abstraction from the deep reservoir in the HPP water-inlets.

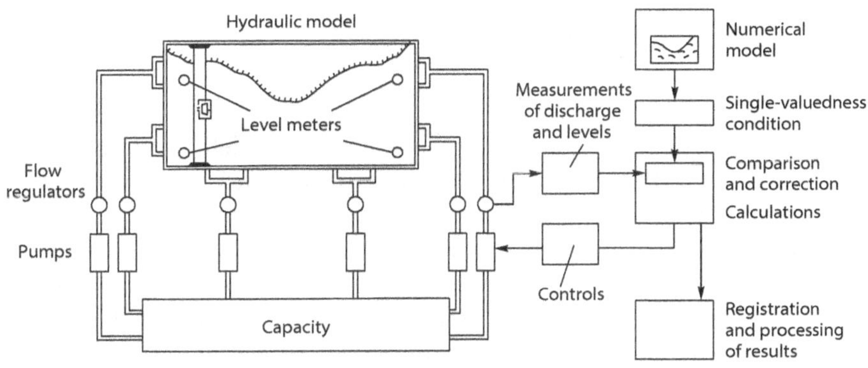

Figure 1.2 Scheme of thermal pollution from nuclear power plants in the coastal area "hybrid" modeling.

(for example, Coriolis forces). In the practice of hydraulic research and there are other cases of distribution between the hydraulic and numerical modeling parts of the phenomenon. For example, in [184] the study reported the load on the vessel in the lock chamber, in which components of the load are defined in different ways, and then made their superposition.

The comparison of the results of the use of such traditional reception of data research proves the appropriateness of the proposed method (Figure 1.3). In Figure 1.3 $F'_s=F_s/(\rho g b_s l_s e_0)$, where F_s – component of load, b_s and l_s - average width and length of the vessel, e_0 – vessel draught in still water.

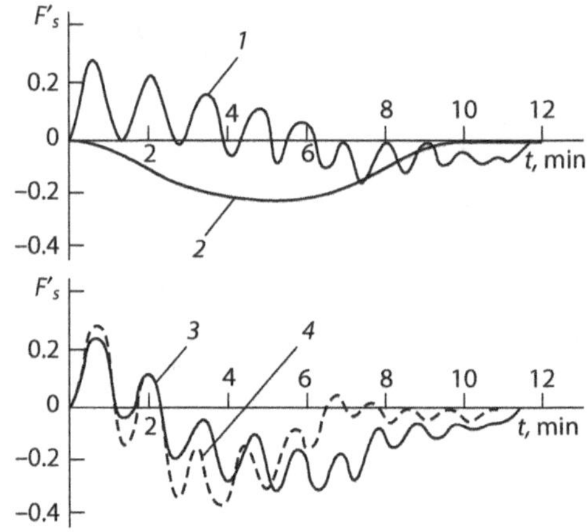

Figure 1.3 Comparison of the results of determination of loads on a vessel in the lock chamber by the means of conventional and hybrid modeling;

1. loads, caused by waves, longitudinal changes of velocity, friction in the uniform flow, form resistance;
2. load caused by the impact jets and local changes of levels;
3. total load, assessed with hybrid modeling;
4. the same with hydraulic modeling.

Many practically important cases of numerical modeling do not prove the convergence of the obtained solutions. If a researcher does not have the necessary in-situ data, the estimation of convergence can be made according to the results of the problem on hydraulic models, which are considered private exact solution of the problem of numerical modeling. Hydraulic models can be used not only to check convergence, but also to clarify the wording of the mathematical model underlying the numerical modeling.

When using hydraulic models to check the results of numerical modeling of the hydraulic model used in the beginning of the study, its main part is made with the use of numerical modeling as a faster and less labour-intensive means. Hydraulic model after the necessary comparisons can be left to check the most responsible decisions. On the other hand, numerical modeling can be used to obtain the basic decisions necessary for the evaluation of the hydraulic conditions of similarity (see Section 1.3). It follows that the ever-expanding use in hydraulic systems of numerical modeling should not undermine the hydraulic modeling.

We propose to use the term "hybrid modeling" in relation to the entire research process when sharing as physical (subject), and numerical modeling. General scheme of research in the use of hybrid modeling are presented in Figure 1.4.

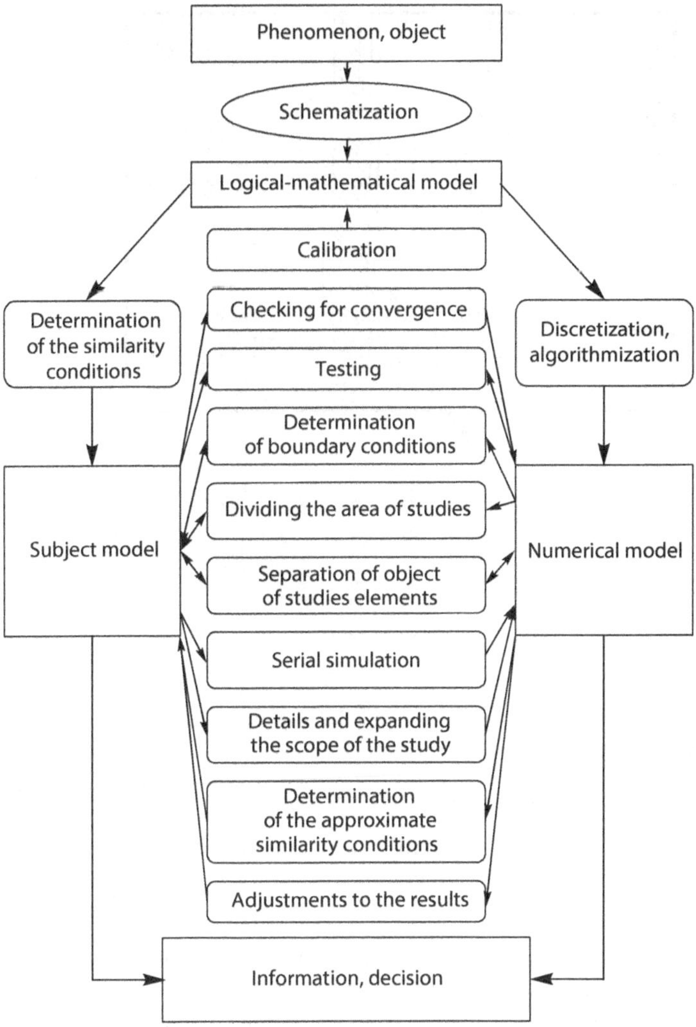

Figure 1.4 Combined implementation of physical and numerical modeling in hydroengineering studies.

A number of fundamental and technical circumstances may lead to inaccuracies in both physical and numerical modeling solutions. Testing of the obtained solutions should be performed by comparing the corresponding modeling results by different methods. Figure 1.5 represents the comparison of forecasts of the spatial currents in the area of bucket water intake from the channel. The research is carried out both on the physical model in geometric scale of 1:20 and by numerical modeling on the basis of the spatial mathematical model. The comparison provides confidence in

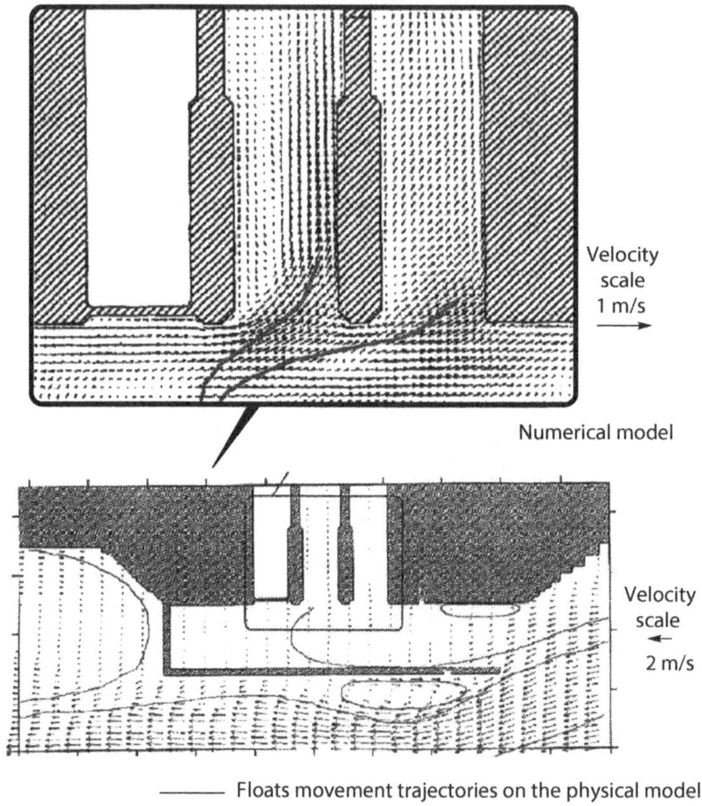

Figure 1.5 Surface currents obtained from numerical models and surface currents trajectories, obtained on the physical model.

the reliability of numerical modeling. When using numerical modeling it is easy to obtain the more detailed data.

Good coincidence of results of physical and numerical modeling is also demonstrated in Figure 1.6, where information is given on the surface currents in the upstream hydroelectric station on the approach to the HPP underground water intakes.

1.3 Dimensions of Quantity

A physical model can be presented as analog device allowing to solve the equations that describe the considered phenomenon. It would seem that in order to solve the equation, you need to know his views. Indeed, the equations view of communication, describing the phenomenon must be

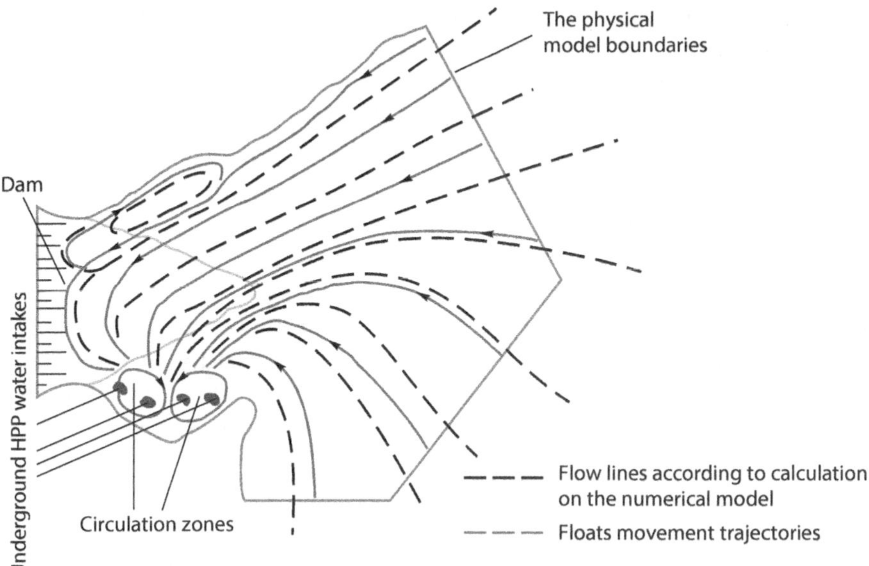

Figure 1.6 Conditions of water abstraction from the deep reservoir to the HPP water intakes.

known to select a phenomenon that plays in the model; on the basis of the equations, communications establishes the rules of modeling (similarity criteria are found).

Consideration of the phenomenon specifics allows for attributing it to the possibly narrower class, and that facilitates modeling. For example, transition from the wide class of "mechanical movement" to the "continuous medium motion," and further to the "fluid flow," "dropping fluid flow," "pressure turbulent flow of the droplet fluid," etc., allows reduction of the number of variables included in the equations, describing the phenomenon.

However, due to the complexity of the phenomena of nature, its lack of knowledge or lack of suitable mathematical methods of its description may be incomplete. Does modeling in this case solve the problem, having a closed system of equations to solve it? This, at first glance, somewhat paradoxical question can be answered affirmatively. This possibility is limited until those cases when the model has the same phenomenon as in kind (on the model and in kind - homogeneous phenomenon). In these conditions, we may assume that both on the model and in kind phenomena are described by the same equations. Then the rules of modeling, providing achievement of natural similarity on the model, can be established on the basis of the theory of dimensions conclusions.

The possibility of solving the problem in the absence of the fully formulated mathematical model may cause doubts in the generality of the scheme of physical modeling, represented above, in accordance with which the physical model and the nature are related through their mathematical model. In fact, there are no exceptions here. This question is considered in [66], which shows "that the dimensional analysis is essentially the analysis of the equations describing the studied phenomenon in General." The smaller the community, the more complete mathematical model of the phenomenon, the more real the implementation of the modeling due to the possibility to evaluate the consequences of the necessary simplifications of similarity. The success of the theory of dimensions to modeling depends primarily on the correctness of the choice of values describing the phenomenon. The concept of the values dimensions forms the basis of the theory of dimensions.

The values, numeric values of which depend on the system of units, are called dimensional, or named. If there is no such dependence, then the quantities are called dimensionless, or abstract. Physical quantities are allied. So if some of them are accepted as "fundamental" and the units are established for them, the units of all other quantities will be expressed in the units of the fundamental quantities in a certain way. Units of fundamental quantities are called basic or primary, and the units of all others are called derived units, or secondary units. In practice in mechanical problems it is enough to establish units for three values, to express through them the units of all the others.

If there are three main units, the units of other mechanical values are obtained from their definitions. The expression derived units via the main unit is called the dimension. The dependence of units of derived values of the items of property values can be represented in the form of formulas, called formula dimension. In this formula the main unit dimensions are as symbols [X]. About the dimension we can talk only with regard to a particular system of units. When using International system of units (ISU) units are symbols of units of length [l], time [t] and weight [m]. Formula dimensions of physical quantities overlook the power of a monomial. In the ISU the formula for the dimension of any mechanical values of X can be represented as

$$[X]=[l]^{m1}[m]^{m2}[t]^{m3}$$

The number of basic units is not necessarily equivalent to three. You can borrow more basic units. For example, if you set independently of each unit four values: time, length, mass and force, the Newton's equation will be:

$$F=c_1 ma$$

where c_1 - is the constant, having $[c_1]=[F][t]^2\times[m]^{-1}[l]^{-1}$ dimension

You can choose independently K each basic units ($K \geq 3$). However, you'll need to enter (K—3) additional dimensional constants. The main units can be rented and less than three. In this case, you must enter (3—K) dimensional constant, and consider them as an absolute constant.

In the study of certain classes of phenomena, it is advisable to use the most typical as the basic unit of those values. The basic units can be different in different private problems. The dimension values can be dependent and independent. Dimension K is a value called independent if each of them can be presented as a combination of the others. For example, dimensions of energy $[m][l]^2[t]^{-2}$, length $[l]$ and velocity $[l]\,[t]^{-1}$ should be considered as independent because none of them can be obtained by a combination of dimensions of other two units.

The constraint equation, that reflects the objective physical law, which does not depend on the choice of system units, can be generally written as:

$$\varphi(X_1,\ldots,X_N)=0 \tag{1.3}$$

The relationship between N dimensional quantities, K of which have independent dimensions, not changing with the change of the system unit, can be replaced by the relationship between N—K dimensionless quantities:

$$\varphi(1,1,\ldots,1,\pi_1,\ldots,\pi_{N\text{-}K})=0 \tag{1.4}$$

or

$$\varphi_1(\pi_1,\ldots,\pi_{N\text{-}K})=0 \tag{1.5}$$

This conclusion of the theory of dimensions is called the Pi-card theorem (Pi theorem). Practical value of the Pi theorem lies primarily in the fact that it can help significantly reduce the number of considered values. Thus simplifies the execution of the study. In particular, if all the values included in the communication, except one, have independent dimensions, use of PI-theorem, this dependence is completely determined with accuracy up to a constant multiplier. Indeed, if $\boldsymbol{N=K+1}$, then

$$\varphi_1\left(\frac{X_{K+1}}{X_1^{m_{11}}X_2^{m_{12}}\ldots X_K^{m_{1K}}}\right)=0 \tag{1.6}$$

or

$$X_{K+1}=C_1 X_1^{m11}X_2^{m12}\ldots X_K^{m1K} \tag{1.7}$$

where C_1 - is the dimensionless constant, which is the root of the equation (1.6), and the exponents m_{11}, m_{12}, . . ., m_{1k} can be easily found from the condition

$$\left[\frac{X_{K+1}}{X_1^{m_{11}} X_2^{m_{12}} \ldots X_K^{m_{1K}}}\right] = [X_1]^0 [X_2]^0 \ldots [X_K]^0 \tag{1.8}$$

Constant C_1 can be defined either by experience or theoretically, solving the corresponding mathematical problem.

Theory of dimensions greatly facilitates physical experiment: reducing the number of variables included in the communication, even one several times reduces the number of experiments needed to establish a link. But it is clear that with only the theory of dimensions it is impossible to determine the functional relationship between the dimensionless quantities for one and the same system of governing parameters, on which the conclusions of the theory of dimensions only depend, there can be different constraint equations (in particular, equations of motion). However, the constraint equations contain the potential of finding solutions mathematically.

If for full analytical solution of the problems of the use of the conclusions of the theory of dimension not enough, then when modeling on these conclusions can be based establish the similarity conditions. The Buckingham's formulation of the Pi theorem reflects this perspective of using theories of dimension: the similarity condition of identical phenomena group, defined by the number of values of N total quantity, consists in the identity of the values of N—3 dimensionless π_i combinations.

Here we should pay attention to the fact that we are talking about the same phenomena, as the fact that mapped phenomena are determined by the same values does not give grounds for attributing them to like. The same phenomena imply that they are described by the equations of communication that have the same type, i.e. the first condition third theorem similarity is automatically performed. The identity of p-members represents the third condition of similarity (consisting of identity criteria of similarity), as they are dimensionless combination of all dimensional quantities, one way or another affect the desired solution.

The identity of part of the π-members provides the second condition of the phenomenon similarity: the requirements of similarity of conditions of uniqueness of the solution because the system of values characterizing the phenomenon must contain the values used to specify conditions of uniqueness.

If you choose among the quantities included in the relation (1.3), as having independent dimensions other values, for example $X_{k+1}, \ldots, X_{2k}$, you will have the dimensionless complexes, other than those obtained using with independent dimensions of values $X_1, \ldots X_k$ and other kind of relation of the dimensionless complexes:

$$\varphi_2(\pi'_1, \ldots, \pi'_K, 1, \ldots, \pi'_{2K+1}, \ldots \pi'_{N-K})$$

Relation

$$\varphi_1(\pi'_1, \ldots, \pi'_{N-K})=0 \tag{1.9}$$

can be replaced by the relation

$$\varphi_i[(\pi_1^{a11}\pi_2^{a12} \ldots \pi_{N-K}^{a1(N-K)})_1, \ldots,$$
$$(\pi^{a\,(N-K)1}{}_1\, \pi^{a(N-K)2}{}_2 \ldots \pi^{a\,(N-K)\,(N-K)}{}_{N-K})_{N-K}]=0 \tag{1.10}$$

If a change of variables in the number of dimensionless units included in the link should remain unchanged, each of the input data must be contained in at least one of the new complexes. We prove the justice of this change from the position of similarity phenomena. The system of similarity:

$$\pi_1=\text{idem}$$
$$\cdots\cdots\cdots\cdot$$
$$\pi_{N-K}=\text{idem} \tag{1.11}$$

is equivalent to the system:

$$\left.\begin{array}{c} \dfrac{M_{N-K}^{m_1(N-K)}}{M_{X_1}^{m_1} M_{X_2}^{m_{12}} M_{X_K}^{m_1 K}} = 1 \\ \cdots\cdots\cdots\cdots\cdots\cdots \\ \dfrac{M_{N-K}^{m_1(N-K)N}}{M_{X_1}^{m(N-K)_1} M_{X_2}^{m(N-K)_2} \ldots M_{X_K}^{m(N-K)K}} = 1 \end{array}\right\} \tag{1.12}$$

or

$$M_{\pi 1}=1$$
$$\cdots\cdots\cdots$$
$$M_{\pi N-K}=1 \tag{1.13}$$

If the scales $M_i \neq 0$, then system (1.13) can be replaced, raising both parts of the equalities in extent and multiplying them on each other, system:

$$\left.\begin{array}{r}\left(M_{\pi 1}^{a_{11}} M_{\pi 2}^{a_{12}} \ldots M_{\pi_{N-K}}^{a_{1(N-K)}}\right)=1 \\ \ldots\ldots\ldots\ldots\ldots\ldots\ldots\ldots\ldots\ldots \\ \left(M_{\pi_1}^{a(N-K)_1} M_{\pi_2}^{a(N-K)_2} \ldots M_{\pi_{N-K}}^{a(N-K)(N-K)}\right)=1\end{array}\right\} \quad (1.14)$$

If the transformation equations (1.12) in the system of equations will be deducted to the extent of all values, scale values X_1, ..., X_N solution of the system (1.14) will be the same extent M_{xi}, that the solution of system (1.12), i.e. the system (1.10) can be replaced by a system of:

$$\left.\begin{array}{l}\left(\pi_1^{a11} \pi_2^{a12} \ldots \pi_{N-K}^{a(N-K)}\right)_1 = \text{idem} \\ \ldots\ldots\ldots\ldots\ldots\ldots\ldots\ldots\ldots\ldots \\ \left(\pi_1^{a(N-K)_1} \pi_2^{a(N-K)_2} \ldots\ldots \pi_{N-K}^{a(N-K)(N-K)}\right)_{N-K} = \text{idem}\end{array}\right\} \quad (1.15)$$

As the dimensionless complexes in dependencies (1.10) have the meaning of the similarity criteria, the record (1.10) corresponds to the relation (1.9), which was to be proved.

Thus, the theory of dimensions can give results in a sense richer than specific mechanical modeling of the phenomenon, which results in obtaining a fewer number of parameters than the number, which could be taken into consideration by the supervisory analysis [218].

If the scales of similar quantities are equal, then, it would seem, when drawing up the criteria of similarity it is insignificant which of the values of this dimension, being included in the uniqueness conditions, should be involved in the criterion. But in fact when modeling it is necessary to assess the impact of the criterion. Therefore, the criterion must enter the values appropriate to the physical essence of the criterion. For example, designing a geometrically undistorted model of open stream received the same scale and speed, regardless of the linear size entered in the Frude criterion (depth or width) of the stream. However, the Frude criterion of gravity (energy provisions) is compared to force of inertia (kinetic energy), and the Frude criterion compiled by the width of the stream will give nothing for the analysis of the communication characteristics of the flow with this complex, as the width of the stream in this case, has no relation to the force of gravity. It is clear that arbitrary choice of values is not possible when using distorted patterns (see Section 3.2), because the scale of similar quantities can be different.

Explain the use of the conclusions of the theory of dimensions on the example. To do this it is advisible to consider the flow of viscous incompressible fluid under the assumption that the surface tension forces do not affect the phenomenon. Believe that the phenomenon is characterized by the following parameters:

1. linear dimensions that define the boundaries of this area: x_1, $x_2, \ldots, x_n$;
2. kinematic and dynamic parameters: velocity U (instead of U could set the flow rate, the time t, pressure drop ΔP and acceleration of volumetric forces;

3. fluid properties: density p, dynamic viscosity μ. Then the equation link quantities responsible for this phenomenon in General we can to present so:

$$\varphi(x_1, x_2, \ldots x_n, U, t, \Delta P, g, \rho, \mu) = 0 \tag{1.16}$$

Choose from the three values that have independent dimensions Such quantities in particular, are $x_1 = l([x_1] = [l])$, $U([U] = [l][l]^{-1})$ и $\rho([\rho] = [m][l]^{-3})$. In accordance with the Pi-card theorem (1.16) can be represented as

$$\varphi\left(1; \frac{x_2}{l^{m_{11}} U^{m_{12}} \rho^{m_{13}}}; \ldots; \frac{x_n}{l^{m_{(n-1)1}} U^{m_{(n-1)2}} \rho^{m_{(n-1)3}}}; 1; \right.$$

$$\frac{t}{l^{m_{n1}} U^{m_{n2}} \rho^{m_{n3}}}; \frac{\Delta P}{l^{m_{(n+1)1}} U^{m_{(n+1)2}} \rho^{m_{(n+1)3}}};$$

$$\left. \frac{g}{l^{m_{(n+2)1}} U^{m_{(n+2)2}} \rho^{m_{(n+2)3}}}; 1; \frac{\mu}{l^{m_{(n+3)1}} U^{m_{(n+3)2}} \rho^{m_{(n+3)3}}} = 0. \right)$$

Thus, the relationship between n+6 dimensional quantities replaced communication n+3 dimensionless complexes. Install them. The first n-1 π -member include the values that have the same dimension, and therefore they have the same structure:

$$[\pi_1] = [\pi_2] = [\pi_{n-1}] = [l]^{1-m_{11}-m_{12}+3m_{13}}[t]^{m_{12}}[m]^{-m_{13}}$$

The exponents of quantities, included in the π -members that can be derived from the fact that the π -members have zero dimension

$$[\pi_i]=[l]^0[t]^0[m]^0$$

Then

$$[l]^{(1-m_{11}-m_{12}+3m_{13})}[t]^{m_{12}}[m]^{-m_{13}}=[l]^0[t]^0[m]^0$$

Having equated the exponents at corresponding dimensions, we find $m_{11}=1, m_{12}=0, m_{13}=0$ и $\pi_1=x_2/x_1, \ldots, \pi_{n-1}=x_n/x_1.$

Similarly for

$$\pi_n=\frac{t}{l^{m_{n1}}U^{m_{n2}}\rho^{m_{n3}}}$$

$$[\pi_n]=\frac{[t]}{[l]^{m_{n1}}([l]/[t])^{m_{n2}}([m]/[l]^3)^{m_{n3}}}=$$

$$=[l]^{3m_{n2}-m_{n1}-m_{n2}}[t]^{1+m_{n2}}[m]-m_{n_3}$$

where $m_{n1}=1$, $m_{n2}=-1$, $m_{n3}=0$, $\pi_n=Ut/l$. In the same way it is easy to obtain, that $\pi_{n+1}=\Delta P/\rho U^2$; $\pi_{n+2}=gl/U^2$; $\pi_{n+3}=\mu/(\rho Ul)$. It is easy to see that $\pi_n = Sh$; $\pi_{n+1}=Eu$; $\pi_{n+2}=1/Fr$; $\pi_{n+3}=1/Re$, i.e., using the theory of dimensions, we come to the same conclusions that when rationing the Navier-Stokes equations.

In using the method of dimensions engineering intuition, the ability to see the main thing in the problem is especially important. It may be more convenient to take from the equations describing the phenomenon in the framework of a particular model, only the variables, and the similarity criteria to be on the principle dimension, given the characteristics of the specific problems [138].

1.4 Conditions of Similarity

The study object (event) in the modeling is possible in that case when there is a correspondence between the characteristics of nature and its model, so knowing descriptions of the model and the form of compliance, you can find the characteristics of nature. Form of compliance can be different [28]. However, physical modeling is mainly used for linear correspondence between the model and in kind: $X_M = M_x X_N$. The coefficient of proportionality M_x is called the scale values of X, and this match we will call likeness. Qualitatively the same phenomenon characterized by the specified line is called uniformly such (or similar), qualitatively different, heterogeneous such (or similar).

Consider what requirements must be presented to nature and models that between them the characteristics existed specified compliance, i.e. establish the similarity conditions. For this study a mathematical model applies to both the mapped objects.

Suppose that the mathematical model of the phenomenon is compiled, i.e. in a written system of equations and the uniqueness conditions ensure the uniqueness of a solution. Here we believe the basic equations and conditions of uniqueness to be complete and correct.

The term "complete" means that there is a sufficient number of independent equations to determine dependent quantities and, moreover, that the mathematical model corresponds to a physical problem with sufficient precision in the investigated range of changes affecting variables.

The term "correctness" characterizes the formulation of the mathematical problems. It, in particular, refers to the uniqueness conditions. It is known that to get only the types of equations there are required conditions for the uniqueness of a certain type. The target is set correctly if there is only one solution of the equation with the system of conditions of uniqueness, from which it depends continuously: small changes of conditions of uniqueness cause small changes in the solution.

However, it may be that the equation has no solution in this sense, but it describes the real situation. For example, the Navier-Stokes equations describe the individual movements of the fluid volumes in the turbulent flow. But it is utterly hopeless to try to compare these individual motions in kind and on the model even in the cases when the boundary and initial conditions are the same. It is because of the non-uniqueness of solutions of the Navier-Stokes equations, for which at high Reynolds numbers is impossible to formulate the conditions of certainty in the usual sense. Here the statement of the problem in terms of the theory of random functions is necessary. The corresponding mathematical problem is very complicated, and a simple physical model often gives practical results. In this case, in the opinion of the author of this guidance, "they should be regarded as certain, anyway reflecting the stochastic nature of the nature reproduction..." In fact there is no fundamental difference between an analog device and any other computational tool, if the mathematical formulation of the problem is executed in the same way.

The reversed situation is possible when equations at given boundary conditions have the only solution, which is not physically implemented, for example, due to its instability. It is clear that by extending these equations, i.e., changing the formulation of the problem, you can get this instability also in the result of calculation. The necessity of such expansion of the problem is not necessarily the obvious one. Physical experiment in this respect could have quickly straightened case.

The mentioned circumstances explain the falseness of indication [28] to the "fundamental incorrectness of the approach to analog and especially physical models as to the calculated units."

Let's assume that the mathematical models of the phenomenon meet the conditions for a model of a viscous fluid described by the equations in the Navier-Stokes equations form. Let's implement the normalization of the basic equations of motion and conditions of uniqueness.

The procedure of regulation resolves into conversion of all values and members of the equations in dimensionless view when selecting the appropriate scale. This can be done, because every equation describing physical phenomena, contains terms that have the same dimension.

The conditions of uniqueness do provide the unique and sustainable solution of the considered equations. In fact, the situation with the Navier-Stokes equations is more complicated, as their solution in many practically interesting cases turns out to be non-unique (under the given initial and boundary conditions) or unstable. This issue is discussed in Section 2.2.

The normalized equations contain dimensionless quantities (in this case x^+_i, t^+, U^+_i, P^+) and dimensionless complexes:

$$\pi_1 = x_0/(U_0 t_0);\ \pi_2 = g_i x_0/U^2_0;\ \pi 3 = \Delta P_0/(\rho U^2_0);\ \pi_4 = \nu/(U_0 x_0)$$

It is easy to notice that the two systems of normalized equations and their uniqueness give the same decisions in relation to dimensionless variables X^+ (for example, P^+ and U^+), if in both systems equations have the same structure and the dimensionless complexes, included in normalized equations, and dimensionless quantities (simplexes) in conditions of uniqueness are equal to π_i –idem, respectively.

If one of the systems describes the phenomenon of nature, and the other refers to the model, then when complying with all these requirements the following relations are set out:

$$X^+_N = X^+_M$$

or

$$X_N/X_{0N} = X_M/X_{0M}$$

and

$$X_{M} = X_{0M}/X_{0N} \cdot X_{M} = M_{x} X_{N}$$

i.e. in this case there is similarity of models and nature. Dimensionless complexes π_i are called the similarity criteria. The numerical value of the π_i complex is called the π_i number Condition

$$\pi_i = X^{m1i}_{01} X^{m2i}_{02} X^{m3i}_{03} \dots X^{mni}_{0n} = idem$$

where X_{0i} – values, from which the criterion is formed, and they can be represented as follows:

$$(X^{m1i}_{01} X^{m2i}_{02} X^{m3i}_{03} \dots X^{mni}_{0n})_{N} = (X^{m1i}_{01} X^{m2i}_{02} X^{m3i}_{03} \dots X^{mni}_{0n})_{M}$$

or

$$(X_{01M}/X_{01N})^{m1i} (X_{02M}/X_{02N})^{m2i} (X_{03M}/X_{03N})^{m3i} \dots (X_{0nM}/X_{0nN})^{mni} = 1$$

i.e.

$$M^{m1i}_{X01} M^{m2i}_{X02} M^{m3i}_{X03} \dots M^{mni}_{X0n} = 1$$

The expression, placed in the left-hand part of equality (1.11) is called the similarity indicator. Thus, you can also say that *the condition of similarity is the equality of indicators of the unit similarity.*

Similarity criteria, obtained by normalization of the Navier-Stokes equations, as we know, have the following names:

$1/\pi_1$ = Sh – the Strouhal criterion (or the homogeneity criterion);
$1/\pi_2$ = Fr – the Froude criterion;
$1/\pi_3$ = Eu – the Euler criterion (or pressure coefficient);
$1/\pi_4$ = Re - the Reynolds criterion.

Equations related to the thread in general (without conditions of uniqueness) do not provide a comprehensive system of criteria. For example, the equations of fluid motion give four criteria: the number of Strouhal, Froude, Euler and Reynolds. Equations of the dynamic capabilities of the motion obtained by applying the operation of the rotor to the equations of motion, give two criteria - number of Strouhal and Reynolds. All others appear when recording conditions of uniqueness (see Section 5.1).

If the conditions of certainty given in the form of equations of the desired function achieve similar phenomena, it is necessary to form similar identity criteria by rationing using these equations. Getting criteria of similarity by bringing the system of equations and conditions of uniqueness to the dimensionless mind can practically be reliable if it is known that these equations and sufficient conditions allow for the existence of clear and sustainable solutions. Criteria that include only the quantities included in the conditions of uniqueness are called determinant. The identity of these criteria is the sufficient condition of similarity. Among the π_i complexes, resulting from the equations rationing, there may be some complexes, which contain values, not included in the conditions of uniqueness. The identity of such complexes represents not the condition, but the consequence of similarity, i.e. the assignment of numerical values of the defining criteria fully defines the numeric values of the non-defining criteria.

Similarity of boundary conditions should be ensured throughout the boundary area, where these conditions can be specified, and the likeness of the initial conditions in the whole area at the initial moment of time. The way to specify the conditions of uniqueness depends on the problem being solved. So, when solving three-dimensional problems, the likeness of the boundary conditions is provided by the identity of simplexes $X(x_1,x_2,x_3)_i/X_0$ on the border region, and the initial conditions (in the study of unsteady flows) - simplexes $X(x_1,x_2,x_3,t_0)_i/X_0$ in the studied area. When solving a scheduled problem, you must ensure at borders and inside the scope of the identity of simplexes, which are averaged over the depth value, and at the solution of one-dimensional problems of simplexes, containing the values averaged over the cross-section.

Thus, *the similarity conditions are:*

1. *the description of the phenomena by the same system of normalized equations;*
2. *in similarity of the uniqueness conditions;*
3. *in equality of criteria, composed of quantities, included in the conditions of uniqueness.*

This is the content of theorem, which is called the third similarity theorem [76].

These conditions of similarity represent the rules of modeling, i.e. requirements that should be complied with when converting the prototype space into the model space in order to obtain the linear correspondence between values in these spaces.

The case of finding similarity criteria for rationing equations that contain the homogeneous function, when constant multipliers can be taken for signs of functions, was considered above. If the equations are heterogeneous functions (transcendent, complex, and so on), then this cannot be realized. In such cases in [28] it is proposed to take the function argument as the criteria. Obviously, you can do otherwise: to take the values from the equations and make one criteria, based on the conclusions of the theory of dimensions, described in Section 1.4.

1.5 About the Newton's Law of Similarity

Two ways of setting conditions for the similarity conditions of phenomena are considered above. The first of them is based on analysis of the equations describing a phenomenon and conditions of their uniqueness, the second - on analysis of dimensions of the quantities characterizing the phenomenon. The method, reasoning from the fact, that similarity is achieved by geometrical and kinematic similarity, is sometimes considered as the third way of finding similarity conditions of mechanical systems, which corresponds to the similarity of the conditions of uniqueness, and dynamic similarity, which is provided by the identity of the criteria of similarity.

The requirement of dynamic similarity is the specificity of the method, based on Newton's law of similarity on the balance of forces in such systems. Implementation of this method includes two operations: 1) the list of forces, which are the most significant in this problem, is formed; each of them is expressed through the values that characterize the phenomenon, through physical representations or using the dimension principle; 2) similarity criteria are represented in the form of relationship of these forces. The number of dimensionless complexes $\pi_{i,}$ representing the relationship of forces is equal to the number of independent forces.

In the classical form Newton's law of similarity is based on the second law of mechanics and in accordance with this law, forces of different nature are correlated with the force of inertia. However, there are special cases where the operational forces are balanced (or their resultant force is small), so that the forces of inertia can be neglected. In these cases, the relation of acting forces between themselves is taken as the criteria of similarity. In [185] the examples of phenomena for which forces of different nature, are balanced so, that the forces of inertia can be neglected, are given. Among these phenomena - uniform surfacing or fall of a body in a viscous fluid (forces of viscosity and gravity are significant), which is related to the Stokes number or its modifications, such as

$$\frac{\rho_s - \rho}{\rho} \cdot \frac{gl^3}{v^2}$$

where l_0 - characteristic size of a body; ρ_s and ρ - density of bodies and fluids; viscous earth's crust and lower mantle interaction, for which forces of viscosity and gravitation are also significant, involvement of air in high-speed flows, determined, according to M. Kenn [185] mostly by viscosity and surface tension forces, which is related to the determining criterion in the form

$$\sigma/(\mu\bar{U}) \text{ or } \rho\sigma l_0/\mu^2$$

where σ - the surface tension coefficient.

The existence of such cases is specified in [186], where these include, in particular, non-pressure filtration in a porous medium, for which viscosity and gravitation forces are substantial, and the determining factor is the Mosheni criterion (Table 1.1).

Between lists of forces, operating in the mechanical system, and values, forming the expressions of these forces, the difference is small, and therefore, there is no principal difference between this method and method of dimensions. Just as when implementing the pi-theorem, this method is applicable in cases when the phenomena compared belong to the same class from the physical point of view, and it is allowed that the equations describing these phenomena have the same form.

However, the method based on Newton's law, indirectly admits the existence of the system of equations, linking the acting forces, i.e. it has common features with the method, using the analysis of the constraint equations. From this point of view there are some advantages over the method of the theory of dimensions, such as the ability to compare the values of the equations members.

S. Kline [64] represents the convenient table, which defines six forces, very common in the fluid mechanics, and where their dimension and 15 independent relations between the forces are given. This table is reproduced here with some change in notations (see Table 1.1).

We may remark, that a number of correlations in Table 1.1 have the same form as the criteria obtained in the analysis of the Navier-Stokes equations. However, the coincidence of these criteria types and relationship of forces does not mean that for this problem, these systems are consistent. If the relation of two forces is small, then the corresponding criterion, composed of randomly selected values, will not always have a very small or a very large value. In each case the values from which it is compiled should be carefully selected in order to provide that one or another criterion really represents the compared forces ratio.

S. Kline [64] proposed the generalization of the method in question. This is the use of the similarity conditions for the analysis of the system of general phenomenological equations or «black box» equations. The Kline's proposal allows, in particular, to eliminate one of the disadvantages of

Table 1.1

Basic forces	Gravitation force F_g, $[F_g]$-$[\rho][l]^3[g]$	Elastic force F_E, $[F_E]=[E][l]^2$	Surface tension force F_σ, $[F_\sigma]=[\sigma][l]$	Pressure force F_ρ, $[F_\rho]=[\rho][l]^2$	Viscosity force F_μ, $[F_\mu]=[\mu][U][t]$
Inertia force F_l, $[F_l]=[\rho][U]^2[l]^2$	Froude number $F_r=\frac{F_l}{F_g}=\frac{U^2}{gl}$	Cauchy number $Co=\frac{F_l}{F_E}=\frac{\rho U^2}{E}$	Weber number $We=\frac{F_l}{F_\sigma}=\frac{\rho U^2 l}{\sigma}$	Euler number $E_u=\frac{F_p}{F_r}=\frac{\Delta P}{\rho U^2}$	Reynolds number $\mathrm{Re}=\frac{F_l}{F_\mu}=\frac{\rho Ul}{\mu}$
$F\mu$	Mosheni number $Mo=\frac{F_g}{F_\mu}=\frac{\rho l^2 g}{\mu U}$	$\frac{F_E}{F_\mu}=\frac{El}{\mu U}$	$\frac{F_\sigma}{F_\mu}=\frac{\sigma}{\mu U}$	Stocks number $St=\frac{F_P}{F_\mu}=\frac{El}{\mu U}$	
$F\rho$	$\frac{F_g}{F_p}=\frac{\rho \lg}{\Delta P}$	$\frac{F_g}{F_p}=\frac{E}{\Delta P}$	$\frac{F_\sigma}{F_P}=\frac{\sigma}{\Delta Pl}$		
$F\sigma$	$\frac{F_g}{F_\sigma}=\frac{\rho l^2 g}{\sigma}$	$\frac{F_E}{F_\sigma}=\frac{El}{\sigma}$			
F_E	$\frac{F_g}{F_E}=\frac{\rho lg}{E}$				

the method, based on Newton's law, as in many physical processes there are values that are not dependent on forces (for example, flows of heat or electricity). Considering complementary the energy balance or other principles, essential in this problem, you can get additional criteria that take into account the effects, missing in the analysis of forces only.

Similarity criteria can be obtained through preliminary grouping of variables into complexes, having any similar dimension, and allocation of these complexes to each other.

Preliminary grouping of values that constitute the problem specification, into complexes, having a particular dimension, is considered by some authors as the procedure, which provides the possibility of choosing the most suitable dimensionless parameters structure. This procedure constitutes a part of the so-called "method of synthesis." For example, D. Barr [218] proposed to group basic values into complexes, which have dimension of length. Grouping is executed by the means of the simple values searching.

However, it can be executed in the same way as when obtaining dimensionless π -members using the dimensions theory. If the values are grouped into complexes, which have the same size $[x_i]$, the relation

$$(x_1, \ldots, x_N)=0$$

between N values, K of which have independent dimensions, can be replaced by relation between N-(K-1) values

$$(x_1, 1, \ldots, 1, \Pi_i, \ldots, \Pi_{N-(K-1)})=0$$

where Π_i - complexes of $[x_1]$ dimension. Type of these systems is easy to define, under equations of the following form

$$\frac{x_{K+1}}{x_2^{m_{12}} x_3^{m_{13}} \ldots . x_K^{m_{1K}}} = [x_1]^1 [x_2]^0 \ldots [x_k]^0$$

Method of synthesis (without application, however, of this term) was implemented in [71] when composing the so-called "internal numbers of similarity" of gas-fluid flows of dimensional quantities, which are mainly the combination of quantities, characterizing the phase's properties.

2

The Mathematical Models of Fluid Motion

2.1 Preliminary Remarks

Analyzing the similarity conditions in a commonly used model of an incompressible viscous fluid and the corresponding system of Navier-Stokes equations, two fundamental questions are raised.

1. In conditions of turbulent flow it becomes necessary to admit the nonuniqueness of solutions of the Navier-Stokes deterministic initial data and corresponding random results. For example, when serving in the tray of some form of a fixed water flow in the turbulent flow regime in the fixed point of the observed changes (fluctuations) of the velocity and pressure, slimming information and considering the average (by chance) values of the velocity and pressure, lose the possibility of practical use of the Navier-Stokes equations, as their averaged similar Reynolds equations are open. The system of criteria of similarity derived from open-loop equations, obviously, may be incomplete. But which way is advisable to seek ways circuit equations: reducing the scale of consideration and increasing the detail of the description by clicking on the molecular level with

the equations of Boltzmann; or on the contrary, enlarging the scope of the consideration by the spatial averaging effects and reducing the number of measurements essential to the problem?

2. Flows in real borders are not clear to the question of boundary conditions for the Navier-Stokes equations with turbulent flow. What is the boundary of the flow in the channel with naturally uneven surface or in the river, where the bed is composed of permeable eroded material? Even in a glass tube with a perfectly flat wall at the turbulent regime is there a need to prevent "sticking" to the wall or slipping fluids?

These issues are significant for detailed studies of turbulent flows. A large number of practical problems can be solved with the help of physical experiment, based on more rough mathematical models of fluid flow.

Consider the following models of real unsteady flow:

1. discrepancy of the fluid;
2. a viscous fluid under the assumption of the completeness of the system (strictly speaking, with small numbers of Reynolds);
3. turbulent fluid, taking hypothesis circuit Boussinesque under different models of turbulent viscosity, recorded through the first statistical moments of hydrodynamic fields;
4. same as in point 3, but with the involvement of the energy balance equations of turbulence and additional hypotheses on the second level of the statistical moments of hydrodynamic fields;
5. same as in point 3 and 4, but with additional fundamental hypothesis on the maximum stability of the probability characteristics of turbulent flows.

In addition to these models, we will consider the equation of turbulent flows, averaged on specially selected volumes (two-dimensional, one-dimensional zero-dimensional equations). We show that the degree of open-ended equations is significantly reduced.

The first model of the flow may be implemented only under the condition of a slip fluid impermeable border. In contrast, all other models allow for the formulation of the problem with both slip and the condition of "sticking" of the fluid to a rigid border.

Modeling of riverbed flows also needs to take into account the deformation of the riverbed by the migration of soil particles. In this regard, the system of equations of fluid should be supplemented by the terms of the start (and stop) strains of the riverbed in sediment transport and the equations that define the process of erosion, weighing and deposition of particles. Here also it is possible (as appropriate) to increase difficulty of models from the model kvazi one-dimensional environment (dispersed), in which the presence of the sediment is taken into account only after the conditional density single-phase environment (water + the soil particles), and ending with complex models of the dynamics of a two-phase medium in which turbulent motion of each phase is described separately, taking into account the interaction of phases.

2.2 Conditions of Mass and Momentum Conservation

The condition of conservation of mass for a multiphase environment can be written in the integral form

$$\frac{d}{dt}\int_{wi} \rho_i dW = 0 \tag{2.1}$$

where the integral is taken by volume W_i changing the shape (and dimensions), but consists of the same particles of the i-th environment, having a density of ρ_i. This condition can be written in the differential divergence form

$$\partial \rho_i / \partial t + \mathrm{div}(\rho_i \mathbf{U}_i) = 0 \tag{2.2}$$

where $\boldsymbol{U}_i$ is the true velocity of the considered phases.

Equations of mass conservation are almost the same for all models of motion. The equations of conservation of momentum, written in stresses for a fixed volume (or mass) and expressing Newton's second law, have the same form for all models of motion too:

$$\frac{d}{dt}\int_{W} \rho_i U_i dW = \int_{W} \rho_i F_i dW + \int_{\Omega} \sigma_n d\Omega \tag{2.3}$$

$$\frac{d}{dt}\int_{Wi} \rho_i U_i dW = \int_{Wi}\int_{t}^{t+dt} \rho_i F_i dW\,dt + \int_{\Omega_i}\int_{t}^{t+dt} \sigma_n d\Omega\, dt \tag{2.4}$$

Here W_i as in (2.4), the volume occupied by the same particle of i-th environment; Ω_i is the surface limiting this volume; F_i is the force per unit mass; σ_n is the stress vector on the site $d\Omega$ with the normal n; $\boldsymbol{\sigma_n}=\{\boldsymbol{\sigma_{kj}}\}\boldsymbol{n}$, where $\{\sigma_{kj}\}$ is the stress tensor.

Usually it is not easy to monitor the volume occupied by the same particle. It is easier to lock in a fixed amount W_{io}, limited surface $\Omega_{i0.}$ In this case, the equation of conservation of momentum becomes:

$$\partial t \int\limits_{W_{i0}} \rho_i U_i dW + \int\limits_{\Omega_{i0}} \rho_i U_i (U_i n) d\Omega = \int\limits_{\Omega_{i0}} \sigma_n d\Omega \tag{2.5}$$

where n is the external normal to the surface Ω_{i0}

Differential analog of equation (2.3) in divergence form does not exist. To move from the surface of the integral in the right-hand side of (2.3) to volume is only differentiability of stress fields σ_n:

$$\rho \frac{d\boldsymbol{U}}{dt} = \rho \boldsymbol{F} + \operatorname{div}\left\{\sigma_{kj}\right\} \tag{2.6}$$

$$\operatorname{div}\left\{\sigma_{kj}\right\} = \nabla\left\{\sigma_{kj}\right\} = \frac{\partial \sigma_{1j}}{\partial x_1} + \frac{\partial \sigma_{2j}}{\partial x_2} + \frac{\partial \sigma_{3j}}{\partial x_3} \tag{2.7}$$

The stress tensor of a fluid can be written as a sum of a spherical tensor $\{\sigma\}$ and deviator $\{\sigma'_{kj}\}$

$$\{\sigma_{kj}\}=\{\sigma\}+\{\sigma'_{kj}\} \tag{2.8}$$

where $\sigma = \dfrac{\sigma_{11} + \sigma_{22} + \sigma_{33}}{3}$ is the first invariant tensor voltage (average normal stress); compression $\boldsymbol{\sigma}$<O.

The value $\boldsymbol{P}=-\boldsymbol{\sigma}$ is usually called pressure. Pay attention to the fact that this pressure is not necessarily the same as the pressure $\boldsymbol{P}$ defined in thermodynamics and characterizing the state of the environment.

In a scalar form, equation (2.6) is:

$$\frac{\partial U_i}{\partial t} + U_k \frac{\partial U_i}{\partial x_L} = F_j + \frac{1}{\rho} \frac{\partial \sigma'_{kj}}{\partial x_L} - \frac{1}{\rho} \frac{\partial P}{\partial x_i} \tag{2.9}$$

On repeated indices the summation is executed.

The difference in mathematical models begins to expand links between the stress tensor of a fluid $\{\boldsymbol{\sigma}_{kj}\}$ and kinematic characteristics of the fluid - velocity fields $\boldsymbol{U(x)}$.

The energy conservation law when considering only one kind of energy - mechanical - does not introduce any additional information, as it is obtained directly from the second law of Newton. This is not the case when taking into account all forms of energy, in particular the internal energy of the fluid. In this case, the equation of energy balance (in all forms) is necessary.

Applying the similarity transformation to (2.2), make sure that it leads to the generalized criterion of Strouhal:

$$\mathrm{Sh}_{\rho} = \frac{U_{0j}t_0}{l_{0j}} \frac{\rho_0}{\Delta\rho_0} \tag{2.10}$$

and criteria that include the extent of the density,

$$\pi_{\rho}=\Delta\rho_0/\rho_0 \tag{2.11}$$

Here t_0, U_{0t}, and l_{0j} are typical values of time, velocity, and length (in j direction); ρ_0, $\Delta\rho_0$ signifies the characteristic values of density of the environment and its changes. Upon receipt of (2.10), (2.11) is accepted that the magnitude of velocity change must be equal to the scale of velocity. On the contrary, for a difference of density and density values it is not the requirement, though possible.

The same transformation of equation (2.9) leads to the following criteria:

$$\mathrm{Sh}_j=U_{0j}t_0/l_0 \tag{2.12}$$

$$\pi_j=(U_{0j}/l_{0j})(l_0/U_0) \tag{2.13}$$

$$\pi_{F=}F_0 l_{0/}U^2{}_0 \tag{214}$$

$$E_u=\Delta P_0/(\rho_0 U^2{}_0) \tag{2.15}$$

$$\pi_{\sigma'}=\sigma'_0/(\rho_0 U^2{}_0) \tag{2.16}$$

$$\pi'_J = \frac{\sigma_{0j}}{l_{0j}} \frac{l_0}{\rho_0 U^2{}_0} \tag{2.17}$$

Equation (2.14) is the criterion of external forces; in the gravity field becomes the Froude criterion; (2.15) – the Euler criterion; the relation (2.16) - criterion internal deviatoric stresses for viscous fluid transformed into the Reynolds criterion. The symbol ΔP emphasizes that if σ=-P, then the pressure in (2.9) is determined only up to a constant.

2.3 Non-Viscous Fluid

Model residual fluid, usually unsuccessfully called "ideal," gives excellent results in the conditions when the energy dissipation (transition mechanical energy into heat) is insignificant, and the main phenomena are related to the inertial forces and the forces of pressure. Inadequcy of the term "perfect" that any mathematical model of fluid in a sense, is ideal.

In residual fluid vector stresses $\boldsymbol{\sigma}_{\mathrm{n}}$ collinear to the vector $\boldsymbol{n}$, normal to the surface Ω in areas where the vector exists, i.e. outside of singular points. This means that at any place, at any point, except for the singular, the instantaneous value of the tangent stress is always zero, and the value of the normal stress does not depend on the orientation of the area. The stress tensor has the ball form.

Believing all off-diagonal components of the tensor $\{\sigma_{kj}\}$ are equal to zero, we obtain instead of (2.6) and (2.9):

$$\partial \mathbf{U}/\partial \mathrm{t} + (\mathbf{U}\nabla)\mathbf{U} = -1/\rho \text{ grad P} + \mathbf{F} \quad (2.18)$$

If you enter the rotor (vortex) velocity rot $\mathbf{U}=\nabla\times\mathbf{U}$, the left part of (2.18) can be converted emitting terms that explicitly depend on vorticity currents:

$$\partial \mathbf{U}/\partial \mathrm{t} + \text{grad } \mathrm{U}^2/2 - \mathbf{U}\times\mathrm{rot}\mathbf{U} = \mathbf{F} - 1/\rho \text{ grad P} \quad (2.19)$$

The use of a calculation of the rotor to (2.19) increases its order, i.e., complicates the formulation of boundary value problems, and allows you to more clearly show the properties of the rotor velocity:

$$\frac{\partial rot\boldsymbol{U}}{\partial t} - \left(\mathrm{rot}\,\boldsymbol{U}\nabla\right)\boldsymbol{U} + \mathrm{div}\,\boldsymbol{U}\,\mathrm{rot}\,\boldsymbol{U} = \mathrm{rot}\,\boldsymbol{F} + \frac{1}{\rho^2}\mathrm{grad}\,\rho\times\mathrm{grad}\,P \quad (2.20)$$

In the case of a barotropic fluid when its density depends only on the pressure:

$$\rho = \rho(P) \quad (2.21)$$

vectors *grad* ρ and *grad* P are collinear, so the last term in the right part of (2.20) vanishes.

If mass forces have the potential f:

$$\mathbf{F}=\text{grad}\, f \tag{2.22}$$

as, for example, the force of gravity, for which:

$$f= -gx_2 \tag{2.23}$$

where x_2 is the vertical coordinate (positive up), (2.19) it is convenient to write in the Lamb form:

$$\frac{\partial U}{\partial t}+\text{rot}U\times U=\text{grad}\, H$$

$$H=U^2/2+P/\rho - f \tag{2.24}$$

If, in addition, a field of velocities in some area of flow has the potential φ, i.e.

$$\boldsymbol{U}= \text{grad}\ \varphi \tag{2.25}$$

then in this area

$$\text{rot}\ \boldsymbol{U}=0 \tag{2.26}$$

and the solution of the equation (2.24) can be recorded immediately in the form of the Cauchy - Lagrange integral:

$$\frac{\partial\varphi}{\partial t}+\frac{1}{2}|\,\text{grad}\,\varphi|^2+\frac{P}{\rho}-f=A(t) \tag{2.27}$$

where the function $A(t)$ is determined from the boundary conditions. In the stationary case of (2.24), we obtain the famous Bernoulli equation, valid not only for potential flow:

$$U^2/2+P/\rho - f=\text{const} \tag{2.28}$$

Dropping fluids usually cannot be barotropic - change in their density is associated with a change in temperature or the content of impurities (e.g. salinity). For this case it is convenient to use the representation (2.19), which is subject to the conditions (2.22), (2.23) and the identities of:

$$\rho\text{grad}f=\text{grad}\rho(f+f_0)-(f+f_0)\text{grad}\rho \tag{2.29}$$

takes the following form:

$$\frac{\partial U}{\partial t}+(U\nabla)U=-\frac{1}{\rho}\text{grad}\,P-\frac{1}{\rho}\text{grad}\,\rho g\left(x_2+x_{20}\right)$$
$$+\frac{gc\left(x_2+x_{20}\right)}{\rho}\text{grad}\,\rho \qquad (2.30)$$

This equation must be completed with the transfer equation of heat or particles, similar to (2.2), but with the additional term, taking into account the molecular transfer of substances:

$$\frac{\partial c}{\partial t}+U_i\frac{\partial c}{\partial x_i}=v_c\Delta c \qquad (2.31)$$

Here V_c is the coefficient characterizing the molecular heat transfer, if c denotes the temperature T, or transfer of a substance, if c denotes the concentration of this substance: $v_c = a$ (a – is the thermal conducticity), or $v_C = D$ (D is the diffusion coefficient).

Applying the similarity transformation to the equation (2.18) with the conditions (2.22) and (2.23), we find the following criteria, supplementing the system (2.12) – (2.17):

$$\pi_{ij}=\frac{U_{0i}U_{0j}}{l_{0j}}\frac{l_0}{U_0^2} \qquad (2.32)$$

the Froude number

$$\text{Fr}=U_0^2/(gh_0) \qquad (2.33)$$

the density Froude number

$$Fr_{\Delta\rho}=\frac{U_0^2}{gh_0\Delta\rho_0/\rho_0} \qquad (2.34)$$

Here h_0 characteristic depth. If as a benchmark figure to take not velocity, and the characteristic velocity gradient $(\partial U/\partial x_2)_0$, then instead of (2.34), we obtain the gradient Richardson number

$$\mathrm{Ri} = -g\,(\partial \rho/\partial x_2)/\rho_0(\partial U/\partial x_2)^2{}_0 \tag{2.35}$$

Applying the similarity transformation to the equation (save) substance (2.31), we obtain new criteria

$$\pi_c = v_c/(U_0 l_0) \tag{2.36}$$

taking into account the processes of molecular transfer of the considered substance.

2.4 Viscous Fluid

The simplest model of a dissipative course, accompanied by loss of mechanical energy of a fluid is the Newtonian model of a viscous fluid. In this case, the stress tensor $\{\sigma_{ij}\}$ is assumed to be a linear function from tensor of deformation $\{l_{ij}\}$:

$$\{\sigma_{ij}\} = (-P - \mu_1 div\mathbf{U})\{I\} + 2\mu\{l_{ij}\} \tag{2.37}$$

Here $\{I\}$ is the unit tensor; μ - dynamic viscosity; μ_1 - a parameter with the dimensions of viscosity.

Opening the designation of the strain rate, we can rewrite (2.37) in the following form:

$$\begin{aligned} \sigma_{ii} &= -P - \mu_1\, divU + 2\mu\, \partial U_i / \partial x_i; \\ \sigma_{ij} &= \mu\left(\partial U_i / \partial x_j + dU_j / \partial x_i\right),\ i \neq j. \end{aligned} \tag{2.38}$$

From (2.38) shows that in a viscous compressible fluid average normal stress and pressure are not the same:

$$-1/3(\sigma_{11} + \sigma_{22} + \sigma_{33}) = P + (\mu_1 - 2/3\mu)\mathrm{div}\mathbf{U} \tag{2.39}$$

This match can be achieved by putting

$$\mu_1 = 2/3\mu \tag{2.40}$$

In general, it is more logical to introduce another parameter of the model - the second viscosity equal to or magnitude μ_1, or $\mu_1 - 2/3\mu$. In problems of hydraulics this question does not arise, as almost always the water can be considered incompressible, i.e. to take

$$\text{div}\mathbf{U} = 0 \tag{2.41}$$

The use of hypotheses (2.38), (2.40) when μ=const leads to the Navier-Stokes equations:

$$\frac{\partial \boldsymbol{U}}{\partial t} + (U\nabla)\boldsymbol{U} = F - \frac{1}{\rho}\text{grad}\,P + \nu(\nabla\nabla)\boldsymbol{U} + \frac{\nu}{3}\text{grad}\,\text{div}\,\boldsymbol{U} \tag{2.42}$$

where $\nu = \mu/\rho$ is the kinematic viscosity.

For viscous fluid it is useful to consider the equation of energy balance. Calculate scalar vector of external forces acting on particles in the selected volume, and the vectors of stresses acting on the surface, fixing the amount allocated by the velocity of the fluid at appropriate points, we get the equation of conservation of pulses equation changes of mechanical energy:

$$\int_t^{t+dt}\int_W FUdWdt + \int_t^{t+dt}\int_\Omega \frac{1}{\rho}\sigma_n Ud\Omega = \int_W d\left(\frac{U^2}{2}\right)dW + \int_t^{t+dt}\int_W \varepsilon\, dW\, dt \tag{2.43}$$

where

$$\varepsilon = \sum\sum \frac{1}{\rho}\sigma_{ij}\frac{\partial U_i}{\partial x_j} \tag{2.44}$$

Obviously, ε is the meaning of the dissipation rate (care) of mechanical energy from the selected individual volume. In a continuous flow of residual fluids

$$\varepsilon \equiv 0. \tag{2.45}$$

In the flow of a viscous incompressible fluid

$$\varepsilon = \frac{\nu}{2}\sum\sum\left(\frac{\partial U_i}{\partial x_j} + \frac{\partial U_j}{\partial x_i}\right)^2 \tag{2.46}$$

Applying the similarity to the Navier-Stokes equations (2.42) provides one additional criterion of similarity – the Reynolds number:

$$Re=U_0 l_0/\nu \tag{2.47}$$

Of course, the form of this criterion depends on the choice of the base units. If, for example, as a benchmark figure we take the rate of energy dissipation $\boldsymbol{\varepsilon}_0$ and velocity $\boldsymbol{U}_0$ or $\boldsymbol{\varepsilon}_0$ and length $\boldsymbol{l}_0$, the Reynolds number will accordingly become modified in following form:

$$\mathrm{Re}_{\varepsilon,U} = U_0^2 \Big/ \sqrt{\nu \varepsilon_0} \tag{2.48}$$

$$\mathrm{Re}_{\varepsilon,l} = l_0^2 \sqrt{\varepsilon_0} \Big/ \nu^{3/2} \tag{2.49}$$

Writing (2.47), (2.48) associated with the choice of coordinate system, and recording (2.49) implies the presence of the characteristic linear scale, which is also associated with a specific boundary value problem. As a base, to take gradient characteristics of the velocity field, you can construct a new number that is not associated directly with the parameters boundary value problem:

$$\mathrm{Re}_{\varepsilon} = \frac{\varepsilon_0^{5/2}}{|\operatorname{grad} \varepsilon|_0^2 \ \nu^{3/2}} \text{ or } \mathrm{Re}_{\mathrm{rot}U} = \frac{|\,rot\,U\,|^3}{|\,rot\,rot\,U\,|^2\ \nu} \tag{2.50}$$

In practice, we often have to deal with non-Newtonian fluids (sand, grain, fluid concrete, slag, coal, concentrated slurry), for which the relation (2.37) is not running or is under some additional restrictions. The most important physical constraint is the emergence of a state of fluidity (the "other status" [47]). These environments are characterized by three qualitatively different states:

limitless when under the influence of the external system of forces, the deformation environment close to the elastic;

limited when in an environment with plastic, permanent deformation, but the velocity of deformation at fixed impacts are considered to be equal to zero; beyond when the deformation is not stabilized and flow occurs.

In the simplest model of such a medium condition of occurrence of the limiting state associated with the critical shear stress $\tau=\tau_c$ on a fixed platform (F.N.Shvedov,1889; Bingham, 1916):

$$dU/dt=0 \text{ при } \tau<\tau_c;$$

$$dU/dt = 1/\mu(\tau - \tau_c) \text{ for } \tau > \tau_c \tag{2.50}$$

Experimental data show, however, that for many materials τ_c is not a parameter environment, and essentially depends on the normal stresses acting on the site. In the general case, the limit state is a complex function of the stress tensor and the parameters characterizing the state of the environment. The most simple conditions, which are in good agreement with the experimental data for granular media in the conditions of plane strain, is a condition limiting state in the form of a law More - Coulon:

$$\tau_c = C - \sigma_n tg\varphi, \tag{2.52}$$

where τ_c - critical stress on some site; σ_n - normal stress at this site (positive tensile); C - adhesion of the material; φ is the angle of internal friction.

In the development of model Shvedov - Bingham in [37] it is suggested to consider the full stress tensor $\{\sigma^{\Sigma}_{ij}\}$ in the environment as a sum of two tensors:

$$\{\sigma^{\Sigma}_{ij}\} = \{\sigma^{1}_{ij}\} + \{\sigma_{ij}\} \tag{2.53}$$

The components of the first tensor $\{\sigma^{1}_{ij}\}$ satisfy the condition limiting state, for example (2.52). The components of the second tensor accepted linearly related to the tensor of strain rate dependency (2.37).

In the analysis of the system of equations corresponding to this model, obtained for the two-dimensional case with some additional hypotheses, additional similarity criteria when selecting the underlying values U_0 and l_0 take the following form:

$$\pi = Cl_0/(\mu U_0) \tag{2.54}$$

$$\pi_{\varphi} = tg\varphi \tag{2.55}$$

Non-Newtonian fluid properties may appear and be counted in various models. Here we will specify only two simplest flow ratios that take into account the elastic properties of a fluid and the delay local reaction environment on the local action of the load [6, 37]:

model Feuchte

$$\{\sigma'_{ij}\} = G\{\gamma\} + \mu(\partial/\partial t)\{\gamma\} \tag{2.56}$$

model Maxwell

$$(\partial/\partial t)\{\gamma\} = (1/G)\,\partial/\partial t\,\{\sigma'_{ij}\} + (1/\mu)\,\{\sigma_{ij}\} \tag{2.57}$$

Here $\{\sigma\rangle_{ij}\}$ is the deviator of the stress; $\{\gamma\}$- deviator relative deformations; μ and G - environment settings. Although the models (2.56) and (2.57) are qualitatively different - the first is close to the viscoelastic "solid" body, the second - of a viscoelastic fluid, both of them are set one additional option - some relaxation time t_0. Using this option, you can make two criteria of similarity, including the characteristic size in the direction of changing velocity h_0 or in the direction of flow 1_0 [6]:
the Wassenberg criterion

$$\text{We}i=t_0U_0/h_0; \tag{2.58}$$

the Deborah criterion

$$\text{De}=t_0U_0/l_0 \tag{2.59}$$

Non-Newtonian fluid properties and criteria (2.58), (2.59) significant in the study of trends in the boundary layer in the presence of polymer additives.

Navier-Stokes equations, usually used to obtain criteria for the similarity, if $\nu \to 0$ pass in the known equations of the "ideal" of a fluid, solution of which, naturally, does not depend on the Reynolds criterion. The difference of these two systems of equations describing the motions of viscous and discrepancy ("perfect") fluids, is due not so much to a difference in equations, but to the difference of the task. No slippage on solid can the border obtain without the introduction of viscosity.

On the contrary, for a viscous fluid, there is a possible problem statement, without specifying the longitudinal velocity in the circuit (see Section 2.5).

On this basis it is considered that with the increase of Reynolds number the effect of this criterion on the solution of Navier-Stokes equations should weaken Indeed, when a solution of these equations exists and it is stable, this effect takes place [70].

For example, the distribution of radial velocities in the flat confuser runoff in the top corner $2\varphi_0$ with relatively large Reynolds numbers ($\boldsymbol{\varphi_0 Re} = \boldsymbol{\varphi_0 q / \nu > 30}$, $\boldsymbol{q}$ - specific discharge, constant along the length of the confuser) shows that increasingly the Reynolds number is becoming more uniform and is committed to the distribution corresponding to the potential for residual fluid (Figure 2.1).

The decline in the relative influence of the Reynolds number as it increases its value is well illustrated by the graph in Figure 2.2, which shows the change in the relative section length unseparated by a viscous fluid in a cone with a uniform velocity distribution in the initial section [70]. The same conclusion can be drawn by changing the length of the zone

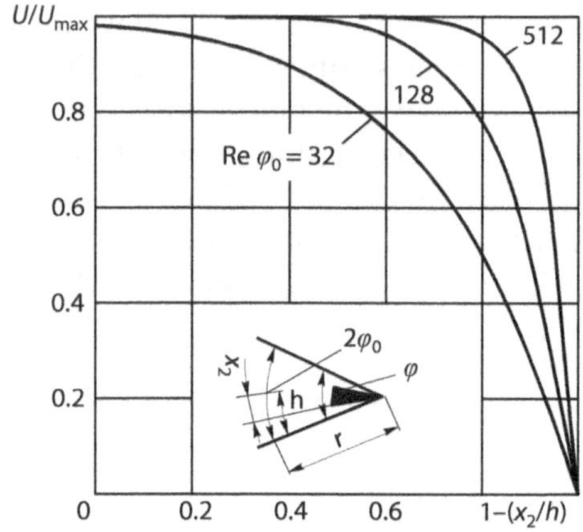

Figure 2.1 The velocity distribution in a flat confuser run off in the top at various values of the Re number.

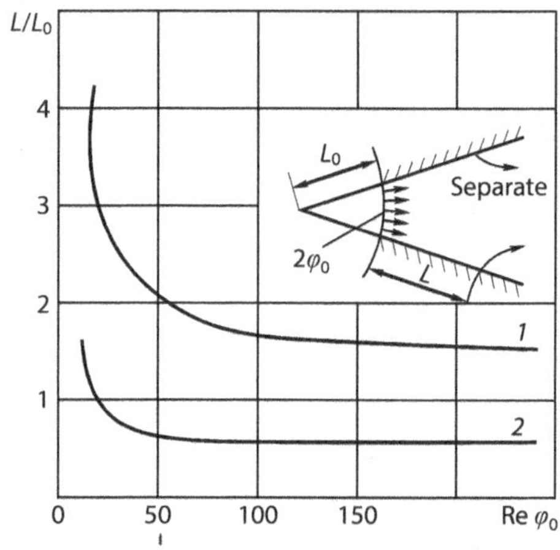

Figure 2.2 The relative length of unseparated trends in diffusers in uniform the velocity distribution in the initial section ($Re= U_0 l_0/\nu$) [143]: 1-flat cone; 2 - cone diffuser.

of separation in the scheme of separated flow past sphere flow of a viscous fluid [220] (Figure 2.3).

It should be noted, however, that this weakening of the influence of the Reynolds number with the growth of its values for deterministic solutions of the Navier-Stokes equations is by no means a constant. For example, it is known [70], that divergent flow in a flat cone with a source in the top of it is possible only for small values of the Reynolds number:

$$Re<(3\pi^2/\varphi_0-12\varphi_0) \quad (2.60)$$

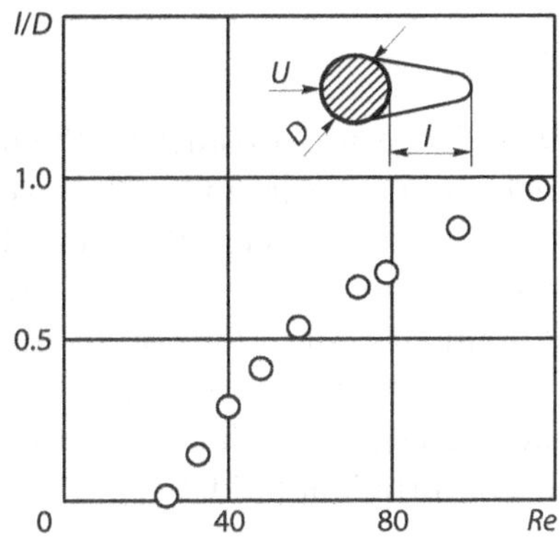

Figure 2.3 The length of the whirlpool areas for field at various Reynolds numbers *Re= UD/v*.

For large Reynolds numbers, part of the cross section of the diffuser is occupied by return currents. Depending on ***Re,*** reverse currents can be one, and include both walls of the diffuser and in its middle part. Such "layered" flow with large velocity gradient is particularly unstable, so that their implementation in practice is hardly feasible. In diffusers with values of the Reynolds number, the larger right side (2.60), apparently, becomes turbulent, and it is important to emphasize that in this example, the influence of the Reynolds number increases rather than decreases.

Self-similarity criterion of Reynolds for deterministic solutions of the Navier-Stokes equations is observed at a very low Re. For example, if Re<1, the velocity distribution in the confuser and the diffuser is given to a single formula, independent of the Reynolds number [70].

The distribution of the velocities corresponding to the Navier-Stokes equations, in some cases formally can use completely self-similar criterion of Reynolds. This distribution, for example, takes place for the flow in a cylindrical pipe, flat channel, the gap between rotating coaxial cylinders [70]. Self-similar distribution of velocities in these cases actually observed only to some (critical) values of the Reynolds number Re_{cr}.

For large Reynolds numbers comes stationary flow, the distribution of averaged velocities in which differs significantly from these "self-similar solutions that explain the instability of stationary solutions of the Navier-Stokes equations [108] and the onset of turbulence.

Instability of stationary solutions of the equations of non-Newtonian fluid is practically not investigated. One can assume, however, that the phenomenon of turbulence in non-Newtonian fluids it is possible and quite widespread.

2.5 Turbulence

The main features of turbulence are, considering the mixing random character of change of velocity and pressure in the flow, vorticity and high dissipativity of a turbulent flow (jump energy flows into heat).

The presence of turbulence means that the repetition of the movement under the same initial boundary conditions of the instantaneous values of velocity and pressure at the same time will be different. You can mark two possible reasons for such behavior of solutions of the Navier-Stokes equations, reflecting features of turbulent fluid motion:

1. instability of stationary solutions;
2. the non-uniqueness of non-stationary solutions.

In the first case, it would seem, you can specify a prescription deterministic solution description - for this you need to expand the number of dimensions of the investigated area, i.e. to enter into the equation of time and initial conditions, and the loss of stability described. Indeed, such an approach proposed by L. D. Landau (1944), helps the understanding of the origin of turbulence. However, the developed turbulence is more complicated. The difficulty lies primarily in the fact that the stationary solution of the problem can be susceptible to stationary perturbations. For example, a small deviation of actual rough surface from the smooth contour in case of large Reynolds numbers can increase the stationary "oscillations" along the border.

It can be shown that the instability of stationary solutions do not lead to the complex and distinct picture of instantaneous States, which is observed in turbulent flow at high Reynolds numbers. This figure giving the turbulent flow the specificity of the space-time random fields connected with the non-uniqueness of non-stationary solutions of the Navier-Stokes equations. In most cases, the mechanism of turbulence seems so: due to the instability of stationary solutions of random spatial or time-space perturbations grow for some time $t \leq t_0$, while remaining clearly and continuously dependent on the initial perturbations, and at the moment $t_1 > t_0$ begins the non-uniqueness of solutions. Source indignation chooses for the further development of the branch solutions, obeying probably accident or some variational principle like the principle of the minimum (or maximum?) energy dissipation.

Such principles were proposed [10, 79] however, most recently in connection with the discovery and study of the "strange attractors" as if it is established that the dynamic system can generate a pseudo-random function of time without the introduction of random initial data or casual external actions [109]. The coincidence of these functions shows that the correlation function of the parameters of motion of decay is infinity. The determinism of the decision is kept in the fact that the result is repeated regardless of the number of the calculation.

On the selected line where the solution lies waiting for a new point of branch, etc., it is proven that the first interval (0, t_0) only exists when the proper solutions of non-stationary problems decrease with the increasing Reynolds number. Looking at every point of branch as a start, this conclusion can be extended to all other interval [t_0,t_1), [t_1 t_2) and so on Thus, for large Reynolds numbers of the stationary flow caused by instability of stationary mode, relatively quickly loses touch with the initial perturbation and "bumping" on a branch point, will develop according to their domestic laws, forming a custom implementation of the random field of turbulence. The behavior of the solution in this case is similar to the behavior of the gas molecules, continually faced with the neighbor. Analog of the mean interval free path in this case will probably be internal (Taylor) turbulence scale, characterizing the average interval of time during which the velocity is changed by about u' and pulse component $\boldsymbol{u}$:

$$\lambda_t = u' / \left(\frac{\partial u}{\partial t}\right)' \tag{2.61}$$

The value λ_t decreases with increasing Reynolds number.

From the positions of modeling, the most important consequence set out is that the turbulent motion of the Navier-Stokes equation and the continuity in the traditional form cannot be used to evaluate the role of the Reynolds criterion, i.e., the Navier-Stokes equations and continuity is not enough to describe turbulent flow, although any of the spatial-temporal distribution of the velocity and pressure in the flow must satisfy these equations. For large values of the Reynolds number and the given initial and boundary conditions of the Navier-Stokes equations together with the continuity equation, provide a set of solutions to pick out which of those implemented at the moment is not possible. For practical use of important statistical characteristics of the set of solutions of the characteristics of the turbulent velocity for the analysis of the similarity conditions, it is important to obtain a closed system of equations linking these characteristics.

It is considered that the only adequate way of describing turbulent flow is an introduction to the consideration of the statistical characteristics of the flow. The field of currents is exhaustively described by the task multidimensional (space-time) probability distribution function of values as a component of velocity and pressure [108]. In many practical cases there are sufficient and more simple statistical characteristics of the turbulent flow.

The desire to build a closed system for statistical characteristics of the flow is traditional to modern fluid dynamics. There is, however, another approach developed independently by O. M. Belotserkovsky with employees [13] and V.M Lyatkher with A.N.Militeev [89]. This approach is to construct a closed system of equations and numerical algorithms for parameters of currents, averaged with some spatial and temporal scope, so that some scale is characterized (It should not be confused with the concept of "scale", introduced in Ch.1).

It turns out that the equations for events of different scales can be significantly different. In particular, many practically important problems can be solved on the basis of the difference in analog of the equation residual fluid. The result of the solution of the problem in this formulation is obtained in the form of individual implementations that with proper choice of scale are informative in themselves. Statistical processing of the ensemble of realizations allows us to estimate statistical characteristics of currents in a given scale. This approach appears in practical terms, the most promising, including for the decision of problems of modeling. However, we first consider the traditional approaches.

Applying the operation of the computation of mathematical expectation to the Navier-Stokes equations, we obtained Reynolds equations linking the first moments - average values of the velocity and pressure:

$$\left.\begin{aligned} &\rho\frac{\partial U_i}{\partial t}=\frac{\partial}{\partial x_j}\left[\left\langle\sigma_{ij}\right\rangle-\rho U_iU_j-\rho\left\langle u_iu_j\right\rangle\right];\\ &\frac{\partial U_i}{\partial x_i}=0,\ i,j=1,2,3.\end{aligned}\right\}\qquad(2.62)$$

Here U_i is averaged (by chance) values of the velocity; u_i is the pulsating components; and the angular brackets denote averaging over the odds. Due to the nonlinear Navier-Stokes equations in the view (2.62) there was a second moment of turbulent stress - $\rho<u_iu_j>$.

Navier-Stokes equations can be written in the Lamb form, highlighting pulsation and averaged components of the movement. Using these equations and the operation of averaging (in probability), we find the equations of the implementing ratio (2.62):

$$\frac{\partial \boldsymbol{U}}{\partial t} - U \times \operatorname{rot} U = -\frac{1}{\rho}\operatorname{grad}\left(P + \rho U^2/2\right)$$

$$+\nu \Delta \boldsymbol{U} - \frac{1}{\rho}\operatorname{grad}\left\langle \rho u^2/2\right\rangle + \left\langle u \times \operatorname{rot} u\right\rangle \tag{2.63}$$

This equation for the averaged velocity field is different from the Navier-Stokes equations in the Lamb form for the instantaneous field presence of the last two terms in the right hand side of (2.63) characterizing the more "normal pressure" $<\rho u^2/2>$ and

$\rho<\boldsymbol{u} \times \boldsymbol{rotu}>$ - "shear stress" turbulence.

Together with the continuity equation, the averages retain the same form as for instantaneous values:

$$\operatorname{div}\mathbf{U}=0$$

Equation (2.63) as well as the Reynolds equations form an open-ended system. The problem of closure of the equations that describe the turbulent motion of the fluid is one of the Central problems of modern science.

The simplest approach is to try to close the system of equations for the averaged velocity and pressure without using the information about the parameters of a turbulent flow. In the case of one-dimensional problem, for example, to find uniform flow in a circular pipe or wide channel, this can be done by having generalized hypothesis of Newton introduction of turbulent viscosity

$$-\left\langle u_1 u_2\right\rangle = \nu_\tau \frac{\partial U_1}{\partial x_2}. \tag{2.64}$$

The turbulent viscosity ν_T should not depend on the kinematic viscosity ν, but may depend on the parameters of the field of the averaged velocity and position. The expression (2.64), first published by J. Boussinesque (1877), closes the system of equations so that even in the simplest case, uniform flow in the channel remains an undefined function ν_T. Classical scheme specifying the functions ν_T belongs to L. Prandtl (1925), and T.Karman (1930). It is stated in all textbooks on hydrodynamics and hydraulics, together with the characteristic inaccuracy in the arguments made by its authors. Consider that these arguments are of direct relevance to the method of similarity. In the model L. Prandtl the amplitude of the longitudinal pulsation velocities rightly taken are proportional to the velocity difference in path length of the mixing $\boldsymbol{l}$:

$$u_1 \sim l\frac{\partial U_1}{\partial x_2}. \tag{2.65}$$

The same (by module) is accepted and for control of pulsation velocities, the sign of which is determined from the analysis of the continuity equation,

$$u_2 \sim -u_1 \sim l\frac{\partial U_1}{\partial x_2}. \tag{2.66}$$

Here

$$-\langle u_1 u_2 \rangle = l^2 \frac{\partial U_1}{\partial x_2} \left| \frac{\partial U_1}{\partial x_2} \right| \tag{2.67}$$

and

$$\nu_\tau = l^2 \left| \frac{\partial U_1}{\partial x_2} \right| \tag{2.68}$$

There are inaccuracies in the reasoning of Prandtl, which are that the uneven distribution of the averaged velocity pulsation velocities are not isotropic and hypothesis (2.66) does not correspond to reality. In particular, concerning trends in the boundary layer in wide canals and pipes, the amplitude of the transverse vertical velocity pulsations is practically constant depth of the flow, little changed on the radius of the pipe and on the thickness of the boundary layer at a sufficient distance from the wall). Taking these circumstances into consideration, the ratio of (2.66) should be rewritten in another form:

$$u_3 \sim -\frac{u_1}{\langle |u_1| \rangle} U_*. \tag{2.69}$$

where $U_* = \sqrt{|\tau|_{\max}/\rho}$ is dynamic velocity; $|\tau_{max}|$ is the maximum value averaged over time tangential stresses in the zone of flow. Taking into account (2.69), repeating the reasoning of Prandtl, we get:

$$-\langle u_1 u_2 \rangle = l U_* \frac{\partial U_1}{\partial x_2} \tag{2.70}$$

and

$$\nu_\tau = lU_* \tag{2.71}$$

In the boundary layer from the reasons of dimension may be write:

$$l = \chi x_2 \tag{2.72}$$

Substituting (2.72), (2.68), or (2.71), we obtain significantly different expressions for ν_T, and the expression following from (2.71), at calculations of the distribution of velocities which gives simpler and more accurate results.

Inaccuracy of reasoning by Karman on the internal similarity of turbulent flows can be detected by comparing these arguments with those given in [108]. The typical value of the shear stress is in the scheme of Karman excluded from consideration and thus we exclude parameter U_*. So the only combination of quantities $\partial U_1/\partial x_2$ and $\partial^2 U_1/\partial x^2_2$, defining Karman velocity profile and turbulent friction (at a fixed density), has the form:

$$-\langle u_1 u_2 \rangle = x_0^2 \left(\frac{\partial U_1}{\partial x_2} \right)^4 \bigg/ \left(\frac{\partial^2 U_1}{\partial x^2_2} \right)^2 \tag{2.73}$$

If you include in the analysis U_*, then, repeating the reasoning of Karman, make sure that they lose their uniqueness and one of the expressions for the turbulent viscosity can be:

$$\nu_T = x_0 U_* \left| \frac{\partial U_1}{\partial x_2} \right| \bigg/ \left| \frac{\partial^2 U_1}{\partial x^2_2} \right| \tag{2.74}$$

It is curious that for conditions of boundary layer with constant voltage turbulent friction in thickness introduced amendments do not affect the results. The difference starts to be shown at a variable value of tangential stresses in the flow.

Scalar relation (2.64) cannot be directly generalized to the correlation tensor of turbulent stress and strain rate. A linear relationship between these tensors, similar to the relation (2.64) with a scalar factor ν_T, can be carried out only when selecting "isotropic" part of the tensor of turbulent stresses. Therefore, with the introduction of the linear association between the tensor of turbulent stress tensor and the strain rate, in general the equation still gets characteristics of the turbulence energy of turbulence e for which you want to enter additional hypotheses:

$$e = \sum \langle u_i^2 \rangle / 2;$$

$$\frac{dU_i}{dt} = g_l - \frac{1}{\rho}\frac{\partial}{\partial x_i}\left(P + \frac{2}{3}e\right) + \sum \frac{\partial}{\partial x_l}(\nu + \nu_\tau)\left(\frac{\partial U_i}{\partial x_j} + \frac{\partial U_j}{\partial x_i}\right); \quad (2.75)$$

$$\nu_\tau = \frac{\langle u_i u_j \rangle - \frac{2}{3}e\delta_{ij}}{\frac{\partial U_i}{\partial x_j} + \frac{\partial U_j}{\partial x_i}} \quad (2.76)$$

Thus, only in the particular case, when $\partial e/\partial x_i = 0$ is the specified path, you can try to close the system without the involvement of information about turbulence.

Another approach to the closure of the equations of turbulent flow consists in construction of equations for senior moments of velocity pulsations [A.Friedman – reference in 100].

A variant of this approach is known as the M.D. Millionschikov [105] hypothesis about cuasinormally distribution pulsation velocities in the flow. This hypothesis allows you to associate senior (even) and younger correlation moments of velocity pulsations under formulas just for multivariate normal distributions. The specific use of this approach with the hypothesis of M.D. Millionschikov or without greater difficulties allows formulation of boundary conditions for those senior moments. For isotropic turbulence this hypothesis leads to physically unrealistic results.

A clearer way to construct a closed system of equations on a similar principle is the proposal of A.N. Kolmogorov (1942) about attraction of the energy balance equation turbulence:

$$\frac{\partial}{\partial t}\left\langle \frac{u^2}{2} \right\rangle = -\sum \frac{\partial}{\partial x_j}\left\langle (U_j + u_j)\left(\frac{P}{\rho} + \frac{u^2}{2}\right)\right\rangle$$
$$+\nu \sum \frac{\partial}{\partial x_i} \sum \left\langle u_j \left(\frac{\partial u_i}{\partial x_j} + \frac{\partial u_j}{\partial x_i}\right)\right\rangle - \quad (2.77)$$
$$-\frac{\nu}{2}\sum\sum\left\langle \left(\frac{\partial u_i}{\partial x_j} + \frac{\partial u_j}{\partial x_i}\right)^2 \right\rangle - \sum\sum \frac{\partial U_i}{\partial x_j}\langle u_i u_j \rangle$$

In fact, the hypothesis of A.N. Kolmogorov concerns the presentation of individual members of the equations (2.77) and (2.62) through the energy of turbulence, the typical scale tour of turbulence L and parameters averaged velocity:

$$\left.\begin{aligned} &\nu_\tau = a_1 L\sqrt{e} \\ &\langle u_i p/\rho\rangle + \frac{1}{2}\sum_j \langle u_j^2 u_i\rangle = -a_2 L\sqrt{e}\frac{\partial e}{\partial x_i} \\ &\frac{\nu}{2}\sum\sum\left\langle\left(\frac{\partial u_i}{\partial x_j}+\frac{\partial u_j}{\partial x_i}\right)^2\right\rangle = a_3\frac{e^{3/2}}{L} \end{aligned}\right\} \tag{2.78}$$

where a_1, a_2, a_3 - some universal dimensionless constants.

The advantage of introducing the new variable L, which has the sense of the scale of the energy carrier part of turbulence, is that this value at different points of the flow at the turbulent should depend on the Reynolds number being less than any other option turbulence. The value of L should be determined mainly by outlines of boundaries of the flow most affecting the low-frequency part of the spectrum [84].

Thus, the system of equations describing the averaged velocity field and pressures in turbulent flow might look like this:

$$\left.\begin{aligned} &\frac{dU_i}{dt} = g_i - \frac{1}{\rho}\frac{\partial}{\partial x_j}\left(P+\frac{2}{3}e\right) + \sum_j \frac{\partial}{\partial x_j}\left(\nu + a_1 L\sqrt{e}\right)\left(\frac{\partial U_i}{\partial x_j}+\frac{\partial U_j}{\partial x_i}\right); \\ &\mathrm{div}\boldsymbol{U} = 0 \\ &\frac{de}{dt} = \sum\sum a_1 L\sqrt{e}\left(\frac{\partial U_i}{\partial x_j}+\frac{\partial U_j}{\partial x_i}\right)\frac{\partial U_i}{\partial x_j} - \sum\frac{\partial}{\partial x_i}a_2 L\sqrt{e}\frac{\partial e}{\partial x_i} + \nu\sum\frac{\partial^2 e}{\partial^2 x_i} - a_3\frac{e^{3/2}}{L} \end{aligned}\right\} \tag{2.79}$$

This system is closed by job function $L(x_1, x_2, x_3, t)$ or more of the equations for its determination.

Using equations for statistical characteristics of the turbulent flow in the form (2.79) or in a more complex form, although not allowing it to fully close the system, and to evaluate the role of certain criteria in this phenomenon, however, allows on the basis of the experiment, the determination of the overall communication component of turbulence, quantitative hypotheses and rules modeling to check their schematized in the conditions applied to more complicated cases, qualitatively similar to those which were considered.

Experimental studies of the spectra of pulsations velocity in the boundary layer and in the pipes show that for large values of the Reynolds number on a fairly large wave numbers $\kappa_1 > \kappa_1'$ in flow manifest properties of the local isotropy. Hence the conclusion is that turbulent voltage of zero in the isotropic flux in a real course will be determined by the structure of the low-frequency component of pulsations. Moreover, if the experiment will show that in some range of values of the Reynolds number of the boundary wave number κ_1' adjudged to be in an area of inertial balance vortices, in which energy is just passed through the cascade wave numbers and the corresponding spectral density pulsations velocity changes proportionally $\kappa_1^{-5/3}$, it is possible to assert with confidence that the distribution of turbulent stresses in this flow does not depend on the Reynolds number. For example, as shown in Figure 2.4, for points separated from the wall approximately $x_2=0,5h$ in a straight tube of rectangular section with smooth walls, isotropy condition is true when these wave numbers are approximately run with the law "minus five of thirds." Thus, in this case, when $Re=\bar{U}h/v=57\ 000$, the range of turbulent stresses should be concentrated mainly on the wave numbers less than 1,5-2 cm^{-1}, so that the relative importance of turbulent friction $-\langle u_1 u_2\rangle / U^2_*$ will not change with increasing the Reynolds number. This is actually measured in the experiments, not only for the middle layer flow, but also for layers, relatively close to the wall (Figure 2.5). The independence of the main energy carrier of the spectrum of the tangent stress from the Reynolds number even in conditions of smooth flow confirms the above considerations about the scale *L*, which is, thus, only additional geometrical parameter.

The choice of model for closing the description of the turbulent flow is complicated by the fact that the "constants," always present in different models, dependent on the conditions of the task and the models themselves, are effective only for the relatively narrow class of problems. From the standpoint of practice of physical modeling, the greatest uncertainty in the use of these models is a priori unknown parameter dependence,

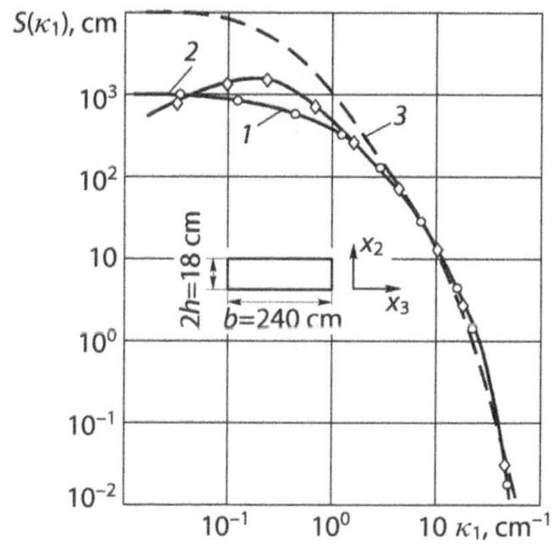

Figure 2.4 Spectrums of cross (1) and lateral (2) of velocity pulsations in the discharge channel in comparison with the calculated (3) measurements of the spectra of longitudinal pulsations in the assumption of isotropy

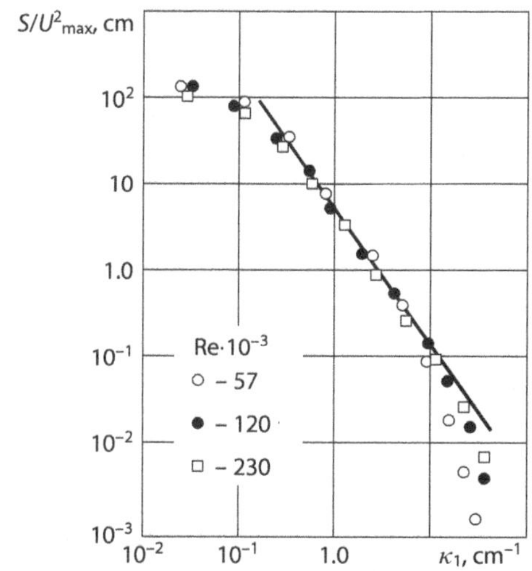

Figure 2.5 Spectral density longitudinal pulsation velocities at different values the number of Re. calculated according to the results of measurements frequency spectra $\kappa_1=\omega/U_1$ in the pressure channel *($x_2/h=0,45$).*

("constants") mathematical models of criteria of similarity, and details of the assignment of boundary conditions, in particular the roughness of the borders. According to the survey [213] 38 models of turbulent flow can be successfully used in various problems of hydraulics. Some of these models will be used below in the analysis of specific problems. Here we will restrict ourselves to the consideration of only the most common models.

The model of turbulent viscosity ν_T, as noted, may not be introduced without increasing the number of unknown functions that you must enter, the energy of turbulence, and another almost unknown function - scale turbulence.

For currents of type of boundary layer, use the effective approximation of the scale of turbulence [54, 100],

$$L/h=\beta_0+\beta_2(x_2/h)^2+\beta_4(x_2/h)^4 \tag{2.80}$$

where

$$\beta_0=0{,}37;\ \beta_2=-0{,}24;\ \beta_4=-0{,}13$$

If the vector Navier-Stokes multiply a scalar separately on pulsation components of the velocity vector in two different locations, the resulting scalar equations folded term by term and averaged by probability will get an equation suitable for the analysis of correlation functions in the flow and, in particular, for the analysis of the integral scale, determined by the correlation function. The transformation of these equations by introduction of additional hypotheses leads to a differential equation for the scale of turbulence and, therefore, to building a closed system for the description of averaged turbulent flow and turbulence energy [40]. Calculations on the obtained equations are considered best in class and give a moderate agreement with the experiment [100]. It is important that this system does not contain new dimensional constants, i.e., does not lead to the emergence of new criteria of similarity. However, from the boundary conditions for this system there are new simplexes similarity characterizing energy ε_0 and scale L_0 turbulent flow in the initial section:

$$\pi_e=e_0/U^2_0;\ \pi_L=L_0/l_0 \tag{2.81}$$

If we neglect the influence of turbulent "pressure" in the equations of conservation of momentum, there is a possible simpler approach - building equations direct subordination to eddy viscosity [100]. The concept of turbulent viscosity in difficult conditions of flow appears very vulnerable - diverters of turbulent stress and strain rate in the general case can be non-coaxial. It is known that non-flows in channels, even if only in one primary direction of the shift of the point where the shear stress and the velocity gradient vanish, can mismatch.

Another serious disadvantage in models of turbulent viscosity, which ν_T is expressed through the energy of turbulence, is a way of reduction of the source of the energy balance equation turbulence. Here are two of the most questionable assumptions:

1. the expression of term, taking into account the energy transfer of turbulence due to the pressure pulsations, through the local characteristics of the flow - second equality in the system (2.78);
2. the expression of the rate of energy dissipation of turbulence through the integral scale of turbulence is the third equality in (2.78).

The incorrectness of the first hypothesis is known. On this issue there are a lot of proposals: A.S. Monin, B. I. Davydov, A. Townsend, J. Lumley, D. Nast, A. Shavit and M. Wolfstein and others (see references in [100]), but acceptable general entries for complicated boundary conditions are not found.

Regarding the second hypothesis (2.78), in recent years, great progress has been made with the so-called two-parameter turbulence model, which for the rate of energy dissipation is issued a separate equation obtained from an equation relative to the rotor velocity pulsation (introducing, of course, additional hypotheses). Taking into account that this model is the most popular in modern literature, let us write it in a simplified form, taking into account, however, possible density heterogeneity currents:

$$\frac{\partial e}{\partial t}+U_j\frac{\partial e}{\partial x_j}=\frac{\partial}{\partial x_j}\left[\left(\frac{\nu_\tau}{a}+\nu\right)\frac{\partial e}{\partial x_j}+\right.$$
$$\left.+\underbrace{\nu_\tau\left(\frac{\partial U_i}{\partial x_j}+\frac{\partial U_j}{\partial x_i}\right)\frac{\partial U_i}{\partial x_j}}_{\Pi}+\underbrace{\beta_c g_j\frac{\nu_\tau}{a_e}\frac{\partial e}{\partial x_j}}_{G}-\varepsilon\right]; \tag{2.82}$$

$$\frac{\partial e}{\partial t}+U_j\frac{\partial e}{\partial x_j}=\frac{\partial}{\partial x_j}\left(\frac{\nu_\tau}{a_\varepsilon}+\frac{\partial e}{\partial x_j}\right)$$
$$a_{1\varepsilon}\frac{\varepsilon}{e}(\Pi+G)(1+a_{3\varepsilon}Ri)-a_{2\varepsilon}\frac{\varepsilon^2}{e}. \tag{2.83}$$

Here:

$$\nu_\tau = a_\nu e^2/\varepsilon \tag{2.84}$$

ν_τ is still turbulent viscosity; Π is the rate of generation of energy of turbulence due to the work of turbulent stresses in the field gradients averaged rate; G is the same at the expense of forces of buoyancy caused by a temperature difference $(c=T)$ or concentrations $(c=c)$ of sediments carried by the coefficient of the β_c rate of dissipation of energy of turbulence; on repeated indices is the summation. Parameters a_k are empirical "universal" dimensionless constants. The versatility of these constants, of course, is relative. Their study in different conditions is the main subject of the hydraulic experiment. In fact, these "constants" there are new similarity criteria, which values to experience the unknown. Some constants have already received their names: a_c is Prandtl number, c if the temperature; a_c is number Schmidt, if c is the concentration of the admixture.

Regardless of equations (2.82), (2.83), and formally completing the system of equations, Reynolds (2.63) with Boussinesque hypothesis (2.76), the value of this circuit should be clarified from the comparison with experiments. [213] provides links to 15 experimental works with different schemes of the currents that have confirmed the feasibility of views (2.82) - (2.84). The generalization of these experiments, mostly related to trends in the boundary layers and jets, gives [192]:

$$a_\nu = 0{,}99;\ a_e = 1;\ a_\delta = 1{,}3;\ a_{1\varepsilon} = 1{,}44 \div 1{,}55;$$

$$a_{3\varepsilon} = 0{,}8;\ a_{2\varepsilon} = 2(\ 1 - 0{,}3\exp - Re_e^2) \tag{2.85}$$

where

$$Re_e = e^2/\nu\varepsilon$$

Note the variation of constants $\boldsymbol{a_{2\varepsilon}}$ depending on the Reynolds number.

An important addition regarding the values of the constants a_y and the questioning of the community equations (2.82) - (2.84), was done by V. Rodi [213]. It was noted that "constant" a_ν depends on the balance between local production and dissipation of the energy of turbulence. If this ratio is not equal to one, i.e. the important processes of energy transfer turbulence, changing Π/ε from 2.5 to 0.25 a_ν value can be increased a hundred times - from 0.05 to 5. This is not unexpected. It can be argued that due to the very sketchy account of turbulence diffusion and the rate of its dissipation associated with the pulsation pressure, a model is presented that in recent years has been implemented in many numerical programs, and its "universal constant" will require significant adjustments in conditions of significant changes in relations between pulse pressure and zero pulsations velocities. These connections in real engineering problems can be very diverse [84].

Flaws in the model of turbulent viscosity associated with the assumption about the alignment of deviators of turbulent stress and deformation field of the averaged velocity are eliminated in models P. Bradshaw and V.Rodi written directly for turbulent stresses [213]. These models are directly connected with equations of Friedman - Keller. In the wording of the criteria of similarity they add only simplexes (turbulence), representing the ratio of turbulent stresses the square characteristic velocities in the initial section (or at the initial moment in the calculation of nonstationary flows):

$$\pi_{ij} = |<u_i u_j>|_0 / U^2{}_0 \tag{2.86}$$

In any case, closure of a system of equations for average (by chance) fields of velocity and pressure of the resulting system, as a rule, comply with the existence, uniqueness and stability of physically implemented solutions. For example, the turbulent viscosity ν_τ in the Boussinesque model is so great that the Reynolds number is very small:

$$\tilde{R}e_\tau = U_0 L_0 / \nu_\tau \ll 1 \tag{2.87}$$

ensuring a sustainable solution that describes the field averaged velocities. Determining similarity criteria derived from these systems usually form the full set of criteria. The exceptions are the cases when the period as a whole, is unstable or non-unique. An example is the course on the flow with the formation of the rolling waves, the failure of down flow waterworks. For such cases, the question of similarity should be specially considered. With just the instability of the steady currents (there is an opinion that it is implemented, in particular, on the chutes with the rolling waves), the similarity conditions are easy to formulate, having considered the task as nonstationary (demanding similarity initial perturbations). If, however, you find that the observed phenomenon is due to the non-uniqueness of the state of flow, which is reflected in the non-uniqueness of solutions of the corresponding equations, the situation with modeling qualitatively more difficult. However, these phenomena in practice, quite rare,

In [47, 79] V.M.Lyatkher suggests that the maximum stability of turbulent flows is evident not only in the fields of the averaged velocity and pressure, as shown by M.A. Goldshtic [41], but concerns the whole population of the probability characteristics that define a turbulent flow. Putting forward the idea that, in principle, complex mechanical systems, especially systems with continual many degrees of freedom, can be in a random state, not predictable deterministically using only the known fundamental laws of nature. The non-uniqueness of solutions of the equations reflecting these laws in mathematically complete boundary conditions, makes it necessary (and possible) to introduce a new hypotheses, generalizing probabilistic as fundamental laws of mechanics. Such a generalization is suggested [79] following the principle of maximum stability: if the system of equations of conservation together with boundary and initial mathematical conditions fully describe the motion of the system, allowing multiple implementations, the probabilistic characteristics of the ensemble of these realizations as stable is possible – see appendix.

From the perspective of building the system of defining criteria of similarity, justice of this principle leads to the following conclusion: the system of criteria derived from the equations has a unique solution and is complete. The fulfillment of these criteria provides the kind of movements, considered in any detail (of course, in the framework of physical and mathematical schemes).

The ways of closing the system of equations describing turbulent flow, began with the introduction of the probabilistic characteristics of the flow and build empirical or hypothetical relationships between them. Such characteristics are:
average (in probability) of velocity and pressure, the mean values of products of the components of velocity fluctuations and their linear combinations $\langle u_i u_j \rangle, e = \frac{1}{2}\sum \langle u_i^2 \rangle$; the average value of the works of the spatial derivatives of the mean and fluctuating component of velocity

$$\varepsilon = \frac{1}{2}\nu \sum\sum \left\langle \left(\frac{\partial u_i}{\partial x_j} + \frac{\partial u_j}{\partial x_i} \right)^2 \right\rangle \qquad \text{etc.}$$

There is, however, another way, briefly outlined in section 2.1. Theoretical basis of this way is still in the stage of formation [89] though the practical results begin to accumulate very intensively. The idea of the approach is closely connected with the method of similarity, which is widely used in hydrodynamics, and consists in the introduction of various scales with consideration of the same objectives in mind. Formalization of this approach can be achieved by different methods. For isotropic homogeneous turbulence, in which the first statistical moments are not specified, there is a natural introduction of spectral representation in the space of frequencies and wave vectors [108]. Here known outstanding observations L. Richardson and theoretical results A. N. Kolmogorov - A. M. Obukhov, singled inertial interval and determined its main feature - cascading transfer of energy from low-frequency anisotropic areas pulsations in another region of higher frequencies and further to the interval pulsation, where the energy dissipation due to the viscosity of the liquid. It is useful in each turbulent flow to define three systems characteristic scales:

integral:

$$L_{ikj}(x) = \int r_{ik}\left(x, x + e_j \xi\right) d\xi; U_0 \tag{2.88}$$

where e_j – axis opt Ox_j; r_{ik} - the correlation coefficient between i-th and k-th components of velocity at the points x and $x+e_j\xi$:

internal Tailor scales:

$$\lambda_{jk}(x) = u_j' / \left(\frac{\partial u_j}{\partial x_k}\right)'; \left(u_j'\right)_0$$
$$\lambda_i \equiv \lambda_{i_1} = u_i' / \left(\frac{\partial u_i}{\partial x_1}\right)'; \tag{2.89}$$

internal Kolmogorov scales:

$$\eta = \nu^{3/4} \varepsilon^{-1/4}; \ U_\varepsilon = \nu^{1/4} \varepsilon^{1/4} \tag{2.90}$$

At high Reynolds numbers there is a clear stratification systems of vortices, each of which is described by introducing the appropriate scale. The most large-scale anisotropic movements, which determine the transfer of energy from the averaged flow turbulence and, in many cases, the main features of the process of transfer of pollutants, summarizes the introduction of the scale L_{ikj} (Figure 2.6). In particular, the scale, introduced in elementary Prandtl scheme can be identified with L_{112} where axis Ox_1 and Ox_2 are directed along a normal to solid border respectively.

The shape of the spectra in the range of vortices (and wave numbers x_i), which gives the greatest contribution to the variance of the corresponding components, is convenient to generalize with the introduction of the scale λ_{ik}, (Figure 2.7). A locally isotropic flow at a relatively low turbulence intensity (for small fluctuations of the dissipation rate of turbulence

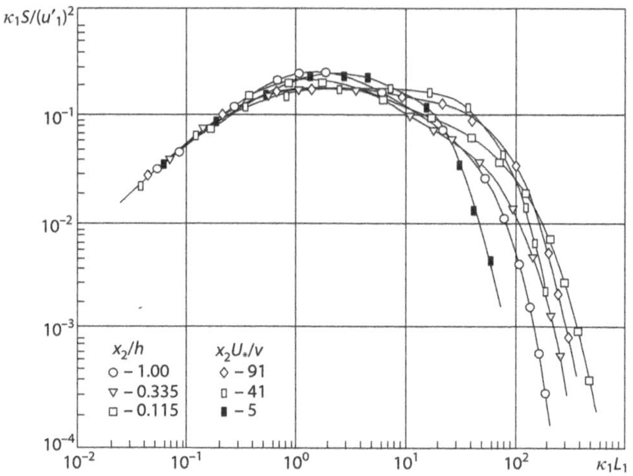

Figure 2.6 The spectral density of the longitudinal velocity pulsations at different distances from the smooth wall in discharge channel at the scale of wave numbers $1/L_1$, $L_1 = L_{111}$ (the radius of the correlation longitudinal pulsations). Re=120000, [67]

energy, $\varepsilon'/\langle\varepsilon\rangle \ll 1$) are summarized in the scale of (2.90). Such conditions are formed only at very large Reynolds numbers $Re_\lambda = u'\lambda/\nu \approx 1000$ and relatively small gradients average rates $\eta/U|\partial U_i/\partial x_k|<1$

For example, in the straight channel with smooth walls at Re=q/v=120000 measurements of the spectra is poorly summarized using scales (2.90) even when $Re_{\lambda 1} = u'_1\lambda_1/\nu = 300 \div 400$ (Figs.2.8, 2.9).

Local isotropy and the law of decreasing of the spectrum proportional to $x_1^{-5/3}$ become clear only when R = 230000 in zones of flow, where $Re_{\lambda 1} > 500$ (Figures 2.10 and 2.11). We note here the common inaccuracy, consisting in the identification of the conditions of locally isotropic flow with the terms of the justice of the "law - 5/3" for spectral component of velocity pulsations. This law is valid only for the specific shape of the flow - in the presence of inertial interval in which there are no other parameters of turbulence, in addition to the rate of energy dissipation. In fact, the class of isotropic and locally isotropic currents is much wider. L.I. Sedov conducted an exhaustive study of self-similar movements of isotropic turbulence, i.e. such movements, the second and third correlation moments which can be considered as functions of the variable from ξ/L, where L is a linear parameter-dependent and time constant parameters that define isotropic for [138]. In particular, L can be associated with Taylor scale turbulence (2.89), and not necessarily with A.N. Kolmogorov (2.90).

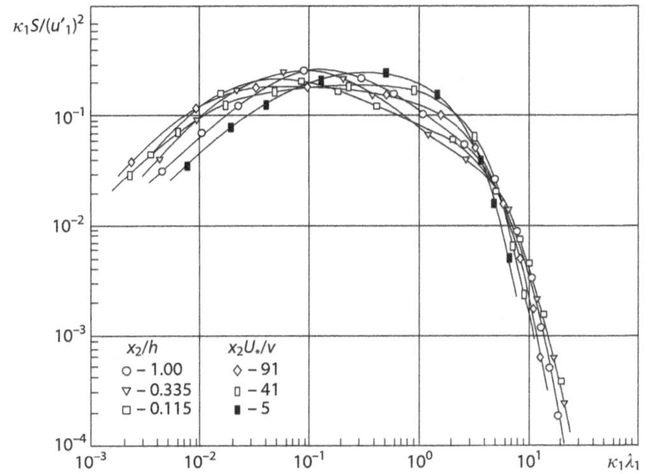

Figure 2.7 The spectral density of the longitudinal velocity pulsations, at different distances from the smooth wall of the pressure in the channel when the scale of the wave numbers $1/\lambda_1$ Re=120000, [67]

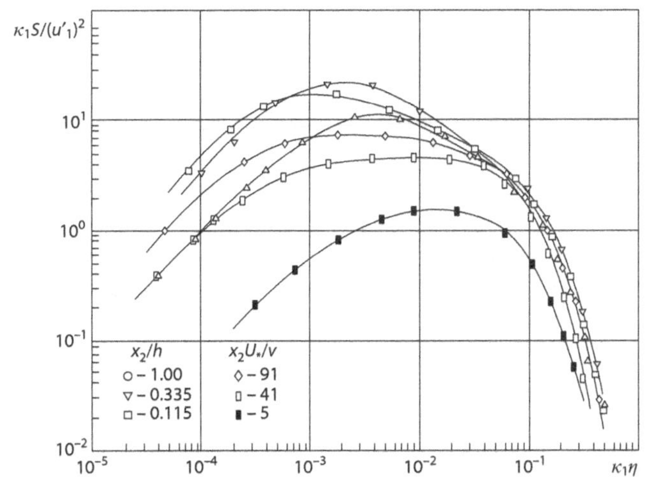

Figure 2.8 The spectral density of the longitudinal velocity pulsations at different distances from the smooth wall in discharge channel at the scale of wave numbers $1/\eta$. Re=120000, [67]

Taking into account the results of L.I. Sedov laws, the "inertial" interval should be considered as important, but a special case of regularities of locally isotropic flow.

The practical importance of this case is that in the presence of the inertial interval in the real spectra of the studied phenomena, there is

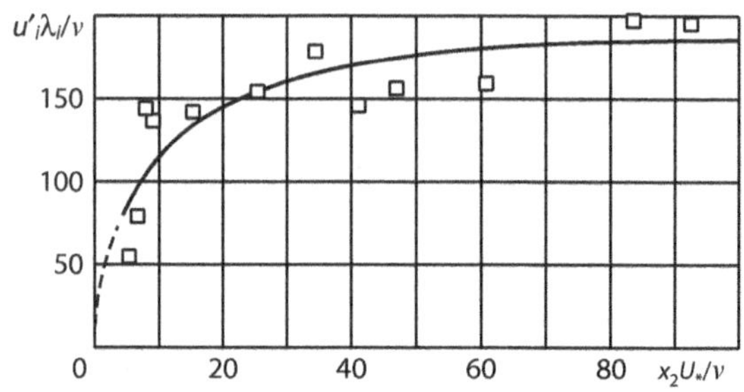

Figure 2.9 The distribution of the sizes of turbulence in the depth of the flow when Re=120000 [67].

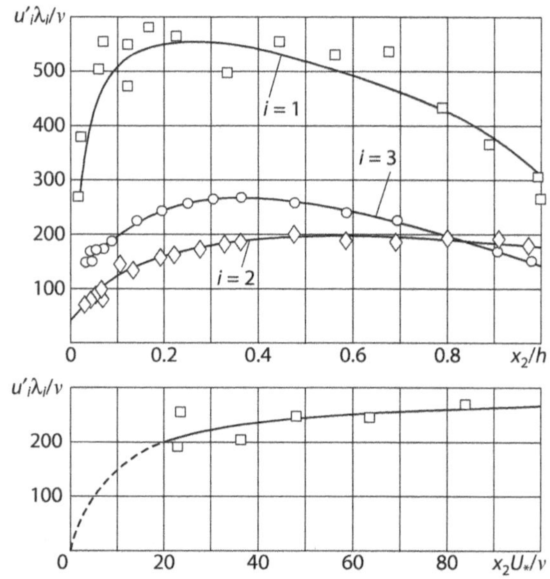

Figure 2.10 Spectrum of longitudinal (1), cross-section (2) and lateral (3) of velocity pulsations in the pressure channel at Re= 230000 (x_2/h =0,45), U_0=42.8 m/s, h=0.09 m and calculation (2) and (3) to (1) the proposal of isotropy (4).

the possibility of distortion of viscous effects (changes in the number of Reynolds) until the moment when this interval will be minimal.

So Figure 2.12, corresponding to the zone of flow in the pipe with the largest local Reynolds number (Re_λ= max), shows that the transition from Re = 230000 to Re = 57000 actually reduces the inertial range (range where parallel lines $\kappa_1^{5/3}$) to zero. This means that when Re<57 000 influence of the Reynolds criterion must be tangible and widespread. This was observed

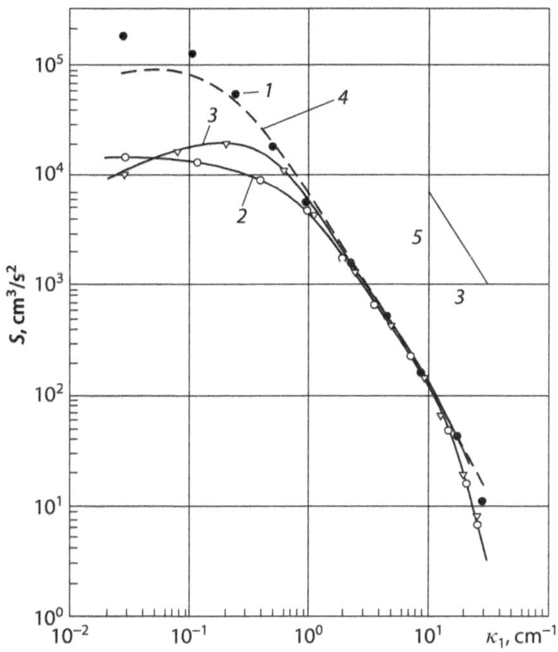

Figure 2.11 Distribution of the scale turbulence in the depth of the flow at Re=230000.

in experiments. It is curious that the inertial range is most striking not on the flow axis, where there are better conditions for isotropy, but at the point $x_2/h = 0{,}335$, where the maximum local Reynolds number $Re_{\lambda 1} = 300$ (Figure 2.13). Thus, viscosity impact on the flow axis is greater than near the wall. The upper bound of the wave number inertial range is determined by the value of Kolmogorov scale:

$$\kappa_1 \eta \approx 0.05 \div 0.08 \tag{2.91}$$

The lower bound is determined by the gradients of the averaged velocity, and if they are small, integral scale of turbulence:

$$\kappa_1 \eta \approx 5 \div 3 \tag{2.92}$$

In the presence of inertial interval change (increase) of scale η through ν within

$$\eta < \eta_{max} = \frac{0.05 \div 0.08}{5 \div 3} L_1, \tag{2.93}$$

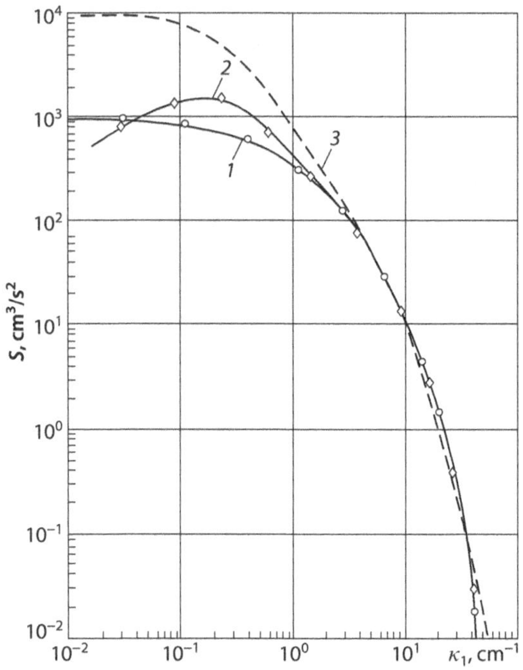

Figure 2.12 Spectra cross (1) and lateral (2) pulsation velocity at Re = 57 000 and calculation of the spectrum of longitudinal pulsations in the assumption of isotropy (3).

Obviously, this should not significantly influence the structure of a turbulent flow, except for a small reduction of dispersion pulsations, determined by the method described in [84].

In connection with the above, it is clear that the study of low-frequency anisotropic velocity field flows with inertial interval in the spectra, can lead, in parameters of currents averaged over an arbitrary space-time scales L_k, to meet the only condition:

$$L_l > L_h > \eta_{max} \tag{2.94}$$

where η_{max} is defined in the field of averaging of flow parameters. This idea is central in the approach developed in [81, 89].

This approach allows us, in particular, to specify requirements to resemble the form of the spectra of pulsations on the model and in kind. It is necessary to provide the sort of shape spectra at:

$$x \leq 1 / L_k \tag{2.95}$$

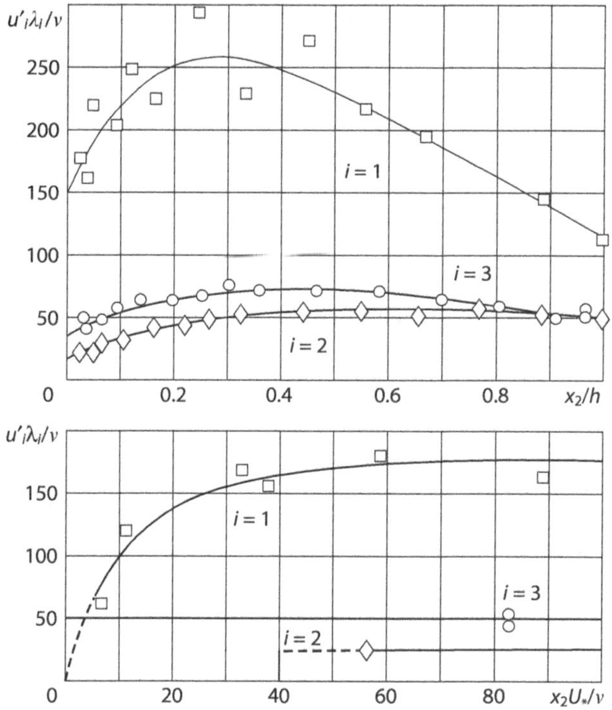

Figure 2.13 The distribution of the sizes of turbulence in the depth of the flow when Re=57000.

and maintaining the cascading process of energy transfer, turbulence, which is controlled by criterion:

$$\pi_e = L_1/\eta_{max} > 30 \div 60 \tag{2.96}$$

If in kind π_e more than this, it is necessary to π_e on the model also was more than a certain number depending on the conditions of flow and determines the presence of inertial range in the spectrum of pulsation.

2.6 Boundary Conditions

Boundary conditions for discharged equations can be quite diverse and are determined by the physical features of the problem under consideration. For example, the boundary of the flow is mobile, but the particles of the fluid do not cross ((impermeable movable boundary). If such an equation of the boundary set

$$\Phi(x, t)=0$$

the normal component of velocity at any point (if grad$\Phi \neq 0$), has the form:

$$U_n = \frac{\frac{\partial \Phi}{\partial t}}{|\operatorname{grad} \Phi|} \tag{2.97}$$

The condition of impermeability (no border crossing particles of fluid) means that

$$\mathbf{U}_\mathrm{n} = \mathbf{U}\frac{\operatorname{grad} \Phi}{|\operatorname{grad} \Phi|} \tag{2.98}$$

Thus, the impermeability condition for the velocity field of the fluid U has the following form:

$$\mathbf{U} \operatorname{grad} \Phi + \frac{\partial \Phi}{\partial t} = 0 \tag{2.99}$$

In particular, if the border is fixed, then $\partial\Phi/\partial t=0$ instead of (2.99), and we get:

$$\mathrm{U}_1 \frac{\partial \Phi}{\partial x_1} + \mathrm{U}_2 \frac{\partial \Phi}{\partial x_2} + \mathrm{U}_3 \frac{\partial \Phi}{\partial x_3} = 0 \tag{2.100}$$

In respect to the tangential velocity component there are various tasks. Some of the considered equations (for example, a model of a viscous fluid) admit the problem with "sticking" of the fluid to the borders, when the rate of border flow and fluid is considered to be the same. Less restrictive condition of the flow "slipping" on boundaries. This condition is usually taken for residual fluid. However, it can be used when more complex rheology environment. For example, Newtonian viscous fluids take on a condition of sliding in the form

$$\mathrm{U}_\mathrm{s} - \{k_1\}\frac{\partial \mathrm{U}_\mathrm{s}}{\partial n} = 0 \tag{2.101}$$

where U_s is projection-difference vector of velocity of the fluid and the velocity of some point smooth boundaries on the plane tangent to the boundary at this point; n is the normal to the boundary at the same point; $\{k_1\}$ is the dimensional boundary value constant.

Numerous proposals to use the same account for turbulent flow can be reduced to three:

$$\{k_1\} = k_m(\Delta) \text{ at } x_2 = \Delta \tag{2.102}$$

$$\{k_1\} = \nu_T + \nu / |U_s| k_b \text{ at } x_2 = 0 \text{ or } x_2 = \Delta \tag{2.103}$$

$$U_s / U_* = f(U_* \Delta/\nu);\ U_s || \tau_0;\ U_* = \sqrt{\tau_0/\rho} \tag{2.104}$$

where Δ is the height of the projection of roughness.

Without dwelling on the review of the well-known proposals (2.102), (V.M Makkaveev, A.V. Karaushev) and (2.103) (A.I. Felzenbaum, T.Simons and others), we note that in many cases anisotropic roughness parameters k_b or k_m can not be considered as scalar functions. A generalization of these hypotheses with the introduction of tensor coefficients is made, just as it is done in the analysis of the plan currents [95].

In accordance with the theme of the book, refer to the considerations of similarity of the underlying records (2.104). Simple considerations underlying the first formula (2.104) are found in one form or another in all modern books on hydraulics. It is alleged that uniformity in length near the boundary of the flow may depend on the "friction velocity" U_*, kinematic viscosity ν and height of the ledge roughness Δ. The only form of the boundary condition can be the first formula (2.104) [(2.102) and (S) are for this formula]. There are even suggestions, based on measurements of Nikuradze that the function $f(U_*\Delta/\nu)$ is universal, but when it reaches full manifestation of roughness this function is constant:

$$U_s / U_* = B \tag{2.105}$$

According to [54] $B = 8{,}5$.

In reality, however, U^*, and Δ are not exhaustive characteristics of the flow near the border. A very important parameter is the fluctuation of the tangent voltage at the wall [85]. Standard and longitudinal range of pulsations of the tangent voltage depending on the spatial characteristics of roughness of the wall can change. In this regard, even in the flow regime with the full manifestation of roughness, "constant" in the right part (2.105) can be significantly different.

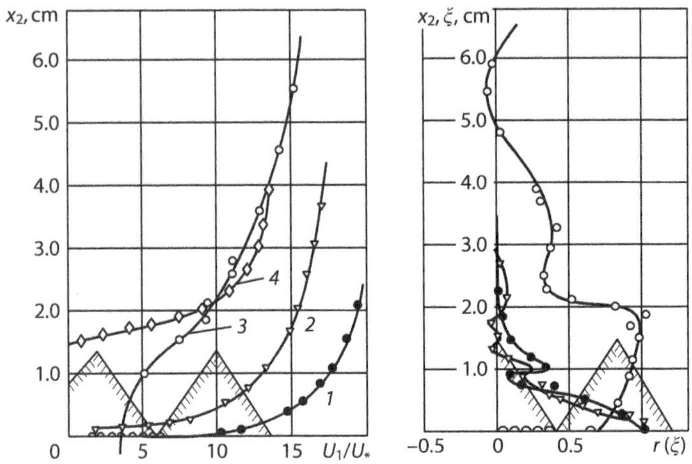

Figure 2.14 The distribution of the averaged velocity (a) and longitudinal correlation pulsation velocities (b) in the flow of water over a smooth (*l*), sand (*2*), semigravel (*3*) base and the crest of roughness (*4*) [25].

Figure 2.14 shows the distribution of averaged (over time and length) velocities in the immediate vicinity of the border of the flow. The measurements were conducted by the electrochemical method [25] using electrodes with a diameter of 0.03 cm wide pressure water flow (ν =0.01cm^2/s).

In one series of experiments the bottom of the tray was glass (line *1*, h_0 = 3.6 cm; U_0=14.5 cm/s; U_* = 0.8 cm/s) and the lower edge is closest to the bottom electrode defended from the bottom 0.02 see the series on the bottom was homogeneous sand average size d_{av}=0.25 cm (curve 2, h = 4.0 cm; U_0=16.6 cm/s; U_*=1.12 cm/s) or gravel d_{av} = 3.0 cm (curve 3, h_0 = 6.5 cm; U_0=25.6 cm/s; {U_* = 2.41 cm/s). Timing distances over rough bottom shows from the middle of the top row of soil particles. Measurements over the gravel averaged 20 vertical separately from the crest and above the valleys of roughness.

Analysis of the plot velocities over a smooth bottom shows that on the border of the turbulent core course and a viscous sublayer (see Section 4.1), determined by the condition δ=(10÷11.6)ν/U_* = 0.125÷1,145 cm, is the ratio U/U_*=12.2÷13, which is not too different from the value of 11.6 adopted in modern hydraulics. On the contrary, over a rough surface relative velocity U/U_* varies in rather wide limits. Between the tabs of the roughness at the level of vertices of the projections ratio (2.105) is about 7, the crest of the fuzz is about 2. On average (by area) this ratio is close to 5.

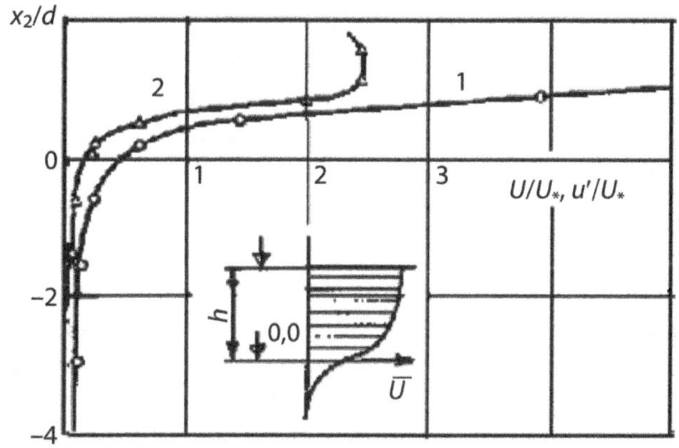

Figure 2.15 The distribution of the averaged velocity (1) and standards longitudinal pulsations (2) on the contact between the water flow (U_*=1.42) cm/s, ν=0.01 cm²/s) and sandy bottom (d_{av} = 0.75 mm, the size of particle in the washed surface layer d=2 mm) [23].

The same result ($U_s/U_{*=}5.6$) was obtained in 1963, I. K. Nikitin [112] by the method of photography. Even earlier, the details of the current over rough bottom were published by B.A. Fiedman [147],

Conditions on the border are complicated when the boundary permeable (for example, the real bottom of the river, folded movable material -Figure 2.15), can deformation or collapse by flow. Similarity criteria here in general should include all dimensional parameters characterizing the state border. However, the formulation of boundary conditions can be different depending on the research objectives.

Description of the flow in the overgrown channel usually does not include the stiffness characteristics of plants, the whole complex picture sets one parameter of roughness, although a detailed study of the phenomenon [88] shows the inadequacy of this approach is the roughness is dependent on the flow rate.

For non-Newtonian fluids a condition of sliding (2.101) can be generalized, for example, in this form:

$$U_s = \{\beta\} \tau_s / \sqrt{\rho \tau_{s,}} \tag{2.106}$$

where τ_s=τ_0-τ_c "overcritical" component shear stress acting on the surface of the border, fluid, τ_s= $|\tau_s|$; $\{\beta\}$ - dimensional scalar or tensor of a special form.

The value τ_s is determined as the difference between the full vector of tangential stresses on the boundary and limit of the vector of the tangent stress corresponding to the condition of flow. The coefficient β, during certain processing experiments with sand and gravel in special units in laboratories and in kind, was quite close to the 0.16-0.20. A detailed study of the phenomena of flow of non-Newtonian fluids near the border section has only just begun.

Modern models of turbulent flow (for example, the e–ε) require the formulation of boundary conditions not only for the averaged velocity, but for the turbulence characteristics. The real-border flow and hypothetical surface on which are put boundary conditions are not always the same - the difference is determined by the properties of mathematical models. For example, the energy flow turbulence e through a sharp line really is equal to zero:

$$\partial e/\partial n = 0 \tag{2.107}$$

However, if the "border" is conducted at the level of the ledge roughness or coincides with the border of a viscous sublayer, it $|\partial e/\partial n|$ may be a maximum (see Section 4.1).

The free boundary of the flow is typically set pressure or the pressure and shear stress, caused for example by wind action. Finding a free surface is, as a rule, included in the research task. Formalization of this part of the problem may be substantially different depending, in particular, on the scale of the studied phenomena. As a rule, the influence of the rheology of fluid at the free surface is minimal. Therefore studying the movements of a medium sized area of the free surface can be an effective and simple model. The presence of a free surface leads to the appearance of the Frude, Euler, Weber criteria (see Section 5.1).

In the calculation of currents in broad, relatively shallow waters and in the boundary layer equation, "scheduled tasks" include shear stresses on the bottom and the surface of a pond [80-83]. Shear stress on the surface of the reservoir is associated with the vector wind velocity over the pond **W**. Shear stress $\boldsymbol{\tau}_i$ at the bottom (averaged probability) is usually considered collinear to the vector average (by probability and depth) flow rate $\boldsymbol{U}_i$.

$$\tau_i = -\frac{\lambda}{2}\rho \mathrm{u}_i\,|\,\mathrm{u}\,|. \tag{2.108}$$

where ρ is the density of the fluid; λ – the coefficient of hydraulic friction, defined typically as a scalar function of the local relative roughness h_s/h

and local Reynolds number is $Re = |u|\, h/\nu$; h the depth of the flow; ν– the kinematic viscosity of the fluid; h_s– height of the projection of roughness.

Relation analogous to (2.108) is written to a surface of a reservoir, but in this case, instead of **U** writing **(W—U)**.

The purpose of this part is to indicate the tensor character of the coefficient of hydraulic friction "planned" problems of hydraulics and consider examples in which considering this circumstance is essential [95]. Tensor generalization record (2.108) is represented in the following form:

$$\tau_j = -\lambda_{ij} u_i \frac{\rho}{2} |u|, \tag{2.109}$$

where τ_j, u_i – are the components tangential stresses on the bottom and average flow velocity in the vertical.

As is known, the proportionality of random vectors in general is possible only when the tensor structure of the coefficient of proportionality. If independent measurements at two, for example, orthogonal directions velocity statistically homogeneous currents known values $\tau_i^{(k)}$ and $u_i^{(k)}$, the components of the tensor λ_{ij} are calculated by solving a system of linear equations corresponding to (2.109), namely:

$$\lambda_{ij} u_i^{(k)} = -\frac{2\tau_j^{(k)}}{\rho |u^{(k)}|} \tag{2.110}$$

When performing the above conditions of orthogonality velocities $\mathbf{U}^{(1)}$ and $\mathbf{U}^{(2)}$ we find in the coordinate system associated with vectors $\mathbf{U}^{(1)}$ and $\mathbf{U}^{(2)}$.

$$\lambda_{ij} = -\frac{2\tau_j^{(i)}}{\rho u_j^{(i)} |u^{(i)}|} \tag{2.111}$$

When $\mathbf{U}^{(1)}$ and $\mathbf{U}^{(2)}$ are not orthogonal, the solution of (2.110) has the following form:

$$\lambda_{ij} = -\frac{\Delta_{ij}}{\Delta} \tag{2.112}$$

where:

$$\Delta = \begin{pmatrix} u_1^{(1)} & u_2^{(1)} & 0 & 0 \\ 0 & 0 & u_1^{(1)} & u_2^{(1)} \\ u_1^{(2)} & u_2^{(2)} & 0 & 0 \\ 0 & 0 & u_1^{(2)} & u_2^{(2)} \end{pmatrix},$$

and the determinant Δ_{ij} is obtained from the determinant Δ replacing the column number $[i\ (i{-}l){+}j]$ in the column:

$$\begin{Bmatrix} 2\tau_1^{(1)} / \rho \,|\, u^{(1)} \,| \\ 2\tau_2^{(1)} / \rho \,|\, u^{(1)} \,| \\ 2\tau_1^{(2)} / \rho \,|\, u^{(2)} \,| \\ 2\tau_2^{(2)} / \rho \,|\, u^{(2)} \,| \end{Bmatrix}$$

Here superscripts indicate the number of measurement, and the lower - coordinate.

The need tensor representation for the coefficient λ will show on the example of three typical situations in the bottom layer of the flow:

I) in the presence of a laminar boundary layer;

II) in the absence of a laminar boundary layer at the bottom roughness with scalar structure;

III) if there is roughness of the bottom with a tensor structure (for the case of a turbulent boundary layer).

Scalar structure of bottom roughness means that averaged (probability) velocity on the border of the bottom layer of δ is collinear with average (by chance) shear stress at the bottom. When there is tensor structure of roughness this collinearity is missing.

In the first two cases shear stress can be considered to be collinear with the "bottom" velocity u_b, measured at the level of border laminar boundary layer (case I) or at the level of the characteristic protrusions roughness (case II), while the tensor character of the coefficient λ is associated with the spectra of the bottom and average depth of velocities.

Case III shows non-collinear shear stress and "bottom" velocity.

As an example, for cases I and II calculate tensor λ_{ij} components within the model of a homogeneous flow on "infinite" turn, considered in

[130,131]. Considering the turbulent viscosity is proportional to the distance z from the bottom $v_\tau = \kappa_0 U.z$, will receive according to [131] formula by which you can express transverse and longitudinal components of the ground velocity u_r and through the components of the average velocity with depth U_ϕ (implicitly through communication U_r and U_ϕ):

$$\frac{u_r}{U_*}\Big|_{z=\delta} \approx \frac{2h}{\kappa_0^2 r}\left\{\sqrt{\frac{2}{\lambda_0}}\left(-\frac{\delta}{h}+\text{In}\frac{\delta}{h}+\frac{3}{2}\right)-\left(\frac{1}{\kappa_0}+\sqrt{\frac{2}{\lambda_0}}\right)\times\right.$$
$$\times\left[\left(\frac{\delta}{h}+1\right)\text{In}\frac{\delta}{h}-2\frac{\delta}{h}+\frac{9}{4}\right]+\frac{1}{2\kappa_0}\left[-\frac{\delta}{h}\left(\text{In}\frac{\delta}{h}\right)^2+\right.$$
$$\left.\left.+\left(4\frac{\delta}{h}+2\right)\text{In}\frac{\delta}{h}-6\frac{\delta}{h}+\frac{25}{4}\right]\right\}, \tag{2.113}$$

$$\frac{u_\cdot}{U_*}\Big|_{z=\delta} \approx \frac{1}{\kappa_0}+\sqrt{\frac{2}{\lambda_0}}+\frac{1}{\kappa_0}\text{In}\ \frac{\delta}{h}; \tag{2.114}$$

For the problem under consideration λ_0 is the coefficient of hydraulic friction in the straight flow with the same physical roughness, depth and average velocity as in the case being considered.

In polar coordinates (r, φ), tensor components λ_{ij} in this example are from the following system of equations:

$$\rho U_*^2 \cos.\text{arctg}\frac{u_r}{u_\varphi}\Big|_{z=\delta} = \lambda_{\varphi\varphi} U_\varphi \frac{\rho}{2}|U|;$$

$$\rho u_*^2 \sin.\text{arctg}\frac{u_r}{u_\varphi}\Big|_{z=\delta} = -\lambda_{\varphi n} U_\varphi \frac{\rho}{2}|U|;$$

$$\lambda_{\varphi\varphi} = 2\left\{\sqrt{\frac{2}{\lambda_0}}+\frac{1}{\kappa_0}.\frac{\text{In}\,h/\delta}{h/\delta-1}\right\}^{-2} \cos\ \text{arctg}\frac{u_r}{u_\varphi}\Big|_{z=\delta}; \tag{2.115-118}$$

$$\lambda_{\varphi r} = -2\left\{\sqrt{\frac{2}{\lambda_0}}+\frac{1}{\kappa_0}.\frac{\text{In}\,h/\delta}{h/\delta-1}\right\}^{-2} \sin\ \text{arctg}\frac{u_r}{u_\varphi}\Big|_{z=\delta};$$

In this case the tensor λ_{ij} has a specific type defined only by two coordinates: λ_{11} and λ_{12}. The other two coordinates can be assigned to any (e.g., zero). This is because the tensor character of the resistance coefficient is determined by the peculiarities of the painting movements, not the physical condition of the rough surface of the bottom. In such cases, there are only two independent parameters to define the relationship between average velocity and shear stress: the angle between the vector and a scalar, which characterizes the ratio of the modules of the bottom and average velocity. Changing the direction of flow in the experiments (saving curvature and other kinematic characteristics), we will not get new information about λ_{ij}

Suppose that for flow you can select the near-wall layer, where the distribution of averaged velocity does not depend on the flow conditions in the rest zone (the core). Then in this case isotropic roughness shear stress is proportional to the velocity u_b on the boundary of the layer:

$$\tau_i = \lambda^b \rho (u_i)_b \,|\, u_b \,|. \tag{2.119}$$

In this case, λ^b is the scalar.

Tensor λ^0_{ij} is determined from the relation between the vectors average and bottom velocity and scalar λ^b:

$$\lambda^b (u_i)_b \,|\, u^b \,| = \lambda^0_{ij} \frac{U_j \,|U|}{2} \tag{2.120}$$

From which:

$$\left[\lambda^0_{ij}\right]^{-1} = \frac{\delta_{ij} U_j \,|U|}{2\lambda^b (u_i)_b \,|\, u_b \,|} \tag{2.121}$$

where $[\lambda^0_{ij}]^{-1}$ is the tensor, inverse λ^0_{ij}; δ_{ij}– is the Kronecker symbol.

Coordinators tensor λ_{ij} in general depends on flow conditions (for example, on the curvature of flow lines). To eliminate this effect, consider again the flow, which can be allocated to the core of current and near-bottom layer. Suppose that the tabs anisotropic roughness is small compared with the thickness of this layer. Then the tensor coefficient of hydraulic friction λ_{ij} is from a system similar to (2.119), (2.120), which, however, λ^b is not a scalar.

In this case it is natural to save the assumption of proportionality tangent voltage module ground velocity with a coefficient of proportionality, which is a function of the vector ground velocity

$$\tau_i = |\mathrm{u}_b| f$$

From the condition of invariance of the vector with respect to a transformation of coordinates, f is the tensor function. Its simplest (linear approximation) –

$$\tau_i = \rho \lambda_{ij} \mathrm{u}_j^{\,b} \, |\mathrm{u}^b| \tag{2.122}$$

When isotropic roughness, as noted above, λ_{ij} degenerates into a scalar λ^b.

Tensor λ_{ij} can degenerate in the scalar also in the case of anisotropic roughness, when τ and u_b are the collinear vectors. This tensor λ_{ij} becomes ball, coordinate of which does not depend on direction.

Here is an example of a roughness of the seabed, for which you need to enter the tensor coefficient of hydraulic friction. Consider in line with specific roughness in the form of alternating furrows and ridges, where along the furrows and ridges the bottom surface is perfectly smooth. In this case, the height of the tabs on 2-3 orders of magnitude less depth, which enables us to count velocity in a layer above the tops of the ridges "bottom." Regardless of the direction, vector of average or near-bottom velocities roughness is "designed" in such a way that it is capable of resisting the only component of the velocity - the normal direction of furrows. For this case the formula can be generalized (2.108) as follows:

$$\tau = -\lambda_n \frac{(\mathrm{Un})\mathrm{n}\,|\mathrm{U}|}{2} \rho \tag{2.123}$$

where λ_n is a scalar coefficient of resistance, which is a function of local relative roughness, h_s/h (h_s is equivalent to the projection of roughness in the direction normal furrow; n = (n_1, n_2) is the unit vector normal to the furrows).

From (2.123) it follows that if the velocity is directed perpendicular to the grooves, the vector τ coincides with the value defined by the formula (2.108); if mutually orthogonal, then it is equal to 0, and the vector τ/[U] linear depends on the velocity vector U.

In matrix form equation (2.123) has the following form:

$$\tau / \rho = -\frac{\lambda_n |\mathrm{U}|}{2} \begin{pmatrix} n_1^2 & n_1 & n_2 \\ n_1 & n_2 & n_2^2 \end{pmatrix} \begin{pmatrix} \mathrm{U}_1 \\ \mathrm{U}_2 \end{pmatrix}. \tag{2.124}$$

The more common case is when friction is present along the furrows, and the equivalent tabs roughness length and breadth of furrows is different. This can be described by the introduction of two scalar drag coefficients:

$$\tau/\rho = -\lambda_n \frac{(Un)n|U|}{2} - \lambda_t \frac{(Ut)t|U|}{2}, \tag{2.125}$$

or

$$\tau/\rho = -\frac{|U|}{2}\begin{pmatrix} \lambda_n n_1^2 + \lambda_t n_2^2 & n_1 n_2(\lambda_n - \lambda_t) \\ n_1 n_2(\lambda_n - \lambda_t) & \lambda_t n_1^2 + \lambda_n n_2^2 \end{pmatrix}\begin{pmatrix} U_1 \\ U_2 \end{pmatrix}, \tag{2.126}$$

where: t=($-n_2$, $-n_1$) is the unit vector of the tangent to the furrow; λ_n and λ_t- scalar resistant coefficient for perpendicular and parallel furrows, respectively. The ledge roughness to identify λ_n and λ_t is taken in the direction of, respectively, the normal and tangential furrows.

Formulas (2.125) and (2.126) go into the formula (2.108) when $\lambda_n = \lambda_t$, and in formulas (2.123), (2.124) when $\lambda_t = 0$.

2.7 Averaging on Space and Time

The account of conservation law in the integral form (Section 2.1) holds for any choice of a volume of space-time coordinate systems. Specifically selecting from this considerable volume can greatly facilitate the task of modeling, although it will reduce the information content of the results of consideration. This has already been discussed in connection with the problem of turbulence and the choice of scale for smoothing (or description) of turbulent pulsations (Section 2.4). Here the issue is considered further:

- averaging over all volume of a river or lake, you can go to "zero-dimensional" tasks (common object hydrology);
- the averaging over "to the living section of the river or canal provides a system of one-dimensional equations;
- the average depth of the flow gives a two-dimensional system of equations ("scheduled task").

In fact, in the last two cases, the averaging is carried out not on the surface and not on the line, and on some volumes, dimensions of which in directions that are stored for research, are small compared with the size in other directions and are chosen depending on specific research objectives, taking into account the considerations set forth in Section 2.4.

Naturally, all three of these cases are described by the equations averaged at some time interval. This smoothing over time is already in transition from the molecular level description of the terms of the continuous medium. In the two-dimensional, non-stationary problems of smoothing naturally lead to a time interval of order:

$$\Delta t_h \geq h_0/U_0 \tag{2.127}$$

where h_0, U_0 is characterized by the depth and flow velocity. In the one-dimensional, non-stationary problems in choosing Δt in the right part (2.127) need not stand the depth of the flow; with uneven distribution of velocities on the width of the flow, effective use of one-dimensional models can be expected by averaging on intervals:

$$\Delta t_b \geq \Omega_0/q_0 \tag{2.128}$$

where Ω_0 and q_0 is a typical cross section of the river and the specific consumption.

In the study of problems in the zero-dimensional, formulation of the unsteady makes sense to look at the scale of large residence time of water in the reservoir, i.e. useful-figuratively averaging of conduct on intervals:

$$\Delta t_W \geq W_0/Q_0 \tag{2.129}$$

Here already W_0, Q_0 is the typical volume element of the system and water consumption. When moving from non-stationary flow to the "equivalent" fixed period of averaging and evaluation of possible errors naturally lead (most of the time) to intervals determined by the equality (2.129).

In the zero-dimensional problems, spatial coordinates do not appear. The working tool of this approach is the balance equation applied to the elements of the system as a whole.

The efficiency of one-dimensional tasks depends on the art of correct choice of the scheme of averaging of flow parameters. In many-dimensional problems it is useful to consider separately the channel from flood flows, etc. One-Dimensional tasks that make up a traditional part of hydraulics help with minimal detail to specify the forecast parameters of currents and water quality in space. These objectives are often solved by using physical modeling.

Significantly more complete information is sufficient in most practical problems, obtained by averaging the true picture of one of the spatial coordinates. Until very recently, these tasks were solved mainly with physical models.

In some cases, you need a complete solution of hydrodynamic tasks and determination of space-time stochastic flow patterns, which currently can only be done on the physical models or in kind.

One-dimensional equations for the wave uneven flow were withdrawn by A. Saint-Venant; for real rivers, taking into account the uneven distribution of velocities along the section, they were refined by J. Boussinesque. In recent years, one-dimensional or two-dimensional equations of hydraulics are obtained by integration along the section or the depth of the river with the Reynolds equation for the averaged (by chance) currents. [61] points to the ambiguity of this procedure, depending on whether weight function is included in averaging. The resulting system of equations is called the Saint-Venant equations, if the pressure on depth accepted is hydrostatic, or it is called the Boussinesque equations, if the curvature of the jets in the vertical plane is taken into account. There are also proposals to the special account of the curvature of the jets in the plan.

To perform the operation of averaging the equations of conservation to a final volume of W are the following [89, 104]:

$$\left.\begin{aligned} &\int_{W} \rho U_i \, dW \Big|_{t_1}^{t_2} + \int_{t_1}^{t_2} dt \int_{\Omega} \rho U_i \left(U_n + \frac{\frac{df}{dt}}{|\operatorname{grad} f|} \right) d\Omega = \\ &= \int_{t_1}^{t_2} dt \left\{ \int_{\Omega} \left(-P n_i + \sigma n_i \right) d\Omega - \int_{W} \rho F_i \, dW \right\}; \\ &\int_{W} \rho \, dW \Big|_{t_1}^{t_2} + \int_{t_1}^{t_2} dt \left\{ \int_{\Omega} \rho \left(U_n + \frac{\frac{df}{dt}}{|\operatorname{grad} \; f|} \right) d\Omega \right\} = 0 \end{aligned}\right\} \quad (2.130)$$

Here U_i is instant component of the fluid velocity along the axis x, U_n - instant component of the fluid velocity normal to the surface Ω; p - is the density of the fluid; P - spherical part of the stress tensor; σ_{ni} - components of the stress deviator; ρF_i - projection mass force per unit volume, on the i-th axis; t - is time; n_i; - projection of the unit normal vector to the surface Ω to the i-th axis (the normal vector, as usual, is directed from the inside of the volume bounded by the surface $\mathbf{\Omega}$).

Equation (2.130) differs from the accepted account of conservation laws, as in this case the surface $\mathbf{\Omega}$, moving in an arbitrary manner, and not associated with particles of fluid or fixed, as it is usually considered. It is assumed that the surface can be expressed by the equation

$$f(x_1,x_2,x_3,t)=0$$

In addition, all variables under the integrals are assumed to be random functions of coordinates and time.

The transition from equations (2.130) to two-dimensional equations of non-traditional species requires the introduction of a series of hypotheses, usually running in fluvial flows and shallow waters. A detailed discussion of these hypotheses that make up the essence of the transition from three-dimensional to two-dimensional task is given in [89]. We give here only the final form of the equations in coordinates, oriented along *(0x₁)* and across *(0x3)*, the priority direction of the currents [89, 104]:

$$\int_{\Omega} \varphi_h dx_1 dx_3 + \varphi_{U_1} dx_2 dt + \varphi_{U_3} dx_3 dt + \int_{W} \varphi dx_1 dx_3 dt = 0 \quad (2.131)$$

$$\left.\begin{aligned} &\varphi_h = \begin{vmatrix} h \\ U_1 h \\ U_3 h \end{vmatrix}; \quad \varphi_{U1} = \begin{vmatrix} U_1 h \\ U_1^2 h + \frac{1}{2} g h^2 \\ U_1 U_3 h \end{vmatrix}; \quad \varphi_{U_3} = \begin{vmatrix} U_3 h \\ U_1 U_3 h \\ U_3^2 h + \frac{1}{2} g h^2 \end{vmatrix}; \\ &\varphi = \begin{vmatrix} 0 \\ gh\partial\eta_b/\partial x_1 \\ gh\partial\eta_b/\partial x_3 \end{vmatrix} + \begin{vmatrix} 0 \\ -\sigma_{21}^b + \sigma_{21}^S \\ -\sigma_{32}^b + \sigma_{32}^S \end{vmatrix} \end{aligned}\right\} \quad (2.132)$$

The system of equations (2.131) is derived from the laws of conservation of momentum and mass without any assumptions on the fluid rheology. To close the system of equations it is enough to specify the relationship between the tangential stresses on the bottom (σ^b_{21} and σ^b_{32}) and on the free surface (σ^s_{21} and σ^s_{32}) with other characteristics of the flow.

Usually it is considered that the bottom of this relationship can be expressed by the ratio:

$$\sigma^b_{2j} = -\rho\lambda_b U_j|U|/2 \quad (2.133)$$

where $\lambda_s=2g/C^2=2gh^2/h^{1/3}$ is the scalar ratio hydraulic friction at the bottom; C is the Chezy coefficient; n - factor group of roughness in the manning formula; U - is the velocity vector in the plan; j=1, 3.

The surface of the flow is issued a similar relationship with the replacement of U_i (V_i— U_i), where V_i is a component of wind velocity, density of water ρ on the air density ρ_0, U for $(V—U)$ and λ_b on λ_s.

The relation (2.133) does not fully reflect the terms of cooperation averaged over the depth of the flow bottom or with the atmosphere. In the general case, the velocity vector is averaged over the depth of non-collinear vectors of the tangent stress on the bottom or the free surface. To establish the correspondence between these vectors we introduce the tensor coefficient of hydraulic friction [95]:

$$\frac{1}{\rho}\sigma_{2j}^{b} = -\lambda_{jk}\frac{U_k\,|U|}{2} \tag{2.134}$$

This need for friction at the bottom is evident in two cases: if the transverse circulation in the flow direction, bottom jets and middle reaches do not coincide; with anisotropic surface bottom.

For a free surface the introduction of tensor coefficient of resistance occurs most often. It is connected with a possible difference in the direction of wave propagation and wind directions in surface layers.

Thus, the system of equations (2.131) is closed, and at its conclusion it has practically not touched upon the problem of turbulence. It is through the specifics of receipt of Saint-Venant equations of conservation laws, and not through integration of the Navier-Stokes equations or Reynolds, that it is usually accepted. The transition to the two-dimensional Saint-Venant equations practically means the transition to the new scale of flow depth h, without any influence of small-scale turbulence.

In the class of generalized functions system of integral relations (2.131) is equivalent to the system of differential equations in divergence form:

$$\left.\begin{aligned}&\frac{\partial q_i}{\partial t}+\frac{\partial q_i U_j}{\partial x_j}+g\frac{\partial}{\partial x_i}\frac{h^2}{2}=-\lambda\frac{U_i\,|U|}{2}-gh\frac{\partial \eta_b}{\partial x_i};\\&\frac{\partial \eta_s}{\partial t}+\frac{\partial q_j}{\partial x_j}=0;q_i=U_i h.\end{aligned}\right\} \tag{2.135}$$

$$\mathbf{i,j}=1,3$$

In the class of continuous functions of equations (2.135) can be written as

$$\left.\begin{aligned}&\frac{\partial U_i}{\partial t}+U_j\frac{\partial U_i}{\partial x_j}+g\frac{\partial \eta_s}{\partial x_i}=-\lambda\frac{U_i\,|U|}{2h};\\&\frac{\partial \eta_s}{\partial t}+\frac{\partial hU_j}{\partial x_j}=0.\end{aligned}\right\}\tag{2.136}$$

The system of equations (2.136) is the most common in the literature form of two-dimensional Saint-Venant equations [61, 74].

The principal difference here is that the values of U_i and h are still random functions averaged by probability. In equations (2.135) or (2.136) formally there are no members, taking into account the shear stress between the jets in the plan. In fact, however, excluded from the equations is only lateral tension associated with the molecular viscosity of no practical value in the conditions of self-similarity criterion of Reynolds. The so-called "turbulent voltage" is fully preserved due to the presence of nonlinear inertial terms. These stresses appear by averaging the equations (2.135) by probability. If such an average is not done, (2.135) can be considered a closed system, which generates (together with the boundary conditions) the full set of criteria of similarity. In addition to the already introduced criteria of (2.135), we can obtain important condition of similarity currents under the "target" task[1]:

$$\pi_b=\lambda b/h=\text{idem}\tag{2.137}$$

The impurity transfer processes are described by the known law of conservation of its weight. Writing the law in the integral form, we get divergent equations for the admixture transfer in the plan:

$$\frac{\partial ch}{\partial t}+\frac{\partial cq_j}{\partial x_j}=f\left(x_j,h,c,t\right)\tag{2.138}$$

Here c is averaged by a depth and a certain element of a surface in terms of the concentration of impurities; f is a function describing impurities' non-conservativeness.

[1] Condition (2.137) was first introduced in the practice of modeling of two-dimensional flow in the works of the authors published in 1956-1958. (See, for example, [92]). To these publications, the condition (2.137) was derived from the one-dimensional equations and had a significantly different meaning (see Section 5.3).

When writing equations (2.138) we used the same hypotheses as in the output system (2.131), which in this case means the neglect of the phenomenon, similar (but not identical) to the phenomenon of the variance associated with the uneven distribution of instant velocity and concentration depth of the flow. The acceptability of this assumption was checked by comparing calculations (2.131) and (2.132) with the results of laboratory and field studies. The defining criteria here, obviously, is the coefficient of hydraulic friction λ characterizing the irregularity of the distribution of velocities in depth, and the relative width of the reservoir *b/h*.

In the real range of changes of these parameters for large and medium rivers, natural lakes and reservoir-coolers consent calculations (2.138), data laboratory-lab and field observations are quite good (see ch. 8 and [89, 90, 104]).

The system of equations (2.130) in certain circumstances, it becomes one-dimensional equations of river [47, 89]:

$$\oint_{\Omega x_1 t} Q dx + (QU + P)dt = \int_{W x_1 t}\int \left(-g\Omega I_{fr} + g\Omega i + J + F\right)dx_1 dt \qquad (2.139)$$

$$\oint Q dx - Q dt = \int_{W x_1 t}\int q_{in}\sigma dx_1 dt \qquad (2.140)$$

where

$$P = \int_{b_s} g\frac{(\eta_s - \eta_b)}{2}dx_2; \Omega = \int_{b_s}(\eta_s - \eta_b)dx_2;$$

Ω - the cross-sectional area of the flow; *Q* is the water flow through all the cross-section of the flow; $U=Q/\Omega$, - average on section flow velocity;

$$I_{fr} = \lambda\frac{U|U|}{2gR} \qquad (2.141)$$

$R=\Omega/\chi$; χ - length of the wetted perimeter; *i* - the average slope of the bottom of the river; *j* - is the specific impulse given to the area together with the consumption of lateral inflow; q_{in} - specific consumption of lateral inflow; *F* - reaction force associated with the channel nonprismaticity:

$$F = g\int_x \int_{\eta_b}^{\eta_s} \left(\frac{d\xi_b}{dx_1}\cos a - \frac{d\eta_b}{dx_1}\sin a \right) db\,dx_2; \tag{2.142}$$

ζ_b - transverse coordinate of the surface of the bottom; a - the angle between the tangent to the bottom and centerline O_{x2} in the plane $x_2 0_{x3}$, averaged normal to the surface of the seabed.

Formula (2.141) is fair in the absence of wind. When taking into account wind ratio (2.141) should be changed.

In native get name equation (2.139) and (2.140) will take the form:

$$\frac{\partial U}{\partial t} + U\frac{\partial U}{\partial x_1} + g\frac{\partial \eta_s}{\partial x_1} = -\lambda\frac{U|U|}{2R} + gi + \frac{J - q_{in}\sigma U}{\Omega} \tag{2.143}$$

$$b_s\frac{\partial \eta_s}{\partial t} + \frac{\partial U\Omega}{\partial x_1} = q_{in}\sigma \tag{2.144}$$

where b_s is width-level flow of the free surface.

The region of applicability of the equations (2.139) and (2.140) are discussed in [89]. The watercourses have the following characteristics: strong meandering channels with a characteristic scale (length) of convolutions L_u significant fluctuations of the bottom levels with respect to average value with a characteristic wavelength L_Δ; significant fluctuations in channel width with respect to average value with the corresponding characteristic wavelength L_b.

All these features lead to the formation of separated flow, distortion of the free surface and sharp unevenness of the flow. In addition, for quite long sections of rivers it is almost impossible to collect morphometric material detailing these features. So all values in (2.139) should be considered as the averaged over the plot:

$$L >> \{L_n, L_\Delta, L_b\} \tag{2.145}$$

all of statistical moments resulting from averaging are included in (2.141).

Values of Q, U, Ω, averaged over sufficiently large sites, usually comply with the terms of the equation (2.139) and (2.140), and relevant statistical moments allow representation (2.141).

In equations (2.139) and (2.140) (as in the related equations) averaging of probability is not assumed. Therefore, strictly speaking, the ratio of (2.141) and others do not coincide with traditional ideas of hydraulics. However, due to the fact that the width of the river is much larger than the characteristic scale of the turbulence, ripple average velocity (or flow rate) can usually be neglected. All information about turbulence is specified via the coefficient wavelength λ. The solution of equations (2.139) and (2.140) for deterministic boundary conditions in a sufficiently wide class of functions is usually also deterministic. However, there are cases when, even on such a large scale, there are still occurances of nonuniqueness of solutions that can be interpreted as a specific form of turbulence.

From one-dimensional equations (2.139) follows additional similarity criterion, comprehensively reflecting the influence of the conditions on the seabed and the surface of the water:

$$\pi_l = \lambda l / R \tag{2.146}$$

The difference between records (2.118) and (2.127) is that the last expression includes the characteristic length of the watercourse and the hydraulic radius. Thus, the scale of the width of the flow in the study of one-dimensional currents can be imposed rather than the scale length. On the contrary, in the studies of two-dimensional problems of the scale, length and width should be the same. In both cases depth of flow is independent of the scale (see Section 5.3).

If you act under the traditional scheme and perform averaging over the probability before averaging, in the depth or in the cross section of the flow, and not to neglect non-uniformity of velocities distribution in depth, two-dimensional equations of conservation of momentum for continuous currents take the following form [61, 91, 213]:

$$\begin{aligned}
&\frac{\partial U_1}{\partial t} + U_1\frac{\partial U_1}{\partial x_1} + U_3\frac{\partial U_3}{\partial x_3} = -g\frac{\partial}{\partial x_1}(h+\eta_b) + \frac{1}{\rho h}\frac{\partial h\sigma_{11}}{\partial x_1} \\
&+\frac{1}{\rho h}\frac{\partial h\sigma_{13}}{\partial x_1} + \frac{\sigma_{12}^S - \sigma_{21}^b}{\rho h} + \\
&+\frac{1}{\rho h}\frac{\partial}{\partial x_1}\int_{\eta_b}^{\eta_s}\rho(u_1-U_1)^2\,dx_2 + \frac{1}{\rho h}\frac{\partial}{\partial x_3}\int_{\eta_b}^{\eta_s}\rho(u_1-U_1)(u_3-U_3)\,dx_2; \\
&\frac{\partial U_3}{\partial t} + U_1\frac{\partial U_3}{\partial x_1} + U_3\frac{\partial U_3}{\partial x_3} = -g\frac{\partial}{\partial x_3}(h+\eta_b) + \frac{1}{\rho h}\frac{\partial h\sigma_{13}}{\partial x_1} \\
&+\frac{1}{\rho h}\frac{\partial h\sigma_{33}}{\partial x_3} + \frac{\sigma_{32}^S - \sigma_{32}^b}{\rho h} + \\
&+\frac{1}{\rho h}\frac{\partial}{\partial x_1}\int_{\eta_b}^{\eta_s}\rho(u_1-U_1)(u_3-U_3)\,dx_2 + \frac{1}{\rho h}\frac{\partial}{\partial x_3}\int_{\eta_b}^{\eta_s}\rho(u_3-U_3)^2\,dx_2;
\end{aligned} \tag{2.147}$$

In both formulas underlined terms reflect the effect of dispersion that appears when the transition to two-dimensional equations is due to the impact of uneven distribution of velocities. Same very important components appear in the two-dimensional and one-dimensional equations of conservation portable substance [213].

Equations (2.147) generally cannot be cast members, including σ_{13}. To close the equations (2.147) hypotheses are needed. Average depth tension can be expressed through derivatives of fields and averaged velocities by analogy with the Boussinesque hypothesis. We introduce the average depth of the turbulent viscosity v_τ, the energy of turbulence $\bar{e}$ and tension of its dissipation $\boldsymbol{\varepsilon}$ [213]:

$$\frac{\sigma_{ij}}{\rho} = (v_\tau + v)\left(\frac{\partial U_i}{\partial x_j} + \frac{\partial U_j}{\partial x_i}\right) - \frac{2}{3} e \delta_{ij}; \tag{2.148}$$

$$v_\tau = a_v e^2 / \varepsilon \tag{2.149}$$

$$\frac{\partial e}{\partial t} + U_1 \frac{\partial e}{\partial x_1} + U_3 \frac{\partial e}{\partial x_3} = \frac{\partial}{\partial x_1}\left(\frac{v_T}{a_v}\frac{\partial e}{\partial t}\right) + \frac{\partial}{\partial x_3}\left(\frac{v_T}{a_v}\frac{\partial e}{\partial x_3}\right) + \Pi_h + \Pi_{ev} - \varepsilon;$$

(2.150)

$$\frac{\partial \varepsilon}{\partial t} + U_1 \frac{\partial \varepsilon}{\partial x_1} + U_3 \frac{\partial \varepsilon}{\partial x_3} = \frac{\partial}{\partial x_1}\left(\frac{v_T}{a_\varepsilon}\frac{\partial \varepsilon}{\partial x_1}\right) + \frac{\partial}{\partial x_3}\left(\frac{v_\tau}{a_\varepsilon}\frac{\partial \varepsilon}{\partial x_3}\right)$$

$$+ a_{1\varepsilon} \frac{\varepsilon}{e} \Pi_h + \Pi_{ev} - a_{2B} \frac{\varepsilon^2}{e}, \tag{2.151}$$

where

$$\Pi_h = v_\tau \left[2\left(\frac{\partial U_1}{\partial x_1}\right)^2 + 2\left(\frac{\partial U_3}{\partial x_3}\right)^2 + \left(\frac{\partial U_1}{\partial x_3} + \frac{\partial U_3}{\partial x_1}\right)^2 \right] \tag{2.152}$$

there are products turbulence; Π_{ev} and $\Pi_{\varepsilon v}$ - sources of turbulence and its dissipation, reflecting the influence of the conditions at the bottom or on the free surface. In particular, for the bottom offered [213]:

$$\Pi_{ev}=a_e U_*^3/h \tag{2.153}$$

$$\Pi_{\varepsilon v}=a_\varepsilon U_*^4/h^2 \tag{2.154}$$

where

$$U_* = \sqrt{\frac{\lambda}{2}\left(U_1^2 + U_3^2\right)}; \tag{2.155}$$

λ - coefficient of hydraulic friction; $a_e = \sqrt{2/\lambda}$; $a_\varepsilon = 3.6a_{2\varepsilon}\sqrt{a_v}\,(2/\lambda)^{3/4}$.

Applying the equations (2.148) - (2.152) a similarity transformation, will find three additional criteria:

$$\left.\begin{aligned}
\pi_{v\tau} &= \frac{e_0 U_0}{\varepsilon b_0}; \\
\pi_{ev} &= \frac{\lambda_0^{3/2} U_0^2 b_0}{e_0 h_0} \\
\pi_{\varepsilon v} &= \frac{\lambda_0^2 U_0^3 b_0}{\varepsilon_0 h_0^2}
\end{aligned}\right\} \tag{2.156}$$

If the velocity fluctuations and the averaged velocity scales are the same, the entry criteria (2.156) is simplified:

$$\left.\begin{aligned}
\pi'_{v\tau} &= \frac{U_0^3}{\varepsilon b_0}; \\
\pi'_{ev} &= \frac{\lambda_0^{3/2} b_0}{e_0 h_0} \\
\pi'_{\varepsilon v} &= \frac{\lambda_0 b_0}{h_0}
\end{aligned}\right\} \tag{2.157}$$

Mapping Π'_{ev} and $\Pi'_{\varepsilon v}$ shows that the criterion $\lambda b/h$ is not the only additional criterion of planned tasks in the model of turbulent flow. It is easy to notice that the output is directly linked to the hypothetical ratio (2.153). If this equality can be rewritten as:

$$\Pi_{ev}=a'_e UU^2_*/h \tag{2.153a}$$

the criterion $\lambda b/h$ will be the only additional criterion of planned tasks.

Criteria Π'_{ev} from (2.157) and Π'_b from (2.118) in general are not equivalent, as the meaning of the coefficient λ varies due to linking in a single random, another mean of the probability of values. In fact, while output (2.118) and (2.138) there is a further assumption that the parameters λ and b/h can be considered as independent.

If average (by chance) field is acceptable (at least for those cases, when it is possible to neglect the tensor structure λ), for a random velocity field, this issue is less clear. This remark reduces the value of reception output (2.137) and leaves the need for more experimental study of areas where conditions (2.137) with the scalar deterministic value λ are enough for similarity plan currents.

From the above consideration, it follows that the structure of the criteria of similarity depends substantially on the accepted mathematical model of the phenomenon. The more simplified the model of the phenomenon are, the easier the similarity conditions that correspond to the accepted description (see Section 3.4).

2.8 Numerical Modeling

One of the Central problems of contemporary hydromechanics is the modeling of a turbulent flow of a fluid. Wide application in the found solution methods, connected with the consideration of equations averaged over the likelihood or time. As you know, beginning from works of Reynolds, this approach leads to the equations of new unknowns, and the task becomes open. Created to date, semi-empirical approaches to the closure of the Reynolds equations are suitable only to a rather narrow class of currents. However, the extension of this framework leads to an increase in the number of empirical constants used in the relevant theories, which reduces their practical value. In this regard, approaches to direct numerical modeling of turbulence using the basic conservation laws for fluids that are written for some finite volume and time intervals, characterizing the scale spatial-temporal averaging, have been developed in the works of several authors [157, 161, 19, 89, 198, 176].

This work develops and specifies the ideas of numerical modeling of large-scale turbulence serial reduction consideration, starting with "zero-dimensional" and "one-dimensional" tasks.

Averaging across all spatial variables with the scale of the depth, width and length, the non-affluent part of the river leads to "zero-dimensional" problems of classical river hydrology, in particular to the formation of a random process of change of the river flow. The averaging time is associated with spatial averaging. The correct results you can expect to receive only when the scale of averaging T, large L/U_0, where L a characteristic linear scale of averaging, U_0 is a characteristic velocity of the flow. In particular, when learning tasks in zero-dimensional the formulation of the scale of averaging time T_0 must meet the condition:

$$T_0 > \frac{W_0}{Q_0} \tag{2.158}$$

where W_0 - is the volume of the reservoir, Q_0 - the water flow, W_0/Q_0- the value is the average residence time of water in the reservoir.

One-dimensional equations of hydraulics are usually obtained by averaging the equations of motion in the living section and some length of a section of the river. The coefficient of hydraulic resistance included loss of momentum, not only related to micro-roughness of the bottom, but with macroscopic changes in the shape of the bottom and shores. Thus, the coefficient of hydraulic resistance λ_L should be different depending on the scale of averaging L, and the use of numerical methods depending on the step differential grid; increasing step, the drag coefficient increases up to a limit, characterizing the river as a whole. The minimum value of this ratio may be determined by the formula:

$$\min\{\lambda_L\} = \frac{1}{LU_{av}^2}\int_L \lambda U^2 dx, \tag{2.159}$$

where λ and U are local values of the coefficient of friction and flow velocity, U is average velocity:

$$\left(x - \frac{L}{2}, x + \frac{L}{2}\right).$$

Pay attention to the fact that the real uneven flow resistance coefficient, which is a one-dimensional equation of momentum, used in the calculations, is not equal to the rate of energy loss that characterizes the "loss" of the mechanical energy of the flow on the same plot. These differences, often wearing a qualitative, are not always taken into account in the formulation of research. This sometimes leads to the publishing of qualitatively different conclusions regarding the effect of irregularity and non-stationarity on the hydraulic resistance [21, 51, 65, 112, 132].

The choice of the scale of averaging the current time is significant. Lower estimates should be added to an upper bound, as measured by physical beings phenomena. So, it is established that the roughness and hydraulic resistance of a sandy riverbed is changing with the change in velocity (with change τ/τ_0, where τ is the shear stress at the bottom, τ_0 - the same corresponding to the beginning of the shift particles) [132]. In this way averaging should be conducted within small changes to river flow, when appropriate implementations assemble.

One-dimensional equations of hydraulics provide a convenient tool of the analysis of the simplest kind of instability - dimensional large-scale turbulence in the form of rolling waves. It is known that the equations of Saint-Venant at a constant width of the channel of rectangular cross-section are of the form:

$$\begin{aligned} &\frac{\partial h}{\partial t}+\frac{\partial q}{\partial x}=0; \quad q=hU, \\ &\frac{\partial q}{\partial t}+\frac{\partial}{\partial x}\left(qU+\frac{gh^2}{2}\right)-ghI+\frac{\lambda U^2}{2}=0, \end{aligned} \tag{2.160}$$

with relatively steep slopes I give oscillating solutions, the amplitude of which increases the length and time. This is the case if:

$$\lambda/I < 5{,}5(1+\beta)^2, \tag{2.161}$$

where β is a parameter in the formula determining the dependence of the depth

There were a series of numerical experiments with the differential equations were approximated system (2.160). It was found that when changing step differential grid or 4 times the wave picture is not qualitatively

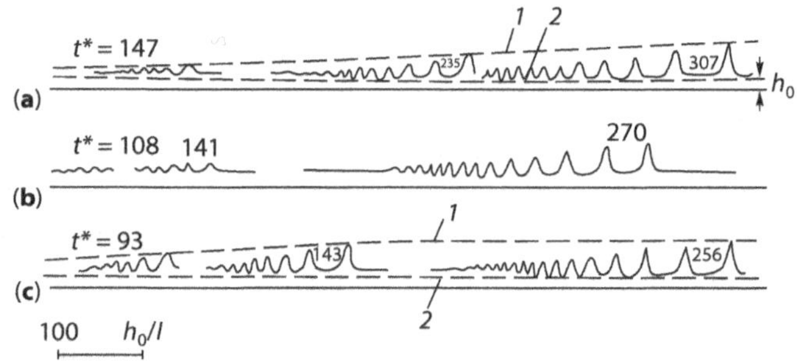

Figure 2.16 Development of the waves on the flow at different amplitude of the initial perturbation $(q_I - q_0)/q_0$ is equal to 0.01 (a); 0.05 (b); 0.25 (c) (λ/I = 0.1; $\beta = 0$; $\Delta x = 2h_0$/I) 1 and 2 envelopes of maximum and minimum depths

changed, although a quantitative assessment in a separate implementations are different. These differences, however, are small: when you change step 4 times (up to $2h$/l) the maximum depth in the first wave h_1 when $t^* = \frac{t}{I}\sqrt{\frac{h_0}{g}} = 106$ changed from 2,86 to 2,41 h_0 Change the step from 1 to 2 (in the same length scales h_0/l) when $t^* = 151$ and gave $h_1 = 3{,}2\ h_0$ and 2,9 h_0 respectively. In both cases, the value of the square of the velocity, averaged over the length of the wave, which had an amplitude of the initial perturbations within certain limits (at least virtually $q_+/q_0 \leq 1.5$) had no effect on the maximum height of a wave, which is mounted on the flow. The only difference is the duration of the process of establishment (Figure 2.16).

The intensity of growth and structure of the generated turbulence is highly dependent on the parameter λ/l, with a decrease in which the wave height is rising sharply, and their length is changed less significantly (Figure 2.17).

With continuous flow of small perturbations in the initial section of the flow rolling waves are generated continuously, showing all the characteristics of a random process. The maximum amplitude of the waves is limited. The depth of the flow will not exceed the values h max, indicated below:

λ/I	0.01	0.02	0.06	0.08	0.10	0.20
h_{max}/h_0	7.9	8.3	3.8	3.3	3.3	3.3
t^*_{max}	45	71	64	12	150	220

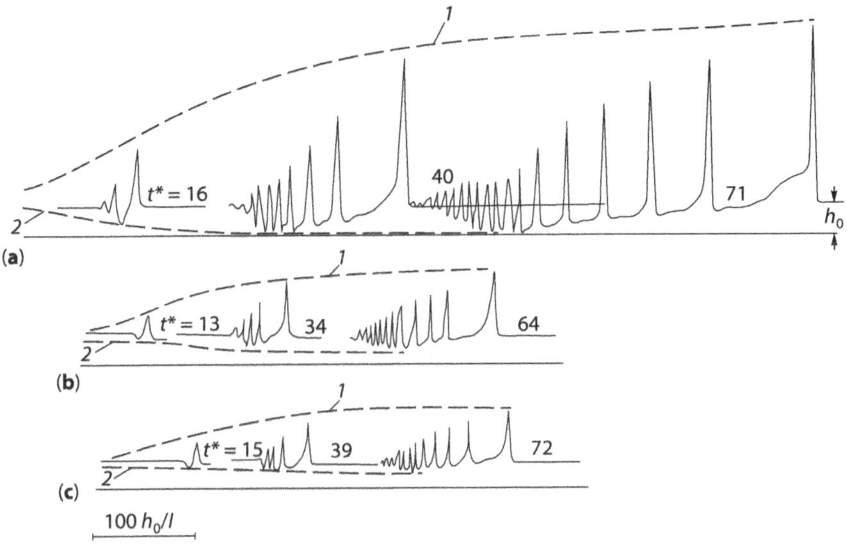

Figure 2.17 Impact of the criterion λ/I and equal 0.02 (a); 0.006 (b) and 0.008(c) on the parameters of the rolling waves ($\beta = 0$; $\Delta x = 0.5\ h_0/\text{I}$; $q + / q_0 = 1.25$; 1,2) see (Figure 2.16).

Definitions and examples of solutions to two-dimensional problems are given in [198, 104, 103, 90, 89, 81, 19, 22]. We note here only features job boundary conditions. On a rough day by averaging the surface of the bottom of the scale, the significantly greater wavelength roughness, conditional bottom surface is below the maximum projections rough edges, but above the minimum rate of the bottom of the watercourse. Thus, averaged on the site $L \times B$, where L, B is a linear scale of averaging, the flow rate in conventional bottom surface should not be zero.

When solving two-dimensional (planned) objectives, the condition at the bottom is used in a different form:

$$\tau_i = \frac{1}{2}\left(\lambda_{ij} U_j\right) \rho U_i, \tag{2.162}$$

where λ_{ij} is the tensor coefficient of hydraulic friction; U_j- the flow rate, averaged over the depth [95].

On the surface of the water can be significant influence of the wind. Analysis of the impact of wind influence on the current field in the conditions of a planned schematization is comfortable to hold for a class of flows with small numbers Froude, such that the change marks a free surface in the continuity equation can be neglected. Then the equations of Saint-Venant will take the form:

$$\frac{\partial q_i}{\partial t}+\frac{\partial U_j q_i}{\partial x_j}+gh\frac{\partial z}{\partial x_i}=-\frac{1}{2}\left(\lambda_{ij}U_j\right)U+\left(\tau_W\right)_i/\rho;$$
$$\frac{\partial q_i}{\partial x_i}=0; \qquad q_i=U_i h. \tag{2.163}$$

We can assume that the shear stress caused by the wind, $(\tau w)_i$ and does not depend on q and h and looks like:

$$\left(\tau_W\right)_i/\rho=\left(\lambda_{ij}^0 W_j\right)W, \tag{2.164}$$

where λ_{ij}^0 is some tensor, W_j- the wind velocity. In the future, for simplicity, let us assume tensors λ_{ij} and λ_{ij}^0 ball with components and λ and λ^0.

Let h = const and $(\tau w)_i$ has potential. Then the first equation of system (2.163) can be written as:

$$\frac{\partial q_i}{\partial t}+\frac{\partial U_j q_i}{\partial x_j}+\frac{\partial P}{\partial x_i}=-\frac{1}{2}\lambda U_i U, \tag{2.165}$$

where $P = ghz + \varphi_i$, φ_i is the potential $(\tau w)_i$. In (2.165) it follows that if in the boundary conditions is not included P, the wind in the specified conditions (in particular, τ_w = const does not affect the velocity field.

Thus, at first glance it seems that taking into account wind influence in many cases is necessary. But it is not.

For differentiable functions the consequence of equation (2.165) is the equation of conservation of the whirlwind:

$$\frac{\partial \omega}{\partial t}+\frac{\partial U_j \omega}{\partial x_j}=-\frac{\partial}{\partial x_2}\frac{\lambda U_1 U}{2h}+\frac{\partial}{\partial x_1}\frac{\lambda U_2 U}{2h}+\frac{\partial}{\partial x_2}\frac{\left(\tau_W\right)_1}{\rho h}-\frac{\partial}{\partial x_1}\frac{\left(\tau_W\right)_2}{\rho h} \tag{2.166}$$

where

$$\omega=\frac{\partial U_1}{\partial x_2}-\frac{\partial U_2}{\partial x_1}.$$

Consider the case where $\lambda = 0$ i.e., friction on the bottom can be neglected. Note that for a potential vector, $(\tau_w)_1$, in particular, τw = const in case of h = const (2.166) it also follows that τ_w does not affect the velocity field. Let now:

$(\tau_w)_1 = 0$, $(\tau_w)_2 = \tau_w$ = conts, $h = h_0 - \xi x_1$ where ξ can be arbitrarily small.

Then (2.166) takes the form:

$$\frac{\partial \omega}{\partial t} + \frac{\partial U_j \omega}{\partial x_j} = -\xi \frac{\tau_W}{\rho h^2}. \tag{2.167}$$

Let's evaluate the course in the pool with waterproof walls. Integrating (2.167) throughout the area, we obtain:

$$\frac{\partial \overline{\omega}}{\partial t} = -\xi \frac{\tau_W}{\rho \bar{h}^2}, \tag{2.168}$$

here the hell are the top represents the averaging

From equation (2.168), it obviously, does not matter how small ξ is, if there is a time t_1, for all $t > t_1$, the deviation $\bar{\omega}$ from $\bar{\omega}|_{t=0}$ will be more of any arbitrarily large, pre-specified value $\delta_w$while:

$$t_1 = \frac{\delta_\omega \rho \bar{h}^2}{\tau_W \xi} \tag{2.169}$$

The solution to the problem proved to be unstable. Even small changes of wind may cause remarkable changes of the plan of water currents and temperature..

This influence is manifested in analyzing the restructuring plan under the influence of the wind (Figure 2.18). A relatively weak wind (4 m/s) over the pond-cooler causes intense vortices in the area where $\partial h/\partial x_i \neq 0$ (the upper and right side of the reservoir Figure 2.18). Change of plan currents driven by wind, despite the increasing heat raises the temperature increase on the water intake (Figure 2.19). The calculated flow has turbulent nature.

In figure 2.20 the results of numerical modeling of turbulence are compared with the data precision experiments of B.A. Fiedman and other authors. It is shown that the averaged (over time) flow patterns in the calculations and the experiments are almost the same when the scale spatial averaging is about 1/10 the characteristic width (depth) of the flow. Standards of pulsation velocities, however, differ. Reducing the size of

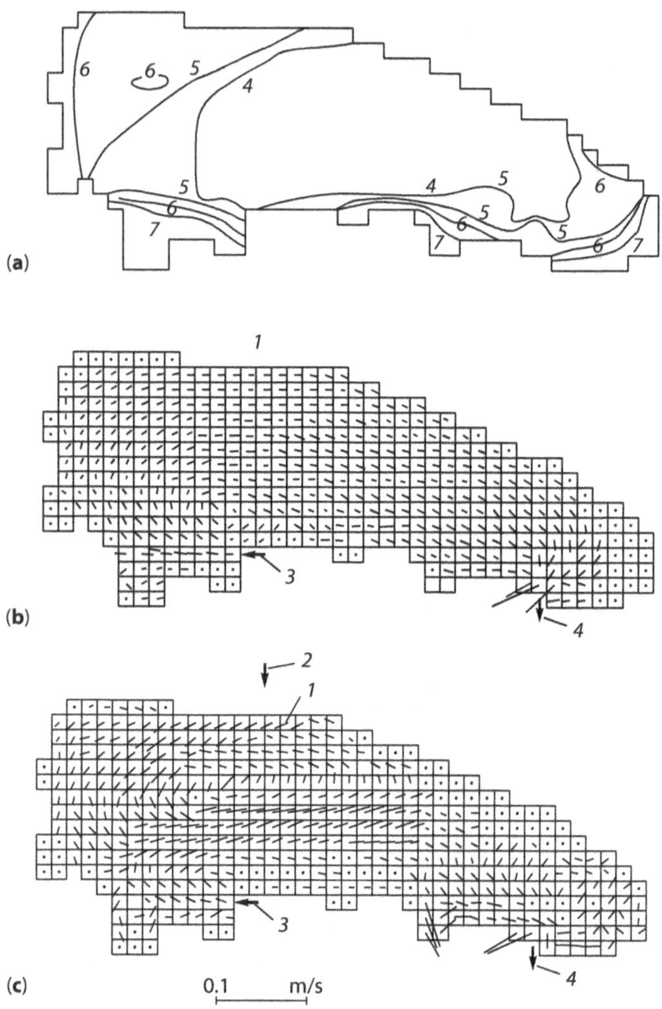

Figure 2.18 The plan contours of the bottom of the cooling pond (a) and plan of currents in the absence of (b) and with action wind (down picture) (water level 9 m) 1 - the instantaneous velocity vectors; 2 - direction of the wind; 3 - the spillway (U_0 = 0.15 m/s; q = 0,6 m²/s; B_0 = 200 m); 4 – water intake.

the volume in the averaging brings together the results of physical and numerical experiments. Here the pulsations spectrum is enriched, which is obtained in numerical experiments.

The success of numerical modeling of turbulence in one-dimensional and two-dimensional problems can be used for description of density currents (turbid flows of stratified water), when it can be effectively applied by

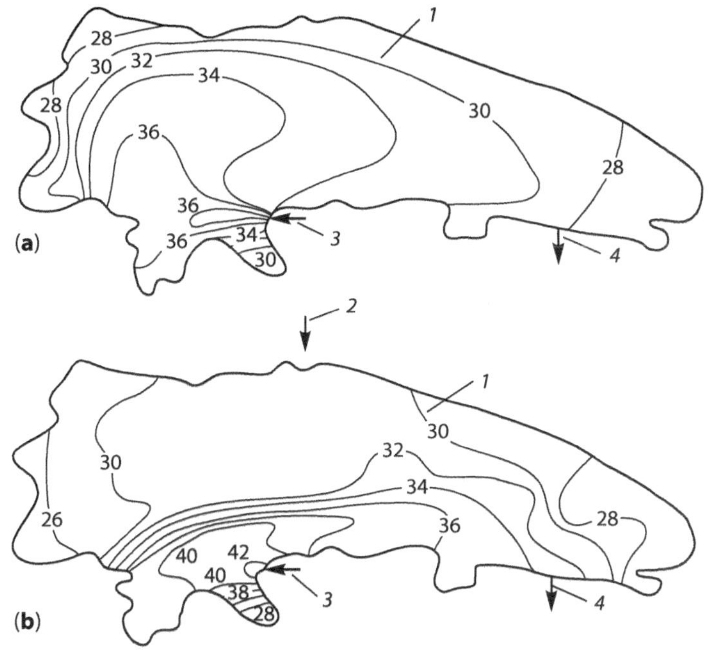

Figure 2.19 Isolines of temperature of water (1) in the absence of (a) and if in (b) wind (2-4-see Figure 2.18).

a two-layer scheme. Each layer describes the one- and two-dimensional Saint-Venant equations. The interaction between the layers is taken into account through the normal pressure, friction $(\tau_0)_i$ and mass exchange. The latter value, which is part of the continuity equation for each of the layers is made proportional $\sqrt{\tau_0 / \rho}$ with the proportionality factor depending on the local number Richardson. For density currents possible effects are described above for homogeneous flows. For example, the analogue of "rolling waves" in bottom density flow will be generated upon:

$$\frac{U_0}{\sqrt{gh_0}} > \frac{2}{1+\beta}\sqrt{\frac{\Delta\rho}{\rho}} \tag{2.170}$$

where U_0 and h_0 is the velocity and depth of bottom density of the flow; $\Delta\rho$- a difference of densities.

The two-dimensional density of the flow of possible instability is of the same type as in open water body under the wind action.

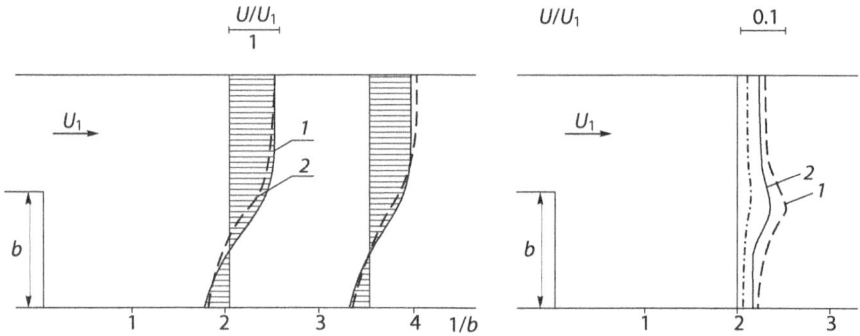

Figure 2.20 Diagrams of averaged longitudinal velocities distribution subcritical flow expansion $U_1 / \sqrt{gh} \approx 0.1$ - tests data from [30a, 148], 2 – computation data.

Numerical modeling of three-dimensional problems is also related to the choice of scale spatial-temporal averaging. For large Reynolds numbers, when in the spectra of pulsations of flows, and there is a wide range of inertial equilibrium, scale of averaging should be selected so that the distortion of the spectrum by smoothing is captured in the inertial range, but does not go beyond the lower limit of wave numbers, in which the shape of the spectrum is determined by the general configuration of flow. The right choice of the scale of averaging in conjunction with the requirements in difference approximations of the equations [89, 198] allows you to simulate the low-frequency part of turbulence, including the largest generation of its energy and parameters of pressure pulsations. High-frequency part of turbulence is completed further on the basis of the hypothesis of the local isotropy on the rate of generation of energy of turbulence in view of its convection and diffusion due to pressure pulsations.

Note that in the calculation of averaged plan currents (2.166), the method of the establishment is almost impossible, since the fluctuations of all hydrodynamic characteristics do not subside. These fluctuations (at constant flow rate in the initial and final sections) are currently studied, but we can already say, that calculations according to (2.166) allow you to detect low-frequency currents and turbulence to consider its influence on formation of transport processes in terms of momentum or impurities. Of course, this statement should be further verified by the analytical study of equations, and comparison of the statistical characteristics of results of numerical and laboratory research.

The question about the impact hypothesis (2.164) is not considered here, as in the proposed formulation of the value α_u, α_υ and $\alpha_{u\upsilon}$ which should be considered as a random function, because there are no experimental data and theoretical assessments, so it requires complex and special analysis.

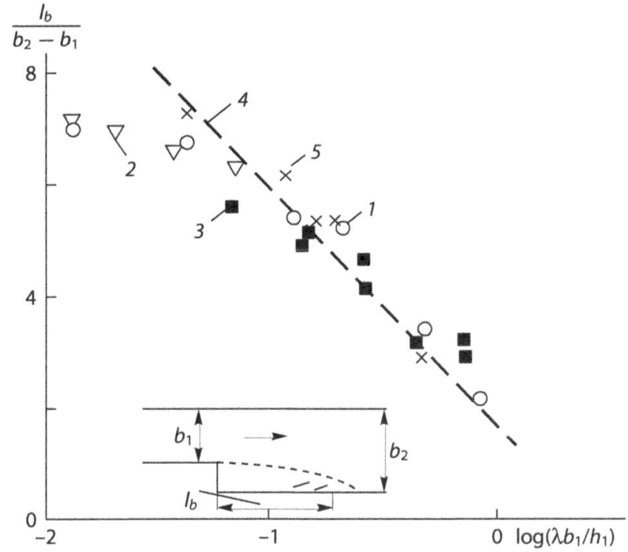

Figure 2.21 The average length of the whirlpool in the scheme sudden expansion 1,2 - air-pressure model $b_2/b_1 = 2$ (1 – D.B. Radkevich, 2 – G.N. Lapshin); 3 - hydraulic model $b_2/b_1 = 1.33$; $U_1/\sqrt{gh_1} = 0.22$ (V.M. Lyatkher and A. M. Proudovsky); 4 - calculation on $b_2/b_1 = 2$; 5 according to data [89, 81].

In deriving the equations (2.166) is also not mentioned previously the hypothesis of a constant (in depth) density of the fluid. The question of the effect of changes in density $\Delta\rho$ is particularly important for water bodies where occurrence of density currents, such as water reservoirs-coolers, in which hot water is discharged. It is shown [78, 86] that sustainable stratified during obviously impossible, if:

$$\frac{\Delta\rho}{\rho}\cdot\frac{gh}{U^2} < 0.1 \tag{2.171}$$

Under the condition (2.171), showing the distribution of temperature and density, the depth of the flow is close to uniform, which indicates the effective use of the system (2.166).

3

Approximate Similarity of Hydraulic Phenomenon

3.1 Inconsistency of Similarity Criterion

On the basis of the Navier-Stokes equation, it is established that similarity criterions for streaming fluid are criterions of Reynolds, Froude, Strouhal and Euler.

It is practically impossible to achieve simultaneous equivalence for all or even part of these similarity criterions. This is explained by the fact that for achievement of similarity criterion against scale of the same values, included in the different criterion, should be put up different requirements. In realistic conditions, which determine possibility for selection of value on the model, these requirements are often unsatisfactory simultaneously (criterions are incompatible).

Impossibility to combine significant conditions of hydraulic similarity in equal characteristics of fluid on the model and actual conditions is presented in Figure 3.1, where is shown dependence of exponent $lg_{Ml}\ M_x$ in linear dimension in the formula of dimension of this value X by exponent $lg_{Ml}\ M_x$ in linear dimension in the formula of time (or velocity) dimension.

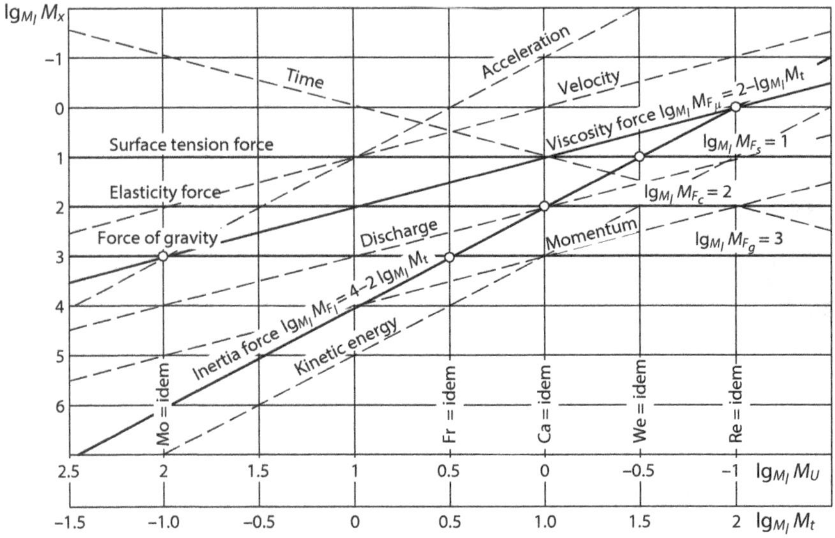

Figure 3.1 Dependence of exponent of linear dimension in formulas of dimension of mechanical values from exponent of linear dimension in formula of time (or velocity) dimension.

There are similar diagrams in [168], where we propose to select a 'compromise" version of time scale for satisfaction of several similarity conditions. But, following this advice without proper evaluation of such "compromise," can lead to significant mistakes.

Incompatibility of similarity criterions defines necessity to deviate from strict similarity of phenomenon in real simulation but in a way that does not lose the most significant study results and does not get large distortion in required values.

Out from four indicated similarity criterions, in a majority of practical problems, Euler`s criterion usually is not determining (ref. Ch. 5), and Strouhal`s criterion falls out from similarity criterion system in studying the field of mean velocities of steady flow. But every experimentalist dealing with simulation of large objects knows about difficulties when it is necessary to take into account two last similarity criterions: Froude and Reynolds.

Indeed, both Froude and Reynolds criterions include velocity and linear dimension. But form of dependence between scales of these values necessary for identity of one of these criterions is inconsistent with other criterions structure. Identity of Froude criterion is achieved at:

$$M_U = M_g^{1/2} M_l^{\frac{1}{2}} \tag{3.1}$$

and identity of Reynolds criterion at:

$$M_U = M_v M_l^{-1} \tag{3.2}$$

Accordingly, to meet simultaneously conditions (3.1) and (3.2), scale of linear values should equal:

$$M_l = M_v^{2/3} M_g^{-1/3}$$

In simulation of large objects, including stream flows, it is always preferable for scale M_l to be as small as possible. Seemingly, this can be achieved by the means of respective values of M_v *and* M_g. But, within the scope of physical simulation of fluid flow almost always M_g=1. Variability of M_v is limited by variability of fluid characteristics. Lowest kinematic viscosity has ethers (ν~0,0033 sm^2/s) or liquid metals (for mercury ν ~0.0014 sm^2/s). In this way in simulation of fluid flow (ν ~0,01 sm^2/s), M_v>1:7, there is a minimal scale of linear values at simultaneous achievement of identical Froude and Reynolds criterions $M_{l\,min}$ ~1:4. It is understandable that to recreate on this scale some large water flow with substitution of water for fluid with significantly lower viscosity is impractical from economic and engineering point of view.

This situation arises upon necessity to fulfill only two similarity conditions. If it is necessary to achieve identity of greater number of similarity criterions, consisting of equal values, it may happen that for similarity achievement, linear dimensions of a model should not differ from prototype dimensions. Input of every additional criterion dramatically complicates simulation.

3.2 Approximate Similarity and Distorted Model

Completeness of similarity conditions depends on completeness of an equation set which describes phenomenon. Because every mathematical description assumes schematization of phenomenon, we can be sure that it does not reflect every factor. At the same time, in solution of practical problems, there may be deviations from true values of desired functions in predicted phenomenon. These deviations are defined by prescribed accuracy degree of the solution. In many cases, especially in studying natural watercourses, the solution doesn`t require high accuracy due to relatively low accuracy of original data (hydrological, geological). Based on this concept, some distortion in phenomenon description does not necessary lead to distortion in the solution, which exceeds tolerable error. Therefore, it can be assumed that in deviation from compliance with some similarity conditions, we can achieve acceptable accuracy of simulation results. In such cases, we can speak about approximate similarity.

Approximate will be considered such similarity which provides definition of predicted function with a desired degree of accuracy at deviations in some similarity conditions.

It is known that achievement of similarity conditions is realized in scale equality of analogous values. For example, condition Re = idem means equality in scales of inertia and viscosity forces, and condition Fr = idem shows equality in scales of gravity and inertia forces, etc. Identity of simplexes, providing for similarity in single-valued conditions, is equivalent to equality of scales of various geometric and kinematic values.

In this way, deviation from condition π_i = idem leads to analogous values having different scales.

Ratio of scales of analogues values is called their distortion, and a model with unequal scales of analogue values is called distorted. This definition widens common perception of distorted model, which foresees only difference in linear scales: $M_l \neq M_b \neq M_h$, where M_b – cross scale; M_l – longitudinal scale (or at $M_b = M_l$ – plane scale); M_h – vertical scale [76, 181]. So it follows that approximate similarity is carried out on a distorted model. We should resort to approximate similarity if it is necessary to reduce the number of similarity criterions and simplexes for the purpose of practical possibility for phenomenon simulation. Reducing the number of similarity criteria (and thus distortion of the model) is acceptable only with appropriate evaluation of its consequences. Disregard of this rule may cause numerous errors in simulation results. Reducing the number of similarity criterions does not principally differ from reducing the number of dimensionless parameters in normal equations, which allows for obtaining an analytical solution.

3.3 Self-Similarity

Hereafter it will be shown how application of dimension theory in some cases allows for reducing the number of similarity criterions through combination. But theory itself does not provide the possibility to disregard some dimensionless group. For this purpose, application of a Newton-like sign, which is close to application of normal equations, possesses some advantages. The final result can be obtained if forces are connected by algebraic equation (ref. Section 3.4).

Let`s consider, for example, unstable falling of mass into incompressible stationary fluid. A dynamic balance equation for such mass is given by:

$$F_g = F_I + F_C \tag{3.3}$$

where F_g — gravity force; F_I — inertia force; F_C — resistance force. In general, resistance force is defined by pressure and friction forces:

$$F_c = F_p + F_\mu \tag{3.4}$$

Then equation (3.3) can be presented as follows:

$$F_g/F_I = 1 + F_\mu/F_I + F_p/F_I$$

Taking into account that $F_g = \rho_s g W$ and assuming pressure force corresponds only with hydrostatic pressure distribution $F_p = \rho g W$, and friction force fully corresponds with viscosity, with regard to what is presented in the Table 1.1 data, equation (3.3) may be given by:

$$\text{Eu} = \frac{1}{\text{Fr}}(1 - \rho/\rho_s) - \frac{1}{\text{Re}} - 1 \tag{3.5}$$

where ρ_s and ρ — respective density of body (particle) and fluid; W — body volume.

Equation (3.5) can lead to conclusion about variation range where it may be possible to disregard impact of one or another dimensionless complex. In algebraic equation such value comparison is obvious, but for differential equation this issue is more complicated.

It is usually accepted that if some term of normal differential equation is smaller or larger than other terms for some order (for example, three), then there is self-similarity by factor of this term. If phenomenon is described by differential equation, than order of one or another equation term cannot be evaluated only by order of dimensionless complex of respective term of normal equation.

Significant variation in order of one of the equation terms in comparison with other terms shows only potential possibility to disregard this term and exclude respective complexity from criterion system. We are interested in the problem's solution, namely the value of a dependent variable, defined by terms of differential equations in some variables domain. In this case, to possess possibility to disregard the term, it is necessary for it to be equally small within the whole domain. If it varies even in one point, then the whole problem solution may be different. Even if the effect corresponding to this term is small, but it is present in a significant part of the variables domain, it also can affect the solution. In this way, in support of the possibility of disregarding one or another term of differential equation and related similarity criterion, it is necessary to show not only that the corresponding effect is locally small, but that it has weak impact on studied integral characteristic. For strict mathematical proof of the possibility to disregard some equation terms as compared to others, it is necessary to find a link between values of differential equations terms and values in solutions for these equations. Searching for this link is quite a complex issue.

But there are some isolated situations, where simple consideration of equations can lead to important results, which allow a reduction of the number of influencing values and correspondingly, number of similarity criterions. Such opportunities are presented when basic equations are homogeneous in relation to one of the variables. Because normalizing of equations is carried out by the means of substitution $X^{+}=X_0$ (X_0 — constant), then dimensionless complex π, containing X_0, falls out from normal equations homogenous in X^{+}. But it may be excluded from a link only when value X_0 is not contained in normal single-valued conditions. Disregarding the value X_0 from single-valued conditions is usually achieved by the means of the respective choice of coordinates.

Possibility to disregard some criterion (one or another equation terms) may exist in specific variables domains. If normal equations describing phenomenon in this domain and single-valued conditions do not contain characteristic criterions, then it can be said that solutions for these equations are self-similar and variables domains, for which such situation is typically occurring, are called self-similar. Conditions for existence of self-similar solutions are considered, for example, by Sedov L.I. [138] and Barenblatt G.I. [10].

In hydraulics two definitions of self-similarity domain exist. In accordance with the first one, self-similarity domain is a range of criterion variations, within which similarity of boundary conditions [76] is enough to achieve the phenomenon similarity – it corresponds with mentioned content of the "self-similarity" term. In accordance with the second one, it is domain, where it is possible to discard an effect of one of the defining criterions. The first definition corresponds, for example, with self-similar in Re number domains (laminar and square) for pressure flows. But for achievement of similarity for effects, taking place in free flows, at self-similarity in Re number (and in hydraulics term "self-similarity" is also used for non-uniform free flows) aside from boundary conditions in general, it is necessary to achieve identity in Froude number.

Often a self-similar domain is defined as a domain of independence of required function from specified criterions. In our opinion, such definition is not quite correct. In most cases, there is no full independence of studied function from the argument in a self-similar domain, but small dependence from it, i.e. dependence, which can be ignored.

For example, it is known that hydraulic friction number λ asymptomatically tends to be constant when Re number tends to be infinity. Boundaries of self-similar domains in well known I. Nikuradze and A.P. Zegzhda curves correspond with Re values, at which measurement error in experiments exceeds λ variations in studied range of Re values.

It is practical to consider argument (criterion) as self-similar domain, if within it argument variations leads to variations of studied function by specified value and no more. Boundaries of self-similar domain for X value in π_i criterion are values of π_{lim} criterion, corresponding with deviations of studied variable from its value X_i (correspondent π_i), equal to tolerable error ΔX_{lim}.

It is understandable that a definition of self-similar domains with the help of common approximation theory methods is quite challenging, because approximation theory compares only equation terms order. For evaluation of consequences of criterion deviation from required value (criterion disturbance) it is necessary to have a solution for the equation. In hydraulic research, for a definition of self-similarity domains following method can be used. Because there is not yet analytical or sufficiently general empirical solution for complex boundaries, it is sought with simple, idealized boundaries. After that criterion impact on such a solution is analyzed, we will name it "basic." It is assumed that though a solution in real boundary conditions may differ from a solution in ideal boundaries, relative errors due to deviations of criterion from given value will be close.

There are different ways for searching for basic solutions. The first one is application of available or specifically obtained analytic dependences, related to simple single-valued conditions. The second way is numerical simulation with the help of ECM. Good results in application of numerical methods can be achieved at admissibility of 2-dimensional schematization. At the researcher's disposal there is an extensive and developing area of modern hydromechanics – computer hydraulics [157]. Possibilities of computer hydraulics allow the analyzing of links between flow characteristics and studied similarity criterion with lesser degree of schematization of boundary conditions of the studied object. Such analysis may be included in an overall research scheme, which uses at the same time hydraulic and numerical simulation (Section 1.2).

And finally, basic solutions (in the first place it is appropriate to use in connection with understudied in theoretical respect dimensional phenomenon) may be obtained as a result of systematic experiments. But, if in usage of analytical dependences and numerical methods, the definition of self-similar domain boundaries does not meet any difficulties, then on the basis of experimental data, this problem is not solved so easily: usually the real criterion value does not fall into study in experiments criterion range. That`s why boundaries of self-similar domains, based on experimental data, in most cases are defined approximately – where the value of derivative $\partial X/\partial \pi$ instinctively seems small.

As a way around this ambiguity we can propose the application of mathematical dependences, approximating experimental data. For example, in the range of larger criterion values where $X \to X_{\pi=\infty} = \lim_{\pi\to\infty} X$, usually good results are achieved by approximation of experimental data by power law. (All the following conclusions also relate to self-similar domains, which occur at $\pi\to 0$).

Among these dependences may be pointed out the following:

$$X=X_{\pi=\infty}+A_1/\pi^{n_1} \tag{3.6}$$

$$X=(X^{1/n_2}{}_{\pi=\infty}+A_2/\pi)^{n_2} \tag{3.7}$$

Dependence (3.7) corresponds with well-known A.D.Altschul formula for hydraulic friction number in transition and square zones of resistance [4]:

$$\lambda_D=0{,}11(\Delta/D+68/Re_D)^{0.25} \tag{3.8}$$

at $n2=0.25$, $X_{\pi=\infty}=(0.11^4\,\Delta/\,D)^{1/4}$; $A_2=0.11^4 68$. Here Δ - effective roughness.

Taking into account that relative error in X definition on the boundary of self-similar domain is:

$$\tilde{\Delta}X_{\lim}=\pm(X_{\lim}/X_N-1) \tag{3.9}$$

it is simple to deduce that boundaries of self-similar domains at correctness of dependence (3.6) correspond with criterion value:

$$\pi_{\lim}=\left[\frac{A_1}{A_1/\pi_N^{n_1}\pm\tilde{\Delta}X_{\lim}(X_{n=\infty}+A_1/\pi_N^{n_1})}\right]^{1/n_1} \tag{3.10}$$

and if dependence (3.7) is satisfied, then:

$$\pi_{\lim}=\frac{A_2}{(1\pm\tilde{\Delta}X_{\lim})^{1/n_2}(X_{n=\infty}^{1/n_2}+A_2/\pi_N)-X_{n=\infty}^{1/n_2}} \tag{3.11}$$

If a life model is characterized by such large values of π_N, criterion that $A_1/\pi^{n1}{}_N \approx 0$ (or $A_2/\pi_N \approx 0$), then dependences (3.10) and (3.11) may be given respectively as:

$$\pi_{\text{lim}} \approx \left[\frac{A1}{\tilde{\Delta} X_{\text{lim}}\, X_{\pi=\infty}}\right]^{1/n_1} \tag{3.12}$$

$$\pi_{\text{lim}} \approx \frac{A_2}{X^{1/n}_{\pi=\infty}[(\tilde{\Delta} X_{\text{lim}}+1)^{1/n}-1]} \tag{3.13}$$

In particular, the boundary of self-similarity of hydraulic friction number defined by (3.8), in Reynolds criterion at $\lambda_N = \lambda_{Re=\infty}$, corresponds with:

$$\text{Re}_{\text{lim}} = \frac{68D/\Delta}{(\tilde{\Delta}\lambda_{\text{lim}}+1)^4-1} \tag{3.14}$$

Calculation results for this dependence at several values $\tilde{\Delta}\lambda_{lim}$ (0.01, 0.03, *0.05)* are placed on well known dependence diagram $\lambda_D = \lambda(\Delta/D, Re)$, presented in Figure 3.2. The figure suggests that usually the defined boundary of square resistance zone approximates: $\tilde{\Delta}\lambda_{\text{lim}} = 0.04$.

The solution obtained on the model, built with consideration of discernment by this method of self-similar domains, can be later checked by input of criterion deviations into this solution (used as "basic").

Usually in hydraulics only self-similarity in *Re* number is contemplated. But simulation is practically possible due to the fact that there are self-similarity domains in other criterions. In studying flows in a square resistance zone there is also an assumed existence of self-similar domain in turbulence criterion K_{ij}. In simulation of open flows, indicative for hydro engineering practice, prototype and model are in self-similar domain in Weber criterion *We*, which includes surface tension of fluid, etc.

Study of flows with an acceptable degree of accuracy can be carried out easier with simulation in self-similarity domains in such criterion, identity of which for model and real phenomenon is usually taken as necessary. Later we will show the availability of self-similar domains in Froude number and several other criterions.

A proposed definition of self-similar domain may be extended on such argument ranges where function is significantly dependent on argument.

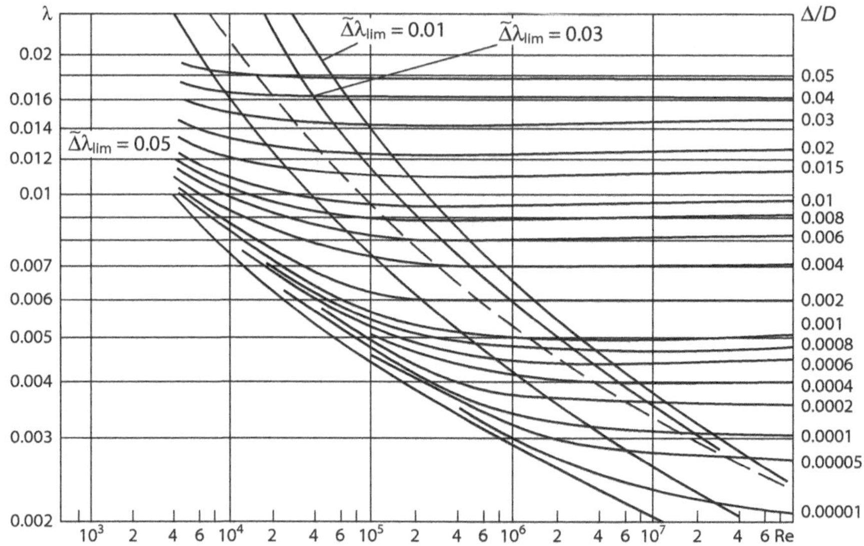

Figure 3.2 Boundaries of self-similar (square) domains of hydraulic friction factor in Re number at steady motion in boundaries with homogenous roughness: usually-accepted boundary of self-similar domain.

The difference between defined on Figure 3.3 self-similar domain, limited by values π'_{lim1} and π'_{lim2}, and domains, which usually are considered in hydraulics (for example, limited by value π''_{lim}), consists of the only fact that required function accuracy corresponds with lesser argument range. H. Einstein and N. Chen [172] consider, without application of the term "self-similar domain," possibility for simulation of flow in alluvial channel with deviations on model from real phenomenon in nine similarity criterions.

From the mentioned above definition it follows that boundaries of self-similar domains depend on research objectives. There is no general advice on boundaries of self-similar domain in required argument (criterion). These boundaries depend on which flow characteristics are studied and also on boundary conditions and required study accuracy.

Success in finding self-similar domains sometimes can be related to the appropriate choice of values which compose criterion. At that are often used is the so-called value`s "inner scale," which usually is not included in single-valued conditions, such as characteristics of boundary layer, dynamic velocity, and turbulent viscosity. For correct application of a phenomenon`s self-similarity in such criterions, it is necessary to have independent links between "inner scale" and values included in single-valued conditions. For example, self-similarity in criterion of bottom particles

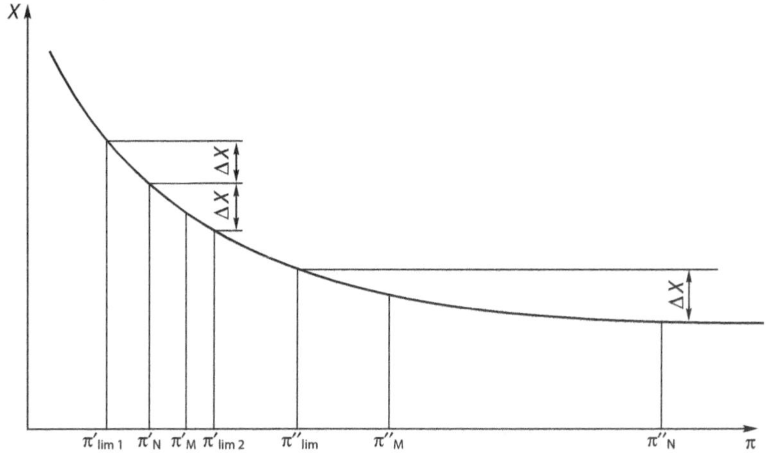

Figure 3.3 Domain of self-similar value X in criterion π.

stability, which includes dynamic velocity, is applied due to a link between dynamic velocity and averaged in depth velocity, given by problem requirements (ref. Section 7.4). Examples of application of "inner scales" are given, in particular, in [71].

3.4 Finding of Approximate Similarity Conditions With Application of Dimension Theory

Dimension theory does not give basis for definition of self-similar zones in one or another criterion. But application of this theory is not possible without taking self-similarity into account. As it is, selecting values significant for studied phenomenon, we assume self-similarity in criterions, which include values not taken into account, i.e. application of dimension theory suggests specific schematization of phenomenon and, as it was noted in Chapter 1, creation of some mathematical models.

In selection of particular problem values that are significant (and assignment of phenomenon to self-similar domains in criterions, not containing these values), attention should be paid to compliance with required phenomenon schematization. A typical example of application of dimension theory in selection of values corresponding with a different level of phenomenon schematization (molecular-kinetic and thermodynamic) is well known as a "Ryabushinsky paradox."

In 1915 Rayleigh applied dimension theory in relation to the problem of steady loss of heat to circulating fluid, which filled all the space around the body. Fluid was assumed non-viscous and incompressible. Rayleigh assumed the that amount of heat, lost by a body per time unit, is defined by a body`s characteristic dimensions l_0, fluid velocity far from body U_∞, difference in body (its walls) temperature and fluid far from body T_b-T_∞, fluid heat capacity c_p and its thermal conductivity λ_T:

$$Q_t=\varphi(l_0,U_\infty,T_b-T_\infty,c_p,\lambda_T) \tag{3.15}$$

In selection of quality of basic units:

$$[l_0]=[l];\ [U_\infty]=[l]/[t];\ [T_b-T_\infty]=[T];$$

$$[c_p]=[Q]/[l]^3[T];\ [\lambda_t]=[Q]/[l][T][t],$$

where [*T*] and [*Q*] — temperature and quantity of heat dimensions, from dimension theory can be obtained dependence:

$$\frac{Q_t}{\lambda_T l_0(T_b-T_\infty)}=\varphi_1\left(\frac{l_0U_\infty c_p}{\lambda_T}\right), \tag{3.16}$$

It follows that heat consumption is proportional to the difference of temperatures T_b — T and has the same value at different U_∞ and c_p, but their constant product $U_\infty c_p$.

In relation with the result obtained by Rayleigh, Ryabushinsky made the following observation. Assuming, that in accordance with molecular-kinetic theory, quantity and temperature of heat possess energy dimensions (kinetic gas theory temperature is defined as mean kinetic energy of molecules in chaotic motion) and their main units have the following dimensions:

$$[l_0]=[l];\ [U_\infty]=[l]/[t];$$

$$[T_b-T_\infty]=[m][l]^2/[t]^2;\ [c_p]=1/[l]^3;\ [\lambda_T]=1/[l][t]$$

Then dependence for heat quantity takes the form:

$$\frac{Q_t}{\lambda_T l_0(T_b-T_\infty)}=\varphi_2\left(\frac{l_0U_\infty c_0}{\lambda_T},c_p l_0^3\right), \tag{3.17}$$

i.e. instead of one defining criterion $\boldsymbol{l_0U_\infty C_p/\lambda_T}$, obtained in accordance with Rayleigh analysis, Ryabushinsky obtained two defining criterions: $\boldsymbol{l_0U_\infty C_p/\lambda_T}$ and $c_p l^3{}_0$.

The difference in Rayleigh's results and Ryabushinsky's results attracted the attention of many scientists but for a long time there was no explanation for it. An explanation for the "Ryabushinsky paradox" was given by L.I. Sedov in 1944 [138]. It amounted to the following. In the system of units, accepted in Rayleigh analysis, there are three regularities:

$$[m][l]^2/[t]^2;\ [T] \text{ and } [Q]$$

Transfer of heat and temperature quantity into mechanical units is related to application of heat mechanical equivalent $j([j]=[m][l]/[t]^2[Q])$ and Boltzmann constant $k([k]=[m][l]^2/[t]^2[T]$. At independent units for mechanical energy, heat quantity and temperature these constants should be considered as physical constants and generally added into consideration in regularity analysis.

From incompressibility and non-viscosity conditions of fluid accepted for this problem, it follows that field of kinematic values does not relate to field of temperatures (they are "untied," as pointed out in Section 8.1), and there is no inter-transformation of heat and mechanical energies in studied phenomenon. It means that fluid density is insignificant for thermal values and the value of heat mechanical equivalent can be discarded due to absence of transformation of heat energy into mechanical. If we accept that density ρ and value j do not affect studied process, then on the basis of dimension theory, the value of Boltzmann constant is also insignificant, because R dimension includes dimension of mass from which dimensions of Q_t and definiens are independent. In this way, studied phenomenon is self-similar in criterions, containing ρ, j and k, as it was given in Rayleigh analysis.

But if we accept that the phenomenon is independent from ρ (Ryabushinsky also accepted this hypotheses), but j and k are significant, then required dependence is:

$$\frac{Q_t}{\lambda_T l_0 (T_b - T_\infty)} = \varphi_3\left(\frac{l_0 U_\infty c_p}{\lambda_T}, \frac{J c_p l_0^3}{k}\right) \tag{3.18}$$

If the phenomenon is self-similar in $Jc_p l^3_0/k$, as it was in the studied in Rayleigh's case, then (3.18) transfers into (3.16).

If we apply value definition through mechanical values as it was done by Ryabushinsky, then J and k should be considered as dimensionless universal constants and (3.18) transfers into (3.17). Because Ryabushinsky analysis does not take into account additional considerations for a phenomenon mechanism, his conclusion appears weaker: he obtained dependence from two criterions and not one, as in Rayleigh's analysis.

In some works on dimension theory [64, 180] as a way to reduce the number of dimensionless complexes it is proposed to increase the number of independent dimensions by means of attribution of different dimensions to values, commonly having the same name but possessing particular differences. With this there should be distinguished segment lengths in directions x_1, x_2, x_3, and every one should be attributed its own dimensions. The above is also true for any vector components. In accordance with such approach, the life of hydraulic processes can be distinguished, for example, from the life of channel deformation and so on. This idea corresponds with affine transformation of space in transition from prototype to model.

As it is known from dimension theory, the lesser the number of dimensionless complexes, the more main measurement units can be chosen. So, attributing independent dimensions to values, which are usually accepted as having the same name, can allow the number of similarity criterions seemingly to be reduced. Obtained in such a way, criterions are combinations of dimensionless complexes relevant to analysis, which does not allow for input of different dimensions for analogues values.

In some publications [15, 64] conditions for application of this method are not stipulated, it is considered as a relatively new proposition, which is called "Huntley addition" [180]. The introduction to the Russian translation of the Cline`s book [64] refers to early works with similar ideas.

It should be noted that the considered method does not possess generality. L.I. Sedov [138] showed that if analogue values, which are being attributed different dimensions, are linked between themselves through dimensional physical constants then at input of additional dimensions it is necessary to input these constants into the link so the number of dimensionless parameters (π-members) will not change. Increase in the number of basic units leads to decrease of criterion number (to criterion combination) when from additional physical considerations follows insignificance of physical constants, appearing at the establishment of new basic units in a particular problem which was used in the supplied explanation of "Ryabushinsky effect." We may assume that in general, at the establishment of different units of analogue values, it is necessary to additionally consider links between these values (not only proportionality with coefficients, amounting to physical constants) and consider in dimension analysis values related to these links. Assignment of different dimensions to analogue values is effective when there are no dependences between analogue values in considered problems or values. Included in the links, are combinations of analogue values, corresponding with accepted phenomenon schematization. Such possibilities arise in space-time averaging of flows.

Let`s explain this statement through the example of application of pi theorem for establishment of dependence for pressure drop in cylindrical tube at laminar steady motion of incompressible fluid. The phenomenon is characterized by the following values: length of pipe segment *l*, its diameter *D*, pressure drop in this segment ΔP, average in section fluid velocity *U*, its density ρ and dynamic viscosity μ. If values *l* and *D* possess identical dimension [/], then, as it`s known '[52, 76], dimension theory gives the following result:

$$\Delta P / (\rho U^2) = \varphi(l / D, \mathrm{Re}_D).$$

Now let`s take into account that the problem can be viewed as one-dimensional (scale of averaging *L.>D)*, and a link between characteristics in directions x_1 and x_2 (x_3) is not considered. So let attach to *D* and *I* different dimensions: *[D]* and *[l]*. Then

$$[\Delta P] = [m][l]^{-2}[D]^{-2}; [U] = [l][t]^{-1}; [\rho] = [m][l]^{-3};;$$
$$[\mu] = [m][t]^{-1} l^{-1}.$$

It is easy to see that in this case in application of dimension theory there is link between two dimensionless complexes

$$\frac{\Delta P}{pU^2} = \varphi_1\left(\frac{l}{D\,\mathrm{Re}_D}\right),$$

which corresponds with well-known dependence

$$\frac{\Delta P}{pU^2} = \frac{C_{\Delta p}}{\mathrm{Re}_D}\frac{l}{D}.$$

In this example application of different dimensions of analogue values is allowed to obtain two dimensionless complexes $\Delta P/(\rho U^2)$ and $l/(DRe_D)$ instead of three $\Delta P/(\rho U)^2$, l/D and Re_D without introduction of additional considerations which usually are taken into account in searching for studied correspondence.

Other examples of application of this method (without indication of its applicability conditions) are contained, in particular, in [15].

Reduction in the number of dimensionless parameters may also be achieved if we introduce additional data on dependence among values contained in problem requirements [52, 76, 218]. Then for consideration there can be introduced known combinations of required values. Such an approach to dimension theory application even more aligns it with similarity theory because the introduced value combinations result from the phenomenon`s schematization. Selection of values, appropriate for applied schematization and creating combination of values, related to more generic case, should be made with great care for the purpose, on the one hand, to obtain maximum simplification on similarity conditions, which is achieved by phenomenon`s schematization, and, on the other hand – to not miss similarity criterions, resulting from links among required values and values in accordance with applied schematization.

Let`s consider efficiency of preliminary value combination, illustrated by establishment of dependence of critical tangent stress on the flat bed consisting of non-cohesive solid matter. We mean tangent stress in the beginning of matter motion at even flow. Problem specifications include the following values: linear dimensions of particles d, free fall acceleration g, fluid density ρ, material density of matter ρ_s, dynamic viscosity μ and critical tangent stress τ_{cr}. Three out of these six values have independent dimensions so connection among them can be replaced by connection among three dimensionless complexes.

Value τ_{cr} corresponds with continuous representation of medium and at its introduction it would be feasible to use such characteristics of particle assembly as internal friction angle ψ and conductivity coefficient k_φ [47]. In connection with the fact that in this particular case there are specified values which characterize a particle, we should apply schematization at discrete level and let`s assume that the effect on the particle is determined by value, proportional to $\tau_{cr}d^2$, and the particle`s drag is proportional to $g(\rho_s\text{-}\rho)d^3$. If we assume that values d, $\tau_{cr,\rho}$ and g are included in connection only in combinations $\tau_{cr}d^2$ and $g(\rho_s\text{-}\rho)d^3$ then, if we take into account that among these combinations and also values ρ and μ two values have independent dimensions, the number of dimensionless complexes can be reduced to two:

$$\frac{\mu}{\rho d\sqrt{\rho^+ gd}} = \frac{\nu}{d\sqrt{\rho^+ gd}} = \frac{1}{\mathrm{Re}_d}.$$

and

$$\tau_{cr}/(\rho\rho^+ gd)$$

where

$$\rho^+=(\rho_s\text{-}\rho)/\rho$$

then

$$\tau_{cr} = \rho\rho^{+}gd\ \varphi(Re_d)$$

i.e. it is enough to study τ_{cr} only in dependence from $Re_{d.}$

In searching for combinations of values which are included in problem specifications, often it is effective to accept for consideration some values as critical (standard), i.e. values, which are related to specific conditions of a studied process. Among these values should be noted non-shear velocity corresponding with the start (stop) of sediment transportation, settling velocity (velocity of particles, corresponding with even fall or floating up into liquid), difference in pressure on the flow boundary and saturation pressure, corresponding with start of vaporization at required temperature (cavitation), critical thermo dynamical parameters (values in critical point). Application of critical values, which are combinations of other values, included in connection, allow us to exclude some of these values from independent parameters, and corresponding criterion - from defining ones. In the studied case in introduced type X/X_{cr} criterion, where X — variable, included in single-value conditions, and X_{cr}, — its critical value. In paragraph Section 7.4 we will demonstrate how due to application of non-shear velocity:

$$\overline{U}_{cr} = \sqrt{2\rho^{+}gd / \lambda h}\ \ \varphi(\mathrm{Re}_d)$$

it is possible after introduction of U/U_{cr} criterion to exclude criterions $Re_{d,}$ ρ_s/ρ, d/h, $Fr_d = U^2/gd$.

3.5 Phenomenon Characterization and Criterions Combination

Above it was noted that obtained in some cases reduction of similarity criterions at application of dimension theory through substitution of part of criterions for their combination is linked to deepening of schematization of phenomenon description. In these cases similarity of schematized phenomenon is obtained not through identity of every criterion individually, but through identity of combination of criterions, related to more generic cases, i.e. dependence $\varphi(\pi_1,\pi_2,..,\pi_n)$ is replaced by dependence $\varphi_1[L_1(\pi_1,\pi_2,..,\pi_m),\ \pi_{m+1},\ \ldots,\ \pi_n]$.

Reduction in number of similarity criterions in the application of dimension theory from insufficient skills of the researcher may lead to significant errors, because phenomenon schematization does not stand out clearly. Much more reliable results can be obtained if a mathematical model is formulated and schematization is reflected in the description of equations and similarity conditions of their solutions. If the mathematical model has satisfactory quality, then definition of similarity conditions from equation analysis and single-value conditions gives the possibility to reliably simplify similarity conditions.

Attribution of the mathematical model to bounded domains of value variations and scale of phenomenon consideration is important for simplification of similarity conditions. Attribution of the mathematical model to bounded domains of value variations corresponds with searching for self-similar domains in criterions containing these values. Exact availability of self-similar domains gives the possibility for creation of corresponding mathematical models, without generality, but necessary for obtaining final results. Criterions define relative impact of variables, characterizing phenomenon, and phenomenon is usually divided into domains accordingly to their value, and then domains are given a mathematical description. For example, a model of non-cohesive incompressible liquid corresponds with self-similar domains in Reynolds, Caushy, and Mach criterions. Evaluation of criterion value at the boundaries of these domains is, in essence, the definition of self-similar zones, in which evaluation is carried out by the way of comparison with experimental data or more complete solution. Mathematical description, related to self-similar domain, does not provide additional possibilities in searching for boundary values of criterion. But comparison of theoretical solutions with experiment allows, at satisfactory match, to estimate self-similarity and define self-similarity boundaries on the ground of systematic difference in results.

Scale, on which phenomenon is considered, impacts the type of similarity criterions, resulting from analysis of respective equations. In enlargement of space and time scales, criterion system is usually simplified and combinations of criterions emerge, related to smaller scales (more generic cases) (ref. Section 2.7). In this work, we mainly study mechanical and thermo dynamical problems, i.e. macroscopic values and processes.

It should be noted, that these variables are functions of values, characteristic for molecular level, i.e. combinations of the latter. That is why similarity criterions, which we address in hydraulic simulation, are combinations of similarity criterions for molecular phenomena. So, making the transition from molecular scales to body dimensions, we obtain different similarity criterions systems. In connection with thermo dynamical similarity this issue is studied in more details in Section 8.1, and in connection with process of particle transportation in Section 6.2.

In the example of macroscopic phenomena, similarity of which is studied in this book, we examine how similarity conditions can be simplified with deepening of their schematization.

In more detail this issue is studied in relation to quasi-steady even flow of viscous liquid in a hard channel. Along with conditions Re =idem (or $Re_M \geq Re_{lim}$, at $Re_N > Re_{\lim}$) and Fr = idem (or $Fr_M \leq Fr_{\lim}$ at $Fr_N < Fr_{\lim}$), which include criterions, containing flow macro dimensions, the similarity conditions system for this phenomenon should include similarity criterions for boundary conditions, related to characteristics of hard boundaries.

Research in Section 4.1 shows that in general, for achievement of similarity in the whole flow domain along with identity of simplexes l_1/l_0,.. . ., l_n/l_0, where $\boldsymbol{l_1}$,-. macro dimensions, is also necessary identity of simplexes l'_1/l'_0,.. . ., l'_n/l_0, where l'_1, — linear variables, characterizing channel irregularity.

Only in the cases when averaging in lateral scale $L'>l'_{imax}$ is permissible, is it possible to introduce relative height of effective roughness peak, which is a combination of simplexes l'_1 / l_0:$\Delta / l_0 = d(l'_1 / l_0,\ldots, l_m / l_0)$, as a singular irregularity characteristic. Functions Δ / l_0 depend on flow schematization, accepted for the solution of a particular problem, and linked to scales of specific averaging for it. At introduction of simplex $\Delta / l_{0,}$ the number of similarity conditions is reduced in m — 1, where m — number of linear dimensions of roughness in the more general case. In self-similarity of phenomenon in Re instead of Δ / l_0 may be used hydraulic friction factor λ.

Averaging of flow by time with sufficiently large scale gives possibility in similarity conditions for axially symmetric flows to replace both simplexes $\boldsymbol{l'_1 / l_0}$ and Re number by hydraulic friction factor:

$$\lambda=\lambda(l'_1/l_0\ldots,l'_m/l_0,Re)$$

And indeed, for example, according to Altshul formula (3.10), distribution of averaged by time velocities over flow section in cylindrical tube is fully defined by $\lambda_{D:}$

$$\frac{U}{U_{\max}} = 1 - \frac{21g[D/2(D/2 - x_2)]}{0.975\sqrt{\lambda_D} + 1.35}$$

where x_2 — distance from the tube axis. In this particular case similarity can be achieved in a distorted model where $Re_{DM} \neq Re_{DN}$ and $(l'_1 / l_0)_M \neq (l'_1 / l_0)_N$; it is only important to sustain correspondence between l'_1/l_0 and Re_D, which supports fulfillment of the condition λ_D =idem.

Averaging of flow by depth by linear scale L/h_0 (with averaging by time scale Δt_h»h_0/U_0) simplifies similarity conditions even more (Sections 2.7,

5.3). Defining criterion in such averaging is $\lambda_h b_0 / h_0$, so it is possible to introduce different scales for lateral and vertical macro dimensions, but linked by the condition (2.118). In this case, the similarity condition is identity of simplexes l_{x2i}/b_0 and l_{x3i}/h_0, where l_{x2i} and l_{x3i} — flow dimensions in the directions x_2 and x_3 and $M_h = M_\lambda . M_b$. Scale of lateral macro dimensions in the problem should equal scale of diagonal ones: complexes, which include lateral dimensions, have the form l_{x1i}/b_0.

Identity of the complex $\lambda_R l_0 / R_0$ (l_0 — characteristic lateral dimension) is a condition for one-dimensional flows, obtained by averaging by diagonal flow section with linear scale $L » b_0$ (b - channel width) and time scale $\Delta t_b = \Omega_0 / q_0$ (ref. Section 2.7). This complex links the scales of lateral, diagonal and vertical dimensions: scales of diagonal and vertical dimensions are introduced through the scale of hydraulic radius R. In such a way, scales of multidirectional dimensions can be attributed differently, but should satisfy correlation (2.127). For wide channels (for more detail ref. Section 5.3) M_h,$=M_R$ and diagonal dimensions do not correlate with flow dimensions in other directions. In accordance with what is mentioned in Section 5.3, scale of diagonal dimensions in this case can be attributed independently, but in the model, the channel should be wide too.

Let`s pay attention to application of criterions, which amount to combination of dimensionless complexes, corresponding with general idea, in problems on channel formation out of cohesion-less material. In the most general case, a criterion system may consist of similarity criterions for fluid flow, containing dimensions and composition of solid particles simplexes, simplex ρ_s / ρ and complex $\mathrm{Re}_d = d_0 \sqrt{gp + d_0 / \nu}$ (d_0 — characteristic particle size). Similarity criterions are simplified in problems, when it is acceptable to schematize soil as particle assembly, which can be characterized by equivalent diameter d.

In some problems, for example, in definition of local abrasions (ref. Section 7.2), it is possible to introduce criterion U/w [$w = w(l_{si}/l_{s0,}\ \rho_s/\rho,\ Re_d)$ – fall diameter] instead of part of simplexes in the mentioned system (l_{si}/l_0 where l_{si} - characteristic particle dimensions; ρ_s/ρ; Re_d).

In the process of solving a planned problem of channel deformation, approximate similarity is achieved due to identity of simplex U/U_{cr}, where $U_{cr} = U(l_{si}/l_{0,}\ \rho_s/\rho,\ Re_d)$. Representation of soil as continuum (Section 2.4) allows us to apply criterions, containing such variables as internal friction angle and filtration coefficient, which are functions of dimensions and composition of particles and Re_d number.

4

Pressure Flows

4.1 Uniform Stream

The central issues of hydraulic modeling of uniform pressure flows are as follows: determination of hydraulic resistance, evaluation of the velocity distribution in the flow, and evaluation of pressure and shear stresses at the boundaries.

In the absence of phase transitions in the study of uniform streams of a simple Newtonian incompressible viscous fluid the determining parameters of the issue are: 1) the shape of the boundaries and conditions at the boundaries; 2) the Reynolds number; 3) the turbulence number.

The effect of the flow boundaries shape is evident and meeting of the similitude requirement (for example, for the flow cross-sections) seems appropriate in the general case. In this case, however, the question of possible acceptable distortions of sectional shape, and in particular the question of the possibility of a one-dimensional description of the flow with introduction of several integral characteristics of the section: cross-sectional area Ω, wetted perimeter χ, hydraulic radius $R = \Omega/\chi$.

The notion of "conditions at the boundaries" is less certain. Usually it refers to the roughness of the boundary. In real channels the roughness can generally be considered as a random function of the coordinates, which have parameters determined by the channel wall's material, design, and manufacturing technology. When formulating the conditions of approximate similitude it is important to clarify the necessary completeness of roughness description (and task) for a particular purpose, the effect of the roughness parameters on the cross section and along the length of the flow. However the overall analysis of the flow conditions at the wall is quite simple and full when using the methods of similitude theory. It is impossible to consider the influence of boundary conditions independently of the effect of the Reynolds number and turbulent flow parameters - all of these factors are closely related. The experiment shows, however, that these relations are significantly different in the boundary layers, where the maximum shift is observed, and in the flow core, where the shear stresses are small and the flows are close to isotropic.

Let's first consider the flow near a smooth wall. Suppose that we are given the mean (in probability) shear stress on the wall τ_0, the fluid density ρ and kinematic viscosity ν. It is required to find the distribution of the mean velocities $U\ (x_2)$ depending on the distance from the wall:

$$U(x_2)=U(\tau_0,\rho,\nu,x_2) \tag{4.1}$$

For fixed x_2 the only combination of initial parameters giving the speed dimension is the dynamic velocity or friction velocity:

$$U_* = \sqrt{\tau_0/\rho}. \tag{4.2}$$

The only dimensionless combination of parameters U_*, ν, x_2 is as follows:

$$x^+_2 = x_2 U_*/\nu. \tag{4.3}$$

Thus, the problem consists in finding a function:

$$U^+=U/U_*=f(x^+_2) \tag{4.4}$$

that seemingly should be universal in the given formulation. Indeed, there are many examples to prove the universality of the function (4.4), including for the liquids with significantly different density and viscosity (Figure 4.1).

The detailed analysis of the experimental conditions, however, shows that all the experiments were carried out under the condition of relatively small variation of the shear stress fluctuation parameters. If this additional condition is not satisfied, then there is no reason to expect the universality of the function (4.4).

In fact, as shown in [85], the shear stress spectrum actually defines all the pulsation processes in the viscous sublayer near the wall. If you take this into account and use a spatio-temporal spectrum of shear stress fluctuations

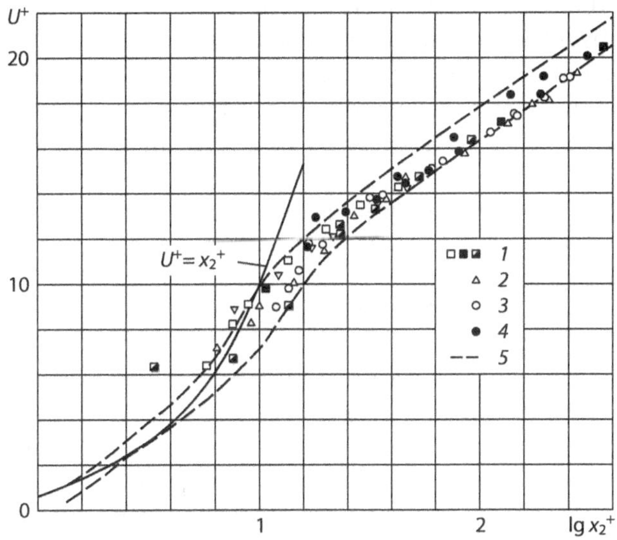

Figure 4.1 Distribution of the mean velocities in the boundary layer at standard conditions [50]:

1. air;
2. water;
3. transformer fluid;
4. glycerine;
5. limits of the scatter of the data obtained in [72].

(in addition to the average shear stress), then at least four parameters will be added to the dimensionless ratios U^+ и x^+_2 under consideration

$$\tau'_0/<\tau_0>; \tag{4.5}$$

$$\kappa_{01}\nu/U_*;\ \kappa_{03}\nu/U_*;\omega_0\nu/U^2_*, \tag{4.6}$$

where τ'_o — shear stress pulsation standard; κ_{01} κ_{03}, ω_o — typical wave numbers and frequency for shear stress spectrum:

$$\kappa_{01} = \frac{1}{\tau'_0}\left(\frac{\partial \tau_0}{\partial x_1}\right)';$$

$$\kappa_{03} = \frac{1}{\tau'_0}\left(\frac{\partial \tau_0}{\partial x_3}\right)'; \tag{4.7}$$

$$\omega_0 = \frac{1}{\tau'_0}\left(\frac{\partial \tau_0}{\partial t}\right)'.$$

It is clear that only in case of the parameters (4.5) and (4.6), one can expect the universality of the function (4.4). Let's try to find a form of this function based on the simplest model of Prandtl turbulent transfer modified subject to the comments made in Section 2.5.

Let's distinguish the viscous sublayer $\boldsymbol{x^+_2 \leq \delta_1}$ in which the turbulent stresses are much smaller than ρU^2_*. It is known [84, 85, 108, 142] that in the viscous sublayer the relative value of longitudinal velocity fluctuations (in fractions of local averaged velocity) remains constant:

$$u'_1/U = \tau'_0/<\tau_0>= 0{,}3. \quad (4.8)$$

Outside the viscous sublayer this value decreases. The transverse component of the velocity fluctuations (which is in the viscous sublayer is about 4 times less than the longitudinal) changes in the same way. In contrast, in the viscous sublayer the relative value of wall-normal velocity fluctuations increases rapidly with increase of the distance from the wall.

The instantaneous value of the viscous sublayer thickness can be determined by introducing a certian averaging time interval, greater than ν/U^2_*, but less than, for example, $1/\omega_0$. In this "quasi-averaged" flow the viscous sublayer thickness fluctuations turn out to be significant. As estimated [158], $\boldsymbol{\delta_1}$ changes in certain periods from 2.3 to 18. According to [142], the period of these fluctuations is of the order of $T=18\nu/U^2_*$. The viscous sublayer fluctuations are closely related to the shear stress pulsations.

Direct measurements of shear stress (Figure 4.2) show that the main energy-carrying disturbances occur in the frequency range $0{,}1\pi\bar{U}/h \leq \omega \leq \pi\bar{U}/h$, where h is a half the channel height [140]. This estimate is consistent with the theoretical results [85] extended in [47] that under standard conditions the maximum spectrum of the shear stress on the wall to be expected at $\omega^+=\omega\nu/U^2_*=4\cdot10^{-2}$ corresponds to the period $150\nu/U^2_*$ that significantly exceeds the period of the viscous sublayer thickness fluctuations determined by visual estimates.

The visible (dominant) fluctuations period of the shear stress calculated using the spectrum

$$T = 2\pi\sqrt{\int_0^\infty S_\tau\, d\omega \Big/ \int_0^\infty \omega^2 S_\tau d\omega}\,.$$

better agrees with visual estimates of the sublayer change periodicity.

The asymptotic behavior of the flow in the viscous sublayer at $x^+_2 \to 0$ can be studied analytically with the introduction of a small number of plausible hypotheses [58, 47, 108].

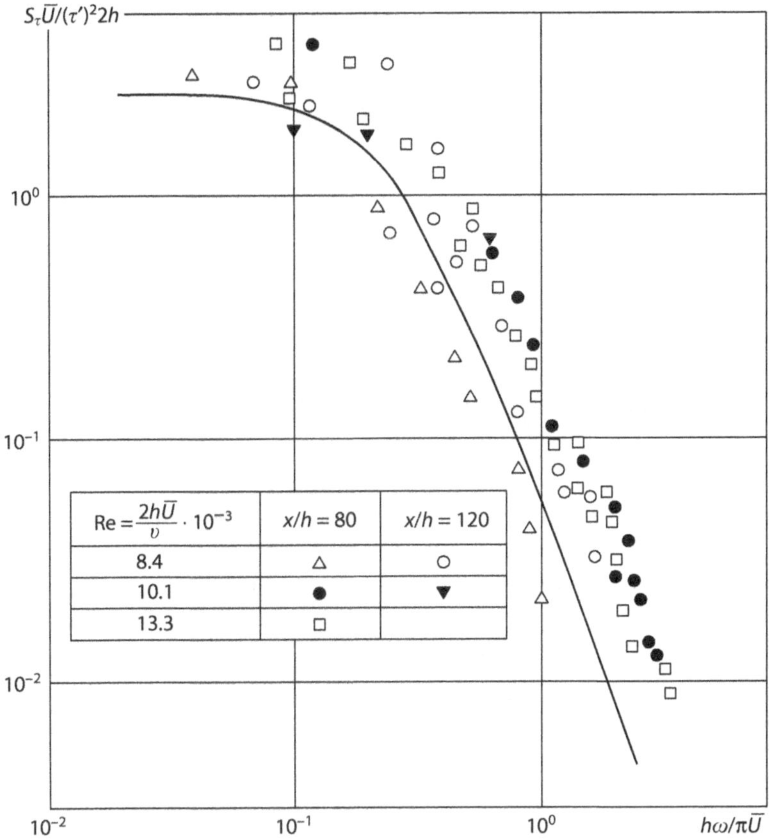

Figure 4.2 The shear stress spectra on the smooth wall in a flow channel at different values of *Re* number [140].

Particularly clear and simple results are obtained for the "flat" turbulence:

$$u'_1/U_* \approx a_1 x^+_2 \tag{4.9}$$

$$u'_2/U_* \approx a_2 (x^+_2)^2 \tag{4.10}$$

$$\langle u_1 u_2 \rangle / U^2_* = -a_4 (x^+_2)^4 \tag{4.11}$$

The estimates (4.9) and (4.10) are valid for any assumptions [108]; the result (4.11) is significantly related to the introduced hypotheses, i.e. it occurs at $\kappa_3 \to 0$ [47].

The most important result of the theory developed in [85] and later improved in [47] is the identification of the relations between the parameters a_i in the formulas (4.9) and (4.11) and the shear stress spectrum at the boundary:

$$a_1 = \tau'_0 / \langle \tau_0 \rangle; \tag{4.12}$$

$$a_z = \frac{1}{2} \frac{\nu}{U_* \langle \tau_0 \rangle} \left(\frac{\partial \tau_0}{\partial x_1} \right)'; \tag{4.13}$$

$$a_4 = \frac{1}{8\langle \tau_0 \rangle^2} \left(\frac{\nu}{U_*} \right)^4 \left\langle \left(\frac{\partial^2 \tau_0}{\partial x^2_1} \right)^2 \right\rangle - \frac{1}{24\langle \tau_0 \rangle^2} \left(\frac{\nu}{U^2_*} \right)^2 \left\langle \left(\frac{\partial \tau_0}{\partial t} \right)^2 \right\rangle. \tag{4.14}$$

Accounting for the three-dimensional nature of the pulsations [47] does not qualitatively change the relations (4.12) and (4.13). There is an additional opportunity to assess the transverse pulsations:

$$u'_3 / U_* \approx a_3 x^+{}_2, \tag{4.15}$$

where:

$$a_3 = (\tau_{03})' / \langle \tau_0 \rangle; \tag{4.16}$$

τ_{03} — instantaneous transverse component of the shear stress at the wall.

As for the changes of the turbulent stresses, in case of flat turbulence the a_4 coefficient is negative [85]:

$$a_4 \approx -2{,}9{\bullet}10^{-4} \left(\frac{\tau'_0}{\langle \tau_0 \rangle} \right)^2 \approx -3{\bullet}10^{-5} \tag{4.17}$$

i.e. for $\chi_3 \to 0$ at the wall the energy flow is directed from the turbulent disturbances to the averaged flow. The inclusion of three-dimensionality [47] allows us to refine this conclusion. It turns out that due to the influence of large wave numbers χ_3, the flow of energy in general, as usual, is directed from the averaged flow to the turbulent disturbances and an additional summand appears in the expression (4.11):

$$\langle u_1 u_2 \rangle / U^2_* = -a_4 (x^+{}_2)^3 - a_4 (x^+{}_2)^4. \tag{4.18}$$

The coefficient $\alpha'_4>0$ is also determined by the spectrum of shear stresses. Contrary to the assertions given in many publications, the coefficients a_j j are not universal constants since they may vary with the shear stress spectrum which depends not only on the local flow conditions. According to experimental data, the coefficients a_j can have the following values (Figure 4.3) [58, 72, 84, 142]:

$$\left.\begin{aligned} a_1 &= 0{,}25 \div 0{,}35;\ a_2 = (0{,}5 \div 2)10^{-2} \\ a'_4 &= (4 \div 8)10^{-4};\ a_3 = (3 \div 7)10^{-2} \end{aligned}\right\} \tag{4.19}$$

Using the linearized equations for pulsating motion in the viscous sublayer, we can frame the exact solution corresponding to the specified shear stress spectrum. The results obtained are lengthy and can be valid only if $x^+_2<\delta_1$. For this reason let's labor the simple analysis developing the known Prandtl ideas.

Since the correlation between the normal and longitudinal pulsations in the viscous sublayer is very small, we can assume that the Prandtl's hypothesis on the linear increase of the mixing length with distance from the wall will be valid if the reference point is selected at the boundary of the viscous sublayer:

$$l = \kappa\left(x_2 - \delta_1 \nu / U_*\right). \tag{4.20}$$

According to S.S. Kutateladze, such a formula was first proposed by B. Hudimoto in 1941 [72]. Using the conventional (as noted in Section 2.9, inaccurate) Prandtl's hypothesis, Hudimoto gets an expression for the shear stress outside the viscous sublayer:

$$\tau = \mu \frac{\partial U}{\partial x_2} + \rho\left[\kappa\left(x_2 - \delta_1 \frac{\nu}{U_*}\right)\frac{\partial U}{\partial x_2}\right]. \tag{4.21}$$

The solution of the equation (4.21) is a rather lengthy formula, which, however, adequately describes the experimental data [72], providing a smooth transfer from the linear velocity distribution in the viscous sublayer to the logarithmic one - in the turbulent boundary layer. The boundary of the viscous sublayer in Hudimoto's model:

$$\delta_1 = \delta_{11} = 6.8 \tag{4.22}$$

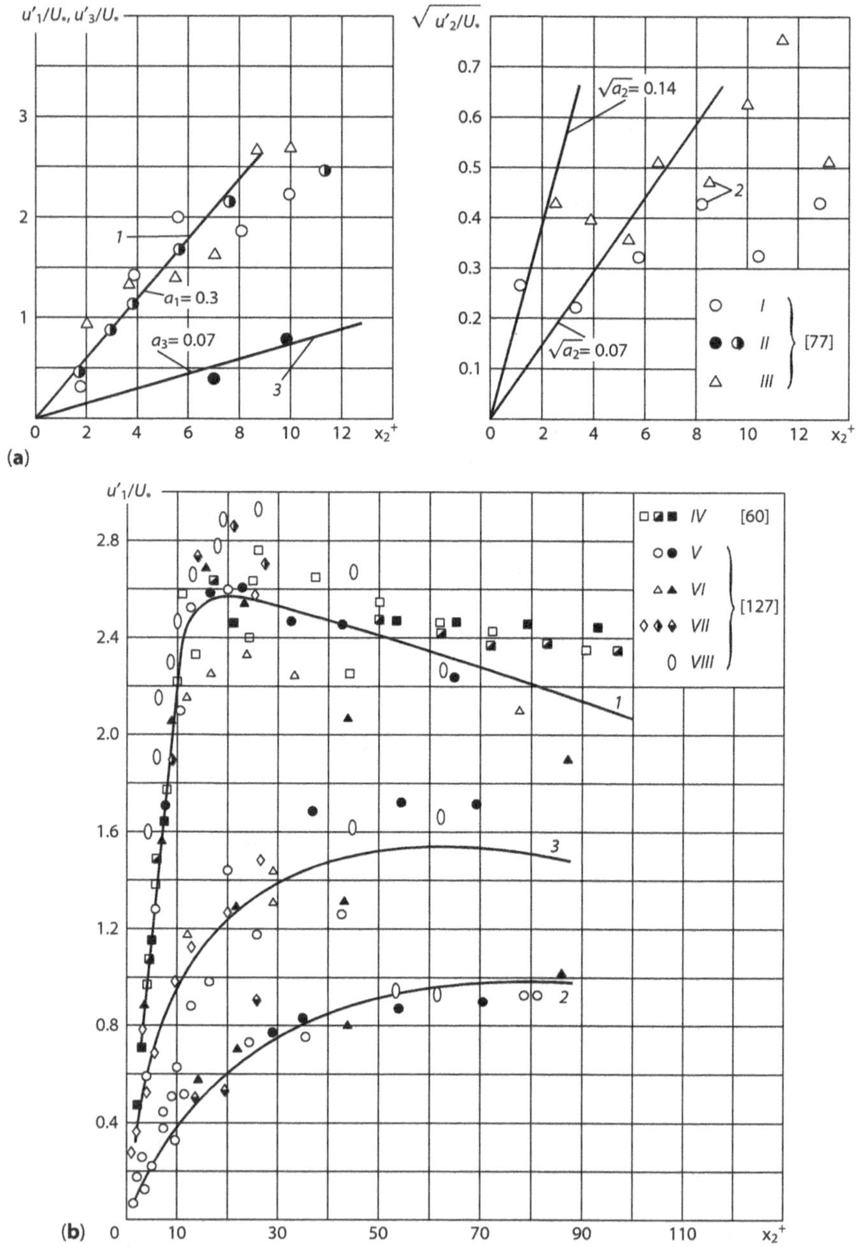

Figure 4.3 The distribution of pulsation standard of longitudinal (1), transverse (2) and lateral (3) velocity components:

ta - in the near-wall viscous sublayer, b – near a smooth wall. Experimental points [142]: *I* – B.A.Fidman; *II* – J.Laufer; *III* – V.V.Orlov; *IV* – J. Kont Bello; *V* – J.Laufer; *VI* – G.S.Tarakanov; *VII* – E.M.Habahpasheva; *VIII* – P.S.Klebanov.

If according to the classical scheme the point of reference is taken on a smooth wall, then, as is well known, using Prandtl's hypotheses one can obtain logarithmic velocity distribution outside the viscous sublayer and linear velocity distribution in the viscous sublayer. The intersection of these functions:

$$\delta_1=\delta_{10}=11.6 \tag{4.23}$$

when $x^+_2<11.6$

$$U^+ = x^+_2 \tag{4.24}$$

when $x^+_2\geq 11.6$

$$U^+ = \delta_{10} - \frac{1}{\kappa} \ln \delta_{10} + \frac{1}{\kappa} \ln x^+_2. \tag{4.25}$$

Imperfection of this model is known. It consists in derivative discontinuity at $x^+_2 = \boldsymbol{\delta}_{10}$ and in δ_{10} and κ variability.

If we return to the anisotropic transfer model discussed in Section 2.5, and take the expression (4.20) for the mixing length, the equation for the mean velocity field will be as follows:

$$U^2_* = \nu \frac{\partial U}{\partial x_2} \quad \text{at } x^+_2 \leq \delta_1 \tag{4.26}$$

$$U_* = \left[\kappa \left(x_2 - \delta_1 \frac{\nu}{U_*} \right) + \frac{\nu}{U_*} \right] \frac{\partial U}{\partial x_2} \quad \text{at } x^+_2 > \delta_1 \tag{4.27}$$

The solution of these equations is as (4.24) for $x^+_2 \leq \delta_1$ and

$$U^+ = \frac{1}{\kappa} \ln \left[\kappa \left(x_2^+ - \delta_1 \right) + 1 \right] + \delta_1 \quad \text{for } x^+_2 > \delta_1 \tag{4.28}$$

Expression (4.28), remarkable for its simplicity, closely corresponds with the experimental data for the pressure channels (Figure 4.4) and boundary layers at

$$\delta_1=\delta_{12}=8 \tag{4.29}$$

The value of parameters, and particularly the value δ_1, depends on the flow conditions - on the dimensionless parameters of the shear stress fluctuations at the wall (4.5) and (4.6), and apparently, the value may vary within wide limits. Indeed, the spectrum of the shear stresses on the wall

S_τ is connected with the spectrum of pressure pulsations on the wall S_p by the equation [47]:

$$S_\tau\left(\omega^+,\kappa^+_j\right)=S_p\left(\omega^+,\kappa^+_j\right)\frac{\left(\kappa_3^{+^2}+2\kappa_1^{+^2}\right)^2}{\left[\omega^{+2}+\left(\kappa_1^{+^2}+\kappa_3^{+^2}\right)^2\right]\left(\kappa_3^{+^2}+\kappa_1^{+^2}\right)^2} \tag{4.30}$$

Here $\kappa^+_j=\kappa_j\nu/U_*$ — dimensionless wave vector component (j=1,3); $\omega^+=\omega\nu/U^2_*$ — dimensionless circular frequency. Since the pressure spectrum can rather sufficiently vary under the influence of the causes that are usually not controlled during hydraulic experiments, it is no surprise that at different plants it is possible to obtain quiet different flow parameters. In (4.25) the constants variability was repeatedly highlighted. If we were to rewrite this as

$$U/U_*=k\lg x^+_2+C \tag{4.31}$$

then the parameter k (even when measured in similar conditions) can vary over the range

$$5.9 < k < 6.6 \tag{4.32}$$

and the parameter C (in accordance with the comment above) can vary even more. According to [67]

$$3.8\leq C\leq 7.1 \tag{4.33}$$

Figure 4.4 shows the results of mean velocities measurements in a 10 cm wide gravity tray with a smooth bottom and walls, water depth h = 3,6 cm, dynamic velocity U_*=0,8 cm/s, speed on the water surface U_s=14.5 cm/s ($Fr=U^2_s/gh$ = 0,06).

Measurements were performed using an electrochemical method and Ø 0.03 cm electrodes [25]. These measurements are compared with the data obtained in the flow channel (2x4x200 cm^3) with smooth walls (metal and organic glass) [72], and also with very careful measurements performed in a 12 m long channel with the section of 18X240 cm^2 in the fan suction line [67]. These results are shown against the background of the experimental data collected by J. Kestin and P. Richardson [108] related to the measurements in pressure flows and boundary layers. Let's note the difference in results that significantly exceeds the possible experimental data errors.

Although in Figure 4.1 and 4.4 it seems that the points are located close to each other, in fact the difference of U^+ (e.g., when x^+_2 = 10) can be up

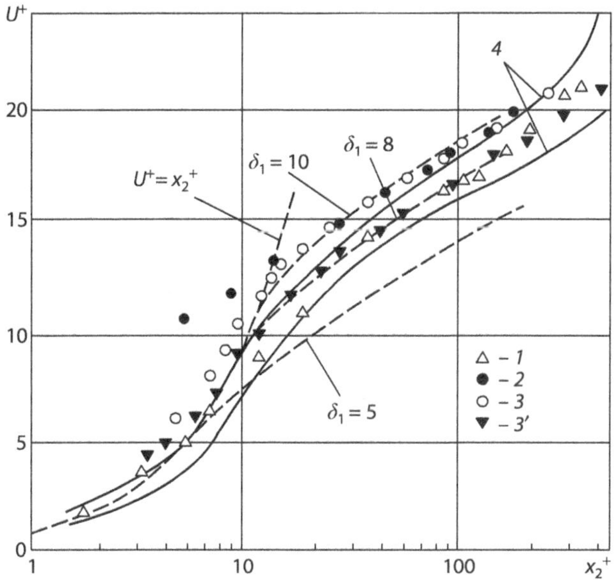

Figure 4.4 Distribution of the flow mean velocities near a smooth wall under various conditions:

1- pressure flow of water [72]; *2* — gravity flow in the channel [25]; *3* — wind tunnel, Re = 2,3.10^5 [67]; *3*' - same as Re-1,2.10^5 [67]; *4* — Kestin and Richardson generalizations for the boundary layer [108].

to 25% in different experiments. Considering the impact of the shear stress spectrum [or pressure spectrum - according to (4.30)], we can expect some differences in the structure of the boundary layer, for example, in pressure and gravity channels, since under these conditions the low frequency part of the pressure may be different [47, 84]. The smaller the Froude number is for the gravity flow, the smaller is the difference in the spectra of the pressure applied to the bottom of pressure and gravity flow. This makes it possible in many cases to widely generalize the results of the measurements in the wall layer. The applicability of these generalizations, however, should be continuously monitored.

Simple relation (4.28) was repeatedly offered by different authors on very different grounds, which do not coincide with the theory proposed here [100]. The parameters offered by different authors give an idea of the possible impact of the criteria (4.5) and (4.6) that were not considered before. It is convenient to make the comparison presenting (4.28) as follows:

$$U^+=k_0 lg(x^+_2-\delta_0)+C_0 \tag{4.34}$$

Where:

$$k_0=2.3/\kappa;\ \delta_0=-1/\kappa+\delta_1\ ;\ C_0=\delta_1-(1/\kappa)\ln(1/\kappa)$$

k_o -constant changes according to the data obtained in different conditions, in the range from 5.5 to 6.0, δ_o - in the range 5 to 7.

The value $\delta_1=8$ corresponds to the qualitative changes in the characteristics of the pulsations in the boundary layer obtained for some standard conditions. Specifically, when $x^+_2>\delta_1=8$ the functions U/U_*, u'_1/U_*, u'_3/U_*, $\sqrt{u'_2}/U_*$ begin to deviate from the straight lines corresponding to the asymptotic solutions of the equations of motion for $x^+_2\to 0$ (Figure 4.3), the Reynolds number of the outside flow starts showing its effect, and the asymmetry of the velocity pulsations sharply decreases (Figure 4.5).

The equation (4.27) and its solution are (4.28) valid in the layer where the shear stress is constant and the turbulence scale increases with the distance from the wall according to (4.20).

It follows from the arguments forming the basis of the model (Section 2.5):

$$\langle u_1u_2\rangle=-u'_2\,l\frac{dU}{dx_2}\approx -U_*l\frac{dU}{dx_2}, \tag{4.35}$$

that the parameter $l(x_2)$ should be closely related to the integral scale:

$$l(x_2)\approx L(x_2)=\int_0^h r_u(x_2,\eta)d\eta, \tag{4.36}$$

The simplest model that approximates the actual graph $l(x_2)\approx L(x_2)$ has the following form in a plane symmetric channel:

$$\left.\begin{aligned} l(x_2)&=\varkappa\left(x_2-\delta_1\frac{\nu}{U_*}\right) \quad \text{for } \frac{\delta_1\nu}{U_*}<x_2<x_{20};\\ l(x_2)&=\varkappa x_{20}=\text{const} \quad \text{for } x_{20}\le x_2\le h. \end{aligned}\right\} \tag{4.37}$$

Noting that the shear stress in the channel decreases linearly with distance from the wall, it is easy to obtain the velocity distribution in the channel central zone where the second condition is met (4.37):

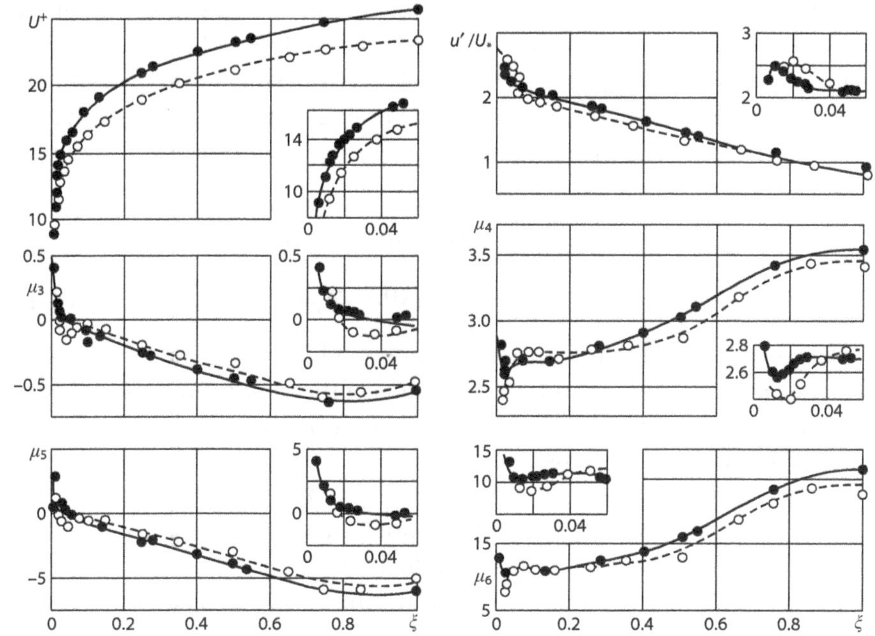

Figure 4.5 Dependence of the statistical moments $U^+, u'/U_*$ and μ_j of longitudinal pulsations on the distance to a smooth wall $\xi = 2_{x2}/D$ in a circular pipe [17]:

------------Re=8·10⁴; – – – –Re=4·10⁴.

$$\frac{U_{max} - U}{U_*} = \frac{\left(1 - \frac{x_2}{h}\right)^2}{2\left[\kappa\left(\frac{x_{20}}{h} - \frac{\delta_1}{\text{Re}_*}\right) + \frac{1}{\text{Re}_*}\right]} \tag{4.38}$$

And in the boundary layer, where the first condition is true (4.37):

$$\frac{U}{U_*} = \delta_1 + \frac{1}{\kappa}\left(1 - \frac{\delta_1}{\text{Re}_*} + \frac{1}{\kappa \text{Re}_*}\right)\ln\left[\kappa\left(x_2 - \frac{\delta_1}{\text{Re}_*}\right) + 1\right] - \left(\frac{x_2}{h} - \frac{\delta_1}{\text{Re}_*}\right) \tag{4.39}$$

Here:

$$Re_* = U_* h/\nu \tag{4.40}$$

Integrating (4.38), (4.39) over the flow depth, we can find the relative value of the maximum velocity $U^{+}_{max}=U_{max}/U_{*}$ and the relative value of the velocity for the average channel depth $\bar{U}^{+}=\bar{U}/U_{*}$. Since the received complete formulas are lengthy, we write here their asymptotic expressions true with an accuracy not lower than 2% for $Re_{*}>200$ and not lower than 0.5% for $Re_{*}>500$:

$$U^{+}_{max}=5.76\lg 10\mathrm{Re}_{*}+\delta_{1}-8 \tag{4.41}$$

$$U^{+}=5.76\lg 3.55\mathrm{Re}_{*}+\delta_{1}-8 \tag{4.42}$$

The relations (4.41) and (4.42) were obtained at $\kappa = 0{,}4$ and $\kappa x_{20}/h = 0{,}07$, that well enough corresponds to the results of the measurements in the turbulent flow core. The formulas (4.41) and (4.42) clearly show that the flow integral parameters are sensitive to the conditions at the boundary - to the value of the viscous sublayer relative thickness $\boldsymbol{\delta}_{1}$.

The analysis shows that in a wide channel with a smooth bottom the local Reynolds number Re_{*} and the relative thickness of the viscous sublayer δ_{1} at the flow boundary are the most significant similitude criteria. The value Re_{*} is directly expressed in terms of the Reynolds number $Re = \bar{U}h/v$ usually considered in hydraulics:

$$\mathrm{Re} = \mathrm{Re}_{*}\bar{U}/U_{*} = \mathrm{Re}_{*}(5.76\lg 3.55\mathrm{Re}_{*} + \delta_{1}-8) \tag{4.43}$$

Taking into account that:

$$U_{*} = \sqrt{gRI_{\mathrm{fr}}} \tag{4.44}$$

and supposing that:

$$I\,\mathrm{fr} = \frac{\lambda R}{R}\frac{\bar{U}^{2}}{2g} \tag{4.45}$$

we obtain the well-known relation for a wide flow channel with the cross-sectional height $2h(R \approx h, \lambda_{n} = \lambda)$:

$$U_{*} = \sqrt{\lambda/2}\,\bar{U} \tag{4.46}$$

Thus,

$$\mathrm{Re}_{*} = \mathrm{Re}\sqrt{\lambda/2}. \tag{4.47}$$

The relations (4.41) - (4.43) and (4.47) associate the integral characteristics of the flow in the flow channel (**U^+_{max}, U^+**) with the hydraulic friction coefficient λ and the Reynolds number Re. These relations show the form of the functions $\lambda=\lambda(Re)$ и $U_{max}/\bar{U}=f(Re)$:

$$5.76 1g\sqrt{2/\lambda}+\sqrt{2/\lambda}=5.76 1g\, 3.55\mathrm{Re}+\delta_1-8; \tag{4.48}$$

$$\frac{U_{\max}}{\bar{U}}=\frac{5.76 1g\, 10\mathrm{Re}+5.76 1g\sqrt{\lambda/2}+\delta_1-8}{5.76 1g\, 3.55\mathrm{Re}+5.76 1g\sqrt{\sqrt{\lambda/2}+\delta_1-8}} \tag{4.49}$$

Thus, the functions λ(Re) and $U_{max}/U=f(Re)$ are not unique even in smooth channels - they contain at least one additional parameter δ_1.

When $\delta_1=8$ and $Re_D<10^5$, the formula (4.48) gives the results that do not differ from the standard Blasius curve: $\lambda_D = 0.3164/Re_D^{0,25}$, where $\lambda_D = 4\lambda$; $Re_D = 4Re$.

The relations (4.48) and (4.49) allow us to solve practical questions concerning the approximate self-similarity of the flows in the channels by the Reynolds criterion. Differentiating the equality (4.48), we find an approximate estimate of the changes of the hydraulic friction coefficient with changes in the Reynolds number

$$-\sqrt{\lambda/2}\left(1/\lambda^2-2.5\right)d\lambda=2.5d\left(1n\mathrm{Re}\right)+d\left(\delta_1\right) \tag{4.50}$$

It is easy to see that the greater the Reynolds number, the greater "distortion" of the Reynolds numbers can be allowed at a fixed "acceptable" error in the definition of λ. A similar situation is observed in the distribution of the averaged longitudinal velocities, turbulence intensity and macrostructure: near the wall with the Reynolds number increase, the flow zone thickness (where v/U_* is the linear scale) decreases steadily as compared with the flow depth or the pipe diameter.

The turbulence microstructure in smooth channels in the near-wall layers and in the flow core depends on the viscosity, even at very high Reynolds numbers. The local isotropy relations are true only for very large "turbulent Reynolds numbers"

$$Re_{\lambda 1}=u'_1\lambda_1/v>500$$

where λ_1 - the Taylor scale of longitudinal velocity fluctuations.

Since in the pipe the maximum value of λ_1 is not on the pipe axis, the lowest influence of the viscosity on the pulsations spectral characteristics will be in the layers located in the middle zone ($x_2/h \approx 0.1 \div 0.2$) (см. Section 2.5).

The velocity fluctuations distribution functions differ markedly from the normal law both near the wall and in the flow core. In the wall layer the choice of v/U_* as the length scale excludes the viscosity influence on the averaged velocity $\bar{U}\ /U$ only, the other parameters of the distribution functions depend on Re (Figure 4.5).

The Reynolds number effect becomes less apparent if we consider the characteristics of "smoothed" fluctuations, i.e. fluctuations averaged over a certain area or volume. Even when the averaging area linear dimension is about 0.05 h, the velocity fluctuations distribution function appear to be close to normal law, and the distribution parameter u'/U_* is almost independent of Re at $Re = U_0 h/v > 3\ 10^4$ (Figure 4.6).

The modeling of flows in channels and pipes with rough walls is complicated since it is necessary to introduce additional criteria defining the shape of the roughness. Furthermore, in this case the notions of the "flow boundary" and "flow velocity at the boundary," require clarification. In many books on hydraulics and fluid mechanics (beginning with L. Prandtl and I.Nikuradze) it is said that the flow boundary is the surface enveloping the boundary irregularities along the outer contour (Figure 4.7). It is difficult to use this definition of the boundaries in actual random uneven surface of pipes channels, where the outer envelope is a random function. In all situations it is more convenient to use the notion of the boundary surface, defined by a certain scale L_Δ of averaging (smoothing).

Let $x_2 = y(x_1, x_3, t)$ be the function (not necessarily a single-value function), which describes the actual flow boundary. Let's call the estimated flow boundary (or simply "boundary" of the flow) the surface

$$y_1(x_1, x_3, t) = \frac{1}{L_{\Delta,x_1} L_{\Delta,x_3}} \int_{x_3 - \frac{L_{\Delta,x_3}}{2}}^{x_3 + \frac{L_{\Delta,x_3}}{2}} \int_{x_1 - \frac{L_{\Delta,x_1}}{2}}^{x_1 + \frac{L_{\Delta,x_1}}{2}} \hat{y}(\xi_1, \xi_3, t)\, d\xi_1 d\xi_3 \tag{4.51}$$

Here $\hat{y} = y$ - in y areas of uniqueness and $\hat{y} = \sup y$ in other cases.

The scales of smoothing in longitudinal $L_{\Delta x1}$ and transverse $L_{\Delta x2}$ directions may be different. When roughness is statistically homogeneous in all directions, it is natural to assume

$$L_{\Delta,x3} = L_{\Delta,x1} = L_\Delta$$

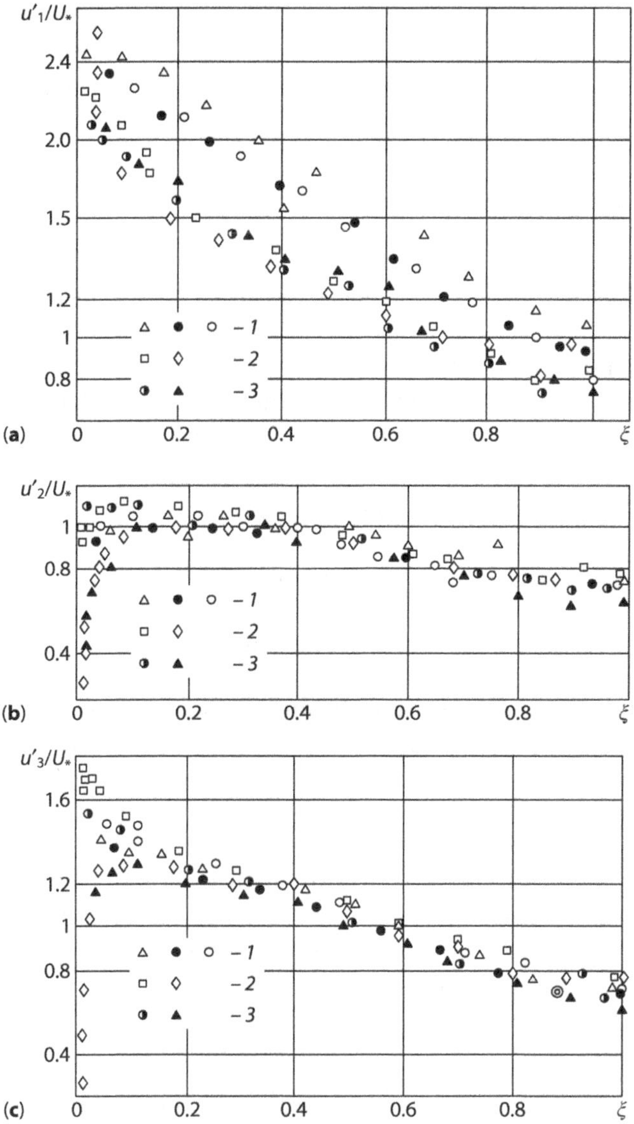

Figure 4.6 The relative value of pulsation standards of longitudinal (a), transverse (b) and lateral (c) velocity components in pipes and pressure channels at Re numbers from $3*10^4$ to $23{\cdot}10^4$. Experimental data [142]:

1 - J. Kont Bello; 2 - J.Laufer; 3 - M.H. Ibragimova, V.I. Subbotin, G.S.Tarakanov.

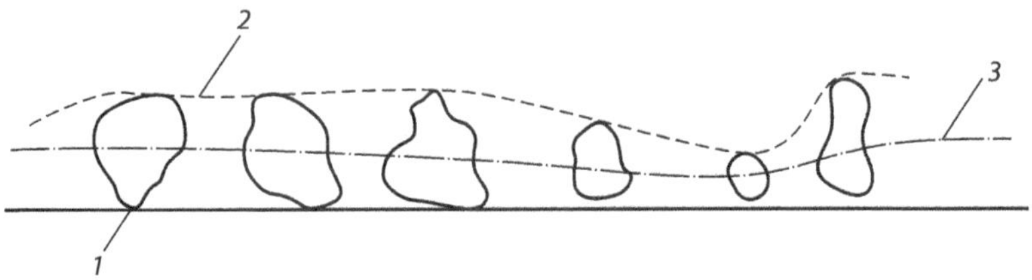

Figure 4.7 Flow boundaries diagram:

1 - outer contour envelope; 2 - inner contour envelope; 3 - average (boundary) surface.

The definition (4.51) corresponds to hydraulic experiment practice when, for example, the inner pipe diameter D is calculated based on the measurements of the water volume W filling the pipe of the length l:

$$D = \sqrt{4W/l\pi}. \tag{4.52}$$

The roughness height is usually as follows:

$$\Delta = \max y - \min y. \tag{4.53}$$

For sand roughness on a smooth surface this value is equal to the diameter of the particles. In the general case it is a random function of the size and position of the site on which max y and min y are defined. When the L_Δ scale is introduced it is natural to determine the Δ value at the site with the dimensions $L_{\Delta,x1} \times L_{\Delta,x3}$.

The similarity of the flow over a rough wall is generally achieved by preservation of dimensionless characteristics of random processes that define the roughness of the model and in actual conditions, and by preservation of the local Reynolds number:

$$Re_{*\Delta} = U_*\Delta/\nu = \text{idem} \tag{4.54}$$

and shape of the spectrum of the shear stress fluctuations [criteria (4.5), (4.6)]. Highly relevant, however, is the question - whether it is possible to reduce the number of the controlled parameters. For example, it is widely believed that at:

$$Re_{*\Delta} < 5 \div 6 \tag{4.55}$$

the roughness shape and dimensions are of no affect (The roughness peaks are "immersed in the viscous sublayer."), the velocities distribution and drag coefficients are the same as in the case of smooth-wall flow. The critical value of the local Reynolds number corresponds to the conditions of flow separation past the sphere of d diameter, which is observed at:

$$Re_{\lim} = Ud/\nu \geq 30 \tag{4.56}$$

If substitute $\boldsymbol{U}$ in (4.56) with the value determined in (4.24): $\boldsymbol{U^2_* d/\nu}$ then, supposing that $\boldsymbol{d} \approx \boldsymbol{\Delta}$, we obtain (4.55) as the condition of no-separation of the flow from spherical roughness. The self-similarity on the basis of $\boldsymbol{Re_{*\Delta}}$ occurs at:

$$Re_{*\Delta} > 60 \tag{4.57}$$

These arguments are plausible and in many cases they are quite exact. However, there may be the cases when the condition (4.55) does not provide the similitude even at of Re = idem. Such "anomaly" can be expected in case of high relative roughness when the hydraulic friction coefficient does not correspond to the classical solution, even at laminar flow conditions, due to jets deflection in the near-wall area.

$$\lambda = 64/Re$$

(here and after $\lambda = 8(U_*/\bar{U})^2 = 4\lambda_R$)

More complete analysis common for filtration tests necessitates the use of the formula (4.57) instead of the relation:

$$\lambda = 64k_\Delta/Re \tag{4.58}$$

or

$$\lambda = 64k_1/Re + k_2 \tag{4.59}$$

k_Δ values can be evaluated by the relation:

$$k_\Delta = 1 + 6(\Delta/D)^{1,5} \tag{4.60}$$

In various experiments with natural and artificial roughness the k_Δ values from 1.05 to 6.2 were obtained (review of the data and references can be found in [144]). The influence of the roughness characteristics under the condition (4.55) should not occur in case of very close or very sparsely located roughness peaks.

In all other cases under the condition (4.55) the difference with the smooth-wall flow regime is that the velocity at the flow boundary (defined by (4.51)) is not zero, and although the velocity distribution at $x_2 - y_1 \to 0$ is close to linear, it has parameters different from the parameters on a smooth wall:

$$U^+ = U/U_* = \beta \quad \text{at} \quad x_2 - y_1 = 0 \tag{4.61}$$

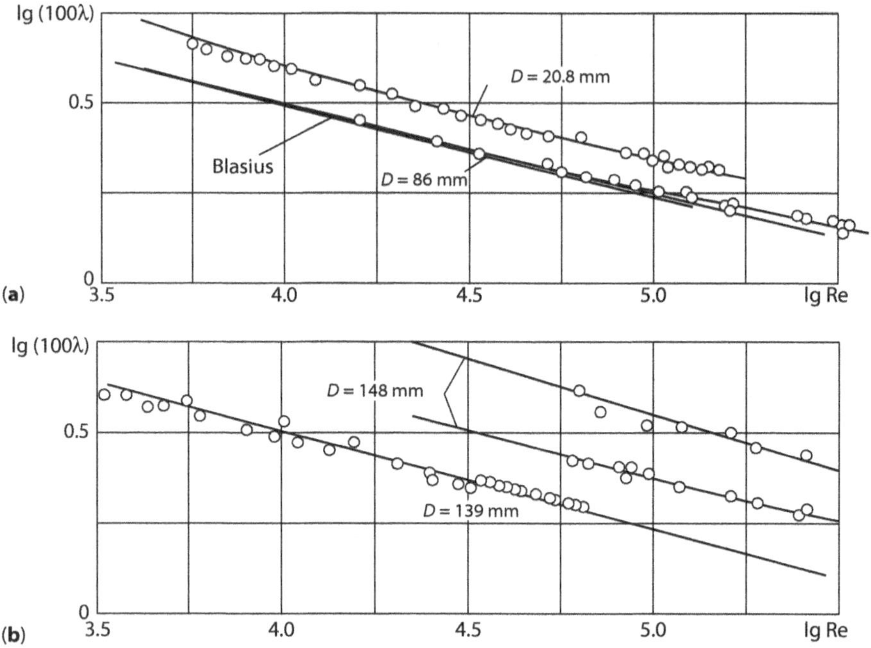

Figure 4.8 Dependence of the hydraulic friction coefficient in plastic (a) and vinylplastic (b) pipes on Re [144].

$$U^{+}=\beta+\beta_1(x_2-y_1)U_*/v \quad \text{at} \quad \delta_1 v/U_* > x_2-y_1 > 0 \tag{4.62}$$

The parameters β and β_1 depend on the statistical characteristics of the roughness and relatively weakly on $Re_{*\Delta}$.

Assuming that the relations (4.37) are valid outside the viscous sublayer, then, considering (4.62) instead of (4.42), we obtain:

$$\bar{U}^{+}=5{,}761g3.55Re_*+\beta+\beta_1\delta_1-8 \tag{4.63}$$

We can expect that if dλ> 0 when calculated according to (4.50) at Re = const, then:

$$d(\beta+\beta_1\delta_1)<0 \tag{4.64}$$

The relations (4.62) - (4.64) show that at the boundary of the viscous sublayer the relative velocity value may be markedly different than for the flow over a smooth wall. Thus, depending on the roughness, even if the smooth-wall regime is established, it is characterized by different (larger) resistance coefficients in comparison to those for smooth-wall pipes with the same Reynolds number (Figures 4.8 and 4.9). In particular, in actual practice the "smooth" pipes of the same diameter may have different resistance values due to the influence of joints and process irregularities.

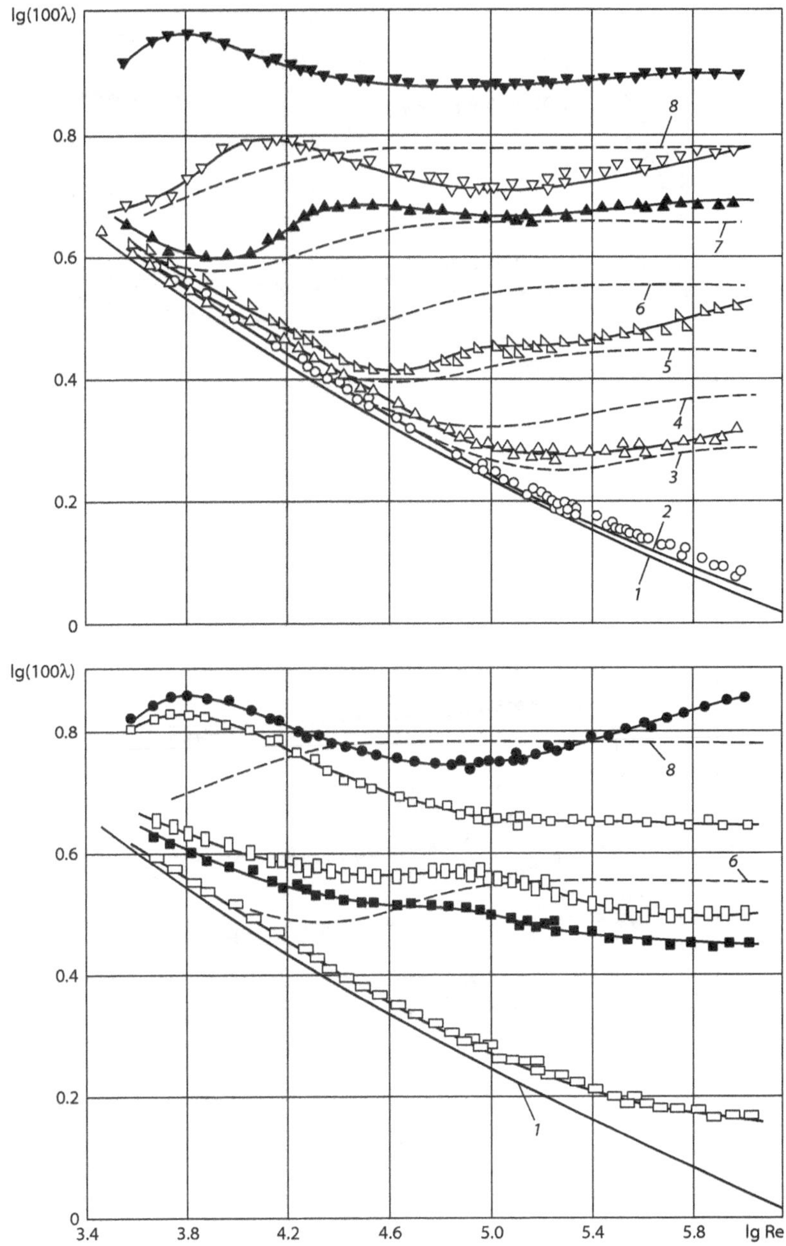

Figure 4.9 Hydraulic friction coefficient in the pipes with artificial roughness:

1 - derived curve for a smooth tube; 2 - averaged experimental curve for smooth pipes; 3-8 - experimental curves for pipes with sand roughness at $D/2\Delta$, respectively equal to 507; 252; 126; 60; 30.6; 15. For points indications see Table. 4.1. (*Continued*)

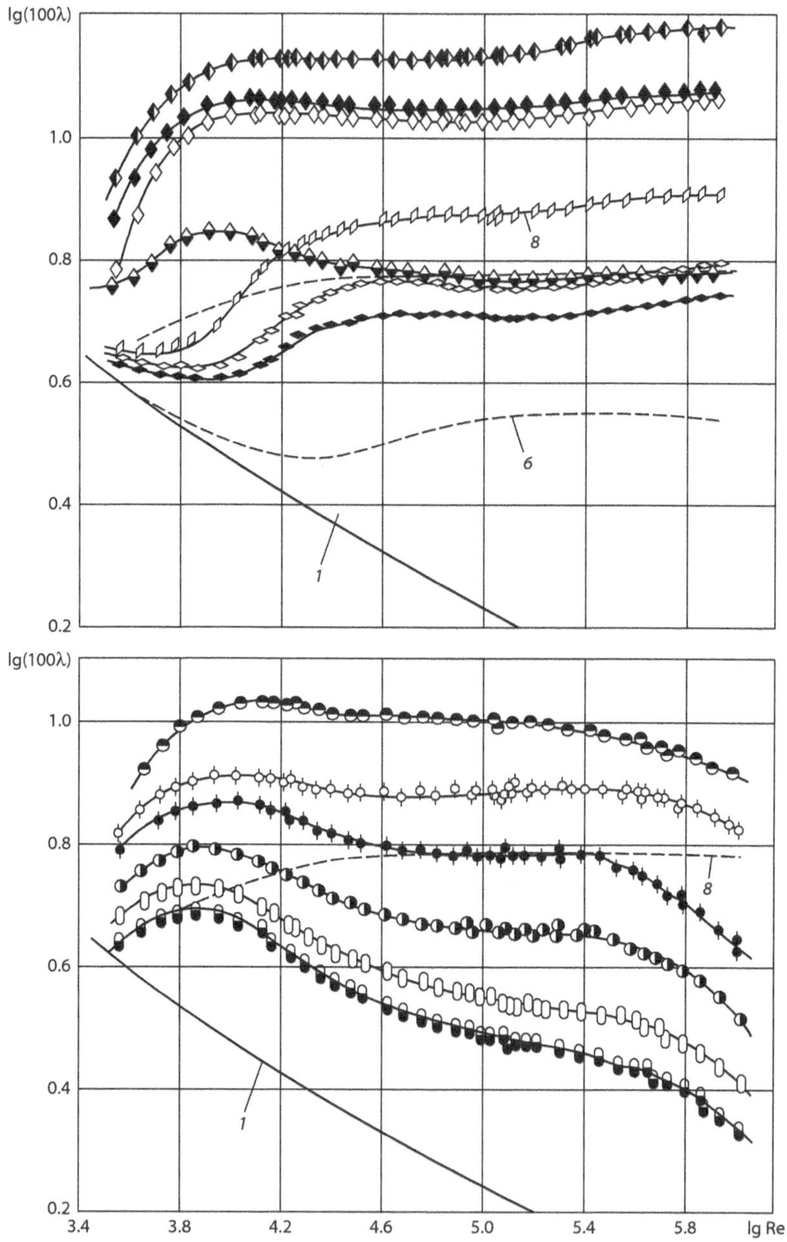

Figure 4.9 Hydraulic friction coefficient in the pipes with artificial roughness:

1 - derived curve for a smooth tube; 2 - averaged experimental curve for smooth pipes; 3-8 - experimental curves for pipes with sand roughness at D/2Δ, respectively equal to 507; 252; 126; 60; 30.6; 15. For points indications see Table. 4.1.

The increase of real tubes resistance compared to the standard Blasius curve means that the relative velocity at the viscous sublayer boundary decreases with increase of roughness.

If the distance from the roughness peak bottom to the surface of the maximum of the longitudinal pulsations standard $\boldsymbol{\delta}_T$ is taken as the characteristic linear scale, it is possible to describe the distribution of velocities and hydraulic resistance of the channels with natural and uniform (sand) artificial roughness with introduction of one or more slightly varying parameters [112]. According to this model, the effect of the Reynolds number becomes apparent only through the relative thickness of the boundary layer (Figure 4.10):

$$\delta_T/\Delta = f(\mathrm{Re}_{*\Delta}) \tag{4.65}$$

The roughness parameter Δ in (4.65) is related (though not uniquely) to the physical irregularity of the boundary. For example, if the roughness of the boundary is formed by uniform sand with a grain size d, tightly attached to a flat base, then:

$$\Delta = 1{,}4d \tag{4.66}$$

If the sand is of a mixed-grained type ($d_{max}=2d_{min}$), then in case of its dense packing:

$$\Delta \approx d_{av} \tag{4.67}$$

Δ value, mm, for some other surfaces:

New steel seamless pipes..0.13-0.20
New cast iron pipes without joints..........................0.15-0.21
Concrete stucco..0.35
Floated with cement concrete surface, carefully
molded plasticine...0.15-0.20

According to this model [112] velocity distribution and hydraulic friction coefficient do not depend on the *Re* number in all cases under the condition (4.57), and for the flows in concrete or steel pipes at $Re_{*\Delta} > 20$ (Figure 4.10).

The generalizations [112] appear to be not sufficient when considering regular roughness. There are experimental data showing that, for example, in the case of a pipe, regular roughness in the form of a fixed height helix the self-similarity of the friction coefficient λ based on Re is not observed up to $Re=2{\cdot}10^5$, while at the same maximum height of irregular roughness the self-similarity is observed at much lower Reynolds numbers [137, 142].

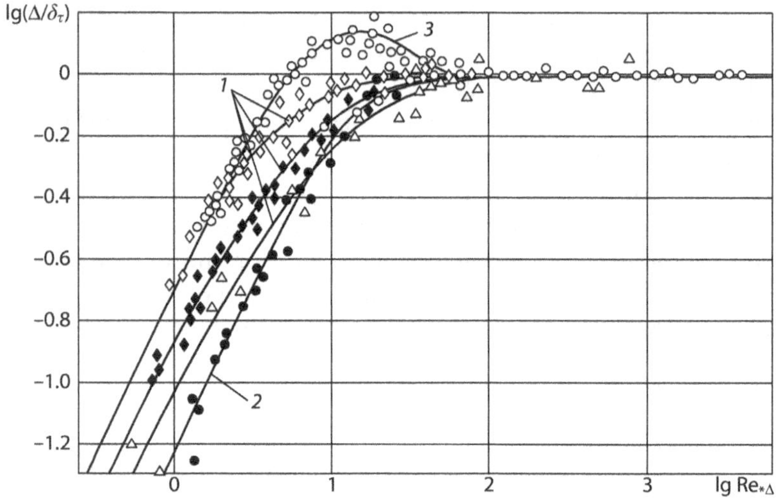

Figure 4.10 Changes of the boundary layer relative thickness δ_τ/Δ depending on local Reynolds number and flow conditions [112]:

1 - non-uniform roughness, steel pipes, concrete; 2 -cast iron pipe; 3 - granular roughness.

The role of irregular roughness is essential not only in a quantitative but also in a qualitative sense. Derating of the hydraulic friction coefficient at the transition from the self-similarity regime based on *Re* to the regime of hydraulically smooth resistance can be observed only at the uniform roughness formed by sharp-edged particles (eg. sand). In recent years the well-known experiments of Nikuradze with glued sand have been repeated with careful registration of received roughness profilogram [142] and pipes diameter determination according to (4.52).

The measurement results generally confirmed the findings of Nikuradze (see Figure 4.9) with the only difference being that the hydraulic friction coefficients in the "smooth-wall" regime are bigger than in smooth pipes at the same Reynolds numbers. The regular roughness of another form can give a variety of relations $\lambda=\lambda(Re)$. The conditions of the experiments, of which results are shown in Figure 4.9, are listed in Table 4.1. It is important that the difference of the functions $\lambda = \lambda\ (Re)$ results from the features of the flow in the boundary layer only. When choosing the coordinates not related to the flow boundary position or the boundary layer structure, the velocity distribution in the flow core turns out to be stable, practically independent of the form of the boundary roughness (Figure 4.11). This means that there is a deep generality (self-similarity) of all turbulent flows away from the areas where intensive generation and dissipation of

Table 4.1

	View roughness	Numbers the height of the protrusion				
		1	*2*	*3*	*4*	*5*
		$\Delta = 0.06$	$\Delta = 0.19$	$\Delta = 0.5$	$\Delta = 1.0$	$\Delta = 2.0$
		$D/2\Delta =$ $= 492$	$D/2\Delta =$ $= 155$	$D/2\Delta = 59$	$D/2\Delta =$ $= 30$	$D/2\Delta = 15$
1	A single triangular thread 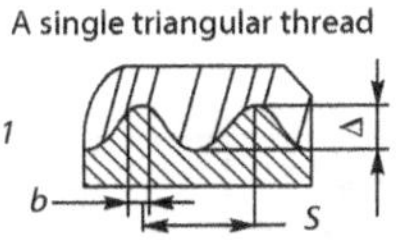	△ *1–1* $S = 0.25$	△ *1–2* $S = 0.5$ $b = 0.11$ $\alpha = 75°$	▲ *1–3* $S = 1$ $b = 0.05$ $\alpha = 40°$	▽ *1–4* $S = 2$ $b = 0.27$ $\alpha = 60°$	▼ *1–5* $S = 4$ $b = 0.54$ $\alpha = 60°$
2	A single rectangular thread 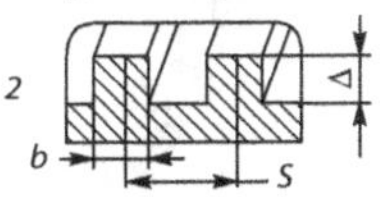					□ *2–5* $S = 4$ $b = 1.7$
3	A single rounded thread 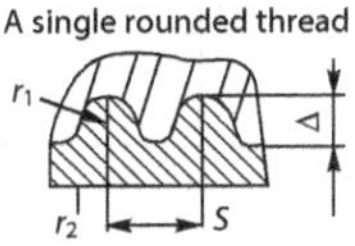					● *3–5* $S = 4$ $r_1 = 0.75$ $r_2 = 1.25$
3	Multiple triangular cross-thread 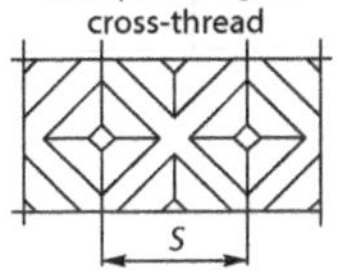			S / N_1 *4–3*: 1 / 80 *4–3–6*: 2 / 40 *4–3–∂*: 2 / 40		S / N_1 *4–5–1*: 4 / 20 *4–5–2*: 4 / 44 *4–5–3*: 8 / 22 *4–5–4*: 16 / 11
5	An annular undercut 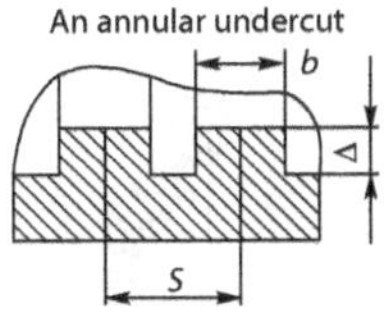			S / b *5–3–1*: 30 / 29 *5–3–2*: 30 / 20 *5–3–3*: 30 / 10		
6	Hemispherical protrusions 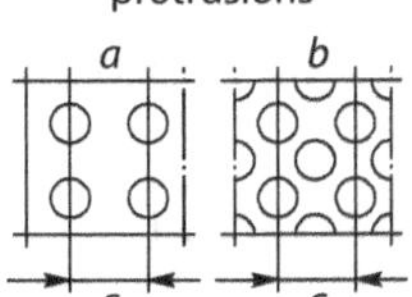					S / N_2 *6–5–1*: a / 32 / 6 *6–5–2*: b / 32 / 11 *6–5–3*: a / 16 / 11 *6–5–4*: b / 16 / 22 *6–5–5*: a / 8 / 22 *6–5–6*: b / 8 / 44

Note. N1 - number of multiple thread entries; N2 - number of protrusions on the pipe section of the length S, the shape of the projections of the variant 1-1 is close to trapezoidal with rounded corners (*a*-90°, *b*≈0, 11).

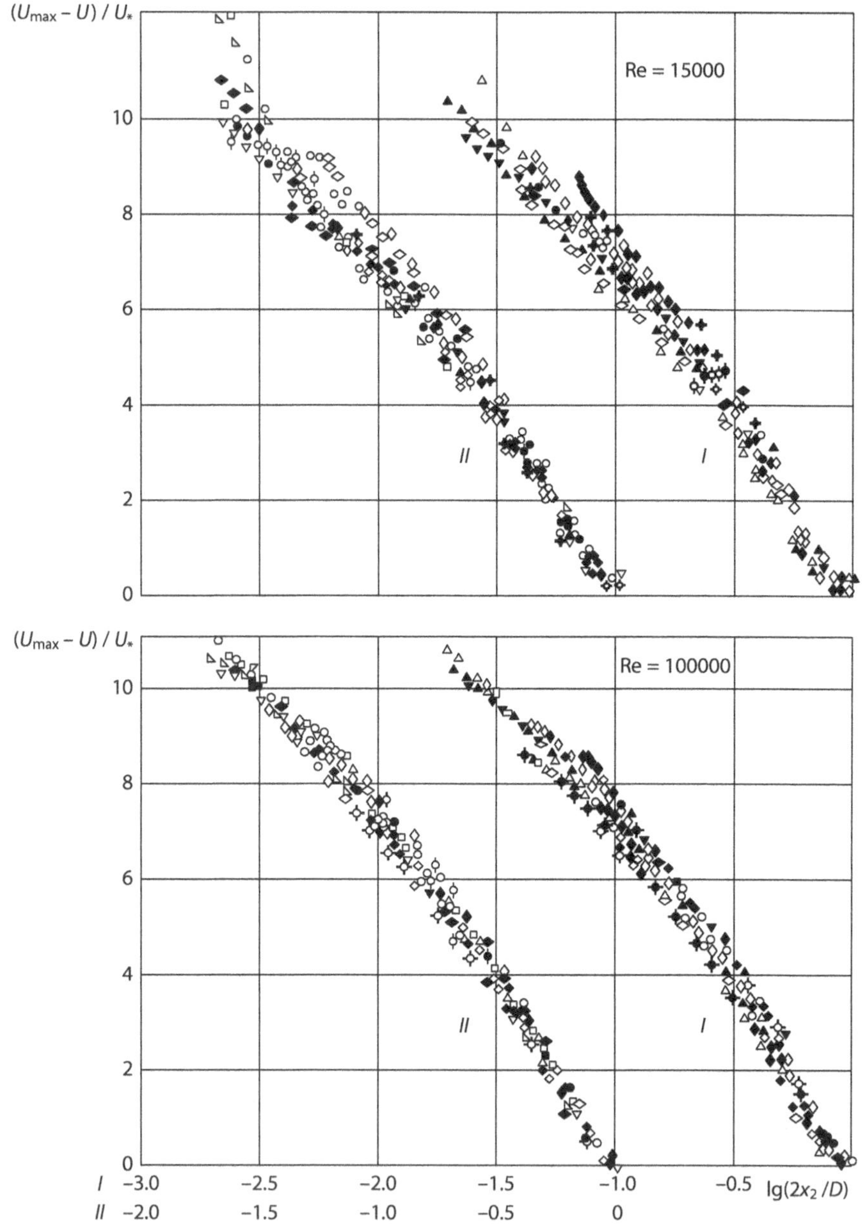

Figure 4.11 Distribution of the velocity deficiency in the pipes with an artificial roughness [142]. For points indications see Table 4.1.

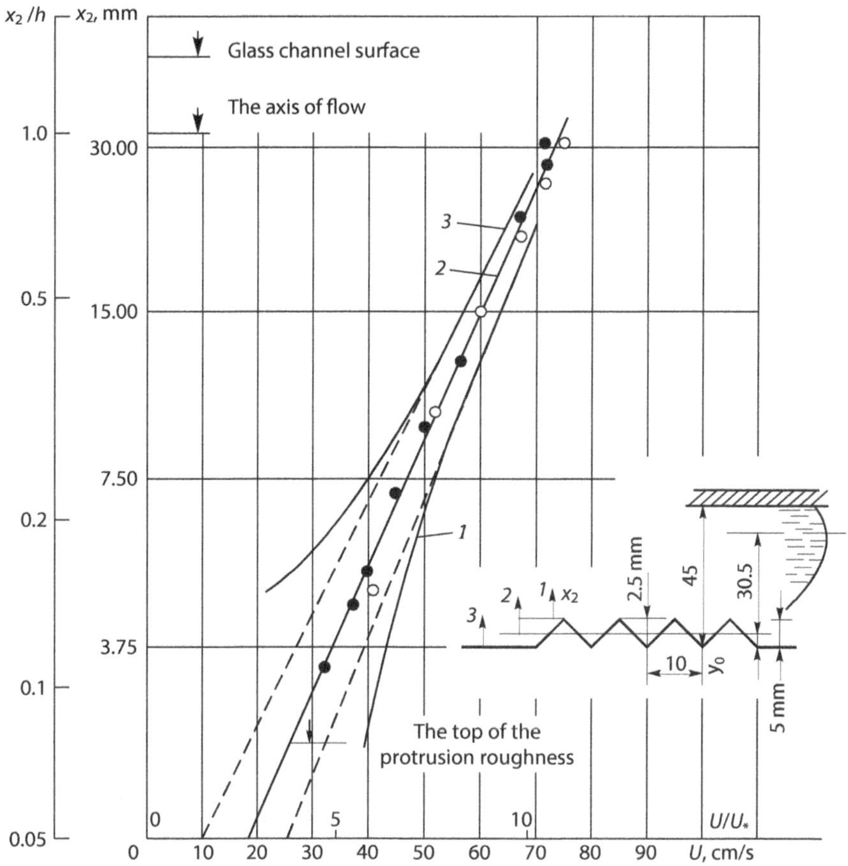

Figure 4.12 Velocity distribution over a rough surface when choosing the point of reference on the crest (*l*), in the middle part (2) and at the base of the roughness (3). Experimental data by B.A. Fidman [147].

turbulence energy occurs. On a smooth wall it is the area at the boundary of the viscous sublayer. On the rough wall it is a zone slightly higher than the maximum peaks of roughness. The rate of the loss of correlation between longitudinal velocity pulsations at the points shifted across the flow (regardless of the roughness) is approximately the same [142]. The foregoing suggests that in case of a reasonable choice of the point of reference [eg. the estimated boundary according to (4.51)] the generalization effectiveness can be significantly higher.

Processing of the experimental data [147] confirms this assumption (4.12). When the point of reference is located in the middle of the roughness peak (line 2), the "universal" logarithmic law (4.31) is valid almost to the crest of the roughness peak. In contrast, the location of the point of reference at the crest (1) or at the base of the roughness (3) causes a significant deviation from the logarithmic curve. A similar result was obtained by processing the data of the experiments, which was carried out by different authors under different conditions [84]. The importance of the choice of the point of reference in the velocity calculations at a rough wall and the variability of the roughness local height was describe by M.D. Millionshchikov in his model of "rolling" vortices [105].

The results of unique measurements in the area of natural roughness location are given in [25]. These data show that at the height of the roughness peaks, the relative velocity U^+ can vary considerably, but outside the wall layer (with a proper choice of the point of reference), the velocity distribution is self-similar relative to the changes in the wall layer, but, of course, dependent on the external conditions: the channel configuration, boundary conditions, parameters instability. The stability of the flows characteristics outside the boundary layer has been noticed in [84] based on the comparison of turbulence parameters, averaged over the length of the separation zone, and the boundary of the wall layer.

All these observations can be summarized by proposing a model in which the rough boundary area is filled with biphasic medium, which has statistical properties given as a function of distance from the surface (4.51). At a certain distance δ_0 from this surface, one can observe the maximum generation and dissipation of the turbulence energy, the maximum relative longitudinal velocity fluctuations u'_i/U_* and the maximum fluctuation of the shear stress $\tau'/<\tau>$. Outside this layer, the turbulent flow structure of it is close to self-similar and mainly depends on external conditions from the channel geometry - the pressure gradient. The value of relative average velocity U^+, turbulent energy $e/(U_*)^2$ and its dissipation rate $\varepsilon h/U^3$on the surface surface $x_2=\delta_{0mm}$ is essential for the flows in the core.

In particular, this parameters setting allows us to use the model «e—ε», and to calculate the velocity distribution in the core [54]. The issue of the effect of the spectral shape of the shear stress fluctuations is less clear. It is likely that under standard conditions this effect can be ignored. However, a sudden change of these conditions (eg. superposition of acoustic oscillations, boundaries elasticity, presence of free surfaces in the flow) can cause a change in the shear stress spectrum and corresponding changes in the flow core. In the wall layer ($x_2<\delta_0$), the shear stress fluctuations can be critical. In this layer the flow is essentially dependent on the features of the boundary roughness, and it is relatively weakly dependent on external factors, such as the averaged pressure gradient and macroinstability parameters.

In the flow core adjacent to the wall boundary layer (where the shear stress varies insignificantly), the hypothesis of the flow local similarity is naturally introduced [105, 108, 112]. This hypothesis leads to the law (4.28) or (4.34), where $x^+_2=x_2/\Delta$ is measured from the surface of $x_2=\delta_0$. In the flow core adjacent to its axis, the assumption of the local isotropy is more real, which leads to a relation similar to (4.38); for the entire flow (at $x_2>\delta_0$), it is possible to introduce a generalized hypothesis of "partial self-similarity," leading to a power-series velocity distribution [10].

Since at the self-similar velocity distribution in the flow core λ is almost completely determined by the value of the relative velocity at the near-wall sublayer boundary, it is obvious that the condition of the coefficients λ equality on the model and in real conditions:

$$\lambda = \text{idem} \tag{4.68}$$

is the necessary condition of the flow structure similitude.

The system of the sufficient similitude criteria is determined by the requirements of the problem under study. The exhaustiveness is almost impossible, however, for example, if it is necessary to ensure only the similitude of the first two statistical moments of the velocity fluctuations. It is enough to supplement the condition (4.68) with the requirements of the criteria (4.5), (4.6) identity and:

$$\left.\begin{array}{l} \mathrm{Re}_{*\delta_{0\tau}} = U_* \delta_0 / \nu = \text{idem} \\ \text{or} \\ \mathrm{Re}_{*\Delta} = U_* \Delta / \nu = \text{idem}, \\ \text{if} \\ \mathrm{Re}_{*\Delta} \langle 60. | \end{array}\right\} \tag{4.69}$$

The self-similarity by *Re* in the new-wall layer is observed at:

$$\mathrm{Re}_{*\Delta} < 60$$

Self-similarity of velocity distribution and pulsation standards in the stream core is specified at more or less Reynolds numbers. Thus the criterion (4.57) gives the evaluation of the complete self-similarity for the channels with natural or artificial sand roughness.

At first glance the identity requirement of the criteria (4.5), (4.6) and (4.68) contradicts the formation principle of characteristic criteria from the parameters set in the experiment or calculation (from the parameters which specify the single-valuedness conditions). However the meaning of the imposed requirements is that many conditions of the single-valuedness which often drop out of consideration in the conventional hydraulic approaches, are the most clearly and fully manifested, namely in these criteria. For example, the first and the second system criteria (4.6) on the roughness boundary characterize the location of roughness peaks along the flow length and in the plan. It is known that under certain conditions, the distance between the peaks gives better roughness characterization than the size of a peak [203]. It's usually enough to ensure the identity of the normalized distribution functions and spatial spectral (or correlation) roughness characteristics on a rough wall instead of meeting the criteria (4.5) and (4.6). It's necessary to pay special attention to the possible tensor character of the roughness when the velocities at the boundary of the wall layer $U_{\delta 0}$ (or even at the stream boundary) and local shear stress τ are collinear [95]. The similitude should be provided for each component of this special tensor connecting the shear stress and the considered velocity.

When making simulation one should set the distribution of the shear stress along the flow boundary in the proper way. Such a job is provided by the macroform similitude of the flow boundaries and distribution along the surface of roughness boundaries. The possibility of effective generalization of the results by the introduction of hydraulic radius R is limited even for cylindrical boundaries of regular shape with a constant roughness. For example, the hydraulic friction coefficient λ in smooth rectangular channels with a ratio of 1: 1 or 20: 1 is different about 1.5 times (Figure 4.13). In channels with complex shape sections even the qualitative behavior may be different in comparison with the circular pipes and wide channels. Geometric similitude of sections is necessary here.

Stationary transverse circulation, causing in some cases the unexpected distortion profiles of the longitudinal velocity, may occur in channels with non-uniform roughness on the cross section, even with a uniform flow.

Velocity distribution in the two-dimensional channels, in which one wall is rough and the other is smooth, was studied in detail in recent years by many authors, with respect to the tasks to be completed on pressure models of open flows [91]. Methodology of elementary calculation of such channels is set out in [121].

Dependencies λ; h_1/h_2; λ_1/λ_2 и $\bar{U}_1/\bar{U}_2$ on Δ_1/Δ_2 and Δ_2/h received by the calculation at square resistance regime are presented in the Figure 4.14. Dependence between λ, $\bar{U}_1/\bar{U}_2$, h_1/h_2 and the *Re* number found by the calculation is shown in the Figure 4.15 for some relation values of the effective height of roughness peaks of parallel surfaces Δ_1/Δ_2. Here λ is a coefficient of hydraulic friction calculated over the total height of the channel h and mean velocity in it; $\bar{U}$; $\bar{U}_1$ and $\bar{U}_2$ are mean velocities in the flow zones

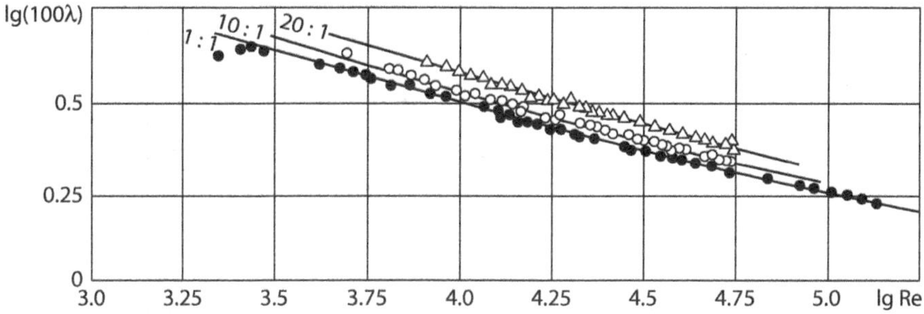

Figure 4.13 Influence of the channel cross-sectional shape on at its hydraulic resistance [144].

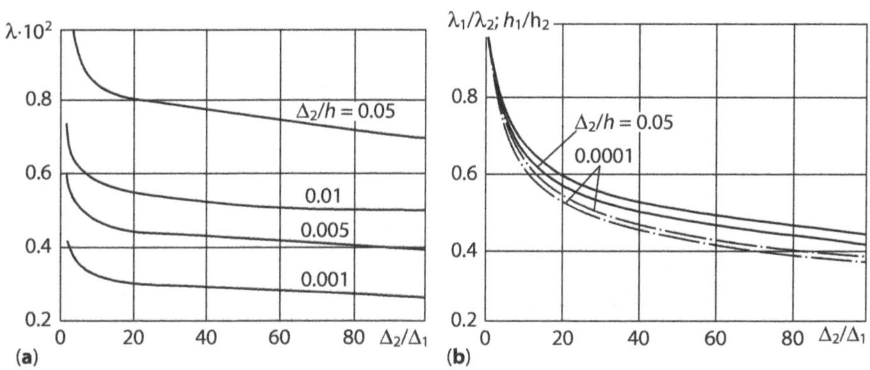

Figure 4.14 Dependencies at square resistance law.

a-$\lambda=\lambda(\Delta_2/\Delta_1;\ \Delta_2/h;)$ *b*- $\lambda_1/\lambda_2,\ h_1/h_2;$ ____________ - $h_1/h_2;$ —·—·—·—·—·—λ_1/λ_2

divided by a subspace going through the maxima of velocity profiles; h_1 and h_2 are the height of these zones; $Re—Uh/v$.

If to match the dependencies $\lambda=\lambda\ (Re)$ for the channel with mixed roughness with the same dependencies for the channel with uniform roughness, it's necessary to mention that with the same λ and Re in a case of the mixed roughness, the derivative $d\lambda/dRe$ is more than it would be in the case of the uniform roughness, and the boundaries of the self-similarity area under Re for the non-uniform roughness move to the side of greater Re values.

Comparison of calculation results with experimental data [38, 177] is presented in the Figure 4.16. Good agreement of the calculation and experimental results shows the acceptability of the calculation model usage. The quoted results are quite logical at different roughness of opposite walls of the rectangular section channel. On the contrary the measurements in the

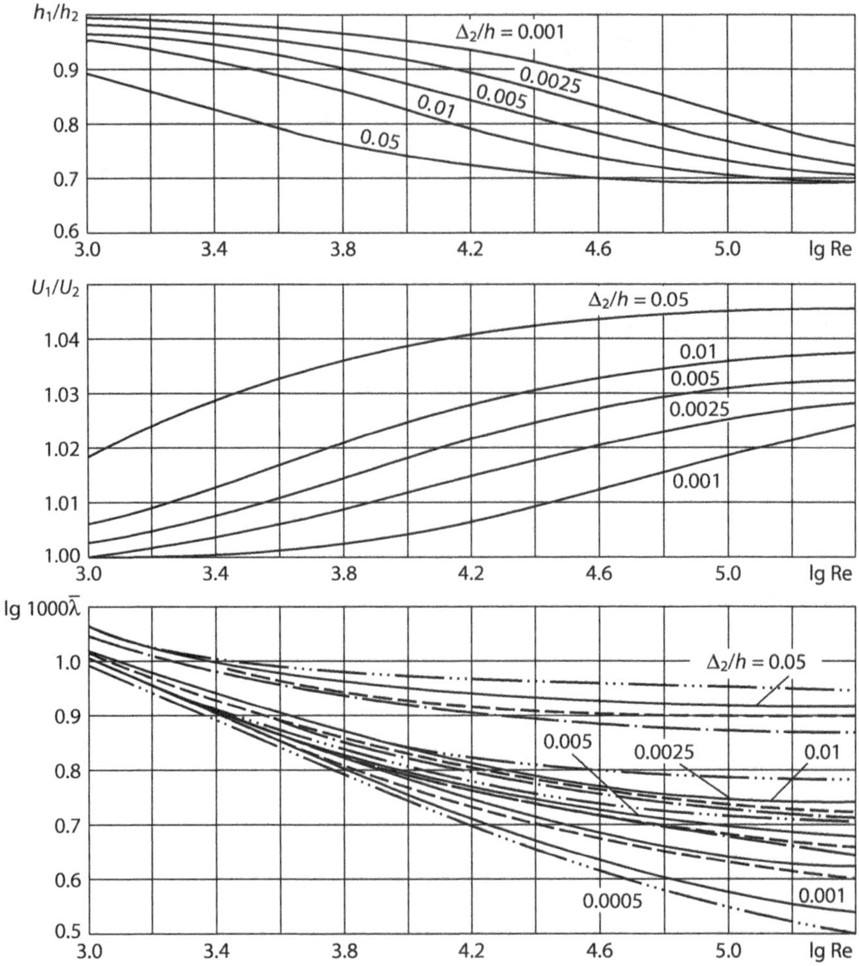

Figure 4.15 Characteristic parameters in the channel with different wall roughness depending on the Re number.

______ $\Delta_2/\Delta_1=10$; - - - - $\Delta_2/\Delta_1=20$;-.-.-.-.-.- - $\Delta_2/\Delta_1=67$; ---...---... $\Delta_2/\Delta_1=1$.

circular pipes, a half of the perimeter of which has an increased surface roughness, provide the opposite picture: velocity maximum is located closer to the rough surface [144]. The position of the maximum and the complete picture of velocities distribution significantly change depending on $Re=UD/v$, even with its values of $(60—90)10^3$ order (Figure 4.17). Self-similarity laws of the wall-adjacent flow (in particular the logarithmic law) in the mentioned conditions have a place at the distance from the walls not exceeding 0,25D.

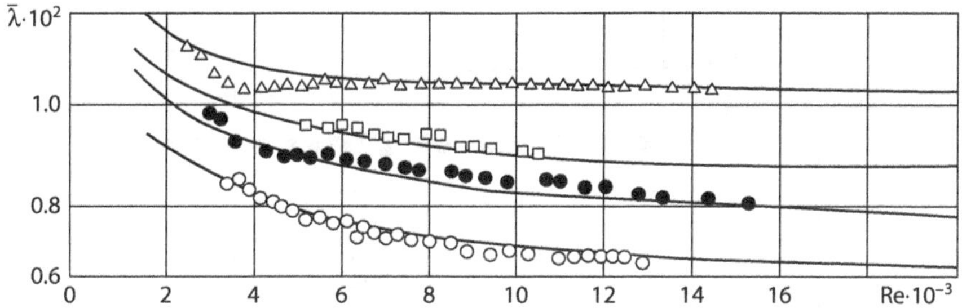

Figure 4.16 Matching of calculated and experimental data:

– at Δ_2/h=0,075; consequently Δ_2/Δ_1=3,5; 12; 100;
– at Δ_2/h=0,015 and Δ_2/Δ_1=20; __________ – results of calculation

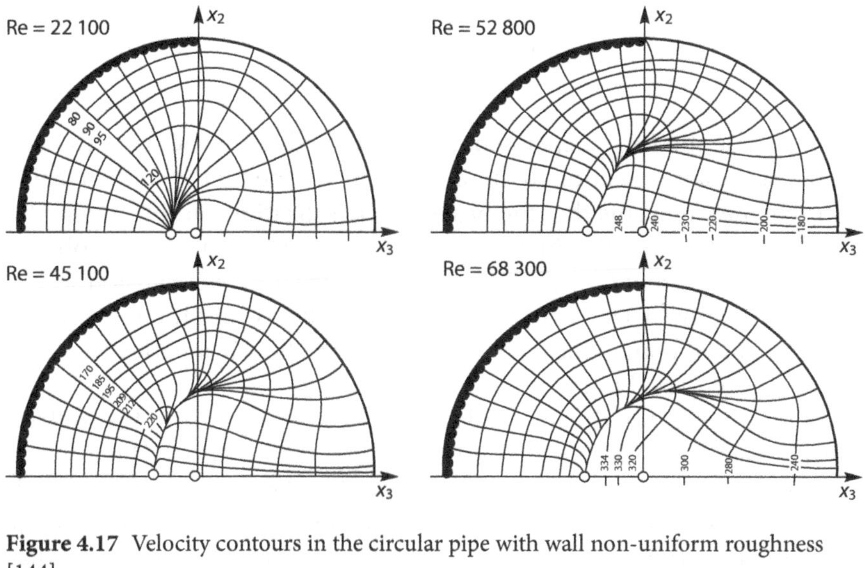

Figure 4.17 Velocity contours in the circular pipe with wall non-uniform roughness [144].

4.2 Non-Uniform Flow

Uniform regime was almost never observed on the model. In most cases there are causes of large-scale perturbations in the flow, which promote the flow turbulence in general. Therefore the boundary values of the Re number are substantially less than in the uniform motion on the flow extension area or obstacle flow-around. In such circumstances the Re_{gr} fundamentally depends on the flow boundary shapes and it's difficult to give any general recommendations on the limits of self-similar areas. A.G. Averkiev

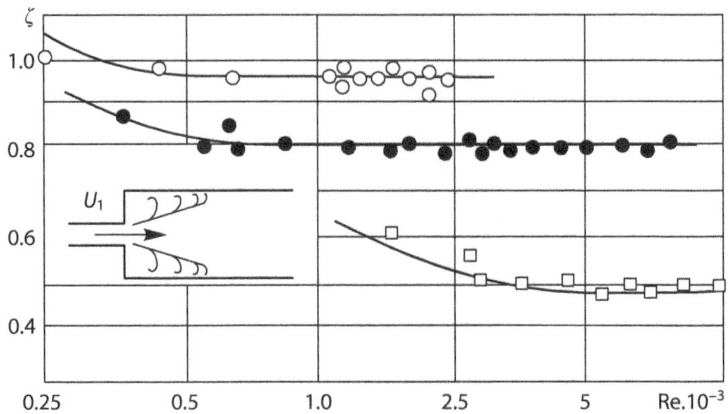

Figure 4.18 Self-similarity ζ under the Re number in the sudden expansion scheme in the pipes:

○- U_1/U_2=3,2; ●- U_1/U_2=11,4; □- U_1/U_2=3,5.

[1] has made the Re_{limit} dependent upon the "bed shape factor" – the ratio of area of the larger section to the smaller one for the for the sudden expansion schemes. It seems that the broader generalization can be obtained by setting the Re_{limit} in the first approximation dependent on the obstacle resistance coefficient ζ. Such dependence on the sudden expansion scheme is built in Figure 4.18. From this picture, it follows that the introduction of even relatively small local resistances into the flow dramatically reduces the Re_{limit} compared to the uniform motion.

As for the effect of the Reynolds number on the friction at the wall, this effect is somewhat weaker than in the uniform flow due to the influence of perturbations penetrating into the boundary layer of the flow core. It's necessary to emphasize the more conservatism of the boundary layer with respect to the external disturbances slightly affecting the range of the shear stress. The distribution of velocities in the layer is determined to a great extent by a local shear stress. For example the Figure 4.19 shows the distribution of the longitudinal velocities and the standards of their pulsations near the wall of the pressure rectangular pipe at different distances from the pipe intake (the pipe intake was smoothly outlined and equipped with a cellular device [67]).

Figure 4.20 shows the distribution of the same values but over the complete flow section (from wall to the flow dynamic axis). As seen, the difference of the flow conditions in the flow thickness had almost no effect on the conditions in the boundary layer at distances up to $x+_2$=10:15. In this example the external flow had the relatively low levels of turbulence and

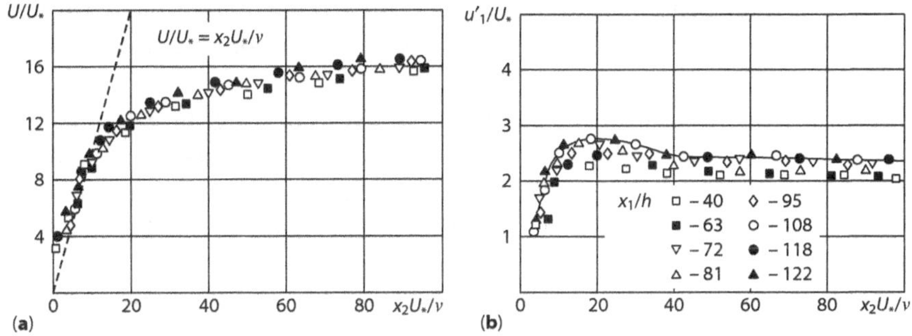

Figure 4.19 Average velocities (*a*) and standards of longitudinal velocity pulsations (*б*) near the wall at $Re= Uh/\nu=1{,}2{\cdot}10^5$ with different distances from the pipe intake x_1/h.

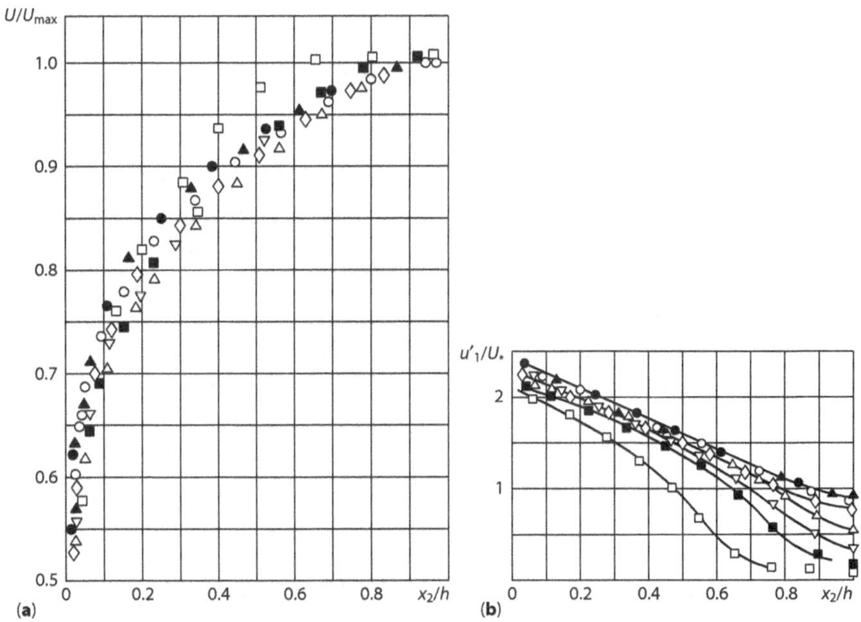

Figure 4.20 Average velocities (*a*) and standards of longitudinal velocity pulsations (*б*) with different distances from the pipe intake (designations are in the Figure 4.19).

the conservatism of the boundary layer may be associated namely with this circumstance. However, a similar result was obtained, for example, also for the diffuser [97], where the external disturbances were rather intense. This means that the relationship between the velocity and shear stress on the outer edge of the boundary layer, in the lack of the abrupt changes of the shear stress spectra, slightly depends on the external flow conditions.

Effect of the Reynolds number under conditions of a two-dimensional problem was studied with different levels of detail for both the unseparated and separated flows.

For the uniform flow at the assigned relative wall roughness the distribution of the averaged velocity with an error less than 5%, as is well known [see Section 4.1], is set by one line in the coordinates $U^+=U/U_*$, $x^+_2=U_*x_2/v$ at small distances from the wall and in the coordinates U_{max}-$U)/U_*$, $\xi=x_2/h$ h in the flow core.

The boundary position between these two zones is dependent on the Reynolds number and the relative roughness of the walls. The second area covers almost the entire flow, and the velocity distribution becomes fully self-similar at the same values of the Reynolds number, in which there is an independence from the Re of hydraulic friction coefficient λ.

Turbulence characteristics are relatively more sensitive to the effect of the Reynolds number. Pulsation standards measured in fractions of the friction velocity in the zone of maximum turbulence generation (near the border of the boundary layer) decreases somehow with the increasing Reynolds number.

For example, according to the data of Laufer [191] at $Re=U_{max}h/v$ $=12.3{\cdot}10^3$, $31\ 10^3$ and $61\ 10^3$ the maximum value of the longitudinal pulsations standard $(u'/U_*)_{max}$ in the rectangular pressure channel with smooth walls is 2.6; 2.2; 1.98 correspondingly. Similar changes were also found by J. Kont Bello [67], though the values $(u'/U_*)_{max}$ in these measurements were somewhat different: at Re = $57\ 10^3$; $120{\cdot}10^3$; $230{\cdot}10^3$ $(u'/U_*)_{max}$ = 2.8; 2.65; 2.5 correspondingly. These values in the flow core are not changed even in the conditions of the smooth-wall regime when the values (a) and the distribution of the average velocities don't vary (see Figure 4.6). Spectra and correlations with the Reynolds number growth significantly change mainly due to the extension of the "inertial" range of wave numbers in which the conditions of local isotropy are fair and the spectral density is proportional to $\kappa_1^{-5/3}$ (Section 2.5). Integral turbulence scale changes slightly and the internal (Taylor) scale decreases proportional to $\sqrt{\nu/(U_*h)}$.

The influence of the Reynolds number in the non-uniform flow should be greater if the nonuniformity of motion contributes to the turbulence weakening (e.g. in confusor) and should be reduced, on the contrary, in the presence of additional sources of disturbances (e.g. in a diffuser or in curved channels). Figures 4.21 and 4.22 show the data of E.V. Zalutsky [51], from which it's seen that the distribution of velocities and velocity pulsations amplitudes in the confusor area don't change greatly with the Reynolds number variation from 10000 up to 20000 at relatively smooth

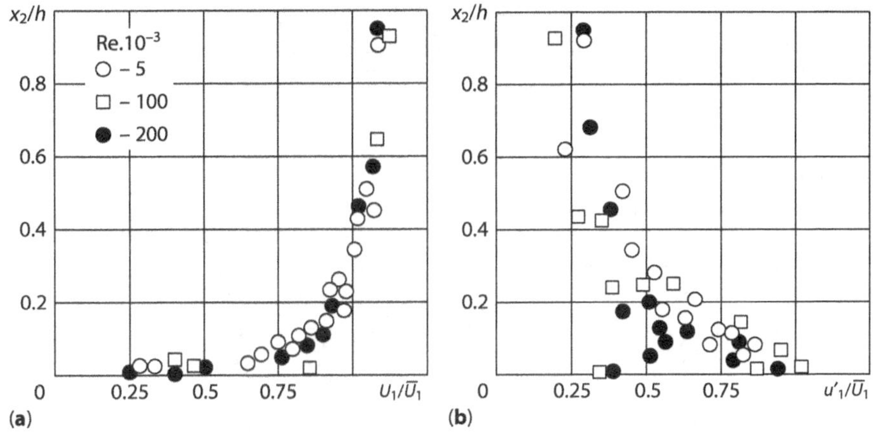

Figure 4.21 Longitudinal average velocities (*a*) and standards of longitudinal velocity pulsations (*б*) in confusor with smooth (iron) bottom at different values of the Re number.

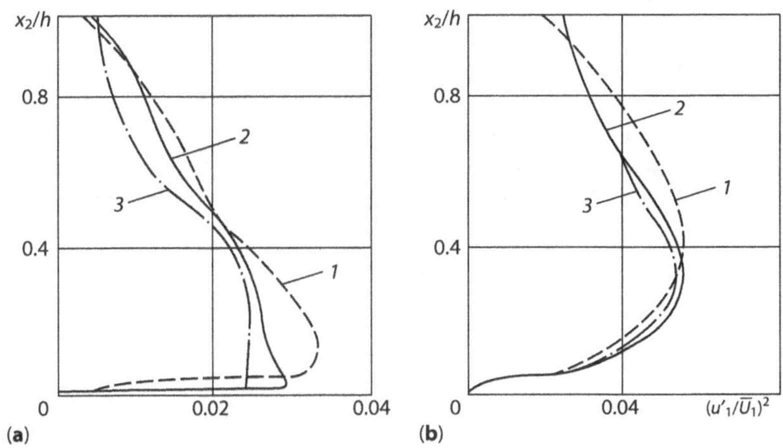

Figure 4.22 Dispersions of velocity pulsation in confusors at different values of the *Re* number:

a – with smooth bottom; *б* – with rough bottom; $h/\Delta = 17 \div 28$; *1*–$Re = 5 \cdot 10^3$; *2* – $Re = 10 \cdot 10^3$; $Re = 20 \cdot 10^3$.

surface of models. This difference is low for the flow in the diffuser even in comparison with the experiment at $Re = q/\nu = 5000$.

Influence of the Reynolds number in the separated flow conditions is relatively small, if the point of flow separation is fixed by the boundary outline. Figure 4.23 shows that the distribution of average velocities in the flow behind the scarp at $Re = U_0 h_0/\nu = 2550$ and 17400 differs slightly though the eddy length changes significantly: from 6 heights of scarps at Re=2550

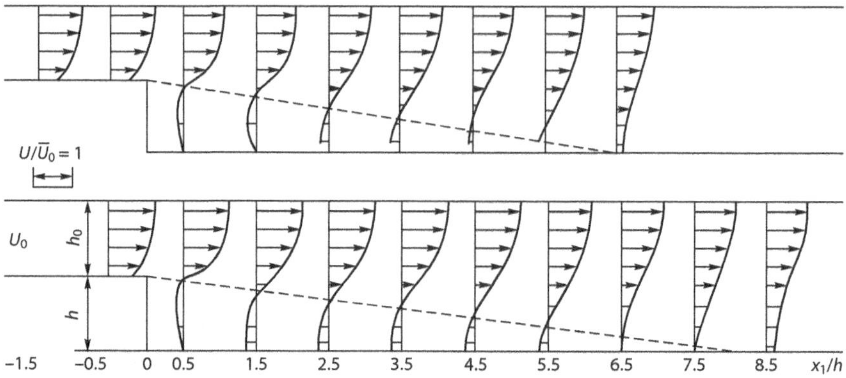

Figure 4.23 Field of average velocities according to the experiments of B.A. Fidman [148]

up to 7.5—8 heights of scarps at Re=17400. The further increase of the Reynolds number (approximately up to $Re=3\cdot10^5$) doesn't cause any perceptible changes of the eddy length or the distribution of average velocities at the extension area [148].

The found eddy length change at not very high values of the Reynolds number becomes clear when comparing the data on the turbulent stresses and standards of velocity pulsations in the same conditions (Figures 4.24 and 4.25). The relative value of the turbulent friction and pulsation standards is more at lower Reynolds numbers. Physically it can be presented as follows: large vortexes, not "diffused" by high-frequency pulsations, and depressed by viscosity will transfer a rather big impulse and cause relatively heavy braking.

If the separation point is not fixed, for example, at the flow-around of obstacle with rounded corners, there could be the anomalous increase in the influence of the Reynolds number at the values of this number, corresponding to the boundary layer turbulence moment formed on these round-ups (Figures 4.26 and 4.27).

Range of anomalously large influence of the Reynolds number is interesting also for the turbulence generation. Namely in these circumstances, when there is a fluctuation of separation points positioned on a smooth cylinder, the maximum oscillation amplitude of the lift force coefficient and resistance coefficient is observed. All these effects are significantly less on a rough cylinder and at the elevated level of free-stream turbulence.

In general it can be noted that in the presence of fixed separation points of the boundary layers, the flow is self-similar under the Reynolds number already at its values of 10^4 order. If the separation points are not fixed, the

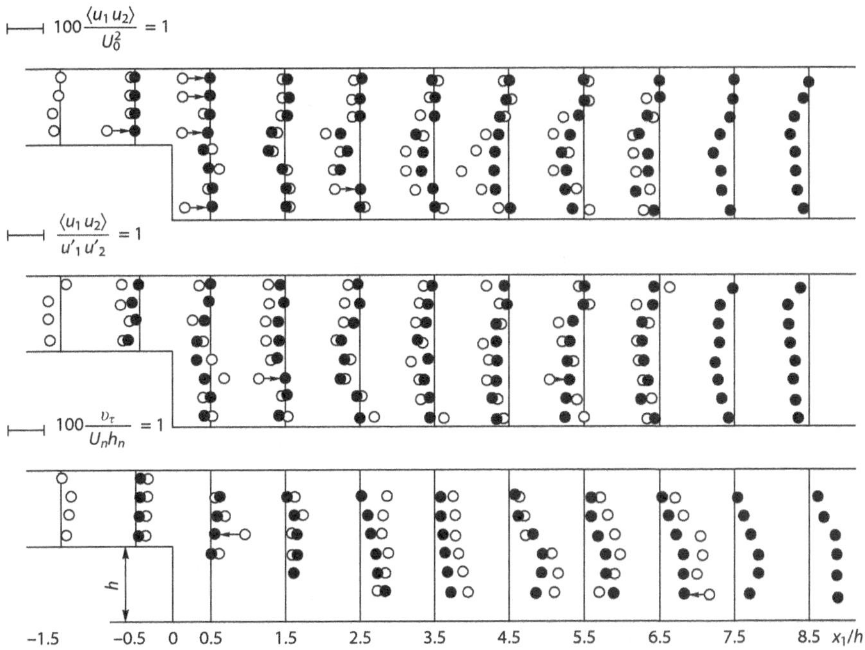

Figure 4.24 Correlation of two velocity components $-\langle U_1 U_2\rangle$ (turbulent friction) and turbulent viscosity $\nu_\tau = \dfrac{-\langle U_1 U_2\rangle}{\partial U/\partial x_2}$ at different Re numbers: o- Re=2550; •- Re= 17400.

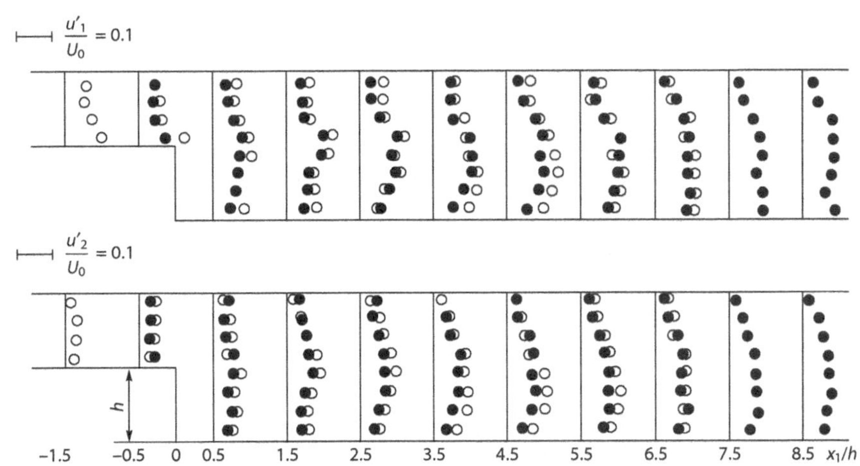

Figure 4.25 Field of velocity pulsation standards u'_1, u'_2 at different Re numbers:

o- Re=2550; •-Re= 17400.

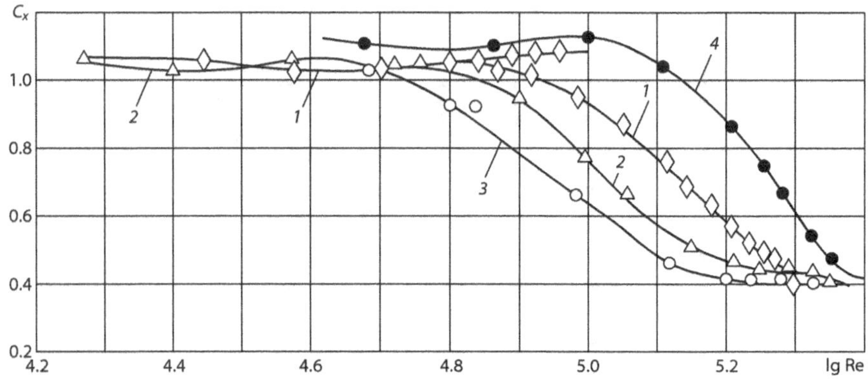

Figure 4.26 The dependence of the drag coefficient of a circular cylinder with a diameter of 155 mm from the Reynolds number at different free-stream turbulence [46].

effect of the Reynolds number can be apparently substantial at the arbitrarily large values of it: the critical region observed by many authors in the study of flow around cylinder when $Re=U_0D/\nu\approx(3\div4)\cdot10^5$ (***U_0***— inflow velocity) is possibly not the only one.

The distance from the turbulizer until cylinder: 1 -1880 mm, 2 -1220mm, 3 – 903mm, 4-∞.

Figure 4.28 shows the oscillation frequency and amplitude of lift forces acting on cylinders. Sharp increase of points dispersion is observed at $Re \approx(2\div5)\cdot10^5$ as well as at $Re \approx(2\div4)\cdot10^5$. Points location at $Re>10^5$ does not allow us to talk about the self-similarity of flow around smooth cylinder. The general problem of the influence of the Reynolds number remains valid, but its specific aspects in relation to the flow around rough surfaces and the formation of separation zones at the fixed separation points are clear enough: we can expect a clear self-similarity at the Reynolds numbers of the 10^4 order, unless the turbulent flow takes place at all model zones.

Modeling of the pressure streams, which is substantial by itself, has acquired in recent years a special significance for the practice of hydraulic modeling, due to the rise and wide development of open flows study method at the pressure models. Sections 5.5, 5.7 as well as [38, 91, 177] are devoted to this method. Here we'd like to mention that many tasks and issues of the pressure flows modeling have occurred thanks to the development of this method. For example, a great influence of conditions on the washing-out character on the model entry was registered with the usage of pressure models with movable bed. In those cases when no special measures were applied, the washing-out intensity at initial areas of the model was usually much lower than at the main area of the model with the same

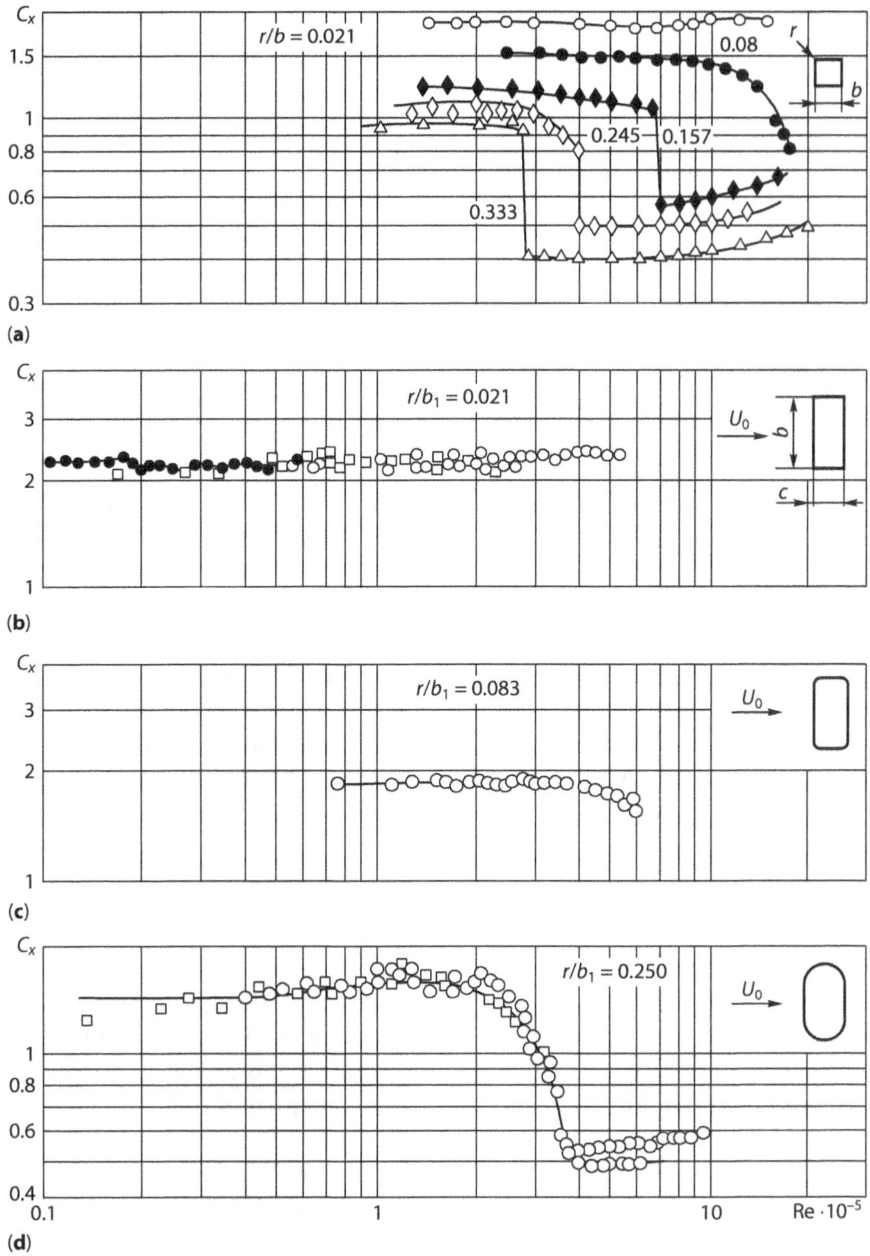

Figure 4.27 Dependence of $C_{\approx}$ coefficient on the *Re* number for square (*a*) and rectangular (*b,c,d*) with the ratio of sides b_1/b_2=2 at different radii of edge roundings rb_1 [46]:

○□•- cross-dimensions equal to 300,100,25 mm correspondingly.

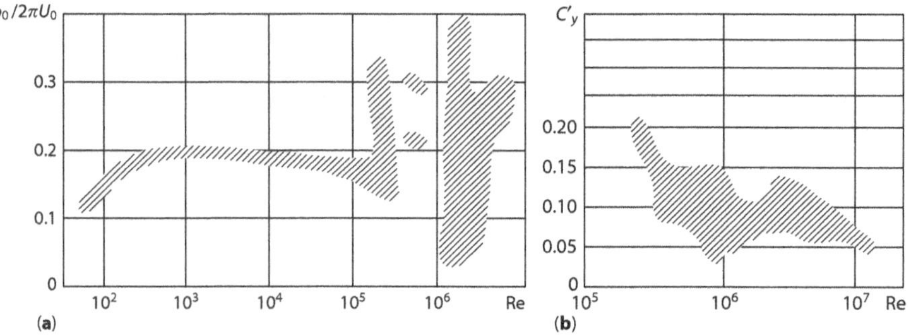

Figure 4.28 Change of frequency (a) and standard of lift force variation (b) at the flow around cylinder (dispersion areas of experimental data are hatched).

cross-sectional area of the flow; this is regardless of the fact that the available measurements show an increase in the shear stress on the bed at the initial area and the distribution of the average velocities in the boundary layer, as was already mentioned, is largely determined by this shear stress. Analysis of the turbulence measurement results shows that the observed effect is associated with the decreased intensity of turbulence at the initial area.

Area which length depends on a wall roughness and pressure gradient is necessary for the turbulence development within the boundary layer at the smoothly contoured entrance into the model. Figure 4.29 shows that the increase of relative pressure along the flow. $\frac{P_{var} - P_1}{\rho U^2{}_0/2}$ contributes to the length decrease of turbulization area of the boundary layer. The similar effect causes the increase of the model bed roughness.

Figure 4.30 shows the change of velocity pulsation standards along the channel length registered in the experiments of J. Kont Bello [67]. A confusor with two cellular devices at its entrance and exit was installed at the channel initial area. Bed and walls of the channel at the first 20 cm of straight section were plastered with rough paper. Friction velocity used in the process of results normalization, illustrated in Figure 4.30, is taken for main area of the flow. Figure 4.30 clearly demonstrates that the longitudinal pulsation standards in the zone of turbulence generation maximum are notedly lower than at the main area of stabilized flow.

In spite of the fact that the difference is less near the wall, it can be assumed that the low-frequency pulsations of shear stress having influence on the stability of bed particles and connected with the longitudinal

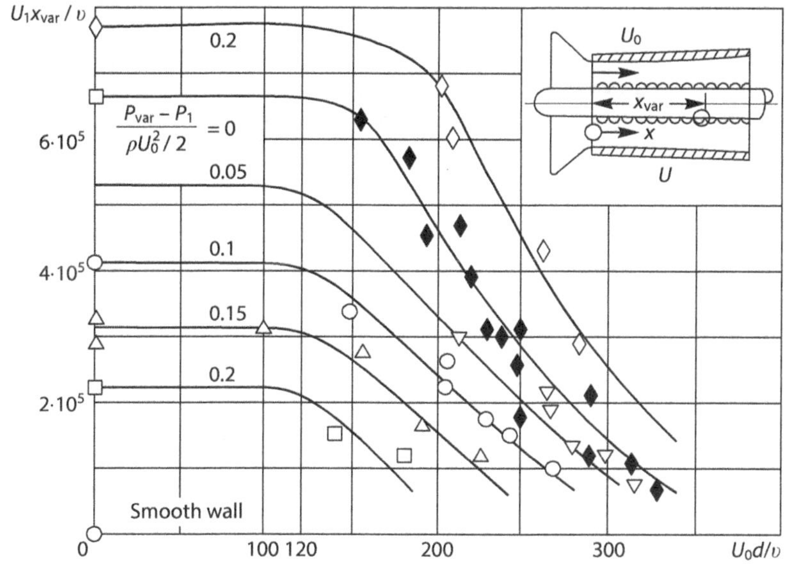

Figure 4.29 Effect of pressure gradient and rough streamlined surface on the position of the transition point in an incompressible fluid according to Find measurements (d – sand grain height).

velocity pulsation in the zone of turbulence generation maximum [84] at the initial area are significantly lower than at the main one. Difference of the turbulence intensity is particularly great in the flow core. This difference decreases approximately in the same way as the difference in the profiles of average velocities. Length of the stabilization area, in which the change of velocity profile has stopped, was not more than 55 – 60 heights of channels at the measurement of Re from 57×10^3 up to 230×10^3 in the considered experiments.

Length of the stabilization area can de decreased by means of the flow initial turbulization. This issue is considered in Section 5.4 in respect to the open flows.

It's particularly important to ensure the similitude of the flow turbulent structure in the study of dynamic effects on the streamlined body. Influence of initial turbulence on the dynamics of the flow around a sphere and a cylinder is widely known (for some time it was assumed to use empirical data on the coefficient of sphere resistance of the ball at the given Reynolds number to estimate the turbulence intensity in the incoming flow). It is believed that a significant effect of $u'_1/U \approx \sqrt{e}/U$

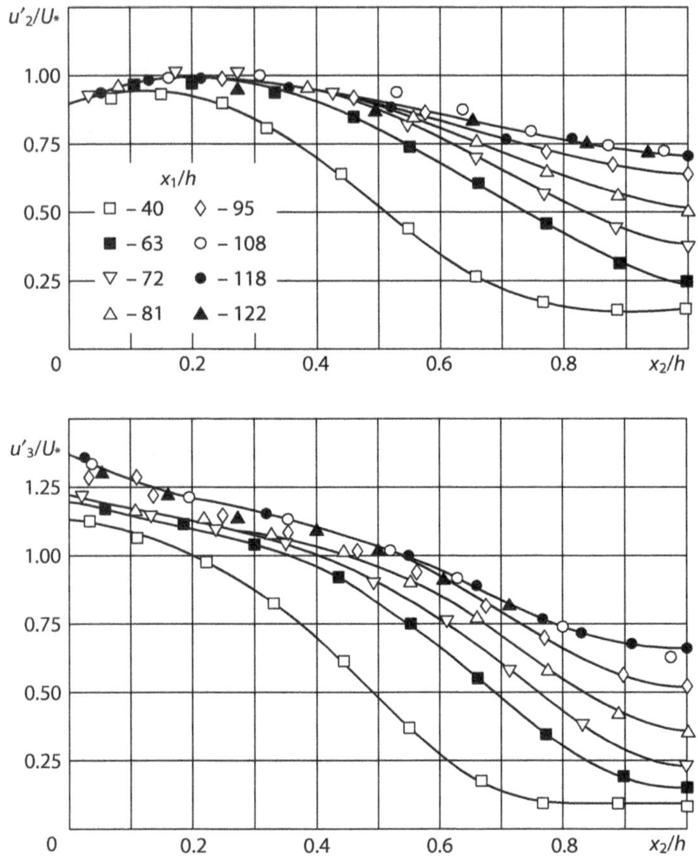

Figure 4.30 Changes of velocity transversal pulsations in the flow core at initial area of the pipe.

is connected with the fact that the flow around a sphere or cylinder in the boundary layer separation point is not fixed, and its position, having effect on the resistance depends on the intensity and spectrum of the initial turbulence.

Influence of the initial turbulence in these cases decreases with the increasing Reynolds number. It is relatively smaller in the flow around a rough cylinder than in the flow around a smooth cylinder (Figure 4.31). If roughness is large enough, for example, a cylinder of the diameter D is covered with racks with height of 1/20D), width of 1/10D) with the distance

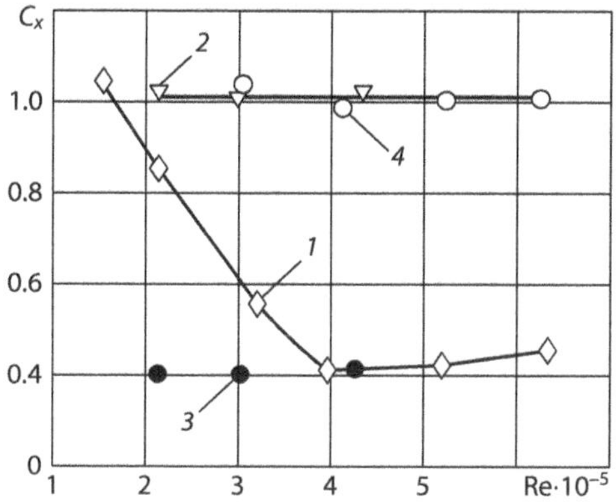

Figure 4.31 Influence of the initial turbulence in the resistance of the cylinder with diameter D=300мм [156] ($Re=U_0D/\nu$);

of 1/20D between racks, the change of initial turbulence level in 25 times (u'_1/U) = 0.2–5%) doesn't alter any results.

In all cases, increased turbulent background contributes to alignment characteristics of the flow. This is clear from the results of research (on physical models and calculations) of jets expiration in a cocurrent flow (Figure 4.32): increased turbulence promotes more rapid expansion of the jet. Data of Figure 4.32 are also an illustration of possibilities of numerical models of e-ε type to reflect the influence of the initial level of turbulence. As you can see, the results of calculations are qualitatively consistent with measurements, however, the quantitative measure of coincidence should be admitted to be relatively modest.

The given data shows that physical modeling of flow reattachment and flow with an indefinite point of separation is a rather complicated problem. The results of modeling (in one part or another) largely depend on the Reynolds number and the characteristics of the turbulent flow. In these tasks, exact reproduction of the streamlined body geometric shape is also very important. The relatively insignificant change of the form (transition from the cylinder to the relation of cone height to diameter of the base h/D =36) significantly changes pressure distribution on the lateral surfaces of these bodies (Figure 4.33) [174]. Further increasing of deviation from the flat flow scheme (transition to the cone h/D=18) changes pressure distribution insignificantly. Large-scale changing of the body shape and emerging spatial effects of flows especially affect turbulence characteristics: intensity of pulsations velocity in the track behind the cone is substantially less than behind the cylinder; integrated whole-scale of spatial

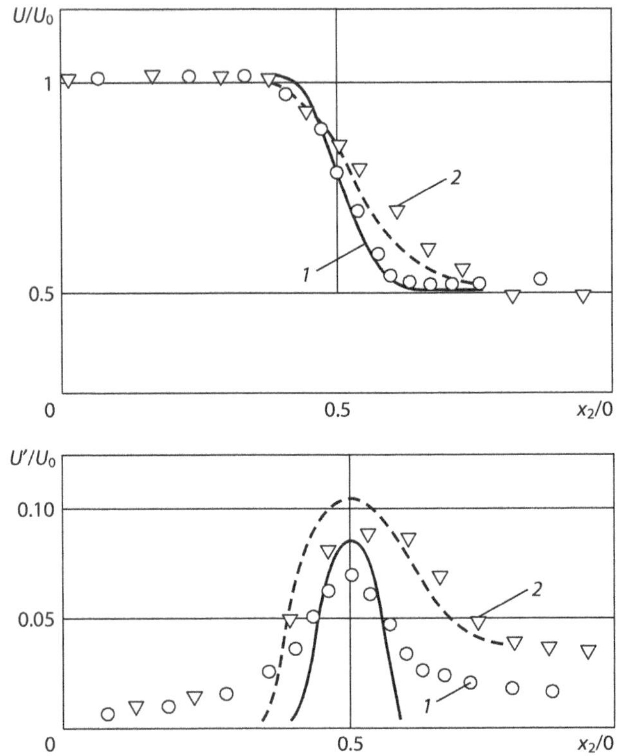

Figure 4.32 Spreading conditions of normal (1) and turbulized (2) jets [196].

correlations of velocities pulsation for cones is 2-3 times less than for the cylinder.

The exact observance of the form and spatial distribution of kinematic variables when testing models is a mandatory condition of similarity. Form of streamlined body strongly influences the characteristics of turbulence track. In [29] measurements in a turbulent wake behind a sphere and a body of revolution with prolongation of 8:1 are described Midsections of compared bodies were the same and their resistance coefficients didn't differ greatly as well. As for the characteristics of turbulence, they were significantly different.

Figure 4.34 shows the intermittency coefficients γ determined by the relative time during which the fluctuations had turbulent nature. Axis abscissa in Figure 4.34 represent relative radial coordinates $r+=r/b$, $r=0$ on the symmetry axis of the track and body; b - characteristic width of the track in the different sections (1-6 Figure 4.34):

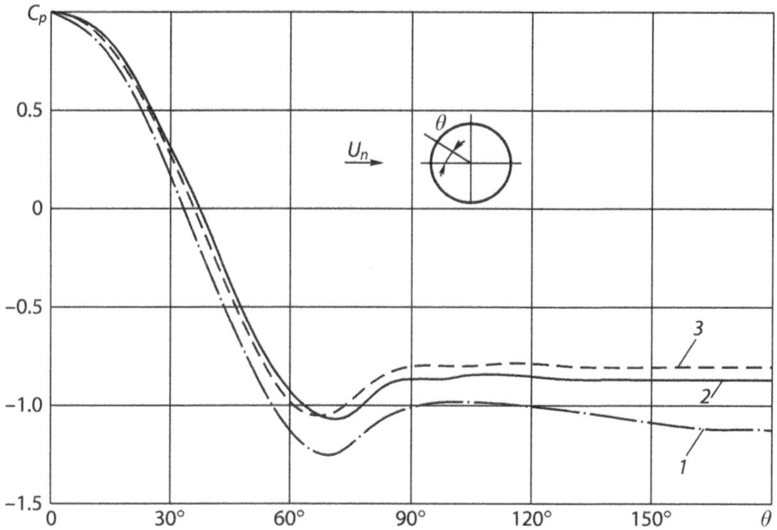

Figure 4.33 Pressure distribution on the lateral surfaces of the cylinder (1) and cones with taper angle 1:36 (2) and 1:18 (3) [174].

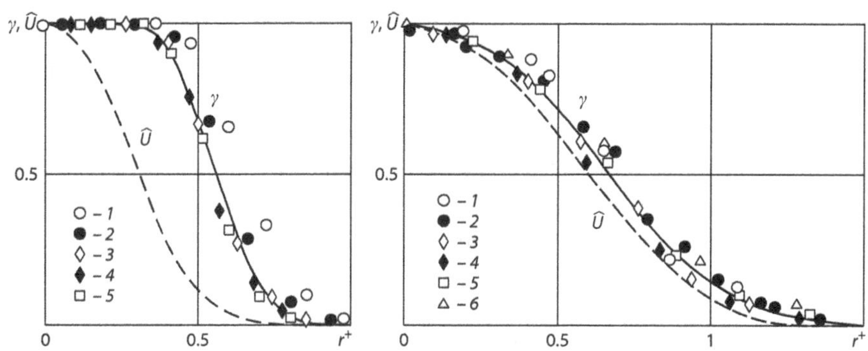

Figure 4.34 Values of the intermittency coefficient in a trace behind a cylindrical body at different distances [29]

$$b = \sqrt{C_x \frac{\pi D^2}{4}} \left[\frac{x_1 - x_{1_0}}{\sqrt{C_x \frac{\pi D^2}{4}}} \right]^{1/3} \tag{4.70}$$

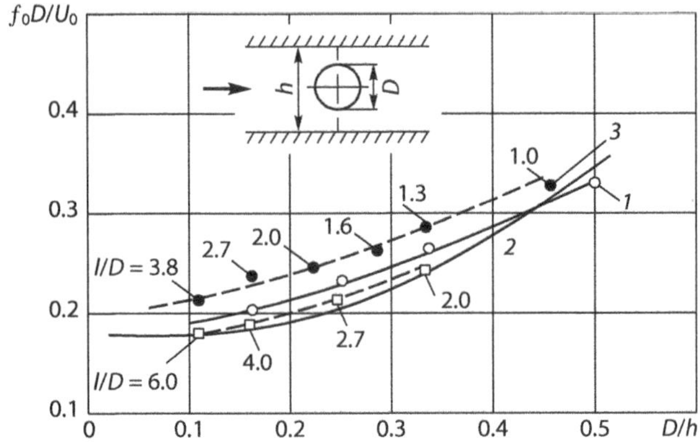

Figure 4.35 Predominant frequency of force action on the streamlined body in the finite width channel [212].

where C_x - is the coefficient of resistance of a body diameter D; x_{10} - is the beginning of self-similar track, which coincides in this case with the center of the sphere or the end of the body of rotation (axisymmetric problem). The dotted line in Figure 4.34 shows a self-similar profile of the averaged velocity deficit

$$\hat{U} = \frac{U_\infty - U}{U_\infty - U_0} \tag{4.71}$$

where U_∞ - flow velocity with $x_1 \to \pm\infty$; U_0 - velocity on the axis of the track.

You can see that in respect of the intermittency coefficient traces behind the analyzed bodies are autosimilar: in the range of $100 \leq x_1/D \leq 250$

$$\hat{U} = \hat{U}(r^+); \; \gamma = \gamma(r^+). \tag{4.72}$$

However, function $\gamma(r^+)$ и $\bar{U}(r^+)$ is considerably different between various bodies.

Undoubtedly, many detached flows are characterized with considerable generality; however, the specific details of the flows structure and quantitative parameters of flows depend on the contours of the zones of separation, on the form of streamlined bodies.

The channel shape is also important (especially for subcritical flow regimes), in which the detached flow is analyzed. In Figure 4.35 [212] the change in the predominant frequency of force action on cylinders in the H height channel (according to different data) is shown. For a flat plate and a round cylinder (at subcritical flow) even when $D/h \approx 0,1$, influence of this parameter practically does not decrease. In a supercritical flow mode [when

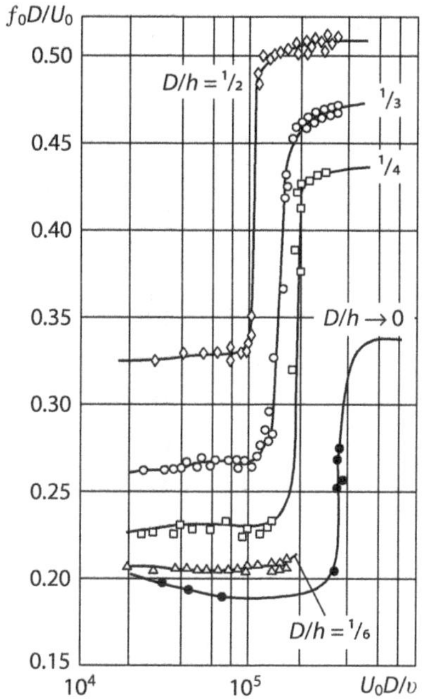

Figure 4.36 Dependence of leading frequency from the Re number

$Re \approx (2 \div 4) \cdot 10^5$], the situation is changing qualitatively - influence of the *D/h* parameter on the Strouhal number significantly decreases (Figure 4.36). Changes in the average value of the resistance coefficient (Figure 4.37) and RMS values C'_x and C'_y are particularly large. Reduction of fluctuations in the supercritical flow mode is accompanied by sharp expansion of their range. If in the pre-crisis flow, approximately 75% of the carrying power variance was concentrated in the frequency band $f_0 \pm 0{,}005 f_0$, then in case of the supercritical flow, it is observed in the frequency band $f_0 \pm 0{,}75 f_0$. The amplitude of oscillations decreases, but the possibility of resonant step-ups increases. Here f_0 is the frequency, corresponding to the spectrum maximum.

4.3 Non-Stationary Flow

Form of additional criteria of similarity that appear in the study of non-stationary motion of the incompressible viscous fluid, naturally, depends on the problem specification. We shall consider the conditions of equivalence of two problems - sudden accelerated motion of a fluid in a hard tube (or hard body in an infinite fluid) and fluid movement with periodically varying flow rate.

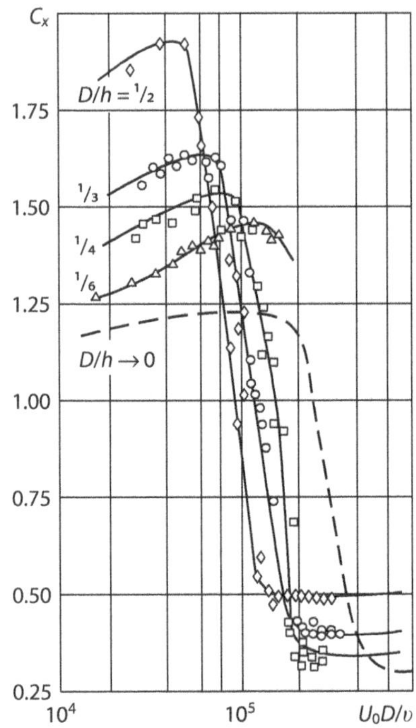

Figure 4.37 Resistance coefficient of the Cx cylinder in the finite width channel [122].

Accelerated motion of the fluid from the state of rest in the case of the suddenly applied pressure gradient *dP/dx* is characterized by the following qualitative characteristics [69]. Most of the time (before occurrence of turbulence) an increase in flow velocity with almost constant acceleration takes place (Figure 4.38):

$$\frac{\partial \overline{U}}{\partial t} = \frac{1}{\rho}\frac{\partial P}{\partial x_1} - \lambda \frac{1}{D}\frac{\rho \overline{U}^2}{2} \tag{4.73}$$

Shear stress on a wall in this period monotonically increases almost linearly with time. Here, movement in all areas of the flow, including the near-wall layer, is laminar. Starting from a certain time moment *t*, the turbulence is observed first near-wall layer, and then through the whole flow. From Figure 4.38 we can see how turbulent fluctuations tangential stresses on the wall at the moment $t=t_{lim}$ appear suddenly and dramatically.

All the parameters of flow in the laminar regime can be found on the known solution I. S. Gromeka (1882). Let us mention only the expression

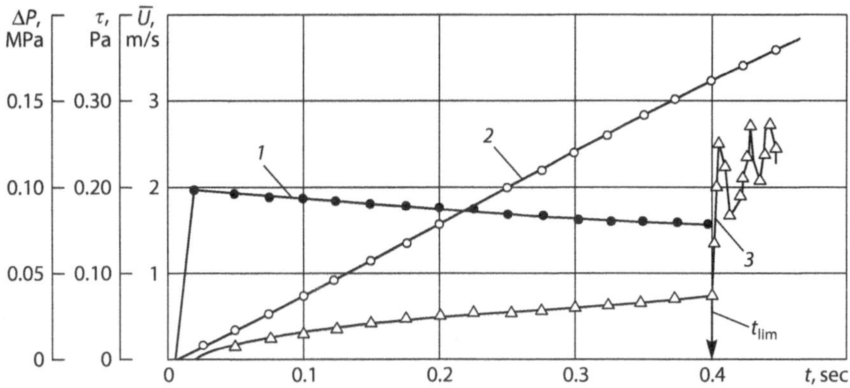

Figure 4.38 Change of the pressure drop (1), flow velocity (2) and tangential stresses on the wall (3) in a round pipe in the starting flow.

for the hydraulic friction coefficient, connecting instant shear stress τ on the wall of the circular pipe with speed *U*, averaged over the cross section:

$$\tau = \frac{\lambda}{4}\frac{\rho \bar{U}^2}{2}; \tag{4.74}$$

$$\lambda = \frac{256}{\mathrm{Re}} \sum_{n=1}^{\infty} \frac{1 - \exp\left(-j_n^2 4 \frac{\nu t}{D^2}\right)}{j_n^2} \tag{4.75}$$

Here $Re = \bar{U}D/\nu$; j_n - the roots of the Bessel functions of zero order (j_1=2,405; j_2=5,520; j_3=8,654). In a case in which the flow turbulence resistance increases, acceleration of the fluid decreases.

In a number of publications the conditions for the occurrence of turbulence are entered via local parameters that are not contained in the boundary and initial problem specification. For example, on the basis of generalization of measurements of tangential stresses on the wall, some studies have indicated that turbulence in case of accelerated flow appears at the t_{lim} moment, satisfying the condition of:

$$\sqrt{\tau t_{\mathrm{lim}} / \mu} = \mathrm{const} \tag{4.76}$$

Record (4.76) is methodologically imperfect, and practically useless, as it doesn't contain the conditions determining the problem. Of course, we can use the solution of Gromeka and find out the t_{cr} value from (4.76). Without carrying out these calculations, we use empirical data shown in Figure 4.38, assuming that:

$$\bar{U} \sim \sqrt{\frac{1}{\rho}\left|\frac{\partial P}{\partial x_1}\right| D}\,\frac{t}{t_0}; \tag{4.77}$$

$$\tau \sim \left|\frac{\partial P}{\partial x_1}\right| D \frac{t}{t_0}, \tag{4.78}$$

where:

$$\begin{aligned} t_0 &= D/U_0 \quad - \text{time scale} \\ \mathrm{U}_0 &= \sqrt{\frac{1}{\rho}\left|\frac{\partial P}{\partial x_1}\right| D} - \text{velocity scale} \end{aligned} \tag{4.79}$$

Substituting evaluations (4.77) and (4.78) in (4.76), we find out that the critical Reynolds number Re_{cr}, when turbulence occurs, should be proportional to the parameter:

$$\mathrm{Re}_P = \sqrt{\frac{1}{\rho}\left|\frac{\partial P}{\partial x_1}\right| D}\,\frac{D}{\nu}. \tag{4.80}$$

Systematic experiments [9] have allowed us to find the coefficient of proportionality between Re_{cr} and Re_p from the condition of occurrence of experimental values deviations λ from the values, calculated on (4.75):

$$Re_{cr} = 4\, Re_p \tag{4.81}$$

if $4\mathrm{Re}_p > 2320$.

$\mathrm{Re}_{cr} = 2320$ otherwise.

As is seen from (4.81), acceleration of movement contributes to the stabilization of the flow and delays occurrence of turbulence. The relation (4.81) allows us to find the values of the Re_p complex in which the impact of the expansion should be considered small. Assuming that $4\mathrm{Re}_p = 2320$, we find a presumptive condition of small impact of non-stationarity:

$$Re_p < 580. \tag{4.82}$$

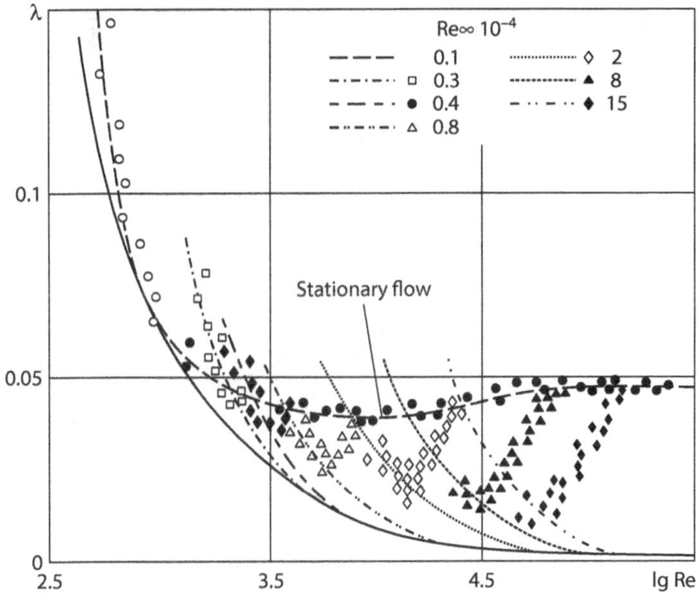

Figure 4.39 Change of the hydraulic friction coefficient λ in the process of liquid acceleration in a straight tube with different values of Re_∞: curves - on the calculation assuming laminar flow; experimental points correspond to non-stationary flow.

If the condition (4.82) is not satisfied, then the non-stationarity obviously affects all the flow characteristics. At this the hypothesis of "quasi-stationarity," consisting in the fact that in each moment of time the movement is determined by the instantaneous flow characteristics, usually does not provide acceptable results. The coefficient of hydraulic friction λ, calculated from (4.73), significantly depends on the non-stationarity parameters (Figure 4.39).

In relation to some integral characteristics it is possible to eliminate the Re_p parameter from the explicit dependencies without major losses in the accuracy of estimates. Such a transformation is proposed in [9, 122] for generalization of experimental data on the coefficient of hydraulic friction in the pipes with natural and artificial roughness (Figure 4.40):

$$\frac{\lambda}{\lambda_{st}} = 1 - 1{,}6\frac{1 - \mathrm{Re}/\mathrm{Re}_\infty}{1 + \left(1 - \mathrm{Re}/\mathrm{Re}_\infty\right)^2} \quad \text{when } \mathrm{Re} > \mathrm{Re}_{cr} \tag{4.83}$$

Here λ_{st} - coefficient of hydraulic friction at the steady state, characterized by the Reynolds number equal to the instantaneous *Re* value at accelerating movement.

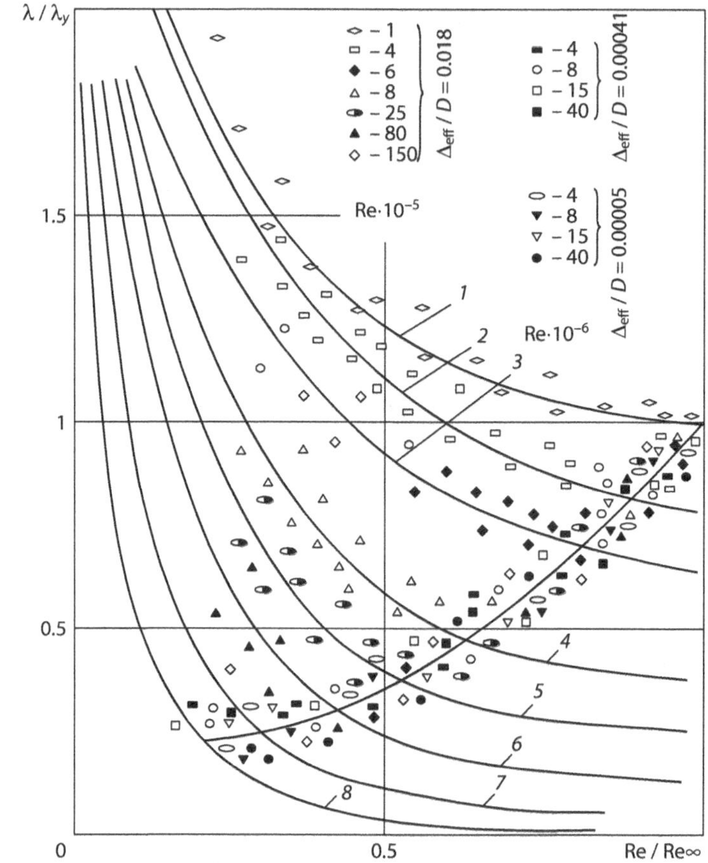

Figure 4.40 Change of the hydraulic friction coefficient λ/λ_y in the process of liquid acceleration: 1-8 calculation for laminar mode when Re_∞: **1**-$1{\cdot}10^5$; **2**- $4{\cdot}10^5$; **3**- $6{\cdot}10^5$; **4** - $8{\cdot}10^5$; **5** - $25{\cdot}10^5$; **6** - $8{\cdot}10^6$; **7** - $1{,}5{\cdot}10^7$; **8** - $4{\cdot}10^7$.

Generalizations like (4.83) are possible only in special cases, in restricted conditions ranges. In the general case, velocity distribution over the cross section is indefinitely determined by the instantaneous value of the *Re* number: the difference of velocity fields with the same *Re*, as a rule, is rather great.

Attempts of making generalizations that include only local (instant) parameters of flows - $\partial \bar{U}/\partial t$, $\partial^2 \bar{U}/\partial t^2$, etc. (Figure 4.41) also seem unpromising. In general the prehistory of motion is important, though in some "standard" conditions such generalizations can be effective.

Estimation of non-stationary flow status by the Re criterion is inconvenient, as the instantaneous value of flow velocity is usually not included in

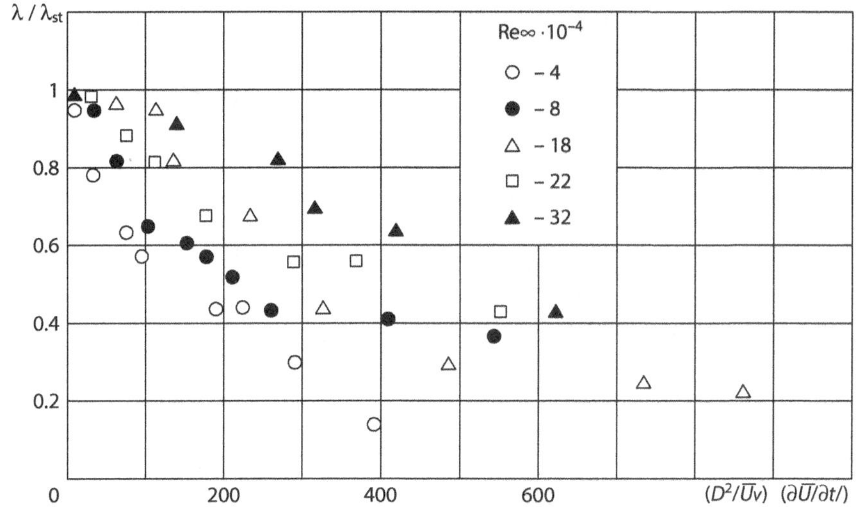

Figure 4.41 Dependence of relative hydraulic friction coefficient λ/λ_{st} from "non-stationarity parameter" $(D^2/\bar{U}\nu)(\partial\bar{U}/\partial t)$, $(\Delta/D{=}0{,}0004)$.

the problem specification, and is the desired quantity. It is more logical to consider the homochronicity criterion together with the defining criterion (4.80)

$$\mathrm{Sh} = \frac{tU_0}{D} = \frac{t}{D}\sqrt{\frac{1}{\rho}\left|\frac{\partial P}{\partial x_1}\right| D} \tag{4.84}$$

Taking into account (4.73) and (4.81), we estimate the Strouhal critical number Sh_{cr}, at which turbulence begins:

$$\mathrm{Sh}_{cr} \approx 4. \tag{4.85}$$

Result (4.85) may seem surprising (and requires additional checks), meaning that the absolute acceleration of the fluid t_{cr} before occurrence of turbulence does not depend on viscosity

$$t_{cr} \approx 4\sqrt{\frac{D}{\frac{1}{\rho}\left|\frac{\partial P}{\partial x_1}\right|}} \approx 4\sqrt{\frac{D}{\left|\frac{\partial U}{\partial t}\right|}} \tag{4.86}$$

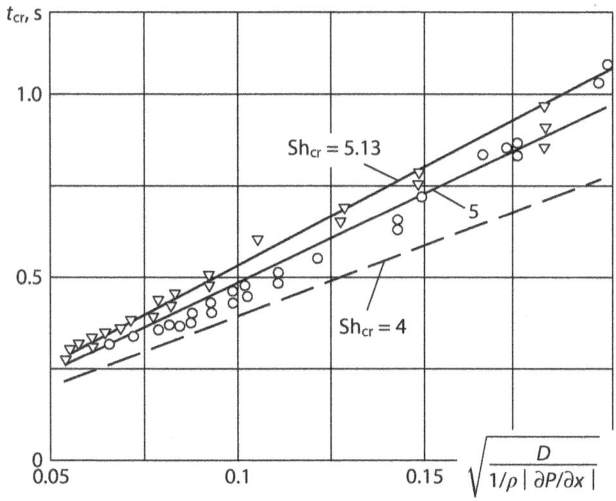

Figure 4.42 Dependence of duration of the laminar regime t_{cr} on the wall from the initial pressure in the tank (experimental and calculated) (4.86): ▽- diameter of 34 mm; o- diameter 61mm.

The calculation on (4.86) for the conditions of the experiments, shown in Figure 4.38 (D=6.1*cm*, $\partial U/\partial t$=8.1 m/s^2), gives the time of the turbulence ocurrence t_{cr}=0.35s. The actual time (t_{cr}=0,4s) differs little from the calculated time.

Processing of the data of the U.R. Liiv systematic experiments, conducted with tubes of different diameters, confirmed the result (Figure 4.42) with a different value of the Strouhal critical number:

$$Sh_{\infty}=4{,}5\div5{,}5 \tag{4.87}$$

Relative duration $Sh_{\infty}=t_{\infty}U_0/D$ of the fluid acceleration in a tube up to a state close to stationary, depends on Re_p and geometrical parameters of the system l/D, Δ/D:

$$Sh_{\infty} = f\left(Re_p, l/D, \Delta/D\right) \tag{4.88}$$

Characteristics of the turbulent flow in a plain tube $\Delta/D \to 0$, when:

$$Sh_{cr} < Sh < Sh_{\infty} \tag{4.89}$$

depending only on two criteria Re_p and Sh, are explored in detail in a series of works of U.R.Liiv [69].

Non-stationary boundary layer in case of pulse movement from the state of rest with the constant velocity V or constant acceleration a was studied theoretically and experimentally [221, 222]. It is found out in [221], that the stationary state of the boundary layer on a flat plate, parallel to the flow, is being set when:

$$\mathrm{Sh} = tU/x_1 > 5, \tag{4.90}$$

if the plate is moving with a constant velocity, and when:

$$\mathrm{Sh} = at^2/x_1 > 8, \tag{4.91}$$

if the plate is moving with constant acceleration. Here x_1 - the distance from the front edge of the plate. Let's pay attention to the fact that, as in the case of pressure flow, the characteristic time of the process does not depend on the viscosity.

Unsteady flow around a flat plate, perpendicular to the flow, cylinder or sphere, suddenly set in motion with the constant velocity U or constant acceleration a, is determined by two criteria - the Reynolds number:

$$\left.\begin{aligned} &\mathrm{Re} = UD/\nu, \text{ if } \mathrm{U} = \text{const},\\ &\text{or}\\ &\mathrm{Re}_1 = a\mathrm{D}^3/\nu^2, \text{ if } a = \text{const}, \end{aligned}\right\} \tag{4.92}$$

and the Strouhal criterion:

$$\left.\begin{aligned} &\mathrm{Sh} = \mathrm{Ut}/D, \text{ if } U = \text{const},\\ &\text{or}\\ &\mathrm{Sh}_1 = at^2/D, \quad \text{if } a = \text{const}, \end{aligned}\right\} \tag{4.93}$$

It is noteworthy that while the Strouhal numbers are less than the certain value Sh_1, the most important flow characteristic - relative length of the whirlpool area behind the body does not depend on the Reynolds number (Figure 4.43). When values Sh_1 are greater, the Reynolds number is greater. When flowing around a flat plate, the effect of viscosity is also not manifested on further, quasi-stationary phases (Figure 4.44).

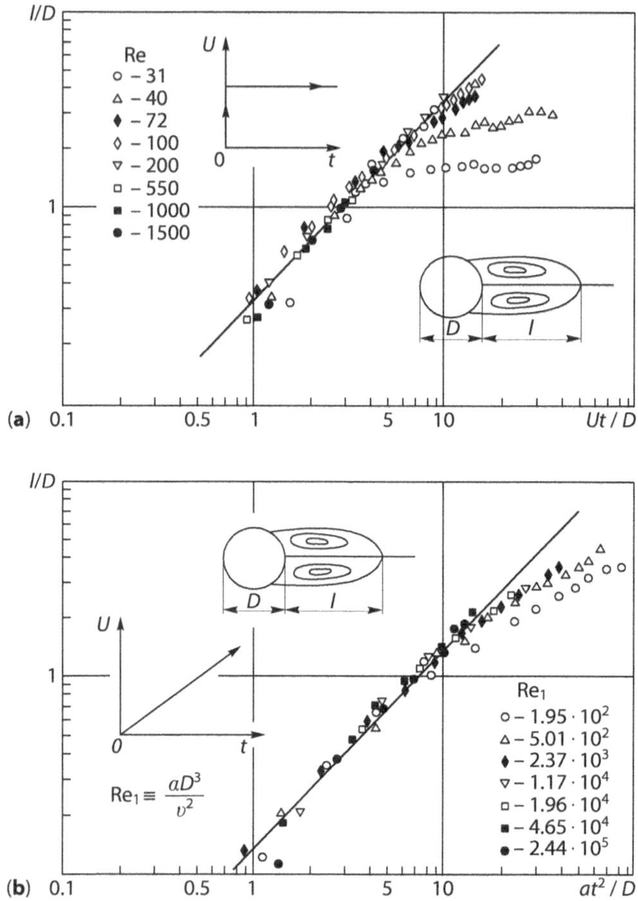

Figure 4.43 The cylinder flow with a deeply non-stationary flow with constant velocity (a) or constant acceleration (б).

All these results are understandable from the perspective of the correlation of forces analysis - in the early stages of movement, inertial forces that dominate and influence viscosity cannot become apparent. Movement here is completely autosimilar, and the only criterion that should be used for modeling or generalization of results is the Strouhal number.

Let's consider the second problem of significantly non-stationary periodic flows. Results typical for this sphere were obtained in research of parameters of turbulence flow in a plain tube of the round cross-section [18] when the flow discharge was varied according to the law

$$Q = Q_0\left(1 + \beta \sin \omega t\right). \tag{4.94}$$

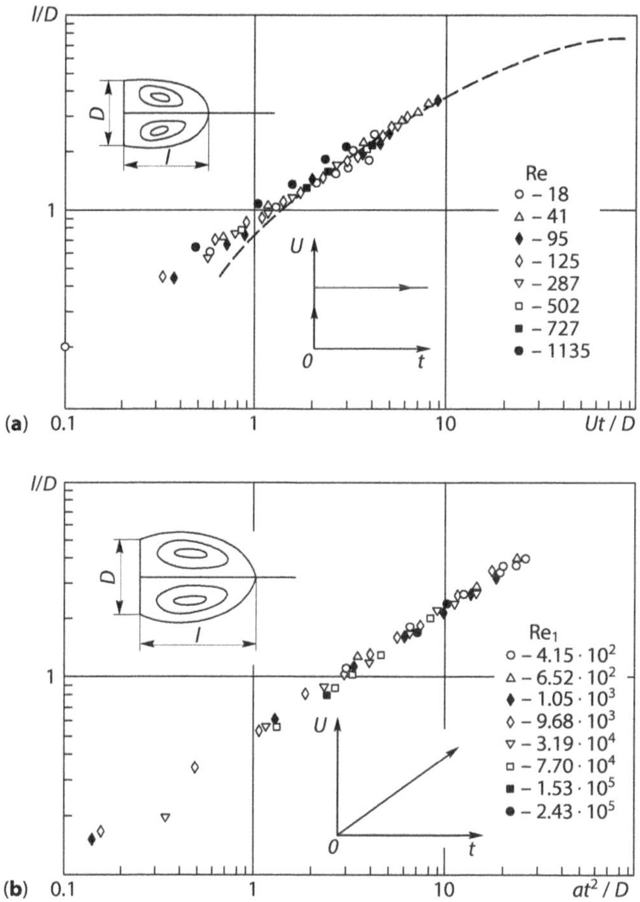

Figure 4.44 Flow of a plain plate with a non-stationary flow with constant velocity (a) or constant acceleration (b); numerical experiment without empirical constants.

Option β in these experiments and calculations varied from 0.2 to 0.5, and the Reynolds number (for Q_0 flow discharge} ranged from $3.2*10^4$ to $6.4*10^4$. Relative frequency:

$$\omega^+ = \omega D_2/\nu \tag{4.95}$$

had two values in the experiments: $2.74{\cdot}10^3$ and $2.74{\cdot}10^4$.

Measurements showed that all the parameters of kinematic and dynamic fields, averaged on probability, in different phases of the oscillations (with $\varphi=\omega t=var$) differ significantly from the values corresponding to the "quasi-stationary" estimates (Figures 4.45 and 4.46). These deviations are decreased with decreasing β and ω^+ and increased with decreasing Re_0.

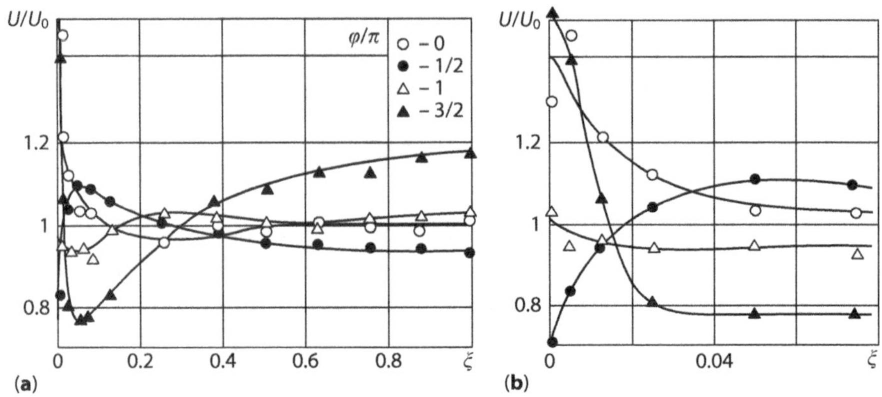

Figure 4.45 Relative av eraged velocity in shares of local velocity U_0 in case of stationary flow with the flow discharge equal to the instantaneous flow discharge in the corresponding phase φ when β= 0,5; ω = 2,74·10[4]

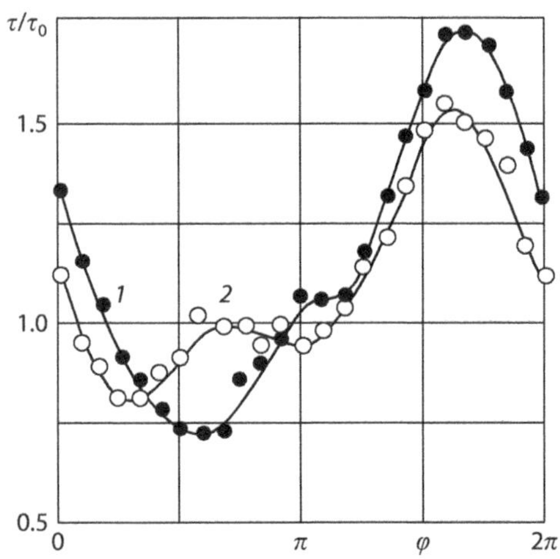

Figure 4.46 Changes of tangential stresses on the wall with frequencies $\omega = 2.74{\cdot}10^3$ *(1)* and $2.74{\cdot}10^4$*(2)*.

Figure 4.47 shows two of the asymptotic coefficients of the hydraulic friction $\lambda=8\tau/\rho\bar{U}^2$: at $\omega^+\to 0$ corresponding to stationary flow ($\boldsymbol{\lambda}$ =0.024) and calculation on "quasi-stationary" scheme ($\boldsymbol{\lambda}$ =0.028).

The same Figure 4.47 shows the change of the coefficient λ', characterizing the relative loss of mechanical energy (per length unit of pipe per time unit). In a stationary flow of λ= λ' in conditions of unsteady flow in the phase of maximum energy losses (φ=1,4π), the coefficient of hydraulic losses λ' may be 2-3 times more than in the corresponding stationary

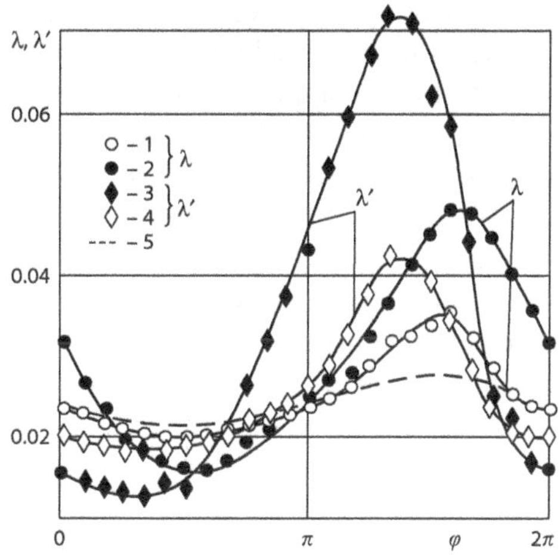

Figure 4.47 Changes of relative tangential stresses λ and energy losses λ' depending from phase fluctuations when $Re_0 = 32\text{-}10^4$ $\beta = 0.5$: 1.3 - $\omega^+=2.74\text{-}10^3$; *2.4* - $\omega^+=2.74\text{-}10^4$; 5 - calculation for quasi-stationary conditions.

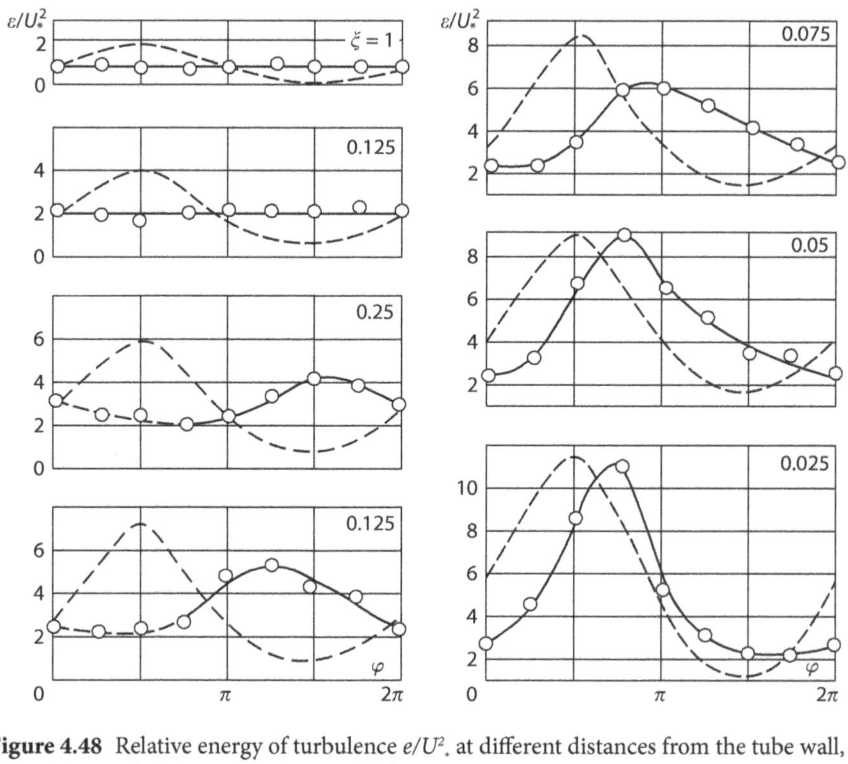

Figure 4.48 Relative energy of turbulence e/U^2_* at different distances from the tube wall, depending on the fluctuation phase φ [18].

conditions. It is noteworthy that the average for the period of oscillations shear stresses and energy loss practically do not differ from the values calculated in the quasi-stationary approximation, even when $\omega^+=2,74_* 10^4$. This is largely due to the fact that in the boundary layer, where nonlinear processes are important, and the relative level of turbulence and velocity of its generation has relatively little difference from the "quasi-stationary" values (Figure 4.48). Boundary layer exerts its "conservative" properties. The given data allows us to select a range of values ω^+ and β, in which the influence of the expansion can be ignored completely or the non-stationarity in quasi-stationary scheme can be taken into account.

5

Open Flow in Hard Channel

5.1 Specific Character of Open Flows. Role of Froude and Euler Criterions

Flows with free external surface are called open flows. Usually as free surface is considered interface of liquid in drops and gas. Such free surfaces are characterized by constant pressure within their boundaries (excluding some specific cases).

Presence of free surfaces significantly complicates prognosis, including simulation of free flow characteristics as compared to pressure flows, examined in Ch. 4, because similarity criterions should include variables, defining free surface.

Equations of motion of viscous incompressible fluid (2.19), written through vorticity, contain single unknown function – fluid velocity – and single free parameter – kinematic viscosity. Out of these equations we can get only two similarity criterions – Strouhal and Reynolds numbers. Two other criterions, resulting from analysis of Navier-Stokes, Froude and Euler`s equations, correspond with determination of boundary conditions for the equation (2.19). This factor sometimes is used for demonstration that Euler criterion is not determining.

It is also obvious that on that basis, Froude criterion may be also classified as non-determining. In reality, depending on problem-specific nature, Euler and Froude criterions can be classified as determining, so non-determining. Let`s give some examples.

Usually pressure on free surface of the open flow is constant and Euler criterion for such flows is not determining. But if to think of open flow, in which surface pressure is varied in area, then it is obvious that *Eu* criterion should be classified among determining ones. In practice it takes place, for example, in hydro engineering of free-flow tunnels at high water velocity. In this case pressure above free surface immediately after dam camera is lower than at the tunnel`s exit.

Another example: in the area of fluid flow with pressure P_1 is supplied gas from area with pressure $P_2 > P_1$, so cavern is formed in the fluid. It is clear that the cavern form and other flow characteristics correspond with *Eu* criterion. (Pressure P_1 is usually not established and *Eu* criterion contains not pressure fall $\Delta P = P_2 - P_1$, but difference between pressure P_2 and pressure in the flow boundary point, where it is known). But this criterion drops out from defining system if we change problem requirements: if we define not pressure fall but gas flow rate.

Criterion *Fr* also is not always determining. First of all, it is true for the above studied pressure flows in hard boundaries. If flow boundaries are non-rigid, conclusions can be different.

Let`s imagine pressure flow where on the axis is a suspended heavy object (for example, plain gate), deflected by the flow from vertical. In this case Fr is defining criterion. But if the object`s location is established as independent, and in the model it`s fixed, then Fr will not be included in the defining criterions system.

For open flow *Fr* criterion is not always defining. So, for similarity of averaged parameters of calm open flows at steady motion, there will be sufficient identity of Re criterion and similarity of geometric characteristics of boundaries, including similarity of free surface location which can be achieved by selection of an appropriate channel angle. At irregular motion with small *Fr* values, flow characteristics are practically independent from it.

Present at the first glance contradictions are easily eliminated on the basis of general conditions of similarity theory. And really, any criterions may be attributed to determining if all contained variables are defined, one way or another, under the problem requirements (for example, on the domain boundary in solution of boundary equation). In the case when fluid boundaries are known, for solving equations (2.42) and continuity, it is necessary and sufficient that boundary and initial requirements contain data only on velocities, and their derivatives in the points are situated in the space-time boundaries of the study object. Therefore, at known fluid boundaries, neither Froude nor Euler criterions can be included in a defining criterions system. Knowing this, of course, solutions of hydraulic problem will be defined ambiguously – pressure will be accurate within some additive function $p_0(\mathbf{x}, t)$, satisfying equation:

$$g = \frac{1}{\rho}\operatorname{grad} p_0. \tag{5.1}$$

If on the flow boundary (on free surface) pressure fall $\Delta P = 0$, then *Eu* criterion does not affect location and form of this boundary and the problem solution. Otherwise it becomes defining.

In many problems boundary form may correspond with pressure through more complex conditions, than on free surface. In those cases new similarity criterions arise which characterize these boundaries, for example deformation parameters in hydro elasticity problems.

If form of gas cavity (flow boundaries) depends on ΔP, then *Eu* criterion should be classified as determining. If the problem is formulated differently and excludes pressure fall from requirements, then result of similarity conditions analysis will be different too.

The abovementioned considerations explain, in particular, the fact that neither Froude number, nor Euler number are included in determining criterions system for pressure flows: liquid boundaries are known for them a priori. But once flow boundaries (location of suspended body) become dependent on gravity forces, the role of *Fr* number changes. On the same basis Froude criterion is not determining criterion for open flow, all boundaries of which (including free surface) are known a priori. The latter factor is used in the method of pressure simulation of open flows: on the known level, corresponding with level of free surface, hard wall is installed on the pressure model [91].

H. Rouse and his personnel [214] have studied characteristics of hydraulic jump by this method. They defined free surface at various Froude numbers in the area of jump in hydraulic flume and then reproduced this surface as hard wall in the air assembly. As can be seen from Figure 5.1, flow averaged characteristics in assemblies (free surface according to pressure measurement on pressure model was obtained in accordance with Section 5.5) is similar everywhere except the relatively thin layer near the upper boundary, where kinematic conditions are significantly different.

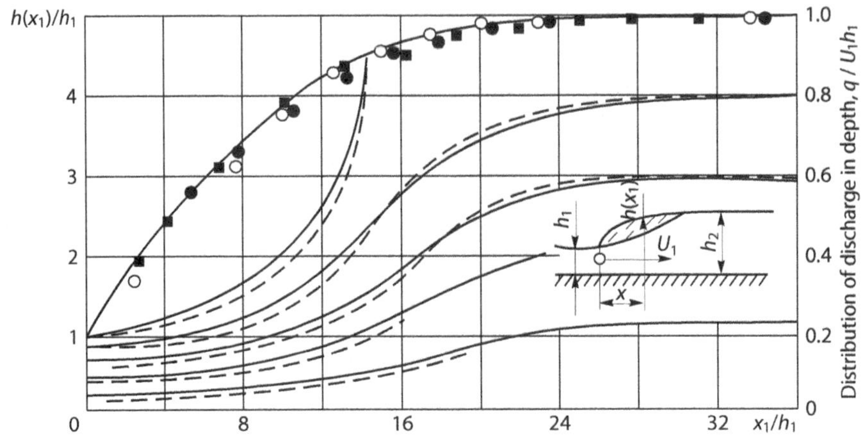

Figure 5.1 Characteristics of hydraulic jump in pressure and free-flow assemblies:

○— Levels in pressure on curved ("free") surface of the pressure model;
●— the same in bottom pressure on air model;
■— the same in hydraulic flume;
________ lines of flow on pressure model;
_ _ _ _ _ the same in hydraulic flume.

Authors studies of submerged outflows were carried out simultaneously on air pressure and hydraulic models [91]. In the air model, free surface after water discharge was represented by plain wall, located at the required mean level of free surface. Figure 5.2 shows results of calculation of water discharge resistance factor in these models. It is clearly seen that at higher water levels (higher jet submergence), when free surface is close to a plane, experiment results for both models are practically identical. In lowering of the lower pool, which results in increase of flow turbulence and deformation of free surface, experiment results start to differ significantly.

One of the experiments approximately represented the form of free surface defined in the hydraulic model. Experiment results coincided with hydraulic model data.

One more experimental fact, pointing out the role of Froude criterion, is data on defining distribution function (ref. Section 8.2) of impurities contained in the water, in time of location within a free-flowing water-supply basin [181]. This function was obtained in real conditions. Evaluating it on a model, in which Froude obtained similarity, resulted in significant difference from real conditions (Figure 5.3). An assumption was made that this difference is explained by low Reynolds numbers in the model. Increase of Re number by means of velocities increasing as compared with required by condition Fr = idem did not lead to similarity in distribution function.

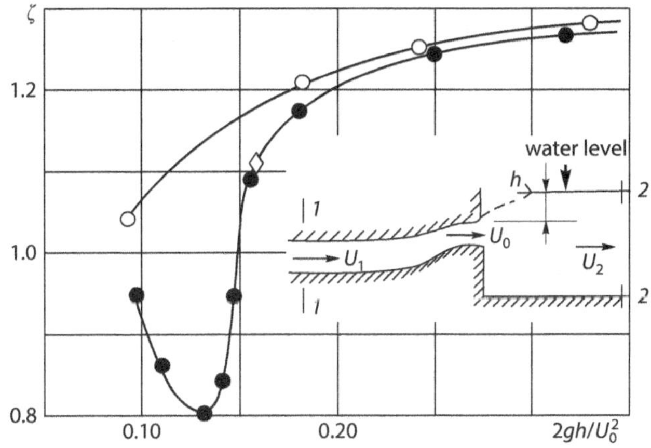

Figure 5.2 Water discharge resistance factor according to the data of free-flow and pressure models:

● Free-flow model;
○ pressure model with plain "free" surface in the lower pool;
◇— pressure model with represented form of free surface;

$\zeta = \dfrac{\Delta E}{\rho U_0^2/2}$; ΔE — difference of specific energies in sections *1-1 and 2-2*

Researchers connected this circumstance with deformation of free surface at Fr = idem: above the drainage hole in the center of a cylindrical tank bottom, in the model there appeared a deep swirl, insignificant at Froude number values, equal to the ones in real conditions. This swirl was eliminated by a flat plate located on the water surface in the swirl generation area. This measure along with increase of Re numbers allowed us to achieve similarity in distribution function in the model and in real conditions.

From the provided examples it follows that Froude criterion affects flow characteristics through change in flow boundaries. If this criterion does not affect free surface location, then it does not affect other flow characteristics, which once more illustrates the thesis that if liquid boundaries are subjects of study and are defined by equations, then a criterion system, obtained from analysis of motion equations, should be completed by criterions, containing new functions and parameters from boundary equations. In many practical problems there are zero pressure falls on free surfaces, and Eυ criterion is not determining. On the contrary, Froude criterion includes variables which compose problem requirements for free surface flows, and formally only at *Fr* = idem equations, is the defining fluid surface invariant. From a perspective of simulation, quantitative estimation

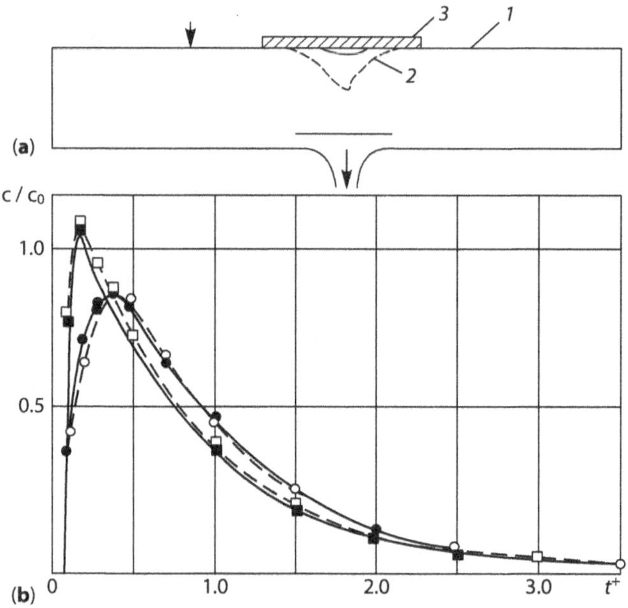

Figure 5.3 Results of definition of water flow distribution functions in time of residence in water-supply basin:

a — basin scheme; *b* — function of flow distribution in residence time;
1 — free surface in real conditions and on the model at Fr = idem; *2* — the same on the model at Re = idem;
3 — plate on the part of free surface on the model; O — real conditions, ● — model with plate on free surface at Re = idem; □ — the same without plate; ■ — model at Fr = idem.

of Fr number effect is very important, because only at availability of self-similarity in this criterion mentioned above, formal requirement can be disregarded.

As was already noted, the role of Froude criterion at presence of free surfaces is not always significant. In given examples it applies to flows, being characterized by small Fr numbers. From works of L.I. Sedov (ref., for example [138]), it is known that even at large Froude numbers there is self-similarity in this criterion (analogous to self-similarity in Reynolds number in quadratic realm).

Such self-similarity is explained by de-emphasis of gravity force in comparison with inertia forces or reducing of respective members in differential equations. Self-similarity at small Froude numbers has another character.

In accordance with the abovementioned, it can be assumed that Froude number impacts flow characteristics through free surface form and location.

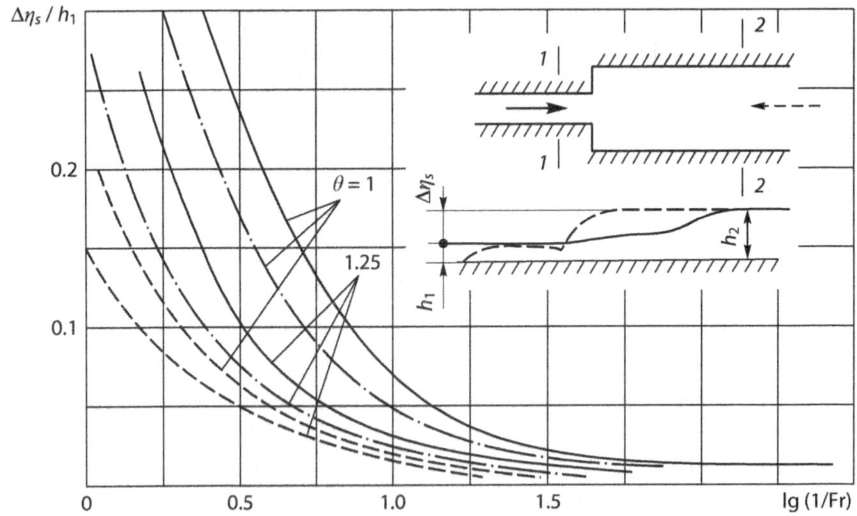

Figure 5.4 Dependence of $\Delta\eta_n/h_1$ from Fr, in the scheme of sudden expansion (or contraction)-·-·-·-·-·- $\xi = 0$;
——— $\xi_p = (1-\Omega_1/\Omega_2)^2$ - - - - - $\xi_{cont} = 0.5(1-\Omega_1/\Omega_2)$.

The most important free surface characteristic is correlation between significant in specific problem level fall $\Delta\eta_S$ and flow depth h. Correlation between $\Delta\eta_S/h$ and Fr in some cases can be obtained analytically.

Contained in [120] solutions can serve as an example. These solutions belong to sudden flow expansion in the rectangular channel with horizontal bottom (Figure 5.4):

$$\frac{2\Delta\eta_s/h_1}{1-\dfrac{1}{\theta^2\left(1-\Delta\eta_S/h_1\right)}\pm\xi} = F_{r_1}, \tag{5.2}$$

where $\boldsymbol{\theta = b_2/b_1}$; $\boldsymbol{\xi}$ — hydraulic resistance factor; to maximal transverse fall on the rectangular channel turn (Figure 5.5):

$$\mathrm{Fr}^2+2\left[2-\frac{\Delta\eta_S/h}{\mathrm{Ln}\,\tilde{r}}-\frac{(\tilde{r}-1)^2-(1-1/\tilde{r})^2}{(\Delta\eta_S/h)\mathrm{Ln}^2\tilde{r}}\right]\mathrm{Fr}+ \tag{5.3}$$

$$+4\left(1-\frac{\Delta\eta_S/h}{\mathrm{Ln}\,\tilde{r}}\right)+\left(\frac{\Delta\eta_S/h}{\mathrm{Ln}\,\tilde{r}}\right)^2=0,$$

where $\check{r} = 1-b/r_{1.}$ These correlations are obtained for Fr<1.

By Figures 5.4 and 5.5 it is easy to ascertain that at small Froude numbers, there can be distinguished wide self-similarity domains $\Delta\eta_S$ /h and Fr.

Sometimes it is possible to analytically search for correlation between relative level difference of free surface $X = X_1(\Delta\eta_S/h)$ (here X — flow characteristic). Having, on one hand, dependence $\Delta\eta_S/h = \eta(Fr)$ and, on the other hand, $X_1 = (\Delta\eta_S/h)$, it is simple to obtain correlation $X = X_2(Fr)$.

Estimations of jet planned compression coefficient provided in [120] at steady flow contraction and relative eddy length at a sudden expansion of such flow in rectangular channel according to the Fr number are presented on Figure 5.6—5.8. Here index Fr = 0 corresponds with limit of studied variable at Fr → 0.

Self-similarity of eddy current length in the scheme of one-sided expansion in Froude criterion is presented in Figure 5.8 at $Fr_1 = U^2_1/gh$ <0,001. Weak impact of Froude criterion can be seen as early as at Fr<0.1.

Figure 5.9 presents experimental dependence of resistance factors C_d of singular free bodies from Fr number, and Figure 5.10 – hydraulic friction factor λ_R in the flume with artificial bottom roughness [59].

From the position of hydraulic simulation self-similarity domains at small Fr numbers are most interesting. Due to presence of such domains, hydraulic model can be implemented with deviation from Froude rule. Simulation in self-similar domains at small Froude numbers corresponds with a known in-laboratory practice method of boosting of flow on model against values defined by Froude rule.

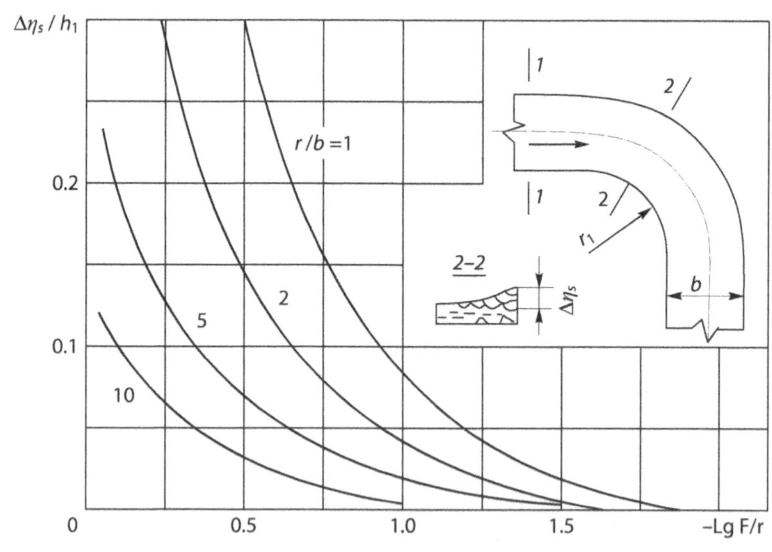

Figure 5.5 Dependence of $\Delta\eta_S$ /h from Fr in scheme of a turn.

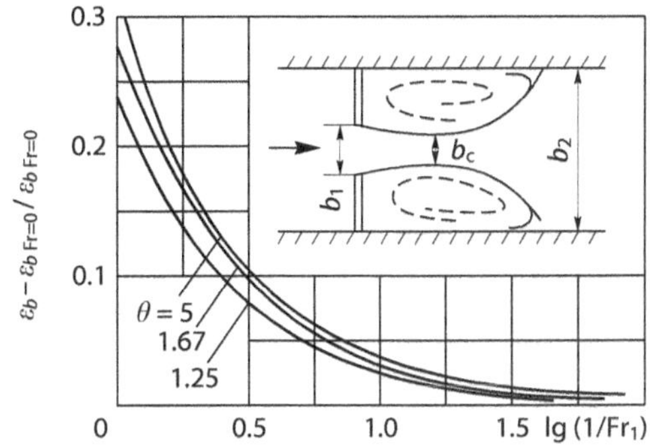

Figure 5.6 Flow turbulence impact on compression coefficient planned contraction: $\varepsilon_b = b_c/b_1$, $\theta = b_2/b_1$

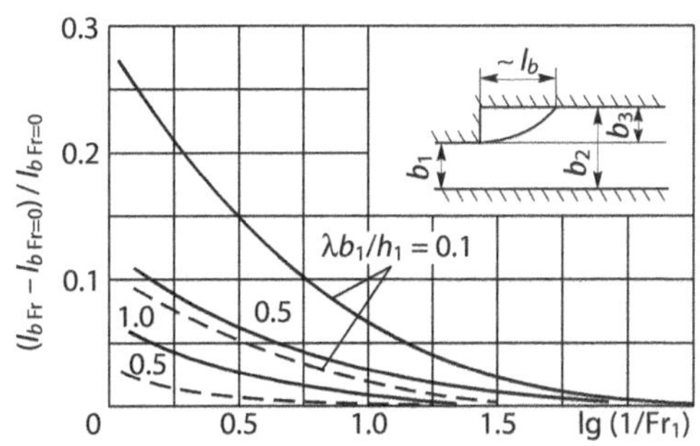

Figure 5.7 Fr number impact on eddy current length of in sudden expansion:
___________ *θ = 1.5; - - - - - θ = 2.0*

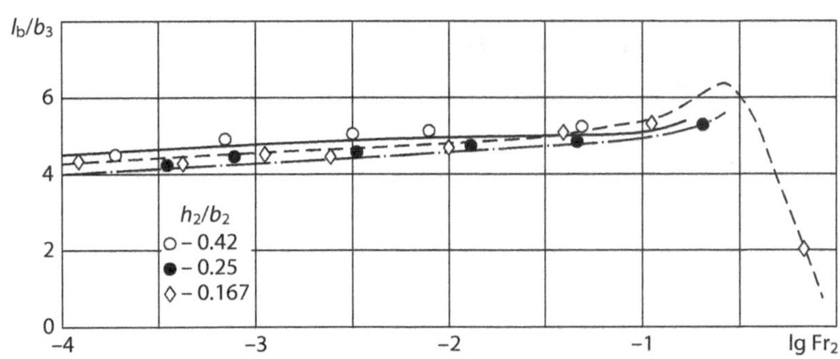

Figure 5.8 Experimental dependence of eddy current length in sudden expansion (b_2/b_1 = 1.25) from *Fr* number, applied as basic solutions.

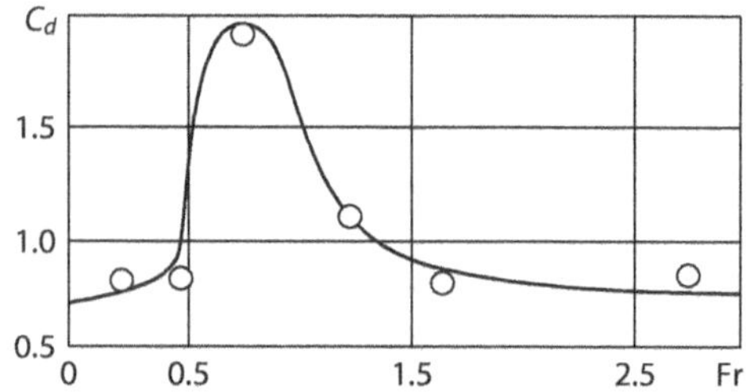

Figure 5.9 Dependence of free body resistance factor from Fr number.

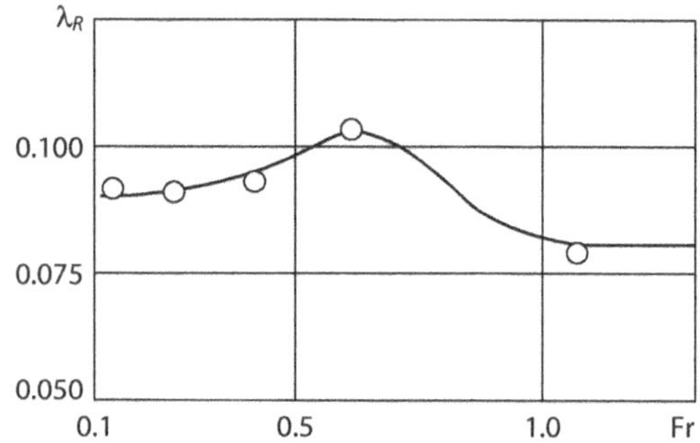

Figure 5.10 Dependence of hydraulic friction at factor increased bottom roughness from Fr number.

It should be noted that impact of Fr number in local phenomena was studied above. If studied area of free flow is long, and friction losses correspond with flow depth, then model distortion by Froude can lead to distortion of similarity of channel filling in different sections, which should be taken into account during organization of research.

5.2 Self-Similarity of Open Flows in Reynolds Criterion. Turbulence Characteristics

In chapter 4 in detail were considered principal conditions of impact caused by liquid viscosity and related Re number on flow characteristics. Here we will study only some aspects specific for open flows and objects, within which happen such flows.

In solving practical problems with the help of hydraulic simulation, in the first place we are interested in estimation of viscosity impact on averaged in time flow characteristics and turbulence characteristics of open flows. Among the former, special placement belongs to hydraulic resistance (or hydraulic friction) coefficients, which, on the one hand, often become a research subject and, on the other hand, in some problems can be used as parameter in correspondence between flow characteristics and Re number. In these cases resistance coefficients may be viewed as some similarity criterions, representing a combination of Re number and simplexes, which contain geometrical characteristics of flow boundaries. That is why first of all we will consider dependence of resistance coefficients from Re number.

Correlation between hydraulic friction coefficient $\lambda_R = 2gRI/U^2$ and *Re* number at steady free flow in the channel with even-granular surface is defined, in particular, in classical experiments of A.P. Zegzhda (Figure 5.11). Dependence $\lambda_R = \lambda(Re, \Delta, R)$, where Δ — effective height of roughness peak, for open flow qualitatively corresponds with what was obtained in Nikuradze`s experiments for pressure tubes.

At sufficiently large numbers of $\mathrm{Re} = \bar{U}R/\nu$ there is self-similar in Re domain λ_R (quadratic domain). In the quadratic domain coefficient λ_R may be defined from the following dependence:

$$\frac{1}{\sqrt{\lambda_R}} = 4\lg\frac{R}{\Delta} + 4.25. \tag{5.4}$$

Boundary of self-similar (quadratic) $\mathrm{Re}_{\lim}$ domain by A.P. Zegzhda corresponds with the following equation:

$$\mathrm{Re}_{\lim} = \frac{63R}{\Delta\sqrt{\lambda_R}}, \tag{5.5}$$

where λ_R is determined by dependence (5.4), Δ – "effective" roughness .

Some researchers propose following condition for determination of self-similar domain boundaries:

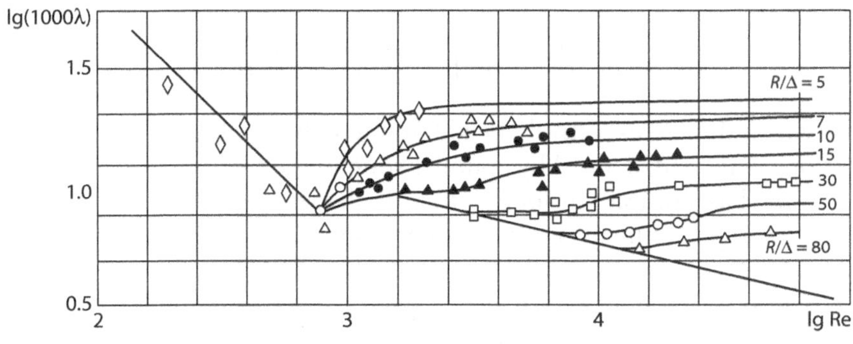

Figure 5.11 Dependence of hydraulic friction coefficient from Re number and evenness at free steady motion in flume with even roughness.

$$U_{*\lim} \Delta/\nu = M, \tag{5.6}$$

where $U_{*\lim}$ — dynamic velocity, corresponding with self-similar domain boundary; M — constant.

Because $U_{*\lim} = \sqrt{\lambda_R/2U}$, then from (5.6) follows:

$$\mathrm{Re}_{\lim} = \frac{M\sqrt{2}}{\sqrt{\lambda_R}}\frac{R}{\Delta}$$

i.e. (5.6) in structure coincides with dependence (5.5). According to different researchers' data, M constant values are 100—70 [218].

At granular roughness in real conditions, approximate exponent of channel evenness R/Δ, defined by such roughness, usually is not less than 10^2 — 10^3. In accordance with (5.5) exponent of values $\mathrm{Re}_{\lim}$ is 10^6 — 10^7. Analogue estimations are obtained in application of Mood`s formula:

$$\mathrm{Re}_{\lim} \sqrt{\lambda}\,\Delta/(42R) = 200 \tag{5.7}$$

Such $\mathrm{Re}_{\lim}$ values are common for natural and artificial open flows in real conditions, but are practically impossible in laboratory environment.

But for largest open water flows (rivers, channels), which usually are objects of hydraulic simulation, it is hard to achieve high Re numbers on models. Along with granular roughness, it is characteristic for them to have large projections on hard boundaries, which serve as additional turbulence sources and a reason for reducing of $Re_{\lim}$.

In the courses of rivers and channels, laying in alluvial soils, there are bottom forms. At ridged bottom structure, quasi-uniform motion, according to V.S. Knoroz [76], is characterized in quadratic domain by hydraulic friction coefficient

$$\lambda_{Rr} = 0{,}2\frac{h_r}{l_r}\left(\frac{h_r}{R}\right)^{0{,}25} + \lambda_R\left(1 - 10\frac{h_r}{l_r}\right), \tag{5.8}$$

where h_r and l_r — respectively height and length of ridge; λ_R — hydraulic friction coefficient, defined by granular roughness.

On the basis of (5.8), it follows that the larger relative (in comparison with flow depth) dimensions of bottom forms are, the lesser is the impact of granular roughness on hydraulic resistance.

V.S. Knoroz recommended to define quadratic domain boundary at ridged structure in accordance with dependence (5.3), inserting there $\lambda_R = \lambda_{Rr}$ and Δ value, determined in dependence (5.4) at $\lambda_R = \lambda_{Rr}$. For sand beds $h_r/R \approx 0.1 \div 0.2$; $l_r/h_r \approx 20 \div 30$ and according to dependence (5.5) R_{lim} equals $10^4 \div 10^5$.

Estimation of coefficient λ_{Rr} at ridged bottom structure is relative procedure, because flow in this case is significantly varied. For assertion of hydraulic resistances we could determine local resistance coefficient within every ridge, related to large-scale disturbances, caused by ridges and contributing to flow turbulence on the whole. It is known (ref. Section 4.2), that Re_{lim} at irregular motion can be tentatively interconnected with local resistance coefficient.

Feasibility of application of local resistance coefficient in Re_{lim} estimation is supported by results of research of straight channel with regular alternate narrowing: channel was composed of intersecting spherical segments [91]. In experiments were studied hydraulic losses, related to one segment. Segments roughness varied. But local resistance coefficient within segments turned out to be dependent mainly on area ratio of maximal and minimal channel sections and on coupling of segments form (sharp

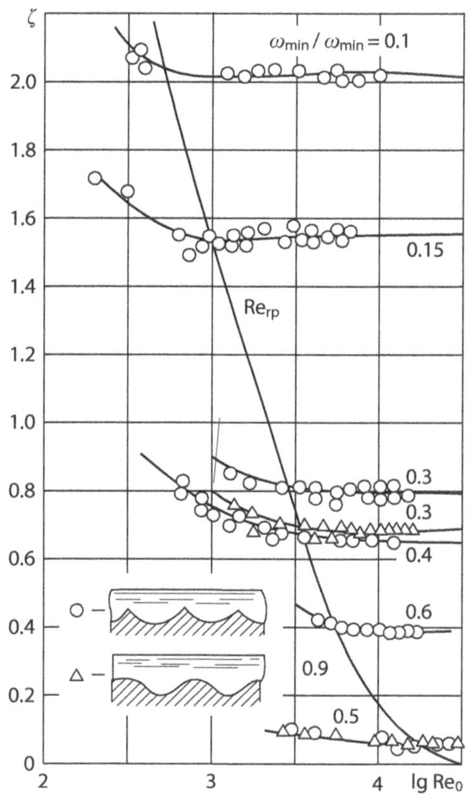

Figure 5.12 Self-similarity of local resistance coefficient ζ in Re number in the channel, constructed from toroidal segments.

edge or toroidal surface). Also it was discovered that Re_{lim} is unmistakable defined by local resistance coefficient ζ, (Figure 5.12).

All that has been explained gives proof that addition of even small local resistances in the flow significantly decreases Re_{lim} as compared with even motion. So we can assume that at presence in the flow of some artificial installations (hydraulic systems, closing dikes, control structures), when local resistance is determined quite clearly, boundary values of Re_{lim} on the areas impacted by these installations have exponent $10^3 \div 10^4$. In [76], for example, it is recommended in such cases accept $Re_{lim} = 5{\cdot}10^3$.

It is hard to schematize a natural riverbed. Here local expansions, constrictions, and turns alternate and combine, affecting each other. Due to the large variety of riverbeds it is practically impossible to give general recommendations for boundary of self-similar in Re domain. But there are some approximate recommendations for Re_{lim} for rivers in references. Various authors propose to accept R_{lim} in the range $400 \div 1000$. Such values Re_{lim} seem to be underestimated. Experiments on channel models reveal distinct tendency: for models of large river sections, there are intrinsic greater values of Re_{lim}, than for models of smaller rivers. For models of such rivers as Volga, Nile, Kama, Dnepr, and Euphrates, middle and low course effect, caused by viscosity on hydraulic resistance, was measured at $Re<1{\cdot}10^4$, but on the models of Ishim, Tura, Daugava and other medium rivers, Re_{lim} values had exponent 10^3. Difference in Re_{lim} values for rivers of different magnitude evidently relates to smaller λ_R values, intrinsic for large rivers, and also greater relative channel width and lesser meandering.

The examined above dependencies of resistance in open flows do not take into account their turbulence (free surface conditions). But presence of free surface technically can affect turbulence characteristics of open flows and energy losses even at not very large Fr numbers.

In [2] on the basis of data generalization for channels, the bottom of which is composed by fine silting sands, with banks out of sand clay or loam at average group roughness coefficient n—0.02, hydraulic radius R = 0.11 ÷ 2.61 m and bottom angle $i = 2.1 \bullet 10^{-6} \div 2{\cdot}10^{-3}$, the following dependence was proposed:

$$\lambda_R = 0{,}004 + 0{,}045 i^{1/3} / R. \tag{5.9}$$

Proceeding of field data shows that this formula gives better correlation of measurements than dependences which do not include angle (mean square error up to 25% against 31-38%, in particular cases up to 46%).

Take into account that at even motion $Fr = 2i/\lambda_R$, (5.9) may be considered as dependence λ_R from Fr. This conclusion, however, is ambiguous because the following equation is possible:

$$i = \frac{\lambda_R v^2}{2gR^4}(\text{Re})^2$$

And, technically, angle impact in (5.9) (at $v \approx$const) can be interpreted also as effect of Reynolds number. But in this particular case special analysis was carried out and it showed that both interpretations are not proved. Most likely in real conditions, generalized by correlation (5.9), there are bottom processes specific for easily erodible channels, directly related to tangent stress on the bottom $\tau = \rho gRi$. For the purpose of practical simulation, correlation with dimension variables of the type of (5.9) are useful only to the extent where they allow us to determine λ in real conditions that are similar to those in which generalization was made with lesser error.

Comparative analysis of turbulence energy generation rate, in the pressure and open flows, determining energy transfer from mean flow to heat through turbulent fluctuations, shows that difference can take place at any Fr numbers in open flow. In particular, vertical velocity fluctuations at Fr→0 near free surface are suppressed and on the axis of respective pressure flow they stay bounded. Regardless of this difference, quantitative impact of free surface can be insignificant because maximal turbulence generation rate in all cases is located near the bottom, where free surface impact cannot be great.

Significant impact of free surface on resistance clearly manifests in relatively great Fr numbers, when free surface even at on average motion significantly differs from plane (ref. Section 5.1).

Achievement of condition $Re_м \geq Re_{\text{lim}}$ on the model at Fr = idem leads to necessity to assign large geometric scales (ref. Section 3.1). Because of that, even modern publications on hydraulic simulations [181] sometimes contain recommendations to provide accordance with condition λ = idem by means of smaller relative roughness of the model, while disregarding condition $Re_м \geq Re_{\text{lim}}$ [i.e. assignment of the model to transition or even smooth-wall area of dependence $\lambda = \lambda(\text{Re})$]. Mentioned recommendations are obtained from description of steady flow. But hydraulic simulation of steady flow in this light is meaningless. If the flow differs from steady, then disregard of at least $Re_м \geq Re_{\text{lim}}$ condition (at $Re_N > Re_{\text{lim}}$) will lead to deviations in form of dependence between flow characteristics in different areas and breakdown of phenomenon similarity.

Up to the present in simulation was considered impact, caused by Re number on characteristics of stable steady flow. Usually question of the flow stabilization amounts to estimation of difference in relative flow characteristics (including energy losses), depending on turbulence (or turbulence characteristics) in irregular or unsteady and steady flows. Such difference always takes place. Quantitatively it relates to variable gradients. In steady flows most of all it manifests in the points of transfer from flow areas with low turbulence level to areas with significantly higher level. From the point of view of hydraulic simulation of open steady flows, at least two problems pose some practical interest.

The first problem relates to estimation of initial model section – a section within which turbulence characteristics not reproduced at the model`s entrance ($Ka_{ij} = <u_i u_j>/U^2 \neq$ idem), fall into accordance with mean flow characteristics and characteristics of its boundaries. It is necessary to determine the length of this section, which in general is dependent from Re_M, in order to take it into account in model designing and add initial section to test section.

The second problem arises at simulation of the most distinct stabilization areas. In hydraulic engineering such areas include entrance into free-flow gates from researches and transfer from energy dissipation zone to mean-stage channel.

In assigning length of initial section impact of *Re*, number is usually not taken into account. In such a way, according to [76], channel model $l_0 = 50h$ approximately corresponds with relevant for pressure channels data [$l_0 = (55 \div 60)h$, where h— channel height, at *Re* variations from $5.7 \cdot 10^4$ to $2.3 \cdot 10^5$]. In reality length of initial section depends not only on *Re* number, but on initial turbulence intensity. According to theoretical analysis [177], with achieved vortex formation of boundary layer, open flow is:

$$1_0 /h = 3.74Re^{0.25}$$

which at $Re \approx 1 \cdot 10^3$ is approximately 3 times less than above estimations.

These estimations apply to cases when along the flow length turbulence increases. For reducing of initial section length it can be rational to artificially create increased turbulence at the model entrance. In [84] it is shown how decay of energy vortexes happens faster if initial specter is of higher frequency. It means that at the entrance of the model it is rational to initiate high frequent, smallscale turbulence, which contains, however, low frequency energy, sufficient for formation of appropriate part of specter of steady flow. In [91] this issue is considered in detail. Also there is provided estimation of initial section length at generation of turbulence in the model entrance with the help of bottom sill. It is showed that at this method of turbulence generation:

$$\frac{l_0}{h} \approx \frac{1}{3}\sqrt{\frac{2}{\lambda_R}}\left(1+2.6\sqrt{\lambda_R}\right)\frac{2.77\sqrt{\lambda_R}+1}{1-1.33\sqrt{\lambda_R}}\mathrm{Ln}\frac{2\left[1-\varepsilon\left(1-h_a/h\right)\sqrt{45\lambda_R}\right]}{\beta} \tag{5.10}$$

where λ_R — hydraulic friction coefficient for steady flow; h_a — sill height; ε—coefficient of flow contraction in the sill flow ($0.61<\varepsilon<1$); β— coefficient, which can be taken up as equal to 0.05.

Correlation between mean flow characteristics with developing of turbulence in entrance sections, between researches and free-flow discharges, should be taken into account in their hydraulic simulation, first, in the context of estimation of discharge capacity. Experimentally this issue is more fully studied for spillways.

Research shows dependence of spillway discharge coefficient from number $Re = q/v$ (where q —specific rate at the spillway crest).

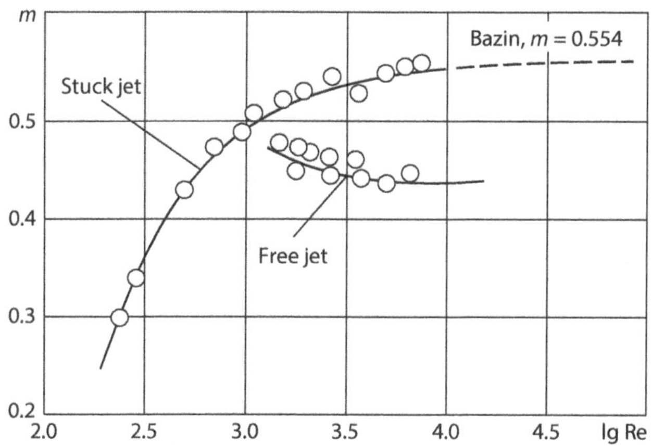

Figure 5.13 Dependence of discharge coefficient т for spillway with thin wall from Re number.

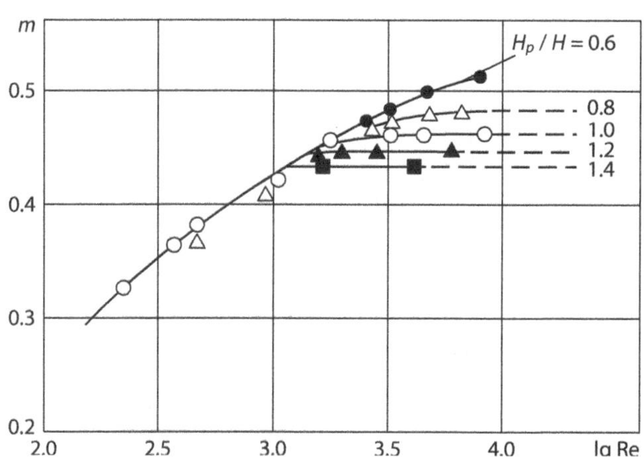

Figure 5.14 Dependence of discharge coefficient расхода m for ogee spillway from Re number at various ratios of rated head at the spillway crest H_p to operating head H.

In the Figures 5.13 and 5.14 are presented results of experiments with overflow over wall with sharp edge and ogee spillway. On the basis of this data in [52] was made a conclusion that for a free jet, overflowing sharp edged wall, there is a weak dependence of discharge coefficient m from Re number at $Re \geq Re_{lim} = 3{\cdot}10^3 \div 5{\cdot}10^3$, but for a stuck jet — at $Re \geq Re_{lim} = 1{\cdot}10^4$. For practic spillway it is accepted that $Re_{lim} = 5{\cdot}10^3 \div 1{\cdot}10^4$.

Results of research of impact, caused by Re number on discharge coefficient m for different spillways, which was carried out by various authors, are presented in [215] as dependencies from Re number - so-called scale correction of the discharge coefficient $\eta_m = m_N/m_M$. Apparently it was assumed that $m_n = \lim_{Re \to \infty} m$. There were also presented dependences, approximating correlation $\eta_m = \eta(Re)$ as:

$$\eta_m = 1 + A/Re^n \tag{5.11}$$

For spillways of different form A varies within range of 7.3-2011, and n — within range 0.58 ÷ 1.145. If we introduce into consideration relative error of discharge coefficient estimation Δm_{lim} and respective boundary value of Reynolds number Re_{lim}, than dependence (5.11) can be reconstructed in the following way:

$$\mathrm{Re}_{lim} = \left[A\left(1\sqrt{\Delta m_{lim}} - 1\right)\right]^{1/n} \tag{5.12}$$

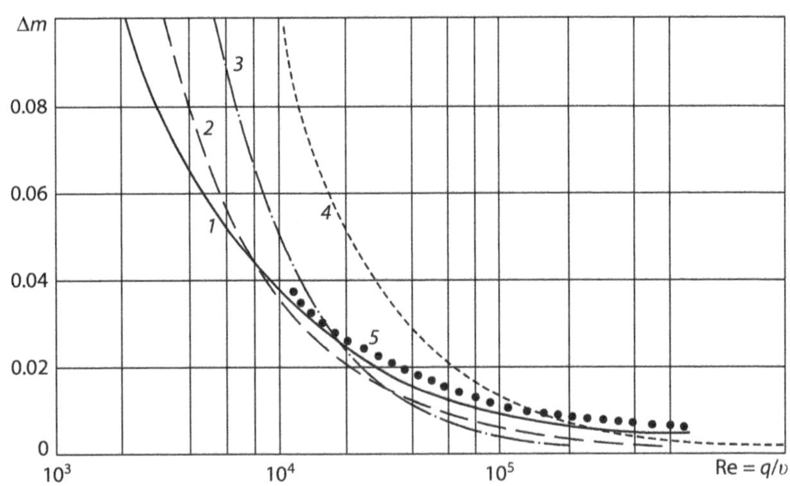

Figure 5.15 Dependence of boundary value Re_{lim} from allowable error of discharge coefficient estimation Δm:
1 — aerated spillway with circular nose; *2* — Krieger-Ofitserov spillway; *3* — non-pressure pipe with non-circular noses; *4* — Norris dam spillway (model and live); 5 — non-aerated spillway.

Presented in the Figure 5.15, dependence for different spillways shows that $Re_{\text{lim}} \approx 1 \cdot 10^4$ corresponds with deviation, close to $\Delta m_{lim} = 0.05$. Upon necessity of determination of discharge capacity with high degree of accuracy, for example, in study of weir gauge, with accuracy of 1%, $Re_{\text{м}}$ should be $>1 \cdot 10^5$. For ogee spillways at $\Delta m_{lim} = 0.05$, overflow height should be $H_{\text{м}} \geq 0.03$m, and at necessity of accuracy, corresponding with $\Delta m_{lim} = 0.01$ - $H_{\text{м}} \geq 0.15$m.

Study of presented in [218] data confirms that at $Re_{\text{м}} < 10^4$ the discharge estimation error of spillways and non-pressure overflows can exceed 5 ÷ 10%.

Weak dependence of discharge coefficient from Re number (and, accordingly, relatively low Re_{lim} value) is caused by the fact that energy losses in the overflow entrance (before critical depth section) are low and not determined discharge capacity. The situation with estimation of Re impact on stabilization zone (at the overflow entrance) characteristics is different, because characteristics are directly related to turbulence. [215] contains data on dependence of scale correction for coefficient of pressure on spillway nose from Re, $\eta_{cp} = C_{PN}/C_{PM}$, where $C_P = (P_{aT} - P_{or})/(\rho g H_0)$ (P_{aT} – atmospheric pressure; $P_{or} = P + p_{max}$, P- mean nose pressure; p_{max} — half of maximal amplitude of pressure pulsation). For correlation is proposed the following approximating dependence:

$$\eta_{Cp} = 1 + 222/(Re - 3000)^{0.71} \tag{5.13}$$

Based on (5.13) dependence between Re_{lim} and ΔC_{Plim} is presented in Figure 5.16. As was expected, directly related to turbulence characteristic for stabilization zone is dependent on Re significantly more, than coefficient m. That is why coefficient C_P can be determined on the models with acceptable scale with low accuracy.

In some practical problems we are interested in characteristics of boundary layer, developing on the surface of free flow. In particular, length of development zone of boundary layer determines location of section, where its aeration starts. Flow characteristics in the development zone of boundary layer significantly depend on Re number. Hydraulic friction coefficient in the particular flow area is linked to this criterion.

According to [187] hydraulic friction coefficient in the development zone of boundary layer is:

$$\sqrt{\lambda_b} = \sqrt{a}\left(\lg \text{Re}_X\right)^{-1{,}19}$$

where $a = a(\Delta)$;Δ— effective height of roughness peak; $Re_x = Ux_B/\nu$; x_B – longitudinal coordinate along the length of spillway face.

It follows that similarity of distribution λ_b along the length of developing boundary layer at $Re \neq$ idem is possible only at appropriate selection of bottom

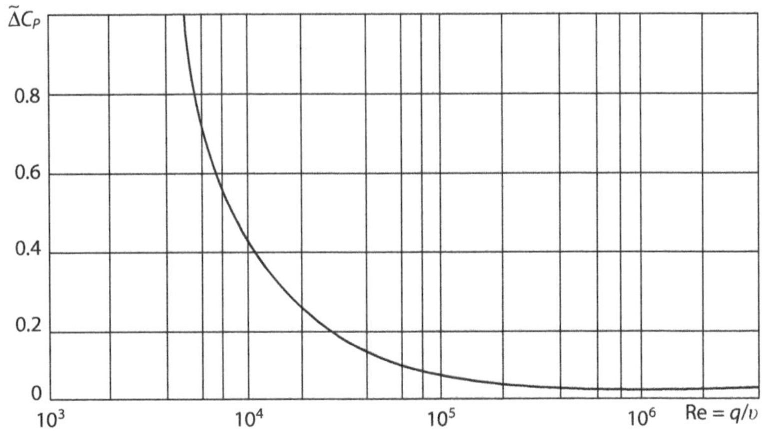

Figure 5.16 Dependence of boundary Re_{lim} value from allowable estimation error of pressure coefficient on spillway nose $\tilde{\Delta}C_p$.

roughness, varying in the development of boundary layer area. Method of such selection is proposed in [187].

Approximate estimation in selection of open overflow roughness constant along the whole length and naturally not providing for similarity of flow details, can be obtained upon research results presented in [76]. On the basis of field research, it was established that losses within spillway faces of the Shastan and Sent-Eten-Cantele dams amount to 20-30% of poll level difference. Length of development area of boundary layer in these dams is (40 ÷ 60)h (*h* — height of overfill layer). A model of Sent-Eten-Cantele dam was made in geometrical scale 1:60, which corresponded with $Re_{\text{M}} = 3_{*}10^4 \div 1_{*}10^5$. Roughness of water spill surfaces on the model varied due to its varnishing, ironing of cement covering and applying sand with size 2 mm.

In Table 5.1 is presented information on energy losses within spillway face, in fractions from total energy in the upper pool in relation to spill layer from spillway $\Delta E/E_0$. Presented in the table, effective height of roughness peak is accepted accordingly to reference data.

Table 5.1

Experiment conditions	Δ mm	$\Delta E/E_0$, %
Field	2.00	35
Model:		
Varnished surface	0.01	29
Ironed surface	0.02	33
Surface with glued sand	0.50	52
d = 2 mm -		

The table shows that correspondence of losses on the model and in real conditions is obtained at ironing of spillway face on the model. Probably, relative roughness at ironing is lower than it should be in accordance with geometrical scale of the model (1.5 – 2 times), which compensated Re number impact.

From the given example we can draw a conclusion that at sufficiently large scale of the model, there is a possibility for estimation of energy losses within overflow. In study of other phenomena, errors can be more significant. For example, disintegration of the jet discharged into the atmosphere significantly depends on turbulence in the jet`s opening. If in the model, turbulence development within overflow will take a different course than in real conditions, or specter of turbulence pulsations approaching short overflow will be distorted, it will affect the jet`s similarity characteristics.

5.3 Simulation of Flow Plan for Channel Flow

Channel flow is usually characterized by shallow (as compared to width) depth and significant variability in coastal line. Relative flow width *b/h* can exceed 100, 200 and more. Such a flow is an appropriate object for planned schematization.

Searching for similarity conditions for distribution of specific flow rate or velocity, averaged by depth, for channel flow is based on equations of planned problem (2.128), written sometimes in special coordinate system with account to flow boundaries form.

Changing of channel form in the plan causes lateral water movement of two types:

1. local mean lateral flow, corresponding with change in special flow rate upon channel width;
2. cross current, directly related to the jet curvature and irregular distribution of velocity upon flow depth.

Cross currents of the first type are fully described by equations of planned problem. That is why in that case, when there is question about stress structures, acting between jets in the plan (i.e. essentially question of equations of turbulent flow closure) doesn`t have significant importance; similarity of cross currents as a similarity of equations for planned problems is defined by conditions, resulting from equation analysis (2.117), including condition (2.118).

If we take into account that practically always $\lambda_M > \lambda_H$, then condition (2.118) proves the necessity for enlargement of the vertical scale in relation to the horizontal in the amount of times the hydraulic friction coefficient on the model is bigger than the one in real conditions: $M_h/M_l = M\lambda$. Knowing this, of course, fulfillment of similarity for coefficient λ distribution in flow length and width should be monitored, which is possible at sufficiently large Reynolds numbers in a hydraulic model. The difference between conditions (2.118) and (2.127) consists in the fact, that at development of condition (2.127) from one-dimensional equations for wide channels, the scale of channel width stays arbitrary. In a planned problem width scale equals length scale. Let`s note that in simulation practice it is allowable to combine bi-dimensional and one-dimensional descriptions of channel in different sections along its length. For example, if in some intermediate river section there is not significant reformation of flow in the plan, then length of this section on the model can be severely reduced, reducing the model by lateral scale for this section with respective increasing of hydraulic friction coefficient (by the means of increasing of model boundary roughness). Width and depth scale stays the same, and accordingly flow rate and velocity scales stay the same. This fact allows practically implementing two different approaches (bi-dimensional and one-dimensional) within one model.

If in studied phenomenon, tangent stress on the surface between liquid jets corresponds with bottom (and surface) stress, then the answer to the question with condition (2.118) is the only similarity condition of the current plan in self-similar domains in Re and Fr criterions, depending on understanding of dependence structure for tangent stress. As it shown in Section 2.7, in some representations of structure of these stresses, the similarity analysis also shows applicability of condition (2.118) in the cases when tangent stresses on vertical surfaces should be taken into account, in other representations of mentioned similarity to this condition, it should be added that there is another correlation, so conditions λ = idem and b_0/h_0 = idem are presented as independent. So, for estimation of applicability of similarity conditions, it is necessary to determine impact of the flow cross current on the currents plan, and for estimation, in particular, of establishment of condition (2.118), it is necessary to determine if this condition holds in the cases when tangent stresses between jets are significant.

In accordance with a comment mentioned at the end of Section 2.3, the question on sufficiency of condition (2.118) can be phrased in another way: can the coefficient λ, linking averaged in-depth instantaneous velocities with instant tangent bottom stress, be the same as in steady flow.

Intensive cross current happens on sharp river turns. For estimation of impact of relative flow width and hydraulic friction coefficient on motion conditions in the turn, special experiments were carried out, which had the results presented in Figures 5.17 – 5.21. The model amounted to flume of rectangular section with constant width and turn of 180°. Average turn radius r_{cp} was accepted as equal to flume width ($r_1 = 0.5b$), and model depth and average roughness of the flume bottom varied independently.

In the course of experiments it was ascertained that with increase of *b/h* and λ, there also can be observed leveling of velocity curve in all section lines. Figure 5.17 shows velocity distribution in two characteristic section lines, obtained in experiments, which significantly differs in *b/h* and λ values. Here we can also apply experiment results of A. Sukri [219] and I.L. Rozovsky [130], carried out on pressure-free models, which have the same correspondence of planned dimensions, as in the authors` experiments on pressure models. On Figure 5.18 is applied average in depth travel velocity in the scale of mean velocity in section ($\bar{U}/\bar{\bar{U}}$).

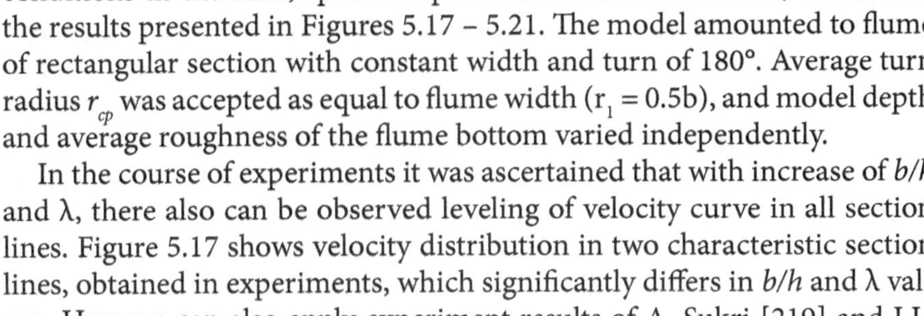

Figure 5.17 Velocity distribution on the turn at $r_2/b = 1.5$ and different λ and *bh*:. *1* — experiments on pressure model ($b/h = 100$, $\lambda = 0.045$); *2* — I.L. Rozovsky`s experiments ($b/h = 13.3$, $\lambda$ -0.012) [132]; *3* — Sukri`s experiments ($b/h = 1.0$, $\lambda = 0.0104$) [219].

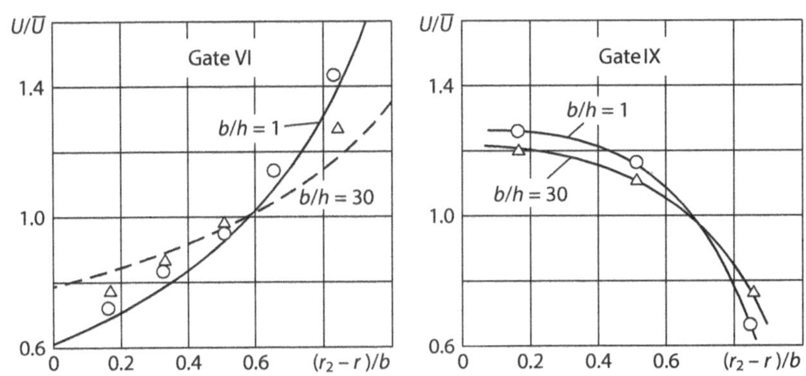

Figure 5.18 Effect caused by b/h on velocity distribution ($\lambda = 0.024$).

Figures 5.18 and 5.19 show the effect caused by b/h and λ correlation on velocity distribution. Comparison of these results makes obvious that increasing of both λ and b/h leads to notable change in travel velocity distribution. Thus allowing us to assume that the main factor in velocity distribution in the plan, on the turn of wide channel, belongs to cross currents of the first type, of which impact is fully taken into account by planned problem equations. In this case, at relatively little significance of cross current and friction forces between jets in the plan, dependence of the current plan from parameters λ and b/h should appear as dependence from $\lambda b/h$ complex. And really, the matching of experiment results at different λ, and b/h, but $\lambda b/h \approx$idem, presented in Figure 5.20, confirms this conclusion.

Little significance of cross current (cross movement of the second type) in these conditions is confirmed by comparison of current plans for pressure and free flow. For comparison were taken experiments of I.L. Rozovsky [130], carried out in hydraulic flume at $Fr = 0.11$ and $b/h = 13.3$,

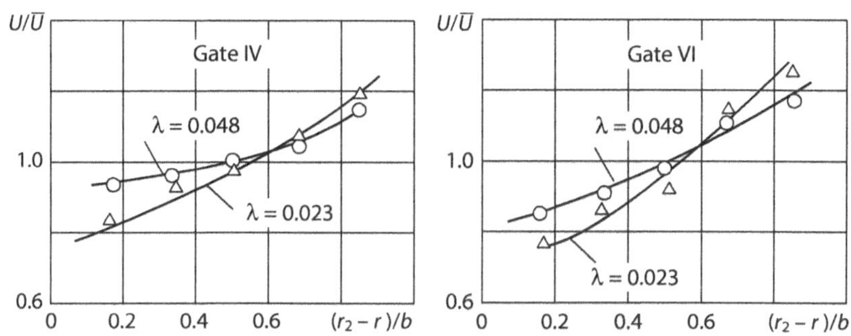

Figure 5.19 Effect of λ on velocity distribution (b/h = 30).

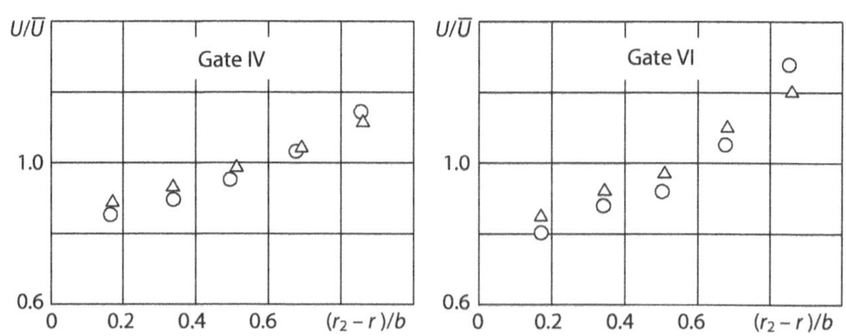

Figure 5.20 Velocity distribution at $\lambda\ b/h = idem$ Δ- $\lambda = 0.048$; $b/h = 30$; O- $\lambda = 0.024$; $b/h = 60$.

and experiments with pressure flows, where, for maximal possible difference in cross currents, was accepted equal roughness of the model`s bottom and cover. Experiments showed that distribution of averaged in depth velocities and transverse slopes on the turn of respective free and pressure flow are almost coincident (Figure 5.21). Little systematic deviation is explained by some difference in hydraulic friction coefficients: for pressure model $\lambda = 0.009$, for free flow $\lambda = 0.007$.

We can overestimate a little the factual impact of cross current on velocity distribution when considering schematized liquid motion in a "closed" turn, without variations in flow length and cross movements of the first type. Such an estimate was carried out in [91].

As a result of performed constructions, the following formula for calculation of distribution of lateral velocities in the plan was obtained:

$$\frac{U}{\overline{U}} = \frac{\frac{1}{\sqrt{r/b}}\left[1+(A_r-1)\exp\left(-\frac{r^2-r_1^2}{2h^2 a_{r/b}}\right)\right]^{1/2}}{\int_{r_1/b}^{(r_1/b)+1}\frac{1}{\sqrt{r_1/b}}\left[1+(A_r-1)\exp\left(-\frac{r^2-r_1^2}{2h^2 a_{r/b}}\right)\right]^{1/2} d\frac{r}{b}} \tag{5.14}$$

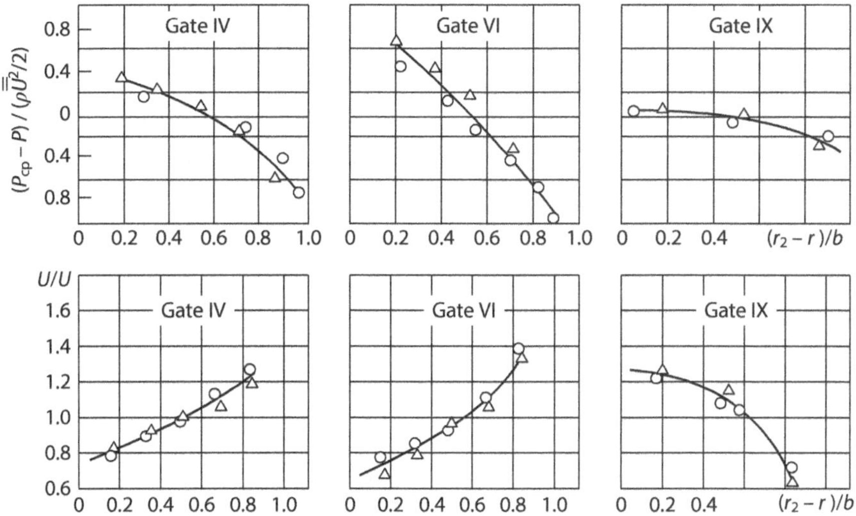

Figure 5.21 Comparison of experiment results on open and pressure models (line sections on the Figure 5.17, $b/h = 13.3$):
a — distribution of piezometric levels in flow width; b — distribution of velocities in flow width; Δ— pressure model, $\lambda = 0.009$; O — hydraulic flume, $\lambda = 0.007$.

Here $A_r = U_*^2(r_1)/ U_{*0}^2$ — correlation of real tangent stress on the bottom of convex shore $(r\text{-}r_1)$ to the tangent stress in steady motion with the same angle and depth. Coefficient $a_{r/b}$ depends on λ [91].

In the Figure 5.22 are presented calculation results according to (5.14) for turn scheme, studied experimentally at $r_2/r_1 = 3$; $r_1/b = 0.5$; $b/h = 10 \div 100$; $\lambda = 0.05 \div 0.005$.

Changing of cross current due to λ impact insignificantly affects distribution of averaged velocities. Impact of b/h is more notable, but it also weakens at $b/h > 20$. In this case, the effect of cross current becomes negligibly small and distribution of averaged velocities in the plan corresponds with the planned problem solution.

To ascertain in which part $\lambda b_0/h_0$ complex defines similarity of the flow plan at significant impact of tangent stresses between jets, in [120] sudden expansion of open steady flow was considered, within which tangent stresses between transfer stream and eddy currents are particularly large. With that was used semi-empirical dependence of mean eddy current length at sudden expansion of a rectangular channel, in which tangent stresses between transfer jet and eddy current are estimated through hydraulic friction coefficient $\lambda_{1,3}$, constant on the interface between jet and eddy current. Boundary estimations are made in assumption of negligible tangent stresses on this interface (l_{B1}) and at value $\lambda_{1,3} = 0.04$, obtained in processing of experimental data (l_B).

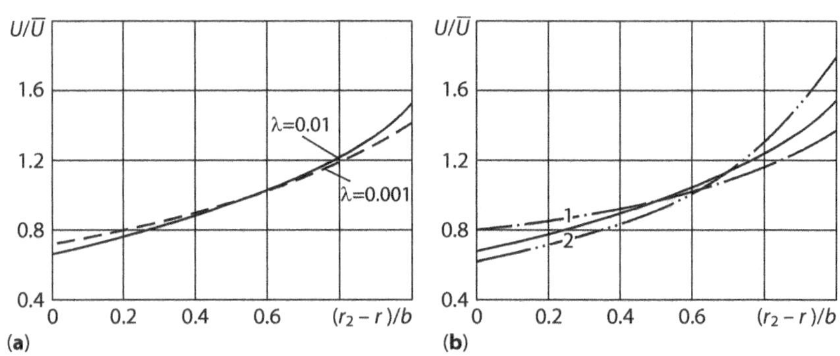

Figure 5.22. Impact of lateral current on width distribution of averaged in depth velocities: a) $\lambda b/h = 10$ b) $\lambda b/h = 0.1$ 1 - Asimptotic $(\sqrt{r_1} + \sqrt{r_2})/2\sqrt{r}$ 2 - potential flow

Dependence of $(l_{B1}—l_B)/l_B$ from complex $\lambda b_1/h_1$ at various expansion degrees is presented in the Figure 5.23. As was expected, at sufficiently large values $\lambda b_1/h_1$, tangent stresses on vertical edges practically have no effects on eddy current length, and otherwise, at very small values of this complex, eddy current length is mostly determined by $\lambda_{1,3,}$ so when there is less impact of tangent stresses, the expansion degree is larger.

In real conditions separated flows are indicative for flows in cooling water ponds in the areas of straightening installations and construction bridges, and in the tail ponds of hydraulic complexes. For cooling water ponds relative flow width in the entrance is usually 30-100 at $\lambda \approx 0.01$, i.e. $\lambda b_1/h_1 = 0.3 \div 1$

For straightening installations on medium and large rivers, $\lambda b_1/h_1 = 0.2 \div 3$, and $\theta = 1 \div 1{,}3$, and for construction bridges on hydraulic complexes in the same conditions $\lambda b_1/h_1 = 0.1 \div 2$ and $\theta = 1.2 \div 3$. From diagrams in the Figure 5.23, it follows that disregard of tangent stresses in estimation of eddy current zones in those cases will not lead to significant errors.

The same conclusion of sufficiency of $\lambda b/h$ = idem condition for flow with separation was obtained in another way – on the comparison basis of calculation of eddy current length in bi-dimensional equations and experimental data.

In analysis of similarity conditions for flow plan in the tail pond of hydraulic complexes two distinctive cases should be noted. Firstly, which is most interesting, in relation to general washing out, maximal water discharge through hydraulic complex, when water release takes place along

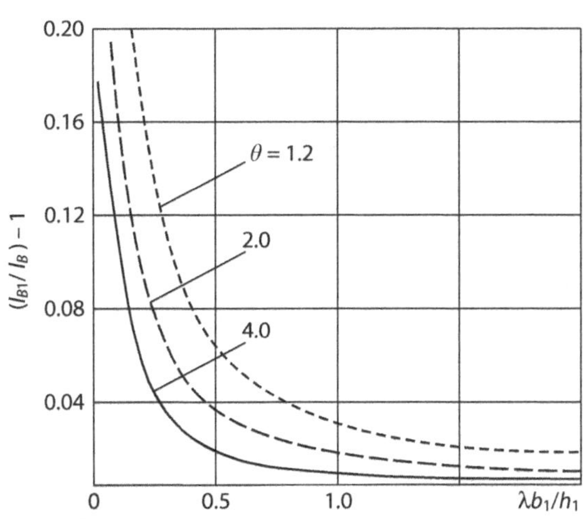

Figure 5.23 Effect of interface stresses on eddy current length at various $\lambda b_1/h_1$ and θ values.

the whole spillway. And, secondly, the case of discharge on the part of spillway should be noted. If in the first case for hydraulic complexes on large plain rivers, relative width is usually within range 50-100, and $\lambda b_1/h_1$ – within 0.2-1, then in the second case complex value $\lambda b_1/h_1$ can be close to $\lambda_{1'3}$ or even smaller. That is why disregarding of tangent stresses on vertical edges at discharge along the whole spillway should not lead to errors exceeding 5-6%. Water release in the part of spillway error can be very large. Nevertheless, even in this situation, condition (2.118) is practically sufficient.

From what is explained above, the conclusion can be made that in solution of the large range of practical problems in the model, when $\lambda \neq$ idem, for achievement of similarity, we can define distortion of geometric scales in such a way so $M_{h'}/M_l$ equals $M\,\lambda$,.

In the Figure 5.7, dependence of relative eddy current length l_B/b_3 from $\lambda b_1/h_1$ at small Froude numbers was presented. From consideration of curves on this diagram we can conclude that at small values of complex $\lambda b_1/h_1$ (when in resistance forces prevail friction forces on the side edges of transfer jet), l_B/b_3 weakly depends on $\lambda b_1/h_1$ and is close to constant at $\lambda b_1/h_1 \to 0$. In such conditions, probably, mixing in the plan plays a major part, so representation (2.134a) becomes true and criterion $\lambda b_1/h_1$ is defining, though its impact is insignificant. (This is true if crosscurrent plays a minor part). So here we can distinguish self-similar domains in $\lambda b_1/h_1$ with small deviation of l_B/b_3 on their boundaries from values within domains. Figure 5.7 allows us to obtain estimation of self-similar domain boundary in $\lambda b_1/h_1$ corresponding with 1≤0≤5 10% accuracy of observations:

$$(\lambda b_1/h_1)_{\lim} = (0.3 \div 0.05)\theta$$

A mentioned fact points out that in the study of objects characterized by small values of the $\lambda b_1/h_1$, complex, assigning scales for λ, b and h can be arbitrary in so much so the value of complex $(\lambda b_1/h_1)$ does not exceed boundary values of this complex:

$$(\lambda b_1/h_1) \leq (\lambda b_1/h_1)_{\lim}, \text{ if } (\lambda b_1/h_1)_N \leq (\lambda b_1/h_1)_{\lim},$$

In such a way, according to different considerations, we can acknowledge that observance of condition $\lambda b/h$ = idem ensures approximate similarity of the plan of separated flows as at quite large values of complex $\lambda b_1/h_1$, so at pretty small values of this complex.

For verification of assumption of uniqueness of dependence of eddy current length from complex $\lambda b_1/h_1$ special experiments were carried out in hydraulic flume with width of 4 m and length of 12m at $Fr = U^2_1/gh_1 \leq 0{,}1$. It was considered a scheme of sudden expansion at 0 = 1.33. In the experiments flow pattern was compared at various values of b_1/h_1 and λ, but stayed constant for every experiment pair value of $\lambda b_1/h_1$. Experiment results are presented in the Table 5.2.

Table 5.2

λ,	b_1/h_1	$\lambda b_1/h_1$	l_B/b_3	$\Delta\left(\frac{l_B}{b_3}\right)/\Delta\left(\frac{b_1}{h_1}\right)$
0.0061	42.0	0.251	4.05	0.30 / 8.5
0.0077	33.4	0.251	4.35	
0.0077	84.0	0.643	2.98	0.24 / 14
0.0098	70.0	0.643	3.22	

From the table 5.2 data it follows that at smaller $\lambda b/h$, relative variation in eddy current length gets bigger with variation of b/h. It means, probably, increasing impact of cross current because deviation from self-similarity of turbulent friction between jets in the plan should be expected with increasing of criterion $\lambda b/h$, and not its decreasing. From presented data it follows that the plan of channel flows, with sufficient accuracy, is defined by single complex $\lambda b/h$, and not by parameters λ and b/h separately.

If we assume that complex $\lambda b/h$ is defining, then, as it seems, similarity of the flow plan can be achieved in any case (when $\lambda_м$ exceeds $\lambda_н$) by the means of appropriate selection of distortion of geometrical scales of the model, i.e. similarity of the flow plan can be achieved (if we do not take into account effect of Re and Fr) at quite small planned scale. But distortion should be limited. It is required by range of circumstances.

Firstly, the affine transformed transverse section of the channel in the model possesses hydraulic characteristics, different from those in the field. One characteristic of transverse section of the channel can be taken as simplex h/R, where R — hydraulic radius. (In particular, at $h/R \approx 1$ channel can be classified as wide.)

If $M_h \neq M_l$, then $h/R \neq$ idem ($M_R \neq M_h$), and on the model, designed on the basis of $\lambda l/h =$ idem condition, losses in length will be distorted even in the conditions of regular flow ($\xi_{ДЛ} \neq$ idem).

For estimation of changes in simplex h/R, at distortion of geometrical scales, there were calculations carried out for channels with rectangular or parabolic transverse section. Maximal depth was accepted as indicative. For rectangular channel

$$h_{max}/R = 1 + 2b/h_{max}.$$

If we consider the allowable value of correlation $(M_h/M_R)_{lim}$, then we can obtain allowable distortion of geometrical dimensions $(M_h/M_b)_{lim}$, corresponding with this value at particular relative channel width in the field $(b/H_{max})_n$:

$$\left(M_h/M_b\right)_{\text{lim}} = (1/2)\left(b/h_{\text{max}}\right)_N\left[\left(M_h/M_R\right)_{\text{lim}} - 1\right] + \left(M_h/M_R\right)_{\text{lim}} \tag{5.15}$$

At two values of $(M_h/M_R)_{lim}$, equal to 1.05 and 1.1, this dependence is shown in the Figure 5.24. For parabolic channel:

$$h_{\text{max}}/R = (1/4)\left(b/h_{\text{max}}\right)\left[4\left(b/h_{\text{max}}\right)^{-1} + 1\right]^{3/2} - 1$$

Obtained from this correlation dependence $(M_h/M_b)_{\text{LIM}} = \varphi[(b/h_{max})_{\text{N}}$, $(M_h/M_R)_{\text{LIM}}$ at the same values of $(M_h/M_R)_{LIM}$ is also presented In the Figure 5.24. It could be noted that for the avoidance of significant difference in scales of depth and hydraulic radius it is infeasible to significantly distort geometrical scales of relatively narrow channels. On the contrary, at wide channels this condition does not pose a practical obstacle for distortion of geometrical scales.

Another (even more important) limitation is the fact that at significant scale distortion large variations in resistances may happen, related

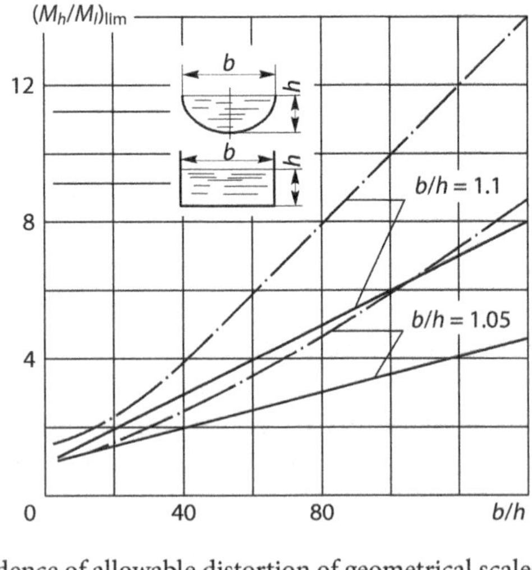

Figure 5.24 Dependence of allowable distortion of geometrical scales from relative channel width in the field:

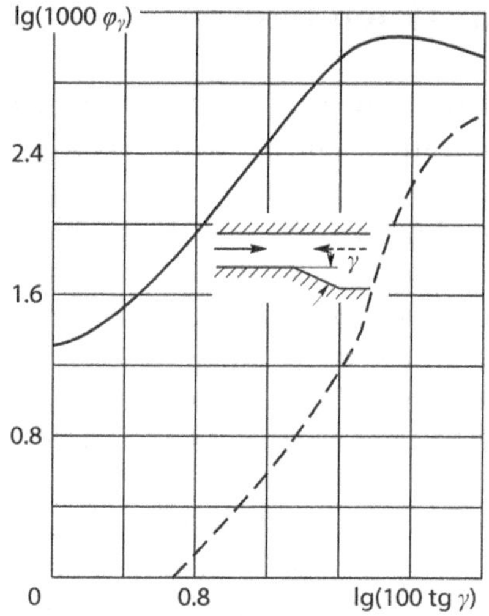

Figure 5.25 Impact of slope steepness distortion *tg* γ on energy losses at depth variations ($\varphi_\gamma = \zeta_\gamma/\zeta_{\gamma = 90°}$)
_________ flow expansion:
_ _ _ _ _ _ _ _ flow constriction.

to change in flow depth due to changing of slope steepness along flow direction.

In Figure 5.25 it may be noted how relatively wide self-similarity domains of local resistance coefficients in the tangent angle of bottom shape (i.e. simplex *h/1)* can take place either at very small values of angle γ or at values close to 90°. But at small values *tg* γ (small values of exponent module $\partial h/\partial x_i$**)**, local resistances due to their smallness make insignificant contribution into total resistance. That is why in the cases when flow depth along stream direction varies insignificantly ($\partial h/\partial x_i \approx 0$), moderate scale distortion does not lead to substantial disturbance of similarity. If module $\partial h/\partial x_i$ has large values, distortion of geometric scales leads to re-distribution of resistance forces and substantial distortion of flow plan.

Distortion of geometric scales should be assigned with great care. Practically we can recommend limiting distortion of geometric scales in study of large and medium rivers by two or three times, and applying greater distortion only in specific cases (for example, at plain bottom shape and for very wide channels).

Let`s note that until present different works suggest to assign distortion of geometric scales either out of concept of some uniform allowable distortion degree or by analysis of some individual phenomenon aspects. Such approaches can lead to significant mistakes.

5.4 Non-Steady Open Flows

Non-steady flows in rivers are usually interesting in long areas, where one-dimensional schematization can be very effective. This is explained by the fact that in short areas (approximately equal to river depth or width) changing rate of flow regimes, even in the problems like distribution of burst waves, for exception of short intervals of passing of the wave front, changes relatively slowly and in many cases can be studied in quasi-steady approximation. One-dimensional equations can have different form of representation (Saint-Venant, Boussinesq, Dressler and others) depending on content of assumptions in relation to pressure distribution in flow section (ref. Section 2.6).

Systematic examination of applicability of one-dimensional models for description of non-steady processes in real rivers became possible with implementation of ECM in hydraulic research. In USSR algorithms and programs were created under supervision of O.F. Vasiliev [19, 22] and V.M. Lyatkher [47, 56, 89, 104]. Examination was necessary for the hypothesis applied in equations. In particular, it was necessary to confirm the question about the possibility of accepting quasi-steady correlations for assignment of boundary tangent stresses and also to assume that all corrections, obtained in transfer from integrals to mean values of integration functions, equal one. With application of the developed algorithm and program comparisons of calculations and field observations of non-steady regimes of short-time storage in tail pond were carried out [44].

In many reports on symposiums of IAHR (Newcastle, 1976 – Non-steady flow in open channels; Bratislava, 1981 – Numerical methods in hydraulics) it was noted that good matching of calculations and experiments can be obtained only in proper adjustment of mathematical model due to roughness coefficient (which was accepted in all calculations as independent from regime), form and area of transverse sections in points, where these sections are of complex form or rapidly vary in length. According to data [160], sufficient matching of calculation and observation in non-steady conditions was achieved only at variation of the Chezy coefficient at 10 -20% as compared to values defined for one of the steady regimes. Inaccurate estimation of resistance severely affects flow discharges (and velocities), especially in the cases when boundary conditions are given in the form of levels mode. According to field data at level variations up to 2.3 – 3.3 m in the channel connecting Lake Barkly and Kentucky, the difference between the calculated and observed level was more than 0.15 m, and at the same time, measured discharge in the flash was 40% less than calculated [167].

Applicability of one-dimensional equations in calculation of severe non-steady flows – distribution of burst wave and wave setup on shores – was analyzed on the basis of comparison with laboratory data [47]. It is ascertained that calculations give satisfactory accuracy though, as a result of undulations and turbulent large-scale fluctuations which appear in repeating experiments. Instant values, for example, of depths, can differ from what is calculated up to 10%, and in separate cases up to 20%, from the calculated maximal level variations in the studied section (Figure 5.26).

In calculations on the basis of one-dimensional equations, the hydraulic friction coefficient was accepted according to the Manning roughness code ($\lambda = 2gn^2_0/h^{1/3}$) with constant roughness coefficient $n_0 = 0.013$, corresponding with steady flow. Experiments, results of which are partly described in [111], were carried out in flumes of rectangular and triangle sections with width of 1 m and length of 129 m with bottom angle $i_0 = 1.1\text{x}\ 10^{-3}$.

It is ascertained that the difference in calculations and experiments is relatively greater for small initial channel filling, at which greater impact of flow non-steadiness on bottom hydraulic resistance is possible, and irregularity of velocity distribution in flow depth is relatively large. Systematic researches of hydraulic friction coefficient λ variations in open flow due to non-steadiness impact were started in the fifties. Then they were continued by I.L. Rozovsky [131 and 132], O.F. Vasiliev and V.I. Kvon [21],

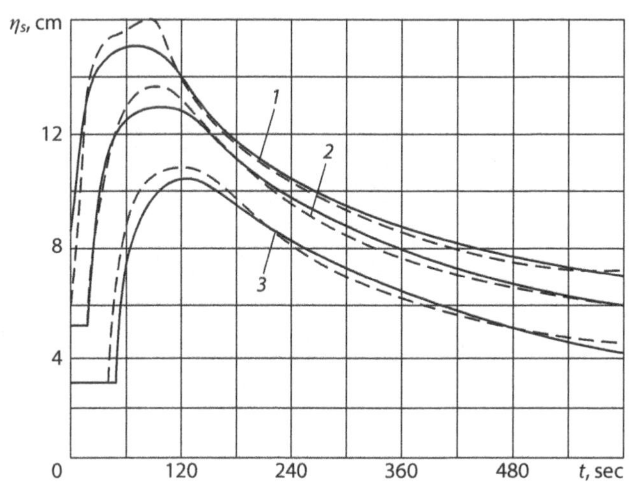

Figure 5.26 Comparison of calculation results (full lines) and experiments (dashed lines) on burst wave distribution in wide flume of rectangular section
$H_0 = 20$ cm, $h_0 = 1$ cm:
1, 2, 3 — distance from dam
respectively 5; 25 and 50 m.

and V.M. Lyatkher with others [47, 111]. On the whole we can acknowledge that with proper selection of the roughness coefficient, calculations by one-dimensional equations and simulation at relevant criterion of any flows in rivers with regular section form (rectangular, triangle, parabolic, with slightly varying roughness by section width) bring results, that have satisfactory corresponding with observations, without special attention to resistance variations due to non-steadiness. This conclusion is relevant for parameters, averaged by sites, significantly exceeding local flow depth.

Less clearly it can be observed for flows in channels with complex form: with turns, developed flood plains, islands, braids. Even in steady conditions, the presence of the flood plain in some cases may manifest as decrease of river flow capacity at an increase in water depth with flow entrance into the flood plain. This phenomenon was called the "kinematic effect" of the flood plain and is described in detail in [49].

In the Figure 5.27 we are shown the dependence of averaged in vertical velocities from depth in 11 verticals in the river Amur channel during flood season in 1958 [11]. The first vertical is located near the flood plain, and ninth in 400 m from the flood plain edge at general channel width 675 m. Clear distinction of functions *U(h)* relates to restraining influence of flood flow, which in this case of the one-sided flood plain, was noticeable at approximately 60% of the channel width.

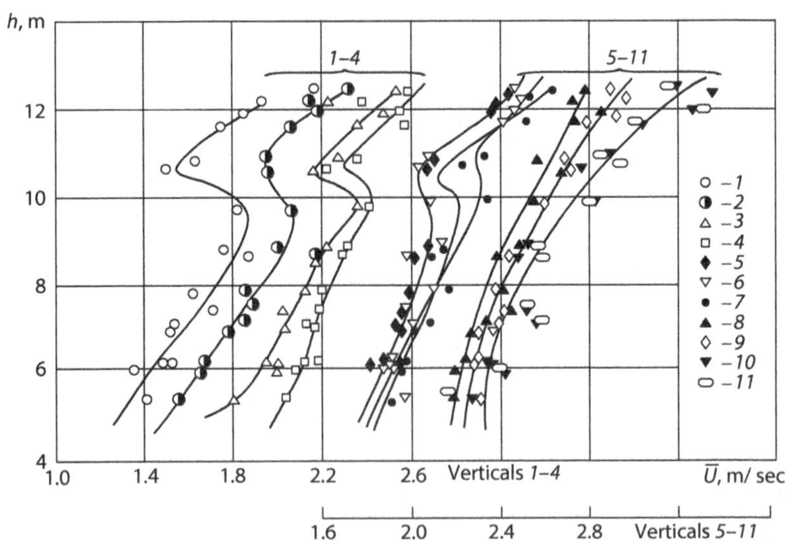

Figure 5.27 Distribution of mean velocities in depth on various verticals in Amur river channel.

Quantitatively this effect is manifested in rapid decrease of the Chezy coefficient, calculated for channel flow, at the exit of water into the flood plain (Figure 5.28). It creates doubts about common recommendations to take account of flood plain only in the equation of mass balance, and to write a dynamic equation only for channel flow. Flood plain impact may be also complicated by the fact, that within bushy or grassy flood plain, group roughness coefficient depends on flow depth and generally on current velocity. Simulation of those phenomena is a complex task.

In [24, 26] a technical approach is described, representing complex characteristics of flood plain roughness in hydraulic models. The point of this approach is to apply plastic shavings of a particular section (for example, 1x3 mm^2), produced in peeling of polyethylene tubes of specific diameter. In this model, roughness in the form of shavings possesses similar qualities with real roughness (Figure 5.29) and, besides that, can be reliably predicted in density, varying in wide range. The roughness coefficient of such a surface varies in accordance with relative depth in simulation flow h/Δ (Figure 5.30) and packing density (Figure 5.31). Greater roughness is observed when flow depth equals thickness of the shavings layer Δ.

Natural non-prismatic characteristics of river valley has some special effect. In Figure 5.32 results of calculations are shown, carried out for real river valley with a slope angle from 3.6_*10^{-4} – in the dam site to 1.9_*10^{-4} in the lower stream, where the river joins the larger river. An event of sudden destruction of the dam was calculated, located in 670 km from the river mouth. The head before dam was H_0 = 90 m. The water basin width was accepted at an average value (in water basin length) with a roughness coefficient of n = 0.03.

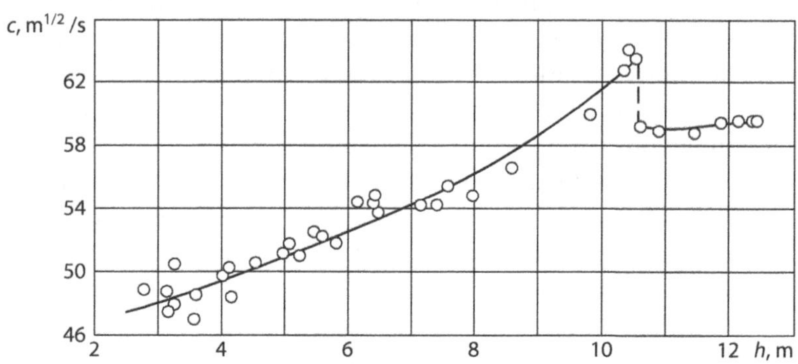

Figure 5.28 Variations in Chezy coefficient C in river Amur channel depending on depth h. Flood plain is flooded at water depth $h \approx$10.5 m.

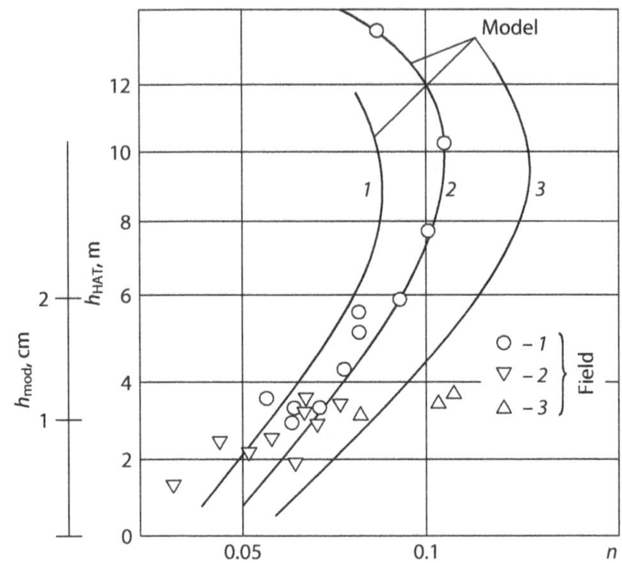

Figure 5.29 Variations of group roughness coefficient *n* of the bushy flood plain, depending on depth *h* according to field measurements and on the model (vertical scale 1:35) with artificial roughness by the means of plastic shavings [26]: *1* — sparse bush; *2* — medium bush; *3* — thick bush.

As can be seen from Figure 5.32, water level between gates R_1—R_4 after the dam destruction rapidly increases, which can be explained by expansion of the valley after gate R_1 and constriction in the gate $R_{4.}$ For verification of this explanation a study of impact was carried out, caused by a roughness coefficient on dynamics of burst wave. The roughness coefficient *n* varied from 0.003 to 0.1. It appeared that such large variations in the roughness coefficient didn`t practically affect wave characteristics. It may be caused by a relatively small effect of the dynamic equation and defining role of continuity equation due to the large volume of area between dam and gate $R_{4,}$ within which velocities are small and the nature of the equation is defined only by a continuity equation.

Another important result consists of the fact that burst wave in 50 hours moved only to 60 km. It may be explained by sudden expansion of the valley in the area behind gate R_1 and consequent severe constriction before gate R_4. Attempt to predict, in this case, levels regime according to general recommendations [57], calculated and verified by experiments for prismatic valley, was absolutely unsatisfactory.

Comparison with solution for bi-dimensional problem and comparative analysis of similar case, studied on physical (hydraulic) model, showed

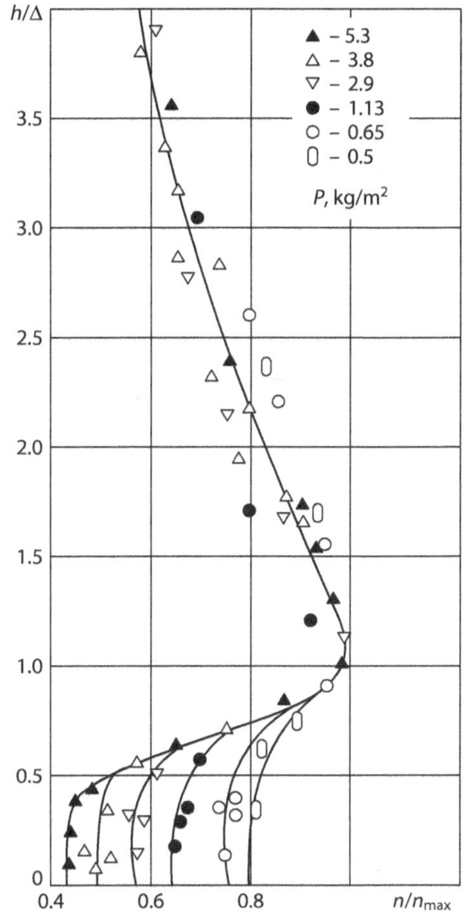

Figure 5.30 Relative variations in group roughness coefficient *n* of the flood plain model, covered by plastic shavings, depending on relative water depth and shavings cover density *P* [24, 26].

that a solution in one-dimensional scenario without any corrections brings estimation, close to reality. This surprising conclusion is a result of small effect of dynamic equation in the zones, where it is recorded with big errors and good accuracy of this equation usage for prismatic, narrow valley areas with "proper" section, where this equation insignificantly defines the phenomena. It is understandable that in the areas where dynamic equation is insignificant, any distortions are allowable with preservation of similarity for volume curve.

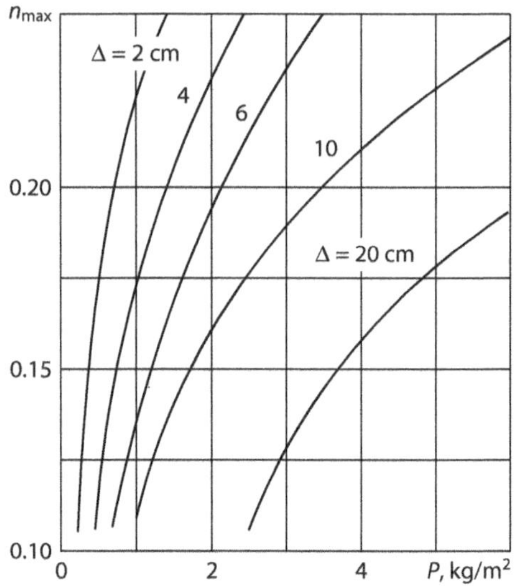

Figure 5.31 Dependence of maximal group roughness coefficient n_{max} of the model, covered by plastic shavings, from thickness of shavings layer Δ and cover density *P*.

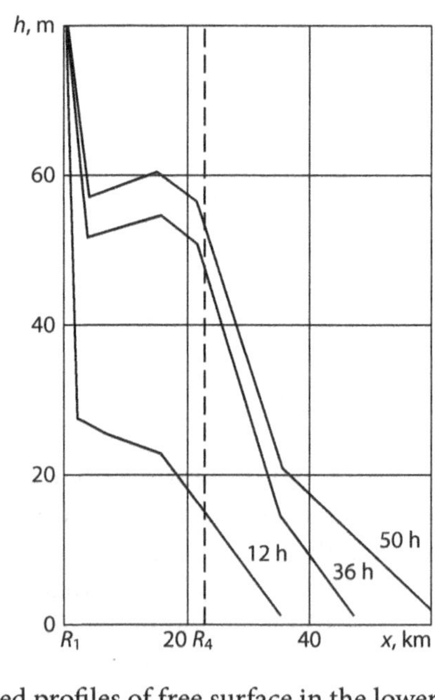

Figure 5.32 Calculated profiles of free surface in the lower pond of hydraulic complex in various time intervals after sudden destruction of pressure front.

Applicability of similarity transformation in Saint-Venant equation system (2.124) leads to appearance of well-known criterion systems:

Froude $$\pi_1 = Fr = U^2_0/(gh_0) \tag{5.16}$$

Strouhal $$\pi_2 = Sh = U_0 t_0/l_0; \tag{5.17}$$

$$\pi_3 = (\lambda/i_0)(U^2_0/gh_0); \tag{5.18}$$

$$\pi_4 = h_0/(i_0 l_0); \tag{5.19}$$

$$\pi_5 = h_0/(i_0 b_0); \tag{5.20}$$

$$\pi_6 = l_0/b_0. \tag{5.21}$$

Here λ_0 — values of λ at $h = H_0$.

Necessary condition is identity of all criterions (5.16) — (5.21) in compared objects. Satisfactory similarity conditions, as always, depend on specific boundary problems and include only criterions and their combinations that contain variables used in definition of boundary or initial conditions. For example, in the problem on full breakthrough of the dam with head H_0 into dry prismatic channel at selection for depth scale value $h_0 = H_0$, the only defining criterion (at $i_0 \neq 0$) will be parameter:

$$\pi'_0 = \pi_3/\pi_1 = \lambda_0/i_0 = 2_{\pi 0} \tag{5.22}$$

Similarity conditions will be:

$$\pi_0 = \text{idem} \tag{5.23}$$

Scales of values, not impacting fulfillment of similarity conditions (5.23), can be selected arbitrarily. Assuming that $\pi_k = 1$ ($k \neq 0$), let`s find characteristic values of velocity U_0, length l_0, and time t_0, which are convenient for generalization of results:

$$U_0 = \sqrt{gH_0}\left(\pi_1 = 1\right), \tag{5.24}$$

or

$$U_0 = \sqrt{gH_0/\pi_0}\left(\pi_1 = 1\right), \tag{5.25}$$

$$l_0 = H_0/i_0 (\pi_4 = 1, \text{ if } i_0 \neq 0); \tag{5.26}$$

$$t_0 = l_0/U_0 (\pi_2 = 1); \tag{5.27}$$

$$b_0 = l_0 (\pi_6 = 1); \tag{5.28}$$

Selection of characteristic values for velocity and time, as can be seen from (5.24) and (5.25), is ambiguous. It is convenient to select such characteristic values so dimensionless results will depend on defining criterion in lesser degree. It appears that in small distances from the dam ($x \leq 0.01H_d/i_0$), it is better to use representation (5.24); in large distances from the dam ($x > 0.02H_d/i_0$) correlation (5.25).

Let`s pay attention to the fact that for un-branched channel selection of flow, width scale does not affect results; requirement (5.28) does not appear and (5.23) is the only similarity condition.

For branched channel selection of flow, width scale matters. If velocity and depth of the side channels are being simulated on the same scale as velocity and depth of the main channel, then additional similarity condition will look like this:

$$\pi_6 = l_d/b_0 = \text{idem} \tag{5.29}$$

which means, in particular, impossibility for width scale distortion in comparison with model length scale.

Figures 5.33 and 5.34 show variations of relative maximum depth $h^+_{max} = h_{max}/l_0$ and relative flow velocity $\boldsymbol{U^+_{max}} = \boldsymbol{U_{max}/U_0}$ with scale U_0 at (5.25) in fixed gates of the tail pond at parameter π_0 variations.

At

$$\pi_0 > (\pi_0)_{lim} \approx 50 \tag{5.30}$$

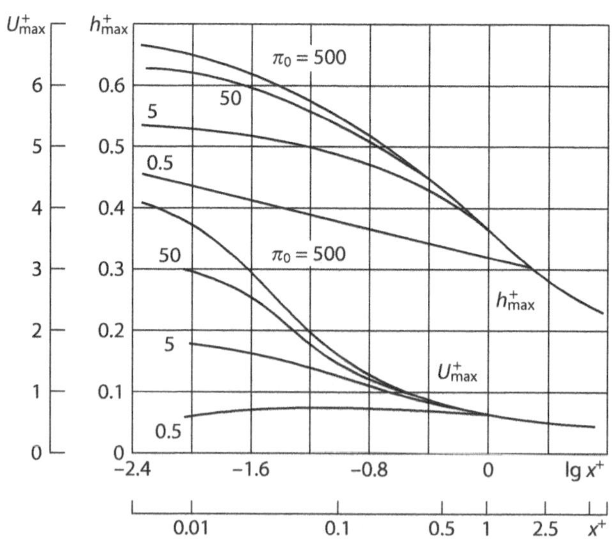

Figure 5.33 Measurement of maximal depth h^+_{max} and velocities U^+_{max} at the tail pond length x^+ at $h_0^+ = 0.05$

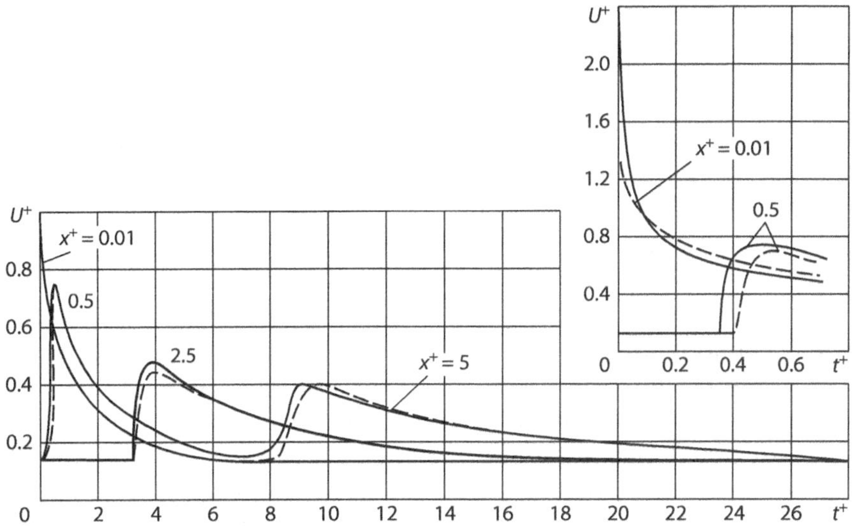

Figure 5.34 Variations in relative velocities $U^+ = U/U_0$ in the tail pond at $h_0^+ = h_0/H_0 = 0.05$ depending on relative time $t^+ = t/t_0$ at instant destruction of the dam:
———— - $\pi_0 = 500$; - - - - - - - - $\pi_0 = 5$.

there is self-similarity in this criterion. Mathematically (and physically) it corresponds with small effect of inertia forces.

Near the dam ($x_{io}/H_0<0.01$) impact of inertia forces is significant. On the contrary, impact of river bottom angle (at $i_0<0.001$) can be disregarded. Applying similarity transformation for equations (2.124) at $i_0 = 0$, we see that a solution for the problem of dam breakthrough into dry channel of rectangular section becomes fully self-similar at selection of scale for length, velocity and time according to formulas:

$$\left.\begin{aligned} l_0 &= H_0/\lambda_0; \\ U_0 &= \sqrt{gH_0}; \\ t_0 &= \sqrt{H_0}/\lambda_0\sqrt{g}, \end{aligned}\right\} \tag{5.31}$$

If water spill takes place into channel with depth h_0, then h_0/H_0 is the only parameter for the problem.

In previous reasoning, of course, it was assumed that in the simulation, flow section form was preserved. A distinctive feature in one-dimensional scenario problem consideration is the possibility to loosen this requirement. It appears that if transverse channel section can be presented in the form:

$$(b/h)_h = Amh^{m-2} \tag{5.32}$$

(where b — river width at maximal depth h; m, A — some constants), then there is similarity transformation, when generalizing results obtained for channels with various sections (with various A *and* m [47, 57].

Many times attempts have been made to simplify Saint-Venant equations. These simplifications, as can be seen from the presented example, disregarding the bottom angle, are very important for estimation of self-similarity domains in individual criterions. We can distinguish two approaches to simplification of Saint-Venant equations: 1) linearization of equations; 2) disregarding of some members.

The first approach was realized by M. Bachet in 1934 and N.T. Meleshchenko in 1940. Many authors came back to it up to the present [207]. Linearization idea is contained, in fact, in application of dominant function and all model options, representing the river system as a "black box" with many exits and entrances. Efficiency of these models up to the present time was not studied systematically, though in many publications, for example, in works on 13th and 15th IAHR congresses, there are examples of successful correlation of calculations, based on linearized equations, and observational data.

In the second approach we can distinguish members, which continue to dynamic equation (continuity equation usually is not changed):

$$\overbrace{\frac{1}{g}\frac{\partial U}{\partial t}+\frac{U}{g}\frac{\partial U}{\partial x}+\frac{\partial h}{\partial x}}^{\mathrm{IV}}+\overbrace{\left(I_{fr}+i_{\sigma}-i_{0}\right)}^{\mathrm{I}}=0. \qquad (5.33)$$

$$\frac{1}{g}\frac{\partial U}{\partial t}+\underbrace{\frac{U}{g}\frac{\partial U}{\partial x}+\underbrace{\frac{\partial h}{\partial x}+\left(I_{fr}+i_{\sigma}-i_{0}\right)}_{\mathrm{II}}}_{\mathrm{III}}=0.$$

The simplest model of "kinematic wave" can be obtained in keeping only the member I. This model is seldom applied.

The most popular in practice is the so-called method of "instant regimes" when members II are kept. Linearized equations in such cases give "diffusive wave." Main ideas of this method were formulated by N.M. Vernadsky in 1932 and later were developed in works of V.A. Archangelsky, Y.D. Guildenblat, M.V. Potapov and others. The main assumption of this method consists of disregarding all inertial terms in dynamic equation, i.e. the application of steady correlations for determination of correspondence between depth and slope angle in every moment of time.

Acceptability of this assumption was verified by comparison of calculated and observed data about flood discharges. This comparison for plain rivers, for example Volga near Kamyshin city [117], on the average brought satisfactory results, though deviations in discharge in particular periods were up to 30%. These deviations were explained not by impact of inertial terms, but errors in estimation of intermediate inflow, for example, incorrect measurement of filtration phenomena in unsaturated flood plain soil, complex interaction of channel and flood volumes, etc. Comparison made by method calculations with field and laboratory data, was presented in many papers of 13th congress of IAHR.

In some works it is claimed that difference between calculation results and observations is small, but factual information shows that often it can reach 15 – 20%.

Relative impact of term $\frac{U}{g}\frac{\partial U}{\partial x_1}$ can be noticeable. According to [223], in value $\frac{U}{g}\frac{\partial U}{\partial x_1} \Big/ \frac{\partial h}{\partial x_1}$ can reach 0.3. It justifies consideration of "convective dynamic wave" – group of summands III in equation (5.33). In [223] there are presented values $\left|\frac{1}{g}\frac{\partial U}{\partial t} \Big/ i_0\right|_{MAX}$ of variable lgi_0. According to this data it appears that with decrease in angle, the relative role of inertial term $\frac{1}{g}\frac{\partial U}{\partial t}$. increases. At very large depths (usually in the river mouth) may be justified approximation of "gravity wave" without friction – IV in the equation (5.33), which is also called "inertial wave."

On the basis of generalization of many ECM calculations results for flood transformations in real rivers, we can give the following estimation for individual terms of equation (5.33) with accuracy up to 1/2 of logarithmic units (Table 5.3) [223].

From the table it can be seen that the difference in exponents of individual terms of dynamic equation, as a rule, does not exceed one, i.e. reliable simplification of equation (5.33) is hardly possible except, maybe in a case of accordance with upper line of the Table 5.3.

Table 5.3

$-\lg\left\|\frac{\partial h}{\partial x} - i_0\right\|$	$-\lg\left\|\frac{1}{g}\frac{\partial U}{\partial t}\right\|$	$-\lg\left\|\frac{u}{g}\frac{\partial U}{\partial x}\right\|$	$-\lg I_{fr}$
4	5	5–4	4
2	5–4	4–3	3
5	6–5	5	5

As was shown above, at $i_0 \neq 0$, impact of angle in motion equations is only noted through values of parameter π_0 (5.22). If boundary and initial conditions would not depend on π_0 (or i_0), then effect of i_0 would manifest only through π_0 and at small i_0 (large π_0) would be singe-valued – with decrease in i_0 (increase in π_0), relative impact of π_0 would decrease. It is clearly seen in results of systematic calculations for transformation of burst wave [57]. In this case initial conditions do not depend on i_0, so with decrease of i_0 (increase of π_0) on relative distance from the dam, bigger than 0.05-0.1, flow parameters stop to depend from π_0 at π_0 >50. Ordinary floods take course in a different way. Here boundary conditions, defining in hydrograph, depend on valley slope and, as it seems, vary in such a way that with decrease of i_0, relative role of inertial terms does not decrease. It is even quite possible that observed impact of i_0 is explained by morphological characteristics of river valley section, also related to valley angle.

Above the possibility of effective decreasing for number of impacting dimensionless parameters by the means of introduction of special scales accordingly to problem setting was demonstrated. But we are interested in the possibility of evaluating the importance of individual members of equation (5.33) in the most general way. It can be done, for example, comparing velocities for distribution of small disturbances in the flow c within period T [176]. Mentioned velocity, measured in fractions of velocity c_0, corresponding with full equation (5.33), appears to be a function of two parameters – Froude number

$$\mathrm{Fr} = Q_0^2/\Omega^2 g h_0 = U_0^2/(g h_0) \tag{5.34}$$

and dimensionless wave period $T^+ = T/T_0$, where

$$T_0 = (2/\lambda_0)\sqrt{h_0/g}. \tag{5.35}$$

At larger T^+ and Fr is the true hypothesis of "kinematic wave" (Figure 5.35) — most important are summands I in (5.33); approximately with the same conditions in T^+, but at relatively smaller limitations in Fr number, is a true diffusion model (Figure 5.35).

Significantly lesser operating possibilities gives inertial model (Figure 5.36), at which in (5.33) continue only summands IV. Minimally limited diffusional model gives relatively faster disturbance decay that solution of full equations. In both cases the solution of linearized equations gives the height of disturbance wave as proportional to *exp(—x/1)*. Value l for diffusion approximation at small Froude numbers is 10-20% smaller than for the full system.

At larger Froude numbers even flow can become unsteady – rolling waves appear. It is believed that satisfactory matching of theoretical steadiness criterion with experiments can be obtained only with correction for

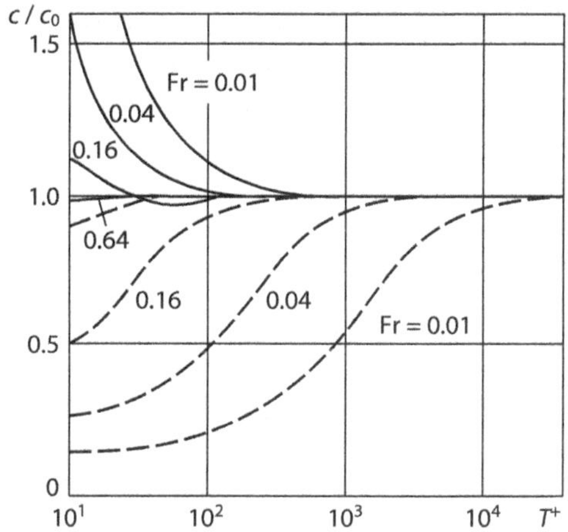

Figure 5.35 Relative distribution velocity of "diffusion waves" (———) and "kinematic waves" (- - - - -) [176].

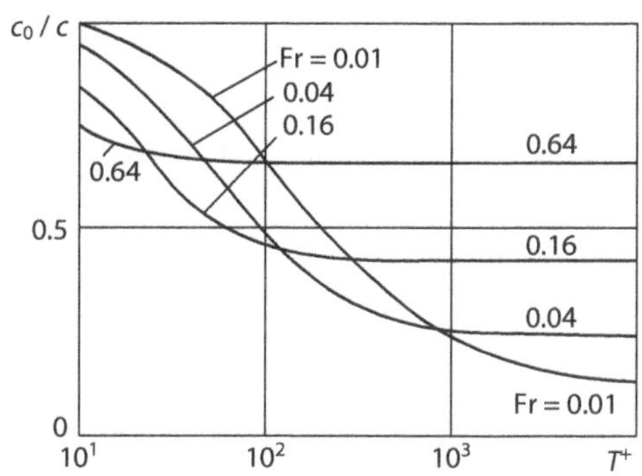

Figure 5.36 Relative velocity of "inertial waves" [176].

momentum and not hydrostatic pressure distribution in depth [31]. The last circumstance leads to a dynamic equation that is more complex than Saint-Venant equation, and general conclusion about strong impact of velocity distribution details complicates the simulation.

In [35] on the basis of systematic experimental material is shown greater impact of high-velocity flow length on appearing conditions and parameters of rolling waves. In particular, it is shown that in the many cases inconsistency in theoretical prediction of unsteadiness and experimental facts may be explained by impact of high-velocity flow length.

Assuming that variations of hydraulic friction coefficient with depth are proportional to $h^{-\varphi}$ and accepting correction for irregularity of velocities distribution $a = 1$, for a wide flow of rectangular section, we can obtain this known condition for flow steadiness:

$$U_0 < \frac{2}{1+\varphi}\sqrt{h_0 g cos\theta} \tag{5.36}$$

where U_0, h_0 — initial flow velocity and depth:

$$U_0 = \sqrt{2gh_0\, sin\theta\lambda_0} \tag{5.37}$$

With application of both equations we can find steadiness condition, represented through bottom slope angle:

$$tg\theta =< 2\lambda_0 / (1+\varphi)^2 \tag{5.38}$$

Because parameter φ and hydraulic friction coefficient λ correspond with each other quite closely, then conditions:

$$\lambda_0 = \text{idem} \tag{5.39}$$

and geometrical similarity of high-velocity flow form are sufficient for achievement of similarity for rolling waves.

It is typical that wave parameters (length l, depth under peak h) in [35] are presented in fractions of critical depth:

$$h_{\text{кр}} = \sqrt[3]{Q^2/(gb^2)} = h_0\sqrt[3]{2l_0/\lambda_0} = h_0\sqrt[3]{\text{Fr}_0}, \tag{5.40}$$

And length scale is accepted as h_{cr}/i_{0}. From a general point of view of similarity theory, selection of these scales is quite natural, since in experiments, discharge Q was the only variable which really changed during tests (at fixed angle of the flume bottom i_0). Experiment results turned out to significantly depend on Froude criterion $Fr_0 = U^2/(gh_0)$. In this case, when impact of resistance force is very important, it is more effective to select calculated depth of even flow h_0 as a depth scale, and h_0/λ_0 as a length scale. With application of these coordinates we obtain estimations, which relatively weakly depend on defining criterion Fr_0. In particular, the length of critical area l_0', outside which the "visible" rolling waves appear, is constant in the assumed coordinates:

$$l'_0\lambda_0/h_0 = 8{,}4 \tag{5.41}$$

Length of initial area l', outside of which the system of rolling waves becomes statistically steady and longitudinally homogenous:

$$l'_0\lambda_0/h_0 = 16 \tag{5.42}$$

In these described cases all information on real flow turbulence is concentrated in hydraulic friction coefficient λ. It is clear, that values of this coefficient will depend on scales for equation averaging. For equation (2.123) this coefficient, defined in accordance with (2.122), is an arbitrary function of flow time, depth, velocity and, possibly, unsteadiness parameter $\frac{1}{g}\frac{\partial U}{\partial t}$ [correlation $\Omega = \Omega(h)$ and roughness characteristics are assumed as preset].

Possible averaging of equations changes the formula for function λ, but does not make this function any more certain. There are two known approaches to practical definition of the function $\lambda(\Omega,Q)$:

1. generalization of data, obtained in steady regimes, supplemented by results of systematic research of unsteadiness impact;
2. solution of inverse problem for finding λ on the basis of data about $Q(t)$), and $\Omega(t)$ for specific river or group of similar rivers.

First approach is traditional for hydraulics (ref. Section 5.2).

Second approach looks especially promising. Its possibilities are significantly expanding, if observations and numeric interpretation are carried out not only for floods, but also for atmospheric currents (winds) in surface layer in periods, when they are oriented along relevant river structures.

Described rules for simulation of non-steady flows considerably rely on Saint-Venant equations. As was noted, these equations are not sufficient for description of uneven continuous flows, for instance, like short waves. In this case are possible various complications of bi-dimensional and one-dimensional equations giving account to jets curve (equations of Boussinesq, Peregrine and others) [161]. All these complicated equations considerably limit possibilities of physical simulation because they provide more severe requirements for correlation of model scales. For example, the condition for continuity of relative jet curve does not allow for distortion of model geometrical scales. This condition makes development of numerical and complex simulation methods, including tests of "non-distorted" models, all the more essential.

Simulation, based on the criterions, derived from averaged (space – time) equations, can be reliably applied only for determination of parameters, averaged by appropriate intervals. Within these not always clearly defined intervals, the actual situation can radically differ from averaged.

For example, actual flow in the dam breakthrough into full tail pond on the length, equal to tens of initial depth, is characterized by widely inhomogeneous velocity distribution by depth (water "slides" over water) [48, 131]. It is clear, that detailed study of models built in accordance with (5.23) and h_0/H_0 = idem will not always give true results. For such studying analysis and continuity of the fuller similarity criterion system is necessary. On the contrary, averaged – macroscopic – process characteristics are represented accurately enough. Correct "upscale" of phenomena obtains corresponding (on the average) with real conditions data even in complex problems, such as prediction of non-steady surging regimes in the river mouth [16].

As discussed above, unsteady flows with free surfaces are interesting from the point of view of hydraulic engineering. There are though, quite a lot of non-steady hydrodynamic problems related to other issues and various technical problems.[1]

Every one of these problems is specific. But two circumstances are common:

1. in the presence of free surfaces the role of compressibility and viscosity of liquid is usually insignificant; many problems on non-steady motion of liquid in drops can be solved within the contest of model for ideal non-viscous, incompressible, weightless liquid;
2. after elimination of the source of non-steadiness, the flow scenario rapidly tends to a steady (in statistical meaning) state. Effects of turbulence and viscosity in non-steady problems are usually a lot smaller than at steady flows in similar conditions.

Let`s point out some characteristic examples of simulation of non-steady flows. Well known phenomenon of appearance and high disruptive action of cumulative jet at initial (very effective) approximation may be considered with the help of M.A. Lavrentev`s method as stationary interaction of incompressible jets. Similarity criterion in this problem at determination of

[1] Partial review of these problems is presented in the classical book by M.A. Lavrentev and B.V. Shabat, *Hydrodynamic problems and their mathematical models*, (M.: Science, 1977). Many problems are considered in the works of L.I. Sedov, G.V. Logvinovich, G. Birkhoff and others. Additional information can be found in the articles of the International symposium, "Non-stationary water flow with high velocity.",(M.: Science, 1973), see also p. 9.2.2 in this book.

perforation depth is correlation of liquid jets density ρ and material being destroyed ρ_M. Perforation depth h is proportional to jet length L:

$$h = \sqrt{\rho/\rho_M} L$$

Next (in importance) effect is compressibility of the liquid and only after that – non-steadiness. Later it is specified that what is considered the simplest model gives reasonable results, if the velocity head of calculated jet is not less than 10 times higher than durability of the destructed material.

If this condition is not met, then barrier continues to be a solid body h, and the problem considerably complicates. A hydrodynamic situation in subsonic liquid jet at impact has three phases [77]. In the first phase during time r_0/a_0, pressure on the barrier varies slightly and is proportional to $\rho U_0 a_0$ [a_0 – sound velocity in liquid, $2r_0$— diameter (or thickness) of the jet, U_0 – jet velocity]. In the second phase with time period about r_0/U_0, unsteady flow develops, which can be reliably predicted by solution of the respective problem about impact of ideal incompressible liquid [then flow scenario, close to steady, is realized. In the first phase effect of barrier, compressibility is noticeable, even if this barrier is granite (Figure 5.37)].

Similar is jet efflux from pressure tank at sudden opening. For two-dimensional jet is ascertained [170] that in the second phase deviation from steady solution decays in time, as exp $(—t/t_0)$, where maximal t_0 is:

$$t_0 \approx \frac{2}{(\pi+2)\left(2-\sqrt{2}\right)} \frac{r_0}{U_0} \approx 0{,}66 \frac{r_0}{U_0}$$

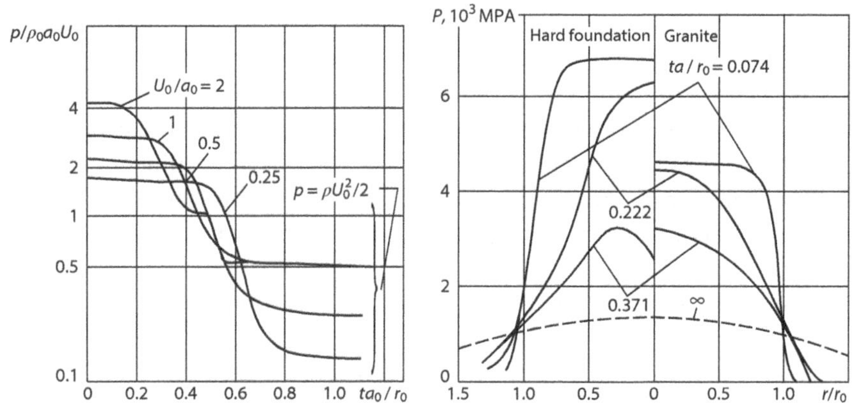

Figure 5.37 Time variations of the pressure in the center of jet during impact with rigid base (**a**) and pressure distribution on surface of rigid base and surface of solid granite (**b**).

Here $2r_0$ — opening width. So, in this case non-steadiness also ceases to appear in time exponent to r_0/U_0.

In absence of free surfaces, for example, in flat-plate flow with width $2r_0$, flow steadies (in statistical meaning) in $(30 \div 50)2r_0/U_0$ after the start of motion with constant velocity Uo, to become perpendicular to its flat surface [221].

5.5 Pressure Model of Open Flow

Limitations in selection of geometrical scales for open flows in hard channel first of all are caused by limitations in distortion of geometrical scales and necessity to simultaneously abide to conditions $Re_м \geq Re_{lim}$ and $Fr_м \leq Fr_{lim}$. If we could neglect the latter condition, disregarding Froude number from defining criterions system, then geometrical scales could be decreased. Such possibility is presented when free surface can be assigned independently from Fr number. Representing free surface by rigid wall, and by this substituting open flow by pressure flow, we can disregard Fr number from defining criterions system, and select velocity scale in such a way, as to satisfy condition $Re_м \geq Re_{\lim}$

The first attempt to apply pressure flow for research of open channel flow is dated at 1941, then under V.M. Makkaveev`s supervision, Y.V. Klimenchich studied schemes for rectifying installations on pressure model. In 1950 A.G. Averkiev also came to an idea about studying of open flows on pressure model.

In the early 50s many hydraulic laboratories of the Soviet Union started to use air pressure models of open flows: LIIVT (V.M. Makkaveev, N.P. Gilyarov), MEI (S.V. Izbash, I.V. Lebedev, B.T. Emtsev), LPI (I.I. Levi, V.S. Knoroz) (in detail ref. [91]).

The scientific research sector of Hydroproject was one of the first organizations that applied pressure models for solution of specific problems of laboratory design. In parallel with the studying of hydraulic engineering objects, work for justification and expanding of the application area of this method was constantly carried out. Results of this work are summarized in [91].

Pressure models of open flow found application aboard USSR. Data on pressure simulation of open flows was published in Romania, Poland, Bulgaria, Czechoslavakia, and Turkey. In the 70s this method was applied in France, FRG, and Portugal (ref., for example, [181]).

Pressure model of open flow amounts to pressure flow, geometrically similar to free prototype, except for boundary roughness. Disruption of roughness similarity in the part of flow boundaries corresponding with real free surface, leads to distortion of tangent stresses in this part of boundaries. In real conditions tangent stresses on free surface may vary, depending on the force and direction of wind. Specifics of pressure flow in the cases, when wind effect is significant, may provide some engineering advantages in hydraulic simulation of cooling ponds, for example.[2]

For river flows with relatively high velocities, impact of tangent stresses on free surface often can be disregarded. In these cases only with ideal wall, used as solid boundary in pressure flow, can there be achieved similarity of boundary conditions of open flow. As we know, such a wall does not exist in the field conditions, and there are always tangent stresses on model free surface.

In studying of open flows, as a rule, preset mean position of free surface level (corresponding curve for levels and discharges) and free surface form is the subject of research. Usually on pressure model the solid wall, corresponding with free surface in the field, is a plain surface, located on known mean free surface level. In open uneven flow, free surface always differs from plane. The more turbulent is the flow, the greater this difference (the greater is Fr_N).

Additional distortion, introduced by rigid "free surface," is caused by difference of boundary conditions of this surface for pressure and velocity pulsations on the model and in the field. The lesser these distortions are, the lesser is *Fr* number for open flow.

So we can state that distortion of boundary conditions on "free surface" in application of pressure model for open flow is as follows:

1. there are tangent stresses on the model free surface, which often can be disregarded in real conditions;
2. free surface form differs from free surface form in the field.
3. velocity pulsations are absent on the model free surface and excess pressure is not zero.

In such a way, pressure model of open flow is distorted: scale of friction forces on free surface does not equal scale of inertia forces, scale of level difference does not equal depth scale, etc. As always in studying of approximate similarity conditions, in this case it is necessary to distinguish appropriate problems.

---

[2] A. c. 135270 (USSR). "Air pressure model for experimental research of water flow in open water basins." V. M. Lyatkher, A. M. Proudovsky. – Published in B.I., 1961. N 2.

Let`s consider how much pressure model is appropriate for solution of planned hydraulic problem, i.e. for estimation of distribution in the plan of averaged by depth velocities and level differences of open flow free surface. For this purpose we apply equations of planned hydraulic problem (2.128) for steady flow ($\partial U_i/\partial t = 0$).

Equations (2.128) are written for open flow, when $\partial P_S/\partial x_i = 0$ (P_S – pressure on free surface). Analogues equations can be written for pressure flow. For pressure flows, geometrically similar to even open flows, free surface is close to plane, usually:

$$g\frac{\partial \eta_s}{\partial x_i} \ll \frac{1}{\rho}\frac{\partial P_s}{\partial x_i} \tag{5.43}$$

If we disregard the difference of distribution in depth kinematic characteristics in pressure and open flows, then equations of planned problem for open and pressure flow will have identical form, at this the term $g\frac{\partial \eta_s}{\partial x_i}$ in equations for open flow will correspond with term $\frac{1}{\rho}\frac{\partial P}{\partial x_i}$ in equations for pressure flow. From analysis of these equations, it follows that similarity condition for flow plan of open and pressure flows is the following formula:

$$\left(\frac{\sigma_{s\,ij} - \sigma_{B\,ij}}{\rho U^2}\frac{b}{h}\right)_0 = \text{idem} \tag{5.44}$$

At achievement of this condition:

$$(g\Delta\eta_0/U^2_0)_N = (\Delta P_0/\rho U^2_0)_M \tag{5.45}$$

(open flow is being assigned index «N», pressure — «M».)

From the formula of condition (5.44), it follows that friction forces distribution between upper and lower flow boundaries is insignificant. Important is total value of these forces and their distribution in the plan. In this respect the very fact of presence of tangent stresses on "free" surface of pressure model is not an obstacle for achievement of similarity for flow scenario in the plan.

Introducing designation $(\sigma_{Sij}\text{-}\sigma_{Bij})_M = \lambda_\Sigma(\rho U^2/2)$, condition (5.44) can be written as follows:

$$\lambda_\Sigma b/h = \text{idem} \tag{5.46}$$

Here coefficient λ_Σ reflects cumulative effect of stresses on the bottom and on surface. It depends on relative roughness of surfaces and *Re* number. For channel flows in real conditions almost always is characteristic self-similarity of λ_Σ in *Re*. At the first glance, condition $Re_м \geq Re_{гр}$ can be always achieved on the pressure model by means of assignment of higher velocities. But for convenience of observations, the free surface of the model is made of glass (smooth wall), and the possibility for achievement of self-similarity in Re is not obvious.

Cited similarity conditions between open and pressure flows are obtained in assumption of insignificant impact of difference in distribution of kinematic characteristics by depth of such flows. This difference, first of all, can be related to mismatch in form and intensity of cross current in the open and pressure flows being compared.

In connection to the fact that in application of pressure model there should be assigned a form of free surface, condition (5.46) should be supplemented by conditions containing values that characterize this form. Such conditions can be obtained from continuity equations for the planned problem:

$$\frac{\partial \eta_s}{\partial x_i}\frac{l}{h} = \text{idem}, \ i = 1,3 \tag{5.47}$$

At representation of free surface by plane $\partial\eta_S/\partial x_i = 0$, the flow plan may be distorted.

Therefore, for validation of possibility for determination of the flow plan on the pressure model it is necessary:

1. to determine correspondence degree for plan distribution of friction forces on pressure model and in real conditions;
2. to find conditions, at which representation of free surface real form by plane does not lead to significant distortion of flow plan characteristics;
3. to evaluate how difference in cross current on the pressure model and in open flow impacts solution accuracy for the planned problem.

For the solution of the first raised question, authors studied dependence of hydraulic friction coefficient from *Re* number and relative surface roughness at even flow between two plain surfaces with different roughness (ref. Section 4.1). As a result of constructions that are using the dependences (4.74) — (4.78), the dependences between thicknesses of flow areas in which this flow is divided by a plane passing through maximum velocity profiles, by average velocities in these areas and hydraulic friction coefficient, calculated by full channel depth and average velocity in it, were obtained:

$$\lambda = hI_{fr}/(\rho \bar{U}^2/2),$$

presented in Figure 4.15 for various surface roughness values and the Reynolds numbers.

From results of these computations, it follows that at analogue values $\lambda_{Re=\infty}$ impact of viscosity is noted at larger Re values and larger difference in model roughness. At surface roughness, characteristic for pressure models with rigid bottom (plasticine and glass), correspondence of effective heights of roughness peaks is about 20. In this case, at common pressure flow depth, about 20 mm boundaries of self-similarity domain, corresponding with required deviation:

$$\tilde{\Delta} \lambda_{\text{lim}} = \lambda_{\text{Re}_{\text{lim}}} / \lambda_{\text{Re}=\infty} - 1,$$

shift to bigger *Re* values for approximately one order. But due to the possibility to depart from Froude rule on pressure models, we can reach *Re* values, exceeding the same on respective free-flow models, at least on two-three orders. On the other hand, impact of large-scale disturbances, leading to significant decrease of Re_{lim} values, manifests in pressure models in the same way, as in free-flow (Section 5.2). In such a way, actual achievement of necessary Reynolds number value on pressure flow is quite simple.

Let`s consider the issue of impact, caused by flow turbulence in real conditions in accuracy of results on the pressure model.

If free surface in the model is represented by plane ($\Delta\eta_S/h = 0$), then we can assume that pressure flow in the model is characterized by number Fr = 0. For estimation of error in the data obtained on the pressure model, we can compare characteristics of flows, for which all similarity conditions are satisfied, excluding Fr = idem (for one flow $Fr = Fr_N$, and for another flow $Fr = 0$).

In some cases error estimation can be made on the basis of the information about flow characteristics correspondence with number $Fr[X = X(Fr)]$, which was presented in Section 5.1.

Other factors being equal, the object is more suitable for study on pressure model with plain "free surface," if it is characterized by lower values of Froude number.

In the first place, such objects are settling basins and cooling water ponds ($Fr<1\cdot10^{-3}$), and also not silted water basins ($Fr<1\cdot10^{-2}$). Free areas of lowland rivers are practically always suitable for study on pressure models ($Fr<5\cdot10^{-2}$). At constriction of rivers by artificial constructions (rectifying installations, construction bridges), flow turbulence in the constriction area can significantly increase. But in navigable rivers there are usually forbidden velocities, exceeding 3 m/s, which corresponds with Fr = = 0.1 ÷ 0.3. In studying of construction bridges for hydraulic systems, the most important characteristics, subject to determination, are flow compression degree and dimensions of appearing eddy current zones. In Figure 5.38 with the help of a diagram, analogues on the Figure 5.6 show how a correspondence is created between flow constriction degree θ and Fr on the way to constriction, correlating with relative deviation of flow compression degree Δε from this variable at Fr = 0: $\Delta\varepsilon = \varepsilon_{Fr}/\varepsilon_{Fr=0} - 1 = 0.05$. Here we are also presented data for bridges on some hydraulic systems on lowland rivers in USSR. From this diagram it follows that representation of free surface by plane in solution of such problems is not an obstacle for prediction with sufficient accuracy.

It is a little more difficult to study flow plan in tail ponds of hydraulic systems. Immediately after, lower spillways flow may be characterized by

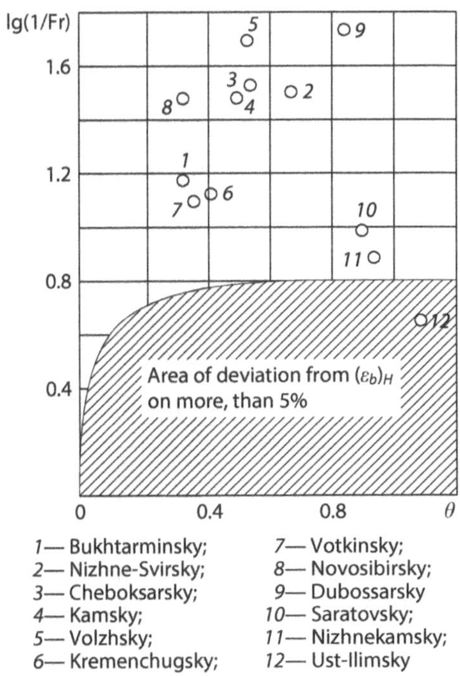

Figure 5.38 Impact boundaries of flow turbulence on planned constriction. Estimation of possibility for study on pressure model with flat free surface of the following construction bridges of hydraulic systems.

larger Froude numbers (close to one and even larger). But spillways installations on the rivers with alluvial channel are usually designed in such a way so by the anchor end the flow becomes calm. If conditions in the gate of anchor end are known, this gate can be accepted as upper boundary for pressure model. For estimation of flow turbulence impact in boundary gate on the flow plan in a tail pond in real conditions for lowland hydraulic systems, the Figure 5.39 shows marked deviation area in 5% of eddy current length at sudden expansion from its value at Fr = 0 and information on some hydraulic systems of Soviet Union. Analysis of this data shows that error in estimation of eddy current length reaches 8% only in isolated cases.

At great immersion of jets of water, discharged through hydraulic system, when free surface is close to plane, the upper boundary of a pressure model may be accepted directly on the exit from installation. In this case, it is necessary to achieve discharge distribution similarity in boundary section. At the first approximation, objects suitable for study on pressure models can be determined on the basis of estimation of flooding impact on free surface level difference far from installations and in the exit [139].

1— Saratovsky;
2— Nizhnekamsky;
3— Votkinsky;
4— Volzhskaya;
5 — *Kievskaya;*
6 — *Kakhoshskaya;*
7 — *Cheboksarskaya.*

Figure 5.39 Impact boundaries of flow turbulence on eddy current length at sudden expansion (in the area, limited by surface and coordinate planes, deviation from $l_{F_2} = 0$ is larger 5%). Estimation of suitability of pressure flow with flat free surface for studying of tail pond of the following HPP:

We can evaluate errors in determining flow plan on the pressure model if they are related to distortion of the cross current, due to the effect of the rigid wall on free surface, and on the basis of the analysis carried out in Section 5.3. It is obvious that in this estimation we can disregard the difference in friction coefficients related to all flow depth, as it is done in determination of similarity conditions for a planned problem, or related to part of the model`s depth – from bottom to maximal longitudinal velocities, as it should be done in estimation of cross current impact on the pressure model. The main source of errors is decreasing of relative "effective" model depth. Relative values of maximal deviation in distribution of mean velocities

$$\tilde{\Delta}\bar{U} = \bar{U}_M / \bar{U}_N - 1,$$

related to introduction of such distortion, were calculated with appliance of the formula (5.14) for the most unfavorable event, when the relative depth on pressure model is twice less than in respective open flow.

Calculation results, presented on the Figure 5.40, allow evaluation of the error in determination of flow plan, caused by distortion of cross current in dependence from relative flow width and hydraulic friction coefficient. Given the fact that with decreasing in turn curve, current intensity is decreasing, it can be concluded that in channel range of conditions ($r_1/b>1 \div 3$ and $b/h>30 \div 40$), this error is insignificant. Compared on the Figure 5.21, measurement results for velocities and pressures (depths) distribution in respective pressure and open flows verify these conclusions.

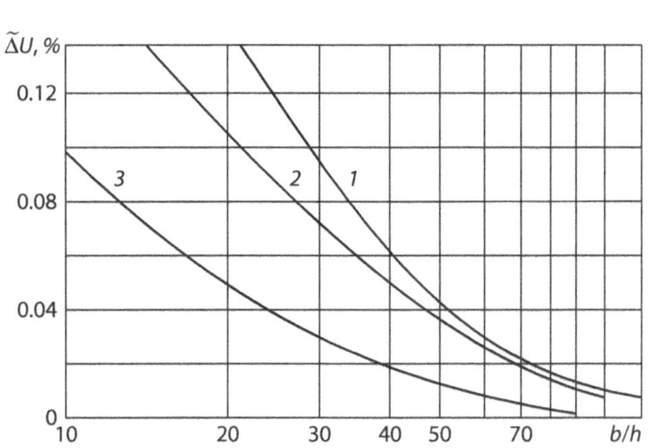

Figure 5.40 Maximal relative deviation ΔU of averaged by depth velocities from symptomless distribution, not taking into effect cross current impact:
1 - $\lambda = 0.01$; $r_1/b = 0.5$; 2 - $\lambda = 0.001$; $r_1/b = 0.5$;
3 - $\lambda = 0.01$; $r_1/b = 1.0$.

So all questions, related to suitability of pressure model for determination of flow plan, can be answered in a positive way: specifics of the pressure model do not lead to significant errors in estimation of flow characteristics.

Geometrical scales of pressure models for free-flow in hard boundaries in the most cases are defined by conditions:

$$\lambda_\Sigma b/h = \text{idem and } \mathrm{Re}_{\text{M}} \geq \mathrm{Re}_{\text{lim}}$$

The second of these conditions can limit selection of model geometrical scales at required characteristics of laboratory pumps (or fans). If achievement of sufficiently high value of air or water discharge (for water pressure models) is not limited by available laboratory equipment, then the only condition, which should provide selection of geometrical scales, is the first condition with account to limitation for distortion of geometrical scales: $M_b/M_h \geq (M_b/M_h)_{\text{lim}}$.

Let`s notice that for achievement of possibility for comparison of pressure model and free-flow prototype, hydraulic friction coefficient for pressure model is calculated by full depth. Representing Chezy coefficient $C = \sqrt{2g/\lambda_\Sigma}$ by Manning, condition $\lambda_\Sigma b/h$ = idem in this case can be rewritten in the following way:

$$M^{1/3}{}_h/M^2{}_n = M_l/M_h$$

Roughness coefficient n in this formula takes into account not only bottom characteristics, but pressure model`s cover too. If the model`s relief is formed from plasticine on metal crossparts, and the cover is made of glass, then $n_M \approx 0.013$. At common for alluvial channels $n_N = 0.021$, the scale is $M_n = 1{:}1.6$. Then at maximum permissible distortion of geometrical scales, equal to 1:3, minimal vertical geometrical scale of pressure plasticine model is $(M_h)_{\min} = M^6{}_n(M_l/M_h)^3{}_{\text{LIM}} = 1/475$, and planned geometrical scale is $(M_l)_{\min} = (M_h)_{\min} \times 1/3 = 1/1430$. For studying of flow plan in the areas of large and medium rivers, adjacent to hydraulic engineering installations, usually there are used pressure models with hard channel and planned geometrical scale 1:1000-1:1500 at two-three times distortion of vertical scale in relation to planned. In such a way, minimal geometrical scales of pressure models are less of an order than respective free-flow models, which allow to fit them on small laboratory sites.

Transfer to pressure flow on the model leads to one more advantage: instead of liquid in drops, atmospheric shroud can be used on it, which allows mostly a simplified model construction, laboratory equipment and experiment conditions, and also the ability to apply measurement equipment, developed in aerodynamic laboratories. Air properties significantly differ from water properties. It is important to note the large difference in compressibility of these mediums. But in real conditions with application of pressure models at velocities up to 50 – 60 m/s, the difference in water and air compressibility does not lead to noticeable errors. Zhukovsky`s prediction on "convenience of study with air will allow to penetrate innermost laws of jet distribution and tightly bond two sciences - hydrodynamics and hydraulics," was proved true by experience of application of pressure models for open flows.

Below are study results of flow plan. Studies were carried out on pressure models in SRC Hydroproject.

On the Figure 5.41 is shown distribution of mean in depth velocities on pressure (M_i = 1:1000, M_h = 1:500) and free-flow (M_l— M_h = 1:85) models of tail pond of Tsimlyanskaya HPP on river Don.

Comparison of results of determination of water level difference in approach channel on Aswan HPP in Figure 5.42 on open (M_l = 1:120) and pressure (M_l = 1:500) models agrees with possibility for quite accurate prediction of difference in free surface levels according to pressure measurements on pressure model at lower values of Fr_N.

Application of hard wall on free surface of the pressure model practically excludes from the range of study objects unsteady flows and flows that are characterized by high Froude numbers. But is it possible to use main advantage of pressure models – departure from Froude rule – in the more general case? The positive answer for this question lies in application of the method of gravity elastic analogue [125].

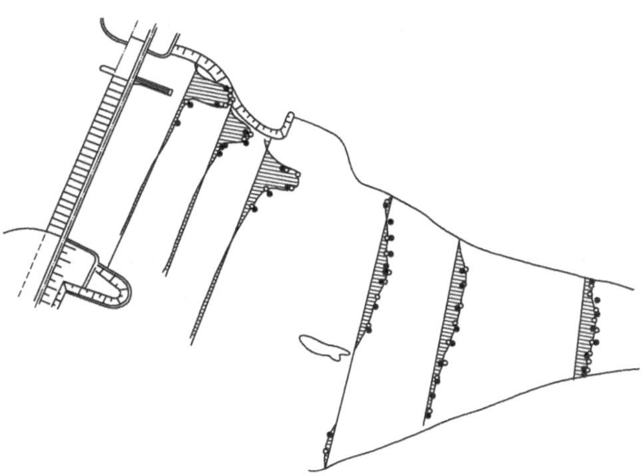

Figure 5.41 Conditions in the tail pond of Tsimlyanskaya HPP
○ — field; ● — field

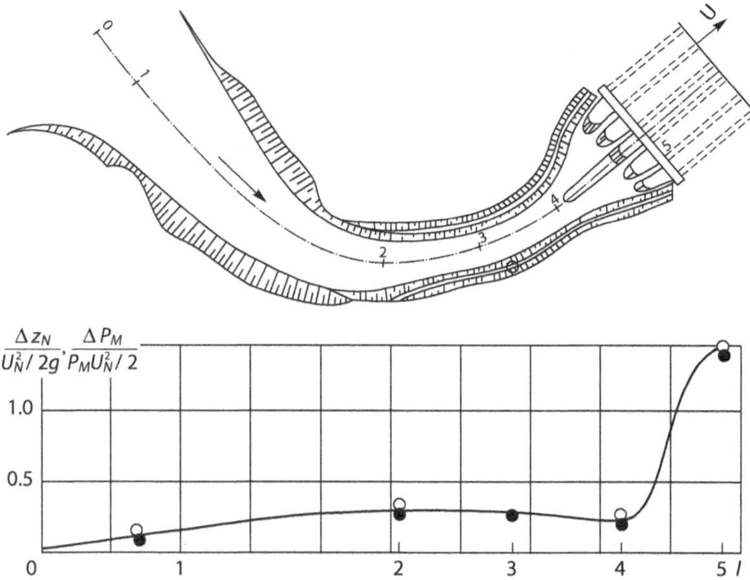

Figure 5.42 Decrease of piezometer level (free surface level) in the approach channel of Aswan HPP in relation to level in water basin, in fractions of velocity head in tunnels: ○ — hydraulic model; ● — pressure air model

For explanation of method essence let`s address equation of continuously varied motion (2.124), which in absence of intermediate inflow and $dP_S/dx \neq 0$ may be written as follows:

$$\frac{\partial \overline{U}}{\partial t} + \frac{\partial}{\partial x}\left(g\eta_s + \frac{P_S}{\rho} + \frac{a\overline{U}^2}{2} \right) + \frac{\lambda_R}{R}\frac{\overline{U}^2}{2} = 0.$$

(For simplicity, the equation is written for a one-dimensional problem, because application of planned schematization, while complicating formulas, does not lead to other results). If on free surface of open flow $\partial\left(P_S/\rho g\right)/\partial x = 0$, then for free flow this equation should be written as follows:

$$\frac{\partial \overline{U}_N}{\partial t_N} + \frac{g\partial \eta_{SN}}{\partial x_N} + \frac{\partial}{\partial x_N}\left(\frac{a\overline{U}_N^2}{2} \right) + \frac{\lambda_{RN}}{R_N}\frac{\overline{U}_N^2}{2} = 0 \qquad (5.48)$$

Here open flow is assigned index "N". For pressure flow, accepted as model, at $\frac{\partial(P_\eta/\rho g)}{\partial x} \gg \frac{\partial \eta_N}{\partial x}$

$$\frac{\partial \bar{U}_M}{\partial t_M} + \frac{\partial}{\partial x_M}\left(\frac{P_{S.M}}{\rho_M}\right) + \frac{\partial}{\partial x_M}\left(\frac{a\bar{U}^2{}_M}{2}\right) + \frac{\lambda_{RM}}{R_M}\frac{\bar{U}^2{}_M}{2} = 0 \quad (5.49)$$

Equations (5.48) and (5.49) look identical except that the term $\frac{g\partial \eta_{S.N}}{\partial x_N}$ in one of them, corresponds with the term $\frac{\partial P_{S.M}/\rho_M}{\partial x_M}$ in the other.

To these equations should be added continuity equations, which, taking into account that $h = \eta_S - \eta_B$ may be written as:

$$\frac{\partial \eta_{S.N}}{\partial t_S} + \bar{U}_N \frac{h_N}{b_N}\frac{\partial b_N}{\partial x_N} + \bar{U}_N \frac{\partial \eta_{S.Ni}}{\partial x_N} + \bar{U}_N \frac{\partial \eta_{B.N}}{\partial x_N} + h_N \frac{\partial \bar{U}_N}{\partial x_N} = 0; \qquad (5.50)$$

$$\frac{\partial \eta_{S.M}}{\partial t_S} + \bar{U}_M \frac{h_M}{b_M}\frac{\partial b_M}{\partial x_M} + \bar{U}_M \frac{\partial \eta_{S.M}}{\partial x_M} + \bar{U}_N \frac{\partial \eta_{B.M}}{\partial x_M} + h_M \frac{\partial \bar{U}_M}{\partial x_M} = 0. \qquad (5.51)$$

If free surface of pressure flow is represented by hard wall, then $\partial\eta_{s,m}/\partial t = 0$, and if the hard wall is flat, then $\partial\eta_{s,m}/\partial x = 0$, i.e. in this case equations (5.50) and (5.51) do not have an equal form, which excludes unsteady flows from the range of objects suitable for study on pressure models or puts limitations on selection of objects among steady flows.

Let`s assume that free surface of open flow is represented on the pressure model by elastic layer surface, with such properties, that movement of this surface in every point is proportional to pressure variations (Winkler`s model):

$$\Delta\eta_S = K\Delta P_S \qquad (5.52)$$

where K — Winkler coefficient.

When on the model, the flow will possess free surface, location and form, which all correspond with flow characteristics. Equation (5.51) may be written as

$$\frac{\partial(KP_{S.M})}{\partial t_M} + \bar{U}_M \frac{h_S}{b_M}\frac{\partial b_M}{\partial x_M} + \bar{U}_N \frac{\partial(KP_{Sl.M})}{\partial x_M} + \bar{U}_M \frac{\partial \eta_{S.N}}{\partial x_M} + h_M \frac{\partial \bar{U}_M}{\partial x_M} = 0. \qquad (5.53)$$

Motion equation for pressure flow can be rewritten as:

$$\frac{\partial \bar{U}_M}{\partial t_M} + \frac{1}{K_{\rho M}} \frac{\partial (KP_{S.M})}{\partial t_M} \left(\frac{a\bar{U}_M^2}{2} \right) + \frac{\lambda_{RM}}{R_M} \frac{\bar{U}_M^2}{2} = 0. \tag{5.54}$$

Equations (5.53) and (5.54) have the same form as equations of free flow: accordingly (5.50) and (5.48), at this derivative $d\eta_{S.N\text{н}}/dx_N$ corresponds with derivative $d(KP_{S.M})/dx_M$, and coefficient g— with coefficient $1/K_{\rho M}$.

Formal analogue for motion equations (5.48) and (5.54), continuity equations (5.50) and (5.54) for open and pressure flows with free surface, possessing required properties, points to the possibility of existence of analogue between these two flows. Because terms related to gravity forces in equations for one phenomenon correspond with terms related to elastic forces in equations for another, such analogue is named gravity-elastic.

From normalized equations (5.48) and (5.54), it follows that analogue is true at achievement of conditions:

$$\Delta P_{s.m}/(\rho_M \bar{U}^2_M) = g\Delta\eta_{S.N}/\bar{U}^2_N \tag{5.55}$$

$$\text{Sh} = \text{idem} \tag{5.56}$$

$$\lambda_R l/h = \text{idem} \tag{5.57}$$

to which should be added condition

$$\Delta P_{S.M}/h_M = \Delta\eta_{S.N}/(Kh_N) \tag{5.58}$$

following from consideration of normalized equations (5.50) and (5.54). Let`s pay attention to the fact that equation (5.55) in this case has meaning of analogue condition and not similarity consequence, as in the case of hard wall on free surface of the pressure model, because in considered situation value $\Delta P_{S.m}$ should be assigned in single-valued conditions.

On the basis of (5.58)

$$\frac{\Delta P_{S.M}}{\Delta \eta_{S.N}} = \frac{1}{k} \frac{h_M}{h_N}$$

and from (5.55), it follows that

$$\Delta P_{S.M}/\Delta\eta_{S.N} = \rho_M g(\bar{U}_M/\bar{U}_N)^2$$

i.e. for achievement of analogue it is necessary

$$K\rho_M U^2_M/h_M = U^2_N/(gh_N)$$

or

$$\mathrm{Fr}_{\mathrm{M}} = \frac{1}{K\rho_{\mathrm{M}}g}\mathrm{Fr}_{N} \tag{5.59}$$

If there is not limit *K*, then on the pressure model with elastic surface, higher values of Fr_{M} (higher velocity values) can be achieved, which helps to achieve other similarity conditions (for example, $Re_{\mathrm{M}} \geq Re_{\mathrm{lim}}$, or $\bar{U}/U_{cr}$ = idem (ref. Section 7.4).

For practical application of the proposed method, first of all it is necessary to determine conditions for meeting the requirements (5.59) at uneven dipping of elastic layer and its real dimensional deformations. This issue was solved [125] by the way of finding relative deviation of movement of elastic layer surface, which was obtained from the solution of spatial problem in elasticity theory for this movement, corresponding with condition (5.58). At this was found correlation between coefficient *K*, elasticity constants and characteristic of uneven pressure distribution:

$$K = \frac{\left(\mu^2{}_0 - \mu_0 - 2\right)\delta}{2\mu_0^2 E(1-\varepsilon)}$$

where δ — layer thickness; E — elasticity module; μ_0 — Poisson number ($\mu_0 = 1/m$, where m — Poisson coefficient); ε - variable, depending on function smoothness $P_u = P(x_1, x_2)$, with increase of smoothness of this function ε value decreases for twice differentiable functions $\varepsilon \leq 0.055$. Research has shown that at smoothness of function $P_n = P(x_1,x_2)$, corresponding with usually smooth flows, coefficient ***K*** may be considered practically constant (with variations not more than 1%) in application for elastic layer of materials, for which $\mu_0 > 10$, $\delta/E < 1$, mPa. Good correlation with requirements gives application of elastic layer made of non-molded latex foam, commonly produced. For such foam, $E = 1.35 \div 1.4{,}10^4$ Pa, $\mu_0 = 11.5 \div 12$. At layer thickness 3 cm, $Kpg = 0.022 \div 0.026$.

In studying of non-steady free flows on the pressure model with elastic free surface this layer stays in the conditions of dynamic dipping, which can lead to difference in correlation between pressure variations and layer deformation with (5.58). But tests with the foam layer at different dipping rate showed that in conditions characteristic for real experiments, at deformation rates 0—28 cm/s, dependence (5.58) stays true.

At application of gravity-elastic analogue test installation amounts to hard leak-tight metal tub, in which is formed (usually from cement mixture) channel of studied flow up to levels, corresponding with maximal water levels. The installation is covered by a flat cover and on the inner surface is fixed an elastic layer. Particular attention should be paid to prevention of cover deformation, so it can be fixed through jacks in the frames, fitted to the tub. If elastic layer material has open pores, it should be isolated from flow by a thin rubber layer. Coefficient λ_R in condition (5.57) can be estimated according to data, presented in Section 5.4 with account to the fact that in application of latex foam, isolated by a thin rubber layer, the height of effective roughness peak on elastic layer surface is, according to experimental results, 0.22 mm.

Possibility for application of gravity-elastic analogue for determination of open steady flows characteristics in a wide range of Froude numbers, and also non-steady open flows is verified by research results for open flows, of which characteristics are known from other sources.

In the Figure 5.43, there are presented research results for dependence of relative eddy current length from Fr at sudden flow symmetrical expansion (expansion rate θ = 1.67). Characteristic bend of a curve gives evidence of hydraulic jump, appearing on pressure installation. Comparison of experiment results with test data for open flows gives good coincidence.

Studies of flat hydraulic jump showed that on installation with elastic free surface at specific Froude numbers and depth relations, hydraulic jump appears with different forms: with or without roll, repelled and overriding (Figure 5.44). Parameters, corresponding with change in the jump form, possess good correlation with known recommendations for open flow.

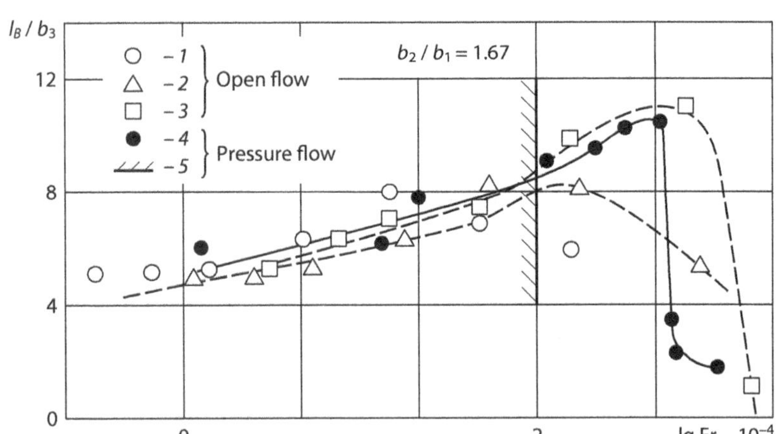

Figure 5.43 Dependence of eddy current length from number Fr_1:
1-h_2/b_2 = 0.42; 2 - h_2/b_2 = 0.25; 3- h_2/b_2 = 0.167;
4 - h_2/b_2 = 0.07; 5 – boundaries for applicability of pressure models with flat free surface.

Non-steady discontinuous wave in pressure flow was created by discharge variation in initial gate by some hydrograph. Its parameters were recorded in several sections by flow length. Experimental results were compared with the parameters of related free flow calculated on ECM under the program that was verified in detail data practically overlaps with calculation results.

Carried out experiments have shown that proposed method can be applied in study of free two-dimensional flows in a wide range of conditions. Application of this method in study of non-steady flows is possible in the cases, when the object of study is general scenario of flow transformation, without emphasis on particularities on the wave front.

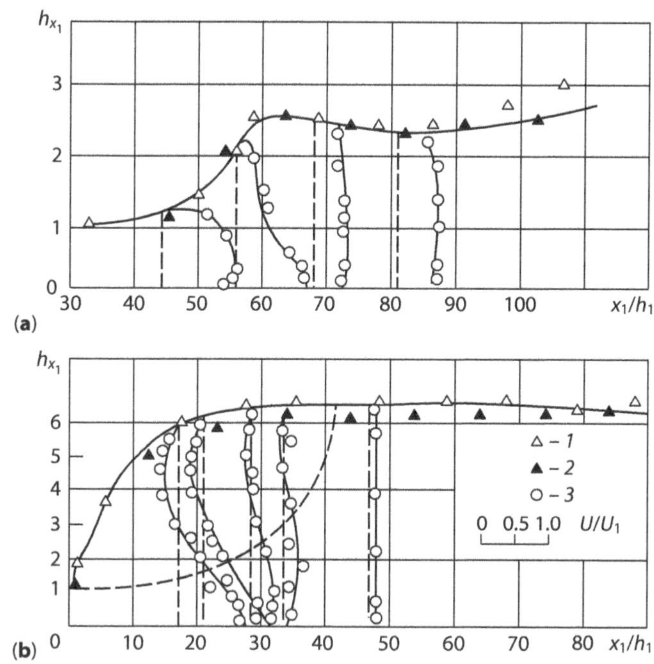

Figure 5.44 Characteristics of hydraulic jump on pressure elastic model:
a — not submerged, without surface roll,
$Fr_1 = 9.4$; $h_1/h_{cr} = 0.82$;
b — submerged, with surface roll, $Fr_1 = 9.6$, $h_1/h_{cr} = 0.47$;
1 — free surface of open flow;
2 — free surface, determined on pressure model;
3 — U/U_1

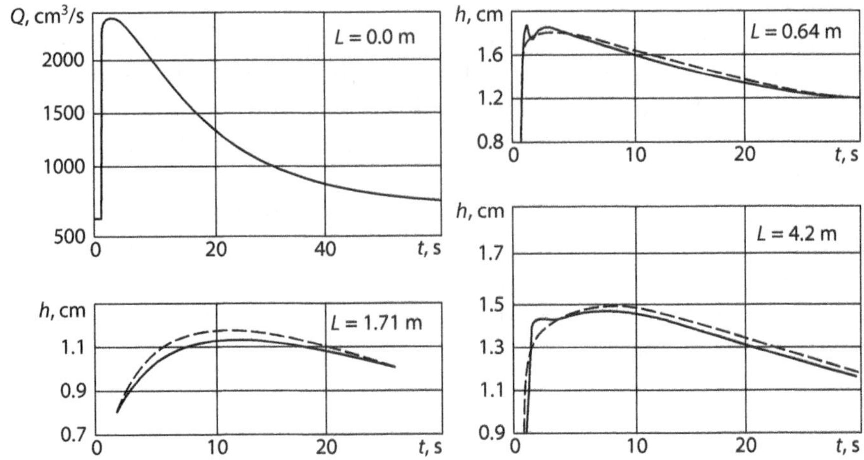

Figure 5.45 Transformation of discontinuous wave on pressure elastic model in various distances from initial gate:
———————model; - - - - - - - - - calculations of free flow.

6

Multi-Component Flows

6.1 General View

Multi-component flows are very diverse - snowstorm, blood in vessels, fuel mixtures in missiles, cement and concrete mixtures, river flows in deformable beds, steam-water mixtures in power plants, debris flows on the slopes - this list of multi-component flows is far from being complete.

Oftentimes you can separate out the flow components, which are very much different in properties: gas, fluid, solid.

Each of these components can be in two qualitatively different forms: carrier environment or carried environment (dispersed phase).

Carrier environment can be absolutely continuous (or just continuous). At any point in this environment a sphere, consisting of particles of this environment can be placed, and it can be moved to any other part of the area, occupied by the environment. On the contrary, carried environment does not have this characteristic. For example, soil particles in a riverbed are completely surrounded by water. It is impossible to get from one of soil particles to the other, bypassing water. Such an environment with small sizes of particles, we propose to be called a continuously dispersed (or uniformly bursting), conditionally solid environment [47].

For the dispersed phase it is not necessary to introduce the conditional hypothesis of continuity. For some tasks, such as introduction of the similarity criterion, it is efficient to keep discrete consideration.

Some area limited with hard surfaces that are occupied with fluid is transferring N solid particles. Motion of each particle is described by six equations: three scalar equations of conservation of a particle motion:

$$m\frac{d^2x_{0i}}{dt^2} = mg_i + \int_{\Omega'}\int \sigma_{ij}n_j d\Omega \tag{6.1}$$

and three equations of angular momentum conservation. In (6.1): m - mass of a particle; x_{0i} - coordinates of its center of gravity; g_i - component of the acceleration of volumetric forces; σ_{ij} - stress in contact of fluid and a particle; n_j – components of normal to the surface of particle Ω'.

If you consider the form of particles to be close to spherical, then there is correlation between its mass and wetted surface Ω':

$$m = \frac{\rho_s \Omega^{1.5}}{36\pi}, \tag{6.2}$$

where ρ_s - density of a particle material; $\Omega = \Omega'/K_s$ - sphere surface area, the volume of which is equal to the volume of the particle; K_s - coefficient of the particle form; for regular particles K_s = 1.1-:-1.2, for sharp grained particles it is substantially larger.

In viscous fluid, the tensor $\{\sigma_{ij}\}$ is defined by the relation (2.37). Equations of fluid motion, boundary conditions on the boundaries of the field and on the contacts between particles and fluid, and conditions of interaction of particles with each other and the border area (collisions) should be added to the equations describing a particle motion. Assuming that these conditions do not contain new dimensional constants or functions, motion similarity criteria of geometrically similar particles in geometrically similar volumes shall be the following:

$$N = \text{idem}; \tag{6.3}$$

$$\rho/\rho_s = \text{idem}; \tag{6.4}$$

$$\bar{d}\ /l_0 = \text{idem}; \tag{6.5}$$

$$F(d) = \text{idem}; \tag{6.6}$$

$$\text{Re}_{l0} = l_0 U_0/\nu = \text{idem}; \tag{6.7}$$

$$\mathrm{Fr}_d = U^2{}_0 / \left(g\bar{d} \right) = \text{idem}. \tag{6.8}$$

Here *F(d}* - relative number of particles, diameter of which in a mixture of *N* particles is less than *d* (granulometric distribution curve); d^{-} - average particle diameter.

Records (6.3) – (6.8), obviously, can be represented in other forms. For example, instead of (6.3), invariance of the volume concentration of particles, equal to the ratio of particles volume to mixture volume can be recalled:

$$c \sim N\bar{d}^{3} / l^{3}{}_0. \tag{6.9}$$

When carried environment is gas or fluid, equations of motion get more complex form: for carried phase its own equations are set up (generating their own similarity criteria system) and, in addition, conditions on the contact between environments are set up, complying with requirements of local equilibrium (including surface tension on phases boundaries), kinematic conditions of motions compatibility.

The system of criteria (6.3) – (6.9), due to possible non-uniqueness of currents, may be incomplete in the same sense as the more simple system of motion similarity criteria of a real one-component fluid. The problem of closure of equations for turbulent multi-component flow is approximately in the same position as for the one-component flow.

6.2 Transfer of Solids by Fluids

Taking into account the interaction of particles of the carried phase, their interaction with the border is specific for a multicomponent environment. For solids this interaction in the simplest case can be represented by two types of phenomena - elastic collision, set by the dimensionless coefficient of collision K_y, characterizing the relative loss of energy upon collision, and inelastic collision - dry friction, set by the friction coefficient $f = arctg\, \varphi$.

These two dimensionless parameters, dependent on material properties of particles and vessel walls and the shape of particles, should be included in the analysis. It is possible to provide the more complete description of particle interactions at collision, leading to appearance of a larger number of parameters that are difficult to set up and control in the experiment.

Individual modeling of absorbing particles is exigeant and in many cases it is not necessary. If conditions for similarity of solid particles structure are provided, as well as:

$$K_y = \text{idem} \tag{6.10}$$

$$f = \text{idem} \tag{6.11}$$

or it is already known that concentration of particles is small, and the impact of (6.10), (6.11) is irrelevant, the main problems of modeling are related to similarity of particle motion in a fluid. As is seen in (6.1), motion of solid particles is determined by the inertia forces affecting it from the side of a fluid. These forces can be found, believing known the particle velocity V(x, *t*), and solving the corresponding boundary problem for Navier-Stokes equations. The fundamental problem in formulation of this problem consists in the necessity of taking into account the real nonstationary and spatial pattern of a turbulent flow, streaming around a particle, influence of complex shape of particles.

Let **U** (x, *t*) be the instantaneous velocity field, and *P*(x, *t*) be the pressure field in the "original" flow without particles. Introduction of a solid particle to the flow will cause distortion of the velocity field and pressures, respectively, on ***u****(**x**, t)* and *p(**x**, t)* values. Thus, the flow that carries a particle, is defined by the equations:

$$\boldsymbol{U}_\Sigma = \boldsymbol{U} + \boldsymbol{u};\ P_\Sigma = P + p \tag{6.12}$$

Having written the Navier-Stokes equations for the original *U (x, t)* and perturbed U_Σ *(x, t)* flows, then subtracting these equations term-by-term one from another, we shall get the equations for field perturbations *u* and *p*. In a real riverbed with the suspended solid particles carrying flow, these perturbations, introduced by the particles, are usually small in comparison with values of the original flow. Members of a relatively nonlinear equation, *u* and *p*, can be discarded in resulting equations:

$$\begin{aligned}&\frac{\partial u_a}{\partial t} + U_\beta \frac{\partial u_a}{\partial x_\beta} + u_\beta \frac{\partial U_a}{\partial x_\beta} = -\frac{1}{\rho}\frac{\partial p}{\partial x_a} + \nu\nabla u_a;\\ &\frac{\partial u_a}{\partial x_a} = 0, a, \beta = 1,2,3.\end{aligned} \tag{6.13}$$

System (6.13) is a generalization of the known equations of Oseen. Boundary conditions for (6.13) are set on a particle surface:

$$u_a = V_a - U_a \tag{6.14}$$

and at a big distance from a particle

$$u_a = 0 \tag{6.15}$$

The equation (6.13) is to be solved together with the equation of particle motion (6.1), which can be rewritten, revealing the value of the integral in the right part:

$$m = \frac{dV_a}{dt} = -P_a - T_a + mg_a, \tag{6.16}$$

where m - particle mass, $m = \rho_s \pi d^3/6$; g_a - projection of gravity acceleration; P_a and T_a - projection of integrals over particles surface from normal pressures and tangential stresses, calculated on the basis of solution of equations (6.13).

Some considerations on the structure of forces can be stated not solving system (6.13) in full.

As in fluid shear stresses occur only in the presence of velocity gradients, it can be assumed that T_a is proportional to the difference of the characteristic speed of environment and a particle:

$$T_a = C_\tau \rho \frac{u_a |u|}{2} \frac{\pi d^2}{4} = C'_\tau \rho \frac{u_a v}{d} \frac{\pi d^2}{4} \tag{6.17}$$

Unlike T_a, force P_a, resulting from normal pressure impact, is determined not only by the relative velocity of flow around the particle, but also by the pressure field, that existed in fluid before introduction of a particle:

$$P_a = \int_W \text{grad}_a P dW + \int_\Omega p d\Omega_a \tag{6.18}$$

First integral in the right part (6.18) is calculated by the volume of fluid W, replaced with the particle. This expression is a generalization of the well-known "Archimedes force" for the moving fluid conditions. The second integral, calculated by the surface of the particle, directly takes into account normal pressures, associated with floating around the particle. This component of force by analogy with the known solutions of a body motion in a static fluid can also be represented by the sum of two components:

$$\int_\Omega p d\Omega_a = p_{aH} + p_{ac} \tag{6.19}$$

taking into account influence of unsteady motion (inertia) P_{aH} and actual resistance force P_{ac}:

$$\left.\begin{aligned} p_{aH} &= C_m \rho \frac{\partial u_a}{\partial t} \frac{\pi d^3}{6}; \\ P_{ac} &= C_P \rho \frac{u_a |u|}{2} \frac{\pi d^2}{4} = C'_P \rho \frac{u_a \nu}{d} \frac{\pi d^2}{4} \end{aligned}\right\} \tag{6.20}$$

"Added mass" coefficient C_m very little depends on viscosity. In contrast, coefficients of resistance C_τ and C_p depend on the local Reynolds number $Re_d = |u|d/\nu$. Coefficient C_τ is the most sensitive to influence of viscosity, decreasing rapidly with the increase of Re.

At small Reynolds numbers, factor Re'_d is also significantly dependant on the coefficient C_p. For example, according to the Oseen decision when $Re'_d < 1$:

$$C_P \approx C_\tau = \frac{12}{\mathrm{Re'}_d} \left\langle 1 + \frac{3}{16} \mathrm{Re'}_d \right\rangle \tag{6.21}$$

In these conditions, coefficients C'_τ and C'_p change very little.

Factors C_p and C_τ significantly depend on particles shape. The form of particles influences the nature of particle sedimentation in stagnant water. If the center of gravity and the center of the action of the surface forces of a particle do not match, the fall of particles comes in a helical line. It is not surprising that even at small Reynolds numbers, ($Re'_d < 10$), coefficients of resistance for particles of different form may differ by 2 times [155]. When $Re'_d \approx 10^3$, the difference may be 5–10 times. The total coefficient of resistance $C_\Sigma = C_p + C_\tau$ depends on the non-stationary flow parameters.

In [155] references are given, pointing to inconsistency of the experimental data on the nonstationarity effects. This is partly due to the fact that in experimental works the resistance force, affecting a particle, is typically represented in the form:

$$\mathrm{F}_s = \Psi \Omega_s \rho \frac{|\mathrm{U} - \mathrm{V}|}{2} \langle \mathrm{U} - \mathrm{V} \rangle \tag{6.22}$$

where ***U*** and ***V*** are velocity vectors, respectively, of fluid and particles; Ω_s – cross-section area of the particles.

In this representation, nonstationary effects that are associated directly with acceleration [the first term in the right part of equation (6.19)], and cases of sudden instability and compression of environment, are not taken into account. Their presence causes significant change in ψ, including under the influence of turbulent pulsations of the oncoming flow. When the amplitude of pulsations is bigger than the coefficient of speed, ψ may be 3 times larger than the standard value. Accounting of the real situation of flow reduces dispersion of the experienced constants values, and in some cases (with a simple cross-sectional shape of a particle) allows you to find the main component of the interaction force (parameter C_p) without introduction of experimental data [8,81].

Values of coefficients C_p and C_{τ}, characterizing resistance for stationary motion of a particle in a stationary fluid, can generally be assessed by one parameter – the hydraulic size of particles, which is defined as the speed of uniform particles sedimentation;

$$-V_2 = w = \sqrt{\frac{2}{3} gd\left(\frac{\rho_s}{\rho} - 1\right)\frac{1}{C_\Sigma}} \tag{6.23}$$

where

$$C_\Sigma = 2C'/\mathrm{Re}'_d$$

Formula (6.23) directly obtained from equation (6.13) - (6.19) when:

$$U_a = 0; \frac{\partial u_a}{\partial t} = 0; grad\, P = \frac{\partial P}{\partial x_2} = -\rho g.$$

Dependence (6.23) is often represented in the following form:

$$w = \varphi(Re_d)\sqrt{g\rho^+ d} \tag{6.24}$$

where $\rho^+ = \rho_s/\rho - 1$; $Re_d = d\sqrt{g\rho^+ d}/\nu$. In [133] value $\theta = d^2/(l_s b_s)$ (where *ls* and *bs* - length and width of a particle) is suggested as the characteristics of the particle shape.

Figure 6.1 shows the received data processing [133] dependence $\varphi = w/\sqrt{g\rho^+ d}$ from Re_d and θ, and in Figure 6.2 - dependence ω quartz particles (q~0.7) in water at 15°C from the given diameter d of these particles.

In real turbulent flow structure of P_a and T_a forces may be assumed to be similar to (6.17) ÷ (6.20). Additional difficulties here include the phenomenon of averaging pulsating pressure on the surface of particles, distortion of the high-frequency part of the turbulent flow spectrum, dependence of coefficients C_p and C_T from the pulsations relative velocities structure, and influence of the velocity gradient dU_a/dx_β [149].

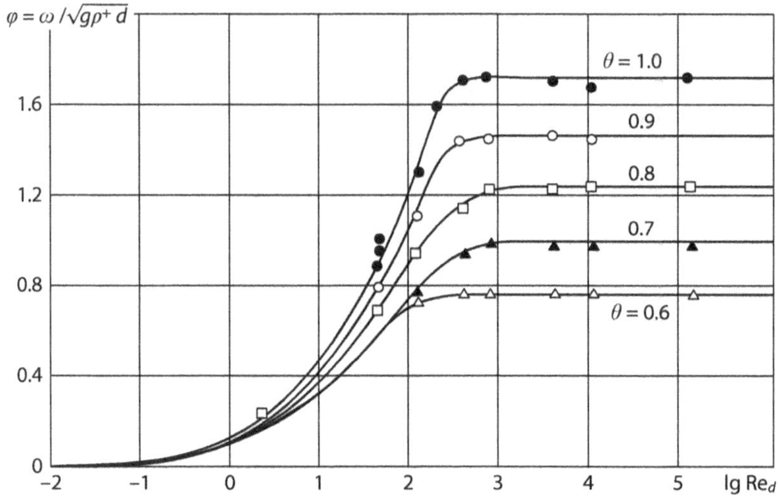

Figure 6.1 Dependance of relative hydraulic size of particles from their form and Re_d.

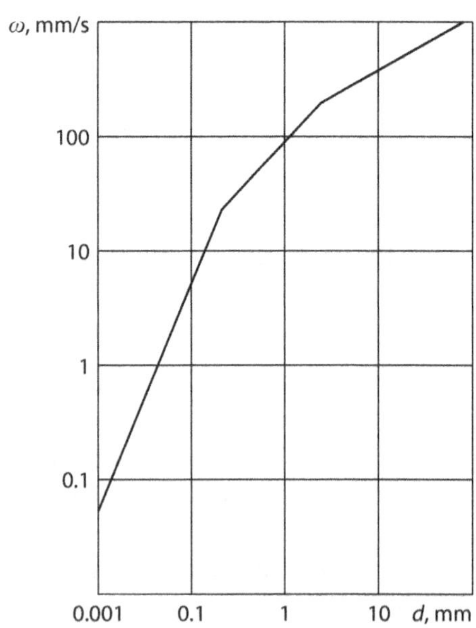

Figure 6.2 Dependence of hydraulic size ω of quartz sand particles from the given diameter *d*.

The influence of these factors is small, and the impact on the particle can be calculated according to the scheme of its nonstationary oscillating motion in infinite fluid with speed $\boldsymbol{u} = \boldsymbol{V} - \boldsymbol{U}$, if the source reaches the following assessment:

$$\frac{Ud}{\nu} \ll 4; \left|\left\langle \frac{\partial U_a}{\partial x\dagger} \right\rangle\right| \frac{d^2}{\nu} \ll 24; \frac{d}{\lambda} \ll 1;$$

$$\text{and also} \qquad (6.25)$$

$$\left|\left(\frac{1}{\rho_s + \frac{1}{2}\rho} - \frac{1}{\frac{3}{2}\rho} \right) \text{grad P}\right| < \frac{\text{U}'}{\lambda_t}$$

Here λ and λ_t - spatial and temporal Tailor scale of turbulence:

$$\lambda = U' \Big/ \left(\frac{\partial U}{\partial x_a} \right)'; \lambda_t = U' \Big/ \left(\frac{\partial U}{\partial t} \right)';$$

Bar (‘) variables means the calculation of standard values.

Assessments (6.25) are seldom implemented in real flows.[1]

If we neglect this fact in the first approximation, the motion similarity conditions for a particle can be written in the following form:

$$\pi_1 = \frac{m\left(1 + \frac{\rho}{\rho_s} C_m\right) U_0 u_0}{C' \rho \frac{u_0 \nu}{d} \frac{\pi d^2}{4} d} = C'_0 \,\text{Re}''_d = C_0 \frac{U_0}{u_0} = \text{idem}; \qquad (6.26)$$

from the correlation of inertia and resistance forces:

$$\pi_2 = \frac{m\left(\frac{1+\rho}{\rho_s} C_m\right) U_0 u_0}{mgd} = C_1 \frac{U_0}{\omega} \frac{u_0}{\omega} = C'_1 \frac{u_0}{\omega} \text{Re}''_d = \text{idem}; \qquad (6.27)$$

---

[1] Assessments (6.25) are obtained from the qualitative analysis of the interaction of particles with turbulent field covered in Lagrangian variables [149].

the ratio of external forces (gravity and pressure gradient):

$$\pi_2 = \frac{\omega|\text{grad P}|}{mg} = \frac{|\text{grad P}|}{\rho_s g} = \frac{\rho U_0^2}{\rho_s gl} = \text{idem}; \tag{6.28}$$

where:

$$\left.\begin{aligned}
&C'_0 = \frac{2}{3}\left(\frac{\rho_s}{\rho} + C_m\right)\frac{1}{C'}; C_0 = \frac{2}{3}\left(\frac{\rho_s}{\rho} + C_m\right)\frac{1}{C};\\
&C_1 = \frac{2}{3}\frac{1}{C}\left(\frac{\rho_s}{\rho} + C_m - 1 - \frac{\rho}{p_s}C_m\right);\\
&C'_1 = \frac{1}{3}\frac{1}{C'}\left(\frac{p_s}{p} + C_m - 1 - \frac{p}{ps}C_m\right);\\
&\text{Re}''_d = u_0 d/v.
\end{aligned}\right\} \tag{6.29}$$

Factors C'_0, C', C'_1 changed little at small Reynolds numbers($\Delta C'/C' < 0{,}1$ when $Re'_d < 10$) the coefficients C'_0, C', C'_1 changed little at high Reynolds numbers ($\Delta C'/C' < 0{,}1$ when $Re'_d > 200 \div 1000$). The function $C(Re'_d)$ is highly dependent on the particle shape. Elongated particle transition from one (viscous) self-similar zones within which $C' = const$ to another (turbulent) self-similar zone ($C = const$) occurs in a relatively narrow range of Reynolds numbers ($20 < Re'd < 80$) than for spherical particles [210].

In relations (6.26) ÷ (6.28) characteristic velocities of the main flow of *Uo* and the relative motion of the particles in the fluid u_0 are used. Particles motions are similar if the scale of these velocities remains the same.

Obviously, all conditions (6.26) – (6.28) are performed, if the diameter of the particles is proportional to the linear scale models, hydraulic size ω - proportionally typical velocity U_0, and the ratio C remains constant. This is possible if the particles are large enough so that models of their size are not less than 1 mm ($Re'_d > 100$). In all other cases it is possible to speak only about close likeness, when one or another criterion impact is relatively small.

Introduction in consideration of the conditions (6.25) and (6.27), related to the structure of turbulence, precludes the ability to accurately reproduce the motion of particles on the model, distinct from nature. Indeed, the reduction of geometric scale hydraulic model requires a reduction in the current velocity and particle sizes. These Tailor scale turbulence wavelengths do not decrease, but increase [84]. In connection with this is the distorted interaction of turbulent field with a particle. For example, smoothing ripple on the surface of the particles in the model is less than in kind.

Impact criteria $\pi 1$ (6.26) can be traced in relation to the characteristic problem of the collision of a particle with an obstacle. This task has a number of works devoted to it, and links to them can be found in [128].

The role of inertia forces in comparison with the forces of resistance is characterized by the coefficient of capture E, defined by the ratio of the number of trapped particles to the number of particles on the approach that falls in the projection streamlined body on the direction of motion. In Figure 6.3 we are shown in the function of the criterion $\pi_1 = \dfrac{4mU_0}{\rho v d^2}$ value of the factor E is calculated excluding the effect of the added masses of particles ($C_{III} = 0$) [128]. The two curves in Figure 6.3 outline the area of possible impact of changes in line currents of fluid from obstacles due to differences of Reynolds number. The point on the graph corresponding to the results of observation of precipitation on the cylinder of air flow shows very small particles (diameter 1.5 and 15 mcm).

According to the data of Figure 6.3, it can be concluded that the criterion π_I has virtually no effect on the motion of the particles in its small and

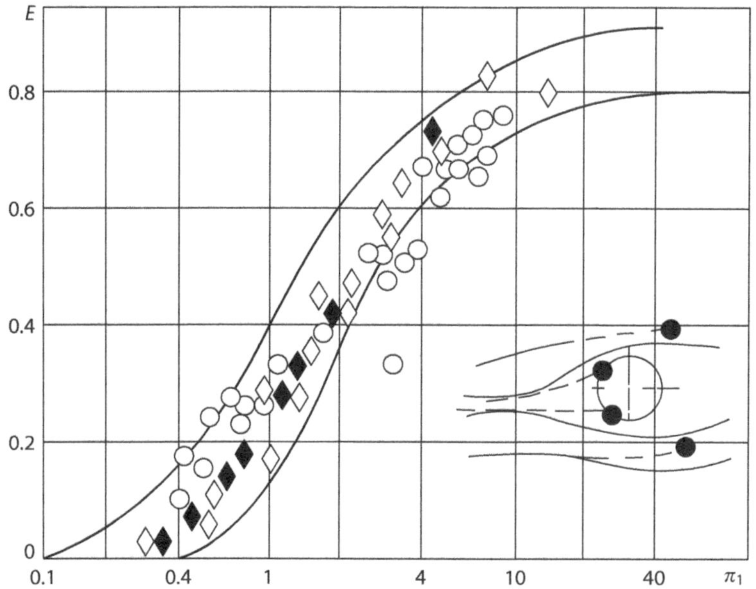

Figure 6.3 Particles capture ratio E by the direct circular cylinder depending on the correlation of forces of inertia and particles resistance.

large values. If $\pi_1 < 0{,}5$, particles repeat lines of a fluid. When values $\pi_1 > 10$, trajectory of the particle will be determined mainly by their collisions with obstacles and with each other.

When the concentration of the particles is large enough for particle collisions to become very likely, it begins to show additional relative sliding of particles and fluid. If the particle diameter d is moving $\mathbf{w}_1$ relatively separate particles of the mix, then, obviously, it will be faced with all particles, the centers of which are located inside the cylinder diameter $2d$ axis collinear speed $\mathbf{w}_{1.}$ In the $\pi(2d)^2L/4$, volume quantity of such particles is smaller than

$$N = \frac{c\frac{\pi}{4}(2d)^2 L}{\frac{4}{3}\pi\left(\frac{d}{2}\right)^3} = \frac{6cL}{d} \tag{6.30}$$

where c - suspended solids volume concentration. Assuming that $N = 2$, we calculate the average path length of a particle in an interval between impulses at minimal mobility of particles

$$L \approx d/3c. \tag{6.31}$$

This estimate is significantly different from the average distance between particles. Indeed, particles located in the nodes of the cubic lattice with L_0 are found from the condition of uniform distribution of these "blocks" in space:

$$c = \frac{8\frac{4}{3}\pi\left(\frac{d}{2}\right)^3}{(2L_0)^3}; L_0 = d\sqrt{\pi/6c} \tag{6.32}$$

The average distance between particles in such a lattice, obviously, is:

$$\bar{L}_0 = \frac{L_0}{26}\left(6+12\sqrt{2}+8\sqrt{3}\right) \approx 1{,}42L_0 \tag{6.33}$$

Pay attention to the fact that the mean free path of particles among relatively slow-moving particles is significantly larger than the distance between the particles. If the particles have a nonzero component of the velocity normal to $\mathbf{w}_{1,}$ then the probability of a collision increases and L is reduced, seeking L_0.

In the adopted assumptions the average motion time t of particle between impulses has the following order:

$$t \approx L/w_1 \approx d/3w_1$$

If this time period is shorter than the characteristic times of a particle free motion (deposition or turbulent transfer with a small change in velocity), then impact of particle collisions is significant. With different particles sizes, collision between them is inevitable even in laminar motion. Collision of particles shows that velocities of hydraulically larger particles decrease, and velocities of hydraulically smaller particles increase. Particles of all sizes reduce velocity when hitting the wall. All these processes have the single-valued effect – they increase energy losses of the carrier fluid. Availability of particles, however, can qualitatively change the flow regime - it causes decrease of intensity of turbulent exchange and due to it, local reduction of energy losses for transport of suspended solids with certain (sufficiently small) concentrations of particles [10].

Individual description of particle collisions requires the introduction of many parameters. For example, the simplest case of symmetric collision of particles requires the introduction of at least two dimensionless coefficients to restore normal $K_n \in (-1,0)$ and tangential $K_\tau \in (-1,0)$ components of the velocity, defined as the attitude of the relevant components of the relative velocity of touching points non-deformable particles [8, 225]. Consideration of the particle collisions phenomena leads to formulation of the similarity requirements of [201], which turns out to be complicated in real conditions. It is almost a requirement of similarity of the processes of particle collisions by some authors to hold constant in nature and on the ratio of the average speeds of solid and fluid phases [211].

For description and simulation of the processes of motion of multiphase media it appears to be more promising now to use the scheme of conventionally solid interlinked and interoperable environments, each of which is specified by its equation of state [47]. Let us consider the equations of two-phase medium encountered particularly often. A more complex three-phase environment is usually needed to lead to the scheme of two-phase flow, neglecting mutual relative motion of one of the vapor phases.

The continuity equations for the two-phase medium, consisting of particles and fluid that fill the space between particles, are in the form of:

$$\frac{\partial c\rho_s}{\partial t} + \text{div } c\rho_s \text{ V} = 0; \tag{6.34}$$

$$\frac{\partial (1-c)\rho}{\partial t} + \text{div}(1-c)\rho U = 0 \tag{6.35}$$

Equations (6.34) and (6.35) do not provide any new significant information for the simulation.

Quantity change equations are more informative:

$$\rho_s c \frac{dV}{dt} = \boldsymbol{F}_{0s} + \mathrm{div}\Pi_s + \boldsymbol{F} \tag{6.36}$$

$$\rho(1-c)\frac{dU}{dt} = \boldsymbol{F}_0 + \mathrm{div}\Pi - \boldsymbol{F} \tag{6.37}$$

Here Π_s, Π - tensors in phase formed by particles and fluids; $\boldsymbol{F}_{0s}$ and $\boldsymbol{F}_0$ - volumetric forces in these phases; $\boldsymbol{F}$ - the power of interphase interaction [47].

The information content of the system (6.36) and (6.37) begins to emerge only in the case if you can uncover the relationship between the tensors Π_s and Π, vector $\boldsymbol{F}$, phase velocity and concentration c.

The most important quality, as a result of using the continuum approach, is to estimate the conditions of appearance and extinction of erosion on the basis of the analysis of immediate-governmental stress state of the environment (see [47], and also part 7).

It is necessary to warn again about the danger of mixing two approaches to the analysis of phenomena. For example, if the continuum approach is used and the critical shear stress τcr is introduced as a characteristic parameter of the task, which corresponds to beginning of soil erosion (or the corresponding critical speed U_{cr}), then parameter of a particle diameter should not be introduced as a linear parameter. It is necessary to form all the criteria from variables related to the same level of a phenomenon schematization. The choice of parameters from different levels of description of phenomena may lead to an unjustified increase in the number of criteria of similarity and the loss of essential criteria. Such mixture of approaches is admitted in the modern book on modeling [216], where the wavelength of rivela on the sandy bottom is measured in fractions of the diameter of the particles, and it is mapped to U/ U_{cr}. On the basis of the continuum concept, it would be more logical to present the results of experiments that have been defined as the length scale ranges, for example,

$$L = \tau_{cr}/g(\rho_s-\rho) \tag{6.38}$$

and as the scale of the flow velocity

$$(U_*)_{cr} = \sqrt{\tau_{cr}/\rho} \tag{6.39}$$

or

$$\left(U_{**}\right)_{cr} = \sqrt{\tau_{cr}/\left(\rho_s - \rho\right)} \tag{6.40}$$

Of course, the continuum approach is optional - an alternative approach as a linear scale, to take the diameter of the particles, and as a zoom rate, for example,

$$U_d = \sqrt{\left(\rho_s/\rho - 1\right)gd} \tag{6.41}$$

The latter approach is used especially widely (see part 7). Combinations of approaches are often found in hydraulic works. For example, the experimenters D. Simon and E. Richardson, trying to find patterns of motion ridges, introduced three parameters U_*/w, U_*d/v and particle diameter in dimensional units [53]. The mixture of approaches and unsatisfactoriness of the size criterion here is obvious.

6.3 Gas Involvement from the Free Surface

If you have an external interface, between fluid flow and gas there are often implemented conditions under which gas takes the form of individual inclusions involved inside the fluid, essentially changing the characteristics of its flow. These phenomena include self-aeration of open thread in gravity spillways and mountain rivers, the capture of gas in the crater formed at the water wells, aeration free jets and so on. The consequences of the involvement of gas can be either positive (decrease in the intensity of impact flows at their borders, improving water quality in natural watercourses, and provision of reactions in processing units) or negative (increase in the size of the flows, lower throughput of spillways, instability of mechanical equipment, and deterioration of heat transfer in the core of a nuclear reactor).

In all cases, the involvement of local mass of the gas is connected with local deformation of the free surface of a fluid flow and non-stationarity of these deformations. Therefore, the process of capturing gas is determined by such properties of a fluid flow and its free surface, such as Burnet, turbulence and surface tension. Although some mechanisms of involvement of gas have a mathematical description, real basis for establishment of a system of similarity of this phenomenon, in most cases, are the results of systematic experiments, which, unfortunately, are often contradictory. As the characteristics of the engagement process, typically a certain value (velocity, Frude number, embedding outlet well level), corresponding to the beginning of the engagement, is used.

Beginning aeration open quasi-uniform flows are typically associated with achieving a sufficiently large (critical) values number and Froude-given roughness bottom of the stream. It is assumed that when the self-similarity criterion hydraulic resistance has self-similarity, there is aeration of the stream.

The general approach to description of the aeration phenomenon, which allows us to draw some conclusions regarding aeration modeling, can be constructed on the basis of analysis of the flow turbulence characteristics, near the free surface [84]. According to a certain plan, Halbrane (1952) aeration flow occurs at the moment of closing the surface of the water after a certain amount of fluid has a large velocity that is normal to the averaged surface water away from the stream, leaving a cavity. In order to assess the frequency of the recurrence of such events and trapped air, you need to know how often the normal component of velocity of the particles under the surface of the water exceeds a certain limit, and depending on the shape and position of the free surface, how long these differences are and what volume of water at the time of departure you can make moving as a unit. Typing Taylor scales of turbulence, evaluating the above values, it is possible to get a fairly common condition of occurrence of aeration [84] that for the scheme uniform flow, on the flow may be specified in the following form:

$$\frac{u'_2}{\sqrt{gh}} \rangle \sqrt[4]{\frac{\nu}{U_* h}} \left\{ C_1 \frac{\sigma}{\rho g h^2} \frac{U_* h}{\nu} + C_2 \cos\theta \right\}^{1/2} \tag{6.42}$$

Here u'_2 - RMS value of a pulse rate normal to the surface of the water ($u'_2 \approx 0{,}5U_*$); C_1 and C_2 are constants; θ is the angle of inclination of the surface water to the horizon. Prescribed ratio is remarkable that the number Weber $We_h = \rho g h^2/\sigma$ is included in the relation with the local Reynolds number $Re_* = U_* h/\nu$. It is clear that in conditions when the number Weber has a significant impact, this will affect the influence of the Reynolds number. The impact of both of these criteria must be large with large gradients of the bottom. In particular, the free fall of the jets must be particularly sensitive to the linear scale of the model. In engineering terms, the non-similarity subtle effects aeration criteria of Weber and Reynolds shows that the hydrodynamic (pulsating) load, operating on small-scale models, in circuits with jet dropped in the low-frequency part of the spectrum, should be generally too high, and in the high-frequency part, underestimated. Fortunately, the high-frequency part of the spectrum usually has little effect on the strength and stability of hydraulic structures.

If we assume that the size of the bubbles of air captured aerated water surface are associated not with Taylor, and on the integral turbulence scale (such a hypothesis is consistent with the model of local buckling of the free surface [30]), that in conditions of similarity aeration, the influence of the Reynolds criterion will sharply decrease. It is important to ensure sufficiently large numbers of Weber. So in this model, it is advisable to make the overall scale of turbulence *L*,

$$We_L = \rho g L^2/\sigma$$

The impact of this criterion is small, if $We_L \geq We_{Lcr} \approx 10^3$.

Self-similarity criterion *We* in this scheme provides no guarantee for the similarity of the fine structure aerated flow (and thus the whole spectrum of pulsation velocities and pressures), but the low-frequency part of the spectrum on the model, based on this description of the phenomenon, can be expected to be close to nature.

Quantitative assessment to establish the similarity conditions of the beginning of aeration on the basis of this concept, gives semiempirical formula [15]:

$$\frac{\mathrm{Fr}}{\cos\varphi} = \frac{44}{\left(1+8.7/C\right)^2 - 13300/\mathrm{We}} \tag{6.43}$$

in which, along with geometrical characteristics (angle of gradient of the φ flow bottom), includes the Shezy coefficient (in quadratic resistance zone) *C* and the Weber number $We = \rho U^2 h/\sigma$. Obviously, this dependence cannot claim to be the sufficient generality, if it doesn't include the ratio of fluids and gas densities: it can be applied only to water and air.

Figure 6.4 shows the link between the numbers Fr_{cr} and *We*, from which it follows that for sufficiently large values of the numbers *We* (the smaller the value, the smaller the Shezy coefficient) there is self-similarity of the beginning of aeration on this criterion. If nature refers to the self-similar region *We*, for inclusion in the same area and models to its geometric scale, subject to the condition *Fr* = idem, it should be required that:

$$M_h \geq \sqrt{\frac{M_\sigma}{M_\rho M_g}\frac{We_{\lim}}{We_N}} \tag{6.44}$$

When modeling for example, chutes, characterized by the values $C = 40 \div 60\ \mathrm{m}^{0,5}/\mathrm{s}$ and $We_{\lim} \approx 1 \cdot 10^5$ minimum geometric scale, selected from

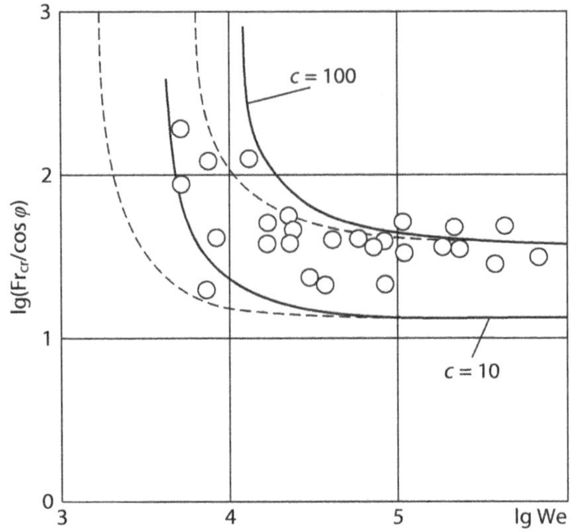

Figure 6.4 Influence of the *We* number on the value of the Fr_{cr} number corresponding to the beginning of aeration:
________ distilled water;
- - - - - - - water with organic impurities;
O - experimental points.

this requirement if the same fluid is in the model and in kind, is 1:10-1:20. Another way of finding areas of the self-similarity of aeration on the criteria *We*, discussed in [15], is where a map of the surface tension force and gravity associated with the deformation of the free surface is determined by the turbulence of the flow. In this paper, the results of that kind of a condition of free surface can be achieved when the depth of the flow on the model is at most, 0.1 m.

The shown data is the fair, of course, to areas outside the initial phase, which is the development boundary layer (see Section 5.2).

With the rapid flow of local obstacles due to the perturbations of the free surface in the area of influence of obstacles, there are additional causes of the involvement of gas. For example, in case of streamlining of a cylinder, involvement of gas is most intensive on the border of a track and a transit flow in vortex structures. Researches of gas involvement in streamlining of single cylinders and their systems (for nuclear reactors on fast neutrons), executed in the Science and Research Sector of Hydroproject (hereinafter – Hydroproject SRS), together with employees of MISI-MGSU [208], pointed to the self-similarity of the beginning of gas involvement by the Reynolds criterion with $Re = UD/\nu > 10^3$ (*U* – running-on flow velocity, *D* - cylinder diameter).

It has been found that in the field of self-similarity in *Re*, beginning of aeration is associated with values of *Fr* and *We* numbers, between which there is the following dependence:

$$Fr_{cr} = 185/We \tag{6.45}$$

where $Fr = U^2/(gD)$; $We = (\rho U^2 D)/\sigma$

According to the obtained data, similarity of gas involvement, in this case, can only be achieved if the following conditions exist:

$$\mathrm{Fr} = \mathrm{idem} \text{ and } \mathrm{We} = \mathrm{idem}$$

In the literature a lot of attention is paid to the involvement of gas vortex cords, formed at the entrance of the underground, below the well fluid level. Only in [171], more than 30 references to the works of foreign authors on this issue are given. According to works of most researchers, beginning capture of the gas vortex cords (critical depth of the hole level) depends on the criteria *Fr, Re,* and *We*; so for each of these criteria there is self-similar area. However, the data on the limit values in the specified criteria vary widely in virtually all the works. Analysis of these data shows the differences caused by the fact that experimental data underlying the recommendations are obtained at different outlines of the borders and different velocity distribution on the approach. The best generalization can be made, if we consider the circulation is relatively from water-intake openings. But with complex geometrical boundary conditions to associate circulation with values included in the conditions of certainty, it is not easy.

Systematic experiments Jane [183] in which, along with other values ranged circulation flow received, show that the boundaries of the self-similar area on Re depend on dimensionless, which includes circulation. The following complex was used:

$$\pi_\Gamma = \Gamma h_{cr}/Q$$

where $\Gamma = \pi D U_\tau$; U_τ - tangential component of the velocity at a distance of D/2 from the axis of the crater; h_{cr} - critical depth of the well fluid level. From [183]:

$$h_{cr}/D_0 = KFr^{0.25} \tag{6.46}$$

where D_0 is diameter of a water intake port; $K = K(Re/Fr^{0,5},\pi_\Gamma)$; $Fr = U^2/gD_0$; $Re = UD_0/v$ (U - velocity in a water intake port). At $Re/Fr^{0.5} \geq 5.10^4$ K - factor self-similarity in this complex.

In [183] it was found that at least $1{\cdot}10^2 < We < 3.4{\cdot}10^4$ ($We = \rho U^2 D_u/\sigma$) start air-involving does not depend on the Weber criterion. However, in experiments, the results of which are represented in [166], where conditions of gas capture similarity have been studied in relation to nuclear reactors on fast neutrons, with variation of fluids from freon to sodium, influence of *We* criterion on gas capture into a funnel was clearly stated. In these experiments circulation flow was clearly associated with consumption of fluid (criterion π_Γ is associated with *Fr*). For a self-similar zone on the *Re* number, there was obtained the following relation for critical submergence of a water outlet port:

$$h_{cr}\Big/D_o = const\sqrt{Fr}\left(\frac{1}{Fr^{0,25}} - \frac{7.6{\bullet}10^4}{We}\right) \tag{6.47}$$

when it follows that:

$$We_{\lim} = \frac{7.6{\bullet}10^4\,Fr^{0,25}}{\left[\tilde{\Delta}\ \left(h_{cr}/D_0\right)\right]\text{permit}} \tag{6.48}$$

where:

$$\left[\tilde{\Delta}\ \left(\frac{h_{cr}}{D_0}\right)\right]_{\text{permit}} = \frac{\left(h_{cr}/D_0\right)we_{\lim}}{\left(h_{cr}/D_0\right)We_{=\infty}} - 1$$

Entering of a free jet beneath the open flow surface (conjugation of upstream walls of a dam, dropped by a stream, fall pits, siphons, ruptures of levels in circulation contours of some heat exchangers) is usually accompanied with gas involvement. And gas involvement in the hydraulic jump is also similar to these cases. Involvement of gas in this situation becomes possible due to both content of gas in a stream and its capture from gas space in place of jet impact on the surface.

Based on a large number of empirical dependencies, connecting the gas content in the flow of water at the jump area with the number Frude, such as Kalinske and Robertson formula:

$$\beta = K_I(Fr^{\,0.5} - 1)^{1.4}$$

Some researchers believe that gas involvement in the cases under consideration is accurately reproduced, provided Fr = idem. According to other researchers, to achieve similarity, in addition, you must provide the big speed in the jet (the influence of *Re and We*) on the model. Thus, according to Willcock and Torny [173] it is necessary that $U_{0M} \geq 0.5$ m/s. From the literature recommendations it seems appropriate to use those as the similarity conditions involving gas features:

$$U_{begin}/U_0 = \text{idem} \tag{6.49}$$

where U_{begin} – flow velocity, corresponding to beginning of gas involvement; U_0 - actual speed in the same section.

In [169] it is recommended to put the U_{begin} ~0.8 m/s (water and air at normal pressure and room temperature). However, in [173], it is established that the U_{begin} can vary greatly (from 0.8 to 3 m/s) depending on the intensity of turbulence in the jet. If additional sources of turbulence are not available, the Ubegin = 0.8 ÷1 m/s.

Proceeding from conditions (6.49), semblance of involving gas jet of fluid in the absence of self-similarity in the number Frude, can be ensured only if the difference between the properties of fluid and gas on the model is from those in nature.

In various sections of technology an urgent task is to forecast the characteristics of the involvement of gas available in spray and decay (spraying) of such jets in the surrounding atmosphere. In the energy sector, for example, this task belongs to spraying of fuel by nozzles, to cooling water by sprinkling devices, and, to coupling of high-pressure dams ponds by dropped jets. Based on the data given in [73] the liquid spraying in gas at very big Froude numbers (in case of self-similarity under the Fr number) is self-similar under the Re number at rather big values of this criterion. Herewith the We criterion and the simplex ρ_{gas}/ρ can be considered as the defining criteria of similarity. Confirmation of this is Figure 6.5, which presents processed data of experiments by L. A. Whitman [73] that show the average diameter of drops, formed by spraying fluid injector. These

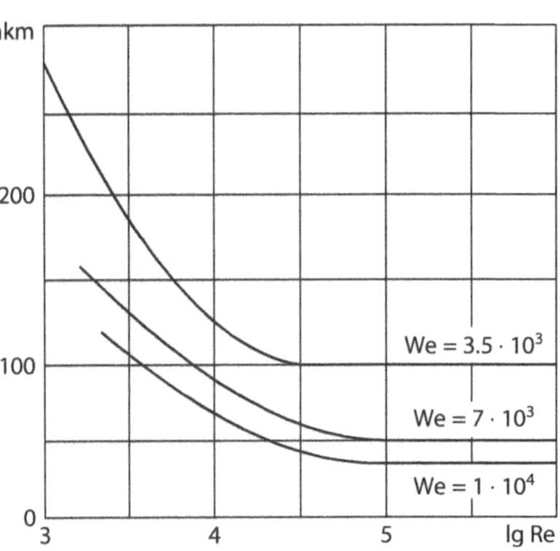

Figure 6.5 Dependence of the mean diameter of drops, formed by spraying fluid with a nozzle, from *Re* and *We* numbers, when *ρgas*/*ρ*~*0,0012.*

data refer to the nozzle of the same structures characterized regularity criteria turbulence. Initial turbulence jet significantly affects the characteristics of the involvement of gas and decay, but its influence is limited to the initial section of the jet. At a sufficient distance from the input section, the jet characteristics stop being dependent on the initial turbulence and are determined by the interaction of moving fluid and gas [39].

A similar result was obtained in the experiments, performed in *Hydroproject SRS*, which included a large experimental setup with a pressure of up to 20 m and a flow rate exceeding 1 m^3/s. The experiments studied the characteristics of free jets coming out of nozzles with rectangular horizontal axis. Figure 6.6 presents the dependence of the relative cross-sectional area of the stream (its borders were determined by the image

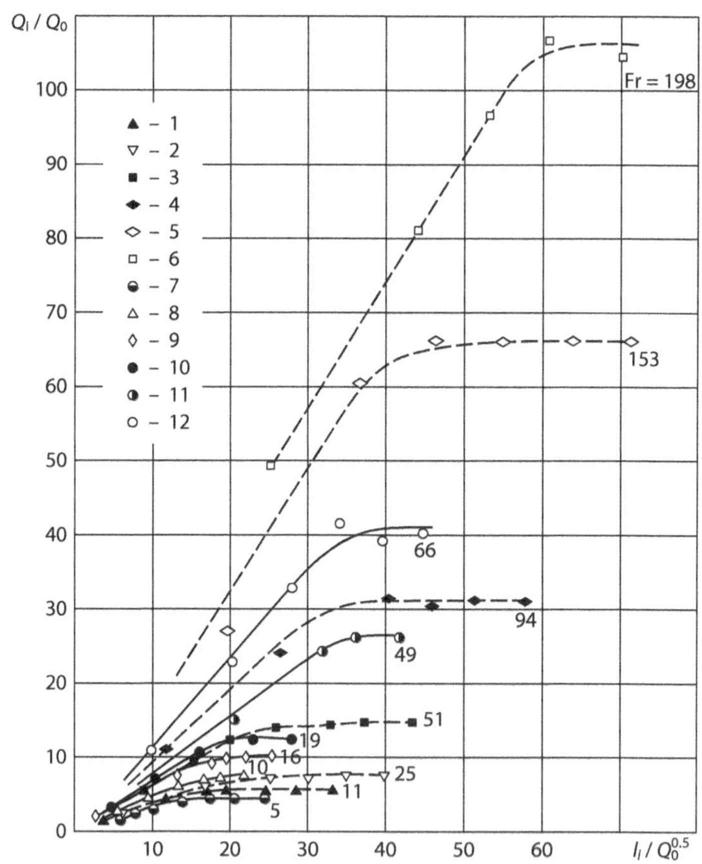

Figure 6.6 Change in the cross-sectional area of the horizontally dropped jet in the air along its length.

processing) from the relative distance of this section, from the exit of the nozzle values with different numbers Fr, Re and We. In this figure, one can note the specified stabilization of the process of expansion of the jets in all considered cases.

Notations	U_0,***m/s***	***Re***	***We***	***Fr***
Nozzle section 500x100 mm				
1	3,3	$3{,}3{\cdot}10^5$	$1{,}5{\cdot}10^4$	11
2	5,0	$5{,}0{\cdot}10^5$	$3{,}4{\cdot}10^4$	25
3	7,0	$7{,}0{\cdot}10^6$	$6{,}8{\cdot}10^4$	51
4	9,6	$9{,}6{\cdot}10^5$	$1{,}27{\cdot}10^5$	94
5	12,2	$1{,}22{\cdot}10^6$	$2{,}05{\cdot}10^5$	153
6	13,9	$1{,}39{\cdot}10^6$	$2{,}65{\cdot}10^5$	198
Nozzle section 500x200 mm				
7	3,1	$6{,}2{\cdot}10^5$	$2{,}6{\cdot}10^4$	5
8	5,1	$1{,}03{\cdot}10^5$	$7{,}2{\cdot}10^4$	13
9	5,7	$1{,}14{\cdot}10^6$	$8{,}9{\cdot}10^4$	16
10	6,1	$1{,}22{\cdot}10^9$	$1{,}02{\cdot}10^5$	19
11	9,8	$1{,}96{\cdot}10^6$	$2{,}63{\cdot}10^3$	49
12	11,4	$2{,}28{\cdot}10^6$	$3{,}56{\cdot}10^3$	66

The study of power equipment components, in which the involvement of gas in free jets and their decay, is not usually a major difficulties, because these items can be played on experimental facilities in full size. The situation is different in the study of spillways high dams, which have models that can realistically be done only in a geometric scale, in substantially smaller units, and the use of these models for fluids other than water (for compliance with the conditions *We* = idem), is almost impossible.

The simulation of such spillway is possible only with the presence of the self-similarity of the studied phenomena in the number *We*. Significant here is the attitude scale turbulence λ_t/l_0 (see part 2). It can be assumed that for the self-similarity of the phenomenon of disintegration of a jet, all the details of this process do not exist, for example, the distribution of water dust in the atmosphere to play on the model of the impossible. However, there is information on the self-similarity of main energy-carrying structures of disintegrated jet at rather big values of the We number and rather big Re numbers. This fact is evidenced by the We number dependence of the normalized intensity of pressure pulsation on rigid horizontal bottom

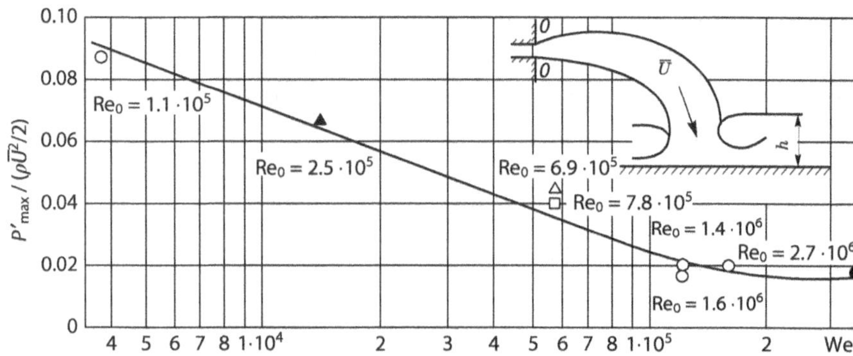

Figure 6.7 Dependence of the normalized maximum pressure pulsation standard at the bottom when flooding by a dropped jet dropped from number *We*, *Fr* = 20 ÷ 30 (*Re*, *We*, and *Fr* numbers refer to the initial section):

● - spillway model of Sayano-Shushenskaya HPP in scale 1:20;

△ - the same in 1:50;

▲ - the same in 1:100;

○ - jet from a nozzle of 500x200 mm cross section;

□ - the same with a nozzle of 357x143 mm section.

from the side of disintegrated jet at its spatial matching with tail water (submerged jump) that is presented in Figure 6.7 Dependence was built by the results in *Hydroproject SRS* experiments on models of real spillway and experimental studies of garbage through horizontal jet nozzles. Based on the data shown in Figure 6.7, you can assume that characteristics such as the impact of the collapsed jets on the obstacle in the low-frequency part of the spectrum could be played on a large-scale model of the spillway high dam. Geometric scale dam height 100-200 m should not be less than 1:20.

Aeration may occur not only from the water surface. It can be a result of the spin-dissolved gases at low pressure in the water coming from the reservoir to the surface, which should be considered when analyzing the simulation of phenomena such as unsteady hydrodynamic influence on the elements of pressure spillways and cavitation.

6.4 Structure of Gas-Fluid Flows

In a joint motion of gas and fluid, a fluid-gas system is formed. Forms of joint motion of gas and fluid are very diverse: from the motion of two continuous flows interacting on the surface of section, to the flow of foam, in which both phases form a complex, delicate and fragile structure. Gas-fluid systems are peculiar to many natural phenomena and technological processes. They differ from the systems of the fluid-solid particles that form the internal interfaces, which are not defined for them. At the interfaces of phases there are the forces, which even under conditions of isothermal flow, significantly affect fields characteristics of flows. There are no reliable theoretical methods for describing such fields in the general case.

Therefore, physical modeling of two-phase flows is given special attention. However, due to the multi-faceted nature of the phenomena of gas-fluid flows, the exact physical modeling, achievable only in special cases and methods of approximate similarity of gas-fluid flows is developed insufficiently.

With basic quantities characterizing fluid-gas system, in the absence of thermodynamic effects, taking geometrical dimensions l, the density of fluid ρ and gas ρ_{gas}, dynamic viscosity of phases μ and μ_{gas}, the coefficient of surface tension on the boundary of phases, given speeds of phases (the ratio of the volume flow phase to full square living section of two-phase flow) U and V, the free fall acceleration g, the defining criteria of similarity can be simplexes ρ_{gas}/ρ, μ_{gas}/μ, $V/\bar{U}$, l/l_0 and complexes, including the characteristics of one of the phases and values that define the interphase interaction: $\bar{U}_0 l_d/v$, $\bar{U}^2{}_d/gl_0$, $\rho\bar{U}^2{}_0 l_d/\sigma$.

Having in mind that these complexes are the *Re*, *Fr* and *We* criteria, it is easy to identify, that modeling of gas-fluid flow in a geometric scale other than one, is very difficult. The difficulties of modeling increase even further when, for technical reasons it is necessary to use fluids and gases on the model, which are significantly different from those in kind, for example, to use water and air at normal temperature and pressure instead of water and steam at high settings.

In partial problems it is sometimes useful to use a combination of these criteria, provided that self-similarity has been proved in other cases. Thus, the criterion of Archimedes can be written as follows:

$$\frac{gl_0^3}{\nu^2_{gas}}\left(1-\rho_{gas}/\rho\right)=\left(\frac{\tilde{U}_0\,l_0}{\nu_{gas}}\right)^2\frac{gl_0}{\tilde{U}^2_0}\left(1-\frac{\rho_{gas}}{\rho}\right) \tag{6.50}$$

This criterion characterizes the ratio of lifting (Archimedes) the force acting on this item under the influence of a difference of densities of phases, and the resistance forces, called molecular viscosity.

Complex

$$\frac{\rho_{gas}\tilde{V}_0{}^2}{g\left(\rho-\rho_{gas}\right)l_0}=\frac{\tilde{V}^2_0}{gl_0}\frac{1}{\rho/\rho_{gas}-1} \tag{6.51}$$

can be considered as the ratio of lifting force and forces of inertia.

When drawing up the criteria of similarity of gas-fluid systems, it is convenient to use the so-called internal linear scale - complexes with linear dimension that include only the properties of the phases [71]. Scale linear sized freely emerging bubbles, drops, and films can serve as a constant Laplas:

$$\delta_s = \sqrt{\frac{\sigma}{g\left(\rho - \rho_{gas}\right)}}$$

Gravitational-viscous interaction for free draining films of viscous fluid can be attributed to a linear scale

$$\delta_v = \left[\frac{\nu^2}{g\left(1 - \rho_{gas}/\rho\right)}\right]^{1/3}$$

The wording of similarity is much easier in cases when the internal inter-phase boundaries are set independently, for example by experimental data. Bubble (or drip) two-phase flows under steady-state size of the bubbles (drops) represent a special case here. An important characteristic is the hydraulic size (speed wool) *w*. As is known, this value is a combination of Weber, Archimedes and Reynolds criteria. With a small contribution of inertia forces as the main similarity conditions, like for systems of fluid - solid particles, in this case, can be taken as follows:

$$U_0/w = \text{idem} \tag{6.52}$$

The acceptability of this condition is demonstrated, in particular, in [173], in relation to the establishment of the gas content in the areas of recycling in the roll of air, taking impinging jet, and transporting it by pressurized water pipeline. For an air-water system under normal conditions, it is recommended to take w = 0.25 m/s. In cases where there is a possibility to derogate from the Froude rules, the condition (6.52) can be performed by setting the scale of *U* as equal to the scale hydraulic size.

The condition (6.52) is used in studies of gas-fluid flow in the elements of the nuclear vapor-generating plants at the water-air models. One of the tasks of the research was to assess the distribution of steam content in the water volume of the horizontal steam separator [124]. Based on the reported data, it was assumed that the average size of bubbles of steam in it in kind (P = 7 MPa, T = 270°C) is approximately 0.3 m/s and for the model (technical water and atmospheric air at normal temperature and pressure) - 0.25 m/s, i.e. M_w~1. Figure 6.8 presents the distribution true volumetric gas content in the water volume on the model depending on the zoom rate M_U. It also displays information about the distribution of steam content obtained on a special stand, the playback section of the steam separator in natural size.

As follows from the chart, rather exact correspondence of results has been obtained at $M_U \approx M_w$. Using water-air model instead of a steam model has allowed simplification of the conduction of studies, to get larger amounts of information, and to choose the optimal engineering solutions [124]. Another example of using water-air model for research of steam-water system is the study of regularities of natural circulation in a shell-type water-watered reactor. The study carried out using the ratio (6.52), allowed us to define the traction circuit characteristics with a significant spatial flow, conditions of steam capturing in surge channels, and to recommend engineering solutions that enhance quality of the natural circulation contour. The main regularities of flows, obtained on the model, have been confirmed by the experience of operation of the shell-type boiling reactor. Some results of the study are presented in Figure 6.9

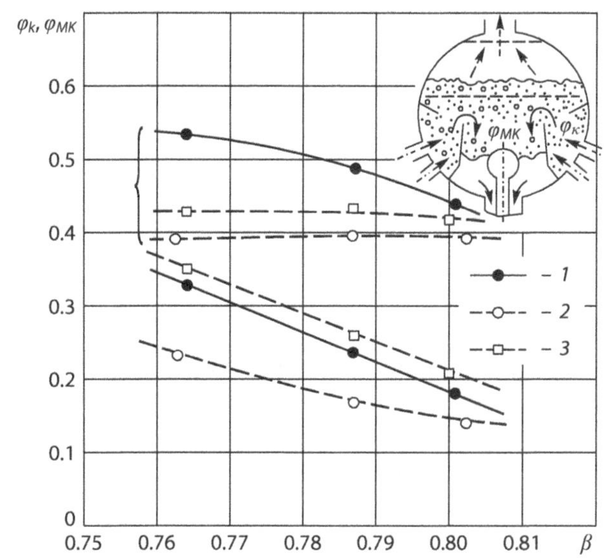

Figure 6.8 Volumetric gas content φ_k in ducts and in the inter-duct space φ_{MK} of a horizontal separator depending on the volume of consumable gas content β in the study of the steam-water and air-to-water installations:
1 - steam-water model, $P = 7\ MPa$, $D = 2300$ mm; 2 - air-water model, $D = 2200$ mm, $M_U = 1$; 3 - same, $M_U = 0.9$.

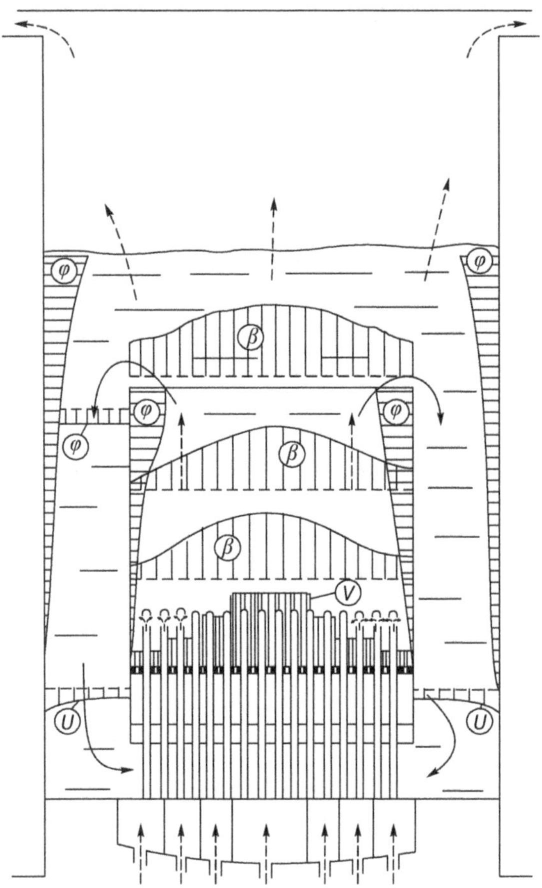

Figure 6.9 Gas content in the natural circulation circuit of a tank reactor according to air-to-water installation data.

The significant part of engineering tasks in the energy sector is associated with gas-fluid flows in pipes. Here many practically important characteristics are connected with the flow regime (stratified, bubble, shell, ring, dispersed, and so on), being realized in the considered case. So when modeling of flows in pipes, first of all, it is important to replicate real regimes. For establishing of the existence of certain regimes areas in the dynamics of two-phase systems, the so-called maps of the flow regimes are used, on which the boundaries of these areas depending on two dimensionless complexes are marked. An example of such a map is Figure 6.10, on which the areas of vertical gas-fluid streaming modes in a cylindrical pipe of D diameter in the coordinates Ku and N are marked:

$$Ku = \frac{\rho_{gas} V_0}{\sqrt{g\sigma(\rho - \rho_{gas})}}$$ - the Kutateladze criterion;

$$N = l'_0 D g^{1/2} \left(\frac{\rho - \rho_{gas}}{4\sigma^{3/4}}\right) \left[\frac{\sigma}{g(\rho - \rho_{gas}) D^2}\right]^{1,25}$$

$$\times \left\{ 1 + \frac{31}{\left\{ \frac{1}{\rho} \left[\frac{\sigma}{g(\rho - \rho_{gas})} \right]^{3/2} \right\}^{0,55}} \right\}$$

If these complexes reliably determine existence of the flow regimes, they can be taken as criteria of similarity.

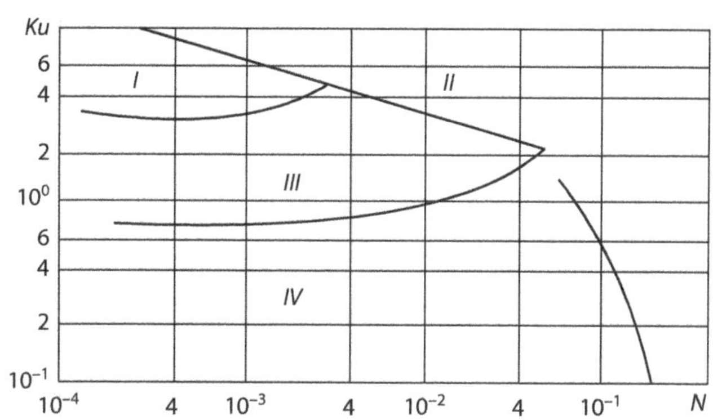

Figure 6.10 Map of stream of the gas-fluid flows regimes in vertical pipes:

I - resistant film flow; *II* - unstable film flow on the wall and emulsion flow - in the center of the pipe; *III* - foamy flow; *IV* - bubble-shell flow.

7

Flow in the Deformable Channel

7.1 Features of Riverbed Deformations Modeling

The study of deformations of the riverbed is one of the most important sections of hydraulic research. Riverbed deformation cause changes of flow characteristics that should be taken into account in the design of river water-development works. Safety of buildings, construction and operating costs directly depend on the riverbed deformations. Most of the phenomena associated with the deformation of a channel, refer to the extremely complex problems of channel flows dynamics, which through intensive study of channel processes and the use of computational methods used in this field of numerical modeling, in recent years have increased considerably. However, at the present stage hydraulic modeling is not less important than in the time of L.J. Fargue, who first used the hydraulic model in a flexible way in 1875, to study river control structures on the Garonne.

However, hydraulic modeling of deformation of a channel meets considerable difficulties, associated primarily with the multifactorial nature of the riverbed evolution process. Along with the characteristics of flow and sediment, it depends on geological and topographical structure of the valley, development of vegetation on the floodplain and in the mainstream, anthropogenic activities, etc., which in the general case, are all factors that affect run-of-river process that can not be reproduced. But the complexity of hydraulic modeling of riverbed deformations is great, and in some cases, it would seem ro be relatively simple.

Consider for in-stream folded cohesionless material, which can be characterized by the size (diameter) of particles d and density ρ_s. The riverbed is limited with coarse shores. Stream transports only the material, forming the bed. It is clear that in establishing criteria of similarity, on the basis of the theory of dimensions, after the introduction of the constraint equations (1.17), values of d and ρ_s will be received as additional similarity criteria d/l_0 and ρ_s/ρ. At first glance, it may seem that ensuring identity of these criteria does not cause complications: when $\rho_м = \rho_n$ enough to $\rho_{sм} = \rho_{sn}$, and scale to the size of particles, cohesionless material, was equal to the geometric model scale. In fact, under normal conditions for lowland rivers, with size bed-formation of sediment equal to 0.2-0.3 mm, and the usual geometric scale model (1:10-1:100), sand will be reproduced on the model of silt and clay particles, for which significant molecular interaction is not manifested in sands. The matter becomes more complicated when attention is drawn to the fact that the hydraulic modeling of open stream is practically possible because of the availability of Reynolds self-similarity criterion. Achievement of self-similar areas with characteristics of the flow in the rigid boundaries for *Re* does not provide the possibility to neglect essential channel processes; the effects of viscosity are manifested around the particles of sediment. So, the effect of viscosity on stability of quartz particles, composing the water flow plain bottom, and on the hydraulic size appears at $d \leq 1,5$ mm.

It is clear that the use of the rolling material on the model with a diameter of particles being large at 1.5 mm, cannot provide the self-similarity for *Re* of all details of the downstream process, as it applies to private events. If to consider this recommendation as appropriate, than in the considered conditions the similarity can be expected in cases, when the life-size of the particle is not less than centimeters, i.e. while investigating pebble and boulder beds. When modeling sandy beds we can hope for an approximate similarity for the distortion on the model of relations of forces on the ground.

Naturally, the approximate modeling of channel process has to dismember the characteristic phenomena, abstracting from other phenomena, relatively less significant for this task. Among the objectives in the area of approximate river bed motion modeling process, you can specify, on the evaluation of local deformations of the reproduced channel, averaged characteristics of the river-bed, looking at the overall planned bed reshaping, the study of channel morphometric forms, study siltation of reservoirs and so on.

7.2 Local Erosion in the Cohesionless Ground

Placing in a natural or artificial water body of various structures (spillway, piers, bridges, piers, thresholds, and so on) leads to formation that there is a high impact on the bottom of the watercourse, associated mainly with the presence of large-scale vortices and turbulence-defined surfaces in the stream. If the flow bottom in these areas is not fixed and the ground at the bottom is unable to resist these influences, there occurs a local scour of bottom, developing (with hydrodynamic effects unlimited in time) to depths, at which hydrodynamic forces and forces, preventing the scour, are balanced.

For cohesionless grounds, execution along with Re = idem and $Re \geq Re_{lim}$ conditions $M_d = M_t$ and $M_{\rho s} = M_\rho$, for sufficiently large amounts of ground particles on the model, provides a semblance of local erosion. This is confirmed, in particular, in [226], where, along with the given conditions of similarity, necessity of observance of similarity of granulometric composition of ground and its use on the cohesionless material model with $d_M \geq 1{,}8$ mm is specified.

The situation is complicated when the bottom of the stream is specifically composed of relatively fine-grained material. In the study of local erosion, compared to other phenomena, there are some that will facilitate the formulation of researching the circumstances related to the fact that there usually are observed sharply uneven flow, kinematic characteristics, determined mainly by microsize boundaries of the stream, the relative sizes of structures and channels, the size of the hole erosion, and poor connection with their roughness. For example, there is reason to exclude simplex d/h from the system of defining criteria and choose the scale of the particle size of the sediment geometric scale object. If you put the phenomenon of local erosion associated only with stability of ground particles to the bottom of the stream (not related to the uneven motion feared particles relatively fluid), then the criterion ρ_s/ρ can be considered insignificant. Vertical weighing particles holding force is proportional to $g(\rho_s - \rho)d^3$, and power of hydrodynamic influence on the particle is proportional to $\rho U^2 d^2 \varphi_1(Re_d)$, where function $\varphi_1(Re_d)$ takes into account the effect of viscosity at particles flow. Then along with the criteria, identity of which provides the similarity of the fluid flow, the following complex should be included in the system of defining criteria:

$$\frac{g(\rho_s-\rho)d^3}{\rho U^2 d^2 \varphi_1(\mathrm{Re}_d)}=\frac{g(\rho_s-\rho)d}{\rho\varphi_1(\mathrm{Re}_d)}\frac{1}{U^2}$$

or (in case of square-rooting) complex:

$$\frac{\varphi_2(\mathrm{Re}_d)\sqrt{\rho^+ gd}}{U} \tag{7.1}$$

where:

$$\varphi_2(\mathrm{Re}_d)=\sqrt{1/\varphi_1(\mathrm{Re}_d)};\ \rho^+=(\rho_s-\rho)/\rho.$$

Note that this result is obtained by using one of the ways of reducing the number of criteria, which is preliminary grouping of units. Determination of the $\varphi_2(\mathrm{Re}_d)$ function is a fundamental problem. You can see that the numerator of the received system is proportional to the hydraulic size: $w=k\varphi(\mathrm{Re}_d)\sqrt{\rho^+ gd}.$

If we take that $\boldsymbol{\varphi_2(Re_d)=\varphi(Re_d)}$, condition of similarity of particles sustainability can be written as

$$U/w=\text{idem} \tag{7.2}$$

Simplex *U/w* has been suggested as a criterion of local deformations similarity by many researchers. There is no direct evidence of functions' $\varphi_2(Re_d)$ identity, related to the flow of a particle, located among other particles at the bottom of the stream, and $\varphi_2(Re_d)$, characterizing free fall of a single particle in a stationary fluid. Furthermore, the recently published data of systematic studies of the cohesionless material erosion with fluid jets [186, 209, 224] show that the condition (7.2) in the general case is not sufficient for erosion similarity.

Figure 7.1 and 7.2 represent results of the experimental study of erosion in the cohesionless material by plain jets of water and air, described in [209]. The given data shows that relations of the erosion depth from the ratio U_0/w, for jets of water and air, are very little the same, especially for plain vertical jets. However, the same fluid data related to the materials of different size, characterized by different w values, practically describes

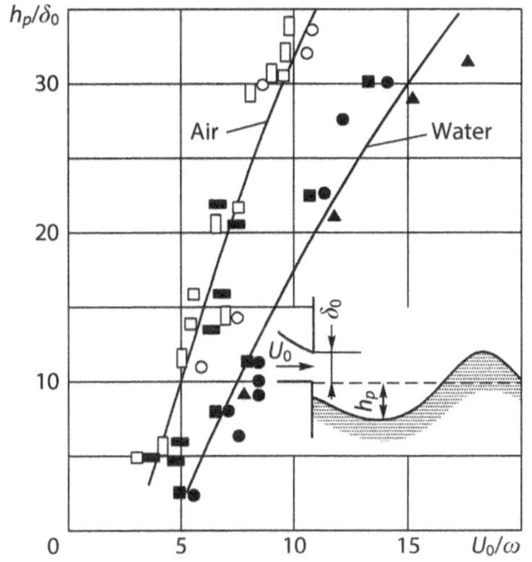

Figure 7.1 Dependence of depth of the cohesionless material local erosion by a horizontal plain water and air jet from the U_0/w relation. Experimental points belong to particles of different density (ρ_s = 1,05 to 2.65 t/m^3) and different values δ_0/d.

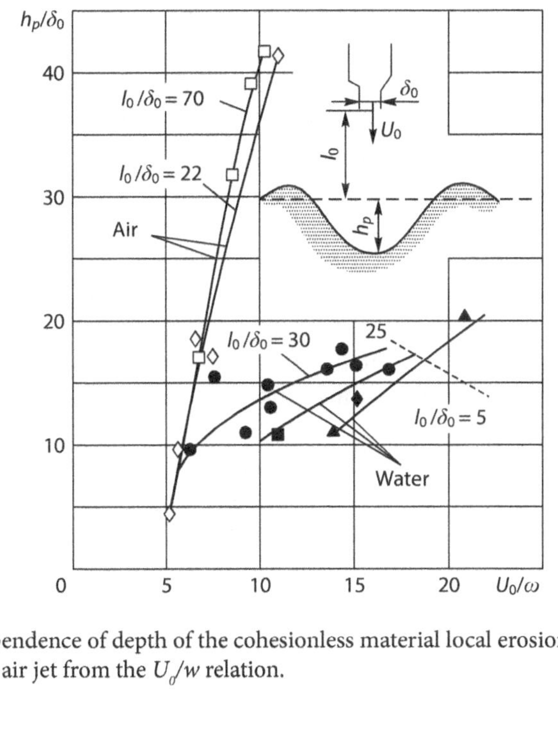

Figure 7.2 Dependence of depth of the cohesionless material local erosion by a vertical plain water and air jet from the U_0/w relation.

common dependencies. The differences between depth of erosion and complexes, similar to U_0/w, with considerable difference ρ^+ (solids in water and air) in [209], differ in these cases; and the mode of moving of a load in hoppers erosion is in dynamic equilibrium, and therefore, in the system of defining criteria of similarity, ground erosion jets should be entered additionally as the value of ρ^+.

Unlike [209] [186] on the basis of the study of erosion of vertical axisymmetric jet similar result is explained by the significant influence of the filtering material, defined particle size and viscosity of the fluid. In this regard, the similarity conditions should contain the criteria Re_d, the influence of which is illustrated by the data given in Figure 7.3

The filtration phenomena role in nonstationary effects on ground, described in [47], was investigated in the Science and Research Sector of Hydroproject in the study of ground erosion by the breakthrough wave [101]. Non-sinchronism of pressure changes on the ground surface and in its column results in deconsolidation of surface layers of cohesionless material and intensive separation of particles from the bottom in the area behind the wave front, even at wave propagation across the smooth riverbed. These effects are exacerbated when flowing with obstacles around.

Systematic study of erosion in the cohesionless ground from vertical cylindrical bodies impacted by breaking waves, have shown, that along with the removal of ground particles from the area near the obstacles with the passage of the wave front, owing to the difference of changes over time pressure on the ground surface and in its mass, leading to the appearance of the weighing forces, there is a significant softening layer of ground. This process is recorded in one of the experiments as shown in Figure 7.4.

The results of studies that indicate the complexity of the dependence of characteristics of local scour away U/w, are applied in case of sharply defined local and transient impact, as well as in cases of very big difference in the ρ_s/ρ value in the compared phenomena. However, according to the results of these studies, the conclusion can be made that in cases other than those specified, the identity of the complex U/w can provide the local erosion approximate similarity.

This is evidenced, in particular, with data of experiments on studying the release rate of flow of water particles of different materials, made with the system presented in Figure 7.5 [216]. The terms of the motion of particles in these experiments are close to conditions of carrying out of the ground from the pit of washout for horizontal mounting of the riverbed. Experimental data satisfactorily summarizes using complex U/w (Figure 7.6).

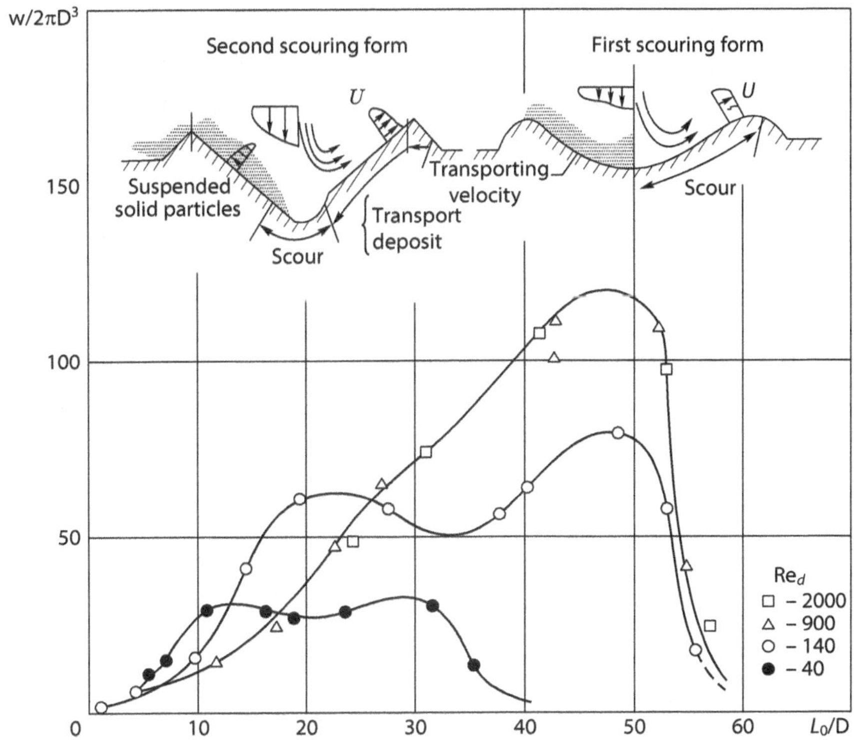

Figure 7.3 Dependence of the relative volume of scour by a vertical jet emerging from the *D* diameter cylindrical nozzle, from the relative distance of the nozzle from the initial bottom with constant relation $U_d/w = 11{,}5$ and various values $Re_{d.}$

Acceptability, in some cases, of conditions (7.2) is confirmed by the results of modeling real objects associated with the nature. Examples of these mappings are contained in [76]. Here we will refer also to the information contained in the work of Dutch specialists [175]. It is a report on the study of local erosion over the spillway, consumption of expiration through which it changes with time in connection with tides (spillway placed in the estuary). The bottom in kind consists of sand d≈0,25 mm. On the model the powder polystyrene is used as the cohesionless material. The hydraulic size scale is $M_w = w_M/w_N = 1{:}5$. The model geometric scale is accepted equal $M_l = 1{:}30$. According to the Froude rule, $M_U = M_l^{0,5} = 1{:}5{,}5 \approx M_w$, i.e. approximately, the condition (7.2) is implemented. The data comparison, represented in Figure 7.7, demonstrates the relevance of the results of local scour determination in kind and on the model.

Condition (7.2) can be done through the appropriate choice of the scale of values w or U. Usually the areas of local erosion are characterized by

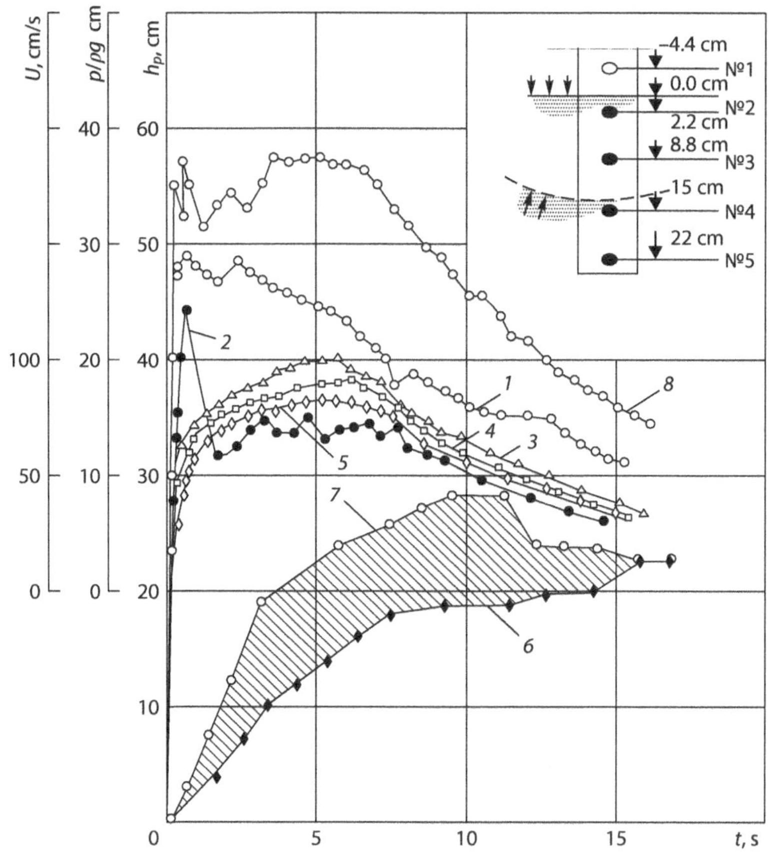

Figure 7.4 Changing of velocity U at the approach to the obstacle in time, pressure p in some points of the cylinder and depth of erosion h_p at the interrupted wave flow of cylindrical obstacles:

1-5 - pressure at points of measurement № 1-5;
6 - depth from the initial bottom to the border of not unconsolidated ground;
7 – the same to the border of unconsolidated ground;
8 – velocity.

relatively high values of the Froude number, so that a substantial distortion of the model on the Froude criterion is impossible, and when using gravity models we have to make $M_U = M_l^{0,5}$. In some cases with relatively small values Fr_N (flooded bodies flow, scour behind fixing elements of low-head dams and so on), there are prospects for the use of pressure models, for which M_u is not associated with M_l.

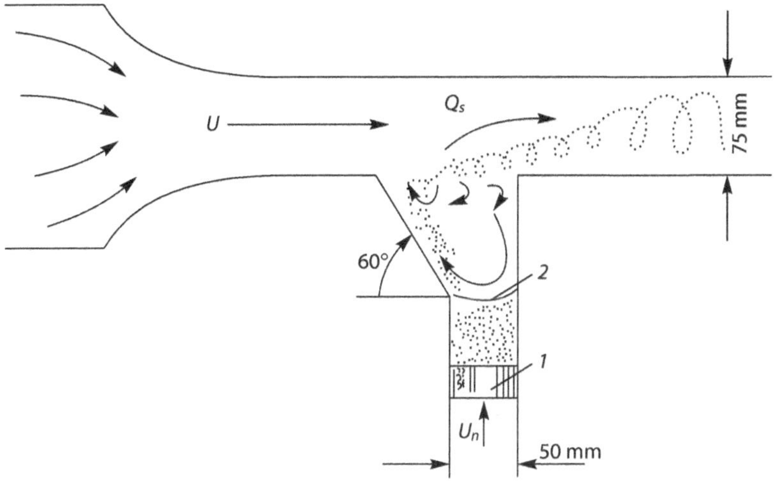

Figure 7.5 The scheme of experiments on determination of intensity of particles removal from a gullet: 1 - piston; 2 - partition level of fluids and solids, supported by matching the piston velocity U_n.

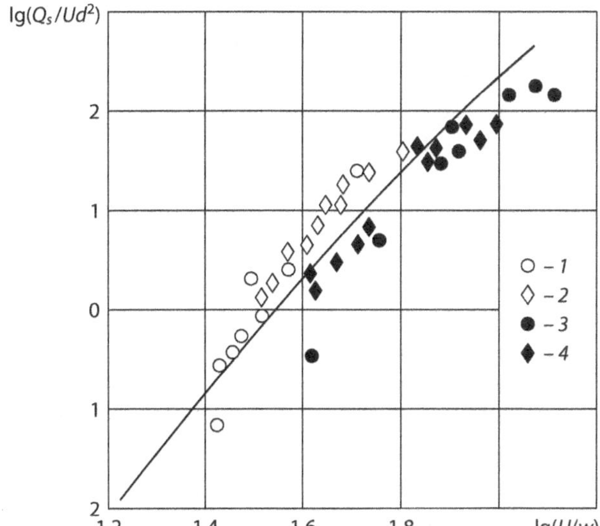

Figure 7.6 Dependence of intensity of particles removal from the U/w relation

1 - nickel (ρ_s =8,75 g/cm³, d= 0,57 mm);
2 - quartz sand (ρ_s=2,63 g/cm³, d= 0.18 mm);
3 - glass (ρ_s=2,46 g/cm³, d= 0,11 mm);
4 - lucite (ρ_s=1.2 g/cm³, d= 0.25 mm)

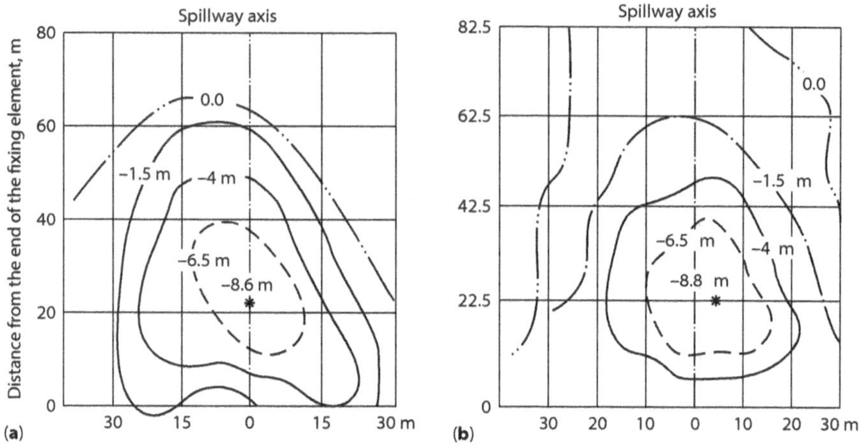

Figure 7.7 Scour well behind the spillway, based on results of determination in kind and in recalculation to the model: a - on the model; b - in kind.

The necessary scale M_w (in particular, $M_w=M_U=M_l^{0.5}$) can be ensured by appropriate selection of the scale M_d and $M_{\rho+}$. The data, necessary for selection of M_d and $M_{\rho+}$, is shown in Figures 6.1 and 6.2.

It would seem that you can always choose the zoom M_d to $M_{\rho+}$ to satisfy condition (7.1). However, this condition is obtained for cohesionless grounds. According to [106], molecular adhesion stress for sandy grounds under water is near $1/(d*10^4)$, $N/m^2([d]=m)$.

The impact of connectivity in problems of stability of the particles at the bottom of the thread can be estimated by the ratio of force molecular adhesion per particle and weight force of his particle. The dependence of such relation from a particle diameter, on the basis of the above-mentioned molecular coupling stress evaluation is represented in Figure 7.8 At this estimation the presence of coupling should be considered in the engineering tasks, at least at $d\leq$ 0,3-:-0,4 mm. In [76] it is alleged that molecular adhesion occurs when d< 0.1 mm, and in [181] – at d< 0.5 mm. Thus, condition (7.1), by choosing M_d, may result in studying of local erosion in small- and medium-grained grounds to an overestimation of the strength of molecular cohesion. So we have to resort to the use of materials with density less than the density of natural materials. In modern laboratory practice there are many artificial powders consisting mainly of polymer materials. When using lightweight materials, $M_d>>M_l$ helps to avoid the influence of molecular cohesion. For example, if the nature of the channel is combined with quartz sand with d_N=0,3 mm (ω~45 mm/s), in a model with M_l=1:50, in accordance with condition (7.2), the quartz sand

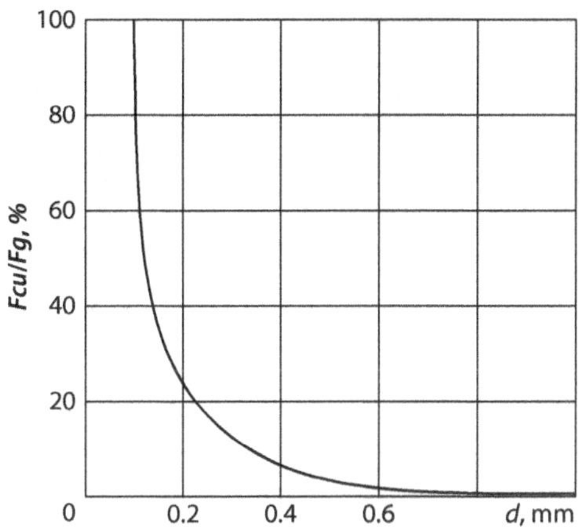

Figure 7.8 Dependence of molecular cohesion forces and particle weight from its diameter.

of particle size should be at Fr=idem, $w_M = w_N M_l^{0,5}$=6 mm/s and d_M=0,06. With such a particle size, the material connectivity will manifest itself very much. If used on the model of the powder with ρ_{SM} =1050 kg/m³ (polystyrene), then condition (7.2) satisfies d_M =0.5 mm. With such a particle size, the material with molecular adhesion can be ignored.

As noted above, fulfillment of the condition *U/w*=idem (or $M_U = M_l^{0,5}$) in low turbulence stream in kind may be provided not only by the appropriate choice of the hydraulic size scale M_w but also the scale of the fluid velocity M_U. The distortion on the Frude criterion when using the non-pressure model provides moderate possibilities. Implementation of pressure models is more about perspective, though in this case it is necessary to reckon with the distortion of the kinematics of spatial currents, due to the presence of a wall on the free surface of the model.

An example of the study of local erosion in the cohesionless ground on the pressure of the model is the definition of washout of the bottom of the channel name of Moscow for fastening one of the gateways in the downstream. On the pressure of the geometric model in scale 1: 200, a nonstationary mode emptying gateway has been reproduced so that the stationary regime corresponds to the maximum flow rate. On the model, the sand of *d*=0,2 mm is used. Scours on the model and in kind have proved to be very similar (Figure 7.9) [91].

In process the of local erosion, change in composition of the ground surface layers occurs - it is a natural revetment, which can strongly affect the scour characteristics. So when modeling a scour in heterogeneous ground it is necessary to reproduce granulometric composition of the

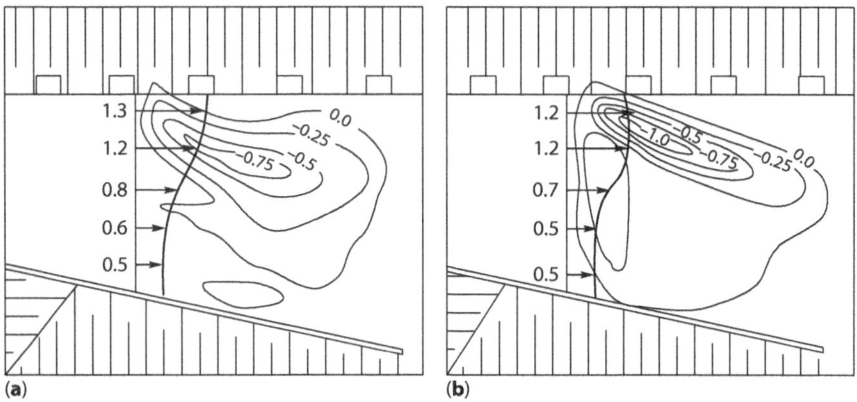

Figure 7.9 Downstream scour of lock in kind (a) and on the air-model (b) and plots of medium-depth velocities at maximum consumption of emptying. Depth of erosion is given in meters.

material. To do this, you should reproduce, at least approximately, distribution of the material on the volume of its hydraulic size. According to Shoklich (see [226]), you should, at least, ensure compliance with the scale hydraulic particle sizes with the d_{50} and d_{90} (d_{50} and d_{90} is a particle size of less is the amount of ground containing 50 and 90% of the material). If a very heterogeneous ground reproduces the material with a low density, with the size of the particles corresponding to the major factions, the model may be comparable with the macroscopic size of the object. In such cases it is possible to use materials with different densities for modeling of different fractions of ground: small fraction fines are reproduced through more lightweight material, coarse fractions – through heavier material. The form of local erosion may depend considerably on the sustainability of the array ground in general. So when modeling, we should pay attention to the identity of the angle of internal friction. Since for non-cohesive soil this value changes, not too much, it is obvious that geometric distortion of the models meant for assessment of the riverbed local deformations is unacceptable. However, geometric distortion is unacceptable because of the significant spaciousness trends in areas of local deformations.

In engineering practice, we can often be limited to a maximum evaluation of local deformations: to get information about their characteristics under the stabilization process in extremal conditions. Here development of deformations in time is not considered, and therefore no question arises about the time scale deformations in modeling. However, there are tasks (related, for example, to the construction conditions) for which the change in strain in time is of interest. The solution of these problems with the use of hydraulic modeling requires time scale deformations.

It is clear that under the conditions $M_d = M_l$ and $M_{\rho s} = M_{\rho}$, which is possible with large cohesionless material in kind, the time scale of deformations $M_{t\partial e\phi}$ is equal to the time scale of hydraulic processes M_t. In particular, subject to the Froude rule $M_{tdef} = M_l^{0,5}$, when $M_d \neq M_l$ and $M_{\rho s} \neq M_{\rho}$ there are no grounds for equality M_{tdef} and M_t, i.e. there is model distortion of characteristic processes in time. In absence of reliable relations, describing non-stationary process of local deformations in the establishing of the time scale, such deformations are significant difficulties and it is optimal to find the time scale to use data received in-kind [181]. However, the ability to obtain such data is very rare. Since for non-cohesive soil this value changes, not too much, it is obvious that geometric distortion of the models meant for assessment of the riverbed local deformations is unacceptable. Thus, in [175] is the dependence of the following type:

$$M_{tdef} = M^{1,7}_{\rho +} M^2_h M^{-4.3}_{(aU-Ucr)}$$

where h - depth; α - dimensionless coefficient associated with the distribution of velocities and turbulence; U_{cr} – velocity, corresponding to the beginning of the ground particles motion.

Considering that on the achievement of similarity $M_{\alpha} = 1$ and $M_{Ucr} = M_U$, this dependence can be rewritten as:

$$M_{tdef} = (M_{\rho +})^{1.7} M^2_h (M_U)^{-4.3}$$

The acceptability of this relationship for assessment of the erosion pit development in time behind horizontal fastening structure of water discharge using polystyrene powered is confirmed by Figure 7.10 showing the time change of the erosion pit longitudinal profile on the model and in natural conditions.

7.3 Local Erosions in Solid and Rocky Grounds

This paragraph is focused on modeling of deformations of the river-bed, formed of materials for which the substantive links between the components of its separate elements are the following: molecular adhesion in cohesive grounds and friction between the blocks of rocky ground. The peculiarity of erosion of these grounds is that in a case of hydrodynamic influence, the structure of the ground in the area of influence may be changed. The presence of these relations makes it difficult to assess the local deformations.

Implementation of numerous empirical dependences, found in literature, for calculation of parameters of erosion in the rock and solid grounds

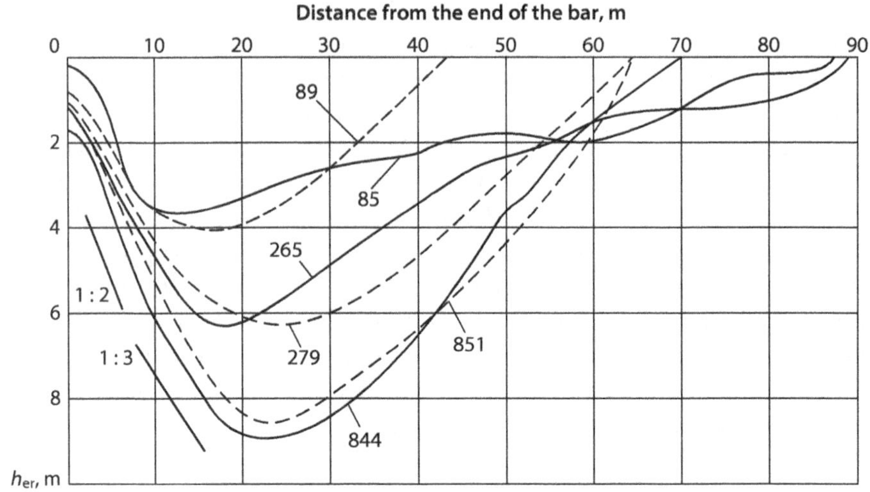

Figure 7.10 Development of the pit erosion over the spillway. The curves indicate the time of the erosion development in hours:

-- in nature; - - - - - on the model.

does not guarantee sufficiently reliable determination of the values, critical for practice. The initial admissions of these dependencies contain significant assumptions, and none of them can provide full preference in comparison with the other; and the results of calculations on them vary considerably. Furthermore, these dependencies were obtained in plain conditions and for the simplest schemes (erosion by a turbulent jet, moving parallel to the bottom, or a jet dropped from a smooth tip of a spillway). Estimations of erosion, for most of them, with significant spaciousness of conditions and complex flow boundaries or evaluation of impact of engineering activities, ensuring the reduction of erosion, are incorrect.

In this situation, there are understandable constant attempts at estimates of erosion in the rock and cohesive grounds using physical modeling. However, due to complexity of the reproduced characteristics of ground mass, influencing erosion (these features are currently not quite accurate identified), experimental evaluation of erosion is purely approximate. The existing methods take into account only some aspects of the interaction between flow and ground, omitting others.

When modeling local erosion in rock and cohesive grounds there are several ways to reproduce ground. Most often it is replaced on the model by the cohesionless material (sand, gravel, crushed stone). This technique is used in both domestic and foreign laboratory practice. As applied to rocky ground one tries to substantiate the validity of this method by the reason that the rock mass endurance fracture occurs and its joints lose their coherency due to dynamic loads caused by water flow.

At the final stage, washout of the bottom of the funnel is usually covered by products from the destruction of rocks, and the sizes lying at the bottom can limit the depth of erosion.

The size of the cohesionless material, that replaces ground mass on the model, is selected on the basis of certain conditions, fulfillment of which, involves similarity of scour depth. When reproducing rocky ground, the dimensions of the cohesionless material particles, are often accepted to be corresponding to the dimensions of the separate elements, for which the rock massif is split by cracks. There are other approaches to determination of the cohesionless material dimensions. For example, the coarseness of this material is chosen in such a way, that the ratio of hydraulic particle size on the model and separate elements of the reproduced massif, was equal to the velocities scale, or so that this scale was equal to the ratio of the noneroding velocities for the ground on the model and in kind, in the conditions of the uniform motion or local erosion in certain standard conditions.

The selection method of cohesionless material for the modeling of cohesive grounds is proposed in [106]. On this proposal, resistance to erosion cohesive ground, characterized by dynamic tensile strength σ_D, size units d and density ρ_s, meets resistance to erosion cohesionless grounds with grain size equal to the size of the units cohesive ground, and with equivalent density:

$$\rho_{sэ}=\rho_s+6\sigma_D/(\pi g d)$$

It is recommended to take $\sigma_D = 2{,}5\,\sigma_p$ (σ_p - static ground tensile strength) and d=3÷5 mm. This "equivalent" cohesionless ground is proposed to be reproduced on the model. Proceeding from the condition:

$$\varphi_2\left(\mathrm{Re}_d\right)\left(\sqrt{\rho + gd}\right)/U = \mathrm{idem}$$

in case of self-similarity on Re_d ([106] for ρ^+=1,65 self-similarity has place when d≥0,5mm) to achieve similarity it is necessary to provide, that:

$$\rho_M^+ d = M^2{}_U \frac{\rho_s - \rho_N}{\rho_N} d_N$$

With significant connectivity to the ground, in order to avoid too large of a particle size and cohesionless material on the model, it is recommended to use material with high density (granulated barite, hematite, light-nets and so on).

In conditions close to the plain, the definition of erosion in a coherent and rocky ground with the right choice of the cohesionless material, sometimes is useful, fairly close to nature. However, in spatial conditions and in particular, the erosion of riverbeds with steep shores, which substantially influence the steepness of natural slopes to make them radically different for the coherent (or rock) and cohesionless grounds, this technique gives misleading results. It should be noted that the conditions of a plane problem of the form of a funnel erosion on the model and in kind may not be the same. This is due both to differences in the steepness of slopes for materials on the model and in kind, and the mismatch of their other characteristics. In [32] it was noted that in certain conditions the pit silt formed dropped jet in fractured or linked material, and may be located closer to the surface than the corresponding hole in the cohesionless material. This fact can be explained by differences in permeability of materials. In the permeable cohesionless material, pressure is averaged by volume. In poorly same permeable material, pressure even in small areas can be distributed significantly unevenly. In particular, the pressure in the space between the jet and a top slope of the crater erosion can be significantly below the pressure at the grassroots surface streams. In case of significant submergence of jets, this results in deviation of the jet in the spillway direction.

Different forms of washout pits in fractured material, reproducing properties of rock massif from that in the cohesionless material, is illustrated by Figure 7.11 Conditions of conducting the relevant experiments are shown at the end of this paragraph. Here we note that with the material, similar to rock, erosion occurs mainly in the area of fall of the jet. In the cohesionless material erosion happens in the fields of currents of high velocity, parallel to the bottom circulation currents near rigid boundaries, etc.

Noting the disadvantages of the method of evaluation of erosion of rock and cohesive ground using cohesionless material, it is necessary to specify its simplicity and mobility, which determines in some cases, the expediency of application of the method for comparative estimation of variants of engineering solutions. The mentioned disadvantages make us to look for the research methods more tightly considering the properties of real soil.

In the study of scours in quasi-homogeneous, non-fractured cohesive grounds, it seems there is a perspective to implement models of artificial easily scouring connected compositions on the basis of sand, plaster and cement binders and some additives.

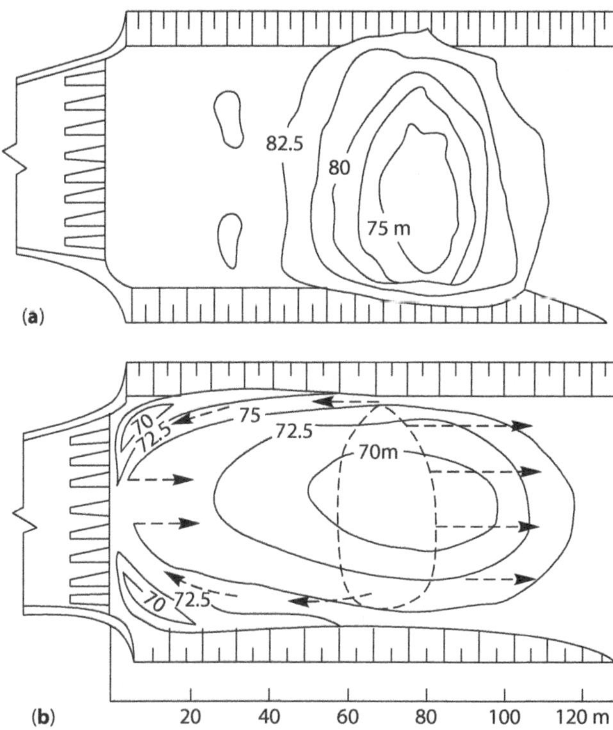

Figure 7.11 Scour, made by the dropped jet in fractured (a) and disjointed (b) materials.

According to [106], forces preventing the cohesive grounds erosion are: pulling ground unit gravity force, characterized by the equivalent diameter d_a ($d_a \approx 3 \div 5$mm); $F_g = g(\rho_s - \rho)\pi d^3_a/6$, adhesive force of the unit with the ground $F_c = \sigma_D d^2_a$, and loading force associated with water pressure in the unit, F_n. The last value, according to the available data, can be neglected. Then in the case of self-similarity in Re_d, the two criteria of similarity should be taken into account:

$$\rho^+ g d_a/U^2 \tag{7.3}$$

$$\sigma_D/(\rho U^2) \tag{7.4}$$

If we assume that the forces F_g and F_c are included in relations, determining erosion, in the form of the sum, the two criteria of similarity can be replaced by one:

$$\frac{(\rho_s - \rho) g \pi d_a/6 + \sigma_D}{\rho U^2} \tag{7.5}$$

Since the values d_a and ρ_s on a model are similar to that in kind, the grip on the model with the identity of the complex (7.5) should be smaller than on the basis of criteria (7.4). Therefore, we use a model with large-scale hydraulic and ground with low connectivity. In connection with the dependence of the properties of artificial songs from their production, to give general recommendations on the formulation of these compositions that meet the specified values σ_D, is not possible. They should be given selection in each particular study.

The study of erosion in the rocky ground is complicated by the anisotropy of its structure, the presence of fracture systems, dismembering the array. In the simplest case, fractured bedrock schematized a set of disjoint blocks and reproduced on the model of the concrete parallelepipeds laid closely to each other. The sizes of these parallelepipeds involve the appropriate size specified separateness of rock massif, and their orientation is the basic system of cracks. This technique has been repeatedly used in domestic [135] and overseas [194] laboratory practice. Model of rock ground, obtained in this way, provides the possibility of the existence of steep slopes and relatively low permeability of the array. Its disadvantages include the following. First, owing to high strength of structural units on the model of their destruction, the process of erosion is excluded, while in kind such destruction occurs. Secondly, due to the lack of links between separate elements, the loss of one separate element results in destabilization of the whole field of the array on the model. Attempt to delete the last drawback can be found in [159] where it is supposed to fill in the gaps with bonding material. However, the gap width recommended is 2 mm, because this width is provided for a maximum of wresting hydrodynamic loads separately. The introduction of binding material significantly approximates qualitative picture of erosion to the reality of erosion of rock ground.

In connection with the fact that rock and cohesive ground are characteristically in areas of high hydrodynamic impacts, there are suggestions to assess rock ground erosion in kind by cohesive ground erosion on the model. This technique is used in some foreign laboratories (for example, in the National hydraulic laboratory of France in Chatou) and in the USSR [7]. As a messenger of the material on the models, we used sand-cement and sand and gypsum composition, causing temporary resistance to compression, which at the moment of carrying out of the experiments was 0.05 - 0.2 MPa. The experiments turn out funnel erosion, often with vertical and even overhanging the slopes. At the bottom of craters is rounded separately-linked material, i.e., the observed pattern is qualitatively similar to that which can be seen in the erosion of rock ground. However, to find the reason for the quantitative determination of the parameters of the pit washout (first of all in its depth), this method does not work. The disadvantages of the method are the lack of similarity to the heterogeneity of the array, non-reproduction of the cracks system and so on. Blurring of the material on the model is destroyed mainly by separation of small units not forming the bar. However, even a qualitative evaluation of pit erosion, in some cases, for example in the task of predicting the slope stability of the narrow canyon, can be very useful. In attempt to overcome some of the shortcomings of the outlined ways of modeling of erosion in the rocky ground, approximate methods of experimental estimation of such erosion are described in [32]. The first is the combination of ways of reproducing the rocky ground with incoherent and coherent materials. Practically this technique is that the shape and position in the erosion well scheme are defined on the model with the riverbed made of sand-cement or sand-plaster solution. The composition of the solution was chosen so that the depth of erosion in it was certainly more than the one corresponding to nature. The erosion pit developed in coherent material is filled with cohesionless material. The size of the cohesionless material is chosen in the same way as for the method of rock erosion assessment based on the erosion in cohesionless material.

At stabilization of erosion, the cohesionless material is placed into the funnel, and from depth of erosion and position of the bar, the water levels are determined.

In the method described above, the combination of the methods eliminates the main shortcomings of each method: distortion of the well form erosion, when using the cohesionless material and uncertainty of the reproduced ground properties, when applying the cohesive material. The second way is that the rocky ground is replaced by the model of a fractured material, reproducing some of the properties of rock massif. Fractured material is obtained from undersized sand and cement mortar. The composition of the solution is adjusted so that its strength corresponded to strength intact rock-scale hydrodynamic pressures $M_{\sigma D}=M_{\rho}M^2_{U}$. The solution is loaded in layers into wooden forms of the largest possible capacity (as far as transport conditions allow). The layers thickness is equal to the distance between the major cracks of one direction. Between the layers of the fresh solution fit the pieces of quicklime, repayment of which leads to the appearance of cracks in the mortar. The wooden casing provides the possibility of deformation of the monolith. Obtained in this way, monoliths prepared the study course.

Scouring of artificial fractured material is regulated by the amount of quicklime, involved in it. Properties of the material are pre-selected in plain conditions so that the depth of erosion in it corresponds to the depth of erosion in the reproduced rock, determined by the most reliable dependencies for the same conditions.

The third technique is different from the second way to set cracks in the ground and bonding of separateness. The model of the array is created from a solution, the strength of which is chosen as in the previous case. To ensure equality of density of the solution and the rocks metal shavings or other heavy fine aggregate are added. Laying solution is made directly on the model of a channel layers, with parallel key cracks closest to the horizontal plane. The thickness of the layers corresponds to the distance between the cracks of this direction. The surface layer is smeared with machine oil. The thickness of a layer of grease is regulated by the adhesion between the layers defined in the samples. Each layer before its hardening, is dissected separately in the direction of major cracks using special knives.

We present the studies of the erosion due to the dropped riverbed jet in the downstream of the Naglu (Afghanistan) and El Mate (Cuba) [32] hydrosystems as the examples of application of the proposed modeling techniques.

Erosion in the hydrosystem downstream of the Naglu river, Kabul, the channel of which is made of granites (the limit of the time compression resistance is of about 100 MPa), divided in the upper layers on blocks with the volume of about 1 m^3, was estimated on the model in scale 1:50 with the first two methods, described above. When using one of them, the bed of one of them was formed of the sandy-cement mortar with the ration of the cement mass to the sand mass 1:30. Temporary resistance of this solution to compression, at the moment of carrying out of the experiments (in 3 days after forming the channel), was about 0.1 MPa.

When reset, consistently increasing up to a maximum expenditure of water, the solution formed a clear pit washout (Figure 7.12). After stabilization of erosion, in the funnel there was laid granite gravel to the level corresponding with the level of household surface of the rock. The size of gravel (approximately 17 mm) was selected on the basis of equality to the hydraulic size of separate rock scale velocity ($M_U = M_l^{0,5} \approx 1{:}7$). The depth of erosion in the gravel, laid down in the crater, turned out to be considerably less than the depth of erosion in skinny solution that is connected, in particular, and with the education of the bar (Figure 7.12).

When using other reception, the temporary limit resistance to compression artificial material had to be:

$$\sigma_{.M} = \sigma_{.N} M_\rho M^2_U = 2MPa$$

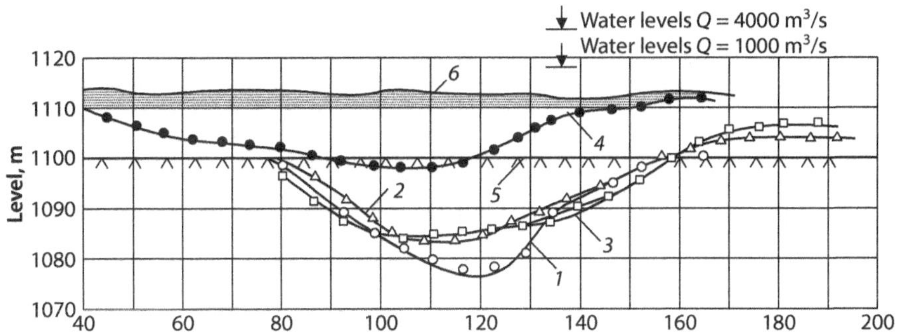

Figure 7.12 The longitudinal profile of the erosion funnel in the downstream of the Naglu HPP:

1 - in the coherent material; 2 - in the cohesionless material; 3- in the fractured material; 4 - in nature when Q=1000 m^3/s; 5 - natural rock surface; 6 - the same for alluvium.

This corresponds to a sand and cement mortar with a ratio of cement mass to the mass of sand 1:10, with water-cement ratio 1:5. The number of input quicklime, were chosen on the basis of matching the depth of erosion in plain conditions in rejection of the jet with the smooth sock, calculated by the formula M.S. Vyzgo [34], and the depth of erosion in artificial material in the same conditions. At specific discharge q=80 m^2/s and the difference of water levels z=70 m, excluding jet aeration depth of water in the pit of washout $h_{er.N} = k_\Sigma \sqrt{q\sqrt{z}} = 40\,m$ (*on model*- 0.8 m). Such depth worked in a plain tray with the introduction of a solution of about 5% by weight of quicklime. In Figure 7.13 it is possible to note quite close agreement outlines funnels washout when using two techniques.

In the evaluation of the erosion over the spillway of the waterworks, El Mate used the third technique. The bottom of the tailrace here is composed of clayey limestone with σ_N =25 MPa.

Depth array splits into layers of 40-50 cm. height and divided by vertical cracks. When the geometric model scale 1:40 requires that σ_M ~0.6 MPa. Relevant material was obtained on the basis of sand (45 parts), building plaster (9 parts) and cement (part 1) with the addition of the sulfite-alcohol liguor. Introduction of engine oil between the layers of the cliff model has provided the linkage between them, equal to approximately 0.02 MPa. Layers of artificial material were cut with knives on separate elements, relevant to units of the rock in kind. Estimations of erosion with the use of artificial material and cohesionless ground was different (see Figure 7.11).

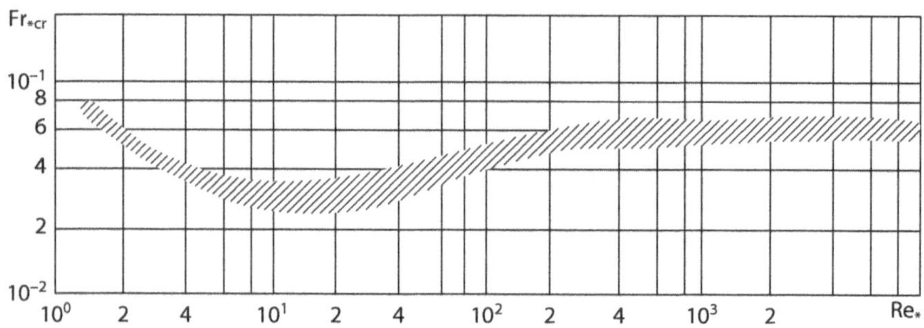

Figure 7.13 The relationship between the Fr_{*cr} and Re_*. [181]

Application of the suggested methods of experimental determination of erosion of the rock bed allows us to obtain an estimate of the local erosion. When conducting research, it is advisable to use several methods that take into account different characteristic effects of the phenomenon.

7.4 Alluvial River-Bed Planned Deformations

Let's consider the case of study of deformations of the channel, formed of the cohesionless material, the development of which is determined not so much by changing of turbulence and transverse circulation in the stream (spatial effects), but by redistribution in terms of medium-depth velocities, i.e., the case for which the flow is quite well described by an equation of the planned hydraulics. Such channel deformations will be called routine.

In this case, to achieve the semblance of phenomena, in addition to the similarity arising from the analysis of the equations planned hydraulics, the condition of similarity that follows from the equation of longitudinal balance of sediments should be satisfied:

$$\frac{\partial Q_s}{\partial x}+b\frac{\partial \eta_b}{\partial t_{\text{def}}}=0, \tag{7.6}$$

where Q_s - consumption of load on the runway width b; x is the coordinate along the course; η_b - coordinate of the surface of the bottom; t_{def} - time deformation of the riverbed. The deposit discharge Q_s can be obtained from the equation of motion of a solid phase, including first approximation characteristics of the water flow. When determining influence the solid phase is not considered. In engineering, estimates are possible to replace the equation of motion for the solid phase by the relation that binds the flow of sediments and parameters of the water flow obtained for the conditions for uniform flow (dependence for carrying capacity). There are lots of such dependencies.

Based on the analysis of dimensions of many researchers (see, for example, [181]) put dimensionless specific consumption of sediment $q_* = q_s/(\rho_s U_* d)$, (here $q_s = \rho_s Q_s/b$, $U_* = \sqrt{\tau/\rho} = \sqrt{ghI_{fr}}$, τ is the shear stress at the bottom in dependence on the value:

$$\mathrm{Fr}_* = \frac{1}{\rho^+}\frac{h}{d}I_{fr} = \frac{1}{\rho^+}\frac{U_*^2}{gd} = \frac{\tau}{(\rho_s - \rho)d}$$

and

$$\mathrm{Re}_* = \sqrt{ghI_{fr}}\, d/\nu = U_* d/\nu.$$

In [181] it is shown that many of the known empirical and semi-empirical relationships for the q_s can be reduced to dependency on these dimensionless complexes. For sufficiently large values of Re_*, there is self-similarity in this complex, allowing to perform modeling in cases, when the nature of the sediment grain size is large enough, as noted in section 7.1. The most empirical and modern semiempirical dependencies for q_s can be represented in the form of links specific consumption of sediments with respect to hydraulic flow parameters (average velocity U, shear stress at the bottom τ, dynamic velocity U_* "attractive power" ghI_{fr}). Critical ("standard") values of these quantities are in typical situations of sediment transport (the beginning of the motion of sediment, the transition in solid attraction, the beginning of particles and so on). More commonly used meanings, refer to the beginning of the motion of particles, for example "noneroding velocity," average depth velocity U_{cr}. As

$$\bar{U} = \sqrt{\frac{2}{\lambda}}U_* = \sqrt{\frac{2}{\lambda}\frac{\tau}{\rho}} = \sqrt{\frac{2ghI_{fr}}{\lambda}} \tag{7.7}$$

then

$$\frac{\bar{U}}{\bar{U}_{cr}} = \frac{U_*}{U_{*cr}} = \sqrt{\frac{\tau}{\tau_{cr}}} = \sqrt{\frac{ghI_{fr}}{(ghI_{fr})_{cr}}} \tag{7.8}$$

and conditions $\bar{U}/\bar{U}_{cr}$ = idem; τ/τ_{cr} = idem; $ghI_{fr}/(ghI_{fr})_{cr}$ = idem are equivalent.

Of the many dependencies specific to consumption of sediment, this structure will point out some formulas, belonging to the Russian scientists, containing the ratio of velocity of flow and velocity of load (to create the generality of these formulas, several are converted in comparison with their originals):

I.I.Levi [75]

$$q_s = K_L d\ \bar{U}_{cr}\ \rho^{+}(\bar{U}/\bar{U}_{cr})^3(\bar{U}/\bar{U}_{cr}-1)\, f(d/h) \tag{7.9}$$

V.N.Goncharov [42]

$$q_s = K_G d\ \ \bar{U}_{cr}[(\bar{U}/\bar{U}_{cr})^3-1](\bar{U}/\bar{U}_{cr}-1) \tag{7.10}$$

K.V.Grishanin [43]

$$q_s = K_{Gr} d\ \ \bar{U}_{cr}(\bar{U}/\bar{U}_{cr})^3(\bar{U}/\bar{U}_{cr}-1) \tag{7.11}$$

Pay attention to the fact that these equations do not include the values that characterize the viscosity of fluid. As will be shown below, the effect of viscosity is taken into account in the size of the U_{cr}.

Now, we substitute the dependence of q_s in the form of I. I. Levy (with the form according to the subsequent, conclusions do not change) in the equation of longitudinal alluviums balance (7.6):

$$\frac{\partial}{\partial x}\left(K_L d\ \rho^{+}\bar{U}_{\mathrm{cr}}\left(\frac{\bar{U}}{\bar{U}_{cr}}\right)^4\right) f\left(\frac{d}{h}\right) - \frac{\partial}{\partial x}\left(K_L d\ \rho^{+}\bar{U}_{\mathrm{cr}}\left(\frac{\bar{U}}{\bar{U}_{\mathrm{cr}}}\right)^3\right) f\left(\frac{d}{h}\right) \cdot$$

$$+\frac{\partial \eta_b}{\partial t_{\mathrm{def}}} = 0 \tag{7.12}$$

After the normalization of this equation, we get the following similarity conditions:

$$\bar{U}/\bar{U}_{cr} = \mathrm{idem} \tag{7.13}$$

and

$$\frac{lh}{t_{\mathrm{def}}\, d\ \rho^{+}\bar{U}_{\mathrm{cr}}\ \ f\left(d/h\right)} = \mathrm{idem} \tag{7.14}$$

The condition (7.14) determines the time scale deformations:

$$M_{t_{\text{def}}} = \frac{M_l M_h}{M_d M_{f\ (d/h)} M_\rho + M\bar{U}_{cr}} \tag{7.15}$$

If the condition (7.13) ($M_{\bar{U}}=M_{\bar{U}cr}$), and when $\rho^+_{\text{M}}=\rho^+_{\text{N}}(M_{\rho+}=1)$ and $M_d=M_h(M_{f(\text{d/h})}=1)$

$$M_{tdef}=M_l/M_{\bar{U}}$$

i.e., the time scale deformations channel M_{tdef}, only in this case, are equal to the time scale hydraulic processes M_t. The condition (7.13) was many times proposed as a condition of riverbed deformations similarity (U/U_{cr} simplex is sometimes called the Lewy criterion) since, among other factors, in the absence of sediments load its fulfillment at $U/U_{\text{cr}} \leq 1$ assures the riverbed stability both actually and on a model, while at $U/U_{\text{cr}} \geq 1$ the compared flows riverbed erosion occurs.

Let us now focus on noneroding velocity U_{cr}. In the modern view, the motion of particles of the cohesionless material begins after dynamic velocity reaches a certain value U_{*cr}. The Shields [181]:

$$\frac{U^2_{*\,\text{cr}}}{\rho^+ gd} = \text{Fr}_{*\text{cr}} = f\left(\beta_{\phi 1}, \beta_{\phi 2}, \beta_{\phi 3}, \text{Re}_{*\text{cr}} = U_{*\text{cr}}\, d/\nu\right),$$

where values $\beta_{\varphi 1}$, $\beta_{\varphi 2}$, $\beta_{\varphi 3}$, take into account the influence of the geometric shape of a particle and its provisions on the bottom. The influence of these values is assumed secondary. Then

$$U_{*\text{cr}} = f\left(\text{Re}_{*\text{cr}}\right)\sqrt{\rho^+ gd}. \tag{7.16}$$

Dependence $\text{Fr}_{*\text{cr}}$ from $\text{Re}_{*\text{cr}}$ shown in Figure 7.12, from which it follows that for sufficiently large values of $\text{Re}_{*\text{cr}}$ is self-similar in this complex. However, in complex $\text{Re}_{*\text{cr}}$ is defined value U_{*cr}, and in this task, it is not determinative. It is better to use the following relationship for the critical values of the dynamic velocity [76]:

$$U_{*\text{cr}} = \varphi\left(\text{Re}_{*\text{cr}}\right)\sqrt{\rho^+ gd}.$$

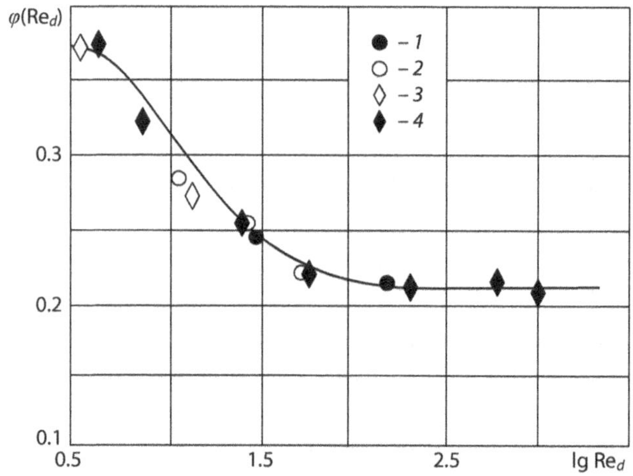

Figure 7.14 The function $\varphi(Re_d)$, formed on the results of the beginning of the particles motion study:

1 - quartz sand in the air;
2 - the same in water;
3 - acrylic powder in water;
1-3 - the authors's data;
4 - the same of V.S. Knoroz [65]

where $\mathrm{Re}_d = d\sqrt{\rho^+ gd}/\nu$, The function $\varphi(Re_d)$ is depicted in Figure 7.13 Here, along with the results of the experiments described in [65], the experimental data of the authors has been included. It can be noted that all points lie on the curve V.S. Knoroz. Results of experiments in compliance with this curve differ substantially in the value of $p+$ (quartz particles in the water and in the air, acrylic powder in water), showing that in the studied range of values of the size of particles ($d \geq 0.2$ mm), the variability in the range specified Re_d function $\varphi(Re_d)$ is primarily driven by the effect of viscosity, not the forces of molecular cohesion, as stated in [106]. From the graph in Figure 7.13 we see that at $Re_d \geq Re_{dlim}$300 has a self-similar magnitude $\varphi(Re_d)$ on Re_d. In a similar area, this value is approximately equal to 0.22.

According to Iwagaki [36a], there are two areas of self-similarity factor $\varphi(\mathrm{Re}_d)$ - for small and large numbers Re_d: $\varphi(\mathrm{Re}_d)$ =0,376 when $\mathrm{Re}_d \leq 2{,}1$ and $\varphi''(\mathrm{Re}_d)=0{,}225$ when $\mathrm{Re}_d \geq 670$.

Express noneroding velocity $\bar{U}_{cr}$, through critical dynamic velocity $\bar{U}_{*cr}$:

$$\bar{U}_{cr} = \sqrt{2/\lambda}U_{*cr} = \varphi(\mathrm{Re}_d)\sqrt{2\rho^+ gd/\lambda_h}$$

or, taking into account that $2/\lambda \approx C^2/g$ (C - Chezy coefficient),

$$\bar{U}_{cr} = \varphi(\mathrm{Re}_d) C \sqrt{\rho^+ d}$$

If taken according to Manning C= $(1/n)h^{1/6}$, then:

$$\bar{U}_{cr} = \frac{\varphi(\mathrm{Re}_d)}{n} h^{1/16} \sqrt{\rho^+ d} \tag{7.17}$$

With h=1 m, we have:

$$\bar{U}_{cr1} = \frac{\varphi(\mathrm{Re}_d)}{n} \sqrt{\rho^+ d} \tag{7.18}$$

The value $\bar{U}_{cr1}$ depends only on the properties of the deposits and fluid. From (7.17) and (7.18), the known dependence of V.N. Goncharov should be:

$$\bar{U}_{cr} = \bar{U}_{cr1} \; h^{1/6} \tag{7.19}$$

Then the condition (7.13) can be written in the form:

$$M_U = M_{Ucr} = M_{Ucr1} M^{1/6}_h$$

If the Froude rule is satisfied:

$$M_U = M^{1/2}_h$$

Therefore, for simultaneous fulfillment of the Froude rules and conditions (7.13), it is necessary that:

$$M_h = M^3_{Ucr1}$$

Proceeding from (7.17), you could choose a fairly small vertical geometric scale model of a movable direction in the study of his scheduled deformations through the appointment of small scale values of p+ and d. However, these values for certain values Re_d influence on the values $\varphi(Re_d)$. For particles with ρ_s =2650 kg/m³ in the water, Re_d corresponds d_{lim} =1,5 mm. Below the boundary derivative $\partial \bar{U}_{cr1}/\partial d$ begins to dramatically

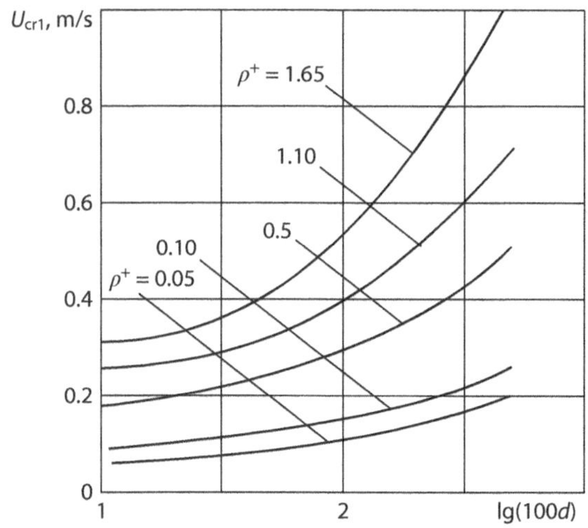

Figure 7.15 Dependence of noneroding velocities of particles with different densities from their diameters, mm, at a depth of 1 m.

decrease (Figure 7.15), so when $d \leq 0.2$ mm U_{cr1} practically does not depend on d. When used on hydraulic model of the natural sands $[(\bar{U}_{cr1})_{min} \approx 0{,}3 m/s]$, a reasonable scale model can be ensured only if there is a large enough load in kind, for example, on model with vertical geometric scale of 1: 50, it is possible to study the object for which $d_н > 4$ mm.

Due to the influence of viscosity reduction, permissible vertical scale of the model by reducing the density of particles of sediment is not as much as it may seem at first glance. For the light material, viscosity starts to affect at higher values of d, for example, if ρ_{SM} =kg/m³ and ρ_M=1100 kg/m³ very weakly depends on d: $d \leq$ 0.4-:-0.5mm $(\bar{U}_{cr1})_{min} \approx 0.13$ m/s. In case of in-kind direction composed of fine-grained sands ($\bar{U}_{cr1N} \approx 0.3$ m/s) when using plastic powders vertical scale model, designed by the Froude rule, should not be less:

$$M_h = (0.13/0.3)^3 \approx 1/12$$

The evaluations are related to the noneroding velocity in the plain bottom of the stream. In actual practice the motion of sediments on the bottom of the stream causes local buildups formation resulting in $(U_{cr1})_{min}$ reduction due to roughness coefficient n increase and Re_{db} decrease. Systematic research in this field is not available, however, to estimate, we can assume that because of the differences between a channel from a plain value, it can be reduced by about 20%. Then, for the most thin materials used on the model, U_{cr1} can be considered close to 0.1 m/s, and in the study of deformations of fine sand bottoms, the minimum vertical scale model -1:30 to 1:40.

The presented approach approximates modeling of river-bed deformations on the basis of conditions (7.13), instead conditions Re_d=idem, ρ^+=idem, d/h=idem (see Section 7.1) is a typical example of the use of distorted models, for which the main criterion of similarity is a combination of criteria in the more general case (Section 3.4). It provides the opportunity to provide an approximate similarity to scheduled deformations of sandy bottoms at relatively large, but in some cases acceptable geometric scale models with the use of thin materials. These materials are widely used in the practice of hydraulic laboratories.

The ways of complying with the condition (7.13) by choosing $U_{\text{сr'ы}}$. as the value have been considered above. The possibility of this condition at a given vertical scale model by selecting an appropriate zoom rate M_u is limited by the need to ensure the identity of the Froude criterion. With relatively small values Fr_N (if self-similarity of nature on Fr) there is some freedom of choice M_{u} due to distortion of the model on the Froude criterion. This applies to case studies on short sections of rivers, in which the increase of the model velocity against certain Froude rule does not lead to significant distortions of differential levels within the study area. If the reproduced area on the model is of considerable length, at the decision of the planned tasks when necessary, equality of the coefficients of the resistance of the longest in kind and on the model ($\lambda l/h$ = idem), and even slightly higher velocities than defined under the Froude rule, lead to the significant exaggeration of the difference of levels of the free surface and therefore distortion of the flow depth. Until recently, this defect sometimes tried to exclude the increase of the longitudinal slope of the bottom of the model (sloping model with movable bottom). However, this may be of interest only with the solution of one-dimensional tasks. In the scheduled task for which the ratio of longitudinal and transverse slopes significantly, this technique is unusable. This has resulted in it not being used in recent years.

Much more perspectives to satisfy the condition (7.13) by setting the appropriate scale M_u provide application for studies of the river-bed deformations of pressure models with movable bottom (see Section 7.6).

When modeling, the riverbed deformations should adhere to the conditions of similarity fluid flow. In the case study of scheduled deformations, these include the condition $\lambda l/h$ = idem. Models with a movable bottom, compared with a rigid model, are extremely complicated by the estimation of the $\lambda_м$, which is determined not only by geometrical characteristics of flow and material channel, as is the case in rigid models.

Resistance of the movable riverbed along with grainy coarseness is determined by bottom-dwelling forms (riffles, ridges, dunes, and so on), and failure of some researchers [76, 181] to take account of this fact, comparing on the model and in kind only bottom grainy coarseness, which can lead to significant errors.

Based on available literature, dependencies to determine the size of the bottom ridges fulfillment of the conditions of similarity scheduled deformations, it would seem, should not lead to a significant distortion of the shape of the bottom of the model.

Thus, in [65]

$$\frac{h_r}{h} = 3.5\,\frac{1-\dfrac{1}{\bar{U}\;/\bar{U}_{\mathrm{cr}}}}{\lg\left(h/\bar{d}\;\right)+6}; \tag{7.20}$$

$$\frac{l_r}{h_r} = 2.8\frac{\bar{U}\;/\bar{U}_{\mathrm{cr}}}{\bar{U}\;/\bar{U}_{\mathrm{cr}}\;-1}, \tag{7.21}$$

where h_r - ridge height; l_r - its length.

In [115], where formation of ridges in natural and artificial materials has been studied, results of the experiments (Figure 7.16) were summarized by the following dependence:

$$\frac{h_r}{h} = 1.25\left(\frac{\bar{U}}{\bar{U}_{\mathrm{cr}}}\frac{\bar{d}}{h}\frac{\mathrm{w}}{\sqrt{gh}}\right)^{1/15} \tag{7.22}$$

Experience in the use of models with movable bottom shows that under the condition (7.14) run-of-river forms on model may not correspond to those in nature, and on the model they are expressed much sharper. Based on the dependencies (7.20) and (7.21), the main reason for the discrepancy between the height of the ridges on the model can be the non-identity simplex *d/h*. At the same time the dependence (7.20) considers the impact of this condition on distortion of ridges dimensions as incidental. Significant influence of simplex *d/h* is formed by calculation on (7.22).

In [226] it was indicated that characteristics of the bottom of the forms along with the complex $Fr_*/Fr_{*cr}=\bar{U}/\bar{U}_{cr}$ significantly influenced Re_{*cr} and *d/h*. In order to avoid significant distortions of the bottom of the form

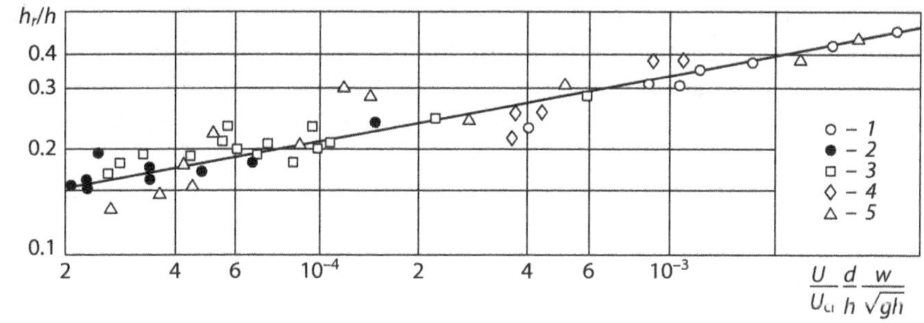

Figure 7.16 Dependence of the relative height of the ridge from the complex.
$\frac{U}{U_{cr}}\frac{d}{h}\frac{w}{\sqrt{gh}}$: 1 - polystyrene; 2-bakelite; 3 - quartz sand d=0.67 mm; 4 - the same for d=0.25 mm;
5 - field data.

when modeling sandy bottoms in [226], it is recommended to accept on model Re_*>25 (which defines the minimum value of d_M) and d/h >50 (which determines the minimum vertical scale model). It is clear that this recommendation is suitable only when modeling a relatively large ground. Actually, when studying scheduled deformations, it is necessary to prevent the distortion of the size of the ridges, offsetting the higher coefficient of hydraulic friction geometric distortion of the scale model.

In some works, for example in [53], characteristics of ridges are made conditional on the Froude number, as evidenced by some correlation between these characteristics and Fr on experimental data. The identified dependence is natural for a turbulent flow, in which such structures as antidunes are formed. For low flows, if to proceed from considerations and facts set forth in section 5.2, this correlation may seem unexpected. In this case, influence of the Froude number can be explained if we consider the stream bottom as the moving boundary between two continual environments. As is known, characteristics of such boundaries are defined by values of criteria, similar to the modified Froude number: $Fr_\rho = \frac{\rho' - \rho''}{\rho''}\frac{U_0^2}{gh_0}$ (ρ' and ρ" - density environments). In connection with the fact that when mapping of threads usually $(\rho' - \rho'')/\rho'' = (\rho_s - \rho)/\rho = const$ (in all cases, the bottom is composed of quartz sand), the influence of the modified Froude number Fr_ρ may manifest as the influence of the conventional Froude number $Fr = U_0^2/gh_0$.

At the present state, the question of the resistance of the channel on the model design can be estimated only approximately. You can do this in the first approximation to use the dependence of (5.8), determining the parameters of the ridges in the example this chapter references.

However, evaluation of the resistance of the channel model is more reliable to perform in conditions of experiment, when it is possibly close to the alleged in the case study.

The scale of the flow of sediments M_{Qs} time and channel deformation $M_{tdef} = M_h M_l / M_{Qs}$ can be, in the first approximation, chosen based on the dependencies for transport lapsed ability [for example, formulas (7.9) - (7.11)]. But it is better to determine these scale values directly using a model. For this purpose the sediments load at the model intake is varied and it is necessary to choose the sediments load value that assures maintenance of the predetermined depths on the model. This is done at selected geometric scale values and liquid discharge scale ratio at known common conditions of the riverbed. This value is taken as Q_{SM}. Comparing Q_{SM} with discharge of sediment in nature, known by results of hydrological studies, or assessed by calculation, we get M_{Qs} and then M_{tdef}.

7.5 The Ratio of the River-Bed Averaged Characteristics in Nature and on the Model

The main characteristics of the rivers in this area of the river, along with geological features of the valley, with the characteristics of vegetation on the floodplain and in the course, depend on the properties of the sediment formed above the study area, the quantity and water consumption. Usually it is considered that the channel is formed by costs, close to the costs of its edges (bed-formation, or the dominant expenses), although there is information that the channel formed by this consumption is not fully consistent with the channel corresponding to a variable flow. If the concept of bed-formation of consumption is fair, in the process of formation of a channel, we are given water flow Q, flow of sediment $Q_{s,}$ and their properties (grain size d, density ρ_s and other characteristics). Hydraulic slope I_{fr}, average depth $-h$, and width of a channel b depend on them. To define these three quantities, there are two equations:
the equation of motion of water:

$$Q = Q\left(d, \bar{h}\ , b, I_{\text{fr}}\right) \tag{7.23}$$

and the equation of sediment transport:

$$Q_s = Q_s\left(d, \bar{h},\ b, \rho, \rho_s, Q\right). \tag{7.23a}$$

For closure of the system we need to have one more equation. However, currently there is no such a physically reasonable equation. In this quality, different authors propose certain empirical relations, often the so-called morphometric dependencies, obtained in the result of processing of the data of field observations and laboratory experiments. As follows from these dependences, with increase in the absolute amount of the cross-section of the stream or water content of the river, the ratio of the channel width and its average depth increases.

Thus, according to Rybkin [136]:

$$bd / \bar{h} = k_1 \quad or \quad b / \bar{h} = k_1 \bar{h} / d; \tag{7.24}$$

according to Leisi [188]:

$$b = k_2 Q^{0.5} \quad \text{or} \quad b / \bar{h} = k_2 I_{fr}^{1/2} \bar{h}^{-2/3} / n^{1/2}; \tag{7.25}$$

according to Galstunskiy [36]:

$$b = k_3 Q^{0.56} / I_{\text{fr}}^{0.16} \quad \text{or} \quad \text{b} / \bar{h} = k_3^{0.23} I_{\text{fr}}^{1/2} \bar{h}^{-1.25} / n^{1.25}; \tag{7.26}$$

according to Altunin [3]:

$$bd/h^2 = k_1 \quad \text{or} \quad b/\bar{h} = k_4^{1/m} \bar{h}^{1/m-1}, \tag{7.27}$$

where, depending on scouring of shores and mobility, channel k_4 varies from 8 to 20, and m - is from 1 to 0.5. When m =0.5 (alluvial plain of the river), this dependence is written in the following form:

$$b = k_5 Q^{0.55} I_{\text{fr}}^{0.275} \quad \text{or} \quad b / \bar{h} \approx k_5^{2.22} \bar{h} / n^{1.22}. \tag{7.28}$$

N.A. Rzhanicyn [127], arranging rivers depending on the water content, places the relative width of a channel in dependence from the river's position in the series.

The first attempt to get morphometric connection with the theory of dimensions belongs to M.A. Velikanov [27]. Believing that Q, d, g, I_{fr}, b, h should be involved in the relation, he has come to the following result:

$$\frac{b}{h}=k_8\left(\frac{Q}{d^2\sqrt{gd}\sqrt{I_{\text{fr}}}}\right)^m \qquad (7.29)$$

In this dependence, same as in many other morphometric relationships the hydraulic slope I_{fr} is included into monovalents. However, in many cases, it is not included in the conditions of the problem, and at the same time, these conditions include the flow of sediments Q_s. If in such cases, the effect of viscosity and honors composition of materials is ignored, and forms a channel and shores, the communication should include the values Q_s, Q, d, ρ_s, ρ, g, b, h, I_{fr}, the first six of which are specified. Then, based on Pi theorem:

$$b/d=k_7 f\left[\bar{h}/d,\rho_s/\rho,\mu_8,Q^2/\left(gd^5\right),I_{\text{fr}}\right], \qquad (7.30)$$

where $\mu_s = Q_s/Q$ - turbidity thread; π -members based, (7.29) can be considered as criteria of similarity, where the ρ_s/ρ, $\mu_{,,}$ Q^2/gd^5 criteria are determinative ones as they are composed of monovalents. In case of these criteria identity we can achieve the identity of other (non-determinative) criteria and similarity of the phenomenon. In particular the b/h=idem condition should be fulfilled.

Condition ρ_s/ρ=idem, for the comparison between natural watercourses, is usually performed as in kind so that ρ_s varies slightly. Turbidity flows can vary significantly. So the rivers, characterized by different turbidity, under other equal conditions, should have direction different forms. For example, the Amu Darya in the middle reaches and the Eye are characterized by approximately the same sediment and bed-formation expenses, but the turbidity of water in the Amu Darya is significantly more than in the eye. Therefore, the slope and the relative width of the Amudarya are far more than the Oka.

The effect of turbidity in the form of a channel indirectly reflects the proposed I. Y. Orlov [3] the dependence of the exponent m in formula (7.27) of the criterion of stability of a channel:

$$M=(\bar{U}/\bar{U}_{cr})^{-0,1}$$

The more $\bar{U}/\bar{U}_{cr}$ (and consequently, more μ_s), the smaller m and the more b/h.

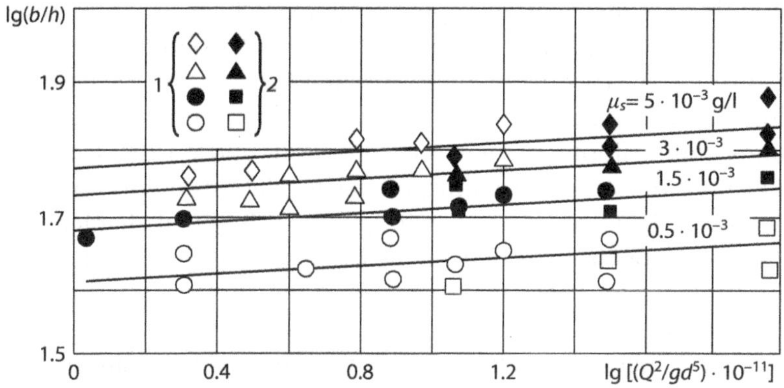

Figure 7.17 Relationship between the relative channel width, complex Q^2/gd^5, and concentration of sediments μ_s: 1 - pressure flow; 2 - non-pressure flow.

Condition Q^2/gd^5=idem for rivers of various sizes are usually not performed, and the shape of their channels can be harmful also for this reason. On this basis, for the conditions to achieve similarity to those of the maps of the rivers, the water content of which is bigger, the load should be larger. However, the nature of the major rivers is usually characterized by the most fine sediment.

From the above analysis it follows that the forms of the cross-sections of the riverbeds belonging to rivers with different water content are not similar since their similarity conditions are not observed in nature.

We attempted to establish the dependence of the relative width of the b/h channel from the defining criteria Q^2/gd^5 and μ_s to watercourses, the shores are of the same broken material as the bottom. Experiments were performed for the study of the development of the pioneer slot at a constant supply of sediment to the pressure and pressure installations. These experiments are shown on the chart, placed in Figure 7.17 Here it can be noted that the experimental points related to different values of turbidity are clearly stratified. As you might expect, ceteris paribus increase in turbidity ratio b/h is growing, and more sharply, than according to I.Y. Orlov.

Data related to the pressure and gravity flows practically coincided. This is obviously due to the fact that in a very rough line the influence of the smooth cover of the pressure of the installation was not significant.

Processing of experimental data has led to the following morphometric relation:

$$b/h^{-} = 63\bar{\mu}_s^{0,17}\left(Q^2/gd^5\right)^{0,033} \tag{7.31}$$

The above considerations apply to alluvial beds with homogeneous geological structure and small influence of vegetation on their formation. In nature the riverbed formation is influenced both by vegetation and by geological heterogeneity of the riverbed, in particular the difference of grounds composition on the riverbed bottom and on the shore. All this should affect the structure of morphometric relationships as noted by M.A. Velikanov [27]. However, he does not put the values that characterize these additional factors in their dependencies. In formula (7.27) such influence indirectly takes into account the fact that the coefficient R_4 is connected with the smearing of shores.

There are suggestions about direct accounting of the shores scouring. [5] in the stable channel velocity equals noneroding velocities for ground composing the shore: $\bar{U}/\bar{U}_{cr.\delta}=1$. Recommendations on the evaluation of the velocity $U_{cr.\delta}$, in conditions of lateral erosion, is not equal to the corresponding value when there is washout of the bottom, thus it is not given.

The same approach is described in [200], where it is supposed, that on a coastal hillside, shear stress $\tau_{=}\ \tau_{kp.\delta}$ ($\tau_{kp.\delta}$ - valid shear stress for the ground, forming a slope). In [190] the ratio between critical shearing stresses on the banks $\tau_{cr.\delta}$ and on the horizontal bottom $\tau_{cr.}$ is obtained:

$$\tau_{cr.\delta} = \tau_{cr} \cos\Phi\sqrt{1-\left(tg\,\Phi/tg\,\varphi\right)^2}$$

where Φ is the angle of the slope, and φ is the angle of repose of the ground.

In [189] an attempt was made to identify the distribution of tangential stresses on the surface of trapezoidal channel. Knowing the distribution of stresses and believing on the slopes of coast $\tau = \tau_{cr.\delta}$, you can find a third dependence linking the middle section properties of a channel.

These proposals for the consideration of the shores scouring are also not universal. They are not appropriate for the same material of the bottom and shores, when the balance of shores is dynamic in nature, i.e. under-adopted through the exchange of particles between the coast and the flow. In these cases, on the slope of the coast can be $\tau > \tau_{kp.\delta.}$ But in most cases, the geological structure of the bottom and shores are sharply different.

As discussed in Section 7.4, when modeling the sandy bottoms usually: $h/d \neq$idem (scale particle size of the sediment is not equal to the geometric scale model). As a consequence, not executed are conditions Q^2/gd^5=idem and μ_s=idem.

The relative width smotrimenya channel on the model $(b/h)_M$, is less than $(b/h)_H$, i.e. violation of the terms of similarity leads to the distortion of the shape of the channel that should be considered when prescribing scale model of a movable course, otherwise, the stream on the model may be the wrong size, in the assumption which built the model. This is sometimes done on the basis of available morphometric dependency [3, 27]. Modeling in which the similarity conditions are obtained using morphometric dependency is called natural. Some researchers, based on the fact that a small channel has a lower relative width, appoint a geometric distortion of scale on the basis of morphological dependencies and for models with rigid bottom. It is clear that to shape models, natural modeling is not irrelevant.

Sometimes mistakes are made when using known methods of natural modeling. The mistakes occur since the same dependences are used for natural river beds and for laboratory streams.

Thus, in [3] on the basis of dependence $b^{0,5}/h=k_4$, it is assumed that $M^{0,5}_b=M_h$. Even if we assume that the structure is used, according to what is fair for lowland rivers in kind and their models in the laboratory, coefficients k_4 have different values. For lowland rivers $k_4 \approx 12$, and for alluvial rivers with depth of up to 10 cm and sediment characterized $d = 0{,}2 \div 0{,}5$ mm, according to the data of K. I. Rossinsky, $k_4 \sim 36$. The difference is explained by the lack of commonality of communication, and the fact that models are usually not reproducing the structure of the shores and vegetation.

In order to take into account the mentioned circumstances, when using formula (7.27), the indicator of similarity should be written as $M^{0,5}_b$ $(M_K M_h)$ [177]. This entry provides only an approximation and not the kind of phenomenon.

Consider the choice of geometrical distortions of scale (M_b/M_h), proceeding from (7.31). This dependence

$$\frac{M_b}{M_h} = M^{0,17}_{\mu_s} \frac{M_Q^{0,066}}{M_d^{0,165}} \tag{7.32}$$

Subject to the Froude rule $M_Q=M^{1,5}_h M_b$. If you take formula (7.10) to evaluate μ_s, which can be written as:

$$\mu_s = \frac{K_L}{\bar{h}} \frac{\bar{U}}{(gd)^3} \left(1 - \frac{\bar{U}_{cr}}{\bar{U}}\right) \left(\frac{d}{\bar{h}}\right)^{0,25}$$

Then with $M_U = M^{0,5}{}_h$:

$$M_{\mu s} = M^{0.75}{}_h / M^{1,25}{}_d$$

After the substitution of expressions for M_Q, $M_{\mu s}$ in (7.32) have:

$$\frac{M_b}{M_h} = \frac{M_h^{0,33}}{M_d^{0,39}} = \frac{1}{M_d^{0,06}} \left(\frac{M_h}{M_d} \right)^{0,35}$$

Given the low degree at M_d and usually small difference of the scale of the unit, as well as proximity used empirical dependencies, you can write:

$$M_b / M_h \approx (M_h / M_d)^{0,33}$$

Now we turn attention to the fact that if you take for Chezy coefficient of a power dependence. $C = k_c (h/d)^{1/6}$, the scale factor hydraulic friction $M_\lambda = \frac{1}{M^2{}_{kc}} \left(M_d / M_h \right)^{0,33}$ and a plain bottom:

$$M_b / M_h \approx 1 / M_\lambda$$

The same result should be expected not only with plain bottom, but not too much difference in performance of channel forms on the model and in kind.

Thus, the geometric distortion of scale models, following from the analysis of morphometric communication, is similar to that which was found from the consideration of the planned tasks hydraulics, which was repeatedly noticed in the studies of channel objects. Note that this result is obtained by $M_{ps} = M_p = 1$ and Fr=idem. It is possible that in other cases, matching may not be.

If the nature of the shores are composed of relatively weak erodible grounds, the value of accounting morphometric ties when modeling decreases. However, the PLA- a new scale model in all cases should be not less than that determined with account of morphometric relations. Otherwise, the width of the channel on the model may be less than the width of the selected scale.

In many engineering tasks, the shore when modeling can be considered non-blurry. If one should consider the stream-bank erosion then it's necessary to reproduce the bank resistance to the erosion on the model. Thus it is possible to proceed from the conditions:

$$\tau_\sigma = \tau_{cr.\sigma}$$

or

$$M_{Ucr.\sigma}=M_U$$

If we understand $U_{cr.\sigma}$ as the average on section velocity at which the ground, constituting shores, is sustainable, this rate is the function of the ground properties, the channel form (in particular, the relationship b/h) and the relative roughness of the bottom ($\Delta_{ef.b}/h$) and shores ($\Delta_{ef.sh}/b$).

Material whose properties on the model correspond to the properties of cohesive ground, forming shores in kind, in our practice, is obtained by adding to fine-stoma sand small amounts of binder (better lime or gypsum), and the recipe is set approximately the same as when modeling a local erosion in a coherent ground (see Section 7.3).

7.6 Determining of Planned Deformations on the Pressure Model

Even at an acceptable deviation from the Frude rule and distortion of geometric scale model of the planned model dimensions, the sandy riverbed should be sufficiently large. This becomes clear if we bear in mind that velocity on a conventional model of open stream depends on the geometric scale models, and the smaller it is, the smaller these scales, and the properties of moving materials on the model (noneroding velocity) are close to those for small - and medium-grained Sands in kind. Modeling of sandy bottoms at acceptable geometric scale models is practically possible using artificial materials. As the cost of artificial moving materials is high, and the size of models, even in the use of such materials, should be very large, the study of deformations of a channel usually require a large expenditure of money, time and effort.

Taking into consideration the identified difficulties of modeling of the deformation bed, it is very tempting to use a pressure model for the purposes of research (see Section 5.5), for which the velocity scale is not associated directly with geometric dimensions. Here velocity scale can be selected in accordance with the scale of noneroding velocity and thereby the condition (7.14) shall be satisfied. This fact was pointed out by A. G. Averkiev [1] in the beginning of air model use. In studies of riverbed deformations on the pressure models, it is necessary to be sure that the equations describing sediment transport and river-bed deformation have the same form for gravity flows in kind as for pressure models.

As shown in Section 5.5, a pressure model is suitable for routine tasks in hydraulics. Therefore, among the objectives focused on defining the deformation of the riverbed, the share of pressure model includes the definition scheduled deformations of the riverbed. When determining similarity, scheduled deformations in section 7.4 are used according to noneroding velocity characterizing the sediment, and for the carrying capacity of the flow. To find these dependencies, with respect to pressure model, we have performed experiments in special units. These units represented pressure trays with lids made of organic glass. On the installation was served fluid (air or water) and sediment (quartz sand average particle size of 0.2 and 0.6 mm). In the experiments with the constant flow of sediment ranged flow rate, and after the stabilization of the bottom of the stream, depth and average velocity was measured.

These experiments placed on the field (*lgh, lgU*), shown in Figure 7.18 - 7.20. It can be noted that most of the points corresponding to the fixed cost of load, lay on parallel lines. Processing of results of experiments showed that the specified rate of sediment average velocity over the stabilized bottom, consisting of these loads, connected with the depth dependence:

$$\bar{U}=C_0 h^{1/6}$$

When $q_s=0$ average velocity represents the noneroding velocity U_{cr}. If the depth h=1 m, then $C_0=\bar{U}_{cr}$. Therefore,

$$\bar{U}_{cr}=\bar{U}_{cr1} h^{1/6}$$

Thus, for pressure water and air flows, there is a link between the noneroding velocity and depth, the same as the dependence of V.N. Goncharov for the open water flow [42]. Test results confirmed that noneroding safe velocities differ noticeably at plain bottom and in the presence of bars on it. Data on average noneroding safe velocities (m/s) in pressure flow at a depth of 1 m are shown in Table 7.1

As follows from the data table, the ratio of proper values of noneroding safe velocity with plain bottom and in the presence of bars on it is 1.17 on the average that corresponds to the data of experiments in open hydraulic flumes [76].

We recall, that

$$\bar{U}_{cr}=\varphi(\mathrm{Re}_d)\sqrt{2\rho^+ gd/\lambda}, \tag{7.33}$$

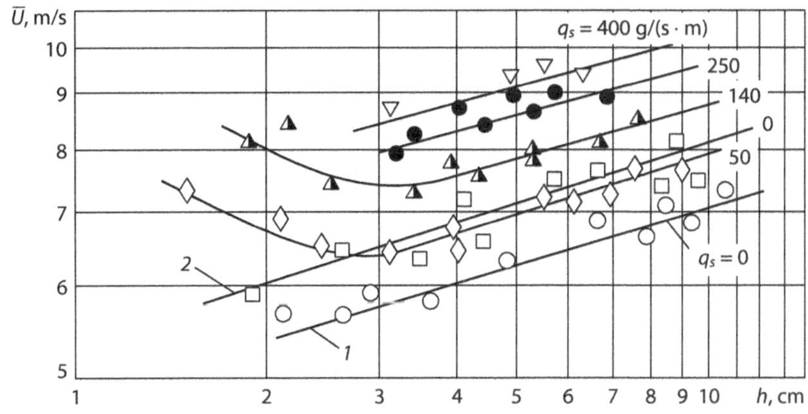

Figure 7.18 Dependence between the average depth velocity, pressure air flow depth and concentration of sediments for sands with an average particle size of 0.2 mm:

1 - at the rifle bottom; 2 - plain bottom.

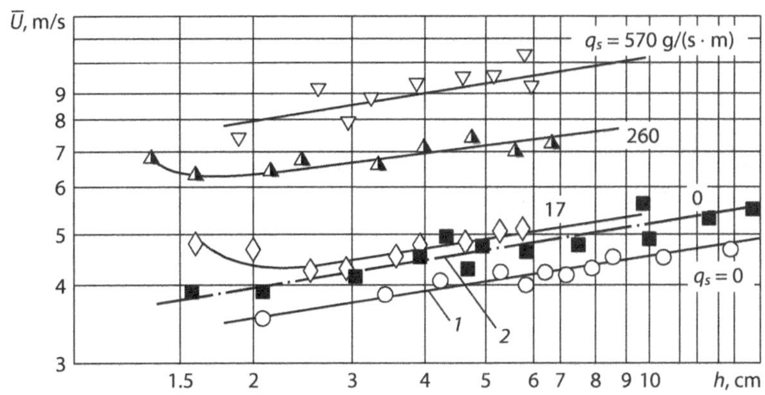

Figure 7.19 Dependence between the average depth velocity, pressure air flow depth and concentration of sediments for sands with an average particle size of 0.6 mm:

1 - at the rifle bottom; 2 - plain bottom.

where $\mathrm{Re}_d = d\sqrt{\rho^+ gd/\nu}$. For the same material at ρ_s = 2650 kg/m^3 and T=15 °C ratio complexes Re_d to air and water is $Re_d/Re_{d\text{вод}} \approx 3{,}5$, i.e., if we keep in mind the nature of the function $\varphi(Re_d)$ (Figure 7.14),

$$\varphi(Re_d)_{air} \leq (Re_d)_{water}$$

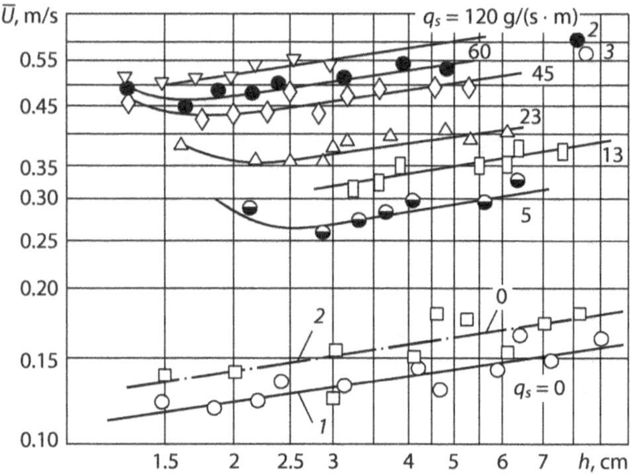

Figure 7.20 Dependence between the average depth velocity, pressure air flow depth and concentration of sediments for sands with an average particle size of 0.2 mm:

1 - at the rifle bottom; 2 - plain bottom.

The experimental data on the basis of dependence (7.33) were defined values $\varphi(Re_d)$ for different sediment and used fluids. Thus adjusted, the hydraulic friction λ, based on (7.26), relied on equal λ (see Section 4.1). Calculation λ was based on the experimentally established fact that in the range of performed experiments, attitude of the lower zone of flow to a total depth h_1/h depends on the particle size of the sediment, and for d=0.2 mm 0.55, and when d = 0.6 mm – 0.65. Experimental points related to the pressure flows located on the schedule of V.S. Knoroz (see Figure 7.14) and closely corresponding to his data, are the average values of the coefficients $\varphi(Re_d)$ calculated in such a way.

In Figures 7.18-7.20, it may be noted that the experimental points associated with constant specific costs of sediments in the field ($1g\bar{U}_{cr}lgh$) went on to direct, roughly parallel to the line $1g\bar{U}_{cr}=1/61gh$. This means that with the constant flow of sediment attitude $\bar{U}/\bar{U}_{cr}$=const, which corresponds to the majority of dependencies for the consumption of the bottom sediments, in particular dependencies (7.2) - (7. 12).

Let us once more turn attention to compliance morphometric connections for pressure and open threads.

From this it follows that the relations between the average characteristics of the flow and characteristics of sediment within the system of equations scheduled deformations of a channel, for pressure and non-pressure water streams have the same view, which is the basis possibility of reaching the equivalence of such deformations. The system scales pressure model with movable bottom is set the same as for conventional models: from the analysis of the equations planned hydraulics and balance of sediments.

With all the freedom in the choice of scale M_U, when using a pressure model, condition $\bar{U}/\bar{U}_{cr}$ can be satisfied by heavier substitutes of sediment than what is provided with a high number *Re* and consequently the validity of small geometric scale pressure models. However, you should still aim at possibly more major planned geometric scale to avoid high geometric distortion of scale.

On the pressure models due to the large value of M_U and small geometric magnitude scale; time deformations are significantly less than conventional models, which provides a short time necessary for carrying out of experiments.

To solve routine tasks, deformations of a channel can be used as water and air pressure model. However, because of the always-present spatial effects, in particular, due to the distortion of the trajectories of motion of solid particles in the fluid, it is preferable to use water models (see Section 6.2).

Construction of air and water pressure models with moving bed and technology of their use is given in [91].

As examples of the results of the use of air models with movable bottom in Figure 7.21 the data related to research erosion of the Volga river, constrained jumper Sarah-Tito HPP. Compare these models with observations in nature proves the reliability of forecasts.

The results of using pressurized water models are shown in Figure 7.22, which presents data on the studies of forming the channel R. Irtysh river on the area of the water intake of the Yermakovskaya TPP.

7.7 "Hybrid" Modeling of River-Bed Deformations

Information provided in this Chapter show the difficulties of research on models with movable bottom because of the problems of research threads in fixed boundaries. They are great even in relatively simple cases: when there is homogeneous composition of the sediment and isotropic geological structure of the channel, if it is possible to allocate in the study process dominant phenomenon. The real process of deformation of a channel is to some extent different from that adopted for modeling schematically. As a rule, the sediment is dissimilar and composition of their deposits changed

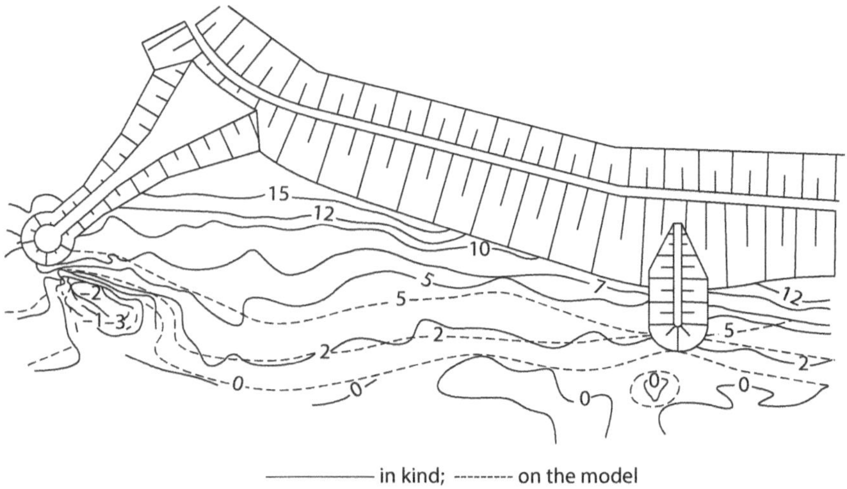

Figure 7.21 The riverbed relief at cofferdams of Saratovskaya HPP:

———in natura; - - - - - - - - - on the model.

Processing of results of experiments show that for investigated pressure threads, the best match between the obtained data and formula has the following structure:

$$q_s = K(\bar{U}/\bar{U}_{cr})^3(\bar{U}/\bar{U}_{cr} - 1)$$

(here $\bar{U}_{cr}$ - noneroding velocity if there are ridges). The coefficient K was for the air flow d = 0.2 mm is equal to 48 g/ (s∗m) and when d =0,6 mm - 260 g/(s∗m) of water flow for d =0.2 mm - 0,48 g/ (s∗m).

in the process of deformation. Geological structure of the riverbed is non-isotropic, and it may be incoherent, and communication grounds on the deformation influence spatial effects, and this changes in the characteristics of turbulence. Because of this, except in some special cases, the determination of the deformation of the rivers in the model with movable bottom is, for almost all important details, impossible.

Deformation of a channel is a process of mutual influence of the stream and its boundaries. One side of this process is that the influence of the channel of the stream is relatively easily estimated at hydraulic models, and if we neglect the fact that the content in water sediment affects the characteristics of the flow, the impact can be defined on a rigid model. When there are relationships between the characteristics of flow and deformation of a channel of information about the characteristics of the stream, this can be used for numerical modeling of deformation. Flow characteristics can be obtained by numerical modeling [47, 157]. Numerical modeling of channel flow is widely used in modern engineering hydraulics, but this

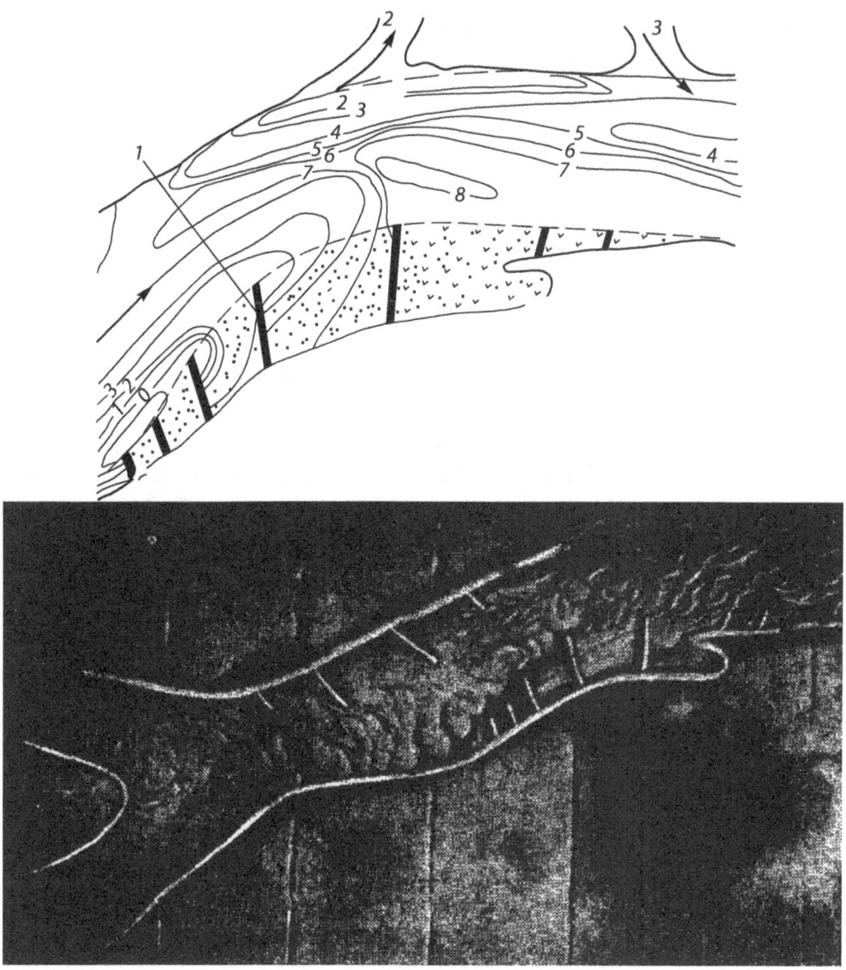

Figure 7.22 Riverbed regulation in the area of the water intake of the Yermakovskaya TPP:

1 - rubble-mound spurs; 2 - water intake channel; 3 – water outlet channel.

possibility with the currently available tools, is limited mainly to one-dimensional and two-dimensional problems. In the three-dimensional case, physical modeling is more preferable (see Section 1.1).

Considerations point to the feasibility of allocating the evaluation of different aspects of the process of channel deformations to different classes of modeling: for non-conforming to determine the impact of a channel for the flow of physical modeling and flow direction - numerical, i.e. on prospects of use in this case hybrid modeling.

This way of modeling in its simplest form is described in [151], where it is called "scraping method." Because the process of deformation of a channel flow is continuously changing, in accordance with the content of the proposal, the process of determining deformations should be divided into several stages, corresponding to different states of a channel when it is deformed. The initial condition of the channel of the rigid patterns are determined by the flow characteristics. These characteristics are calculated to show deformation of the riverbed for a certain period of time. The relief of the channel of the rigid model varies in accordance with the calculation results. The model identifies the characteristics of the flow, calculating deformation for the next period, and so on, until the stabilization of deformation or achieving a specified time.

In [151] the use of a method is proposed for determining scheduled deformations. When solving the tasks, the stream can be divided into turbostreams in accordance with the results obtained on hydraulic models, and along each turbostream, starting with the section where the Deposit discharge is specified, to determine deformation of the riverbed during t_{def}, using the equation of the balance of sediments. This may be accounted for and sharing load between turbostreams. Currently, with the widespread use of computers, this part "hybrid" modeling of river-bed deformations technically greatly relieved, allows us to solve not only planned, but also other more complicated tasks associated with deformations of the bed. "Hybrid" modeling of deformation with the use of modern computer technologies is used, in particular, in the national hydraulic laboratory of France in Chatou.

Unfortunately, the second side of the process hybrid modeling - determination of characteristics of the flow remains very time consuming. With this purpose, the riverbed is constructed from the lean mortar, which is "scraped" (or built up) after each measurement of the flow characteristics, and that is complicated when using large dimensions of hydraulic models. As the area, occupied by pressure models, is small in comparison with the areas of open hydraulic models, and the material from which rigid aircraft models (plasticine) are usually made of, can be easily deformed mechanically, these models are very suitable for "hybrid" modeling. It is very easy to determine some characteristics that are directly included in the dependencies used in the calculation of deformation on the pressure models [91].

Movable material markedly differing in color from the rigid surface of the model is laid in a thin layer on rigid relief of pressure model. Then the air is passed through the model which consumption is stepwise increased. Particles at this air consumption are removed from areas where the velocities exceed the safe ones for material laid on the relief. Given the fact that $\bar{U}_{cr}=\bar{U}_{cr1}h^{1/6}$, on the border region flushing material $\bar{U}_{b.м}=\bar{U}_{cr1м}h^{1/6}$ m.

As $M_U = M_Q/(M_l M_h)$ velocity in kind on the border of the area corresponding to the field flushing material on the model:

$$U_{b.N} = U_{b.m} \frac{M_Q}{M_l M_h} = \tilde{U}_{cr1} \ h_N^{1/6}$$

where:

$$\tilde{U}_{cr1} = U_{cr\ 1m} \frac{MQ}{M_l M_h^{7/6}}$$

As a result of experiences, we obtained a number of areas, corresponding to different M_Q on the borders with known values U_{cr1}.

In the absence of transit, sediment erosion will occur where $\tilde{U}_{cr1} > U_{cr1N}$. If nature is the transit of sediment for determination of deformation of a channel, you should know the value carrying capacity flow in different areas of the riverbed. As $q_s = f(U/U_{cr1})$, the form of information received on the air model set forth is very handy:

$$\frac{\bar{U}_{b.N}}{\bar{U}_{cr\ N}} = \frac{\tilde{U}_{cr1}}{\bar{U}_{cr1N}}$$

i.e., the region with the same values U_{cr1}, which are characterized by the same specific costs of load.

The use of the considered, in taking measurements of the characteristics necessary for determining the deformation of a channel that allows you to indirectly assess the deformation, is not related to changes in medium-depth velocities, e.g. in the areas of whirlwinds that occur when flowing around obstacles. By the erosion of the material, laid on a hard terrain model, one can judge the position and size of such area and the intensity of erosion by the deformation of the riverbed. This reception accurately determined, for example, areas of erosion in the heads spurs or protective tip jumpers. On the basis of measurements, only mean velocities of these zones can be identified, which sometimes leads to serious errors, threatening accident structures.

Hybrid modeling of riverbed deformations using air pressure models has been repeatedly used in the practice of research Hydroproject SRS, and in many cases gave results that are well-proven in-situ observations.

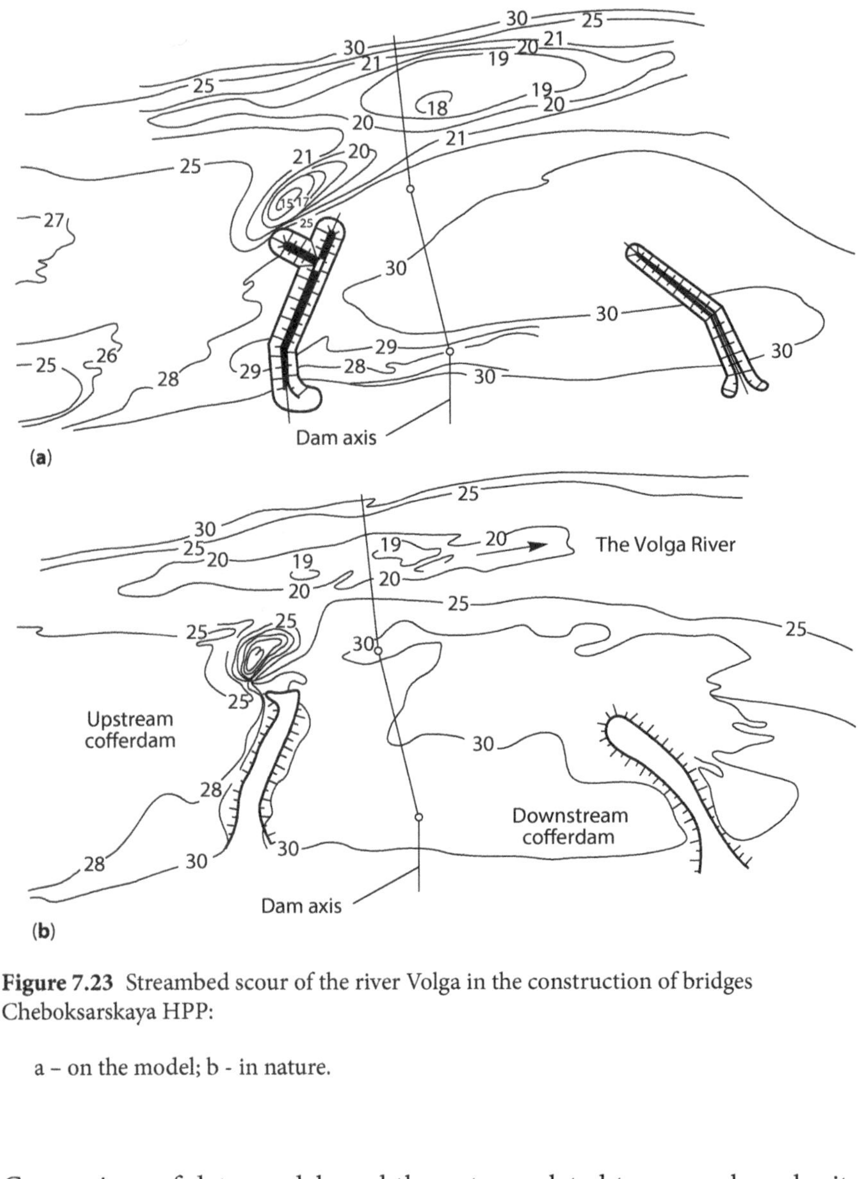

Figure 7.23 Streambed scour of the river Volga in the construction of bridges Cheboksarskaya HPP:

a – on the model; b - in nature.

Comparison of data models and the nature related to research on hesitation of the Volga dams in the construction of bridges Cheboksarskaya HPP, and ceremony of a channel of the Euphrates building dams of hydroelectric Tabka (Syria), is shown in Figures 7.23 and 7.24 [91].

Precision hybrid modeling of riverbed deformations is almost completely dependent on the reliability of links used by numerical modeling.

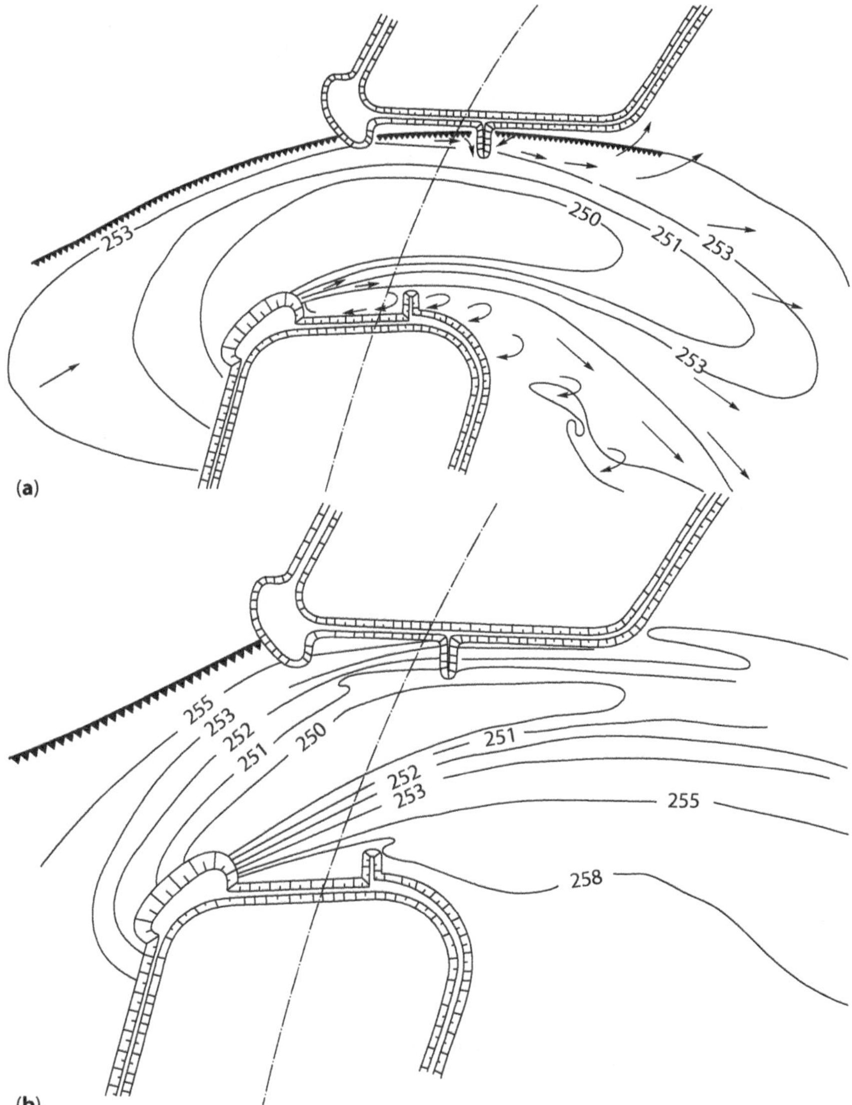

Figure 7.24 The Euphrates riverbed erosion, restrained with dams of the Tabka hydrosystem:

a – on the model; b - in nature.

Since the dependencies existing in modern channel hydraulics are imperfect (this relates to the dependencies used for sedimentation estimation in particular), one should either determine the deformations together with the usage of hybrid modeling on the model with movable bed or execute the combined experiments. For example, defining the erosion in the hybrid modeling, then fill the field of erosion of rolling material and determine its motion.

7.8 Flow in the Channel with Grassy Vegetation

In engineering practice it is often necessary to determine the resistance of the surface covered by vegetation, for example, the calculation of currents in wide channels and floodplains, as well as in the calculation of will to break through hydraulic engineering structures.

Grass cover protects the bed and the slopes of canals from erosion, allowing increase of noneroding velocity in a channel, which can serve as cheap slopes fixed hydraulic structures (for example, dry slopes of dams).

The resistance of the channel with grassy cover was studied in [93a and 43a], where there are different models for calculation of such motions. In [4a, 87, 43a, and 97a] there is various consideration of the deformation of vegetation that caused the average shear stress.

Significant influence, however, has a ripple tangential stress. The proposed model takes into account the effect of averaged and pulsation component stress.

To describe the motion of the fluid above, the vegetation will use the equation of turbulent boundary layer in an open stream with a small slope [21]:

$$\frac{\partial U}{\partial t}+U\frac{\partial U}{\partial x}+V\frac{\partial U}{\partial y}=g\left(\sin\alpha_0-\frac{\partial h}{\partial x}\cos\alpha_0\right)+\frac{1}{\rho}\frac{\partial \tau}{\partial y}, \qquad (7.34)$$

where U, V are the longitudinal and transverse (normal to the surface of the bottom) components average rates; α_0 = the acute angle between the axis normal to the averaged surface of the bottom, and the direction of gravity; ρ - density of the fluid; τ- turbulent friction; t is time; x - longitudinal coordinate.

Use regular representation for the average shear stress and turbulent viscosity [84], given the fluctuations in the bottom of the thread associated with the presence of vegetation, only in the boundary conditions:

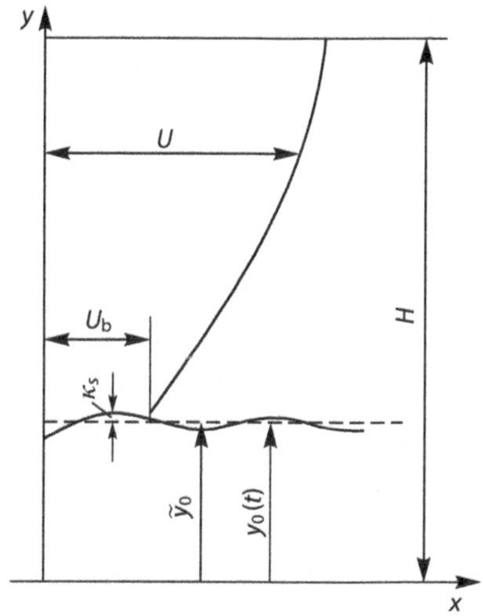

Figure 7.25 Scheme for computation of the flow over the grassy vegetation.

$$\tau = \rho \nu_T \frac{\partial U}{\partial y},$$
$$\nu_T = \kappa_0 U_* (y - \tilde{y}_0)\left(1 - \frac{y - \tilde{y}_0}{H - \tilde{y}_0}\right), \tag{7.35}$$
$$(y - \tilde{y}_0) > k_s.$$

Here U_* is dynamic velocity; κ_0 - Karman constant; $\tilde{y}_0 = \tilde{y}_0(t)$ - averaged vegetation height (Figure 7.25); k_s- coarseness ledge height.

The ledge size roughness proportional to the difference in local level surface vegetation y_0(x, t) and a certain average level surface vegetation.

$$\tilde{y}_0(t) = \frac{1}{2\xi}\int_{x-\xi}^{x+\xi} y_0(x, t)\,dx,$$
$$k_s = y_0(x, t) - \tilde{y}_0(t). \tag{7.36}$$

The scale longitudinal averaging ξ is chosen by large integral characteristic scale longitudinal correlation in pulsations and tangential stresses on the boundary.

Neglecting nonlinear members and taking into account the nonstationarity only parametrically, through fluctuations borders $\tilde{y}_0(t)$ and changing the roughness parameter k_s (t), will provide for quasi-uniform motion, the velocity distribution vertically as a function of the fluctuations of the border.

$$U(y,t) = \frac{U_*}{\kappa_0} Ln \frac{y - \tilde{y}_0(t)}{k_s(t)} + U_b \tag{7.37}$$

Where U_b is the velocity at the height of the projection of roughness k_s.

Having integrated (7.37) by the depth of the stream, we obtain specific consumption over the oscillating surface as the function of time.

$$q(t) = \int_0^{\tilde{y}_0} U_b\,dy + \int_{\tilde{y}_0}^{H} \left(\frac{U_*}{\kappa_0} \ln \frac{y - \tilde{y}_0}{k_s} + U_b \right) dy$$
$$= \frac{U_*}{\kappa_0} \left[\left(H - \tilde{y}_0 \right) \left(\ln \frac{H - \tilde{y}_0}{k_s} - 1 \right) + U_b \frac{H\kappa_0}{U_*} \right]. \tag{7.38}$$

To determine the average time-specific consumption, it is necessary to average q (t). We arrange q (t) in a Taylor series in the vicinity $\overline{\overline{y}}_0$, k_s- and will find its mathematical expectation. Hereafter, to refer to the average for time values, we have used a feature above the symbol to denote variables related to the thread in which the vegetation is not deformed, which are the two features above the symbol. As for variable $\tilde{y}_0(t)$, it is responsible for (mostly) large-scale disturbances, and as for fluctuations k_s (t), and short-wave perturbations, it can be assumed that the correlation between values $(k_s - \bar{k}_s)$ and $(\tilde{y}_0 - \bar{y}_0)$ will be close to zero. For the average specific consumption, we obtained the following expression:

$$\bar{q} = \overline{\overline{q}} \left(1 - \frac{\overline{\tilde{y}_0 - \overline{\overline{y}}_0}}{H - \overline{\overline{y}}_0} \right) + \frac{U_* H}{\kappa 0} \left[\frac{\overline{\tilde{y}_0 - \overline{\overline{y}}_0}}{H} + \frac{\overline{\tilde{y}_0 - \overline{\overline{y}}_0}}{H - \overline{\overline{y}}_0} \frac{U_b \kappa_0}{U_*} + \right.$$
$$\left. + \frac{\overline{\left(\tilde{y}_0 - \overline{\overline{y}}_0 \right)^2}}{2H \left(H - \overline{\overline{y}}_0 \right)} + \frac{\overline{\left(1 - \bar{y}_0 / H \right) \left(k_s - \bar{k}_s \right)^2}}{2\bar{k}_s^2} \right] \tag{7.39}$$

where:

$$\overline{\overline{q}} = \frac{U_* H}{\kappa_0}\left[(1-\overline{\overline{y}}_0/H)\left(\ln\frac{H-\overline{\overline{y}}_0}{\overline{k}_s}-1\right)+\frac{U_b\kappa_0}{U_*}\right].$$

Since, $\overline{(\tilde{y}_0-\overline{y}_0)}/H \ll 1$ and $U_*H/\kappa_0 \ll \overline{\overline{q}}$, the second term in the right-hand side of (7.39) is unimportant. Given this and noticing that the value $\overline{(\tilde{y}_0-\overline{\overline{y}}_0)}$ has a negative sign, as the instantaneous value of the height of the vegetation may not be greater than the height of the vegetation without deformation, we received the obvious conclusion that fluctuation of vegetation increased the flow above the surface under other equal conditions and thereby reduced the coefficient of hydraulic friction.

Let's see how it changes the distribution of average velocity on the depth of the stream. To do this, $U(y, t)$ is put in a number of Tailor in the neighborhood $\overline{\overline{y}}_0$, $\overline{k}_s$ and average time. Keeping those terms of smallness, we obtain:

$$\overline{U}(y)=\frac{U_*}{\kappa_0}\left[\ln\frac{y-y_0}{\overline{k}_s}-\frac{\overline{y_0-\overline{\overline{y}}_0}}{y-y_0}+\frac{U_b\kappa_0}{U_*}\right] \tag{7.40}$$

Here and below the sign ~ in the designation, $\tilde{y}_0$ is omitted.

From (7.40) we see that the fluctuations of surface vegetation lead to increase of average velocity, and the more than closest point to the surface vegetation.

Introducing maximum velocity $\overline{U}_0$, at $y = H$ equal

$$\overline{U}_0=\frac{U}{\kappa_0}\left[\ln\frac{H-\overline{\overline{y}}_0}{\overline{k}_s}-\frac{\overline{y_0-\overline{\overline{y}}_0}}{H-\overline{\overline{y}}_0}+\frac{U_b\kappa_0}{U_*}\right]$$

can be freed from the constants U_b/U_* in (7.40), by calculating the difference:

$$\frac{\overline{U}_0-\overline{U}}{U_*}=\frac{1}{\kappa_0}\left[\ln\frac{H-\overline{\overline{y}}_0}{y-\overline{\overline{y}}}+\overline{(y_0-\overline{\overline{y}}_0)}\left(\frac{1}{y-\overline{\overline{y}}_0}-\frac{1}{H-\overline{\overline{y}}_0}\right)\right] \tag{7.41}$$

For computation of the flow over a grassy vegetation in equations (7.39) - (7.41) it is necessary to know the characteristics of deformation of a surface vegetation $\overline{y_0 - \overline{\overline{y}}_0}$ and $\overline{(y_0 - \overline{\overline{y}}_0)^2}$

On vegetation in a fluid flow, there are two variables of stress: the tangent τ and normal *ρ*

Spectra of pulsations of the tangent stress $S_\tau(\omega)$ and pressure $S_\rho(\omega)$ are connected by the relations obtained in [47].

$$p = -\frac{\partial \tau}{\partial \tau}\frac{\nu}{U_*^2}, \quad S_\tau = \frac{S_p(\omega)}{\omega^2}\left(\frac{U_*^2}{\nu}\right)^2 \tag{7.42}$$

The equation (7.42) is obtained for smooth walls. For rough walls instead of kinematic viscosity *ν*, according to the recommendations [47], it is necessary to take the turbulent viscosity $\nu_T = \delta U_* \kappa_0$, where δ is typical thickness of the boundary layer.

(100 implies that range ripple tangent stress has lower frequency than the corresponding range of pressure $S_\rho(\omega)$.)

The pressure acting on the surface vegetation is evenly distributed on the depth of plants, because of the large (τ) and normal (ρ) stresses acting on one stalk, when believing that all tangent load is perceived by the grass stems. The power associated with the action of shear stress is $P_1 = \tau/N$, where *N* is the number of stems per unit area attached to the top of the stem.

The pressure on the stem surface provides resultant

$$P_2 = -\frac{\partial P}{\partial x}\overline{\overline{y}}_0 d^2_{\text{av}}$$

where d_{av} is the average diameter of the stems of plants.

For comparison, we shall calculate the ratio of the spectra of existing forces.

$$S_{p1} = \frac{1}{N^2} \cdot \frac{S_p(\omega, \kappa)}{\omega^2}\left(\frac{U_*}{\delta \kappa_0}\right)^2,$$
$$S_{p2} = \kappa^2 S_p(\omega, \kappa) d_{av}^4 \left(\overline{\overline{y}}_0\right)^2. \tag{7.43}$$

Where $S_\rho(\omega, \kappa)$ is a two-dimensional spatial-temporary spectra of pressure pulsations, then κ is the wave number. Assuming a non-zero value of the two-dimensional spectrum is concentrated along the line $\omega = -\kappa U_{av}$, that corresponds to the well-known hypothesis of frozen turbulence. Turning to the one-dimensional spectra, we find:

$$\frac{S_{p1}}{S_{p2}} \approx \frac{U_*^2}{\kappa^4 \overline{U}_{av}^2 \ \delta^2 N^2 \ \kappa_0^2 \ d^4{}_{av} \left(\bar{\bar{y}}_0\right)} \tag{7.44}$$

Introducing dimensionless quantities: $\kappa' = \kappa\left(H - \bar{\bar{y}}_0\right), \delta' = \delta\Big/\left(H - \bar{\bar{y}}_0\right)$; $y'_0 = \bar{\bar{y}}_0\Big/\left(H - \bar{\bar{y}}_0\right)$ and substituting them into (7.44), we obtain:

$$\frac{S_{p1}}{S_{p2}} \approx \frac{\lambda}{8(\kappa')^2 \ (\delta')^2 \ N^2 d_{av}^4 \ (y_0')^2 \ \kappa_0^2} \tag{7.45}$$

where $\lambda = 8U_*^2/\bar{U}_{av}^2$ is the coefficient of hydraulic friction.

Substituting in (7.44) characteristic values of the corresponding values: λ=0.1 [87a], N=8000 m^{-2} [4a], d_{av} =2 10^{-3} m, $y'_0 \approx 1$, $\delta' \approx 0{,}1$, we get:

$$\frac{S_{p1}}{S_{p2}} \approx \frac{76760}{(\kappa')^4} \tag{7.46}$$

From (7.44) - (7.46) we see that by increasing κ', the role of pressure increases. High-range pressure range tangential stresses are in the field $\kappa' < 3$. So in the above example, the role of efforts related to shear stress, is substantially more than the role of efforts related to pressure pulsations. So, when the wave number $\kappa' = 2$ (maximum range pressure) $S_{p1}/S_{p2} \approx 475$.

At wave numbers $\kappa' > 5$ role of pressure pulsations sharply increases, however, the absolute value of the spectrum of pressure pulsations in these wave numbers is small [84]. That is why in further calculations the pressure is neglected in comparison with the effect of shear stress.

For calculation of a flow and vegetation, we adopted the following scheme: on vegetation valid variable shear stress is equal to the sum of averaged $\bar{\tau} = \rho U_*^2$ and pulsation shear stress τ; deformation of vegetation is proportional to the total shear stress.

$$y_0 - \bar{\bar{y}}_0 = \frac{\bar{\tau} + \tau}{k'_0} \tag{7.47}$$

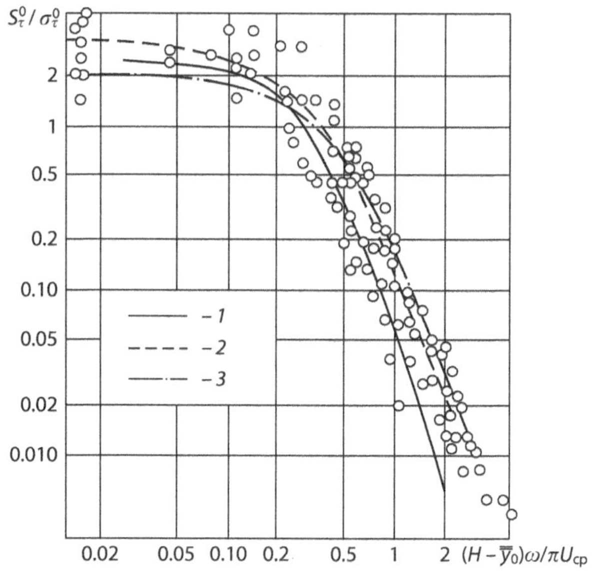

Figure 7.26 Spectra of tangential stresses on the vegetation borders. Points - experimental data; *1*- the Buckwell curve, Re=8700 [72] 2,3 - calculation using equation (7.43) for $\delta/(H-\bar{\bar{y}}0)$ = 0,10 and 0.01, respectively $\left(S_\tau^0 = \dfrac{U_\bullet}{2\left(H-\bar{\bar{y}}_0\right)} S_\tau \right)$

Where is the coefficient for the walls, vegetation cannot stretch under the influence of negative ripple tangential stresses, but only sags under the action of effort, i.e. the height of the vegetation is always less than the height of the plants in the undeformed state.

Range of pressure pulsation can be calculated according to [84], based on kinematics of flow. For its calculation, as in [84], the data of B.A. Fidman, E.M. Minskiy and I.K. Nikitin on the parameters of the vertical velocity pulsations were used. Spectra of the shear stresses, calculated with respect to (7.42), in good agreement with the known data was obtained with the smooth mode (Figure 7.26).

The dependence of the dispersion of tangential stresses σ_τ^2 from thickness of the lower layer is shown in Figure 7.27 For further calculations, this dependence is approximated by the expression:

$$_0\sigma^2{}_\tau = 2{,}95\,\mathrm{arctg}\,85\left|0{,}055-\delta/(H-\bar{\bar{y}}_0)\right| + 7.9, \qquad (7.48)$$

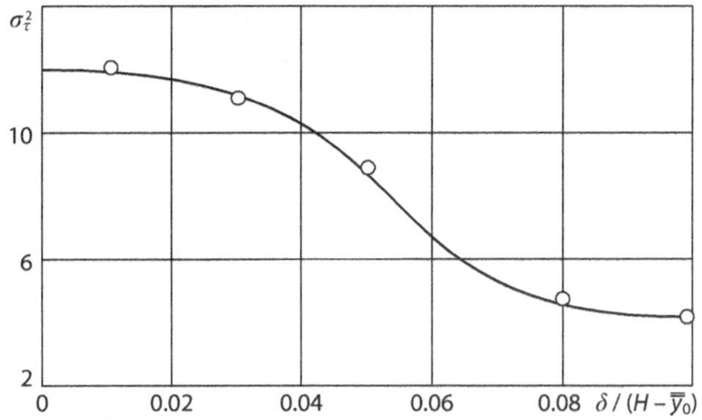

Figure 7.27 Dependence of the pulsations tangential stresses dispersion on the bottom layer thickness

Points - calculated values; line - approximation by the expression (7.48)

where:

$$_0\sigma_\tau^2 = \frac{\sigma_\tau^2\,\overline{U}_{av}^2\,V_T^2}{\rho^2 U_*^6\,\sigma_V^2\left(H-\overline{\overline{y}}_0\right)^2}$$

δ- thickness of the bottom layer; σ_υ^2 - dispersion of the pulsations of the vertical component of the velocity on the boundary of the near-bottom area; according to different authors, $\sigma_\upsilon^2 = (1{,}1 \div 1{,}2)U_*^2$

When calculating the dispersion of surface oscillations of vegetation, it is necessary to remember that a negative ripple tangential stress, larger in absolute value than the average shear stress, can't stretch the stems of plants. Taking for pulsations of the tangent stress of normal distribution law [72], we get the following expression for the density of distribution $f(y_0)$ of the surface oscillations:

$$f(y_0) = \frac{K_0}{\sqrt{2\pi}}\exp\left[-\frac{(y_0-y_b)^2}{2\sigma_\tau^2}K_0^2\right], \quad \text{if} \quad y_0 < \overline{\overline{y}}_0;$$

$$f(y_0) = 0, \quad \text{if} \quad y_0 \geq \overline{\overline{y}}_0.$$

At the accepted assumptions, the average deviation from the non-state and dispersion oscillations are determined as follows:

$$\overline{y_0 - \bar{\bar{y}}_0} = \bar{y}_0 - \bar{\bar{y}}_0;$$

$$\overline{\left(y_0 - \bar{\bar{y}}_0\right)^2} = \overline{y_0^{2}} - 2\bar{y}_0\bar{\bar{y}}_0 + \bar{\bar{y}}_0^{\,2};$$

where:

$$\bar{y}_0 = -\frac{\sigma_\tau}{K_0\sqrt{2\pi}}\exp\left[-\frac{(\bar{\bar{y}}_0 - y_b)^2 K_0^2}{2\sigma_\tau^2}\right] +$$

$$+\frac{y_b - \bar{\bar{y}}_0}{2}\Phi\left(\frac{\bar{\bar{y}}_0 - y_b}{\sigma_\tau\sqrt{2}}K_0\right) + \frac{y_b + \bar{\bar{y}}_0}{2};$$

$$\overline{y_0^{2}} = -\frac{\sigma_\tau(\bar{\bar{y}}_0 + y_b)}{K_0\sqrt{2\pi}}\exp\left[-\frac{(\bar{\bar{y}}_0 - y_b)^2 K_0^2}{2\sigma_\tau^2}\right] +$$

$$+\frac{y_b^2 + \sigma_\tau^2 / K_0^2 - \bar{\bar{y}}_0^{\,2}}{2}\Phi\left(\frac{\bar{\bar{y}}_0 - y_b}{\sqrt{2}\sigma_\tau}K_0\right) + \frac{y_b^2 + \bar{\bar{y}}_0^{\,2} + \sigma_\tau^2 / K_0^2}{2};$$

$$\Phi(x) = \frac{2}{\sqrt{\pi}}\int_0^x \exp(-t^2)\,dt;$$

y_b- the height of the vegetation under the action of only average shear stress:

$$y_b = \bar{\bar{y}}_0 - \frac{\bar{\tau}}{K_0}.$$

Knowing $\overline{y_0 - \bar{y}_0}$ and $\overline{(y_0 - \bar{\bar{y}}_0)^2}$ using equations (7.39) and (7.40), one can calculate the distributions of velocity, specific consumption and, therefore, all the hydraulic characteristics of the flow.

To verify found correlations in the laboratories of the Novocherkassk Engineering and Melioration Institute, the series of experiments was

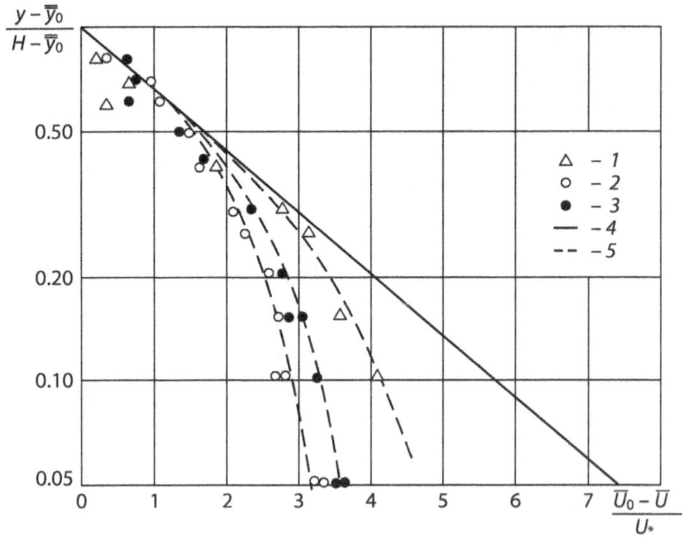

Figure 7.28 Distribution of the averaged velocity, depth of the stream (series 4, $(H—\overline{\overline{y}}_0) = 0.173$ m, $K_0 = 1100$ n/m^3, $\overline{\overline{y}}_0 = 0.088$ m^2). *1-3*-$U_* = 0.23$; 0.0542 and of 0.075 m/s, respectively; 4 - calculation on logarithms at $\kappa_0 = 0.4$; 5 - the average value of the corresponding dynamic velocities.

conducted in which different values of dynamic velocity obtained distributions of velocities and pulsation characteristics of the longitudinal component of velocity. The measurements were carried out in the tray with the length of 6 m and width of 0.58 m.

Measuring the target is located at a distance of 15 $(H—\overline{\overline{y}}_0)$ from the entrance to the tray. The bottom of the tray was filled with ground in which wheat was planted. The experiments were conducted after the shoots of wheat were a certain height.

Distribution of average velocity deviates significantly from the logarithmic law. Figure 7.28 shows the dependence of the deficiency of velocity on the logarithm relations $(y_0—\overline{\overline{y}}_0) / (H—\overline{\overline{y}}_0)$.

From (7.40) we see that the value:

$$\psi + \frac{\overline{U}_0 - \overline{U}}{U_*} \text{ that } \psi = -\frac{\overline{y_0 - \overline{\overline{y}}_0}}{k_0}\left(\frac{1}{y - \overline{\overline{y}}_0} - \frac{1}{H - \overline{\overline{y}}_0}\right),$$

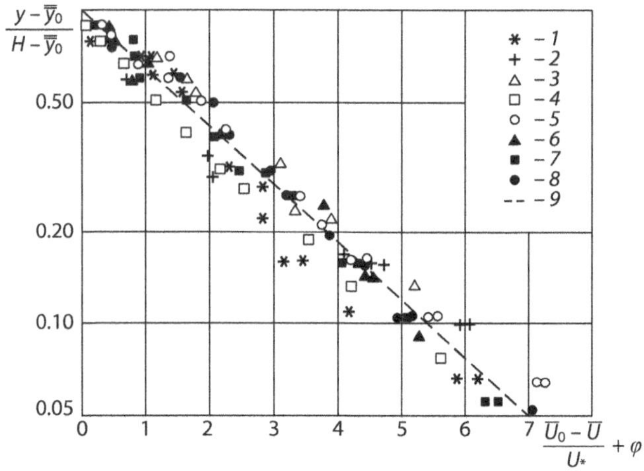

Figure 7.29 Distribution (Ū0–Ū)/U.+φ on the flow depth

should be linearly connected with the value $\lg[(y_0—\bar{\bar{y}}_0) / (H—\bar{\bar{y}}_0)]$. Dependence on (7.41) for the distribution of deficit average velocity is well confirmed by experimental data (Figure 7.29).

The distribution of the standards of pulsations of the longitudinal component of velocity takes place as the distribution medium velocity differs from distribution in flows with solid wall. There is a significant dependence of the distribution of the absolute value of the dynamic velocity.

$1-U{\bullet}=0.055m/s, H-\bar{\bar{y}}_0=0,16m, N=8.10^3m^{-2}, k'_0=596N/m^{-3}, \bar{\bar{y}}_0$
$=0.14m$

$2-U{\bullet}=0.326 \quad H-\bar{\bar{y}}_0=0,187 \ N=8.10^3 \ k'_0=2760 \ \bar{\bar{y}}_0=0,0713$

$3-U{\bullet}=0,016 \quad H-\bar{\bar{y}}_0=0,153 \ N=8,10^3 \ k'_0=745 \ \bar{\bar{y}}_0=0,148$

$4-U{\bullet}=0,374 \quad H-\bar{\bar{y}}_0=0,175 \ N=13,8.10^3 \ k'_0=745 \ \bar{\bar{y}}_0=0,148$

$5-U{\bullet}=0,571 \quad H-\bar{\bar{y}}_0=0,193 \ N=13,8.10^3 \ k'_0=745 \ \bar{\bar{y}}_0=0,148$

$6-U{\bullet}=0,23 \quad H-\bar{\bar{y}}_0=0,175 \ N=10^4 \ k'_0=1100 \ \bar{\bar{y}}_0=0,088$

$7-U{\bullet}=0,0542 \quad H-\bar{\bar{y}}_0=0,173 \ N=10^4 \ k'_0=1100 \ \bar{\bar{y}}_0=0,088$

$8-U{\bullet}=0,075 \quad H-\bar{\bar{y}}_0=0,234 \ N=10^4 \ k'_0=1100 \ \bar{\bar{y}}_0=0,088;$

$9-\text{calculated by }(7.41)\text{for } \kappa_0=0,44$

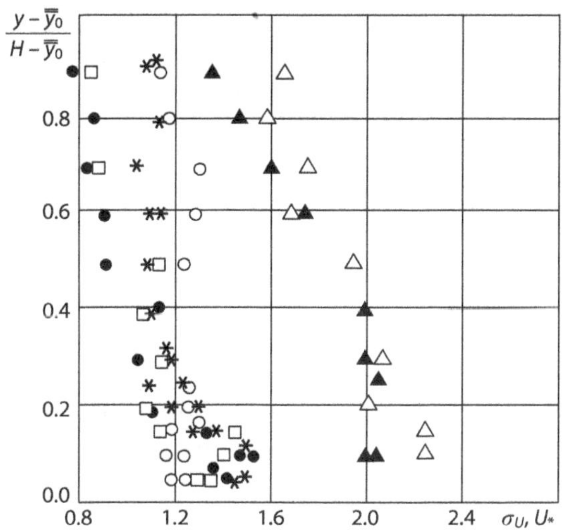

Figure 7.30 Distribution of standards pulsations of the longitudinal component of velocity in the flow depth (see legend in Figure 7.29).

Figure 7.30 shows the distribution of the different values U_*. It can be seen that the increase in dynamic velocity ratio σ_u/U_* decreases. Apparently, this is due to a reduction of the mean velocity gradient $|\partial U/\partial y|$ and, consequently, reducing the generation of turbulence energy from averaged flow:

The existence of oscillations of the surface vegetation is confirmed by the appearance of local maxima in the spectra of the longitudinal velocity pulsations (Figure 7.31). For the analysis of these spectra, we use the equations for finding wave components of velocity $\underset{\sim}{u_i} = U_i—\underset{\sim}{U_i}$ and pressure $p = P—\underset{\sim}{P}$, where $\underset{\sim}{U_i}$, $\underset{\sim}{P}$ shows velocity field and pressure on the rolling surface; Field velocity and pressure over the rigid wall is shown by [84]:

$$\begin{aligned}
&\frac{\partial \underset{\sim}{u}_1}{\partial t} + \bar{U}\frac{\partial \underset{\sim}{u}_1}{\partial x_1} + \underset{\sim}{u}_2 \frac{\partial \bar{U}}{\partial x_2} + \frac{1}{\rho}\frac{\partial p}{\partial x_1} = 0, \\
&\frac{\partial \underset{\sim}{u}_2}{\partial t} + \bar{U}\frac{\partial \underset{\sim}{u}_2}{\partial x_1} + \frac{1}{\rho}\frac{\partial p}{\partial x_2} = 0, \quad \frac{\partial \underset{\sim}{u}_1}{\partial x_1} + \frac{\partial \underset{\sim}{u}_2}{\partial x_2} = 0.
\end{aligned} \tag{7.49}$$

Boundary conditions for the solutions of this system:

$$\underset{\sim}{u}_2 \bigg|_{x_2=0} = \frac{\partial \eta}{\partial t}, \quad \underset{\sim}{u} \bigg|_{x_2 \to \infty} = 0, \tag{7.50}$$

where η is the displacement of the surface vegetation.

Applying to the system (7.49) the two-dimensional Fourier transform (coordinates x_1 and t), will provide for the definitions of "image" ripple $\underset{\sim}{u}_2^*$ in the following equation:

$$\frac{\partial^2 \underset{\sim}{u}_2^*}{\partial x_2^2} - \left(\kappa^2 + \frac{\bar{U}''}{\omega/\kappa + \bar{U}} \right) \underset{\sim}{u}^*_2 = 0,$$

where U'' is the second derivative of the averaged velocity coordinate x_2, κ-parameter Fourier transform.

The expression $U''/(\omega/\kappa + \bar{U})$ defines the interaction of averaged motion of wave perturbations. Neglecting these interactions, we get to determine $\underset{\sim}{u}_2^*$ the equation:

$$\frac{\partial^2 \underset{\sim}{u}^*_2}{\partial x_2^2} - k^2 \underset{\sim}{u}_2^* = 0,$$

which with the boundary conditions:

$$\underset{\sim}{u}^*_2 \Big|_{x_2=0} = i\omega\eta^*, \ \underset{\sim}{u}_2^* \Big|_{x_2 \to \infty} = 0$$

has the following resolution:

$$\underset{\sim}{u}_2^* = i\kappa U_c \eta^* \exp[-\kappa x_2],$$

where U_c is the velocity of drift of the disturbances, equal to (0,8 ÷ 0,9) $\bar{U}_{cp}$ of the continuity equation, we define $\underset{\sim}{u}_1^*$

$$\underset{\sim}{u}_1^* = \kappa U_c \eta^* \exp[-\kappa x_2].$$

Multiplying complex-conjugate "images" pulsation of the longitudinal component of the "wave" components and computing mathematical expectation, we obtain the spectrum of the wave velocity:

$$S\underset{\sim}{u}_1 = \kappa^2 U_c^2 \exp[-2\kappa x_2] S_\eta \tag{7.51}$$

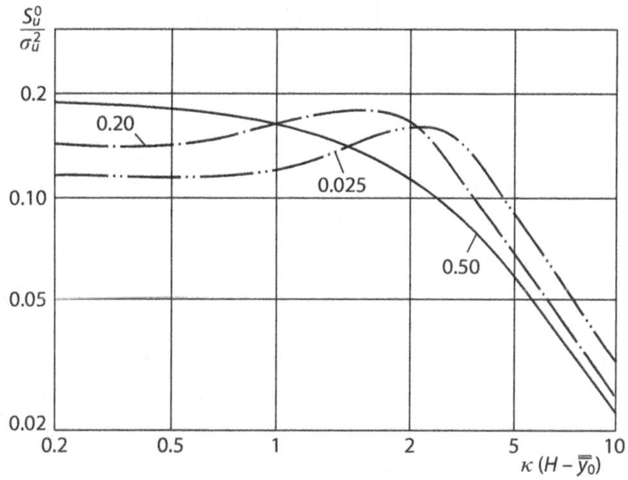

Figure 7.31 Range of pulsations of the longitudinal component of velocity (series 4, test 2). $U_* = 0.0542$ m/s, $H - \bar{\bar{y}}_0 = 0.173$ m, $K_0 = 1100$ n/m³, $y_0 = 0.088$ m, $s_u^0 = \frac{U_c}{2\pi\left(H - \bar{\bar{y}}_0\right)} S_u$ (figures near the curves represent the relation $\frac{y - y_0}{H - y_0}$ =)).

Define the range of fluctuations of surface vegetation S_η through the range of shear stress, expressed through a range of pressure S_p (7.42):

$$S_{\underset{\sim}{u}1} = \frac{U_*^2 \exp\left[-2\kappa x_2\right]}{\delta^2 K_0^2} S_p$$

Here x_2 is measured from the surface vegetation.

It is obvious that $x_2 = 0$, in the range of wave components, has a similar range of pressure to the increasing of x_2 value $S\underset{\sim}{u}_1$ of damped exponential dependence and the fastest-shortwave fade components.

Thus, the fluctuations of surface vegetation make an additional contribution to the range of pulsations of the longitudinal component of velocity, and this contribution maximum is at wave numbers k′ = 2 (maximum range of pressure).

Thus, fluctuations of the surface vegetation give an additional contribution to the uctuation spectrum of the longitudinal component of velocity, and this contribution is observed in the zone of maximum wave umber spectrum of the pressure pulsations. Figure 7.31 local maxima are visible in the spectra of the longitudinal velocity component due to the variation of the boundaries under the influence of the flow. It is possible in the first approximation to accurately calculate deformation of vegetation and their impact on the distribution of average velocity, specific charges and all hydraulic flow parameters

The problem reflects only one of the possible schemes of the trends covered in the course - when the height of bottom vegetation is small compared with the depth of flow. Vegetation has a low inertia - its properties are determined by the average diameter dav of the rods of plants and the number N of rods per unit area of the surface of the seabed. The deformation of the bottom of the thread, with such a coating, is defined by the stiffness coefficient K_0, connecting the vertical offset of the border with shear stress at the boundary flow. It is important that ripple and shear stress, and not pressure, determine the deformation of the boundaries of the stream covered with vegetation. In the considered conditions, additional criteria are the relative density of the surface of bottom plants:

$$Nd_{av}^{\ 2} = \text{idem} \tag{7.52}$$

and its relative stiffness:

$$y_0\, K_0/\rho U_*^{\ 2} = \text{idem} \tag{7.53}$$

or

$$hK_0/\rho U_*^{\ 2} = \text{idem} \tag{7.54}$$

The preservation of these criteria in the simulation is an additional requirement to the condition of similarity of the relative roughness of the bottom, in which the height of the roughness should take the average height y_0 of the plants, covering the bottom. Self-similarity of the flow takes place at sufficiently small and, perhaps, at sufficiently large values of the criterion (7.53) - see Figure 7.28

8

Heat and Mass Transfer and Phase Transitions

8.1 Heat Transfer in the Equipment Elements

When determining the similarity conditions of heat transfer in fluids along with the equations of motion (for example, in the form of the Navier-Stokes equations) there should be considered the heat transfer equations with their conditions of uniqueness in the general case - the equations of state. If it is possible to ignore the effects of compressibility, then it is sufficient to add the heat transfer equations, which for the single-phase are chemically homogeneous and isotropic fluid can be written in the following form:

$$\rho c_p(\partial T/\partial t + U\nabla T) = \mu/2(\partial U_i/\partial x_i + \partial U_j/\partial x_j)^2 + \lambda_T \Delta T + q_n \quad (8.1)$$

where c_p is the heat capacity at constant pressure; T - temperature; λ_T - conductivity; q_n - internal heat sources of power. Flows without internal heat sources in cases of negligible specific heat of friction, which is released in fluid [the first term in the right part of equation (8.1)], in two-dimensional schematization of the course of the transfer equation of heat are written as:

$$\frac{\partial T}{\partial t}+U_1\frac{\partial T}{\partial x_1}+U_2\frac{\partial T}{\partial x_2}=a\left(\frac{\partial^2 T}{\partial x^2{}_1}+\frac{\partial^2 T}{\partial x^2{}_2}\right) \tag{8.2}$$

Here $\alpha = \lambda_T/c_p\rho$ - the thermal diffusivity. When $p = const$, you can assume that $\alpha =$ const. In the problems under consideration, temperature (like pressure) is included in the equations under the sign of the derivative. So the changes of these values are significant. When rationing equations of heat transfer as a measure included in the conditions of certainty, we may adopt, for example, the difference between the set temperature solid wall (T_w) and the fluid in the primary section of the $T_w—T_0$. Then the relative temperature $T^+ = (T—T_0)/(T_w—T_0)$ shall be included in the normalized equations:

$$\frac{U_0 t_o}{a}\left(\frac{\partial T^+}{\partial t^+}+U_1^+\frac{\partial T^+}{\partial x^+{}_1}+U_2^+\frac{\partial T^+}{\partial x^+{}_2}\right)=\frac{\partial^2 T^+}{\partial\left(x_1{}^+\right)^2}+\frac{\partial^2 T^+}{\partial\left(x_2{}^+\right)^2} \tag{8.3}$$

It follows from (8.3), that along with dimensionless complexes, resulting from the analysis of the equations of motion, in the considered case, the list of criteria of similarity should be complemented with the complex:

$$Pe = U_0 l_0/a, \tag{8.4}$$

called the Pekle criterion.

It is conventional to include combination of the Pekle and Reynolds criteria, instead of Pe in the system of defining criteria – the Prandtl criterion:

$$Pr = Pe/Re = \nu/a \tag{8.5}$$

In this criterion only the parameters, characterizing the properties of the fluid are included:

$$\mu,\ \rho,\ \lambda_T,\ c_p.$$

Thus, if for in kind and on the model the same fluid is used in close thermodynamic parameters, the condition of Pr = idem is satisfied automatically.

The numbers Pr for dropping fluids are highly temperature dependent, and for most fluids, this dependence is essentially the same as the dependence of viscosity on temperature because the heat capacity c_ρ and conductivity λ_T are less dependent from temperature. The dependence of the Pr number on the water temperature at saturation line is shown in Figure 8.1. At temperatures from 130 to 310°C the Pr values for water are slightly changed and are near to 1.

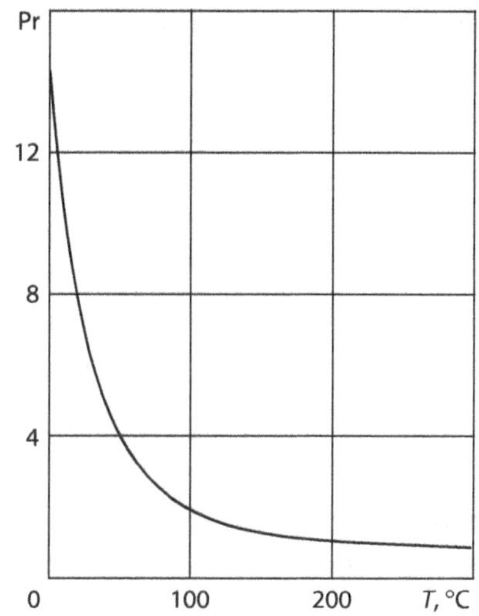

Figure 8.1 Dependence of the *Pr* number on the water temperature at saturation line.

The *Pr* number for gases virtually does not depend on temperature or pressure. It is near 1, and for this, gas is a constant defined by gas atomicity.

The *Pr* number for heavy and alkaline fluid metals, used as heat transfer fluids, changes within 0,005 – 0,05. Small values of the *Pr* number for such fluids can be explained by their high thermal conductivity. This feature of fluid metals makes simulation of heat transfer in their flows with the use of other fluids difficult. When setting the research of heat transfer in fluid metals, finding of the areas of self-similarity for *Pr* is especially important.

In the flow of incompressible fluids without free surfaces, the similarity of the fields of temperature in general case is reached, when Re = idem and Pr = idem:

$$T^{+} = T(Re, Pr)$$

In studies of heat transfer from rigid boundaries of the research problem there can be determined the heat transfer coefficient:

$$a = q_T/(T_w - T)$$

Where q_T - is the heat flow; T - average flow rate of the fluid temperature.

The normalized coefficient of heat transfer is presented as the Nusselt number:

$$Nu = \frac{a}{\lambda_T / l_0} \tag{8.6}$$

The *Nu* number characterizes the ratio of the total heat flow from the wall to the flow, defined by thermal conductivity:

$$q_T / q_\lambda = a \frac{\left(T_W - \overline{T}\right)}{\lambda_T \left(T_W - \overline{T}\right) / l_0}$$

The *Nu* criterion usually is not determinative, as it includes the value of alpha, which is not specified in the conditions of uniqueness. The *Nu* number expresses the resulting effect and is obtained in the function of the numbers *Re* and *Pr*:

$$Nu = f(Re, Pr)$$

It is necessary to pay attention to the fact that in the processes of heat transfer, conventional self-similarity of results (including the Euler criterion *Eu*) on the criterion of Reynolds is usually absent even when there are high levels of turbulence. In Figure 8.2 dependence of the *Nu* and *Eu* numbers from *Re* are identified from studies of transverse air flow of five-row corridor and chess tube bundles, is shown. As follows from the figure, in the case of achievement of the self-similarity of *Eu* on *Re*, the *Nu* number continues to change with the growth of *Re*: the molecular mechanism of heat transfer that remains comparable with the molar one. If the fluid can be considered as incompressible (conductivity, viscosity, density and heat capacity of the fluid are constant), then equations of fluid motion turn out to be decoupled ("disengaged") with equations of heat transfer, as a result of it, solution of equations of motion does not depend on the field of temperatures. This incoherence between equations of motion and equations of heat transfer, occurring at constant values of μ, ρ, λ_T, and c_p, is essential for the estimated-theoretical solution (or at numerical simulation) of respective problems and allows us to outline a relatively easy (at least in principle) way of calculating heat transfer in fluid flow. For this it is sufficient to solve equations of motion, and to substitute the obtained velocity values to the heat transfer equation.

From positions of physical modeling, the specified "disengagement" of equations gives the possibility in the absence of external heat exchange to use the analogy of heat transfer with conservative impurities transfer. This is possible due to formal similarity of records of the Fourier heat equation and the Fick law [see equation (2.31)]. In this analogy, gradient of substance concentration matches temperature gradient, and thermal diffusivity gradient α matches the diffusion coefficient D. Condition (8.4) in this case is replaced by the following:

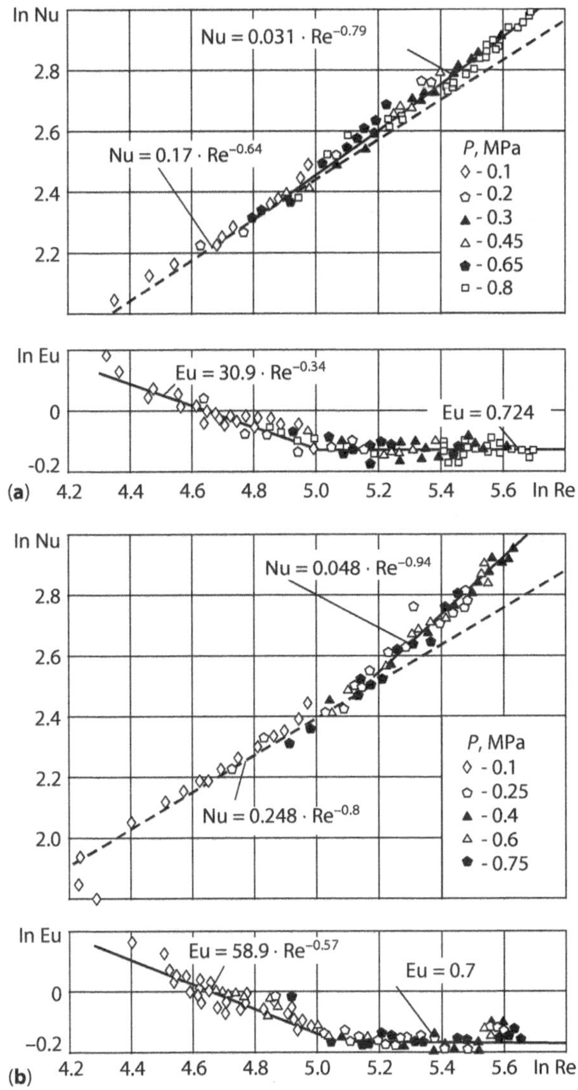

Figure 8.2 Dependences $Eu = \varphi(Re)$ and $Nu = f(Re)$ for cross air streamlining five-row corridor (a) and chess (b) beams with relative distances between pipes $l_1/D = 1.28$ and $l_2/D = 1.5$ [73].

$$(U_0 l_0/a)_N = (U_0 l_0/D)_M$$

The transition from a field of concentration on the analogue to the field of temperatures in kind, is based on the ratio of:

$$(\Delta T_i/\Delta T_0)_N = (\Delta c_i/\Delta c_0)_M$$

By using this analogy in [118 and 123] we performed a study of the time variation of the temperature field at the entrance into the active zone of the tank water reactor under pressure-population, with a sudden connect one of the heat transfer loops through which heat carrier temperature was dramatically different from its temperature in other loops. Through one of the loops the salt solution was supplied on the model. Its concentration was measured by conductivity sensors.

Part of the results of this study in the form of contour value $T^+ = \dfrac{T - \overline{T}}{\overline{T} - T_0}$, where T is the temperature at point: $\overline{T} = \dfrac{\int_Q T dQ}{Q}$; Q is the flow of heat-carrier; T_0 is the temperature of the heat carrier into plug-loop presented in Figure 8.3.

The presence of external heat exchange (for example, in the ponds-coolers or other heat exchangers) complicates the use of the considered analogy. In such cases, physical modeling can be combined with numerical, i.e. to implement hybrid simulation. The use of "hybrid" model with a distribution time of water consumption within cooler is described in Section 8.3.

All of the above holds when the fluid can be considered as incompressible. If it cannot, then at the analysis of similarity, the thermodynamic relationships should be added to equations (8.1) and (8.2). This will allow

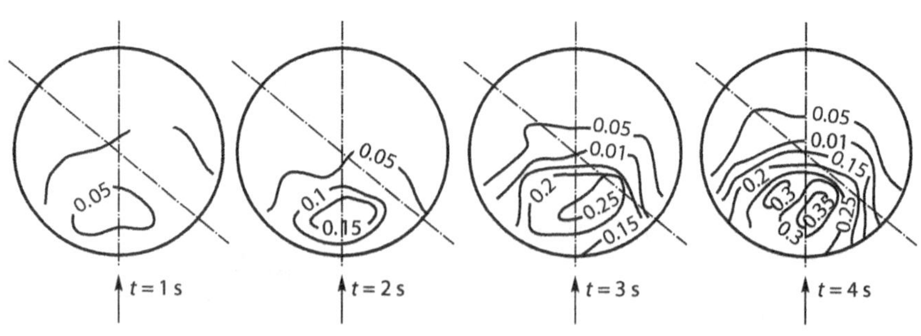

Figure 8.3 Changing of the field of temperatures in time at the inlet into the active zone of the reactor with a sudden connection of the loop, containing the heat-transfer with - lower than in other loops – temperature.

consideration of a number of values and ratios related to the molecular structure of the fluid. This applies primarily to the kinetic coefficients of heat capacity, and equation of the state of a fluid. Variability of kinetic coefficients, like fluid density, depending on temperature and pressure, leads to a change in velocity distribution of temperatures and concentrations in the fluid flow, thus, affecting the intensity of the processes of transfer of momentum, heat and mass.

Changing of the local properties of the fluid particularly affects characteristics of the boundary layer. In [50] it is stated that in case of insignificance of effects of buoyancy, the main reason for adjustment of velocity profile at wall is the heterogeneity of the viscosity field, and the reason for reconstruction of the temperature profile is inhomogeneity of the thermal conductivity field. The impact of the variability of the properties of the fluid on the velocity distribution depends on the direction of the flow of heat. When the flow of heat from walls of the velocity profile in the boundary layer is more uniform, and in comparison, with isothermal for the frictional resistance reduced, the flow of heat to the wall grows.

Zukauskas and Shlanchauskas [50] invites us to consider the variability of the properties of the fluid introduction into the system of defining criteria along with Re and *Pr* relations Pr/Pr_{ω} (Pr - Prandtl number, composed from the values corresponding to the temperature of the unperturbed flow of fluid, and Pr_{ω} - the same number composed from the values corresponding to the wall temperature). Figure 8.4 demonstrates changing the velocity profile of glycerin in a flat wall depending on this relationship with the direction of the flow of heat to the wall, as in Figure 8.5 – the profile changes the water flow rate depending on relations in different directions of the flow of heat.

In general, the system of criteria, corresponding to the motion of a viscous and heat conducting fluid, should contain molecular characteristics of fluid or directly associated macroscopic parameters. In [114] it is shown that these quantities are critical parameters, i.e. values of pressure, temperature and density are critical points. Strictly speaking, thermodynamic similarity is possible if substances on the model and in kind are in the appropriate states, when the simplexes P/P_{cr}, T/T_{cr}, $\bar{U}/\bar{U}_{cr}$ ($\bar{U}$ - specific volume) for them are equal, and these substances meet one and the same reduced equation of state (equation of state of the real fluid or gas, in particular the Van-der-Waals equation, in which thermodynamic parameters are normalized with their critical values).

Strict observance of conditions of thermodynamic similarity leads, in most cases, to insurmountable technical difficulties of modeling. Therefore,

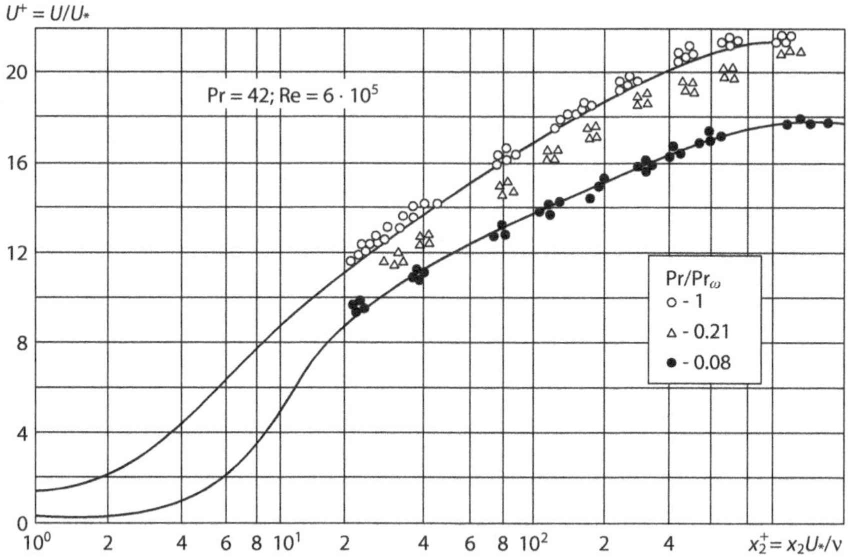

Figure 8.4 Changing of the glycerin flow velocity profile near a flat wall when it is heated at different Pr/Pr_ω relations

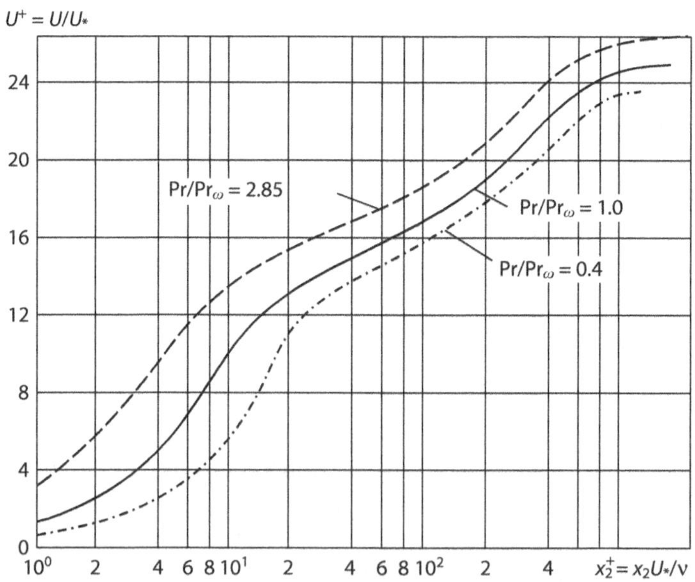

Figure 8.5 Changing of the profile of water flow velocity at the plate when it is heated ($Pr/Pr_\omega<1$), cooled ($Pr/Pr_\omega>1$) and in isothermal conditions ($Pr/Pr_\omega = 1$).

usually the studies are limited to the achievement of the approximate similarity with the assumption that in the studied range of changes of thermodynamic parameters of change, part of the characteristics of the fluid can be neglected. For example, in case of materiality of the buoyancy effects due to changes in density, fluid viscosity, its heat capacity and thermal conductivity are accepted to be constant. Here the system of defining criteria along with hydrodynamic criteria and the Prandtl number (or Pekle) includes the Archimedes criterion:

$$Ar_{\Delta T} = \frac{gl_0}{U^2{}_0} \beta_T \Delta T_0. \tag{8.7}$$

where β_T - temperature coefficient of fluid expansion, and with free convection (with circulation, defined by density gradients, associated with non-isothermality) – the Grasgof criterion:

$$G_r = \frac{gl^3{}_0}{U^2{}_0} \beta_T \Delta T_0. \tag{8.8}$$

If in conditions of uniqueness, the heat flow q_{TO} is set, and the temperature difference ΔT_0 is not, then Archimedes and Grasgof criteria can be rewritten in another form:

$$Ar_q = \frac{gl_0}{U^2{}_0} \frac{\beta_T q T_0}{c_\rho}; \tag{8.9}$$

$$Gr_q = \frac{gl^3{}_0}{\upsilon^2} \frac{\beta_T q T_0}{c_\rho} \tag{8.10}$$

Sometimes it is believed that to ensure similarity of turbulent free convection, it is necessary at least that convection current on the model is turbulent. This requires $Gr>10^7$. In investigation of problems of forced and mixed convection, the role of criteria (8.7) and (8.8) is continued, and such criteria should be considered in conjunction with other criteria of equivalence determining the relevant flow (Ch. 4 or 5).

With free convection, effective generalization in some cases, is achieved by the introduction of the Rayleigh criterion:

$$Ra = Cr \Pr = \frac{g\beta_T}{\nu a} l^2{}_0 \Delta T_0 \tag{8.11}$$

For the current along the plate, the Nusselt number, for example, is uniquely determined by the *Ra* criterion [114]:

$$\mathrm{Nu} = 0.135\mathrm{Ra}^{1/3} \tag{8.12}$$

Using the above considerations, hydro-thermodynamic modeling of water-filled metal blocks through a compartment of the external borders of which the heat comes, was executed in Hydroproject SRS. These blocks are of differing designs, position in space and heat flows supply scheme. The main problem of the study was the choice of such a circulation scheme for each block, which would provide valid temperature gradients in the metal structures to avoid dangerous deformation and damage to the blocks.

In Figure 8.6 the temperature distribution, obtained in the experiments, is shown (contours of $\frac{T-T_1}{T_2-T_1}$ value, where T is the temperature at a point, T_1 - temperature on entering the block, T_2 is the same on exit) of steel structures of one of the blocks in different water circulation schemes in it.

8.2 Transport Processes in the Fluid

Transfer of water masses with any impurities or heat in a fluid under the known hydraulic mode, is determined by the corresponding conservation equation [see (2.119)].

The similarity criteria of transfer processes are significantly dependent on whether the portable substance is passive or active. Passive impurity in definition, does not affect the hydrodynamic picture in the pond. In all other cases, the impurity is considered to be active. Strictly speaking, passive impurities do not exist. Even if the impurity of the properties are indistinguishable from water, it modifies the source of the hydrodynamic field. Introduced classification makes sense (as already repeatedly noted above) when fixed as valid differences in compared settings. Simulation of transfer of a passive admixture is automatic, while ensuring equivalence of hydrodynamic fields, boundary conditions and preservation of the condition of passivity in kind and on the model.

Recalculation of results of measuring the concentration of the admixture $c(x,t)$ is done by the formula:

$$c/c_0(x_1/l_{10}, x_2/l_{20}, x_3/l_{30}, t/t_0) = idem \tag{8.13}$$

Here c_0 is defined concentration in the characteristic point; l_{10} - a characteristic linear scale; and t_0 is the characteristic time scale, when modeling with geometric distortion of scale is not straightforward and depends on the specific research objectives.

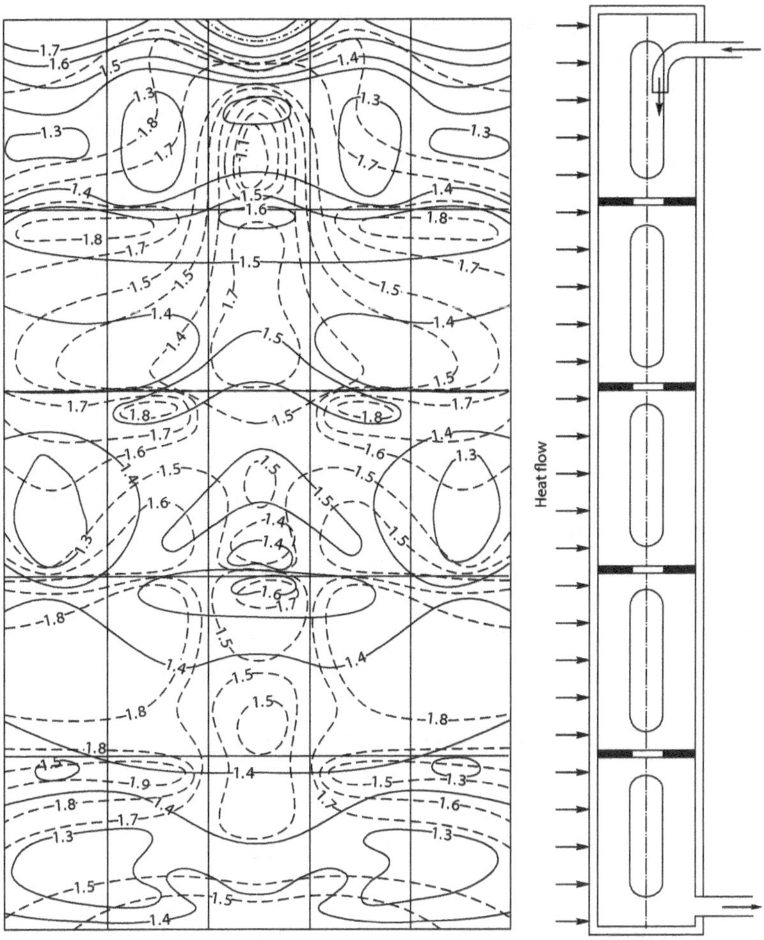

Figure 8.6 The temperature distribution along the metal wall of the heat insulation block in different water circulation schemes in it:
________-water supply to all compartments; - - - - - - - - - - supply in the central compartment.

Practically, when modeling the transfer of a passive admixture, special attention should be paid to monitoring the implementation of boundary conditions for impurities. Admixture can be absorbed by the border or can rebound from it. The corresponding boundary condition in the general case can provide additional similarity criteria.

Study of mass transfer models (and in kind), in many cases, can be facilitated by the use of the Lagrangian coordinates. A variant of this approach is consideration of the distribution function of a certain amount of fluid to time in one or another part of the considered flow regions. The basic idea is that marking a small amount of fluid will fix the time of his pre-tenure varying selection. For example, consider that the water, which is discharged (and from which it is taken), is a fluid flow Q. The task is to estimate the mass transfer within the reservoir. We will tag the water received by the pond in the period (0,0 + Δt) with mass m_0 aiming substances and fix in time *t* the concentration aiming substances *c(t)* at the output of the pond.

Function

$$p(t) = \frac{c(t)}{m_0} Q = \frac{c(t)}{c_0 \Delta t} \tag{8.14}$$

Here $c_0 = m_0/Q\Delta t$ - initial concentration aiming substances.

The function *p(t)* was first proposed and studied by the authors in 1957 applied to the water reservoirs-coolers TPP [82 and 93]. It was named the distribution function of the flow rate for the time spent in reservoir. More exactly it should be called the density of the fluid distribution over time. The value of $p(t)\Delta t$ characterizes the relative volume of the fluid located in the reservoir during a time $(t, t + \Delta t)$. The flow of fluid coming out of the reservoir at a given moment τ, is made up of items that fall into the pond in the interval $(\tau, \tau\text{-}t)$, where *t* is changed from 0 to ∞.

Therefore

$$Q = \int_0^\infty Q p(t) dt \text{ and } \int_0^\infty p(t) dt = 1. \tag{8.15}$$

Depending on the conditions of water exchange the form of *p(t)* functions can be quite varied [82].

In particular, two critical situations are possible: "the ideal displacer," when the incoming water, without stirring, displaces water that was in the pond previously; and the "ideal mixer," when the incoming water immediately, fully and uniformly, is mixed in the pond.

In the first case the function *p(t)* has the form of the Dirac Delta-function:

$$p(t) = \delta(t\text{-}W/Q) \tag{8.16}$$

In the second case:

$$\left. \begin{aligned} p(t) &= \frac{Q}{W} \exp - \frac{tQ}{W}, t \geq 0; \\ p(t) &= 0\,, t < 0 \end{aligned} \right\} \tag{8.17}$$

Here W is the reservoir volume.

The function $p(t)$ has an important property, arising from the condition of conservation of mass and mass transfer in a water body:

$$\int_0^\infty t\, p dt = W/Q \tag{8.18}$$

The proof of (8.18) is available in [82]. Ratio (8.15) and (8.18) show that the typical time scale for description of the mass transfer processes is the value:

$$t_0 = W/Q \tag{8.19}$$

It is rational to consider density of distribution $p(t)$ in the dimensionless form (in function of the relative time $t^+ = t/t_0$) with the time scale is t_0. In this case the condition (8.15) does not change, and (8.18) takes the following form:

$$\int_0^\infty t^+ p\left(t^+\right) dt^+ = 1 \tag{8.18a}$$

The function $p(t^+)$ is dimensionless.

For the particular body of water conditions, the $p(t)$ function most reliably can be obtained from laboratory tests of the hydraulic or air-pressure model of the reservoir. For this you need to mark any amount, getting into the reservoir, and to determine what time its certain parts are located within the reservoir.

The model of this operation can be made uniform by dissolving a substance in the volume of water entering the model over time, which is negligible compared with t_0, and then registering in time concentration of the substance in water which is taken away from the model of the reservoir.

Time is measured from the moment of inlet of the labeled water volume in the reservoir, until its parts get to the water intake in shares t_0. It is easy to see that in this case:

$$\left.\begin{aligned} p\left(t^+\right) &= \frac{W}{m_0} c\left(t^+\right); \\ p(t) &= \frac{1}{t_0} p\left(t^+\right), \end{aligned}\right\} \tag{8.20}$$

where W is the volume of water within the model; m_0 is the mass of the solute; $c(t)$ is the concentration of the substance in water, registered at the water intake.

You can put the experiments on determination of $p(t)$ in a slightly different way. Having filled the reservoir model with water with constant concentration of dissolved substances, without changing water consumption, from a certain point of time, we start to supply clean water to the model. Measuring the concentration of substance $c(t)$ in water at the water intake, we obtain values proportional to the value of:

$$c(t) = k\left(1 - \int_0^t p dt\right) \tag{8.21}$$

where you can find:

$$P(t) = \int_0^t p dt$$

and calculate:

$$p(t) = \partial P / \partial t$$

The first of the proposed method of determining the function $p(t)$ should be used in experiments on large-scale hydraulic models, where time t_0 is relatively high and where the inlet to the model labeled water volume is easy to produce over time, and negligible compared to t_0.

The integral method of determination of the $p(t)$ function, is used primarily in cases where the time of water location on the model t_0 is short. This method is used, in particular, for conducting research on the air-pressure models.

The weak solution of salt, floats (confetti) and others are used as the marking substance on hydraulic models. In the air-pressure models it is convenient to use, for example, the low-temperature smoke, concentration of which can be taken as proportional to the optical density of the medium.

The relation (8.15) allows us to neglect the specific value of the constant, linking the concentration of the marking substance $c(t)$ and the registered signal $A(t)$:

$$\rho(t) = k_1 c(t) = k_2 A(t) \tag{8.21a}$$

Really, if you know that marking substance was injected into a stream fast enough, you can use the value (8.15), specifying:

$$\left.\begin{aligned} k_2\int_0^{\infty} A(t)dt = 1 \\ p(t) = \frac{A(t)}{\int_0^{\infty} A(t)dt} \end{aligned}\right\} \tag{8.22}$$

The relation (8.18) or (8.18a) can be used to determine the actual volume (*efficiency*) of the reservoir W_{ef}, actually participating in the exchange:

$$W_{ef} = Q\int_0^{\infty} tA(t)dt \Big/ \int_0^{\infty} A(t)dt \tag{8.23}$$

On the contrary, if you know (or set up) a certain amount within a water body and you want to determine the flow Q_l of water exchange between the volume of W_l and the rest of the water somewhere, marking the water in the volume and locking concentration marking substances c_l *(t)* on the surface, separating the considered part from the rest of the pond, we find from (8.20):

$$p_1(t) = -\frac{1}{c_1(t=0)}\frac{d}{dt}c_1(t) \tag{8.24}$$

$$Q_1 = \frac{W_1}{\int_0^{\infty} t\,p_1(t)dt} = \frac{W_1 c_1(t=0)}{\int_0^{\infty} c_1 dt} \tag{8.25}$$

While ensuring hydrodynamic similarity normalized function *p(t)* or *P(t)* is apparent in kind and models should be the same. For example, as shown in Figure 8.7, plans flows in hydraulic and air-pressure models differ little. Accordingly, the function *P(t)*, defined in different ways on different models, is also very close (Figure 8.8). Hydraulic model scaled $M_l = 1/200$; $M_h = 1/75$ for n = 0.012; air-pressure model $M_l = 1/2500$; $M_h = 1/450$ for n = 0.013; however, it was made a condition $\lambda b/h = idem$, providing the approximate similarity plan currents. The similarity of functions *P(t)* indicates, in particular, that the main processes of migration in the reservoir are connected with transfer and mixing of the mass of fluid in the plan. The function *p(t)* or *P(t)* reflect what we usually mean by turbulent mixing.

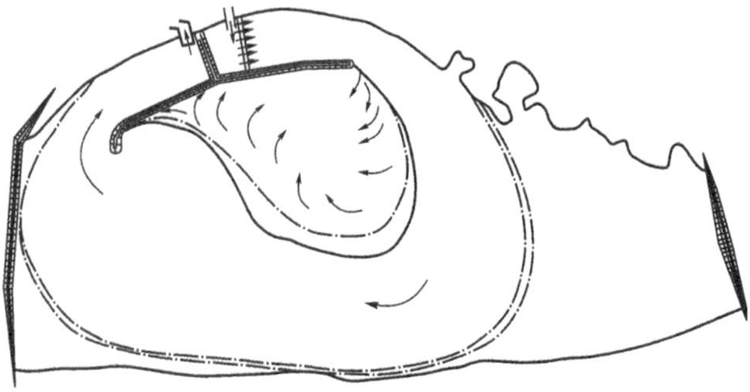

Figure 8.7 Transit jet outlines in the Zmiyivskaya GRES pond-cooler
________________ hydraulic model;
-- *----*----*----*----*--- air model.

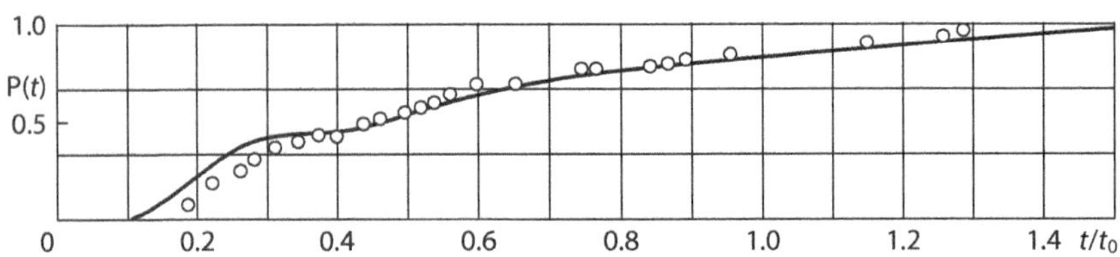

Figure 8.8 The integral distribution function *P(t)* of water volumes, withdrawn from the Zmiyivskaya GRES pond-cooler, on the time of staying in the pond:
———— air model (registration of smoke concentration); O - hydraulic model [numerical integration of the p(t) function].

Therefore, the repetition of experiments under constant external conditions should give various types of these functions. It is clear that the registration of *p(t)*, on the intake of high-frequency pulsations, are smoothed out and what can be noticed is only disturbance to the scope of the order of t_0.

In fact, such variations are observed in the experiment (Figure 8.9). It is important that differences in the results have not been associated with a lack of passivity marking substance or changing any of the conditions of flow. For example, when used to mark a water hydraulic model, floats get the picture mixing distorted due to the fact that in the surface layer (where the floats are) velocity, even when well-mixed in the depths of the waters, is somewhat more than the average depth current velocity. The maximum of the function *p(t)*, calculated from measurements of the number of floaters, comes earlier and is more important than using completely passive tags.

When used to mark a water solution of salt, another possible inaccuracy is if the initial concentration marking solution is small enough, the

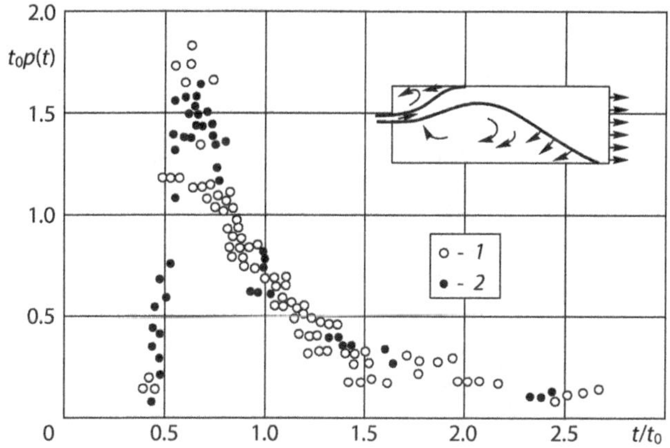

Figure 8.9 Re-determination of the p(t) function in experiments with invariable conditions:
/ - first determination; 2 - second determination.

density stratification and concentration at the outlet from the model can be secured with a higher concentration of salt at the bottom than at the surface (Figure 8.10). Even if in the output of the model (in the alignment of registration), this is not observed, but somewhere in the feed area, labeled solution stratification occurs, the function *p(t)* can be distorted and not satisfy the conditions (8.15) and (8.18). If labeled solution is heavier than water, it will move in the bottom layers, the consumption of which, of course, is smaller than the total flow. Therefore, it appears that:

$$\int_{n}^{\infty} c\frac{W}{m_0}dt < t_0 \tag{8. 26}$$

Here *c (t)* is the concentration marking substances in water out of the cistern; m_0 is the mass marking substances introduced into the water at the entrance to the reservoir; *W* is the volume of the reservoir.

But since the average movement velocities of layers, bearing solution, are less than average flow rates, the average time of motion of the solution in water is more than the average time of water movement:

$$t_{av} = \frac{\int_0^{\infty} tc\frac{W}{m_0}dt}{\int_0^{\infty} c\frac{W}{m_0}dt} > t_0 \tag{8.27}$$

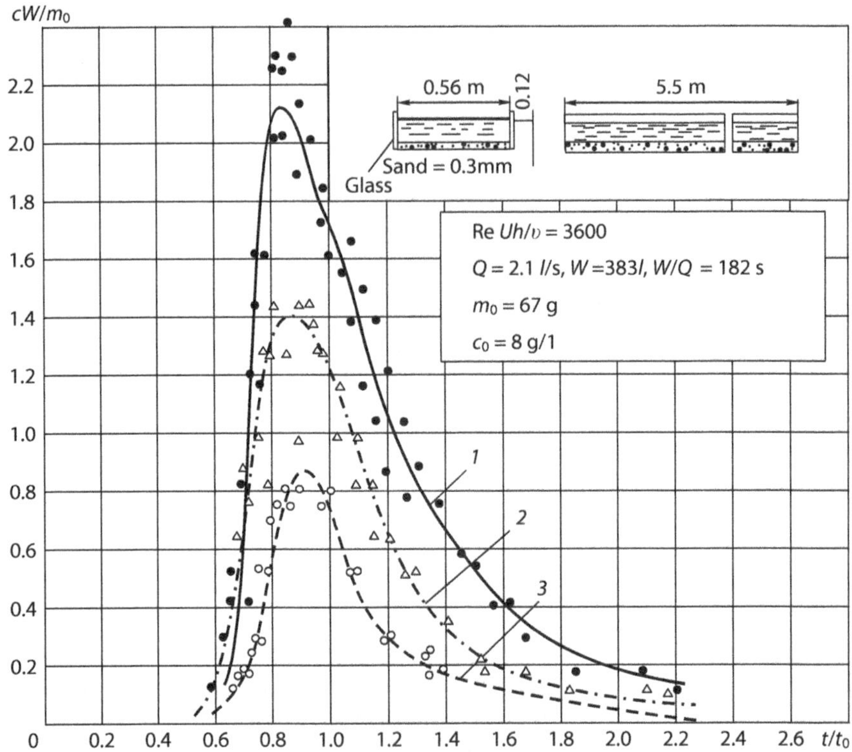

Figure 8.10 Changing of the salt concentration in time at the direct tray outlet:
1 - in the bottom layers with a large initial concentration;
2 - in the middle layers;
3 - at the water surface

If the marking solution is lighter than water, the inequality sign in (8.26) and (8.27), obviously, will change its direction.

The ultimate concentration, providing that the solution movement together with water is at its uniform distribution on depth, is connected with instability of density flow and is characterized by the critical value of the Richardson number:

$$Ri = \frac{\Delta\rho_0}{\rho_0}\frac{gh_0}{U^2_0} \tag{8.28}$$

where $\Delta\rho_0$ - initial difference of densities; h_0 - typical water depth; U_0 – flow velocity.

With the increase of *Ri*, density stratification of the flow also increases and vice versa. Figure 8.11 shows the character of change of the function

$p(t) = cW/m_0$ at change of the flow velocity, flow depth and initial solution concentration separately. As can be seen in Figure 8.11, the increase of concentration, decrease of velocity or increase of depth are acting in one way, and that corresponds to the structure of the *Ri* number.

Stability of density currents that occur when supplying salt solution, may be estimated by the average time of stay of the solution in the reservoir. As stated above, in the presence of density stratification, the relative average time of movement of salt solution is excesses 1. The relative average time of movement of clean water is strictly equal to 1. In Figure 8.12 the summary of results of the experiments, shown in Figures 8.10 and 8.11, held in direct 20-metre rectangular tray (tray width 4.2 m), is represented. The uniform distribution of velocities across the flow width was provided by installation of the overflow flow-distributioning dam at the head of the tray. As can be seen in Figure 8.12, with rather large points dispersion,

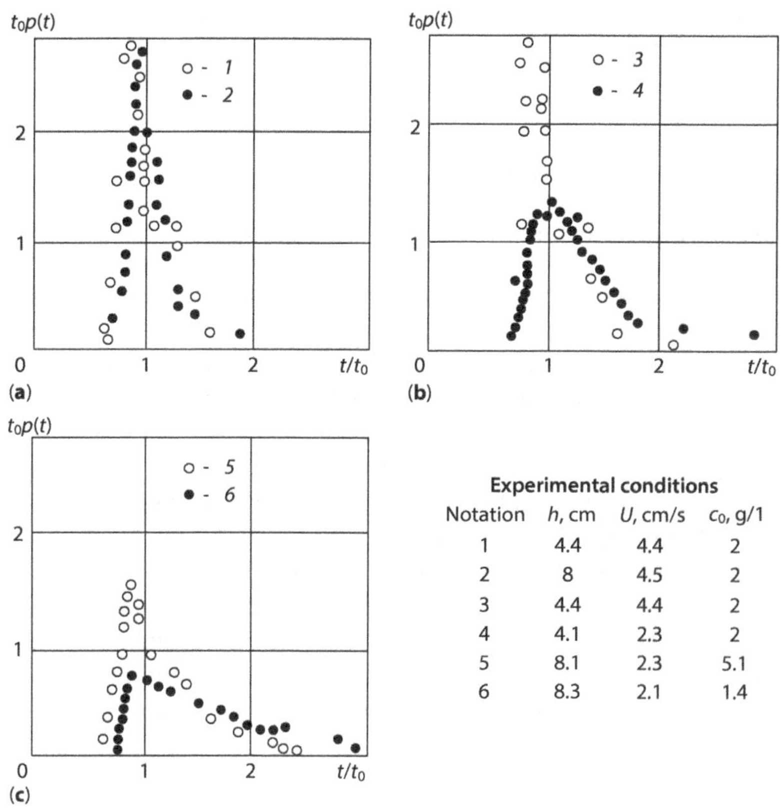

Experimental conditions

Notation	*h*, cm	*U*, cm/s	c_0, g/1
1	4.4	4.4	2
2	8	4.5	2
3	4.4	4.4	2
4	4.1	2.3	2
5	8.1	2.3	5.1
6	8.3	2.1	1.4

Figure 8.11 The influence of depth (**a**), velocity (**b**) and initial concentration (**c**) on the results of the p(*t*) experimental determination.

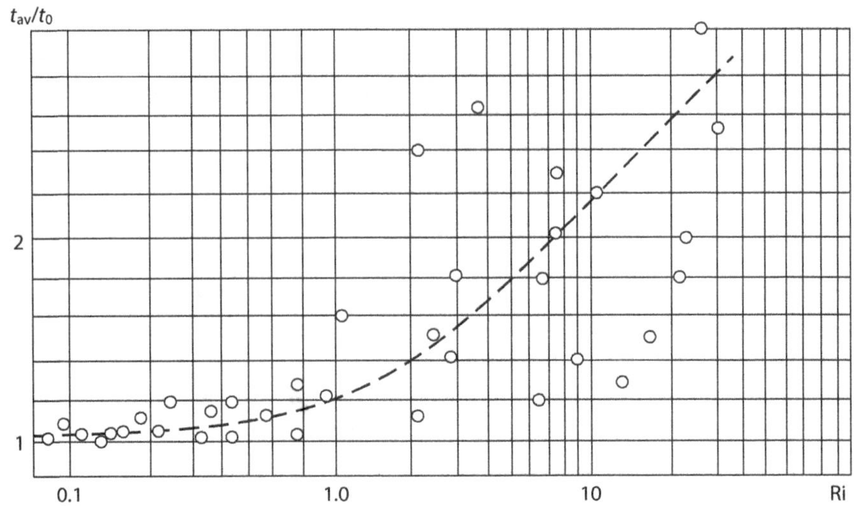

Figure 8.12 The dependence of the relative time of staying of the salt solution in water t^{+}_{av} from the *Ri* number.

probably resulting from differences in the conditions of the salt solution supply, the downward trend in the relative time $t_{av} / t_0 = \int_0^\infty t\, pdt / t_0 \int_0^\infty pdt$ at the decrease of the Ri number, is clearly traced. In some experiments salt was poured into the stream. In other experiments the concentrated solution was supplied. The salt solution, in certain cases, was supplied directly in the forward part of the tray, sometimes in the mixer in front of the jet-distributing dam at the head of the model.

When *Ri* <0.09 ÷ 0.1, the relative time is practically equal to 1 and does not depend on the *Ri* number. In this range, movement of the salt solution is realized only together with water masses.

In the study of mass transfer in the non-stationary flow densities of distribution $p(\tau, t)$ and distribution functions $P(\tau, t)$, considered as functions of two variables, - τ time of input (or output) of marking water in a reservoir with the flow rate Q_+ (or from a reservoir Q_-) and *t* time of stay in the pond, can be used. From the condition of conservation of the marking substance mass, we obtain:

$$m_0(\tau) = \int_0^\infty c(\tau+t)Q\_(\tau+t)dt \tag{8.29}$$

where m_0 - mass of dissolved marking substances; $c(\tau_1)$ - its concentration at the outlet of the water body; $Q_{-}(\tau_1)$ - water flow at the outlet from the water body.

We define p and P:

$$\rho(\tau,t) = c(\tau + t)Q_{-}(\tau + t)/m_0 \tag{8.30}$$

$$P(\tau,t) = \int_0^t p(\tau,t)dt \tag{8.31}$$

Just as in stationary conditions, the functions $p(\tau, t)$ and $P(\tau, t)$ are characterized by mass transfer in the pond.

Consider that the function $p(\tau,t)$ is essentially the green function for the equation of mass conservation. Described techniques for obtaining this function easily converted to the algorithm of the numerical model when setting the coefficients of the equation, are defined in the picture of the current.

The time scale, under non-stationary conditions, must be equal to the scale of values of $t_0 = W/Q$. In particular, when modeling the distortion scale: $(M_1 \neq M_h)$

$$M_t = M_l/M_U \tag{8.32}$$

The duration of the experiment on the study of mass transfer must be at least a few t_0. In stationary conditions, assessment of necessary duration of the experiment will receive from the consideration of the function, P(t) for "the perfect mixer":

$$P(t) = \frac{1}{t_0}\int_0^t \exp(-t/t_0)dt = 1 - \exp(-t/t_0) \tag{8.33}$$

Value

$$1\text{-}P(t) = \exp(-t/t_0) \tag{8.34}$$

can be considered as the relative error of the experiment on the study of mass transfer due to the limited duration of the experiment. In [181] it is recommended that the maximum duration of the experiment, is equal to t_0. Formula (8.34) shows that the use of this recommendation can give the error in the estimation of mass transfer as around 40%.

The above map, confirming the self-similarity of transfer processes under the conditions of similarity plan flows, should be classified, characterized by the sticks, averaged over sufficiently large volumes with the linear size equal to several depths. The processes of mixing within these volumes in kind and models can be different due to the influence of parts of boundary conditions, significantly different Reynolds numbers, and identical relations between the internal and external scale of turbulence (see Section 2.5). In particular, important phenomena can take place directly in the area of water discharge and intake structures. These zones should be studied for some models without distortion geometric scale, showing the art of the choice of boundary conditions on the basis of the full model, usually done with distortion of scale. The choice of scale for undistorted fragmented models depends on how detailed we should study the processes of mass transfer. Here it is particularly important to ensure the similarity (or controlled self-similar) on the Reynolds criterion. Specific limits, decreasing the value of the Reynolds criterion, should be selected based on the arguments given in Chapter 2, in connection with the discussion on the structure of turbulence. In practice, in the absence of special requirements for the details of modeling, it is usually enough to $Re_{м} = q/v > 1500$ ([96, 99] reported lower limits).

In the presence of stratification, the similarity conditions become more complicated. Density stratification in the water bodies may occur due to the non-uniform distribution of temperatures such as: summer heating of the surface layers of deep lakes or reservoirs [134]; discharge of warm waters into reservoirs-coolers of TPP or NPP [96, 116], due to the different salinity of sea and river waters [107]; and under the influence of the water saturation with fine particles of sand or silt ("turbidity" current – according to the terminology of I. I. Levy, who is the first in the USSR to start their systematic study).

The simultaneous implementation of temperature and turbidity stratification is also possible, as in the case of the Nurekskoe reservoir. The question of stratified flows is of great current importance. Significant results in the framework of the traditional models of semi-empirical theory of turbulence were obtained by the group of specialists headed by G. I. Marchuk, O.F. Vasilyev, N. N. Moiseev, and A.S. Monin.

Presentation of the outcomes at different stages of the research is given in reviews [81, 94, 141], books [10, 99, 107, 113, 134, 154, 213], and publications in *Water resources journal* (1981, № 3; 1976, № 4; 1975, № 2); materials of the Symposium IAHR on stratified flows, Novosibirsk, 1972.

All of these models describe the statistical characteristics of the fields, and in the works, in which the equations for the first moments are widely used, the hypothesis of quasi-hydrostatic pressure distribution in depth of the reservoir is considered. The resulting three-dimensional flow patterns reflect the three-dimensionality only through the continuity condition of the stream. The practical significance of these computational models may be finally evaluated only when there are at least some exact solutions that do not use the hypothesis of quasihydrostatic character of occurrences.

However, the presence of the sufficiently convincing mappings with field data [213] allows us to believe that, for example, the system of equations (2.30) may serve as the basis for formulation of rules of physical modeling and may help to find the areas of self-similarity on individual criteria. Accounting of stratification introduces into consideration the Ri criterion or its modifications, depending on the problem.

The above experiments with salt solution in a thread that is close to uniform, allowed us to estimate the critical value of a number (8.28), describing the boundary to the realm of self-similarity:

$$Ri_{cr} \leq 0{,}1 \tag{8.35}$$

The specific value Ri_{cr} depends on the conditions of the problem. However, laboratory tests with two different threads and natural observations, undertaken in the area of discharge of warm water in a large river, confirmed the possibility of using the conditions (8.35) as sufficient conditions for the absence of stratification.

Sufficiency conditions (8.35) are confirmed by the data of many publications related to different objects. So, when researching the mixing of water in rivers, in case of simultaneous administration, reset warm water (downstream) and the fence cold floating warm water to the water intake (as in the stratification) not observed already in $Ri < 1{,}6$ [96]. This example shows that there are situations where $Ri > 0{,}1$, and stratification is observed, which is usually under the action of external additional turbulizer. Most important in this turbulization is the breeze. In Figure 8.13 the distribution of the temperature measured on the basin-cooler of the Sredneuralskaya GRES in the flow cross section of the spillway is shown. In both cases (with the calm and the wind) $Ri > 0{,}1$, but in Figure 8.13, b stratification is absent due to the intense wind mixing. It is essential that stratification (large temperature gradients in this example) ambiguously depends on wind velocity (Figure 8.14).

Necessary conditions of absence of stratification or sufficient conditions of its existence are highly dependent on the details of the task, the shape of the borders of the reservoir and schematic reset and water intake. The intensity of natural (background) flows occurred before the beginning of the water heating in the reservoir, which was due to the effect of the station and other hydrothermal conditions.

The detailed study of stratification stability in relation to long-wave disturbances, which do not have the effect of viscosity, but essentially the ratio of flow depths, was carried out in [30].

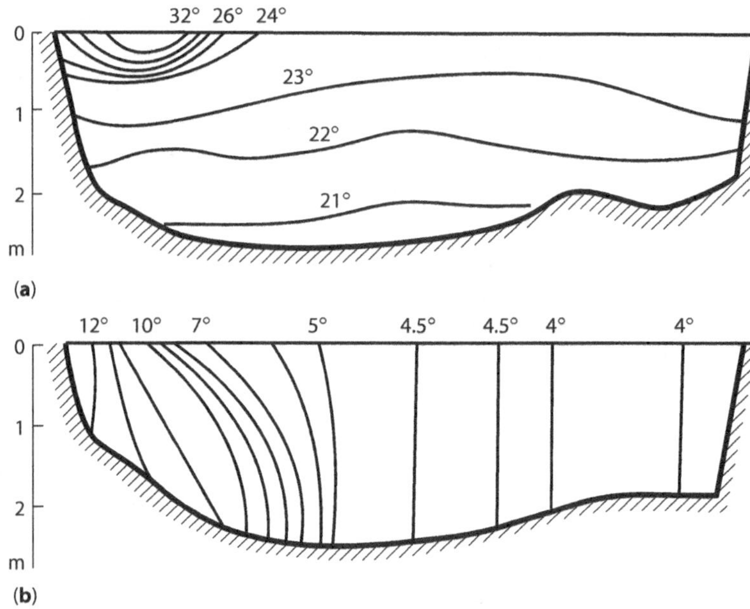

Figure 8.13 Isotherms in the cross section of the flow at the outlet of the cooling reservoir at the Sredneuralskaya GRES with the maximum flow rate of 0.6 m/s:
a - in calm conditions; б- when the wind with a speed of 4 m/s.

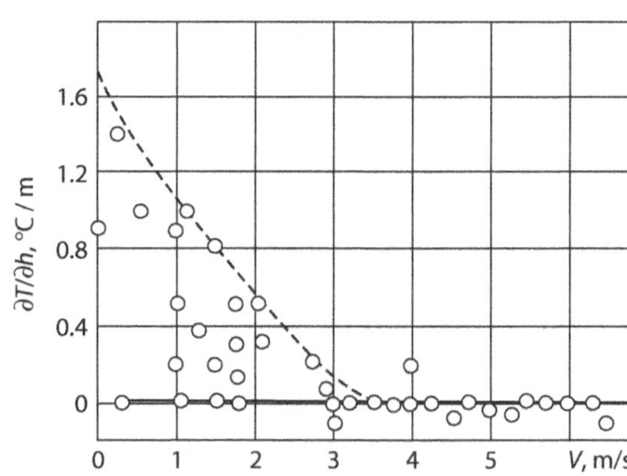

Figure 8.14 The maximum modulus of the temperature gradient depending on wind velocity over the pond:
——————— from calm to the wind: - - - - - - - - - - from wind to calm.

If the flow is such that the impact of bottom and free surface is deliberately low (for example, for a light fluid over a stationary heavy fluid, after a light fluid from a ledge in "unlimited" water, water intake from cold or heated layer near the surface of the section in deep water, and others), then in those cases when the boundary condition is not characteristic linear size, the only dynamic indicated is that the decisive criterion is the complex:

$$C = \frac{\mathrm{Re}}{Ri} = \frac{U^3{}_0}{gv\Delta\rho_0 / \rho_0} \tag{8.36}$$

or its modification:

$$C_* = \frac{\mathrm{Re}_*}{Ri} = \frac{U^3{}_*}{gv\Delta\rho_0\rho_0} \tag{8.37}$$

where U_* - friction velocity on the section surface.

According to [110 and 154] the values of the C criterion determine the shape of the section surface. In particular, formation of the "scoured" boundaries of layers should take place at:

$$C > 1650,$$

and saving of the plain, clear boundary of the section is provided at:

$$C < 150.$$

The section surface "scouring" does not mean the absence of stratification. For example, in [62] the data are given, according to which the stratified flow is held when values C range up to 15600 ($Re_1 = 60{\cdot}10^3$; $\Delta\rho_0/\rho_0 = 0{,}05$; $U^2{}_1/gh_1 = 1{,}3{\cdot}10^{-2}$). The non-uniformity of temperature distribution in the depth of the reservoirs-coolers on field data, is observed even when C = 64 500 (Shchyokinskaya GRES pond), though the clear "jump" in temperature on depth was fixed only when C = 2600 (Barabinskaya GRES pond). Also the conditions, ensuring steady position of the surface section, were identified as:

$$U^2{}_1/gh_1 \le 0.12\,(\Delta\rho_0/\rho_0)^{0{,}7} \tag{8.40}$$

In fact, in the main experiments, the depth of the upper warm water layer h_1 is changed within small limits, so the condition (8.40), probably, can be represented as follows:

$$C = \frac{U^3{}_1}{g\nu\Delta\rho_0 / \rho_0} \le (0{,}12)^{3/2}\left(\frac{\Delta\rho_0}{\rho_0}\right)^{0{,}05}\frac{h_1\sqrt{gh_1}}{\nu} \approx 850 \tag{8.41}$$

This estimate agrees with the estimate (8.38)

Criteria Ri and C (or C_*) allows us to evaluate the behavior of the surface section in relation to perturbations of different scale.

In the absence of stratification effective results can be obtained by solving the two-dimensional (planned) problem by numerical methods or physical modeling on the basis of the above rules. At the conclusion of the two-dimensional transport equation, without prior averaging on probability (see Section 2.7), we used the hypothesis for neglect of the phenomenon, which is similar (but not identical) to the phenomenon of the variance associated with the uneven distribution of instant velocity and concentration depth flow [213]. The acceptability of such assumptions, liberating you from the necessity of imposing additional restrictions on the distortion scale, was checked by comparing the calculations that do not take into account this phenomenon with the results of laboratory and field measurements. Decisive here, obviously, is the coefficient of hydraulic friction λ (characterizing the irregularity of the distribution of velocities in depth), the relative width b/h and the form of the reservoir in the plan.

In Figure 8.15 the results of calculations [90] of the p(1) function for the part of the cooling reservoir at the Sredneuralskaya GRES with the data

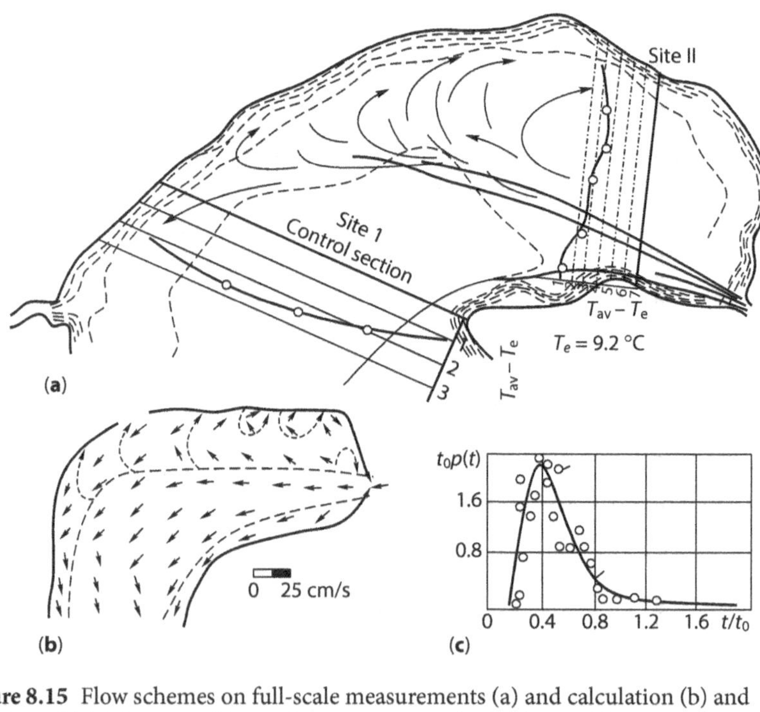

Figure 8.15 Flow schemes on full-scale measurements (a) and calculation (b) and function *p(t)* (c) for part of the cooling reservoir at the Sredneuralskaya GRES: points – datum of nature measurements; line – on calculation.

of measurements in kind [83] are mapped. In the calculations, only one empirical parameter - the coefficient of hydraulic friction $\lambda = 0.007$ was used. The results of calculations and field measurements are essentially the same.

The study of the object was produced in connection with the increase of the power plant capacity and, consequently, the cooler heat load.

Laboratory study was preceded by in-situ observations on the existing stations that allowed us to reliably validate methods subsequent experiments by comparing fixed in kind modes with the relevant regimes for the model. In connection with the fact that the large size of the pond was difficult to study, detailed study in kind has been mainly performed on its bay in the area of the spillway. On this site plan currents, thermal regime and the distribution function of the flow of time-in the mouth of the bay were defined.

When choosing a geometric scale, pressure model range is planned by its scale and roughness of the bottom. Figure 8.16 shows the outlines of transit streams recorded on the model with the planned scale $M_l = 1:5000$, vertical scale $M_h = 1:400$, and clay with smooth bottom ($\lambda = 0.018$). On a model with $M_l = 1:2500$ and $M_h = 1:400$, clay with smooth bottom is ($\lambda = 0.018$);

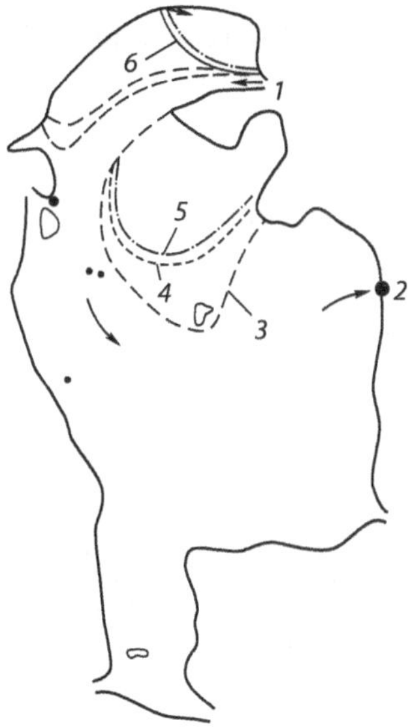

Figure 8.16 The transit jets outlines in the reservoir-cooler of the Sredneuralskaya GRES: 1 - spillway; 2 – water intake; 3 – for measurements on the model with Mh = 1:400, Ml = 1 : 5000, $\lambda = 0.018$; 4 – the same, Ml = 1 : 2500; 5 - the same, $\lambda = 0.04$; 6 – on full-scale observations.

on the same model, at the label on the bottom of coarse sand (λ ~0.040), and the outlines of transit streams in kind is (λ ≈0.007) the study area.

Here it is possible to establish, that expansion of the transit jet least intensively takes place on the first of these models $M_{\lambda b/h}$ = 0.4 and most intensely – in a case of mounting additional coarseness. Due to the fact that in the latter case $M_{\lambda b/h}$ = 1, outlines of a transit stream on this model and in kind have coincided. For the northern part of the pond, calculation of currents scheme was performed, which allowed us to identify the whirlpool border, practically coinciding with measurements in kind and on the model.

The calculations were carried out for the conditions of the models of cooling reservoirs of the Verhnetagilskaya and Cherepetskaya GRES, which have fairly complex form in the plan and noticeably different depths in the water reservoirs [89 and 90]. As in the previous case, the calculations equations, average instant velocity field (and temperatures or impurities), and the depth of the stream, well coincide with the data of measurements (Figure 8.17) [87]. Note in figure. 8.17 the different experimental implementations of the functions $p(t)$ associated with the above-mentioned that influence large-scale fluctuations.

The submitted materials and other existing mapping [154 and 178] confirm the possibility of the direct conversion of the characteristics of mass transfer with in kind models in the real range of affecting while choosing scales, providing a sort of current plan.

If the flow pattern is complicated by wind action, modeling of transfer processes still remains unresolved. For registration technique of transfer processes, the distribution function $p(t)$ and $P(t)$, described above, are particularly useful as they reflect all the features of the currents. In Figure 8.18 the distribution functions $P(t)$ and the density function $p(t)$ are compared

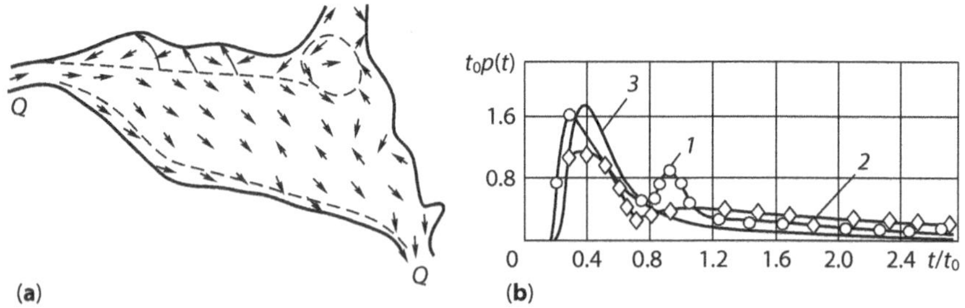

Figure 8.17 The plan of the velocity vectors (a) and functions p(t) (b) for the Verhnetagilskaya GRES cooling pond on measurements at hydrothermal models 1, 2 [87] and calculation 3 [90].

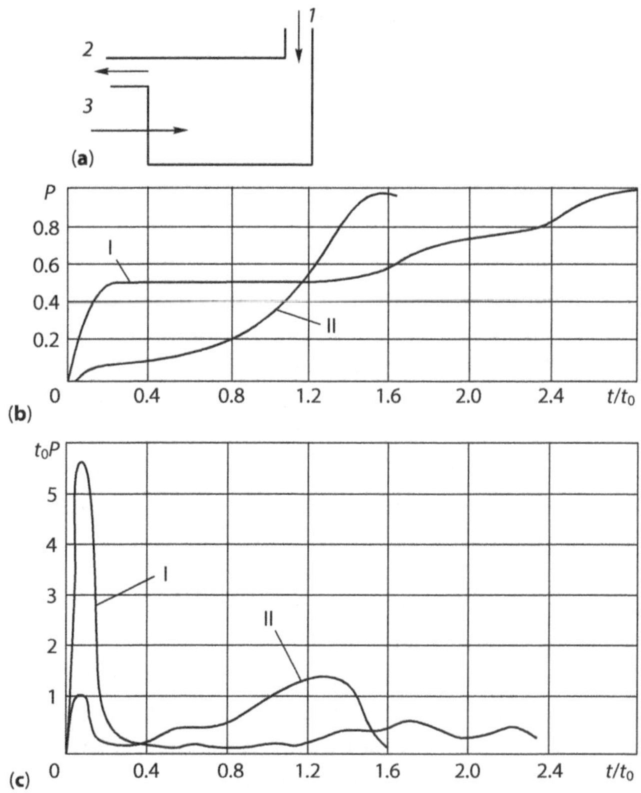

Figure 8.18 The pressure model scheme for study of mass transfer with the influence of the wind (a), results of determination (in experiment) of the integral function *P(t)* (b) and its recalculation into the function $p(t)$ (c). Velocity of line, simulating the wind action, on the model 8 m/s; air speed on the model 8m/s. Approximate natural conditions: water velocity - 0.1 or 0.2 m/s, wind speed - 5 or 7.3 m/s, respectively:
I - no wind; *II* - wind; *1* - the spillway; *2* - water; *3* - the direction of the line motion on the model.

by being registered on the air-pressure models with mobile tape under cover, imitating the wind action (model description is given in [91]). As you can see, the effect of wind on transfer processes is very significant.

In the absence of self-similarity, according to the criterion Richardson (the density), the simulation becomes much more complicated. Two questions are especially important, and the answers can qualitatively change with the advent of stratification:

first, the influence of the Reynolds criterion and the relative roughness of the bottom in terms of stratified flow;

and secondly, features of the planned tasks, the possibilities and limitations of geometrical distortions of scale models.

The influence of the Reynolds criterion can be presented in two ways:

1. due to the effect on traffic conditions in layers separating baseplate fluid, and boundary layers adjacent to hard (or loose) the boundaries of the reservoir;
2. due to the effect on the distribution of averaged and pulsation velocities in the thickness of the thread.

In our production, the main result of the study is the evaluation of the boundaries of the self-similarity, The first case, apparently, can be limited to consideration of flat, stationary and homogeneous areas along the length of the stream. The investigation of this case gives the value of the Reynolds number Re'_{lim} limiting self-similar area. In real conditions the imposition of perturbations of different origin will cause additional flow turbulization and will expand the scope of the relatively small influence of the Reynolds criterion ($Re \underset{\text{lim}}{<} Re'_{\text{lim}}$). Experimental proof of this provision for destratification of flows is provided in Sections 4.1 and 5.2.

Experimental data on the influence of the Reynolds criterion in terms of stratification is contradictory. According to the data collected in [110 and 154], the influence of the criteria *Re* and *Ri* is reflected by one criterion *C*. And influence of this criterion is very great: *C* (*C*<150)

$$\lambda = 2(U_*/U_1)^2 = 9{,}7C^{-0.9} \tag{8.42}$$

when large *C* (*C* > 1650)

$$\lambda_1 = 0{,}32C^{-0.54} \tag{8.43}$$

According to the conclusion [62 and 116] the self-similarity criterion $Re = q/v$ (top layer) is observed at $Re > 20000$ regardless of the values of the criterion *Ri* (but under condition of preservation of stratification).

The closer examination of the data that formed the basis of this conclusion, shows, however, that the coefficient λ_1 when $\Delta\rho_0/\rho_0 = 0.05$ is systematically (on 30–40%) less than, for example, when $\Delta\rho_0/\rho_0 = 0.02$ ($\lambda_1 = 0.004$). Theoretical analysis, performed by the method [30] for the scheme with three layers (two layers of homogeneous fluids separated by a layer of variable density), has shown that at small Reynolds numbers in the bottom layer, coefficient λ_1 for the upper layer depends on the *Re* number being somewhat stronger than in the "smooth" mode. Impact of criteria *Ri* in this analysis was relatively weak. The obtained result is an intermediate in relation to conclusions [62 and 110] given above.

These and other results [96] however, agree as to the amount λ_l, which at the Reynolds number of the order $(2\div10)\times10^4$ and stable stratification, is changed within $\lambda_l = 0.002\div0.006$. Apparently, in this case there is no possibility to achieve self-similarity on the Reynolds criterion on the conventional model.

Even more significant is that practically the only convenient way to control the friction coefficient of the upper layer of the open stream is associated with the change in his Reynolds number. Significant expansion of modeling capabilities can be achieved by using pressure models (air or hydraulic). However, you can change λ_l, due to changes in the roughness cover model. Change the coefficient of friction on the model you want for models with distortion (enlargement) of vertical scale in relation to the scale of the plan.

Such distortion, as a rule, is necessary for investigation of ponds-coolers and river objects, for which the ratio of the flow width to the depth is very high and almost non-reproducible on the model. It was shown (Sections 2.7 and 5.3), that the study of the distribution medium-depth velocities in the schedule (scheduled task) should be done with performance of the following conditions:

$$\lambda b/h = \text{idem} \tag{8.44}$$

where b is the reservoir width; h - average depth.

In relation to the stratified reservoir (8.44) should be included in the values related to the layer mainline (usually to the top layer). In the study of the effects of transverse circulation, more significantly influenced by the relative width of the stream b/h, values λ play a secondary role, and modeling by condition (8.44) leads to some errors (Section 5.3). Study of stratified flows on distorted models is additionally complicated by the uncertainty of the choice of the form of entry criteria of similarity in field densities (in particular, hydrothermal).

If you rely on the equation, closed at the level of the first moment (with the introduction of turbulent viscosity ν_T (Section 2.5), in a case when a major role in shaping currents is determined by the ratio of Archimedean force and turbulent friction forces between the horizontal layer of fluid, the similarity criterion and thermal stratification take the following form ($\nu_T \sim U_l h_l$) [78]:

$$\frac{g\beta_T \Delta T h^2{}_1}{\nu_\tau U_1} = \frac{g\beta_T \Delta T h_1}{U^2{}_1} = \text{idem}, \tag{8.45}$$

similar to the Ri criterion.

If the most significant forces acting between the jets in the plan are ($\nu_T \sim U_1 b$), the criterion of a similarity-distorted model takes a different form:

$$\frac{g\beta_T \Delta T b^2}{\nu_\tau U_1} \approx \frac{g\beta_T \Delta T b}{U^2{}_1} = \text{idem}. \quad (8.46)$$

With the same general conditions, but with the decisive role of mixing depth in the formation of the temperature field ($\nu_T \sim U_1 h_1$), criterion of hydrothermal similarity takes the third form:

$$\frac{g\beta_T \Delta T b^2}{U^2{}_1 h_1} = \text{idem}. \quad (8.47)$$

Here $\beta_T = 1{,}5 \times 10^{-4}$ 1/°C.

Similarly, the criteria of density currents similarity can be written (and will be different) as not related to temperature.

Conditions and results of modeling on criteria (8.45) – (8.47) are significantly different (Figure 8.19). The specific conditions of applicability of this or that criteria cannot be formulated yet. It can be noted that in the absence of whirl zones or at:

$$\lambda_1 b/h_1 \gg \lambda_{\text{jet}} \quad (8.48)$$

mixing in the plan practically has no effect on the total hydrodynamic picture in the pond and the simulation should be carried out under the condition (8.45). On the contrary, if there are whirl zones, the requirement (8.46) is significant.

Here $\lambda_{\text{jet}} = 2|\tau|/\rho U^2{}_{max}$ is the coefficient of friction on the boundary between the jets in the plan; $|\tau|$ - shear stress on the lateral surfaces of the jets; and U_{max} - maximally average speed in this section of the flow. According to the data collected in [91],

$$\lambda_{\text{jet}} \sim 0.05 \div 0.07 \quad (8.49)$$

The stated rules allow the approximate reproduction of the phenomenon on the hydrothermal model.

For the study of mass transfer in a stratified water basin, there can be applied a somewhat more complicated procedure than for destratification of the reservoir. In this case it is advisable to distinguish the volume moving in different layers. We define, for example, the distribution density $p_1(t_1, \tau_1, \tau)$ volume of water in time of stay in the top layer of a stratified lake. The value $\rho_1 \Delta t_1$ characterizes the share of the volume of water that had been in the top layer at the time $t_1 \pm \Delta t_1/2$.

Let us assume that the transition of the volume of the top layer to the bottom in the τ_1, is mainly due to the cooling of this volume and precedes

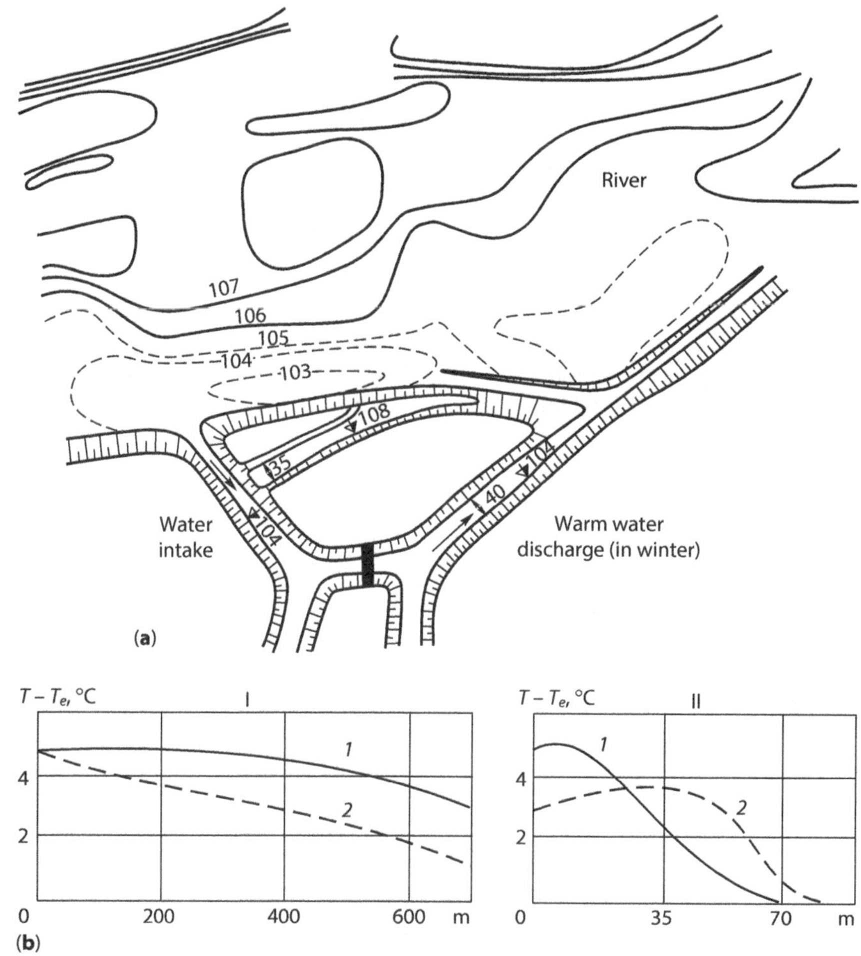

Figure 8.19 The scheme of arrangement (a) and the results of recalculation of measurements in kind (b) temperature in the area of the warm waters discharge in the river: / - along the line of maximum temperatures in the river; // - across the stream (110 m below the point of warm waters discharge); 1 - when assigning temperature on the model (8.45), $T_0 = 17°C$, $T_e = 14°C$; 2 - the same according to (8.47); $T_0 = 23.4°C$, $T_e = 14°C$.

its release from a reservoir. During the motion of the element $t_2 = \tau - \tau_1$, bottom layer temperature (and density) is not changed. Then by definition, at stationary state:

$$\int_0^{\infty} p_1(t_1)dt_1 = 1$$

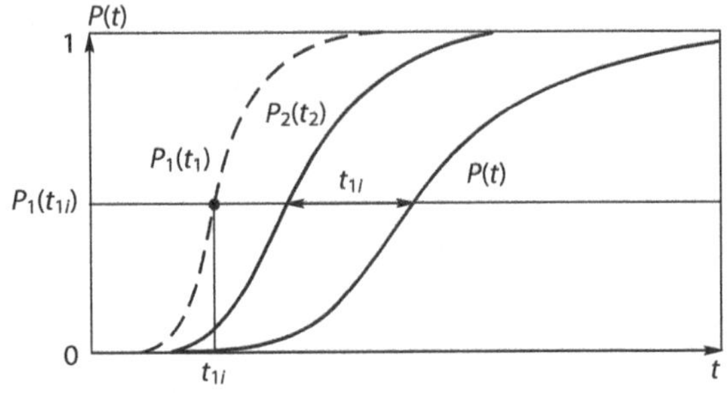

Figure 8.20 Scheme of determination of the cumulative distribution function for the "active" part of the pond $P_1(t_1)$ based on the function $P(t)$ for all the stratified reservoir and $P_2(t)$ for its "passive" part.

but

$$\int_0^\infty t_1 p_1(t_1)dt_1 = W_1/Q$$

where W_1 - volume of the zone is occupied with the top layer.

The definition of the function $p_1(t_1)$ requires some sophistication of the experiment. As stated above, the function $p(t)$ can be found, for example, by marking the fluid in all volume of the pond and registering changes in the relative concentration marking substances with $c^+ = c/c_0$ at the exit of the pond (intake):

$$P(t) = 1 - c^+(t) \tag{8.50}$$

To determine $p_1(t)$ have the same (or other) experiences aiming to distinguish substance entered, for example, in "passive" part of the pond. The time difference is stay around the pond and its "passive," which characterizes time job share of water consumption in the active (top) frequent the pond (Figure 8.20). This assessment of the cumulative distribution function $P_1(t_1)$ is true if all consumption that comes to the water intake only through "passive" bottom layer. In another important special case when all the consumption comes from the "active" upper layer, distribution function $P_1(t)$ is calculated in the same way as for the shallow pond-cooler in general.

8.3 Heat Transfer in the Water Reservoirs-Coolers

Thermal and atomic power engineering is essential to forecast hydrothermal regime of watercourses and water bodies, which are reset with warm water that has passed through the turbine condensers. Such forecasting is important both from the point of view of assessment of thermal pollution of water environment, and from the point of view of definition of temperature of water used for capacitors. If, at direct-flow scheme of water supply, the temperature of water at water works on natural, mainly connected with the hit parts of spent water intake, and at a small distance between the spillway and water intake, usually weakly depends on the heat transfer in the atmosphere. The reverse scheme is based, in particular, on the water reservoirs-coolers and the temperature of the inflowing water, which is completely determined by the heat in the atmosphere. It is possible, of course, to have an intermediate situation, when the water is partially cooled by heat emission to the atmosphere and partly mixed with fresh, cold water.

Due to the non-isothermality phenomena, first, the conditions of mass transfer in the water are because of the appearance of the difference between densities associated with the temperature difference between the water; second, the question arises about the rules of modeling of the temperature regime of water bodies on the appointed water temperature and terms of measurement results with the model in kind under given conditions of heat transfer in the atmosphere; and third, there is need for modeling not only the process of heat transfer in the water, but of mass - and heat transfer in drive layers of the atmosphere, determining the heat transfer of the water body.

The question about changes in flow patterns, under the influence of density inhomogeneities, caused by changes in water temperature, is discussed in Section 8.2.

Considering the similarity of processes of migration in the reservoir-off, also consider the terms of modeling of thermal regime of the reservoir. The heat equation in a traditional form, obtained using gradient hypotheses for representing turbulent and molecular heat transfer, results from the application of this equation of similarity transformation that gives, in addition to the previously reviewed, the new criterion (Pekle):

$$Pe = U_0 L_0 / a_\Sigma \tag{8.51}$$

Here α_Σ - total (turbulent + molecular) thermal diffusivity of the reservoir.

Conditions on the free surface of a pond usually reflect three processes that determine the mode of heat transfer of water and atmospheric radiation, evaporation and the heat transfer [80, 98, 146].

With a relatively small change in temperature on the surface of a pond (usually not more than 10 to 12 °C) all processes of heat exchange can be linearised and represent the flow of heat q_T per unit area of the free surface in the form:

$$q_T = \alpha_0 (T - T_e) \tag{8.52}$$

Here α_0 - the total heat transfer coefficient, which depends primarily on the speed of the wind over the pond V and relatively weakly from absolute water temperature T [82, 146]; T_e are the natural temperature of the water, which would be under the same weather conditions in the absence of dumping heat into the pond.

Boundary condition (8.52), when using the above-mentioned traditional forms of these equation migrations, allows introduction of the determining criterion Bio for consideration:

$$Bi = \alpha_0 l_0/\lambda_\Sigma \tag{8.53}$$

where λ_Σ - total thermal conductivity (turbulent + molecular); l_0 - some linear scale.

In the calculations of temperature distribution in depth $l_0 = h$; in the analysis of heat transfer in the plan, l_0 is the characteristic size in the plan. The Pekle and Bio criteria, in the form presented, are often used in practice (including normative documents, for example [146].

In this case, however, there was found insuperable difficulty correcting job a_Σ and $\lambda_{\Sigma,}$ reflecting turbulent currency whose parameters are usually the subject of study and cannot be reliably measured during the experience or after it. More promising seems to be the approach described in Section 2.5 that does not require the introduction of turbulent exchange coefficients. In this case, the value of a_2 in the Pekle criteria should be replaced by molecular thermal diffusivity and the criterion of influence on the processes of heat exchange should be approximately as much as the Reynolds criterion. Sufficiently large Reynolds numbers on the model ensure that in the spectra of pulsations of the inertial interval (see Section 2.5), the impact of the Re and Pe criteria may not be given through.

The Bio criterion in the frame of this approach is divided into two criteria, one of which takes into account the molecular thermal conductivity and usually can be neglected. The other criteria that can be considered as the combination of the Bio and Pekle criteria, is very important. In the study of cooling reservoirs, and it is convenient to write it in the form:

$$\Pi = \alpha\Omega/Q \tag{8.54}$$

Here $a = a_0/\rho c_p$ - the ratio of the total heat transfer, which is hereinafter referred to as the heat transfer coefficient of size $[a] = [l]/[t]$; c_p - specific heat of water; Ω - the surface area of the reservoir; Q - circulating water flow.

The special criterion of Bio (8.54) for reservoirs-coolers was published in [82], where the influence of this criterion, in particular, the "utilization of the water body," coefficient was investigated.

The ratio between the flow of heat through the free surface and convective transfer, as the defining criterion in the more general (and less efficient) form, is used in the methodology, published in [12].[1] Before these publications, and in some laboratories nowadays, recalculation of the temperature plan from hydrothermal models is executed on the basis of the hypothesis about the similarity of the isotherms location [98], i.e., accepting that in special points of nature and models:

$$(T - T_1)/\Delta T = \text{idem} \tag{8.55}$$

regardless of the Π criterion values. Here T_1 - characteristic temperature in the reservoir; ΔT - specified (in nature) or measured (at model) temperature difference between the surface and the water intake.

As shown below, the hypothesis (8.55) at $\Pi_N \neq \Pi_M$ is only true for highly superheated water bodies in stationary conditions.

In the general case, recalculation on (8.55) is permitted only under the following condition:

$$\Pi = \text{idem} \tag{8.56}$$

The criterion of Π affects the efficiency of the cooling pond, characterized by the coefficient of use of the area of the reservoir k. The value k is usually prescribed under equal temperature of water at water intake in a real reservoir with an area of Ω and the "ideal" of the reservoir area $k\Omega$, in which depth is the same as in real pond, but the speed is evenly distributed in the volume of the reservoir.

By setting up the mass exchange in the reservoir with the function $p(t)$, *the* actual cooling water in a real reservoir can be calculated by the formulas [82, 83, 87].

$$\left(T_2 - T_e\right)_\tau = \int_0^\infty \left(T_0 - T_e\right)_{\tau - t} \exp\left[-\int_{\tau - t}^{\tau} \Pi(t)\frac{dt}{t_0}\right] p(t)\,dt \tag{8.57}$$

for stationary hydro meteorological conditions:

$$T_2 - T_e = \left(T_0 - T_e\right)\int_0^\infty p(t)\,exp\left(-\Pi\frac{t}{t_0}\right)dt \tag{8.58}$$

or

[1] In [12] the symbol Π identifies the reversed value (8.54)

$$T_0 - T_e = \frac{\Delta T}{1 - \int_0^{\infty} p(t) exp\left(-\Pi \frac{t}{t_0}\right) dt} \qquad (8.59)$$

Correctness of calculations (8.57) is well confirmed by the results of measurement in kind (Figure 8.21) and on the models (Figure 8.22 and 8.23).

In the "ideal" water body with the area kΩ, the temperature at the water drainage line T_0 and at the water intake T_2 are related through the ratio:

$$\left(T_2 - T_e\right)_{\tau} = \left(T_0 - T_e\right)_{\tau - kt_0} \exp\left[-\int_{\tau - kt_0}^{\tau} k\Pi(t)\frac{dt}{t_0}\right] \qquad (8.60)$$

Or in stationary conditions:

$$T_2 - T_e = (T_0 - T_e)\exp(-k\Pi) \qquad (8.61)$$

The ratio of (8.58) and (8.61) allow one to calculate the values of k that are dependent not only on the conditions of mass transfer [the function $p(t)$], but the parameter Π.

Figure 8.24 shows how great the influence of Π (Π < 4) may be. Therefore, the recommendation that the value k is associated only with the hydraulic

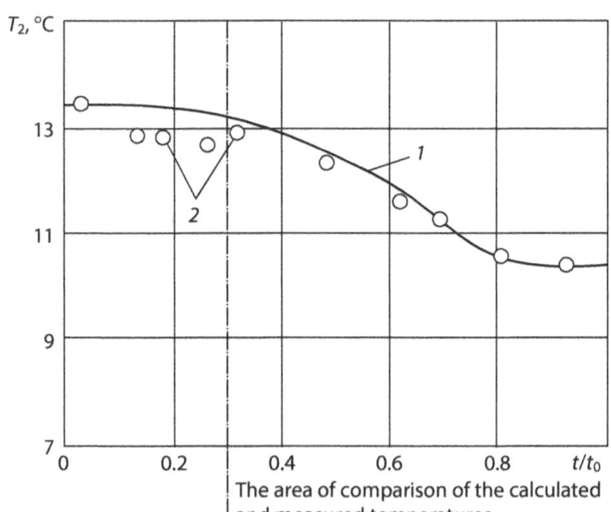

Figure 8.21 Temperature water in the control target, limiting the northern part of the cooling reservoir at the Sredne-Uralskaya GRES: 1-calculation on p(t), defined in nature; 2 - measurement in nature [83].

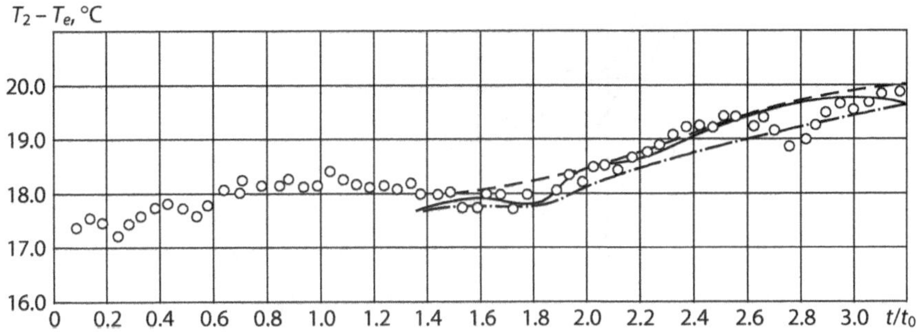

Figure 8.22 The water temperature near the intake on the model of the cooling reservoir at the Verhnetagilskaya GRES:
—• — • — •— — calculation on the functions p(t), determined experimentally (see Figure 8.17) at constant (averaged) heat transfer coefficient a;
------ the same on function 1 in Figure 8.17 with variable a;
O — results of measurements on the model [87].

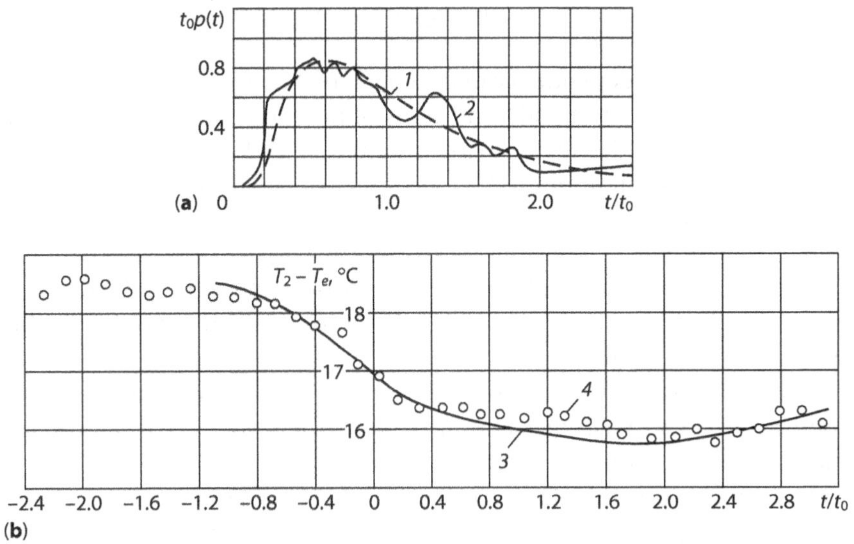

Figure 8.23 The distribution function p*(t) (a)* and water temperature *(b)* at the intake on the model of the Cherepetskaya GRES pond-cooler:
1 - on the calculation; 2 - according to experimental data; 3 - calculation (8.57) with the use of p(t) on experimental data; 4 - measurement data [87].

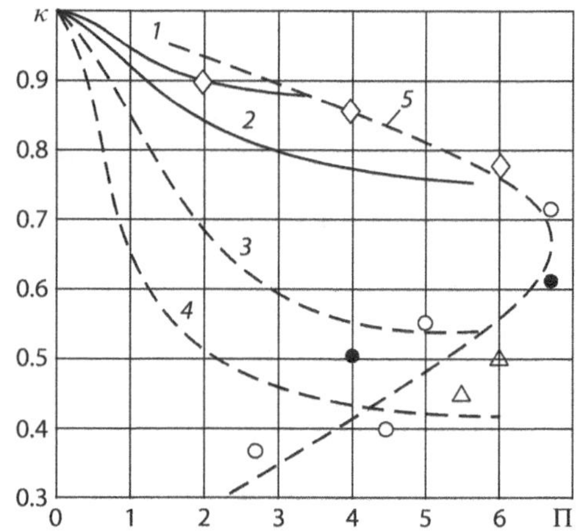

Figure 8.24 Dependences of the "coefficient of the reservoir area use" from Π criterion: 1, 2, 3, 4 – schemes of organization of the circulation flow in reservoirs at Zmiyivskaya, Sredneuralskaya, Verhnetagilskaya and Cherepetskaya GRES, respectively; 5 - self-similar zone boundary on Π criterion; points - minimum values *k*.

regime of the reservoir (with the ratio of the area of transit streams to the area of the reservoir) can be true only under small thermal loads on water (large values of Π).

There is possible dependence of the coefficient of use in the cooling pond of the thermal load Q/Ω and conditions of heat transfer, as mentioned in the publications of the thirties (for example, in [14]), but in subsequent years, this fact is often ignored. Approvals available on the admissibility identify *k* in the hydraulic model with the subsequent calculation of the temperature on the heat balance equations [96, 98, 99, 145], as can be seen in Figure 8.24, and can lead to a significant overestimation of the design temperature in the reservoir and unjustified understatement of the cooling capacity of water bodies.

In the sixties, the hypothesis of similarity of isotherms form [33] was proposed by G.V. Vostrzhel and A. G. Averkiev, who have contributed much to the evolution of hydrothermal modeling.

According to this hypothesis, using the model takes only plan isotherm (without taking into account the specific marking temperature). This plan is transferred (scale) on a full-scale reservoir. Specific values of temperature for each isotherm are calculated from the equation of thermal balance. The validity of this hypothesis currently can be proven at least for the conditions of stationary meteorological h-unit over the pond and according to the local conditions of heat transfer, only on the temperature of the water.

The idea of the proof is connected with the results of [102, 103, 198], keeping the possibility of converting equations of heat transfer to self-similar in mind, and on this basis of the rules of mutual conversion of data obtained for different values of the criterion Π . Equation of heat transfer, integrated over a depth of flow (without averaging on chance), taking into account the equations of conservation of mass of water, and with a disregard of molecular processes of transfer and phenomena of small-scale dispersion, is:

$$\frac{\partial(T-T_1)h}{\partial t}+\frac{\partial q_i(T-T_1)h}{\partial x_i}=\frac{q_T}{c_p\rho} \tag{8.62}$$

or in the areas of continuity: h и $q_i = U_i h$

$$h\left[\frac{\partial(T-T_1)}{\partial t}+U_i\frac{\partial(T-T_1)}{\partial x_i}\right]=\frac{q_T}{c_p\rho}$$

Here T_1 - some characteristic temperature, constant or variable outside connection with the processes in the reservoir; U_i - projection on 0_{xi} averaged depth h instantaneous flow rate; q_T - the flow of heat from one surface of a pond.

Dividing the left and right side (at 8.62) on q_T, enter the conversion:

$$\partial\theta=\frac{t_0 c_p\rho}{h_0}\frac{\partial(T-T_1)}{q_T} \tag{8.63}$$

i.e. we define a new variable:

$$\theta=\frac{t_0}{h_0}\int_{T_0-T_1}^{T-T_1}\frac{c_P\rho d\xi}{q_T(\xi)} \tag{8.64}$$

where T_0, T_1 temperature in characteristic points.

New variable θ is associated with temperature T, i.e., contours T essence contours θ. However, the equation for the function θ:

$$\frac{\partial\theta\bar{h}}{\partial\bar{t}}+\frac{\partial\bar{q}_i\theta}{\partial\bar{x}_i}=1 \tag{8.65}$$

does not depend on the criterion Π, which is included in implicit form only in the boundary condition for θ (via a temperature drop on the water body). Here: $\bar{t}=t/t_0$; $\bar{h}=h/h_0$; $\bar{x}_i=x_i/l_0$; $\bar{q}_i=q_i/U_0 h_0$; $t_0=l_0/U_0=W/Q$. Index 0 marked characteristic size (scales).

If without prejudice to the generality of the few to change the problem statement, schitaya specified values θ_0 in the area of the spillway, the decision (8.65), in particular the shape and position of isolines θ = const, will not depend on Π. It is the proved "hypothesis" of Vostrzhel-Averkiev, which has caused discussions for many years.

Practically, if we take the approximation (8.52) for $T_1 = T_e$ and a = const, from (8.64), we obtain:

$$\theta = \frac{1}{a}\text{In}\frac{T - T_e}{T_0 - T_e} \tag{8.66}$$

where:

$$\bar{a} \equiv \frac{a\Omega}{Q} \equiv \Pi$$

Thus, if on the model for some $\Pi = \Pi_M$ fixed field relative isotherms $\left(\frac{T - T_e}{\Delta T}\right)_M$, you have from this field of isotherms to go to the field contour θ:

$$\theta_M = \frac{1}{\Pi_M}\text{In}\left(\frac{T - T_e}{\Delta T}\right)_M \left(\frac{\Delta T}{T_0 - T_e}\right)_M \tag{8.67}$$

and this is the save any other value Π, in particular, for the conditions of life if $\Pi = \Pi_N$:

$$\theta_N = \theta_M \tag{8.68}$$

$$\left(\frac{T - T_e}{\Delta T}\right)_N = \left(\frac{T_0 - T_e}{\Delta T}\right)_N \exp\left\{\frac{\Pi_N}{\Pi_M} \times In\left(\frac{T - T_e}{\Delta T}\right)_M \left(\frac{\Delta T}{T_0 - T_e}\right)_M\right\} \tag{8.69}$$

In the trivial case ($\Pi_N = \Pi_M$), we obtain:

$$\left(\frac{T - T_2}{\Delta T}\right)_N = \left(\frac{T - T_2}{\Delta T}\right)_M$$

where $\Delta T = T_0 - T_2$; T_0 is the temperature of the discharge; T_2 - the temperature at the water intake.

If $\Pi_N \neq \Pi_M$, then from (8.69), we obtain:

$$\left(\frac{T-T_e}{T_0-T_e}\right)_N=\left(\frac{T-T_e}{T_o-T_e}\right)_M^{\Pi_N/\Pi_M} \tag{8.70}$$

At the temperature T_0, in this case, it would be convenient to take the temperature on the spillway, which in natural conditions is associated with the temperature T_2, and water and temperature difference ΔT, supported on the capacitors stations constantly (at constant power station and cooling water consumption). In experiments on model temperature T_0, control (specify) directly when setting up models, choosing it mainly from the similarity conditions of the regime of density currents.

In natural conditions, there is not usually a set water temperature discharge, and the temperature difference on the capacitors stations is ΔT.

By entering this value into (8.70), you can obtain the conversion formula of simulation results in a different form [102]:

$$\left(\frac{T-T_e}{\Delta}\right)_N=\frac{\left(\frac{T-T_e}{T_o-T_e}\right)_M^{\Pi_N/\Pi_M}}{1-\left(\frac{T_2-T_e}{T_o-T_e}\right)_M^{\Pi_N/\Pi_M}} \tag{8.71}$$

We can show [102], that when:

$$\left(\frac{T_0-T_e}{T_0-T_e}\right)_M<1 \tag{8.72}$$

and

$$\frac{1}{2}\left|\left(\frac{\Pi_N}{\Pi_M}-1\right)\left(\frac{T_0-T}{T_0-T_e}\right)_M\right|\ll 1 \tag{8.73}$$

from (8.71) is the translation rule temperatures (8.55), which is widely used nowadays as an empirical hypothesis.

If several strengthen the requirements (8.72) and (8.73), replacing T temperature with T_2, close to the minimum (for this water body), then we obtain the conditions of the self-similarity of the plan temperatures on the criterion of Π as follows:

$$\left(\frac{\Delta T}{T_0-T_e}\right)_M<1 \tag{8.72a}$$

$$\frac{1}{2}\left|\left(\frac{\Pi_N}{\Pi_M}-1\right)\left(\frac{\Delta T}{T_0-T_e}\right)_M\right| \ll 1 \tag{8.73a}$$

With these inequalities, the temperature distribution in kind can be calculated, for example, by the formula:

$$\left(\frac{T-T_2}{\Delta T}\right)_N = \left(\frac{T-T_2}{\Delta T}\right)_M \tag{8.74}$$

with a relative error $\delta T/\Delta T$, not to exceed (by module):

$$\frac{\delta T}{\Delta T} = \frac{1}{2}\left|\frac{\left(\frac{\Delta T}{T_0-T_e}\right)_M\left[\frac{\Pi_N}{\Pi_M}-1\right]}{1-\left(\frac{\Delta T}{T_0-T_e}\right)_M}\right| \tag{8.75}$$

Obviously, the modern practice of translation plan temperatures (8.55) or (8.74) are effective for heavily loaded reservoirs. In these cases, the relative overheating of water at water intake in kind and on the model are linked by the approximate ratio of the following (8.70):

$$\left(\frac{T_2-T_e}{\Delta T}\right)_N \approx \left[1+\left(\frac{T_2-T_e}{\Delta T}\right)_M\right]\frac{\Pi_N}{\Pi_M}-1 \tag{8.76}$$

Under these conditions, the comparison of the data field and model test is satisfactory [102].

If necessary, to increase the accuracy of the forecast temperature, you can use the value (8.64), taking into account the nonlinearity of links q_T (T, in kind and on the model. The condition (8.68) is a necessary condition of similarity and non-stationary thermal mode of the reservoir that is associated with changes in water consumption without changing weather conditions.

Under non-stationary meteorological circumstances, to ensure similar isotherms, a necessary condition is (8.56). In these cases, using the defined on the model of the functions $p(t,\tau)$ with the subsequent allocation of a temperature mode in kind could be especially effective. This case is an example of the efficiency of hybrid simulation.

Figure (8.71) shows that when modeling hydrothermal and in kind on the model, it is important to know that the total heat transfer is coefficient *a* and the natural temperature of water T_e.

These parameters can be calculated, for example, on the recommendations of regulations [98 and 99]. In practice, however, these important values for existing formulas are defined with a big mistake. In this regard, it is recommended with models and in kind, to organize a special dimension, taking into account local features of the site of testing models and area, where there will be built or reconstructed water. On the model of natural water, temperature is measured directly during the experiment, creating a stagnant pond with parameters close to the current model next to the existing model. On this body of water or on the operating model were systematically conducted measurements of the total heat transfer coefficient. In [87] the detailed examples of such tests are represented.

As for the coefficient *a*, this option is difficult depending on the processes of mass transfer over the pond, the state of the surface water, and other factors. Physical considerations and detailed analysis of the phenomenon (see below) leads to the assumption that the main factor determining *a*, must be the wind speed over the pond in drive layers. Dimensional analysis gives the following simple formula for *a*:

$$\alpha = \alpha' + k_w|V| \tag{8.77}$$

This formula is quite well confirmed by measurements on models [87] and in kind [80]. Data for a relatively long channel with hot water at different directions and wind speed is measured at a distance of 2 m from the surface (see Figure 8.25). The constants in (8.77) have the following meanings:

for models:

$$\alpha' = 0{,}16\ m/day;\ k_w = 0{,}29\ sec/day \tag{8.78}$$

in nature:

$$\alpha' = 0{,}18 m/day;\ k_w = 0{,}22\ sec/day; \tag{8.79}$$

(here day = 24 hours)

The relatively small difference between constants, found in experiments on models and in nature, is remarkable.

The more detailed analysis of changes in the atmosphere over the heated reservoir was started in [80]; essentially this question was thoroughly studied in the cycle of works, generalized in [113].

Despite the obvious scientific value of these works, practical conclusion for the current state of questions on hydrothermal modeling is that

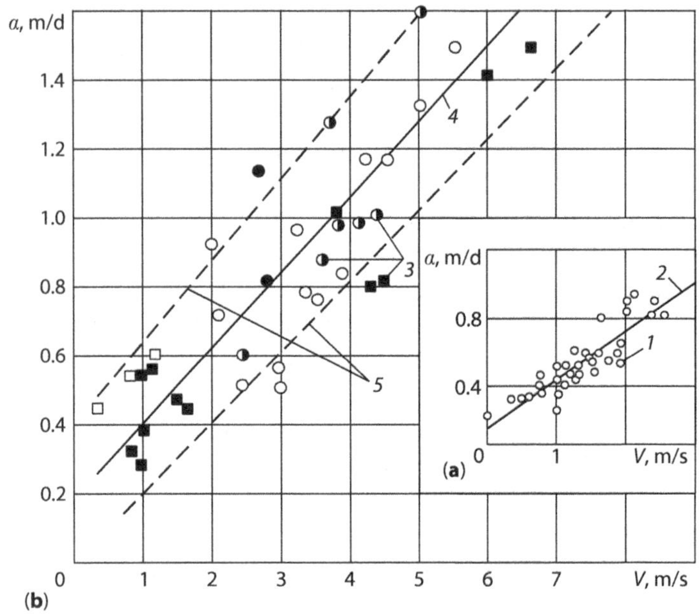

Figure 8.25 The relative ratios of the total heat transfer *a*:
a – for measurements on the models; b)-the same for measurements in kind [80];
1- experimental data [87]; *2* - the calculation on (8.78); *3* - experimental data [153];
4 – calculation on (8.79); *5* – boundaries of maximum deviations, associated with measurement errors.

specifically addressing the transformation of air masses over the pond and the corresponding change of the parameters *a* and T_e in a function coordinate is impractical. The effects of non-stationarity of meteorological regime over the pond are much more significant [80].

If you still try to take into account changes in the state of air in process of its motion over the pond, then doing it on a physical model is impossible. These changes in the atmosphere are considered calculated using plan isotherms obtained on models [68]. This technique is another example of the "hybrid" model.

8.4 Phase Transformations

In the presence of phase transitions of the conditions on the phase boundaries, there are not boundary conditions for the system of differential equations describing heat and mass transfer, and therefore they not included in the terms of the uniqueness of the whole system. The conditions on the phase boundaries include the physical properties of both media and the gradients of temperature and speed for each phase. The gradients of temperature and velocity during boiling and condensation are determined by the thermal load of the surface of heating (or cooling) system in general. Regularities of thermodynamic similarity are connected with the physical properties of the medium. Therefore, the system of differential equations, in general, can be closed only if the joining of analytical relations reflect the law of corresponding states, which allows transferring the conditions on the interfaces (these terms are sometimes called [73, 114] offline, boundary conditions) in the boundary conditions of the whole system. Thus, the conditions of similarity (as well as in the general case, considered in section 8.1) should include two simplexes, representing the ratio of the given values of thermodynamic parameters to their critical values (for example, T/T_{cr}, P/P_{cr}).

The versatility of these complexes is confirmed in Figure 8.26, where the coordinates of P/P_{cr}, T/T_{cr} present border boiling regimes, obtained for different fluids under different conditions. Here the bottom line 2 corresponds to the saturation temperature of T_{sat}, the top 1 - rated temperature of spinodal, i.e. the temperature, corresponding to limiting overheating in the fluid phase. The area below the saturation line corresponds to the existence of single-phase flow, the area between the lines responding to possible a temperature of the heating surface, providing bubble boiling. The area above the spinodal is the area of the temperature of the wall, which when possible is only film boiling. More detailed proof of the correctness of such simplexes as criteria of similarity of phase transformations are presented in [73].

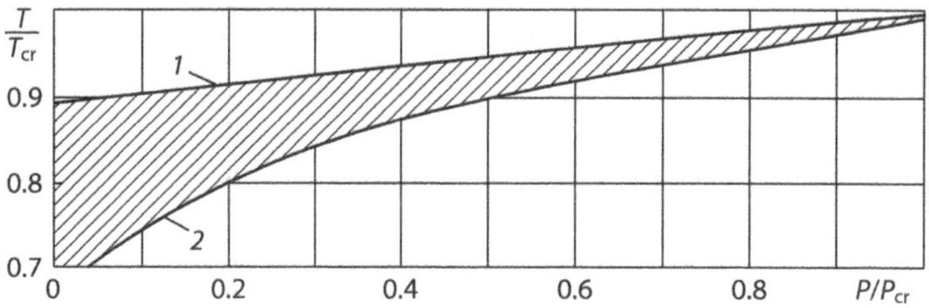

Figure 8.26 Boiling regimes boundaries.

If you know any characteristics of the environments, and their interaction on the phase boundaries, then the similarity conditions of phase transformations are considerably easier. In these cases:

Along with the criteria composed of phase parameters, typical for fluid flows in the absence of phase transitions (see Ch. 6), are based on the terms of thermal interaction of phases:

$$T_b = T_{g.b};\tag{8.80}$$

$$-\lambda_T\left(\frac{dT}{dn}\right)_b = rq_a - \lambda_{T_g}\left(\frac{dT_g}{dn}\right)_b$$

Where index g belongs to the gas phase, index b marks the boundary between phases, q_a - phase transformation mass velocity; r - latent heat of phase transformation, and it is possible to obtain the following similarity conditions:

$$\lambda_{Tg}/\lambda_T = \text{idem}\tag{8.81}$$

$$rq_a l_0(\lambda_T \Delta T) = \text{idem}\tag{8.82}$$

As $q_a = \rho g \omega_n$ (ω_n - volumetric rate of phase transformations), the following change can be performed:

$$\frac{rq_a l_0}{\lambda_T \Delta T} \sim \frac{U_0 l_0}{a}\frac{r}{c_p \Delta T} = Pe\frac{r}{c_p \Delta T}\tag{8.83}$$

Thus, accounting of phase transformation leads to the expansion of the defining criteria due to the $Ku = r/(c_p \Delta T)$ complex, first introduced by S.S. Kutateladze [73]. This criterion characterizes the volumetric heat generation in homogeneous reactions, if the r value is the reaction heat.

In some cases it is more convenient not to use the temperature difference ΔT, but the density of the heat flow. If in conditions of uniqueness the parameter of density of heat flow q_T is introduced, then the determining criteria Ku is not determinative any more, but its combination with the criterion of Nusselt becomes so:

$$\frac{Nu}{Ku} = \frac{q_T l_0}{r\rho g a}\tag{8.84}$$

or with the Nusselt and Prandtl criteria:

$$\frac{Nu}{Ku\,\mathrm{Pr}} = \frac{q_T l_0}{r\rho g \nu} \tag{8.85}$$

The value $q_T/r\rho_g g$ has the velocity dimension and may be called the condensing rate. Criterion (8.84) should be considered as a special form of the Pekle criterion, and the criterion (8.85) as a form of the Reynolds criterion.

A large number of factors, determining heat and mass transfer at change of the substance state of aggregation, usually exclude the possibility of accurate modeling of phase transitions. The approximate modeling is possible to implement in relatively simple cases.

This case is considered in [73], where there are similarity conditions of the film-type condensation of pure steam on the horizontal tube bundle.

A typical case of phase transformations is cavitation in the moving fluid. At lower absolute pressure in the flow to a saturated vapor pressure of the liquid, bubbles occur, the collapse of which causes a local increase of the pressure. This phenomenon is called cavitation, and is especially considered when designing high-pressure spillways and hydraulic machines [181, 198, 217, 29a, 37a, 31a, 104a].

8.5 Cavitation

A typical case of phase transitions is cavitation in a moving fluid. As a result of lowering the absolute pressure in any area of isothermal flow to the saturated vapor pressure *Psat,* there starts formation of vapor bubbles confined to the nuclei associated, mainly, with not fully wetted surface or suspended particles, which significantly reduces resistance of intermolecular forces to the formation of fluid breaks. Formed in the low-pressure areas bubbles are carried by the flow into areas of higher pressure, where they are destroyed as a result of vapor condensation. This process is called cavitation.

Destruction («collapse») of bubbles is accompanied by a sharp local increase in the pressure up to 10^3 MPa (depending on the size of the bubbles, content of non-condensable gases and the like) and spreading of pressure waves, which can lead to periodicity in the process of vaporization and condensation. Material of solid walls, located in the zone of cavitation, suffers impact of variable loads and may be destroyed due to fatigue effect. Other negative effects of cavitation - noise, maximum range of which falls in the ultrasonic frequency, shock and vibration of structures - so engineers typically seek to prevent cavitation. However, there are examples of useful cavitation: cavitation in the metering nozzles, in restrictive inserts which are employed as safety elements at atomic power stations and so on.

The most important parameter characterizing the possibility, stage of development and the intensity of cavitation is the so-called cavitation number (Thoma criterion):

$$Th = \frac{P_0 - P_{sat}}{\rho U^2{}_0/2} \tag{8.86}$$

where P_0 — pressure at a given point; U_0 — velocity under uniqueness condition.

Because usually the absolute pressure in the fluid cannot be below saturated vapor pressure, the increase in velocity (pressure reduction) to a value corresponding to the start of cavitation causes a change in the pressure distribution in the fluid due to expansion of zone of vapor bubbles or relatively stable cavitation cavern. The value of the cavitation number corresponding to its formation is called the critical number Th_{cr}.

The objective of the study is often to establish the possibility of cavitation occurrence. This task is not much different from the comparison of Th_{cr} number with minimal value of the pressure coefficient:

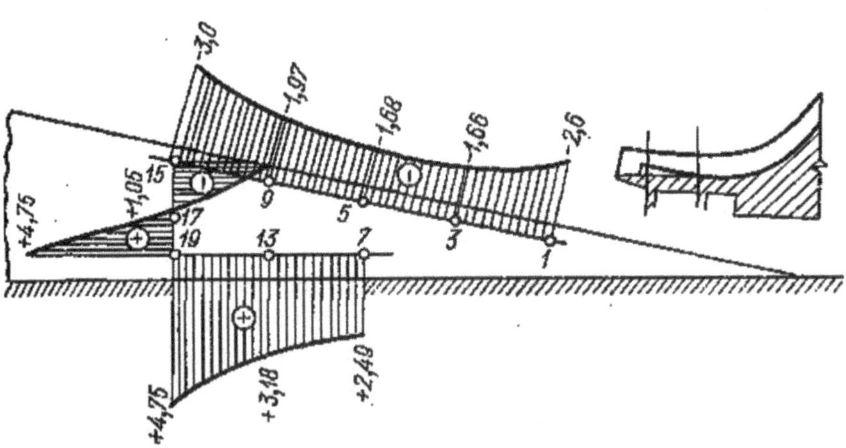

Figure 8.27 Pressure distribution on the splitter faces according to the conventional model test data

$$C_{P_{min}} = \frac{P_{min} - P_0}{\rho U_0^2 / 2} \tag{8.87}$$

It would seem that the assessment of possibility for cavitation is simple with usage of conventional model (without cavitation simulation), provided detailed measurements of pressure field (which is usually the case in a laboratory). However, with this approach, researchers can encounter errors such as occurred in our practice.

In assessing the risk of cavitation in the flow splitter, mounted on the descent from the spillway face of the dam, on the conventional model was made detailed pressure measurements on the splitter surface and multipoint measurement of the pressure pulsations (Figure 8.27). The measurement results, recalculated in the field, allow us to conclude that a significant pressure margin never drops to the saturated vapor pressure. However, at the first discharge of water in the field was discovered cavitation damage to splitter faces. Control experiments, carried out on the vacuum bench, confirmed presence of cavitation. It is obvious that the study error was related to the fact that cavitation was associated with a decrease in pressure within the fluid. Cavitation led to a restructuring of the entire structure of the flow. The foregoing suggests that if the cavitation may occur, then the simulation should provide a semblance of this phenomenon.

In studying the effect, caused by cavitation on the pressure distribution, dynamic loads on the structure or other characteristics of cavitating flow, it is necessary, along with other similarity conditions, ensure the fulfillment of condition Th = idem - for example, by selecting either a corresponding value U_{0m} or R_{0m} values. The first way to fulfill specified condition is applied in the study of cavitation in the pressurized flow, with cavitation pipes, where P_{0m} may be varied.

If selection of velocity scale is associated with any other conditions (for example, Froude rule for study of open flow), then we have to use a second path. In the study of open flow experiments are conducted in vacuum trays where pressure in the gas space above the liquid flow is regulated. However, it should be noted that condition *Th* = idem is insufficient to guarantee the achievement of similarity. The reason for this is, firstly, the impact on the cavitation caused by pressure pulsations. Unlike other phenomena for which there is *Re* self-similarity for non-uniform motion, in this case at relatively small values of this criterion it is important to simulate small-scale turbulent structures where there is minimal pressure, i.e., for a sufficiently complete cavitation simulation (especially when it occurs) Re_m numbers should be close to Re_n. Secondly, there are certain difficulties

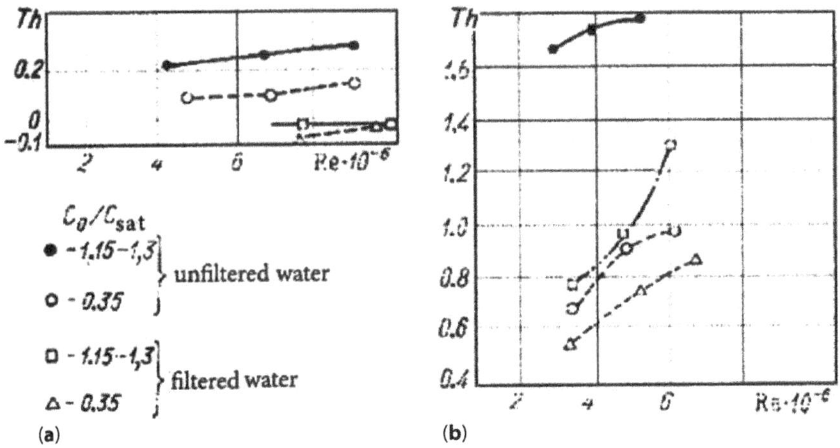

Figure 8.28 Dependence of cavitation number *Th* corresponding to its appearance in the body at attached (**a**) and detached (**b**) flow, on the Re number at different contents of cavitation nuclei and gas (filtered and unfiltered water and a different ratio of measured c_0 to the limit gas concentration C_{sat} of dissolved gas)

in the assessment of the pressure P_{sat} which is affected by the surface tension, concentration of dissolved gases, such properties of inclusions as their size, amount and shape.

Systematic studies [181] have shown that the onset of cavitation behind a body depends greatly on the composition of cavitation nuclei present in the liquid, and that the degree of influence of the nuclei composition is associated with the flow characteristic gradients (Figure 8.28). The research also showed that the value of *Th* cavitation number is strongly influenced by "prehistory" of the studied fluid. For example, it is revealed that for the same body, at the same gas and nuclei concentration, cavitation number Th_{cr} varies widely depending on whether the fluid was at rest before the experiment, moved under cavitation or was under pressure.

Described circumstances indicate the need for a thorough analysis in the cavitation simulation. In particular, in each individual case properties of a liquid should be comprehensively studied, using, for example, cavitation tests in standard conditions. It should be noted that if there is a free surface involved, liquid properties on the model may change during the experiment due to the gas involvement and not correspond to the field due to this circumstance. However, most often such discrepancy provides some margin in assessment of cavitation risk.

Typically, cavitation on the model appears at lower values of Th and its effects are weaker than in the field. The differences between the model and the field are smaller at larger geometric scale of the model and greater

Experiment conditions

$U_\infty/U_{cr\infty}$	$U/U_\infty = f\left(\xi_c \frac{U_\infty(t)}{l_0}\right)$		Th experiment	$U_\infty/U_{cr\infty}$	$U/U_\infty = f\left(\xi_c \frac{U_\infty(t)}{l_0}\right)$		Th experiment
	calculation	experiment			calculation	experiment	
	Nozzle diameter 14.6 mm				Nozzle diameter 25 mm		
0,45	1	○	6	2,42		○	6
0,6		●	7	0,53	1	◊	7
1,15	2	△	8	0,68		●	8
1,33	3	□	9	1,2	2	△	9
1,82	4	▲	10	1,48	3	□	10
3	5	■	11	1,6	4	▲	11
				1,87	5	■	12

Note: ζ_c—nozzle resistance factor for stationary process; l_0—nozzle typical size; U_{00}, U_{cr00} – ref. § 4.3

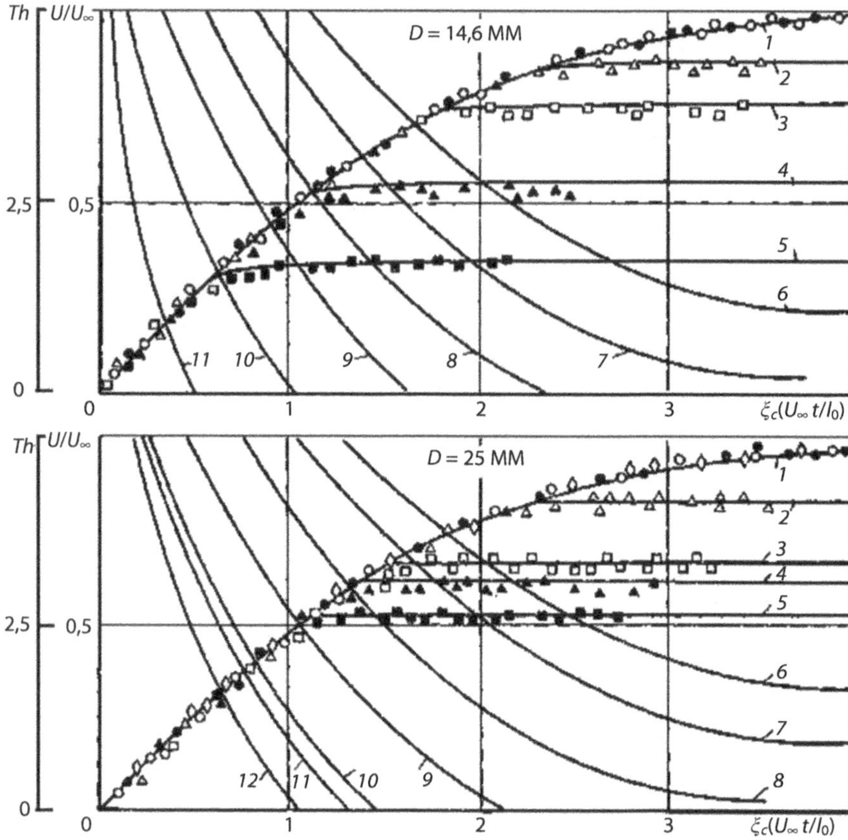

Figure 8.29 Conditions of flow through the nozzle of different diameters for accelerated fluid motion.

velocity: the Reynolds number should be as much close to the field as possible.

In the study of partially or fully developed cavitation specified modeling complexity is less significant than in the assessment of its occurrence. But the greater cavitation cavern is, the more significant are buoyancy effects. In these cases, the system of determining criteria should include Froude number - particularly if it is relatively small or if the cavern is located close to the free surface, where there are waves.

In addition to these circumstances, some concern from the point of cavitation modeling could cause finiteness of time for phase transitions

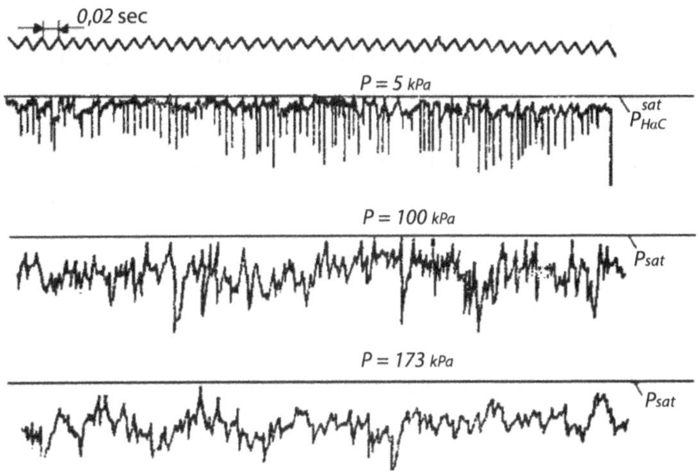

Figure 8.30 The pattern of pressure pulsations at different absolute pressures

(relaxation time): mismatch of its scale with time scale for hydraulic processes. This applies, primarily, to transient cavitation processes. However, the results show that at achieved in experiments values of acceleration, phase transitions can be considered as instantaneous.

This is evidenced by the results of our experiments on accelerated motion through standard nozzle at accelerations up to 25 m/s^2. In the Figure 8.29 may be noted that cavitation occurs immediately at achievement of saturated vapor pressure: there is virtually no transition sections from *1* curves, corresponding to flow without cavitation, to the horizontal lines, corresponding to cavitation flows. Another proof of the above statement is a pressure pulsation waveform (Figure 8.30), which it can be established that the minimal values of the absolute pressure do not fall below P_{sat}.

Noted above features should be considered as the tasks for which flow can be assumed as isothermal. In practice such flows occur at cavitation in water at normal temperature and in liquid metals (except mercury). In other cases, the process of cavitation can be significantly affected by thermodynamic effects, which occur at high values of density of vapor and phase transformation heat. Such effects were observed in the study of cavitation in hydrocarbons, cryogenic liquids and water at high pressures (at high temperature).

Influence of thermodynamic effects is related to the fact that the heat, spent on evaporation, is taken away from the surrounding fluid. At this, in the area adjacent to vapor bubbles or top of the cavern, temperature of the fluid falls. Therefore, further evaporation is possible only at a lower pressure, corresponding to reduced temperature: cavitation is "late" compared to those cases where the thermodynamic effects can be neglected.[2]

In simulation of cavitation including thermodynamic phenomena can be used given in [198] typical scales:

Temperatures

$$\Delta T_0 = \frac{\rho''}{\rho'}\frac{r}{c_p} \tag{8.88}$$

where ρ'' and ρ' — vapor and fluid density on the saturation line; r — latent heat of vaporization; c_p—isobaric specific heat capacity of the fluid; differential pressure

$$\Delta P_0 = \frac{\rho'' r}{\rho' c_p}\frac{dp_{sat}}{dT} \tag{8.89}$$

where dP_{sat}/dT — derivative of the saturated vapor pressure by temperature in the phase transition area;

time

$$t_0 = \frac{\rho'}{\rho''}\frac{\lambda_T}{r\, dP_{sat} dT} \tag{8.90}$$

where λ_T — thermal conductivity of the fluid.

In cavitation study may be set objective to not only evaluate hydrodynamic characteristics, but also identify possible cavitation damage. In these cases, to ensure hydrodynamic characteristics similarity to achieve a cavitation erosion similarity, it is necessary to select a material, reproducing studied structure on the model and possessing appropriate characteristics. At the present, issues of cavitation erosion similarity are not sufficiently studied.

---

[2] This issue is considered in the [217] review, which contains a detailed bibliographic information on the work in this area.

9

Hydrodynamic Loads

Hydrodynamic loads onto a rigid construction (river-bed protection in the tailrace, for instance} may be represented as the sum of the averaged (in the probabilistic sense) and pulsating components. In many cases of practice the averaged load may be determined on conventional type hydraulic models. Estimate of pulsation components of load is a more difficult problem. Usually in the first stage of research only the amplitude and the predominant period of pressure pulsation are determined. The first tests of pressure pulsations under hydraulic jump were published by N.A. Preobrajenskiy [98a] and M.S Fomichev [33a]. The regular measurements performed by G.A.Yuditskii [119a] provide information on the amplitude of pulsation of forces acting on the downstream apron slab and the downstream riverbed protection at various relative dimensions of slabs and various flow parameters. A. S. Abelev et. [1a, 2a] studied in detail the amplitudes of pulsating load on gates. However, in spite of the practical importance of these studies, the data of maximum amplitudes and on the predominant period of pulsation are still inadequate for prediction of the structural vibrations, and the results of the studies may be applied only in a case in which the commutation model of the construction under design is similar to the computation model of the construction on which the experiments have been carried out. The modern statistic methods for description of pressure pulsation in hydrotehnickal structures were used by S.P. Bojich [11a, 12a]. The approach, which is based on the analysis of the interrelation between the pressure pulsation and the kinematics of the flow, is more promising. Yu. D. Gorodkov (1940) was the first researcher who pointed out the important part that size of the area of averaging plays and he has also given a structural formula for the amplitude of the pressure pulsation on a uniform flow boundary [26a]. D.I. Koumin [46a] has drawn attention to the important part played by turbulent waves forming on the free surface of flow. The rigorous treatment of the problem of interrelation between the pulsation of velocity and of pressure was started by A.M. Oboukhov [98a] and R.H.Kraichnan [48a].

9.1 The Structure and the Variants of Loading Schemes

For rational design of hydraulic structures, it is of great importance to correct account dynamic, time-varying forces of water flows on structures. Implementation (recording) of pressure pulsations on the border of the flow are presented as periodic rapidly varying functions of time (Figure 9.1).

The study of pulsation pressure directly on implementations is difficult. To describe the process we should involve the methods of theory of random functions. Physical sources of pressure pulsations on a solid border flow can be:

1. Turbulence, arising at this boundary, or available in the stream;
2. Fluctuations connected with the wave processes in the water, and vibration border of flow.

The pulse pressure directly related to the turbulence can be considered as a random process. The immutability of the flow and head on the structure provides that this process is statistically stationary. There are two classes of stationary random processes that are the most wide, representing the pulsation pressure.

1. The random processes with continuous derivative, appropriate for relatively regular pulsations caused by a small number of the micro sources. Distribution function in such

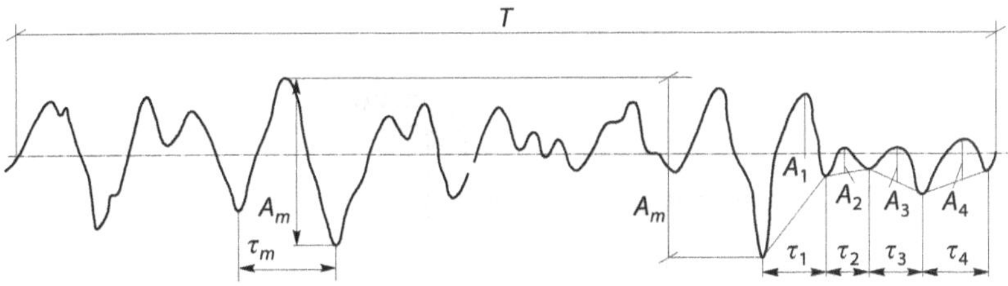

Figure 9.1 Example of pressure pulsation.

processes can be a different view. In particular, the functions of the distribution can follow the normal law. For example, the values of the pulsating pressure at the entrance of the spillway with the tip poorly streamlined, are normally distributed (Figure 9.2)

2. Random processes with independent increments have corresponding chaotic pulsations from many independent micro sources. This surge can occur on an evenly rough surface, sometimes in the stream at the end of the long fastening downstream with several rows of small energy dissipaters. Distribution function of a process with independent increments is infinitely devided. The distribution of the pressure value here strictly follows the normal law, and the distribution of the extremes - law Poisson.

Pressure pulsations on hydraulic structure are of interest as the reason that causes the following hazards: vibration elements and fatigue of structures; cavitations in the stream and cavitations destruction of the surface of the construction element; and sudden (fragile) structural failure.

Information about the pressure pulsation should be sufficient to resolve the end tasks, usually in assessing the risk of one or each of the named phenomena, or in the development of the event that reduces this risk. The solutions of practical problems do not always need full knowledge of the characteristics of the process. For example, if you find the probability of low pressure at the point below a certain limit, it can be limited to a consideration of only one-dimensional distribution of the minimum values of the pulsating pressure. To link pulsating forces with a movement's buildings, you should have a function of the spectral density of the process.

In the beginning, research assessment of the amplitude of fluctuations was made with the magnitude (A_m) observed during the relatively short period of observation. However, the value of the A_m is unsTable and can vary widely even in the same fixed duration of observations (Figure 9.3). [55a]

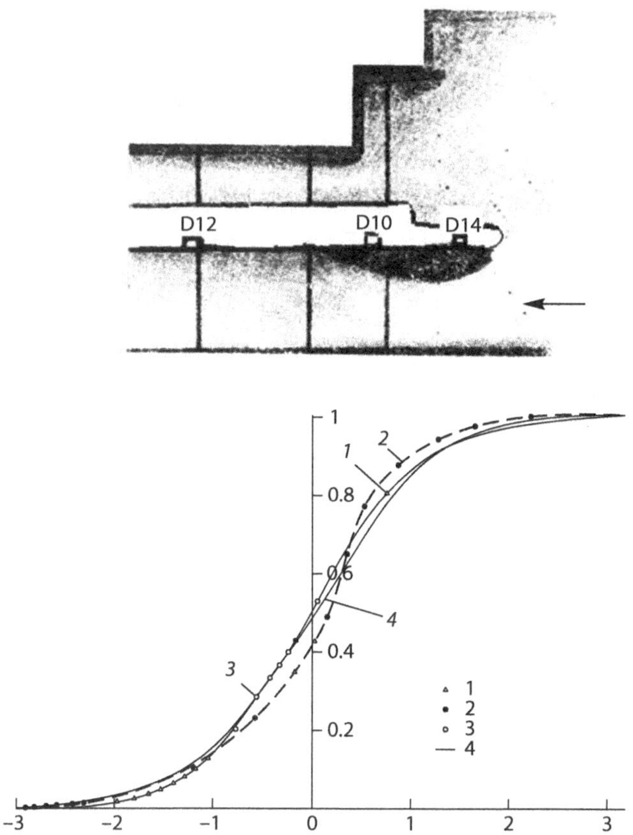

Figure 9.2 The function of a probability distribution of pressure pulsation on the ceiling discharge spillway. 1, 2, 3 – points D10, D14, D12, RMS (root mean square) 2.95, 1.55, 0.33 cm.water, 4-normal law.

To obtain sustainable values of the maximum deviation or the maximum of the scale, there should be monitoring in very long duration. Many researchers were limited to only log scale pulsation, not paying much attention to the duration and repeaTable results. This data, of course, has a certain value to give an idea about the influence of the main factors (Figure 9.4).

A more sTable amplitude characteristic is the standard deviation of pressure from the mean (RMS – root mean square). The characteristic of the process, possible to directly assess the risk of resonance oscillations and vibrations design, is a function of the spectral density [18a]. The function of the spectral density S (ω), or otherwise power range, is the result of applying the Fourier transform to the autocovariation function R(τ).

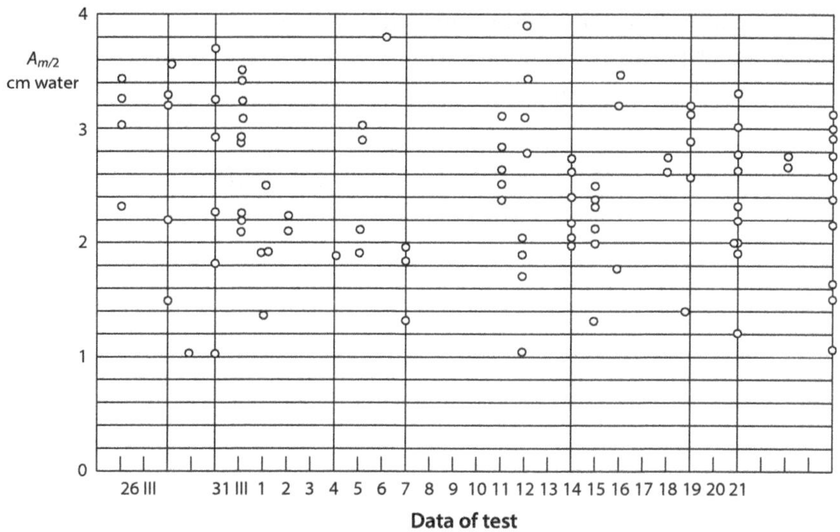

Figure 9.3 The maximum deviation of pressure from the mean (A_m) by repeating the experiments in the same conditions. The recording time T=25 sec, average interval between zero pulsations 1.8 sec.

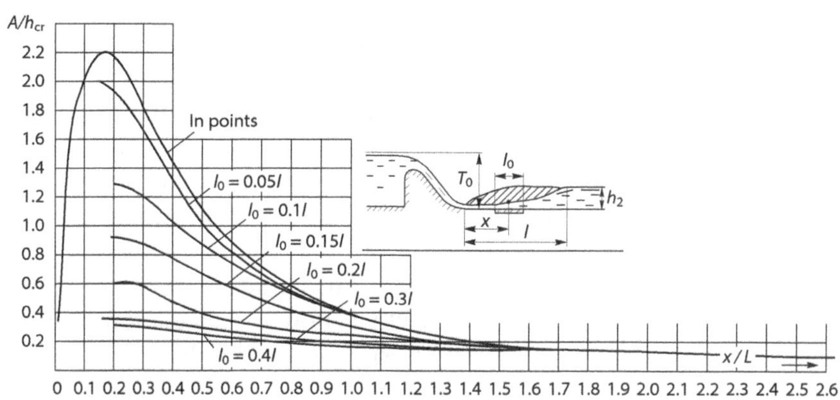

Figure 9.4 The amplitude ripple load on the plate under the hydraulic jump depending on the length of the unit and its provisions. The load is measured in fractions of a critical depth of flow [120a].

Autocovariation function is determined by averaging the result of the multiplication of the pulsation's deviations from the average value measured with a time shift in the interval τ:

$$R_x(\tau) = \lim_{T\to\infty} \frac{1}{2T} \int_{-T}^{+T} x(t)(t+\tau)dt.$$

$$S_x(\omega) = \frac{1}{2\pi} \int_{-\infty}^{+\infty} R_x(\tau) e^{-j\omega\tau} d\tau.$$

$$R_x(\tau) = \int_{-\infty}^{+\infty} S_x(\omega) e^{j\omega\tau} d\omega.$$

$$S_x(\omega) = \frac{1}{2\pi} \int_{-\infty}^{+\infty} R_x(\tau) \cos\omega\tau d\tau,$$

$$R_x(\tau) = \int_{-\infty}^{+\infty} S_x(\omega) \cos\omega\tau d\omega.$$

The function of the spectral density S (ω) has the meaning of the mathematical expectation of the square of the amplitude wave with circular frequency ω=2πn/60 in the Fourier expansion, representing the pulsation pressure as an infinite sum of periodic oscillations with the frequency n and random amplitude. In the transition from pressure pulsation in the separate points of a design to load on the element of construction necessary information on mutual correlation functions or mutual spectra of pressure pulsations.

Regardless of completeness, the statistical characteristics determined to implement the pressure must be objective enough. Calculation of statistical characteristics of pulsation can be errors of two kinds:

- Errors caused by the inaccuracy of calculation of statistical characteristics of a particular implementation, and
- Errors associated with insufficient duration of implementation.

If in the overall process of experience, we choose the location of the site implementation duration T randomly, we can assume that the statistical characteristics of the same process, for example, the average value $\langle x \rangle$ and variance σ, some of the different implementations of the same duration, will follow normal law with mathematical expectation equal to the mathematical expectation of the calculated characteristics. Knowledge dispersion of this characteristic will find probabilistic border scatter, and it is reasonable to set the record length, providing necessary accuracy of results.

The dependence of the dispersion medium pressure value and variance of the standard variation from the recording time is determined only by the form of the correlation function.

The probability of the small dispersion of results of processing by increasing the length of the recording increases. The large variability of the results of determining the magnitude of average quadratic deviation (standard, root mean square – RMS) is more sTable amplitude characteristic pulsing than the maximal amplitude of pulsations.

In the study of dynamic loads, on the hard turbulent boundary flow, it is most simple to register a pulsation pressure gauge, having a relatively small area of a receiving device. Information obtained from such a sensor, well illustrates the level of turbulence and peculiarities of the flow structure. This can be directly used in assessing the local structural strength and risk of cavitations and erosion.

In some cases, however, it is of interest to load element of design in general. The dimensions of the surface of the item, on which you want to fold pulsating pressure, can be quite large. If in laboratory conditions, the load on the item as a whole is often possible to determine experimentally, in natural conditions, such determination is very difficult. This clearly shows the expediency consideration of the problem of the calculation of the statistical parameters of pulsation pressure force on known parameters of pressure pulsation in the individual points of the surface of the item [84, 17a, 18a, 56a]. Mathematically, the problem can be formulated as follows: find the parameters of a stationary random process on known parameters of the process $p(x,y,t)$ defined on the space D.

$$\mathrm{P(t)} = \iint_{D} p(x, y, t)\,dx\,dy \tag{9.1}$$

Mathematical expectation, calculated integrating mean values of pressure on this particular site, will be considered known. Without loss of generality we can take:

$$\langle \mathrm{P(t)} \rangle = \iint \langle p(x,y,t) \rangle\,dx\,dy. \tag{9.2}$$

$$\langle \mathrm{P(t)} \rangle = 0. \tag{9.3}$$

For the known limit theorem of A. N. Kolmogorov [108] the distribution function of the pulsation pressure force in all cases should be closer to the normal law distribution function of pressure pulsations in points. So correlation function is almost enough to be a characteristic of the pulsation pressure force. To set the torque, obviously, is enough to calculate the statistical characteristics of random processes:

$$M_j(t) = \iint_D jp(x, y, t) > dxdy, j = x \text{ or } y \tag{9.4}$$

The *ox* axis is chosen along the stream. The axis *oy* is perpendicular to *ox* and lies in the plane D.

Covariance of pulsation pressure force, using the condition (9.3), can be written in the following form:

$$R_\Sigma(\tau) = < \left[\iint_D \mathrm{p}(x, y, t)\right]\left[\iint_D \mathrm{p}(x, y, t+\tau)\, dxdy\right] > \tag{9.5}$$

Replacing the product of the integrals multiple of integration, we can transfer the operation of averaging under the integral.

$$\mathrm{R}_\Sigma(\tau) = \iiiint < \mathrm{p}(x,y,t)\ \mathrm{p}(\xi,\eta,t+\tau) > dxdyd\xi d\eta \tag{9.6}$$

Under the sign of the integral in (9.6), is the cross-covariance pulsation pressure p and p' at points with coordinates (x, y) and (ξ, η). The dispersion of the pulsation pressure force on the plane D will be determined by (9.6) when $\tau \to 0$. Thus, the problem reduces to finding mutual covariances of pressure pulsations $R(x, y, \xi, \eta, \tau)$ by known autocovariance $R(x, y, \tau)$ and averaged picture currents.

The Covariance Function of Pressure Strength in Conditions of a Plane Problem

There are experimental data showing that in the conditions of a plane problem, specific load on a plate of water fight under the hydraulic jump practically does not depend on the width of the plate. This means that in the conditions of a plane, there is a problem with the pressure pulse at various points along the width of the stream simultaneously.

In this case,

$$p(x,y,t) = p(x,t) \text{ and } R_{\Sigma}(\tau) = B^2 \int_0^L \int < p(x,t)p(\xi,t+\tau) > dxd\xi \quad (9.7)$$

Here L is the length of plate D.

Homogeneous Turbulence

If turbulent flow adopts uniformity along the length of the stream, the value of cross-covariance at constant t would depend only on the distance between points correlation. In this case, it is convenient to introduce the change of variables, putting x = x, and $\xi = x + \eta$.

Calculation of the integral (9.7) held by the area D network:

$$R_{\Sigma}(\tau) = B^2L^2 \int_0^1 \left(1 - \eta/L\right)\left[R(\eta,\tau) + R(-\eta,\tau)\right] d(\eta/L) \quad (9.8)$$

Turbulent flow, uniform in length, is observed in cases where the disturbance sources, providing a distinctive "chaotic" change of the velocity and pressure in the stream, is distributed evenly along the course'. Homogeneous turbulence is possible in the case of sources of disturbances in the survey area no. It is necessary that the disturbances, porTable averaged over, did not change in length. In conditions of homogeneous turbulence, mutual covariance simply is expressed through the autocovariance and averaged velocity of the demolition of the perturbation U [84, 105, 108]:

$$R(\eta,\tau) = R(\tau - \eta/U) \quad (9.9)$$

Substituting the expression (9.9) into the formula (9.8), we obtain the relation, suiTable for direct calculations:

$$R_{\Sigma}(\tau) = B^2L^2 \int_0^1 (1-z)\left[R(\tau - \tau_L z) + R(\tau + \tau_L z)\right] dz \quad (9.10)$$

where R (t) - the autocovariance of pressure pulsations; τ_L = L/U - the running time of outrage over the plane. The integral (9.10) can be written in an explicit form, if you ask any expression for autocovariance. The appropriate expression for the autocorrelation function of pressure pulsations of the turbulent and wave nature under the hydraulic jump can serve as an expression of the following type proposed by Serge Bojich [11a]:

$$R(\tau) = \Sigma\sigma_i^2 \exp(-\alpha_i|\tau|) \mathrm{Cos}\beta_i\tau \tag{9.11}$$

Figure 9.5 shows that the autocorrelation function r(τ)=R(τ)/R(0) of pressure pulsation under the jump and right behind it, is well summarized by the introduction of these two options ascension and topically .

The results of calculations according to (9.10) for the representation (9.11) are shown in Figure 9.6 in the form of the dispersion relations of the specific load on the stove to the dispersion of pressure pulsations in the points of the surface of the plate in the function parameter $\alpha\tau_L$, characterizing the decay of correlations between pressure pulsations on the length of the plate.

Figure 9.7 shows a reduction in the standard of pulsation of the specific load on the plate with increasing the length of the plate. It is seen that already during the length of the plate with 5 times smaller length of the hydraulic jump L_0, standard pulsations of the specific load on the plate, in general, are 2.5 times less than the average standard of pressure pulsations in individual points of the surface of the plate.

There are two approaches to the task of hydrodynamic load, determined in the laboratory:

1. You build a model to directly register interest engineer values (the force or moment acting on the design element);
2. You can register a pulsation pressure and shear stress at certain points of a design to determine (or set) the multivariate probability distributions and the multidimensional covariance function.

In practical calculation between the pulse point and likely uploading design there is another stage - definition of the burden on small element of design, the size of which, however, may be considerably larger than the "spot" of the sensor. In that case, if ripple load is connected, for example, with the motion of vortices, demolished with velocity U, a fair assessment is:

$$\sigma_i^2 \approx \sigma_a^2 \left[\frac{1-0,35\sqrt{\Omega_i}\,\dfrac{a}{U}}{1-0,35\sqrt{\Omega_0}\,\dfrac{a}{U}} \right]^2 + \sigma_0^2 - \sigma_a^2, \tag{9.12}$$

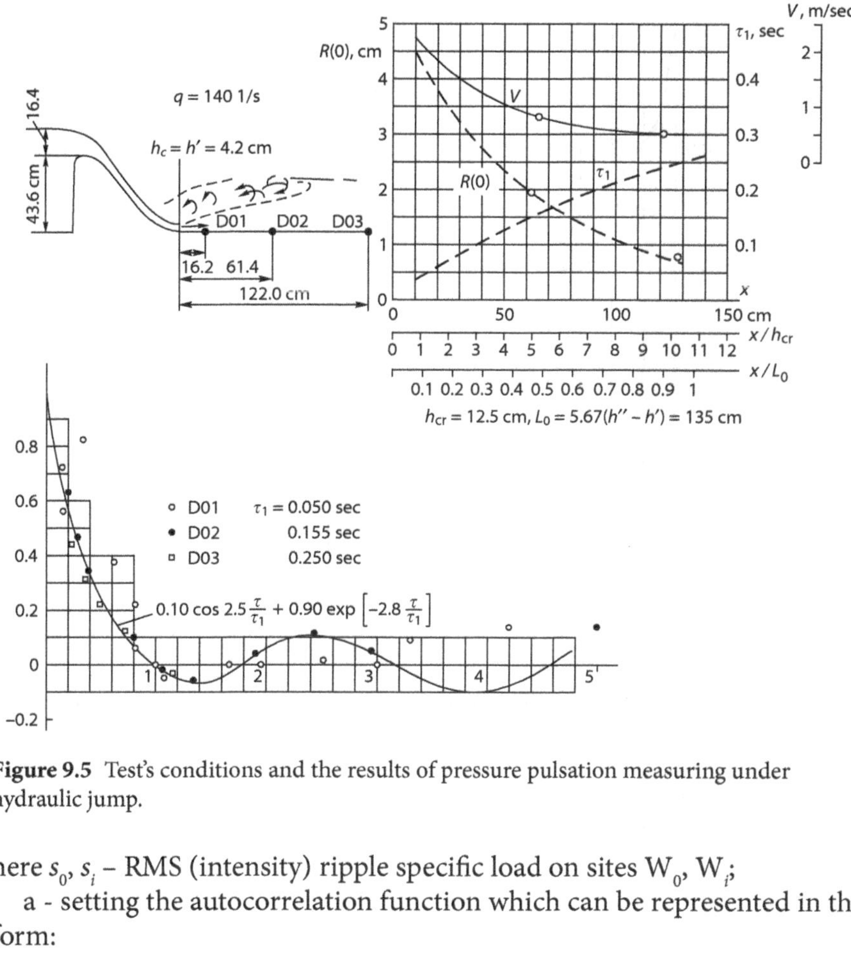

Figure 9.5 Test's conditions and the results of pressure pulsation measuring under hydraulic jump.

here s_0, s_i – RMS (intensity) ripple specific load on sites W_0, W_i;

a - setting the autocorrelation function which can be represented in the form:

$$r(\tau) = \frac{\sigma_a^2}{\sigma_0^2}\left(\exp - a|\tau| + 1 - \frac{\sigma_a^2}{\sigma_0^2}\right). \quad \text{for} \quad 0 \le \tau \le \frac{\sqrt{\Omega_i}}{U} \tag{9.13}$$

Mutual correlation between specific loads on structures differs from mutual correlation calculated according to the records of "pixel sensors" located in the centers of these elements. However, covariate specific loads on the sensors and on platforms in general, in many cases turns out to be almost the same.

As an example, compare the covariance of specific loads on the left and the right half of the beam loaded uniform pulse load intensity σ_0 (single-point sensors) and the spatial correlation:

$r(\xi,\eta)=\exp-\alpha|\xi-\eta|$, where ξ and η - the coordinates of the points $(0<\xi<1, 0)$.

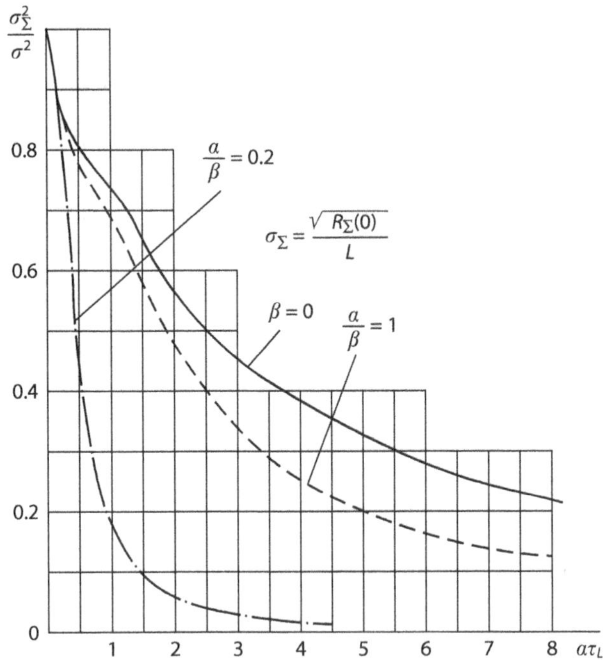

Figure 9.6 Changes in the relative dispersion load depending on the relative range of smoothing.

Unit load on the left half of the beams is determined by the integral of:

$$P_{\Sigma 1} = 2\int_0^{0.5} p(\xi,t)\,d\xi$$

and on the right half of the beam – integral:

$$P_{\Sigma 2} = 2\int_{0.5}^{1} p(\eta,t)\,d\eta$$

The covariance between these loads is written as:

$$< P_{\Sigma 1}P_{\Sigma 2} > \; = 4\int_0^{0.5} d\xi \int_{0.5}^{1} <p(\xi,t)p(\eta,t)> d\eta \qquad (9.14)$$

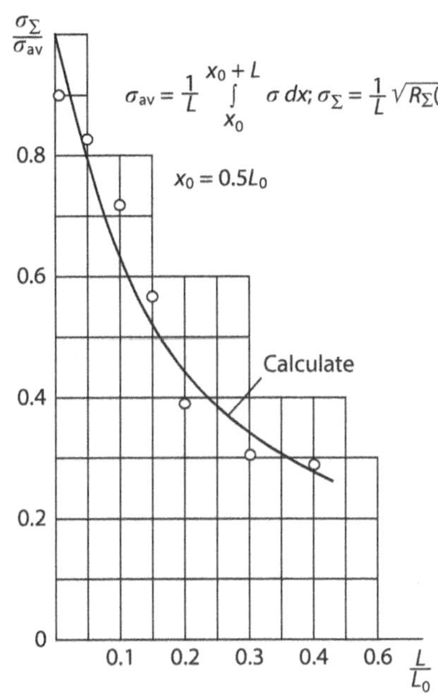

Figure 9.7 RMS of the load pulsation on the plate with length L under hydraulic jump with length L_0.σ_{av}- averaged RMS of pressure pulsations on the points of plate.

The expression staying under the integral is the covariance ripple load at points ξ and η:

$$<p(\xi,t)p(\eta,t)> = \sigma_0^2\, r(\xi,\eta) = \sigma_0^2 \exp{-\alpha|\xi-\eta|} \quad (9.15)$$

Calculation (9.14) using (9.15) gives:

$$<P_{\Sigma 1}\, P_{\Sigma 2}> = \sigma_0^2 8\exp(-0.5\alpha)[\text{ch}0.5\alpha - 1]/\alpha^2 \quad (9.16)$$

This expression is comparable to the covariance of pressure pulsations in the centers of the left and right halfbeams, remote from each other at 0.5.

$$<p(0.25,t)p(0.75,t)> = \sigma_0^2 \exp{-0.5\alpha} \quad (9.17)$$

The results of calculations by formulas (9.16) and (9.17) coincide to values α=4-5 (Figure 9.8). Figure 9.8 also shows the value of the correlation between specific loads on halfbeams. As we can see, the correlation between loads is significantly different from the correlation between the pulsations in the point - in centres halfbeams.

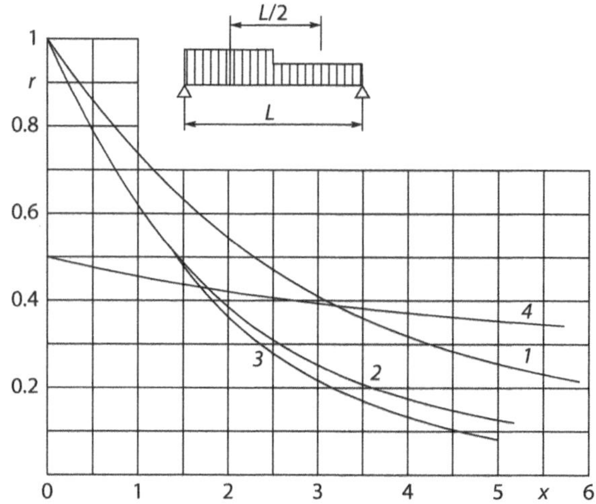

Figure 9.8 The results of the calculation of covariances and correlations. 1-correlation between the forces, acted on the left and right halves of the beam; 2-covariance between the forces, acting on the left and right halves of the beam (in shares of ¼ $\sigma_0^2L^2$); 3-the correlation between pulsations load in the centers of the left and right half beam; 4-intensity pulses force acting on half beams (in shares $\sigma_0 L$).

The example proves overall assessment given by the formula:

$$r_{ij}\sigma_i\sigma_j \approx \left(r_{ij}\right)_0\left(\sigma_i\right)_0\left(\sigma_j\right)_0. \tag{9.18}$$

Dynamic analysis of the structure under the load is not dependent on the reactions of the structure, just the job of the reciprocal spectral density loads $S_{kj}(w)$ in different areas of construction and the transfer function matrix.

The spectral density of the i-th reaction of the construction is determined by the product of three matrices:

$$S_i(\omega) = \left(y_{i,1}y_{i,2},\ldots,y_{i,n}\right)\left(S_{k,j}\right)\begin{pmatrix} y_{i,1} \\ y_{i,2} \\ \vdots \\ y_{i,n} \end{pmatrix} = \sum_{k=1}^{n}\sum_{j=1}^{n} y_{i,k}y_{i,j}S_{k,j}. \tag{9.19}$$

$Y_{i,j}$ - (i-th) reaction structures under the action of periodic load applied with the amplitude of 1 by j-th site design.

For dynamic calculation, job spectral density loads $S_{kj}(\omega)$ of different areas of construction and the transfer function matrix is usually enough. If all the natural frequencies lie outside the essential values of the spectral density - natural frequencies higher frequency ripple load dynamic calculations are reduced to the calculation of hazardous instant loading applied statically. Extreme load is implemented at one of the sites, and others implement the most probable value defined multidimensional function of a probability distribution. If one of the sites' designs resulted in extreme deviation from the mean, on other sites, it is most likely that its extreme deviation was multiplied by the coefficient of correlation between the fluctuations of the stress on the considered stations.

$$\frac{x_k - \bar{x}_k}{\left|x_k - \bar{x}_k\right|_{MAX}} = r_{mk}. \tag{9.20}$$

Figure 9.9 presents an example of the likely rare loading water boards (at surface mode). Distribution of the instant of loads taken for each site as the average of those values that were observed at the moment of occurrence of the maximum load on the first site. It contains the probable distribution of instant exertion, calculated using data on the spatial correlation. The coincidence between calculations and observations are quite satisfactory.

Experimental data on the real extreme uploading water boards in this example are consistent with the estimated uploading according to the described procedure.

The above can formulate the following recommendation for modeling technology as the amplitude characteristics of the pulsed process. It is advisable to use the standard deviation that allows less change when changing the duration of the registration process than the scope of the oscillations allows. When you register pressure, pulsations are set to the size of the receiving area of the pressure sensor. Under constant flow conditions, when the ripple amplitude is smaller, the larger the parameter d/l, where d is the diameter of the receiving area of the sensor, and l is the characteristic linear scale of turbulent perturbations. The sensor distorts the shape of the spectrum of pulsation and correlation functions in area $\omega > U/d$ or $0 < \tau < d/U$.

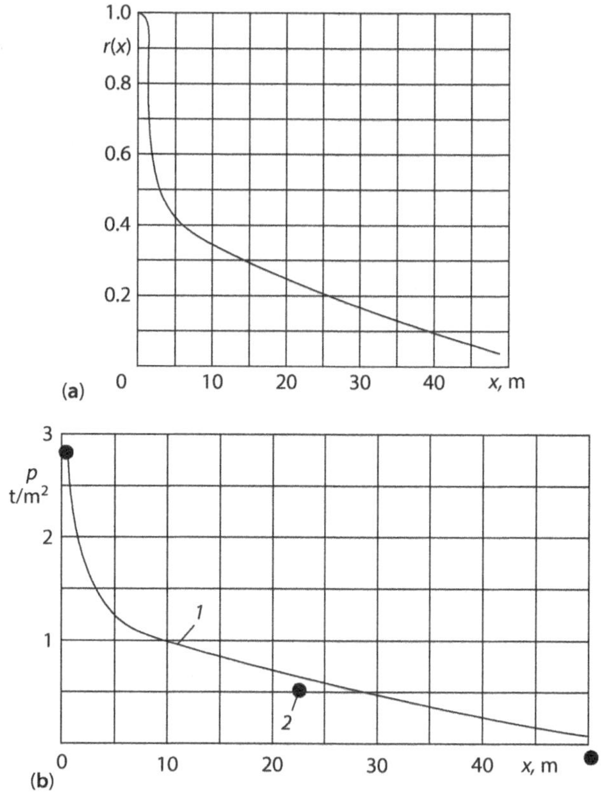

Figure 9.9 Spatial correlation loads on water fight for the hydraulic power unit with horizontal units and surface weirs (a) and one of the variants of extreme loading of water fight (b). 1 - the calculation according to Figure a) with the use of information about the intensity of pressure pulsations in specific points; 2 - experimental data.

9.2 Pressure Pulsations at the Points of Border Flow

Statement of the Problem and Solution Methods

Applying the operation of the divergence to the Navier-Stokes equations and highlighting the averaged value of pressure obtain a differential equation of elliptic type relative pressure pulsations [84, 64a, 73a]:

$$-\frac{1}{\rho}\Sigma\frac{\partial^2 p}{\partial x_i^2}=\underbrace{\Sigma\Sigma\frac{\partial^2\left(U_i u_k+U_k u_i\right)}{\partial x_i \partial x_k}}_{1}+\underbrace{\Sigma\Sigma\frac{\partial^2 u_i u_k}{\partial x_i \partial x_k}-\Sigma\Sigma\frac{\partial^2 < u_i u_k >}{\partial x_i \partial x_k}}_{2} \quad (9.21)$$

Studying the pulsation pressure, it is natural to assume all the information about the kinematics of the turbulent flow is known. Thus,

$$\Delta p = -\rho f\left(x_1, x_2, x_3, t\right), \tag{9.22}$$

Here f is a given random function of coordinates and time (kinematic function).

Design of parameters of pressure pulsations at the flow boundary become possible while taking into account the relation between the pressure pulsation and flow kinematics. Developed theory allows us to consider separately flow "kinematic function" ***f*** which little depends on dynamic boundary conditions and Green function G which depends mainly on the boundary conditions:

$$\mathrm{p}(\mathbf{x},\mathrm{t}) = \int \mathrm{f}(\xi,\tau)\mathrm{G}(\mathbf{x},\mathrm{t},\xi,\tau)\, d\xi d\tau \tag{9.23}$$

Here and below, except for special cases, symbol p indicates the pressure divided by the density. Influence of disturbances arising in points with coordinates ξ (vector) on pressure pulsation in points with coordinates $\boldsymbol{x}$ (vector) is characterized by Green function, which may be determined analytically or by electric analogy methods. Kinematic function for the flow slowly changes along the x axis, which consists of two components;

$$\mathrm{f} = \mathrm{f}_1 + \mathrm{f}_2 \tag{9.24}$$

The first of which is linear – {1} in (9.21), and the second one is nonlinear relative to the pulsation velocity u_i - {2} in (9.21). To flow, slowly changing along the longitudinal axis x_1 [73a, 34a]:

$$-f_1 = 2\frac{\partial U_1}{\partial x_2}\frac{\partial u_2}{\partial x_1}$$

$$-f_2 = 2\left[\frac{\partial u_2}{\partial x_1}\frac{\partial u_1}{\partial x_2} - <\frac{\partial u_2}{\partial x_2}\frac{\partial u_1}{\partial x_2}>\right] + 2\left[\left(\frac{\partial u_1}{\partial x_2}\right)^2 - <\left(\frac{\partial u_1}{\partial x_2}\right)^2>\right]$$

The most significant low - and medium frequency components are formed mostly due to the influence of the linear component of kinematic function f_1. Dispersion of this component is proportional to dispersion of the derivative with respect to the fluctuating velocity.

$$< f_1^2 > \approx 4\left(\frac{\partial U_1}{\partial x_2}\right)^2 < \left(\frac{\partial u_2}{\partial x_1}\right)^2 >$$

Dispersion of the nonlinear component is proportional to the dispersion of derivatives with respect to fluctuating velocities squared. For example if small whirls are isotropic:

$$< f^2 > \approx 15\left[< \left(\frac{\partial u_2}{\partial x_1}\right)^2 > \right]^2$$

Therefore $<f_1^2>$ would be much larger than $<f_2^2>$.

$$\left(\frac{\partial U_1}{\partial x_2}\right)^2 \gg \frac{15}{4} < \left(\frac{\partial u_2}{\partial x_1}\right)^2 >$$

The infinite isotropic flow of mutual covariance of pressure pulsations in the points at distance x (vector) determines by the space correlation function r(ξ) and RMS of the longitudinal velocity pulsation σ_u:

$$1/\rho^2 < p(\mathbf{x}_0)\ p(\mathbf{x}_0 + \mathbf{x}) > \ = 2\sigma_u^{\ 4}\int_x^{\infty}\left(\xi - x^2/\ \xi\right)\left[dr(\xi)/d\xi\right]^2 d\,\xi$$

Here r(ξ) - correlation function longitudinal velocity pulsation along the line between points $\mathbf{x}_0$ and ($\mathbf{x}_0$+ **ξ**), **ξ**-distance between $\mathbf{x}_0$ and ($\mathbf{x}_0$+ **ξ**).

For isotropic turbulence:

$$1/\rho\ \sigma_p = (0.58 \div 1.0)\ \sigma_u^{\ 2}$$

The smaller coefficient is for middle Reynolds numbers, larger - for highest Reynolds numbers.

In a limited flow of boundary conditions, equation (9.22) can be very diverse. The most simple are the following:

1. the case of border flow as a peaceful open water surface

$$p\big|_{\Gamma_1} = 0; \qquad (9.25)$$

2. case of solid sloping boundary, committing specified fluctuations in the direction normal to the surface. From the Navier-Stokes equations we obtained:

$$\frac{1}{\rho}\frac{\partial p}{\partial n}\bigg|_{\Gamma_2} = \nu\frac{\partial^2 u_n}{\partial n^2} - \frac{\partial^2 \zeta}{\partial t^2}, \tag{9.26}$$

Here u_n – projection of velocity pulsation is normal to the boundary surface;

ζ - moving of the boundary of the flow;

ν - the coefficient of kinematic viscosity.

If, on the border there is laminar sublayer of finite thickness, in which the velocity fluctuations are equal to zero, all interior points of this sublayer will be:

$$\frac{\partial^2 u_n}{\partial n^2} = \frac{\partial^2 u_2}{\partial x_2^2} = 0. \tag{9.27}$$

The assuming the presence of a laminar sublayer is not mandatory. Experimental measurements show that already in the turbulent boundary layer closer to the wall the rate of energy dissipation decreases, i.e. it decreases the value derived from the speed. Direct estimates of the variance component of the pressure gradient in a turbulent boundary layer show that the pressure gradient along the wall is much higher than the gradient in the transverse direction:

$$< \left(\frac{\partial p}{\partial n}\right)^2 > = 0.34 \cdot 10^{-3}\frac{\tau_0^3}{\nu^2 \rho} < \quad < \left(\frac{\partial p}{\partial s}\right)^2 > = 2 \cdot 10^{-3}\frac{\tau_0^3}{\nu^2 \rho}. \tag{9.28}$$

Considerations allow us to take on the hard wall of the normal projection with instant pulsating pressure gradient equal to zero,

$$\frac{\partial p}{\partial x_2} = 0. \tag{9.29}$$

On the oscillating boundary, it must be:

$$\frac{\partial p}{\partial x_2} = -\rho\frac{\partial^2 \zeta}{\partial t^2} = \phi(x_1, x_3, t). \tag{9.30}$$

Often, moving boundaries are directly connected with the pulsation pressure on the border. One of the most simple forms of this relationship is evident in the conditions when the part of the boundary varies as a rigid body along a normal to streamlined surface:

$$-\int_{\Omega} p(t,x_1,x_3)dx_1dx_3 = \Omega m\left[\frac{\partial^2\zeta}{\partial t^2} + \omega_0\beta\frac{\partial\zeta}{\partial t} + \omega_0^2\zeta\right], \tag{9.31}$$

Here Ωm – the mass of the oscillating part of the border.

From the conditions (9.31) and (9.30), moving boundaries can be excluded:

$$\int_{\Omega}\frac{\partial^2 p}{\partial t^2}dx_1dx_3 = \frac{\Omega m}{\rho}\left[\frac{\partial}{\partial x_2}\left(\frac{\partial^2 p}{\partial t^2}\right) + \omega_0\beta\frac{\partial}{\partial x_2}\left(\frac{\partial p}{\partial t}\right) + \omega_0^2\frac{\partial p}{\partial x_2}\right]. \tag{9.32}$$

Considering statically stationary processes, we can escape from the initial conditions and study the spectral images of pressure pulsations. Applying the Fourier transform in time for the equations (9.22) and (9.32) we find:

$$\Delta p^* = \rho f^*(x_1,x_2,x_3,\omega), \tag{9.33}$$

$$\int_{\Omega} p^* dx_1dx_3 = \frac{\Omega^m}{\rho}\left[1 - \frac{\omega_0}{\omega}\beta i - \frac{\omega_0^2}{\omega^2}\right]\frac{\partial p^*}{\partial x_2}, \tag{9.34}$$

Here p^*, f^* - images of the functions p and f for the Fourier conversion; ω - the conversion parameter on time;

$$i = \sqrt{-1}.$$

If the area of spatial averaging of the load is small enough, the expression (9.34) turns into the usual condition for the mixed boundary value problem:

$$p^* + a\frac{\partial p^*}{\partial x_2} = 0. \tag{9.35}$$

Methods for constructing solutions of the Poisson equation (9.22, 9.33) for boundary conditions (9.25), (9.29), (9.30) or (9.31) are well studied.

The linearity of the basic equation allows you to find the solution as a sum of two parts

$$p = p_1 + p_2, \tag{9.36}$$

Here:

p_2 – component of pressure pulsations associated with vibration borders, a solution of the Laplace equation with inhomogeneous boundary conditions (9.30 or 9.31);

p_1 – the main part of pressure pulsations solution of the complete equation with homogeneous boundary conditions.

Pressure Pulsations at the Bottom of the Open Flow

For open flow, uniform in the direction of the axis x_3, the solution of equation (9.22), with boundary condition on the surface of the water (9.25) and at the bottom (9.30), has the following view (for points on the bottom of the stream, when y=-1

$$p(x,t) = \int_{-1}^{0} d\xi \int_{-\infty}^{\infty} G(l,\xi) f(x-l,\xi) dl + \frac{\partial^2}{\partial t^2} \int_{-\infty}^{\infty} \xi(x-l) G_0(l) dl \tag{9.37}$$

Included in (9.37) weight function $G(l,\xi)$ and $G_0(l)$ are:

$$G(l,\xi) = \frac{1}{2\pi} \text{In} \left[\frac{ch\frac{\pi l}{2} + \sin\frac{\pi\xi}{2}}{ch\frac{\pi l}{2} - \sin\frac{\pi\xi}{2}} \right] \tag{9.38}$$

$$G_0(l) = -G(l, \xi = -1). \tag{9.39}$$

Weight functions .G, G_0 with increasing l and ξ rapidly decrease. Perturbation, deleted from the bottom more than 0.6 depth of the flow and shifted up or down by more than 1.5 depth, has virtually no effect on pulse at this point (at the moment).

When approaching the point under consideration $l \to 0$, $\xi \to -1$, the function weight increases (by module) about as much as:

$$\frac{1}{2\pi} \text{In} \frac{l^2\pi^2}{16} \text{ or } \frac{1}{2\pi} \text{In} \frac{\pi^2(1+\xi)}{16}$$

The Fourier transform of pressure on the longitudinal coordinate in this case is written especially simply:

$$F_x = \frac{1}{\kappa ch\kappa}\int_{-1}^{0} f_x * sh\kappa\xi d\xi + \frac{th\kappa}{\kappa}\frac{\partial^2 \zeta_x *}{\partial t^2}. \qquad (9.40)$$

Here κ - wave number normalized by the depth of the flow

A further calculation of the spectral density of pressure pulsations significantly depends on the form of communication between moving the boundaries of the $\zeta_x(x, t)$ and the pressure $p(x, t)$. If the move does not depend on the main part of pressure pulsations at this point, then:

$$S_p(\kappa) = \frac{1}{\kappa^2 ch^2\kappa}\int_{-1}^{1}\int_{-1}^{0} S_{f_{\xi,\eta}}(\kappa) sh\kappa\xi sh\kappa\eta d\xi d\eta + \frac{th^2\kappa}{\kappa^2} S_{\ddot{\zeta}}, \qquad (9.41)$$

where $S_p(\kappa)$ - longitudinal spectral density of pressure pulsations (cosine Fourier transform of the longitudinal correlation functions);

$S_{f\xi,\eta}$ - the reciprocal spectral density pulsations of kinematic functions in layers flow with coordinates ξ and η;

$S_{\ddot{\zeta}}$ - longitudinal spectral density of the acceleration of the border.

From the equation (9.41), there should be an important conclusion: if moving boundaries statistically does not depend on the main part of pressure pulsations and does not change, the total amplitude of pressure pulsation, recorded by the sensor on the oscillating boundary is greater, and that leads to greater acceleration and the frequency of oscillation. This phenomenon is analogous to the effect of the inertial resistance of so-called added masses of water. In practice, this effect takes into account the introduction of the added masses, shaken with boundary flow. Such a situation occurs, for example, at the end of the water fight, where the main part of the pulsation pressure is low and vibration water fight, caused by intensive effects of flow on the home stretch of water fight, is relatively high [52a].

The main part of pulsation pressure depends on the kinematic structure of the flow. Let us consider the simplest cases, when there is a small area of high-intensity turbulence, beyond which the second derivatives of the works component of velocity and therefore, kinematic function, can be considered equal to zero. If this region lies in the vicinity of the point $y = a$, and has a thickness of b, then the spectral density of the main part of pressure pulsations on the bottom approximately can be written as:

$$\tilde{S}_p(\kappa) \approx S_f \frac{sh^2\kappa a}{\kappa^2 ch^2\kappa} b^2. \qquad (9.42)$$

At long waves (κ → 0), the value of the coefficient in front of S_f in the right part (9.42), is not depend on the frequency. With the increase κ the role of short waves components to a spectrum of pressure pulsations is relatively less than in the spectrum of the kinematic functions S_f.

Kinematic function is the sum of the second derivatives of the works component of velocity. It is known that the differentiation of the spectrum of random functions is expanding and is derived from random functions, approaching a Markov process. Suppose that

$$\tilde{S}_f = \frac{\sigma_f^2}{\pi} \frac{a}{\kappa^2 + a^2}. \tag{9.43}$$

This corresponds to the longitudinal correlation function:

$$< f(x) f(x+l) >= \sigma_f^2 \exp - al \tag{9.44}$$

From (9.42) and (9.43) we can calculate the dispersion of pressure pulsations:

$$\sigma_p^2 = 2\frac{\sigma_f^2}{\pi} \int_0^\infty \frac{ab^2}{\kappa^2 + a^2} \frac{sh^2 \kappa a}{\kappa^2 ch^2 \kappa} d\kappa \approx \frac{2\sigma_f^2 b^2}{\pi a} \int_0^\infty \frac{sh^2 \kappa a}{\kappa^2 ch^2 \kappa} d\kappa. \tag{9.45}$$

The expression (9.45) can be used to explain changes in the intensity of high-frequency components of pressure pulsations at the bottom.

If the intensity of the high-frequency components of pressure pulsations at the bottom should be per unit, the intensity of the high-frequency pulsations on the bottom surface mode, with the same specific consumption and identical to the ratio of conjugated depths, will amount to about 0.25 [54a, 63a, 64a]. To determine the spectral density of the S_p and the absolute values of the intensity of pressure pulsations, you must use the ratio of (9.42). Spectral density kinematic functions are expedient to be calculated separately for plot moderate intensity of turbulence when:

$$|\text{grad U}| \gg (\text{grad u})' \tag{9.46}$$

and for a site of high intensity of turbulence, when inequality (9.46) changes direction. In the first case, using data on the averaged velocity field and keeping only the members of approximately the same order you can record:

$$S_{f\text{I}} \approx 4\left\{S_{\upsilon}\left[\left(\frac{\partial^2 U}{\partial x \partial y}\right)^2 + \kappa^2\left(\frac{\partial U}{\partial y}\right)^2\right] + \kappa^2 S_u\left[4\left(\frac{\partial U}{\partial x}\right)^2 + \kappa^2 U^2\right]\cdot\right.$$

$$\left. + 2\kappa^2 S_{u\upsilon}\left[U\frac{\partial^2 U}{\partial x \partial y} + 2\frac{\partial U}{\partial x}\frac{\partial U}{\partial y}\right]\right\}. \quad (9.47)$$

In the case of turbulence high intensity:

$$S_{f\text{II}} \approx \kappa^4 S_{u^2} + 4\kappa^2 S_{\frac{\partial u\upsilon}{\partial u}} + S_{\frac{\partial^2 \upsilon^2}{\partial y^2}}. \quad (9.48)$$

Here S_{φ} is the operation of calculating the spectral density over function φ.

Comparing expressions (9.47) and (9.48), it is easy to see that in the field of high-intensity turbulence, standard pressure pulse is proportional to the square of the standard of velocity pulsations:

$$\sigma_p \approx k_1^0 \sqrt{I(a)}(\sigma_v)_{\max}^2 (ab)\sqrt{ah}. \quad (9.49)$$

In the field of low intensity of turbulence, intensity of pressure pulsations is proportional to the first degree of intensity of velocity pulsations.

$$\sigma_p \approx k_2^0 \sqrt{I(a)}\left|\frac{\partial U}{\partial y}\right|_{\max} (\sigma_v)_{\max} b\sqrt{ah}, \quad (9.50)$$

Range of pressure pulsations in the zone of intensive turbulence is shifted to the area of high frequencies. When registering pressure pulsations in this area, the effect of spatial averaging of the load and impact of compliance of the pressure sensor - hydro-elastic distortion pressure can be manifested. The impact of rigidity on the main part of the existing hydrodynamic loads is seen in the loads acting on the structure as a whole. This influence is manifested only in areas of increased turbulence, and can be explained by the nonlinear interaction of the main turbulent flow and currents induced by movement of construction. In the kinematic role, defining the main part of pressure pulsation, includes works derived from a component of velocity ($\frac{\partial u_i}{\partial x_j}\frac{\partial u_j}{\partial x_i}$).

Put
$$u_i = \tilde{u}_i + \underset{\sim}{u}_i,$$

where $\tilde{u}_i$ is a component of the instantaneous velocity, not associated with the motion of boundaries; $\underset{\sim}{u}_i$ - component of velocity, caused by the moving boundary. It is easy to see that the mentioned product of derivatives fall into the amount of works, a part of which has the form:

$$\frac{\partial \tilde{u}_i}{\partial x_j}\frac{\partial \underset{\sim}{u}_j}{\partial x_i}.$$

If the turbulence intensity is high enough, even with a very small second factor of the work itself, the sum of the products of such type can be significant. Data practice is particularly important when studying the load on the vibrant design on the length of the stream turbulence. Experimental determination of these loads should play into the deformation of the structure. Here is an especially desirable integrated method of stress designs directly on the hydraulic model.

The General approaches will look at specific examples.

Pressure Pulsation on the Bottom of the Uniform Flow

This examines uniform non-pressure turbulent flow of an incompressible fluid in a channel large width (plane). For turbulent flow, in the term "a flat problem," in addition to the usual content, there are embedded assumptions about the presence of a single cross-correlation between the same pulsating variables.

In the core of the turbulent flow, the first two members in the right part (9.21) are certainly less than the last. This ratio will continue in the near-wall layer. Keeping in the right hand side (9.21), there are only linear members that for the considered conditions can be recorded as:

$$\frac{1}{\rho}\left(\frac{\partial^2 p}{\partial x^2}+\frac{\partial^2 p}{\partial y^2}\right)\approx -2\frac{\partial U}{\partial y}\frac{\partial \upsilon}{\partial x} \tag{9.51}$$

The y axis is directed upwards from the surface of the water, the x - axis along the stream. The information needed for the statistical description of the kinematic function f (x, y, t) in the right part of (9.51), we assume known. Boundary conditions for equation (9.21) are the following:

on the free surface: (9.25)

$$y = 0, \qquad p = 0$$

on the hard (fixed) the bottom of the flow of the equations of motion and continuity: (9.26)

$$\partial p / \partial y = \nu \partial^2 u / \partial y^2, \quad y = -H = -1 .$$

If, on the border, there is laminar sublayer of finite thickness, and inside vertical ripple equal to zero, this condition turns into homogeneous:

$$\left. \partial p / \partial y \right|_{y=-1} = 0. \tag{9.52}$$

When laminar sublayer is *no*, the condition (9.52) is taken as a first approximation that is not contrary to the experimental data.

The solution of the equation (9.51) satisfies the boundary conditions, and limited for

$x \to \pm \infty$ in the points, located on the bottom of flow is:

$$p(x,t) = \int_{-1}^{0} \int_{-\infty}^{\infty} G(x,\xi,\eta) f(\xi,\eta,t) d\xi d\eta$$

$$G(x,\xi,\eta) = \frac{1}{2\pi} \ln \frac{ch \frac{\pi(x-\xi)}{2} + \sin \frac{\pi\eta}{2}}{ch \frac{\pi(x-\xi)}{2} - \sin \frac{\pi\eta}{2}}. \tag{9.53}$$

In the expression (9.53) the symbol p is saved to indicate pressure pulsations, divided by the density of the liquid; on the x-coordinate, settings x and h are measured in fractions of flow depth H.

Using the equality (9.53) of the Fourier transform with complex conjugate parameters, multiplying images and computing mathematical expectation, we find longitudinal spectral density of pressure pulsation:

$$S_p(\kappa) = \frac{1}{\kappa^2 ch^2 \kappa} \int \int S_{f_{\eta\eta'}}(\kappa) sh\, \kappa\eta\; sh \kappa\eta'\, d\eta d\eta'. \tag{9.54}$$

Here $S_{f,\eta\eta}$ - the reciprocal spectral density pulsations of the function f in the points: $y = \eta \;\; y = \eta'$

$$S_{f_{\eta\eta'}} = 4\kappa^2 \left(\partial U / \partial y\right)_{y=\eta} \left(\partial U / \partial y\right)_{y=\eta'} S_{\upsilon'_{\eta\eta'}}. \tag{9.55}$$

The calculations made on the basis of known experimental data on the spectra of pulsations speed showed that when calculating the integral (9.54) of the reciprocal spectral density, $S_{\upsilon,\eta\eta}$ may be replaced by the product of normalized spectral density:

$$\tilde{s}(\kappa) = \sqrt{s_\eta s_{\eta'}},$$

averaged over the layer ($\eta\eta'$), and covariances $\upsilon'(\eta')\,\upsilon'(\eta')\tilde{r}_{\eta\eta'}$, here $\tilde{r}_{\eta\eta'}$- the value of correlations of vertical velocity pulsations, averaged on the interval ($\eta\eta'$)

$$S_{\upsilon_{\eta\eta}} \approx \upsilon'(\eta)\upsilon'(\eta')\tilde{s}(\kappa)\tilde{r}_{\eta\eta'}. \tag{9.56}$$

Distribution of standard pulsations of the vertical component of the velocity along the depth of uniform turbulent flow may be described, considering the magnitude of what is changing is linear in the area at the bottom:

$$\upsilon' = 0{,}95\,\upsilon_{\max}'(1 + y) \qquad (-1 \le y \le -0.94),$$

and the constant in the rest of the thread:

$$\upsilon' = 0{,}95\upsilon_{\max}' \qquad (-0.94 \le y \le 0)$$

Cross-correlation $r_\upsilon(\eta, \eta')$ with the increase $|\,\eta - \eta'\,|$ from 0 to 0.08 sharply decreases from 1 to 0.5 ÷ 0.3, with further increase$|\,\eta - \eta'\,|$ the value of r is slow to change, not falling below the values of 0.25 ÷ 0.15.

The longitudinal gradient of the averaged velocity is

$$\frac{\partial U}{\partial y} = 2.8U_* \left[\frac{1}{1+y} + \frac{\delta}{(1+y)^2}\right] \quad (\delta\text{-}1 \le y \le 0),$$

$$\frac{\partial U}{\partial y} = 5.6\frac{U_*}{\delta} \quad (-1 \le y \le \delta - 1), \quad U_* = \sqrt{\frac{\tau}{\rho}} = \sqrt{gHI}.$$

Here U* "speed friction" at the bottom; I - "pitch friction" in the stream, g = 9,81 m/sec^2, δ - the thickness of the bottom layer in shares depth of flow [5].

Computing these datum to (9.54), may be fined:

$$S_p(\kappa) = U_*^2 \left(\upsilon_{\max}'\right)^2 S_p^0(\kappa) \tag{9.57}$$

The results of calculations of the relative spectral density of pressure pulsations $S_p^0(\kappa)$ point to the relatively small influence of the thickness of the boundary layer at δ < 0.01 (Figure 9.10)

Function $S_p(m)$ for δ < 0.01 has one maximum value of the dimensionless wave number as $\kappa = 2\pi\, H/1 = 2.4$. When $\delta \rightarrow 0.06$ increases altitude, u_d ¢/u ¢$_{\max}$, and the impact of the turbulence in the bottom layer is rapidly increasing, the spector of pressure pulsation expands in the direction of higher frequencies.

Dispersion of pressure pulsations calculated from Figure 9.10, were:

$$\left\langle p^2 \right\rangle = 2\int_0^\infty S_p(\kappa)d\kappa = 29U_*^2\left(\upsilon_{\max}'\right)^2 \text{ for } \delta = 0.01$$

$$\left\langle p^2 \right\rangle = 25U_*^2\left(\upsilon_{\max}'\right)^2 \text{ for } \delta = 0.001$$

The maximum RMS of the vertical velocity pulsations according to experiments in trays, pipes, boundary layer on a plate and atmospheric surface layer is the matter from 0.6 to 1.1 U_*. Smaller Figures are for the flow of over a smooth bottom, larger - current over the rough bottom.

According to this estimation, the RMS of pressure pulsation is:

$$p' = (3.24 \div 5.92)U_*^2$$

According extensive American experiments, standard pressure pulsation at the bottom in terms of subsonic flow is:

$$p' = (3.0 \pm 0.5)U_*^2$$

In a supersonic flow, in streams with low Reynolds numbers, standard pulsation pressure according to the data of experiments increases to:

$$p' = (4 \div 6)U_*^2$$

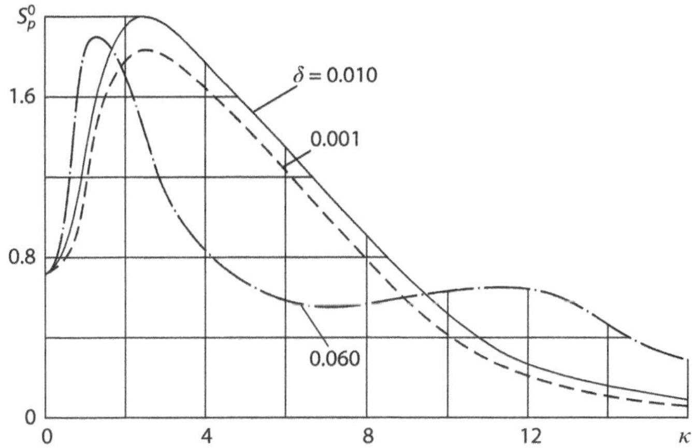

Figure 9.10 The relative spectral density of pressure pulsations on the bottom of uniform flow.

Our estimate (9.57) and these results are of the same order.

Measurement of pressure pulsations on the bottom of the steep canal, made by the author and Mrs. N.V. Halturina, shows:

$$p' = 2{,}71U_*^2.$$

These measurements are performed on the model of flow width 175 cm; length of flow - 420 cm; the slope of the bottom - 0,1; the slope of the line of energy in the area of pressure sensor - 0,025 (moving rapidly); the depth of the water - 3.25 cm; average depth current velocity over the sensor - 160 cm/sec (Reynolds number Re = 52 000); the diameter of a landing sensor - 0.8 cm, $U_* = 9.25$ cm/sec.

Figure 9.11 shows the normalized autocorrelation function of pressure pulsations obtained in this experience [63a].

Figure 9.11 is clearly, the low-frequency component (dotted line in Figure 9.11). A more detailed analysis and comparison with the data of observations over the surface water suggest that this is part of the wave of origin. Figure 9.12 is a normalized turbulent component of the correlation functions obtained experimentally, (3) associated with correlation function (line 1), calculated from the spectral density $S_p(\kappa)$, and shown in Figure 9.10 (for the $\delta = 0{,}01$).

Experimental data are in good agreement with the theory, if we accept that the speed of demolition perturbation U_{trans} (specific rate used in the transition from temporal scale of the autocorrelation function for longitudinal scale lengths) is 0.48 average depth of the flow velocity. On the same

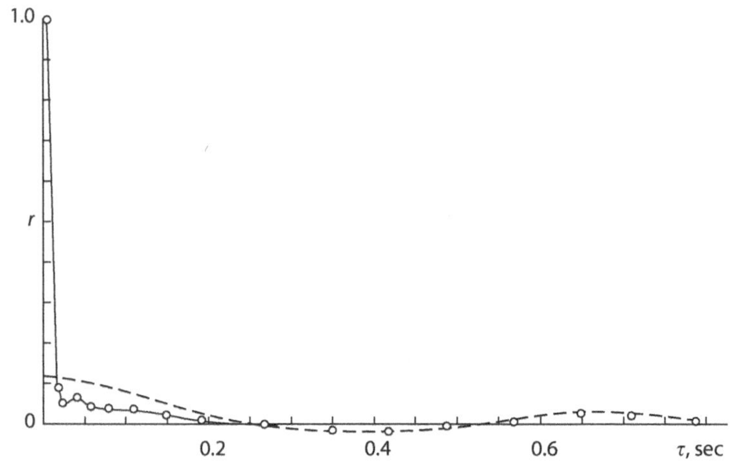

Figure 9.11 Autocorrelation of pressure pulsation on the bottom of water flow with free surface.

Figure 12, the dotted line (line 2) shows the result of the restatement of Willmarth and Wooldridge relating to boundary layer on a plate [118a].

The speed of demolition perturbations here is accepted as equal to 0.8 U_{max} (as is actually received in experiments is [63a]), where the thickness of the layer displacement is δ^*, adopted in the [6a] as a characteristic linear dimension, expressed through the depth of the stream:

$$\delta^* = \int_0^1 \left(1 - \frac{U}{U_{max}}\right) dy \approx 0{,}17.$$

Comparing the theory of the experimental data obtained with the help of sensors with the end (sometimes relatively large) linear size landing L, we should take into account the distortion of the spectrum, and especially dispersion pressure pulsations introduced by this sensor, by averaging turbulent pressure on the surface of the landing.

In conditions of a plane problem of distorted spectral density, $\tilde{S}_p(\omega)$ is associated with a real spectrum $S_p(\kappa)$ ratio:

$$\tilde{S}p(\omega) = \frac{2}{L^2} \frac{(1 - \cos \kappa L)}{\kappa^2} S_p(\kappa),\ \omega = \kappa U_{tr} \tag{9.58}$$

When the size of the receiving area of the sensor is (0.10 ÷ 0.25)H, an understatement is that dispersion pressure pulsations can reach 15 - 25 %.

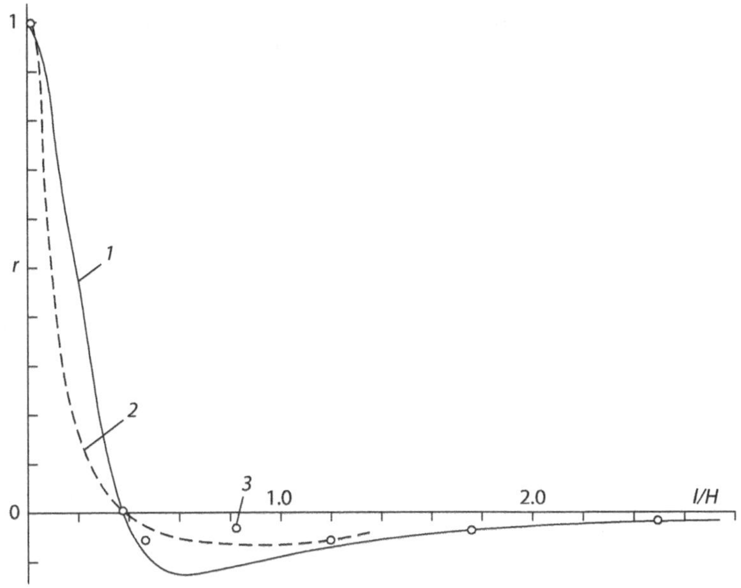

Figure 9.12 The Longitudinal correlation, calculated for δ=0.01 (line 1), tested by Willmarth and Wooldridge in the air boundary on the flat plate (2), and recalculated from the tests with open water flow (Figure 9.11) for transfer velocity 0.48 of averaged speed (3).

In particular, received on the flow, the value of σ_p should be increased to $3U_*^2$. As distortions are greatest in the high-frequency part of the spectrum, the overall progress of the normalized correlation of the function is changed relatively little.

Oscillations of Surface Water and Pressure in Flow with Large Froude's Numbers

With increasing kinetics of uniform flow i.e. increasing the Froude number Fr = U^2/gH, where U is the velocity on the surface of the water and H - depth of flow, under other equal conditions, the open water surface is covered by the gentle waves, the height of which increasing, causes the Froude number to increase, so that when Fr > 1, the uniform thread acquires a peculiar species, given grounds to be called the turbulent mode (or critical) mode. A further increase in the Froude's number can lead to the establishment of a supercritical regime with rolling waves [31, 35, 61, 80a]. In the works [15, 22, 61, 157, 63a] the mechanism was discussed that causes these changes on the free surface flow; there were regularities of the effect of free surfaces on the kinematic characteristics of a turbulent flow of water near it. The solution of this problem was conducted based on the following experimental data:

1. Kinematic characteristics of turbulence in some "bottom" area of a thickness:

$$(1 - \delta/H)\, H$$

   does not depend on conditions on the surface of water.
2. Beyond the bottom area is "basically the core of flow," which at a sufficiently high Reynolds number after a turbulent pulsations speed, can be considered irrational.

The border of the "core," of course, is expedient to take so that within the "core," standards transversed and longitudinal velocity pulsations changed monotonically. At the lower end of the kernel, given the pulsations of the vertical component of the velocity:

$$y = -\delta,\ \upsilon = \upsilon_0(x,t). \tag{9.59}$$

Inside the core of flow:

$$\left.\begin{aligned} \frac{\partial^2\phi}{\partial x^2} + \frac{\partial^2\phi}{\partial y^2} = 0; \\ \upsilon = \frac{\partial\phi}{\partial y};\ u = \frac{\partial\phi}{\partial x}. \end{aligned}\right\} \tag{9.60}$$

Linearization condition on the surface of the water is so:

$$\frac{\partial\phi}{\partial y} = -\frac{1}{g}\frac{\partial^2\phi}{\partial t^2} - \frac{2U}{g}\frac{\partial^2\phi}{\partial t\partial x} - \frac{1}{g}\left[\frac{\partial U}{\partial t} + U\frac{\partial U}{\partial x}\right]\frac{\partial\phi}{\partial x} - \frac{U^2}{g}\frac{\partial^2\phi}{\partial x^2} + \frac{a}{\gamma}\frac{\partial^3\phi}{\partial y\partial x^2},$$

(9.61)

Here U – flow velocity near water surface;
α – the surface tension of water;
γ – specific weight of water;
g – acceleration of gravity.

The equation of the surface water:

$$\zeta+\frac{1}{g}\left[\frac{\partial\phi}{\partial t}+U\frac{\partial\phi}{\partial x}\right]-\frac{a}{\gamma}\frac{\partial^2\zeta}{\partial x^2}=0, \qquad (9.62)$$

Here ζ – vertical coordinate of the surface of the water.

Applicable to equations (9.60) and the boundary conditions of the two-dimensional Fourier transform coordinates t and (ω) and $x(\kappa)$.

$$\phi^*(y,\omega,\kappa)=C_1(\operatorname{ch}\kappa y+\operatorname{th}\kappa\delta\operatorname{sh}\kappa y)+\frac{\upsilon_0{}^*(\omega,\kappa)}{\kappa}\frac{\operatorname{sh}\kappa y}{\operatorname{ch}\kappa\delta} \qquad (9.63)$$

From equation (9.62) we get the image of oscillations of the surface of the water:

$$\zeta^*=\phi^*\frac{i}{g}\frac{\omega+\kappa U}{1+\frac{a}{\gamma}\kappa^2}. \qquad (9.64)$$

Spectral density of fluctuations of surface water:

$$S_\zeta(\kappa)=\frac{(U_p-U)^2}{g^2\left(1+\frac{a}{\gamma}\kappa^2\right)}S_u(\kappa)\Big|_{y=0}, \qquad (9.65)$$

The spectral density of the longitudinal velocity pulsations $S_u(\kappa)$ in a uniform stream is determined by the expression:

$$S_u(\kappa)=\frac{S_{\upsilon_0}(\kappa)}{\operatorname{ch}^2\kappa\delta}\left\{\frac{g\left(1+\frac{a}{\gamma}\kappa^2\right)\operatorname{ch}\kappa y+\kappa(U_p-U)^2\operatorname{sh}\kappa y}{\kappa(U_p-U)^2-g\left(1+\frac{a}{\gamma}\kappa^2\right)\operatorname{th}\kappa\delta}\right\}^2; \qquad (9.66)$$

$$S_{\upsilon}(\kappa)=\frac{S_{\upsilon_0}(\kappa)}{\mathrm{ch}^2\,\kappa\delta}\left\{\frac{g\left(1+\frac{a}{\gamma}\kappa^2\right)\mathrm{sh}\,\kappa y-\kappa\left(U_p-U\right)^2\mathrm{ch}\,\kappa y}{\kappa\left(U_p-U\right)^2-g\left(1+\frac{a}{\gamma}\kappa^2\right)\mathrm{th}\,\kappa\delta}\right\}^2; \quad (9.67)$$

On the border of the kernel thread when y =- δ:

$$S_{u}(\kappa)=\frac{S_{\upsilon_0}(\kappa)}{\mathrm{ch}^2\,\kappa\delta}\left\{\frac{g\left(1+\frac{a}{\gamma}\kappa^2\right)\mathrm{ch}\,\kappa\delta-\kappa\left(U_p-U\right)^2\mathrm{sh}\,\kappa\delta}{\kappa\left(U_p-U\right)^2-g\left(1+\frac{a}{\gamma}\kappa^2\right)\mathrm{th}\,\kappa\delta}\right\}^2; \quad (9.68)$$

$$S_{\upsilon}(\kappa)=S_{\upsilon_0}(\kappa). \quad (9.69)$$

The expression (9.69) is useful for a reasonable choice of the thickness of the core course δ. The border kernel is desirable where the ratio between the component spectra of pulsations approximately follows the equation (15B). The calculations made for $\delta = 0$ and Fr << 1, showed that the condition (9.69) at $\delta = (0.75 \div 0{,}80)$H.

On the free surface flow at y = 0:

$$\left.\begin{aligned} S_{v}(\kappa)&=\frac{S_{v_0}(\kappa)}{\mathrm{ch}^2\,\kappa\delta}\frac{g^2\left(1+\frac{a}{\gamma}\kappa^2\right)^2}{\left[\kappa\left(U_{\mathrm{tr}}-U\right)^2-g\left(1+\frac{a}{\gamma}\kappa^2\right)\mathrm{th}\,\kappa\delta\right]^2};\\ \frac{S_{v}(\kappa)}{S_{u}(\kappa)}&=\frac{\kappa^2\left(U_{\mathrm{tr}}-U\right)^4}{g^2\left(1+\frac{a}{\gamma}\kappa^2\right)^2}\end{aligned}\right\} \quad (9.70)$$

Equation (9.70) shows that when the spectral density pulsations of the vertical velocity near water surface in comparison with the spectrum of horizontal pulsations is greater, the greater the Froude number. It is important that the ratio of the spectra does not depend on δ. In conditionality model it is only necessary that: $U_{tr}/U < 1$.

From equation (9.70), we obtain the spectral density of fluctuations of surface water:

$$S_{\varsigma}(\kappa) = \frac{S_{v_0}(\kappa)}{\mathrm{ch}^2 \kappa\delta} \frac{(U_{\mathrm{tr}} - U)^2}{\left[\kappa(U_{\mathrm{tr}} - U)^2 - g\left(1 + \frac{a}{\gamma}\kappa^2\right)\mathrm{th}\,\kappa\delta\right]^2} \tag{9.71}$$

Water surface tension plays a role only for large wave numbers ω, when:

$$\frac{a}{\gamma}\kappa^2 \geq 0,1 \cdot \tag{9.72}$$

At a temperature of 20° C at the contact of water - air $\alpha/\gamma = 0{,}071$ cm^2. Thus, the surface tension to consider when

$$\kappa \geq 1{,}19\ 1/cm.$$

The dimensionless form of this condition is equivalent to the inequality:

$$\frac{\kappa\delta}{\sqrt{We}} \geq 0{,}316, \tag{9.73}$$

Here $We = \gamma\delta^2/\alpha$ – criterion Weber.

Using the upper estimate of the frequency spectrum through the inner turbulence scale, the condition (9.73) can be given a particularly clear view:

$$\frac{a}{\gamma\lambda_\varepsilon^2} \leq 0{,}1. \tag{9.74}$$

Suppose that the boundary of the "core course" dissipation rate is 0.1 from dissipation rate, averaged over the cross section of the flow, i.e.

$$\bar{\varepsilon} = 0{,}1U_{av}\,Ig = 0.1\frac{U_{av}U_*^2}{H} \tag{9.75}$$

Here U_{av} - average depth H flow rate;

U_* - dynamic speed at the bottom;

I - slope of the stream.

In this case, labeling $\frac{U_{av}H}{\nu} - \text{Re}$ and believing $\sigma_{\upsilon} \approx U_*$, will get:

$$\lambda_\varepsilon = 12H\,\text{Re}^{-0,5}.$$

$$\frac{\delta}{\lambda_\varepsilon} = \frac{\delta}{H}\cdot 0.8\sqrt{\text{Re}}. \tag{9.76}$$

Substituting the maximum value $\delta\kappa = \delta/\lambda_\varepsilon$, calculated by (9.76), in the condition (9.73), you can find the minimum value of the Weber number (or stream depth), in which the influence of surface tension obviously does not appear.

$$\delta/\lambda_\varepsilon \approx 8,\ We_{\text{min}} = 620.$$

Surface tension is essential for the study of conditions of occurrence of aeration. Given the spectrum of a longitudinal ripple, the surface of the water surface tension, as can be seen from (9.65), always has a stabilizing effect. However, in a more natural setting, speed pulsations are only in the bottom layer, and the role of surface tension can be more complex. For very large Froude numbers, standard oscillations of the surface water will be proportional to the depth of the stream, and the shape of the surface water does not depend on surface tension and the Froude numbers. With very small Froude numbers:

$$S\varsigma(\kappa) \approx \frac{S_{v0}(\kappa)}{U^2\text{sh}^2\kappa\delta}\cdot\frac{\left(\frac{U_{\text{tr}}}{U}-1\right)}{\left(1+\frac{a}{\gamma}\kappa^2\right)^2}4\left[\frac{U^2}{2g}\right]^2 \tag{9.77}$$

Here, the picture was completely different; in small numbers of Froude, standard fluctuations of the water surface is proportional to velocity head of the stream, and the stabilizing effect of surface tension can manifest itself fully. However, in this case the shape of the surface water is not directly dependent on the Froude number. Here again is manifested remarkable property of the Froude number as the similarity criterion - the phenomena of "Avtomodelling on Froude," for very large and small values of this criterion [Chapter 5 of this book, 138, 199].

Table 9.1 The results of the calculation of the standard of turbulent waves

$\lambda = 2g/C^2$	0,0218	0,0123	0,0079	0,0055	0,0040
Rough stream, σ_ζ^H / H	0,052	0,043	0,037	0,032	0,028
The quiet flow, $2g\sigma_\varsigma^H / U_{av}^2$	0,054	0,042	0,034	0,028	0,024

This method allows us to calculate the standards of oscillations of the surface of the water for very large and very small Froude numbers in uniform flow. (Table 9.1)

In cases of non-uniform motion of dispersion and oscillation spectrum, results can be significantly different. Neglecting surface tension, we get:

Rough stream. σ_ζ^H / H

$$S_\varsigma(\kappa) = \frac{S_{v_0}(\kappa)}{\mathrm{ch}^2\kappa\delta} \frac{U^2\left(\frac{U_{\mathrm{tr}}}{U}-1\right)^2}{\left[\kappa U^2\left(\frac{U_{\mathrm{tr}}}{U}-1\right)^2 - g\ \mathrm{th}\,\kappa\delta\right]^2 + \left[\frac{\partial U}{\partial t}+U\frac{\partial U}{\partial x}\right]^2} \tag{9.78}$$

The expression (9.78), in contrast to the corresponding formulas for the uniform flow, ensures maximum spectral density $S_\zeta(\kappa)$ of modulation $\kappa > 0$, as in low uneven averaged currents along the x-axis, spectral density $S_{\upsilon_0}(\kappa)$ at $\kappa \to 0$ decreases, and the denominator in (9.78) seeks to constant number. In this case, when $\kappa \to 0$ should subside, the spectral density $S_\zeta(\kappa)$ should too.

The maximum spectral density $S_\zeta(\kappa)$ can be expected if $(\kappa\delta) < 1$, where the denominator in (9.78) increases dramatically.

Thus, it is highly likely that the turbulent waves on the surface of uneven flow should have correlation function with negative values for the τ reason it is possible. Figure 9.13 shows the autocovariation function of the wave components of pressure fluctuations, obtained by Mrs. N.V. Halturina. The measurements are performed on the model of flow width 175 cm from

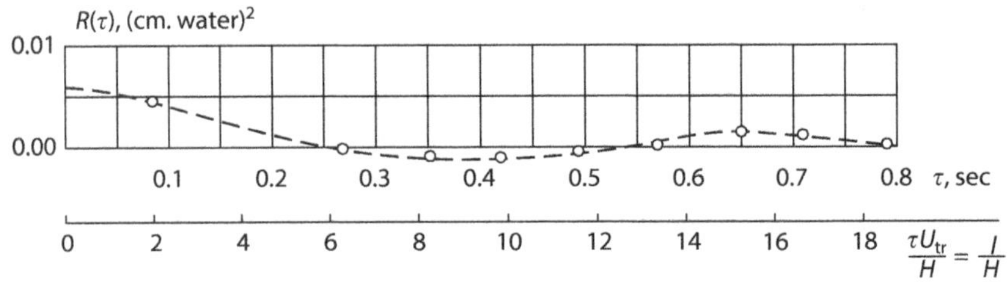

Figure 9.13 Autocovariation function of the wave components of pressure fluctuations.

laid concrete slab size 25 × 25 cm^2. When the length of the flow is 420, we see the Slope of the bottom is: I = 0,1. The slope of the line energy is: I_{fr} = 0,025. The water depth is 3.25 cm, and the average depth of the flow rate at measurement of vibrations 160 cm/sec, with velocity on the surface of the water, is 170 cm/sec.

The function in Figure 9.13 is kind of typical for the process with a narrow spectrum. Leading the frequency of the process about 1/0.7 = 1,43 Hz, which corresponds to:

$$\kappa\delta = \frac{2\pi \cdot 0,8 \cdot 3,25}{0,7 \cdot 0,48 \cdot 160} = 0.30 < 1.$$

Dispersion wave component of the pressure in the experiments was 0.006 (cm of water). This corresponds to $\sigma\zeta/H = 0.024$, which is slightly less than the values calculated by the formulas for the uniform motion, but using actual data on the amount of U_{tr}/U_{av} ($\sigma_\zeta/H = 0.028$). The difference can be explained by the influence of the uneven flow.

Pressure Pulsations on the Boundary of the Open Flow with the Abrupt Expansion

The most significant low and medium frequency components are formed mostly due to the influence of the linear component of kinematic function f_1. Dispersion of this component is proportional to dispersion of the derivative with respect to the fluctuating velocity.

Dispersion of the nonlinear component is proportional to the dispersion of derivatives with respect to fluctuating velocities squared.

The most intensive disturbances arise at the boundaries of wakes due to abrupt expansions. The usual hydraulic jump, flowing behind the ledge with abrupt expansion by width, may be considered approximately as two-dimensional flows with the wakes. A characteristic feature of such a flow is relatively slow variation of the mixing layer width. In this layer the sharp increase of longitudinal velocity gradient is observed and the velocity pulsations are most intense. The first part shows that in such a flow, at the flow boundary parallel to the mixing layer, spectral density of pressure pulsation may be defined by multiplying of velocity spectral density and transfer function Π:

$$S_p(\kappa,\eta) = \rho^2 4b^2 \left(\frac{\partial U_1}{\partial x_2}\right)^2 S_{u_2}(\kappa)\Pi^2(\kappa,\eta) \qquad (9.79)$$

here, in a case where the Froude number is much less than unity:

$$\Pi^2 = \frac{\mathrm{ch}^2 \kappa\eta h}{\mathrm{sh}^2 \kappa h} \qquad (9.80)$$

and if the Froude number is much larger than unity:

$$\Pi^2 = \frac{\mathrm{sh}^2 \kappa\eta h}{\mathrm{ch}^2 \kappa h} \qquad (9.81)$$

The Froude number Fr is calculated using the value of flow velocity under the surface and the flow depth - h, κ - wave number, b - "effective" width of mixing layer, and η – ratio, between the mixing layer submergence below the surface and the depth h.

Spectral density of vertical velocity component u_2 can be approximated with the expression satisfying the measuring data in free jets:

$$S_{u_2}(\kappa) = \frac{2}{b\pi} \frac{\kappa^2}{\left(\frac{1}{b^2} + \kappa^2\right)^2} \left(u_2'\right)^2 \qquad (9.82)$$

Here u'_2 is RMS of fluctuating vertical velocity component, and b is effective thickness of mixing layer. According to the experimental data, b= 0.15 ÷0.20 h, and the longitudinal correlation is:

$$r_u(\xi) = \left(1 - \frac{\xi}{b}\right) \exp - \left|\frac{\xi}{b}\right| \qquad (9.83)$$

In the case when the mixing layer is normal to the rigid boundary (for instance, at the abrupt expansion by width), spectrum of pressure pulsation in the most intensely loaded points, just under the mixing layer, equals:

$$S_p(\kappa,\omega)=\rho^2 4\pi^2\left(\frac{\partial U_1}{\partial x_3}\right)^2 b_c^{\,2} S_{u_3}(\kappa,\omega) \tag{9.84}$$

I.e., the spectrum of pressure pulsation in this region is similar to the one of velocity pulsation. It must be mentioned that the expression (9.82) is held for the spectrum of velocity pulsation for the flow with stagnant wakes. Self-oscillating disturbances that are due to the whirls swept by the averaged flow and return to the initial section by the return current of wake are negligible. But in some cases this condition is not satisfied. For instance, on the shortened hydraulic jump, limited by pier-baffles, local peaks connected with the surface roller rotation may appear in the velocity spectrum and therefore in the pressure pulsation spectrum. In this case, one can expect the appearance in the spectral density of vertical velocity pulsation of local maximums associated with the rotation of a roller over the jet at the frequency:

$$\omega = 2\, U_1/(h_2 - h_1) \tag{9.85}$$

Here U_1 is velocity in the contracted section; and h_2-h_1 is hydraulic jump height. A similar effect can be observed also with the developed short swirls at the expansion by width. The velocity spectrums are rarely measured in practice of hydraulic investigations. The velocity spectrum correspondence with the expression (9.82) is conveniently checked for the layer, normal to the rigid boundary. The abrupt expansion of supercritical flow (by width) illustrates the case when the flow considerably differs from the round jet expansion in infinite space. The jet flow out of the bottom outlet is B=0.7m wide and 0.17m high into the flow 2B= 1.4m wide. The water level of a flume with horizontal bottom was chosen in such a way that the transit jet on the section under consideration was not submerged and the interface between the jet and the swirl was near the flume axis (Figure 9.14a); Fr= $U^2/gh=5$; U= 2.9m/sec.

The velocity of disturbances sweep was calculated from comparison of time correlation and longitudinal correlation at the distance x = 1.57 B = 1.1m) from the contraction section U_{tr} = 0.67 U. In conformity with the hypothesis of the "frozen" turbulence, the interval until the first zero of the autocorrelation function, corresponds to the distance to the first zero of the longitudinal correlation function: τ_0= b/U_{tr}, b = 11.8 cm = 0.17 B.

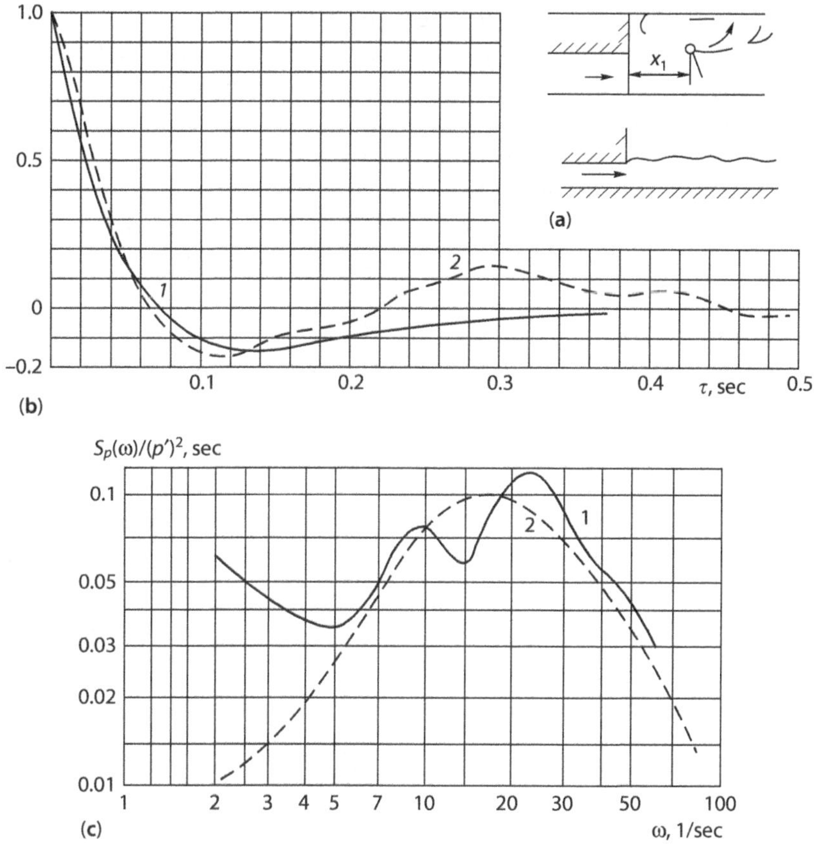

Figure 9.14 Abrupt expansion by width.

a) Location of the transducer.
b) Autocorrelation function.
1. Experiment.
2. Calculation.
c) Spectral density of pressure pulsation.
1. Experiment.
2. Calculation.

At $\tau < \tau_0$, the agreement between correlation (9.83) and the experiment is good (Figure 9.14b). The comparison of spectrums (Figure 9.14c) shows that in experiments, quasiperiodicity is evident, which seems to be associated with the returning disturbances in a complex lateral roller.

Another example refers to the field measurement of pressure pulsations at the Saratov hydroelectric station downstream apron. The hydroelectric station bottom outlet with the cross-section of 12 x 8m^2 passes water at low downstream water level with the operating gate entirely open. The adjacent bottom outlet to the left is closed. The gate of the outlet, isolated by a blank span, is opened at *2.85m* ($a=0.355a_0$, $a_0= 8$m). Downstream the outlet, the current assumes the type of the jet expansion by width in the infinite space; at the depth - in the finite one (Figure 9.15a).

The average velocity along the jet section above the transducer in the cross-section under consideration is 9m/sec. The jet width is about 35m. The largest gradient of longitudinal velocity over the depth is:

$$|\partial U/\partial x_2| = 0.54 \ 1/\text{sec}$$

The averaged by depth longitudinal velocity gradients maximum by width is:

$$|\partial U/\partial x_3| = 0.79 \div 0.66 \ 1/\text{sec}.$$

Pressure pulsation below the central jet zone can be considered as superposition of disturbance effects from the lateral and bottom mixing layers of the jet. The disturbance effect from mixing layers that is normal to the rigid boundary is governed by the Green function G in conformity with the general results. At Fr >> 1:

$$G = -4\kappa h \sum_{m=0}^{\infty} (-1)^m \frac{\exp - \left| \frac{x_3}{h} \sqrt{\frac{\pi^2}{4}(2m+1)^2 + \kappa^2 h^2} \right|}{(2m+1)\sqrt{\frac{\pi^2}{4}(2m+1)^2 + \kappa^2 h^2}} \tag{9.85}$$

And the spectrum of pressure pulsations at the distance x_3 from the mixing layer is:

$$S_p(\kappa h, x_3/h) = \rho^2 S_f(\kappa) b^2 |G|^2 \tag{9.86}$$

The functions G have the maximum at $\kappa h = \text{I} \div 1.5$, and they decrease with the increase of the distance x_3/h from the mixing layer (Figure 9.16).

Due to local conditions expansion of the jet flowing out of the outlets is nonsymmetrical relative to its axis, where transducer recording pressure pulsations is located. Distance from the transducer to the centre of the right-hand mixing layer amounts to about 0.7h and to the left-hand one, – h (h=15m). These components' contribution into the pressure pulsation spectrum according to (9.85) and (9.86) is shown in Figure (9.15b)

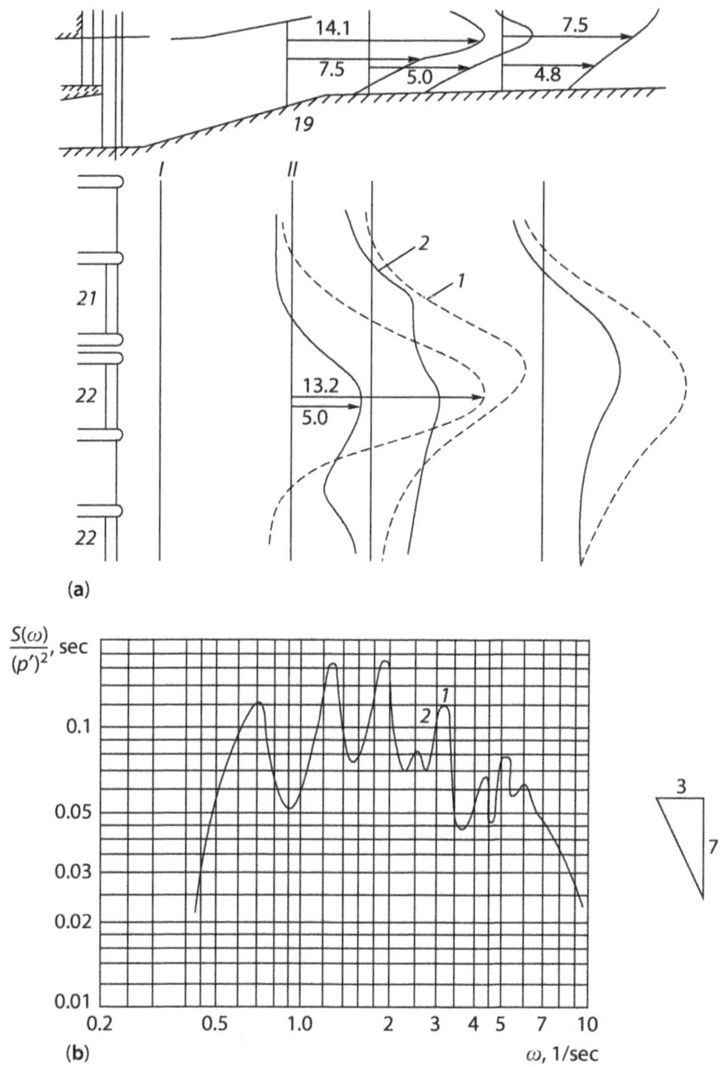

Figure 9.15 Flow downstream the hydroelectric station outlet.

a) Flow velocities (horizontal components).
1. Under the surface.
2. Near the bottom.
3. Distribution by depth along the flow dynamic axis.
b) Spectral density function.
1. In prototype.
2. Calculation.

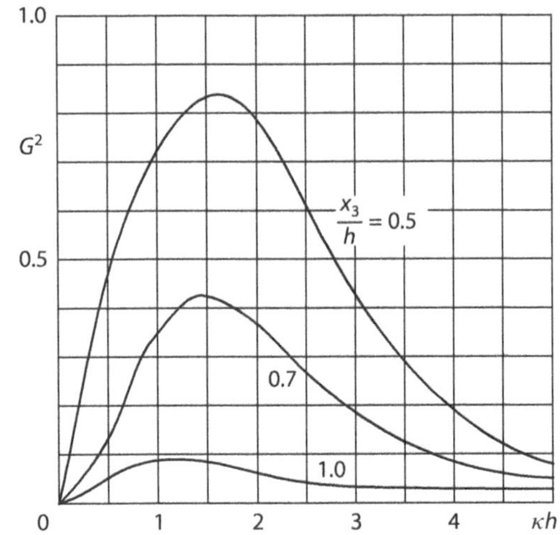

Figure 9.16 Decrease of Green function due to increasing distance from mixing layer normal to the bottom.

by small dash lines. In this case the main disturbance source is the mixing layer at the lower boundary of the jet. The transducer is placed just in the mixing layer. In the calculation, we adopt the value $\eta = 0.9$, with effective width of the mixing layer $b \sim 0.2$ h. The measured spectrum in the average is rather satisfactorily approximated *by* the theoretical relation (9.82), after the low—frequency component associated with the slow level oscillations in the adjacent regions is excluded.

Larger measured spectrum values in comparison with the calculated results are observed in the frequency region higher than about 5 I/sec. The field spectrum is decreased approximately according to the law of minus 7/8, characteristic of the "interval of the velocity spectrum dissipation"[108]. The Reynolds number in the considered cross-section is calculated over the thickness and average velocity of the jet is $Uh/\nu \sim 6.9 \times 10^7$.

Pressure pulsations below the mixing layer, normal to the bottom, were recorded in the above-mentioned hydroelectric station at the complex space flow regime (Figure 9.17-a). Water was discharged through the 22 left-hand outlet, entirely opened, and the 21 right-hand, where the gate was opened by 5.83m. Flow deflection to the left resulted from specific features of the construction period. The flow is deflecting to the left and the transducer under consideration occurs at the boundary of the main jet.

In this case the measured spectrum (Figure 9.17b) is more sharply resonant than the one calculated from the expression (9.82). This effect seems to be connected with the existence of intensive local swirls, and hence with

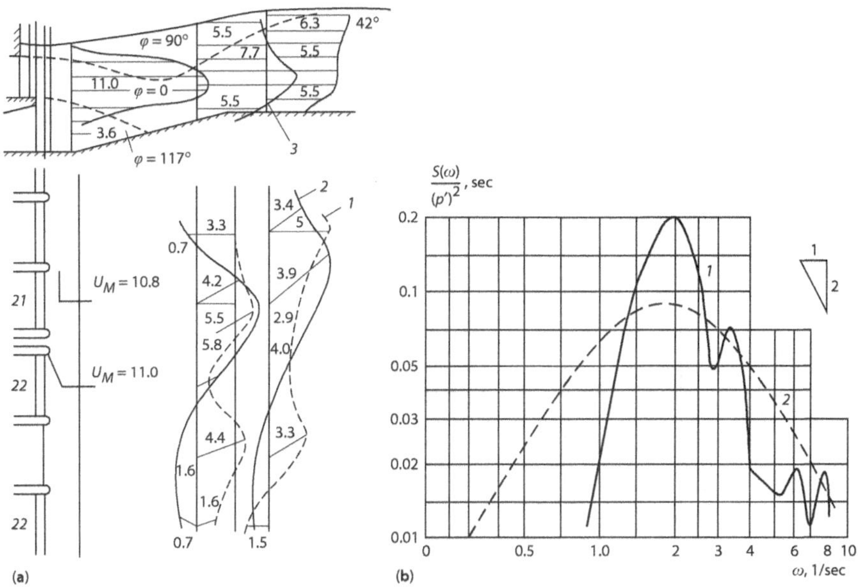

Figure 9.17 Flow downstream the hydroelectric station outlets.

a) Flow velocities.
1. Under the surface.
2. Near the bottom.
3. Distribution by depth along the flow dynamic axis.
b) Spectral density function of pressure pulsation.
1. In prototype.
2. Calculation.

the variation of the kinematic function proper. Bottom regime downstream of the hydroelectric stations combined with spillways differs from the bottom regime downstream of the spillway dams, mainly in the fact that in the former case, the hydraulic jump is much submerged and the Froude number Fr, composed on the basis of flow velocity at its surface and at the depth, is less than unity.

The theoretical spectrum of pressure pulsations (for η=0.7) has a non-significantly pronounced maximum and it fails rapidly with the frequency increase. According to model measurements (N.V. Halturina, [34a], model scale I:40, Re=1.9 10^5) the maximum of the spectra is pronounced more markedly and at frequency in excess of 2 1/sec, the experimental spectrum decays slower than the theoretical one (Figure 9.18).

In this case, a need is generated to take into account that the second (nonlinear) component of the kinematic function f_2 (9.21) is not related

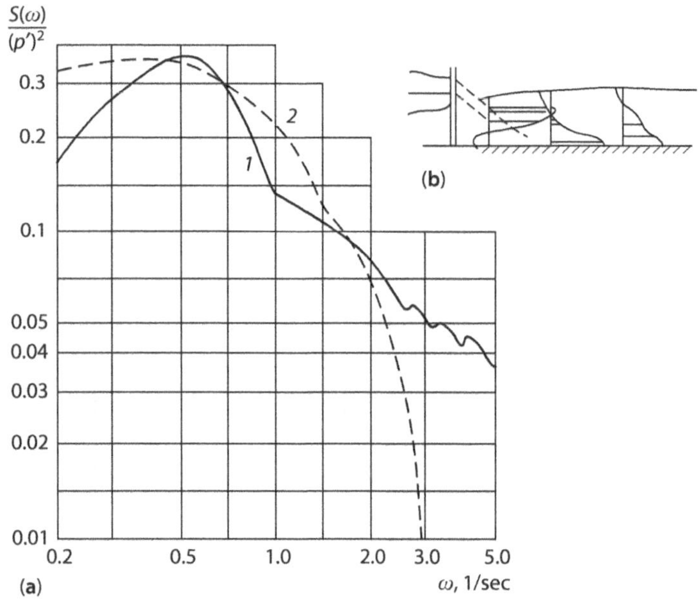

Figure 9.18 Flow downstream the ledge.

a) Distribution of velocities by depth.
b) Spectral density.
1. Experiment.
2. Calculation.

with the gradient of the averaged velocity, dependent mainly on the fluctuating velocity components. Despite the fact that in the field of large-scale turbulence, f_2 is significantly smaller than f_1, as the rigid boundary moves from this region (mixing layer), the values of these high frequency components can increase. Usually the natural frequency of the structural members (for instance of the downstream apron plates) are much larger than the predominant frequency of the load. This necessitates treating the high frequency spectrum part with special attention.

Pressure Pulsations on a Separate Wall Downstream

In many cases, the pulsation pressure on a separate wall can be represented as a sum of statistically independent turbulent and wave component. For the calculation of the turbulent components, it is advisable to use the problem formulated in p.9.2.1

Boundary conditions for equation (9.21) in this case are the following:

$$\begin{aligned} &\text{Ha on the surface of water } p=0 \quad \text{for} \quad z=0; \\ &\text{on the bottom} \qquad \frac{\partial p}{\partial z}=0 \text{ for } \ z=-1; \\ &\text{on the separate wall} \qquad \frac{\partial p}{\partial y}=-\frac{\partial^2 \xi}{\partial t^2} \text{ for } y=0. \end{aligned} \tag{9.87}$$

The decision as pressure pulsations on the wall is the sum of the main part and vibration components.

For pressure pulsations in the middle part of the long wall in the tail-water of the big width of the following applies spectral representation:

$$\begin{aligned} p^*(\kappa,z,t) &= \int_0^\infty \int_{-1}^0 f^*\left(y-l,\kappa,\zeta,t\right) G_1\left(l,\kappa,z,\xi\right) dl d\xi - \\ &-\sqrt{\frac{2}{\pi}}\frac{\partial^2}{\partial t^2}\int_{-1}^0 \xi^* G_1\left(l=0,\kappa,z,\xi\right) d\xi + \\ &+\int_0^\infty \int_0^z f^*\left(y-l,\kappa,\xi,t\right) G_2\left(l,\kappa,\xi\right) dl\, d\zeta - \sqrt{\frac{2}{\pi}}\frac{\partial^2}{\partial t^2}\int_0^z \xi^* \\ &G_2\left(l=0,\kappa,\xi\right) d\xi, \end{aligned} \tag{9.88}$$

Here:

$$G_1 = \sqrt{\frac{2}{\pi}}\int_0^\infty \frac{sh\sqrt{\kappa^2+\mu^2}z}{\sqrt{\kappa^2+\mu^2}\, ch\sqrt{\kappa^2+\mu^2}} ch\left(1+\xi\right)\sqrt{\kappa^2+\mu^2}\cos\mu l\, d\mu$$

$$G_2 = \sqrt{\frac{2}{\pi}}\int_0^\infty \frac{sh\left(z-\xi\right)\sqrt{\kappa^2+\mu^2}}{\sqrt{\kappa^2+\mu^2}}\cos\mu l\, d\mu$$

p^* и f^* - the results are applied to pressure pulsations and kinematic functions cosine Fourier transform on the longitudinal coordinate *x*.

Wave component of the dynamic loads on the wall in the first approximation is determined by ordinary linear wave theory. Using this theory and assuming for a single sine that waves probability density phase angles in the range from 0 to 2π is a constant, you can find expressions for the spectral density of the load, acting on the element of length *L* and the height of the unit, buried under the water level on the value of *z*:

$$S_1(\omega) \approx S_0(\omega)\exp\left(-\frac{4\pi|z|}{\lambda}\right)\frac{2\lambda^2}{L^2\pi^2}\sin^2\frac{\pi L}{\lambda}\left[\frac{1}{2}-\frac{1}{\pi^2}\sin^2\frac{\pi L}{\lambda}\right], \qquad (9.89)$$

Here $S_0(\omega)$ - frequency spectral density of fluctuations of surface water; $S_1(\omega)$ - spectral density of pressure pulsations; λ - wave length associated with frequency and phase velocity of wave propagation. For waves on deep water at a relative low speed flow:

$$\lambda = \frac{2\pi g}{\omega^2}.$$

Pressure Pulsations on Overlapping Discharge Spillway

Consider a two-dimensional task, assuming the bottom and ceiling spillway are oscillating by the known law $\zeta_1(t)$ and $\zeta(t)$.

The main part of pulsation pressure is determined by the solution of boundary value problem:

$$\frac{\partial p_1}{\partial y} = 0 \text{ for } y = 0 \text{ and } y = 1 \qquad (9.90)$$

$$p_1 = 0 \text{ for } x = 0 \text{ and } x = a$$

for the equation:

$$\Delta p_1 = f(x, y, t). \qquad (9.91)$$

Here and everywhere below, all variables are expressed in dimensionless form. As basis variables taken: the density of water is, the depth of the stream (height spillway) h, the characteristic velocity U.

The fundamental functions of the Laplace equation under conditions (9.90) will function:

$$\psi_{m,n} = \sin\frac{m\pi x}{a}\cos n\pi yz.$$

Decomposing the function $f(x, y, t)$, $p_1(x, y, t)$ in double rows function is $y_{m,n}$, substituting these expansions in (9.91) and equating the coefficients of the relevant members of the series, we'll find:

$$p_1(x,y,t) = \int_0^a\int_0^1 G(x,y,\xi,\eta)f(\xi,\eta)d\xi d\eta, \qquad (9.92)$$

Here:

$$G(x,y,\xi,\eta)=-\frac{4a}{\pi^2}\sum_{m,n=1}^{\infty}\frac{\sin\frac{m\pi x}{a}\cos n\pi y\sin\frac{m\pi\xi}{a}\cos n\pi\eta}{m^2+a^2n^2}$$

$$-\frac{2a}{\pi^2}\sum_{m=1}^{\infty}\frac{1}{m^2}\sin\frac{m\pi x}{a}\sin\frac{m\pi\xi}{a}. \tag{9.93}$$

If a number (9.93) converges everywhere except for the point $x = \xi$, then $y = \eta$ is where the function G is in infinite logarithmic order (order $\frac{1}{\pi}\ln r$, if r is the distance from a given point, located on the border). The function $G(x, y, x, h)$ at a fixed point (x, y) describes the contribution to the pulsation pressure at this point with values of kinematic features (characteristics of the turbulent flow) at the point with coordinates ξ (on the x-axis) and η (on the y-axis).

Changing weight function depending on ξ and η will allow study for a point located on the ceiling of the spillway ($y = 1$).

Weight function (9.93) in this case, is possible to present in the form of a single row:

$$g(x,\xi,\eta)=G\Big|_{y=1}=-\frac{2}{\pi}\sum_{m=1}^{\infty}\frac{1}{m}\frac{ch\frac{m\pi\eta}{a}}{sh\frac{m\pi}{a}}\sin\frac{m\pi x}{a}\sin\frac{m\pi\xi}{a}. \tag{9.94}$$

Almost everywhere the row (9.94) quickly converges.

Figure 9.19 presents the results of calculating the weight functions for the point $x = 0{,}5a$ (middle of the spillway)

$$g_1(\eta)=g(x=0{,}5a,\xi=x,\eta)=-\frac{2}{\pi}\sum_{k=0}^{\infty}\frac{1}{2k+1}\frac{ch\frac{(2k+1)\pi\eta}{a}}{sh\frac{(2k+1)\pi}{a}},$$

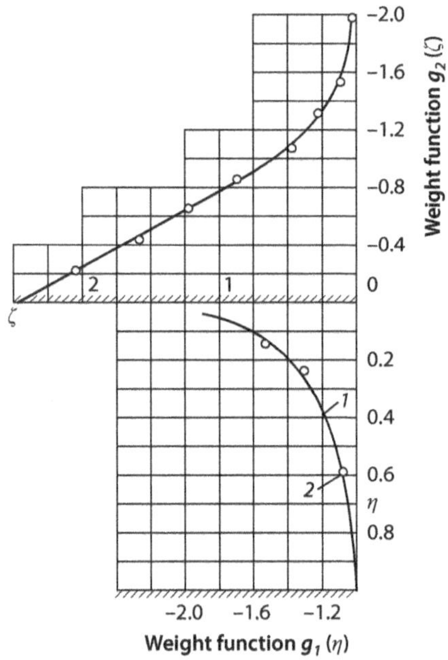

Figure 9.19 Weight function for the middle point on the ceiling spillway (relative length of the spillway a=5) .1- theoretical calculation, 2 – dimension on model with electrolyte.

$$g_2(\xi) = g(x = 0{,}5a, \xi, \eta = 1) = -\frac{2}{\pi}\sum_{k=0}^{\infty}\frac{(-1)^k}{2k+1} cth\frac{2k+1}{a}\pi \sin\frac{(2k+1)\pi\xi}{a}.$$

As you can see in Figure 9.19, weighting function with increasing distance from the considered point decreases. Function $g_1(\eta)$ at $\eta < 0{,}5$ decreases very slowly. Disturbances in the middle and lower sections of the spillway are, with the same contribution to the pulsation pressure on the ceiling, almost regardless of their vertical position.

Deterministic solution (9.92), obviously, is enough to get all of the statistical characteristics of the main part of pressure pulsations on the known characteristics of the velocity fluctuations. For example, mutual covariance function of pressure pulsations on the ceiling of the spillway at the points $\boldsymbol{x}$ and $\boldsymbol{x}_1$ has the form:

$$R_{x,x_1}(\tau) = \iiiint G(x,\xi,\eta)G(x_1,\xi_1,\eta_1) f(\xi,\eta,t) f(\xi_1,\eta_1,t+\tau) d\xi d\xi_1 d\eta d\eta_1. \tag{9.95}$$

Let us now consider the effects of fluctuations in the borders of the spillway and pressure pulsation in the initial and final sections.

If moving ceiling spillway to designate the ζ(x, t), moving floor is ζ_1(x, t), pulsation pressure in the initial section $p_0(y, t)$, and the surge in end-section - $p_k(y, t)$. The additional component ripple obtained as the solution of the Laplace equation for the corresponding mixed nonhomogeneous boundary-value problem has the form:

$$p_1 = \sum_{n=1}^{\infty} \frac{(-1)^n}{sh n\pi a}\left[(p_0)_n sh\pi n(a-x) + (p_k)_n - sh\pi nx\right] -$$

$$-\frac{\partial^2}{\partial t^2}\sum \frac{a}{\pi n sh\frac{\pi n}{a}}\left[(\zeta)_k ch\frac{\pi n}{a} - (\zeta_1)_n\right]\sin\frac{\pi nx}{a}$$

$(p_0)_n$, $(p_k)_n$, $(\zeta)_n$, $(\zeta_1)_n$ is the Fourier coefficient of the corresponding functions:

$$\left.\begin{aligned}(p_k)_n &= 2\int_0^1 p_k(\eta,t)\cos\pi n\eta d\eta,\\ (\zeta)_n &= \frac{2}{a}\int_0^a \zeta(\xi,t)\sin\frac{\pi n\xi}{a}d\xi.\end{aligned}\right\}$$

Often with vibration bottom, you can ignore $\zeta_1 = 0$, and pulse pressure at the inlet spillway is very small. In this case, pressure pulsations on the ceiling of the spillway, caused by vibration and pressure variation at the output, is determined by the expression:

$$p_2(x,t) = \int_0^1 G(\eta,x)p_k(\eta,t)d\eta - \frac{\partial^2}{\partial t^2}\int_0^a G_1(\xi,x)\xi(\xi,t)d\xi, \quad (9.96)$$

$$G(\eta,x) = 2\sum_{n-1}^{\infty}\frac{(-1)^n sh\pi nx\cos\pi n\eta}{sh\pi na,}$$

$$G_1(\xi, x) = \frac{2}{\pi}\sum \frac{\sin\frac{\pi n x}{a}\sin\frac{\pi n \xi}{a}}{n} cth\frac{\pi n}{a}.$$

The second term in formula (9.96) is very important: it evaluates the impact of vibration on the surge in first approximation, without taking into account changes in the main part of pressure pulsations. In the presence of turbulent flow however it mainly reflects the impact of water on the fluctuation in construction, which is usually associated with the term "attached" to the masses. This member directly characterizes the inertial resistance of the water. The value of the inertial resistance is little changed in the absence of flow. Because kinematic function f is derived from the works component of the velocity, with small fluctuations of the border in stagnant water the value of f can be considered close to zero. Note that with the value of "attached" mass determined from the expression (9.96), the resulting solution of the Laplace equation with boundary condition (9.90) exactly coincides with the results obtained for the perfect residual liquid.

Calculating the weight function G is easy to make on electrointegrator intended for solution of Poisson's equations, such as the model electrohydrodynamic analogy. Calculating a weight function that is included in the expression for the main part of pressure pulsations can be made particularly easy. The fixed boundaries of the spillway are made of dielectric; areas of zero pressure pulsations that are grounded. In point (ξ, η), probe is current $I(\zeta, \eta)$; at the point (x, y) is fixed potential $\upsilon(x, y)$.

Green function (weighting function) is calculated by the formula:

$$G(x, y, \xi, \eta) = -\frac{c\upsilon(x, y)}{I(\xi, \eta)}, \tag{9.97}$$

where c is the electrical conductivity of electrolyte on the model of electrohydrodynamic analogy.

The expression (9.97) is sometimes more convenient to present in some form, using the principle of reciprocity and replacing the current strength of its expression through the gradient of potential:

$$G(x, y, \xi, \eta) = \frac{\upsilon(\xi, \eta)}{\int \frac{\partial \upsilon}{\partial n} ds}. \tag{9.98}$$

The integral in the denominator of the right-hand side of (9.98) is calculated on any closed circuit covering the considered point (x, y), which in this case is current:

$$I(x,y) = -c\int \frac{\partial v}{\partial n} ds. \tag{9.99}$$

Data of the elektrolit model practically coincide with results of theoretical calculations (Figure 9.19). Knowing the function of weight and having fairly complete information about the kinematics of flow, they can calculate all necessary data on pressure pulsations.

In a two dimensional flow with the little changing depth solution of the equation (9.91), the points at the bottom of the stream have the following form:

$$p(x,t) = -\int_{-1}^{0} d\eta \int_{-\infty}^{\infty} G(\xi,\eta) f(x-\xi,\eta) d\xi. \tag{9.100}$$

The longitudinal range of pressure pulsations on the bottom flat thread can be simply calculated, if known mutual longitudinal range of kinematic functions in different layers flow $\mathbf{S}_f(\kappa, \eta, \eta')$:

$$S_F(\kappa) = \langle p * \overline{p} * \rangle = \int_{-1}^{0}\int_{-1}^{0} S_f(\kappa,\eta,\eta') G^*(\kappa\eta)\overline{G^*}(\kappa\eta') d\eta' d\eta'. \tag{9.101}$$

Further calculation of the integral in (9.101) can be performed, involving experimental data and plausible hypotheses about the structure of the kinematic functions. The results of semi empirical calculation of the spectrum of pressure are consistent with data from direct measurements.

For hydraulic engineering practices an interesting case is sharply non-uniform motion. The main difficulty preventing theoretical calculation is insufficient study of the velocity field. In this regard, it is necessary to use the approximate representation, based on indirect observations comparing the results of calculations with the data of direct measurements of pressure pulsations.

Calculation of pressure pulsations on the border of the flow in the presence of the interface and narrow "mixing zone" with high vorticity (Figure 9.20) can be simplified by assuming the variance kinematic function equal to zero only within this zone of mixing.

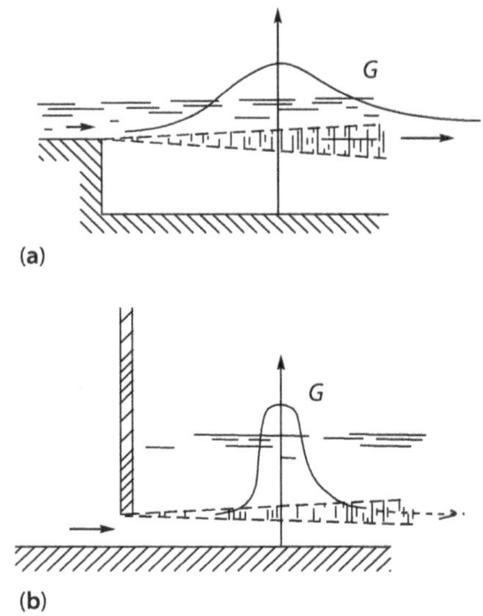

Figure 9.20 The mixing zone where the intensity of velocity pulsations (and kinematic function) max. The form of the weight functions for pressure points on the bottom of the stream.

Using this condition leads to the following relation for the spatial-temporal covariations of pressure on the bottom of the thread:

$$R_F\left(x,x',\tau\right)=\left\langle p\left(x,t\right)p\left(x',t+\tau\right)\right\rangle =$$

$$=\int\int b(\xi)b(\xi')G(x,\xi)G(x',\xi')R_f\left(\xi,\xi',\tau\right)d\xi d\xi' \qquad (9.102)$$

Here b is the width of the mixing zone, **G**(***x***, ξ) - the value of the weight function in the mixing zone, $\boldsymbol{R_f}$(ξ, ξ', τ) - longitudinal temporary covariations kinematic functions in the mixing zone.

Further calculations in unchanged form of kinematical correlations functions R_f lead to different results depending on how quickly or slowly varying function of the weights along the mixed layer happens. If the mixing zone is located at the surface and the weight function is changed relatively slowly (Figure 9.20a), spatial-temporal correlation of pressure pulsations on the bottom is significantly different from the correlation kinematic functions.

In particular, if in the kinematic functions can be traced property frozen turbulence, the pressure pulsations at the bottom of it practically do not occur. If, on the contrary, the function of weight quickly changes the length of the mixing zone (rib), all features of kinematic features are brightly reflected in the properties of pressure pulsations on the bottom. This conclusion was confirmed, in particular, in the experiments on special high-pressure setting, created on the territory of the complex in Istra of Moscow region.

Figure 9.21 shows a diagram of this installation (b) and model diagram spillway (a), which examined the spread of correlations and standards of pressure pulsations in the zone of separation.

Figure 9.22 shows the results of measurements correlations of pressure pulsations on the ceiling spillway at different locations of the base of the measuring point.

As can be seen from Figure 9.22, for different points shown by different symbols (except triangles), there is a high correlation at large distances between points. This means the presence in the given pressure system of long-wave fluctuations is not directly associated with turbulence. These vibrations to some extent managed to suppress, having arranged in front of the entrance gate system pneumatic surge tank. Correlation of pressure on distances was significantly decreased (triangles Figure 9.22).

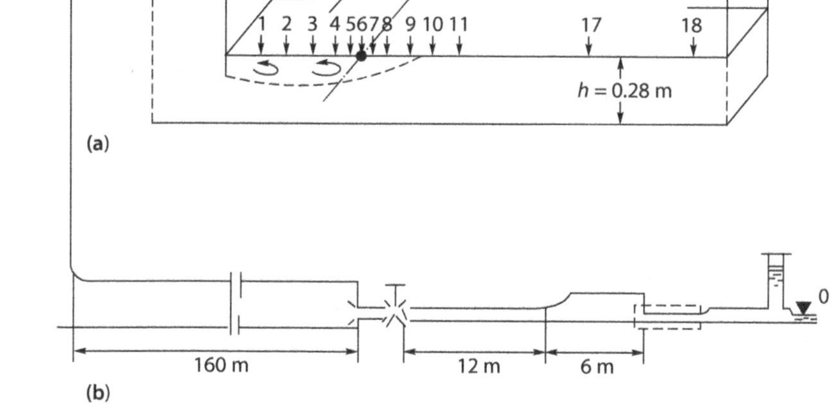

Figure 9.21 High-pressure testing system on the territory of the complex of Istra Hydro Power Plant in Moscow region. Pressure sensors (a), the General scheme (b).

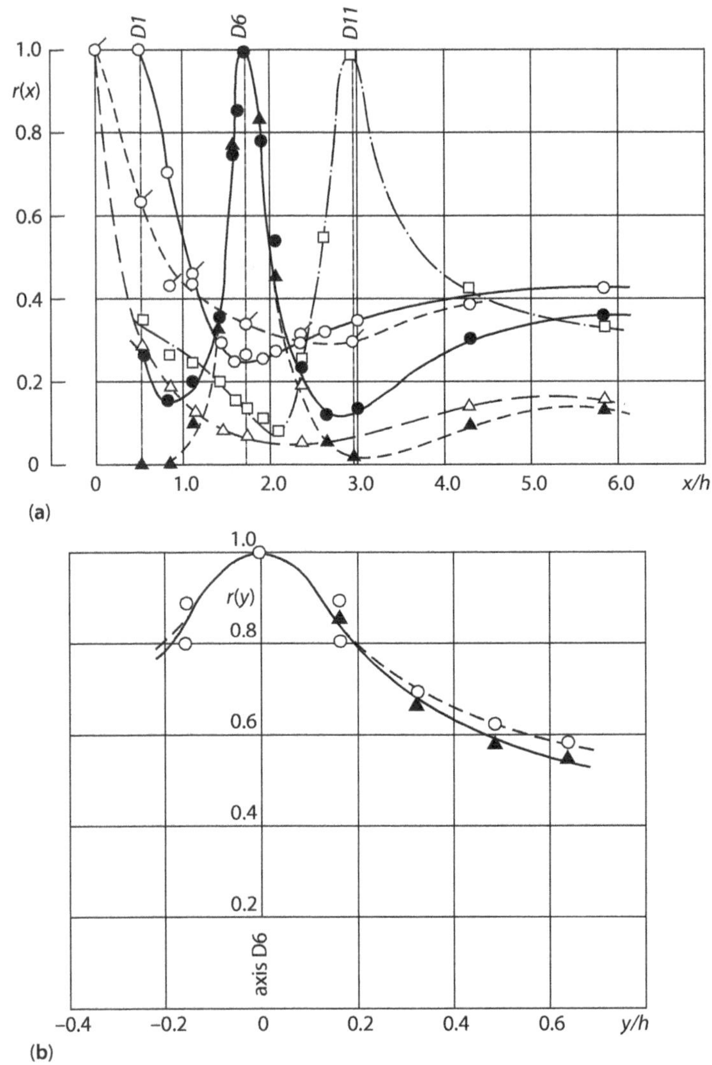

Figure 9.22 The longitudinal (a) and transverse (b) correlation of pressure pulsation from sensor by Figure 9.21a.

Pressure pulsations on the ceiling of the spillway were experimentally studied under different absolute pressures in the stream with different numbers of cavitation $K = \left(\langle p \rangle - p^0\right) / \left(\rho U_1^2/2\right)$ -Thoma criterion.

Here p^0 - saturation vapor pressure of water (usually about 1 atmosphere = 10 m water). It was found that decreasing K, beginning with its certain value, standard pressure pulsation rapidly at first increases and then decreases rapidly (Figures 9.23 and 9.24).

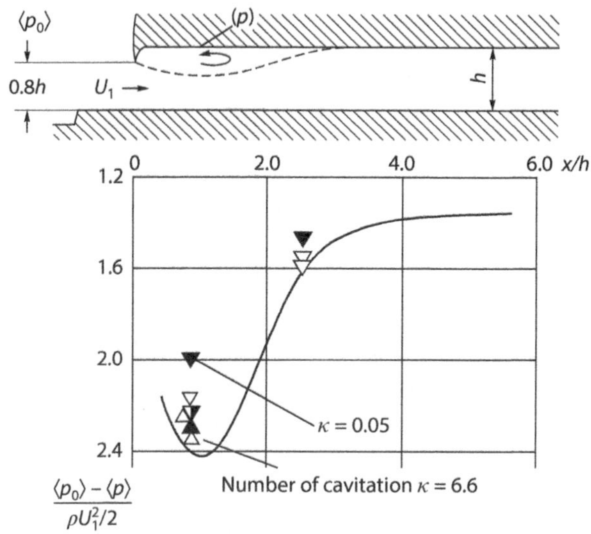

Figure 9.23 The averaged relative pressure on the ceiling spillway with different numbers of cavitation.

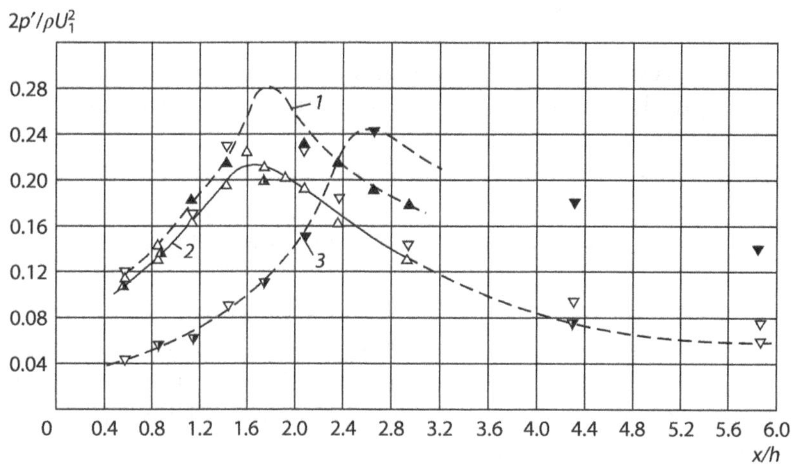

Figure 9.24 The relative standards of pulsation pressure in the zone of separation on the ceiling spillway at different modes of cavitation.1- In the absence of phase transitions; 2 -Internal aeration flow; 3 - Developed cavitation.

A similar effect is described by Naudasher [87a]. This is due to the qualitative changes in the structure of pulsations. In the experiment, when the numbers of cavitation were less than 0,5, there began to be an intensive selection air flow (internal aeration flow). The amplitude of pressure

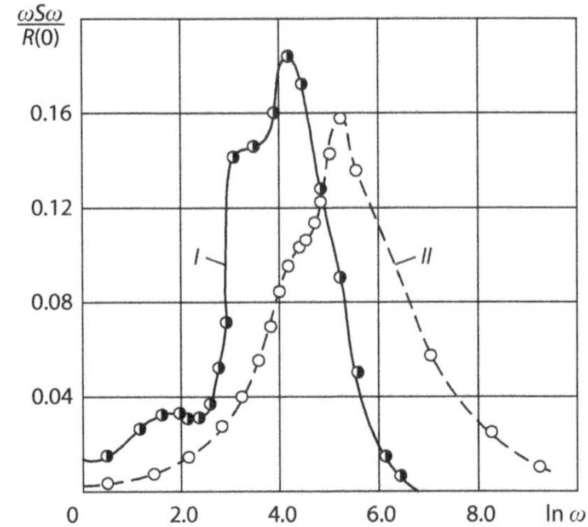

Figure 9.25 Spectra of pressure pulsations at point 6 in Figure 9.213 in the absence of cavitation (I – K = 6.6) and in the presence of cavitation (II - K = 0.31).

pulsations sharply increased. Directly on the waveform there could be seen the emergence of high-frequency pulsations. Further decrease in the number of cavitation is the reduction of the standard of ripples due to "cut" depressions pressure below the cavitation threshold. However, dramatically changed, the shape of the spectrum of pressure pulsations is shifted towards higher frequencies (Figure 9.25).

Regarding the impact on structural elements that change the spectrum may be much more important than some decrease in the standard of pulsations. Indeed, the voltage at the plate, which formed part of the boundary of the flow and had a frequency of natural oscillations about 200 Hz, in the presence of the cavitating flow, was approximately 2.5 times more than in the absence of cavitation (with data conversion experience on the same dynamic pressure). Waveform analysis shows that these changes are mainly related to the high-frequency excitation of oscillations in the design (resonance swinging design).

These effects are often the direct cause of the destruction of the lining of structures under the action of cavity flow.

The pulsation pressure at specific points cladding, sealing camera tunnels change with shutter, change of water flow and absolute pressure in the zone of separation.

If the absolute pressure in the zone of separation is $<\boldsymbol{p}>$, then the number of cavitation is: $K = \dfrac{\langle p \rangle - p_0}{\rho U_1^2/2}$ more 1,6, phase transitions in liquid stream is not observed and the water can be considered incompressible. In this case, when the pressure reaches sufficiently large Reynolds numbers, hydrodynamic loads depend only on velocity head and flow configuration. Load, measured in fractions of a high-speed flow pressure in the section under the shutter is characterized variance, spatial correlations and frequency spectrums.

If the highest frequency spectrum is less than 0.4, frequency in lower forms of natural oscillations of the design found loads should be made "quasistatically," summarizing pulsation component averaged. This can be considered different schemes dynamic loading under the assumption that the maximum ripple is realized on a particular piece. In other parts of the structure, during the construction of the scheme, instant loading should be made of local extremum of pulse load multiplied by the coefficient of correlation between the surge in the given point and the point of the expected peak load.

Characteristics of pressure pulsations on the ceiling and bottom spillway in the absence of phase transitions can be calculated with the introduction of the following assumptions:

1. for a flat;
2. all the turbulence is concentrated in a relatively narrow layer mixing, located in the zone of maximum gradients average rates between the border transit streams and the line of zero velocity in the maelstrom (Figure 9.26);
3. is considered a low-frequency part of turbulence in the layer blending, for which the gradient of the averaged velocity is much more than mean-square values of the gradient of pulse speed:

$$\left|\frac{\partial U}{\partial y}\right| >> \left(\frac{\partial u}{\partial y}\right)' ;$$

4. characteristics of turbulence in the layer blending smoothly vary in length, so pulsation velocities can be considered locally homogeneous and be represented in the form of two-dimensional Fourier integral:

$$\upsilon(x,t) \approx \int_{-\infty}^{\infty}\int \exp i(\omega t + \kappa x) d\Phi(\omega,\kappa), \tag{9.103}$$

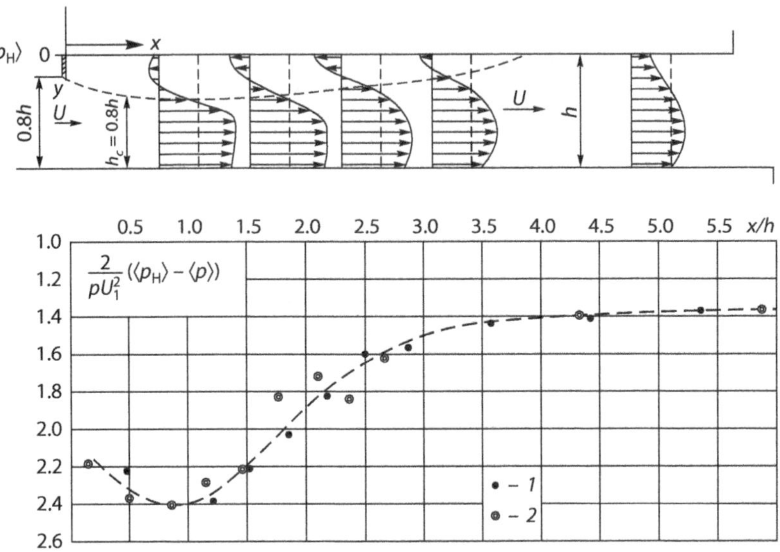

Figure 9.26 The distribution of the averaged velocity and pressure in the spillway at the partially open gate. 1 – Re= q/ν =4.5 10^5; 2 – Re= 14.4 10^5. No cavitation.

where random differential dΦ is associated with two-dimensional spectral density $\mathbf{S}_\upsilon(\omega, \kappa)$:

$$\langle d\Phi(\omega,\kappa)d\bar{\Phi}(\omega,\kappa_1)\rangle = S_\upsilon(\omega,\kappa)\delta(\kappa-\kappa_1)d\omega d\omega_1 d\kappa d\kappa_1,$$

where δ(z) - Delta-function;

5. the ceiling and the bottom of the bolt fixed camera that lets you take to pressure pulsations on this boundary condition:

$$\frac{\partial p}{\partial y} = 0 \text{ for } y = 0 \text{ and } y = h. \qquad (9.104)$$

The equation relating the pressure pulsations and speed, flat low turbulence of two-dimensional flow has the following form ($\boldsymbol{\upsilon}$ -vertical pulse rate).

$$\frac{\partial^2 p}{\partial x^2} + \frac{\partial^2 p}{\partial y^2} = -\rho\frac{\partial U}{\partial y}\frac{\partial \upsilon}{\partial x}$$

The solution with respect to “images” of pressure pulsations (Fourier) is written in the first part of this point. Multiplying complex-conjugate images and calculating the mathematical expectation of the work, we find the spectral density pulsations on the bottom $S_{p1}(\omega,\kappa)$ and on the ceiling $S_{p2}(\omega,\kappa)$ of the bolt camera:

$$S_{p1} = \rho^2 b^2 \left(\frac{\partial U}{\partial y}\right)^2_{\max} \frac{\mathrm{ch}^2 \kappa (h - h_T)}{\mathrm{sh}^2 \kappa h} S_\upsilon; \tag{9.105}$$

$$S_{p2} = \rho^2 b^2 \left(\frac{\partial U}{\partial y}\right)^2_{\max} \frac{\mathrm{ch}^2 \kappa h_T}{\mathrm{sh}^2 \kappa h} S_\upsilon. \tag{9.106}$$

$\left(\frac{\partial U}{\partial y}\right)_{\max}$ the gradient of the averaged velocity in the layer blending width b; hт - thickness of transit streams; $\boldsymbol{S_\upsilon} = \boldsymbol{S_\upsilon}(\omega, \kappa)$ is the spectral density of the vertical velocity pulsations in the layer blending.

The solution (9.105) and (9.106) have a singularity at $\kappa \to 0$ (sh $\kappa \boldsymbol{h} \to 0$), which disappears when you consider that the vertical displacement of particles in the layer blending uniform in κ.

$$S_\upsilon(\kappa,\omega) \underset{\kappa \to 0}{\to} h^2 \kappa^2 (\upsilon')^2 L_\upsilon, \tag{9.107}$$

$\boldsymbol{L_\upsilon}$ -some of the characteristic linear scale pulsations

For specific calculations of the spectra $\boldsymbol{S_p}$, we need to know spectra $\boldsymbol{S_\upsilon}$.

Use of empirical data [66a] obtained for the mixed layer streams, resulting in infinite space. Our data processing [70a] showed that the range of transverse velocity pulsations in the layer blending can be represented as follows:

$$S_\upsilon(\kappa) = (\upsilon')^2 \frac{2}{b\pi} \frac{\kappa^2}{\left(\kappa^2 + \frac{1}{b^2}\right)^2}.$$

The thickness of the mixed layer b is determined from the condition:

$$\int_0^\infty \left(\frac{\partial U}{\partial y}\right)^2 dy = b \left(\frac{\partial U}{\partial y}\right)^2_{\max},$$

where reference is selected on the axis of the jet.

Using these relations and integrating by ω and κ in the range from - ∞ to + ∞, will find the standards of pulsation pressure in the sealing chamber: at the bottom:

$$p_1^{'} = \rho b \left|\frac{\partial U}{\partial y}\right|_{max} (h - h_T) \upsilon' A \sqrt{\frac{2}{\pi}\frac{b^3}{h^3}} \tag{9.108}$$

on the ceiling:

$$p_2^{'} = \rho b \left|\frac{\partial U}{\partial y}\right|_{max} h_T \upsilon' A \sqrt{\frac{2}{\pi}\frac{b^3}{h^3}} \tag{9.109}$$

$$A = \sqrt{2\int_0^{\infty} \frac{\frac{h^4}{b^4} x^2}{\left(x^2 + \frac{h_2}{b_2}\right)^2} \frac{\text{ch}^2 zx}{\text{sh}^2 zx} dx};$$

$$z = \frac{h - h_T}{h} \text{ for calculate } p_1^{'},\ z = \frac{h_T}{h} \text{ for calculate } p_2^{'}.$$

Calculations by these relations show that the change of standard pressure pulsations on the floor or the ceiling spillway when changing the shutter opens (Figure 9.27) is not only due to changes in provisions of the mixed layer carried coefficient ***A***, but also due to changes kinematic characteristics in this layer.

Changes of kinematics of the mixed layer should be taken into account in the analysis of changes in the standard of pressure pulsations on the length of the zone of separation. With the approach of the mixing zone to the ceiling (with the expansion of the jet), standard pressure pulsations grow due to the increase in A in equation (9.109). However, as offset downstream value decreases, $b\left|\frac{\partial U}{\partial y}\right|_{max}$, so because of this, starting from a certain distance (about 0,8 - 0,9 on the length of the zone of separation), standard pressure pulsations decrease (Figure 9.27). A similar effect of reducing the standard of ripples due to the decrease $b\left|\frac{\partial U}{\partial y}\right|_{max}$, can be expected, at a very low relative extensions flow.

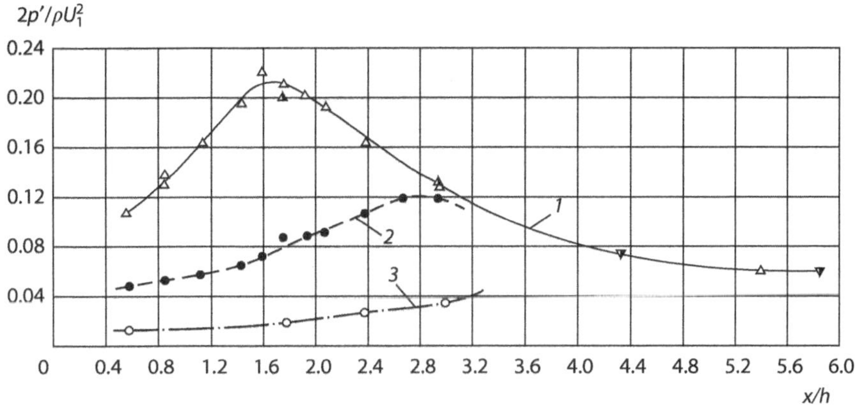

Figure 9.27 The distribution of the standards of pressure pulsations on the ceiling spillway at different open shutter. 1- ***a=0.8h, Re= (1.3÷1.9)10⁶, σ>1.6;*** 2 – ***a=0.5h, Re=1.15 10⁶, σ=2.42;*** 3 - ***a=0.2h, Re=6 10⁵, σ=0.82;***

By applying the ratio of (9.105) or (9.106) to cosine Fourier transform, you can find the longitudinal correlation function of pressure pulsations on the border. The normalized longitudinal spectra pressure on the border have the form:

$$S_p(\kappa)=\frac{1}{A^2}\frac{\mathrm{ch}^2 z\kappa x}{\mathrm{sh}^2\kappa h}\frac{\frac{h^4}{b^4}(\kappa h)^2}{\left[(\kappa h)^2+\frac{h^2}{b^2}\right]^2}h. \tag{9.110}$$

Note that if the mixing zone is very close to the surface on which the pulsation pressure is studied, then considering $\boldsymbol{S}_p(\chi)\approx(1-\boldsymbol{z})\,\boldsymbol{h}\exp-2\chi\boldsymbol{h}(1-\boldsymbol{z})$, a simple asymptotic formula for the longitudinal correlation [1] can be found:

$$r(\xi)\approx\frac{1}{1+\left[\frac{\xi}{2h}(1-z)\right]^2}, \tag{9.111}$$

Turning to the experimental data (Figure 9.28), you may notice that the longitudinal correlation (along the stream) decreases faster than the cross: vortex disturbances are stretched across the stream.

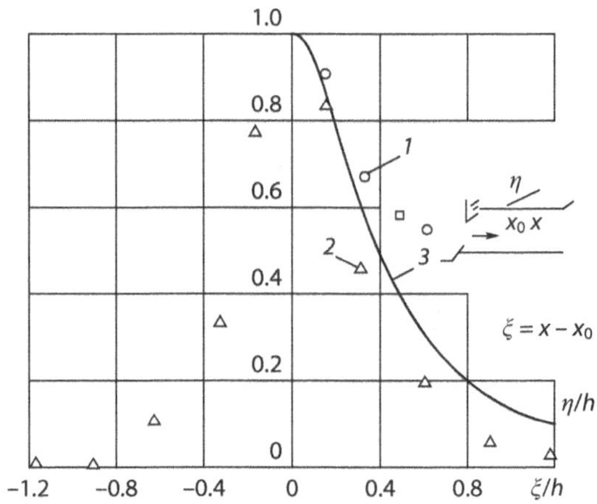

Figure 9.28 Transverse (1) and longitudinal (2) correlation pressure pulsations on the border of the flow in the zone of separation and the result of calculation of the longitudinal correlation (3). The shutter is open for 0.8h.

If we accept that the mixing zone is separated from the ceiling camera on the value shutter, it appears that the tightness at low flow (Grand opening) has a satisfactory agreement with the experience and even gives the limit relation (9.111) (Figure 9.28).

Formulas (9.105) and (9.106) can be used for discussion of the properties of the frequency spectrum pressure pulsations at the border. According to the measurements in the layer blending free-jets of two-dimensional array of velocity pulsations, $S_v(\kappa, \omega)$ can be approximated, associated with frequency $S_v(\omega)$or longitudinal $S_v(\kappa)$ one-dimensional spectra, using the hypothesis for frozen turbulence:

$$S_v(\omega,\kappa) \approx S_v(\omega)\delta\left(\kappa - \frac{\omega}{U_{tr}}\right) \approx S_v(\kappa)\delta(\omega - U_{tr}\kappa), \quad (9.112)$$

where U_{tr} is the speed of drift waves in the layer blending, in the early and middle part of the zone of separation, approximately equal to the rate under the shutter U_1.

Integrating the equation (9.105) or (9.106) at χ, taking into account (9.112), we find:

$$S_{p1}(\omega) = \rho^2 b^2 \left(\frac{\partial U}{\partial y}\right)^2_{\max} \frac{\mathrm{ch}^2 \dfrac{\omega(h - h_T)}{U_{tr}}}{\mathrm{sh}^2 \dfrac{\omega h}{U_{tr}}} S_v(\omega); \quad (9.113)$$

$$S_{p2}(\omega) = \rho^2 b^2 \left(\frac{\partial U}{\partial y}\right)^2_{\max} \frac{\mathrm{ch}^2 \frac{\omega h_T}{U_{tr}}}{\mathrm{sh}^2 \frac{\omega h}{U_{tr}}} S_{\upsilon}(\omega). \tag{9.114}$$

The expression for the normalized frequency spectrum remains the same as (9.110), but instead of κ, we should write ω/U_{tr}. The results of calculations and measurements are compared in Figure 9.29

Coordinates axes, in Figure 9.29 are selected so that element of the area between the graph of the spectrum and the abscissa axis corresponds to the contribution of pulsations in the considered frequency range (ω_1, ω_2) to the total dispersion of the process:

$$\int_{\omega_1}^{\omega_2} \omega S_p(\omega) d(\ln \omega) = \int_{\omega_1}^{\omega_2} S_p(\omega) d\omega,$$

in particular:

$$\int_0^{\infty} \omega S_p(\omega) d(\ln \omega) = 0,5.$$

The difference between the results of theoretical calculation (line 1 in Figure 9.29) and experiment (line 2 Figure 9.29) in the high-frequency part of the spectrum may be due to the influence of the nonlinear components of kinematic features thrown at the problem statement. A role is also played in the choice of the thickness of the mixed layer $b = 0,20h$ and speed of drift of indignation $U_{tr} = 0,8U_{max} = U_1$ (the last by analogy with the flow in a free jet).

Spectrum (9.114) (line 1 Figure 9.29) was calculated as the average interval between adjacent zeros of pressure pulsation:

$$\langle \tau_0 \rangle = \pi \sqrt{\frac{\int_0^{\infty} S_p(\omega) d\omega}{\int_0^{\infty} \omega^2 S_p(\omega) d\omega}} = \frac{\pi}{2,55} \frac{h}{U_1} = 1,23 \frac{h}{U_1}.$$

This value is determined directly on the waveform of pressure pulsations, was equal to $< \tau_0 > = 1,17\, h/U_1$ (experience U_1 = 8.38 m/s, h = 0,28

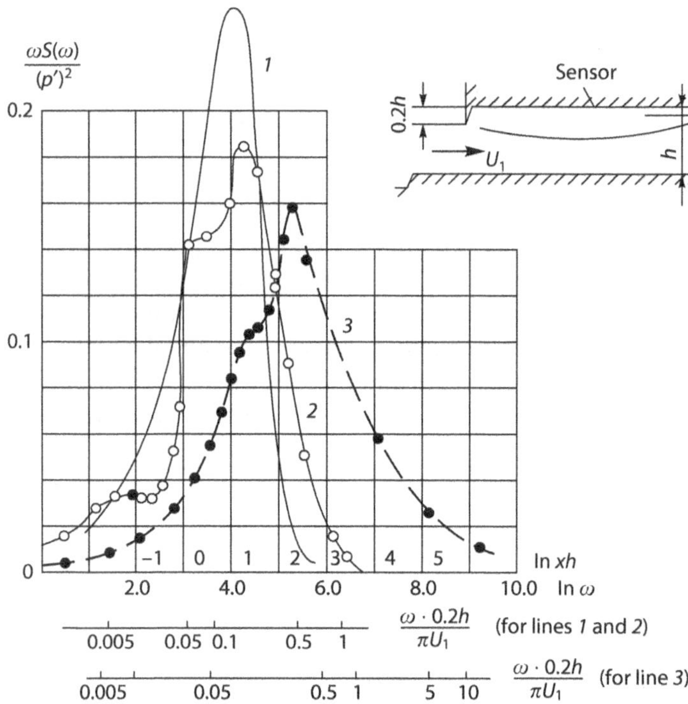

Figure 9.29 Spectral density of pressure pulsations.1 – calculation, 2 – test result K =1.6, Re = 1.9 10^6, 3 – the same for K =0.31, Re = 2.3 10^6.

m, < τ_0 > = 0,039 sec). The match is better than one would expect based on the Figure 9.29

On the same Figure 9.29 shows the range of pressure pulsations in the zone of separation in the presence of developed cavitation in the stream. As you can see, when cavitation spectrum is shifted to higher frequencies, phase transitions that occur in the flow under a certain amount of cavitation change the structure of pressure pulsations. Locking ripple at some point in the zone of separation is possible to distinguish the characteristics of the influence of phase transitions (Figure 9.30).

An internal aeration flow increases relative frequency and amplitude of pulsations in the entire zone of separation (line 2 Figure 9.24).

With a further increasing number of cavitation, standard pulsations at the beginning of the zone of separation are reduced by the emergence of cutting deep depressions pressure (total pressure is not lower than vapor pressure p^0). However, in the end zone of separation, where the kernel cavitation goes to the borders of the stream, standard pulsations increase dramatically (line 3 Figure 9.24). Changes in the structure of pulsation is

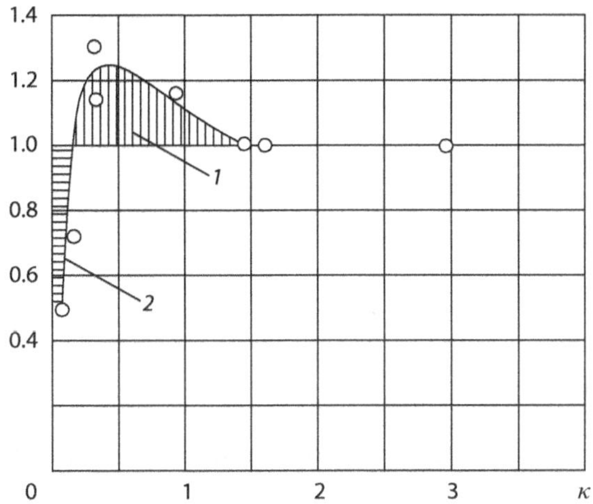

Figure 9.30 Changes in the relative values of standard pressure pulsations in the zone of separation (x= 1.6÷1.8 h), depending on the amount of cavitation. 1 - the influence of internal aeration, 2 - influence of cavitation.

important, as a maximum range of pressures approaching relatively high natural frequencies of the structure and intensity of resonance oscillations of constructions may increase substantially.

In the presented theoretical analysis of the influence of phase transitions, air and cavitation were not taken into account. Experiments have shown that this effect could be significant. Let us consider this problem in more detail.

A flow with the zone of separation on one side of which fluid with a relatively low gas content is flowing and on the other one there is relatively long cavity filled with a mixture of vapors, gases and liquid is usually call ed supercavitating flow (Figure 9.3I).

High velocity gradient and high turbulence intensity in the zone of separation is typical for such type of flow. This fact as well as a relatively slow change of flow parameters along the cavity permit idealization of the real phenomenon and consideration of the flow as being uniform in the longitudinal direction. Low-frequency components of turbulence, in which flow may be assumed two-dimensional, are of most importance for dynamic analysis.

Considering the above given limitations, pressure pulsation can be obtained from equation:

$$\frac{\partial^2 \mathrm{p}}{\partial x^2}+\frac{\partial^2 \mathrm{p}}{\partial y^2}-\frac{1}{C^2}\frac{\partial^2 \mathrm{p}}{\partial t^2}=\rho f\left(x,y,t\right) \qquad (9.115)$$

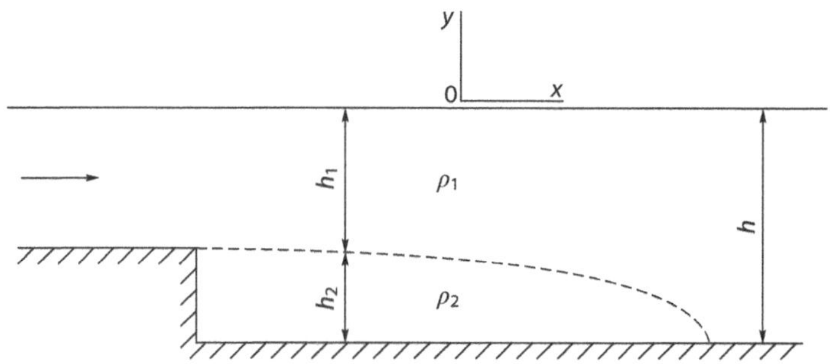

Figure 9.31 Flow pattern.

where C - velocity of elastic wave propagation in gas-fluid medium.

$$C = \sqrt{\frac{1}{\rho\left|\frac{\partial w}{w\partial\rho}\right|}} \approx \sqrt{\frac{1}{\rho\left[a/\mathrm{p}_0 + (1-a)/\mathrm{E}_{\mathrm{fl}}\right]}}$$

$\rho \approx (1-a)\rho_w$ - density of this medium;

a - air concentration;

p_0 - absolute pressure inside gas and vapour bubbles;

E_{fl} - modulus of elasticity of fluid;

(9.116)

The kinematic function f(x,y,t) in the right part of equation (9.115) is expressed in terms of derivatives of velocity with respect to coordinates /I/ . In case of two-dimensional uniform flow in the longitudinal direction and low-frequency pulsation components:

$$f(x,y,t) = -2\frac{\partial u}{\partial y}\frac{\partial v}{\partial x}$$

where:

U - local averaged velocity in the longitudinal direction ***x***,

v - transverse pulsation velocity component. Kinematic function f is assumed to be equal to zero within the whole zone of flow excluding a layer at the separation boundary zone. In this layer, with the width "b," the longitudinal spectrum of vertical velocity pulsations is represented in the following form, which corresponds to the test data /3/ and to the condition of stationary vertical velocity pulsations:

$$S_v(\kappa) = (V')^2 \frac{2}{b\pi} \frac{\kappa^2}{\left(\kappa^2 + \frac{1}{b^2}\right)^2}$$

where,

κ - wave number,

v'- standard of velocity pulsation.

Therelation of longitudinal and space-time spectra of velocity pulsation is in agreement with the well-known Taylor's assumption about the so-callad "frozen" turbulence /l,3/:

$$S_v(\kappa,\omega) = S_v(\kappa)\delta(\omega - \kappa U_{tr})$$

δ - Dirac delta-function.

Equation (9.115) is solved assuming the following boundary condition is written for the "images" of pressure pulsation:

$$P^* = \frac{1}{2\pi}\int\int_{-\infty}^{\infty} p\exp - i(\omega t + \kappa x)\mathrm{dtdx}$$

$$\frac{\partial p^*}{\partial y} = kP^*$$

$$k = \frac{(\omega + U_0\kappa)^2 - i\frac{\partial U_o}{\partial x}(\omega + U_0\kappa)}{g\cos\theta - iV_0(\omega + U_0\kappa)}$$

where

U_0, V_0 - longitudinal and transverse velocities on the water surface,

θ - angle of inclination of water surface to the horizon.

On a watertight boundary, *k*=0 and in case of a large Froude number, *k*= ∞ (p*=o) on the free surface of flow. On the zone of separation between the supercavitation zone and the uniform flow, the pressure is continuous while the pressure gradient undergoes the function discontinuity:

$$\frac{1}{\rho_2}\frac{\partial p_2}{\partial y}=\frac{1}{\rho_1}\frac{\partial p_1}{\partial y} \tag{9.117}$$

Applying the two-dimensional Fourier transform (with respect to time and longitudinal coordinate) to equation (9.116), while boundary conditions and conditions on the boundary between two layers are taken into account, it is possible to derive expressions for the images of pressure pulsation. After multiplying complex-conjugated values of images and calculating the mathematical expectation, spectra of pressure pulsation will be found. In particular for points at the bottom of the flow:

$$S_p(\kappa,\omega)=4\rho_1^2\left(\frac{\partial U}{\partial y}\right)^2 b^2 S_v(\kappa,\omega)\Pi^2(\kappa,\omega) \tag{9.118}$$

Here the assumed kinematic function structure is taken into account:

$$\Pi^2(\kappa,\omega)=\frac{\rho_2^2}{\rho_1^2}\frac{\kappa^2}{\kappa_2^2\left[sh\kappa_2 h_2+\frac{\rho_2}{\rho_1}\frac{\kappa_1}{\kappa_2}A\,ch\,\kappa_2 h_2\right]^2} \tag{9.119}$$

where parameters κ_2 and κ_1 are connected with the wave number κ and frequency ω by means of relations:

$$\kappa_2=\kappa B_2=\kappa\sqrt{1-\frac{\omega^2}{C_2^2\kappa^2}};\kappa_1=\kappa B_1=\kappa\sqrt{1-\frac{\omega^2}{C_1^2\kappa^2}}$$

$$A=\frac{\text{k}\text{ch}\kappa_1 h_1-\kappa_1\text{sh}\kappa_1 h_1}{\text{k}\text{sh}\kappa_1 h_1-\kappa_1\text{ch}\kappa_1 h_1}$$

where the velocities C_1 and C_2 arc different in various layers of fluid.

In particular, if cavitation cavity is located at the flow bottom and above the cavity the fluid is not aerated (noncompressible),
$A=th\kappa h_1$ for pressure flow (k=0) and:

$A=\frac{1}{th\kappa h_1}$ for free surface flow at very large Froude numbers.

Integrating the two-dimensional spectrum (9.118), it is possible to proceed to one-dimensional longitudinal and frequency spectra:

$$S_p\left(\frac{\omega h}{U_{tr}}\right) \approx S_p(\kappa h) = 4\rho_1^2\left(\frac{\partial U}{\partial y}\right)^2 b^2 S_v(\kappa)\Pi^2(\kappa) \qquad (9.120)$$

For the function: $\Pi^2(\kappa)$, formula (9.119) remains valid; the coefficient B can be expressed as follows:

$$B = \sqrt{1 - u_{tr}^2 / C^2}$$

If representation (9.116) is valid, then:

$$B = \sqrt{1 - \frac{a(1-a)}{K}}$$

where:

$$K = \frac{P_0 - P^0}{\rho_w U_{tr}^2}$$

is the cavitation number, and P_0 - mean pressure in the supercavitatien zone, P^0 - the vapor pressure of water. The relations derived permit us to follow the influence of the degree air saturation ***a*** and the cavitation number *K* or the parameter *B* on pressure pulsation. If the velocity spectrum in the separation layer is assumed not to depend on the above given parameters, then by differentiating the denominator of formula (9.119) it is found that:

$$\frac{\partial \Pi}{\partial a} < 0$$

in case if:

$$\frac{B}{1-a}\text{shB}\kappa h_2 + \frac{\partial B}{\partial a}\left[\text{shB}\kappa h_2 + B\kappa h_2 \text{chB}\kappa h_2 + A\kappa h_2 \text{shB}\kappa h_2\right] > 0 \quad (9.121)$$

From equation (9.121) it follows, in particular, that within the range of variation of concentration ***a***, when $\frac{\partial C}{\partial a} \geq 0$ an increase of air concentration always leads to a decrease of pressure pulsation. Such conclusions are valid for the cases conforming with the relation (9.116), if ***a***>0. 5. But in this

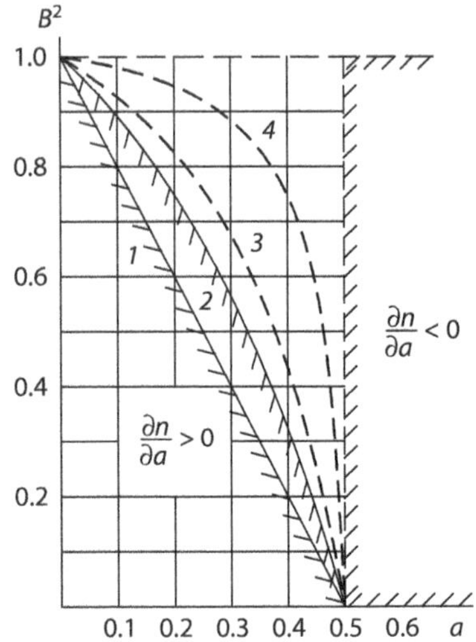

Figure 9.32 Location of limits of domains different effects of air concentration (explanation in the text).

case, however, there is a domain of values ***B*** and ***a*** , at which the pressure pulsation increases with the increase of saturation with air. This takes place at all frequencies if:

$0<B^2<(1\text{-}2a)/(1\text{-}a)$ (line 2 in Figure 9.32).

The above-mentioned conclusions are valid for pressure pulsation on the opposite wall (beyond the supercavitation zone), if:

$0<\boldsymbol{B}^2<1\text{-}2a$ (line 1 in Figure 9.32).

In the zone:

$$(1\text{-}2a)/(1\text{-}a) < B^2 < 1$$

the low frequency part of the spectrum diminishes with the increase of ***a*** , and the high frequency part - enlarges. It is possible to calculate the corresponding dividing line ***B*** (***a***) if the wave number value separating these parts of spectrum is assumed to be given.

In the Figure 9.32, line 3 corresponds to the value:

$$\kappa h_2 \approx \frac{2}{B^2+1-a}$$

and the line 4 - to the value:

$$\kappa h_2 \approx \frac{11}{B^2+1-a}$$

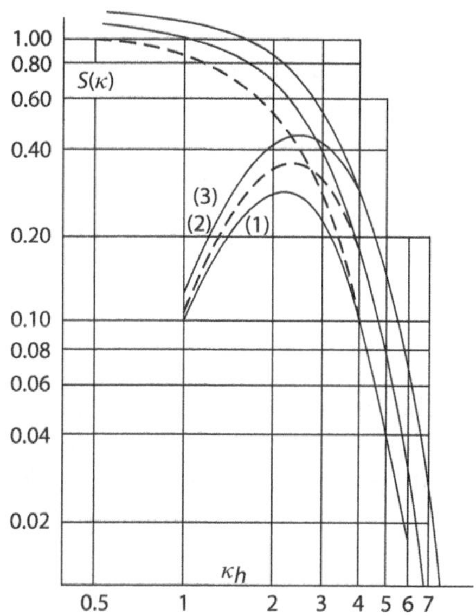

Figure 9.33 Configuration of pressure pulsation spectra at the boundary as a function of air concentration in the supercavitation zone adjacent to pressure cells.

The character of spectrum variation with the change of "**a.**" in the zone, where:

$$\frac{\partial \Pi}{\partial a} > 0$$

is illustrated in Figure 9.33

$$S_1(\kappa) = \frac{1}{(v')^2} S_v(\kappa)\Pi^2(\kappa)\frac{\pi}{2b} = \frac{\pi}{2b^3 (v')^2 \left(\frac{\partial U}{\partial y}\right)^2} S_p(\kappa)$$

$$\mathrm{I} - a = 0 \quad \text{(incompressible fluid)} \qquad = 4.67(1.56)$$

$$2 - a = 0.\mathrm{I};\ \mathrm{B}^2 = 0.8 \qquad 2\int_0^\infty S_1(\kappa)d\kappa = 5.76(2.09)$$

$$3 - a = 0.25;\ B^2 = 0.6 \qquad = 7.16(2.88)$$

It can be noticed that spectrum values become relatively higher in the zone of large wave numbers (in high frequency zone); this has been proved in the tests.

It should be emphasized, that in the developed theory, only one aspect of supercavitating flow - the appearance of a layer of compressible medium - is taken into account. Besides this fact, limitations of pressure decrease by a certain physical limit, variations of turbulence in the separation zone and new sources of high frequency pressure pulsations, which are connected with impact effects in collapsing microcavities, and are of great significance under real conditions.

9.3 Jet Impact

It is well known that the impact breaking of rocks by a jet is a very economical method. Machines, in which nonstationary impulse jets are employed, are especially promising ones. Some of these machines make use of super speed water jet obtained by the impact of a heavy piston on a certain volume of water. The performance of such a plant is of a pronounced cyclic nature. An extremely high pressure is developed during a short period of time in the impulse chamber of the plant, resulting in formation of a super speed water jet which is capable of destroying the strongest rocks as well аз metals [117a].

The impulse method of generating high-speed water jets is utilized in some other installations too, the most perfect of them being hydro-impulsators, where a periodical jet is produced by the action of the pressure wave, which in its turn, is the result of a water hammer (USSR patent 244991, 1969). Hydraulic installations of other types are based on employment of a high-pressure pipe, and breaking of the rocks is carried out by a thin water jet.

Despite the fact that the methods employed to produce the jets in the above-mentioned installations are different, the common feature of installations of both kinds consists in breaking the rock by action of the jet velocity head onto an obstacle. Although an illusion may arise that the shock action of the jet is being utilized in the impulse installations, actually the share of the shock action is incompatibly small in comparison with the stationary action of the jet, taking into account the fact the jet may be considered practically as infinitely long (the water propeller jet length equals to about 200 to 300 diameters of the nozzle). In particular, as it is known [8a], that the duration of the initial shock peak pressure on the obstacle amounts to:

$$t_i = (5 \div 10) x l0^{-6} \text{ sec},$$

while the duration of the stationary action in installations already known is usually in excess of:

$$t_\Sigma = (1 \div 10) \times 10^{-3} \text{ sec.}$$

Low output of developed installations belongs too among their shortcomings.

The only practical way of development of such installations, which are capable to meet the requirements of industry both in respect to productivity and specific energy consumption per unit volume of crushed rock, is the more efficient utilization of energy of the jet under optimum conditions (in respect to rock breaking) of dynamic action of jet on the obstacle.

The theoretical analysis of effect exerted by individual volumes of fluid striking a rigid surface [197a] demonstrates the presence of two fundamentally different kinds of action:

the dynamical one with a high shock pressure peak (providing the obstacle is rigid enough) and

the stationary one, depending on the velocity head.

The presence of a sharply defined peak pressure and a subsequent "shelf" in the velocity head is convincingly confirmed by experimental studies -- both carried out in the tests (Figure 9.34 –[8a]).

The approximate analysis of the "shock" part of the process may be accomplished on the base of solution of the problem in hydrodynamics relating to the impact of a jet of an incompressible fluid on a deformable foundation. It was found [197a], in particular (on the basis of solution of the problem about the impact of a jet of an incompressible fluid onto a rigid foundation, the jet length being considered as a finite value), that the "shock" impulse I_i absorbed by the obstacle at an impact of an individual volume of fluid is little depending on the length of this volume (in the impact direction), in case the volume length exceeds the jet diameter (Figure 9.35).

As applied to an actual diagram of pressure (Figure 9.34), the value of the shock impulse should be calculated from the formula:

$$I_i = \int_0^{t_i}\int_\Omega p d\Omega dt \tag{9.122}$$

where: p - is the pressure on the obstacle; Ω- is the surface area over which the jet is acting; t_i - duration of the impact process.

The analysis of the entire process as a whole (with due consideration of the foundation pliability and the effusion of the volume of fluid) may be performed by numerical methods, for instance, by the "tracer particles" method (see Second Internat. Conference on Numerical Methods in Fluid

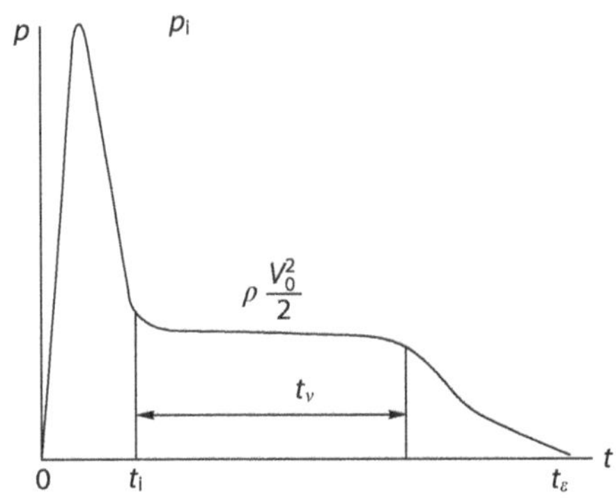

Figure 9.34 Variation of pressure on the obstacle in the centre of the jet impact.

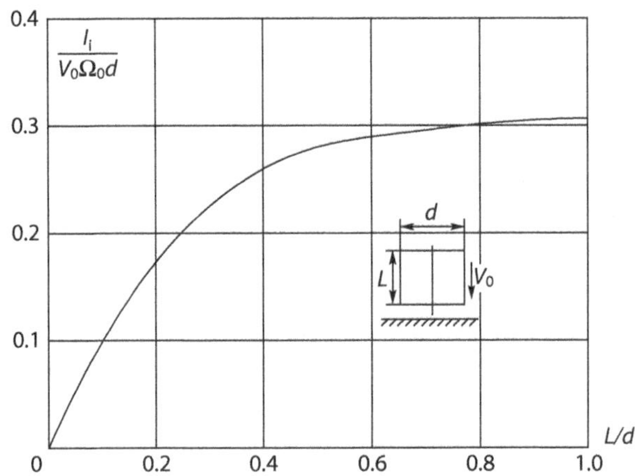

Figure 9.35 Effect of jet length on the value of the shock impulse (results of solution of the two-dimensional problem [197]; (Ω_i - cross-sectional area of the jet prior to shock; d – jet diameter).

Dynamics, Springer-Verlag, 1971). Simplified methods may be used too, these methods being based on the fact that the dynamical stressed state of an elastic medium proved to be independent on the distribution of pressure in the loading zone at the distance of about 1/4 of this zone width from its edge. Therewith only the value of the total acting effort and the variation of this effort with time are of importance. Corresponding simplified equations are obtained by integrating the equations of motion and continuity over the jet cross-section. The summary reaction of the elastic semi-space controlling the variation of the effort in the contact between the jet and the obstacle can be expressed in a compact form with the help of the solution [50a].

The analysis shows that the kind of dynamical action of jet and the curve of pressure variations with time may be quite different depending on the ratio between the acoustic stiffness of jet and obstacle:

$$(\rho C)_{jet}/(\rho C_1)_o$$

and Poisson's ratio for the obstacle material. The value of the maximum ("peak") pressure in the centre of the jet impact can be determined, as a first approximation, from the equation of conservation of momentum at fronts of shock-waves induced in the obstacle and fluid.

$$p_i = \frac{(\rho C)_{jet} V}{\left[1 + \frac{(\rho C)_{jet}}{(\rho C_1)_o}\right]} \tag{9.123}$$

In this formula index "jet" denotes fluid jet, index "o" - the obstacle; ρ - is density; C, C_1 - velocity of compression shock wave propagation; V - jet velocity prior to shock.

The formula similar to formula (9.123) is given in [30a]. The assessment (9.123) is true in case the obstacle is not too much destroyed after the shock. In case a return jet of the obstacle material is formed, the maximum pressure on the obstacle may increase 2 to 2 (ρ_o/ρ_{jet}) times.

If we prefer to make use of the shock effects ("peak" pressure), it is evident that the action of a jet, separated by intervening air spaces into individual volumes of a certain length, will be more effective than the action of a continuous jet. In case of a discontinuous jet the obstacle is exposed to the action of a number of shocks and if the length of an individual volume exceeds one or two diameters of the jet, the shock impulse and peak effects received each time by the obstacle are practically equal to respective parameters of shock of a semi-infinite jet. However the process of breaking of strong materials depends not only on the magnitude of the impulse and the peak pressure but — in certain limits — also on the curve of variations of pressure with time, i.e., on the duration of action of given loads.

Figure 9.36 shows the shape of zones of the super-limit state (destruction zones) in the rock semi-space under the action of a constant concentrated force P.

Calculation – by the formula (9.134) where:

$$I_2' = \frac{1}{6}[(\sigma_z - \sigma_r)^2 + (\sigma_r - \sigma_\theta)^2 + (\sigma_\theta - \sigma_z)^2 + 6\tau_{rr}^2],$$

$$\sigma = \frac{1}{3}(\sigma_r + \sigma_z + \sigma_\theta).$$

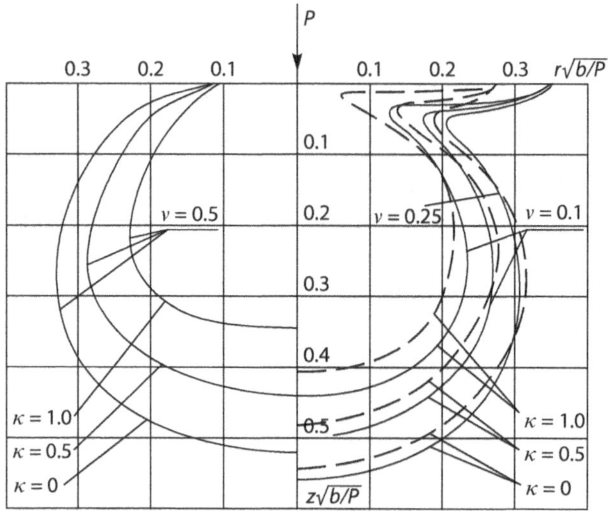

Figure 9.36 Boundaries of zones of super-limit state of rock under the action of statical concentrated force *P*. The zones are axial-symmetrical. The lines in the left and right parts of the Figure relate to different values of the Poisson's ratio ν and strength parameters *K* of the rock.

The values σ_j $(j = r, z, \theta)$ were found by the solution of the Boussinesq's statical problem.

The zone boundaries are governed by the strength condition.

$$\sqrt{I_2^1} + k\sigma - b = 0 \tag{9.124}$$

where: I_2' is the second invariant of the deviator of stresses in the rock; $\sigma = 1/3\ \Sigma\sigma_{ii}$ is the first invariant of stresses tensor; k and b are the rock strength parameters ($0<k<\sqrt{3}$). The condition (9.124) was well confirmed for a number of materials with the most different structures. The acceptability of this condition for rocks at high pressures is illustrated by diagrams shown in Figure 9.37; these diagrams were plotted on the basis of processing experimental data given in the book [108a].

Figure 9.38 shows the change of the relative depth of zone of destruction with time at a sudden application of the force P at the semispace boundary at the instant of time t = 0.

Calculation by formula (9.124); the values of σ_j were found by solving the Lamb's dynamical problem ($\nu = 0.25$); *h* - the depth of zone at statical loading (from data of Figure 9.36).

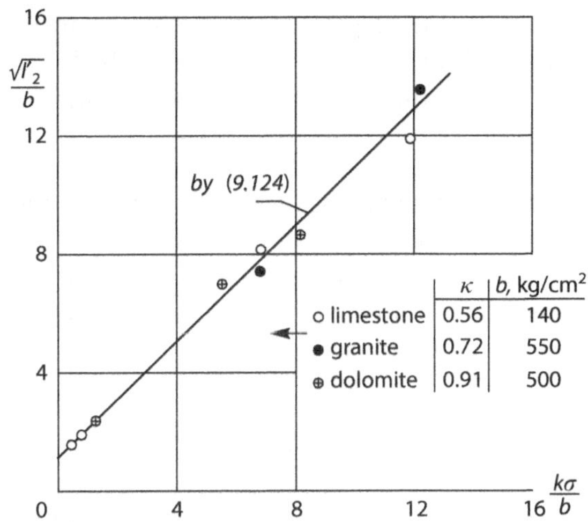

Figure 9.37 Conditions of rocks breaking (from experimental data)

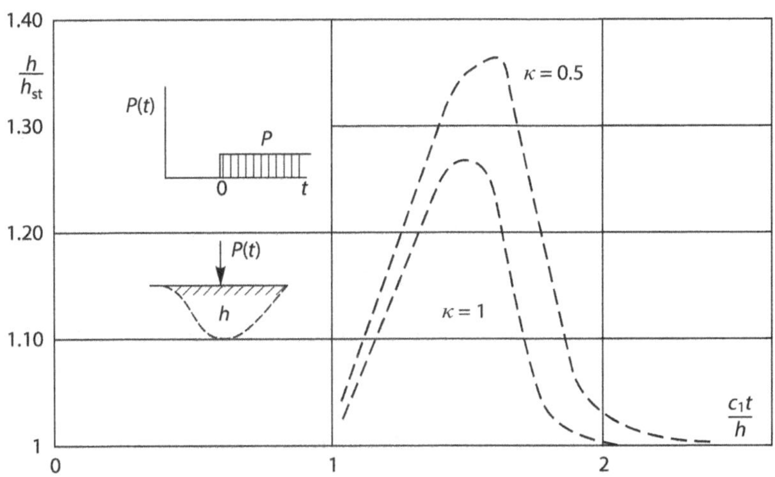

Figure 9.38 Relative depth $\frac{h}{h_{st}}$ of the super-limit zone at sudden application of force *P*.

The magnitude of force remains constant after the instant of its application (the calculations proceeded from the results of solution of the problem in the dynamic theory of elasticity [23a]). As may be seen even the simplest dynamical loading can increase the super-limit state zone about 30 to 40 per cent.

Let us evaluate the value of pressure p_h acting upon the obstacle and ensuring such a depth h of the super-limit zone which would be α times more than the jet initial diameter d (prior to the shock), i.e.,

$$h = \alpha d.$$

Let us too assume for average conditions: the Poisson's ratio $\nu = 0.25$, the strength parameter $k = 0.5$ and

$\alpha > 1.25$. Under such conditions the substitution of the actual load by a concentrated force will be quite justified and taking into consideration the data given in Figure 9.36, we obtain:

$$h_{st} = 0.48\sqrt{\frac{P_h}{b}} \tag{9.125}$$

$h = h_{st}(h/h_{st})$ for the adopted regime of destruction, where h/h_{st} is taken from Figure 9.38

Since:

$$P_h = \frac{\pi d^2}{4}\beta p_h \tag{9.126}$$

where the factor $\beta <$ I introduces an allowance for the non-uniformity of distribution of pressure over the jet cross-section in the instant of impact, we can find that:

$$\frac{p_h}{b} = \frac{4\alpha^2}{0.48^2 \pi\beta} \tag{9.127}$$

The volume W of zone of possible destruction is geometrically related to the depth h by the following formula:

$$W \approx \frac{1}{6}\pi\alpha^3 d^3$$

If the length of jet is equal-to L, then the ratio between the water volume W_0 and the volume of destroyed rock W will make:

$$\frac{W_0}{W} = \frac{6}{4}\frac{1}{\alpha^3}\frac{L}{d} \tag{9.128}$$

The energy of the water volume W_0 [m^3] flying with velocity V (corresponding thus to the pressure

p_0 [kg/cm^2]= $\rho V^2/2$) may be estimated as E = 98/3600 $W_0 p_0$ [kW hour]. Assuming:

$$p_0 = \beta_1 p_h \qquad (\beta_i \leq 1)..$$

and taking into account (9.127) and (9.128), the specific energy consumption for breaking rock will be equal to:

$$\frac{E}{W} \approx 0,02 \frac{\beta_1 b}{\alpha\beta} \frac{L}{d} \qquad \left[\frac{kWh}{m^3}\right] \tag{9.129}$$

The strength parameter "b" in this formula has the dimensionality of kg/cm^2. Formula (9.129) shows that it is desirable to take the parameter as great as possible, taking care however, to avoid an excessive increase of initial pressure since such an increase may result in a considerable increase in the equipment cost and a decrease in the relative value of the peak pressure (v_i/p_0). For instance, at $\alpha = 1.25$ and $\beta = 0.5$, the following values of the quasi-steady pressure p_h may be practically found, this pressure p_h being necessary, for destruction of rock for the depth h, which is 1.25 times more than the jet diameter:

$$p_h = 17.3\ b \tag{9.130}$$

The p_h value will be equal:
for granite $p_h = 8\,650$ kg/cm^2,
for limestone $p_h = 2\,410$ kg/cm2.

Taking into consideration the simplest dynamical procedure of loading (Figure 9.38), the needed pressures p_h may be decreased √ 1.35=1.16 times. In this case, we prefer to make use of the "shock" effects taking $p_h = p_i$, and the initial pressure P_o in the jet may be considerably less (2 to 3 times) than the given values.

It is necessary, in order to convert the zone of the material super-limit state into the destruction zone, that the super-limit state exists in the rock over such an interval of time which would permit an adequate propagation of failure joints. A generalization of experimental data carried out in [31a] demonstrated that under average conditions of rock the velocity of joints propagation amounts approximately to $0.6C_2$, where C_2 is the velocity of shear waves propagation. The ratio between the depth of destruction h and the length of the joint travel L_T makes, about $L_T/h = 3.5$ for destruction surfaces which were shown in Figure 9.36 Thus, the duration of destruction may be estimated as:

$$t_d \approx \frac{h}{C_2}\frac{3.5}{0.6} = 5.8\frac{h}{C_2} \tag{9.131}$$

A conclusion may be drawn from the Figure 9.38 and (9.131) that the efficiency of destructive dynamic stresses, even at a relative long duration of impact load, will be manifested only at repeated shocks, ensuring accumulation and gradual development of joints. A similar approach may be applied too to the evaluation of efficiency of action of individual impulses with various duration, of action of a series of impulses separated by various time intervals and of other kinds of dynamic loads.

An adequate analysis shows that the efficiency of dynamical processes of loading and destruction are likely to be close to the optimum one if the duration of an individual shock impulse will be of an order of :

$$t_i = (1 \div 1{,}8)\ h/C_1,$$

and the duration of the subsequent quasi-steady action of the velocity head will amount to:

$$t_v = (10 \div 15)\ h/C_1.$$

With a fractured rock the mechanism of destruction may change — the wedging effect of water as well as the phase shift of the dynamical pressure in the pores and on the rock surface gain greatly in their importance. The optimization of destructive effect may be attained in other ways in this case, but the absolute efficiency of the hydro-impulse action will be higher.

The theoretical prediction of the more severe destructive action of a discontinuous jet, as compared with a continuous one, is confirmed by published experimental results [109a].

The possibility of a substantial increase of the efficiency of rocks destruction due to optimization of non-stationary jets parameters is illustrated by results of experiments carried out by the author (Figure 9.39):

In Figure 9.39 the volumes of material (characterized by strength parameters $b = 6{,}5$ kg/cm^2, $\kappa = 1.1$, compression waves propagation velocity $C_1 = 1200$ m/sec), destroyed under the action of a water jet with a constant average discharge, are correlated for two cases: at the pressure in the shock chamber (before the nozzle) pulsating with the frequency 85 to 100 Hz (line I) in the first case, and with the frequency 330 to 400 Hz (line 2) in the second case. The average pressure at the nozzle was about the same ($p_0 = 70$ kg/cm^2) in both cases; the distance from the obstacle also remained constant equaling to 25 diameters of the jet. The nozzle diameter was equal $d = 4$ mm. Although in both cases the parameters of jets (the nature of which was close to discontinuous) were by no means optimum ones ($L/d \sim 200$ for line I and $L/d \sim 50$ for line 2), the trend of increase of productivity with decrease of the relative length of jets was obvious nevertheless.

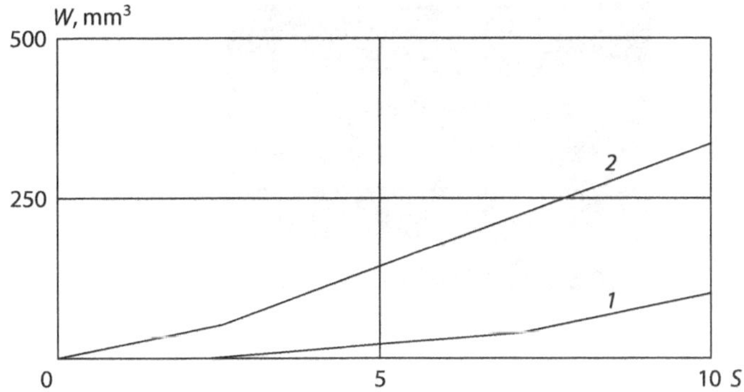

Figure 9.39 Relation of the destroyed volume of the obstacle and the duration of non-steady jets action. 1- the pressure pulsates in the shock chamber with frequency 85÷100 Hz; 2 – ditto for 330÷400 Hz.

Development of methods of creation of discontinuous jets is an important stage in the realization of the hydroimpulse method of rock breaking. One of the ways to accomplish this resides in utilization of the natural instability of the jet investigated too by Raleigh.

Figure 9.40 shows oscillograms of variations of pressure recorded by a mosaic consisting of piezo-ceramic pick-ups under the action of a jet from the nozzle, which is a common cylindrical pipe (curves "a" — usual turbulent "noise"), and the oscillograms obtained for a jet formed in a nozzle, the inside surface of which is complying with the condition of the disturbances superposition; the growth of the velocity of these disturbances is at the maximum on the free surface of the jet (curves "b").

Sharp pressure overshoots (peaks) is characteristic for the jet discontinuity; the effect was recorded by three pick-ups at a time. The calculation of the summary impulse experienced by the obstacle also demonstrated that a discontinuous jet produces a larger impulse as compared with the continuous one.

It is evident that the creation of sTable and dependable discontinuous high-velocity jets is a rattier complicated engineering problem. But employment of such jets must enable a sharp increase in the productivity of existing hydraulic installations and the development of new installations. The shown way of a more efficient utilization of the jets energy will result in development of maçhines that are competitive with conventional methods of rocks breaking.

Presenting the general analysis of the structure of the dynamic flow effects on border, detects various components of the impacts associated with the turbulence pulsation of the velocities, the impact of waves on

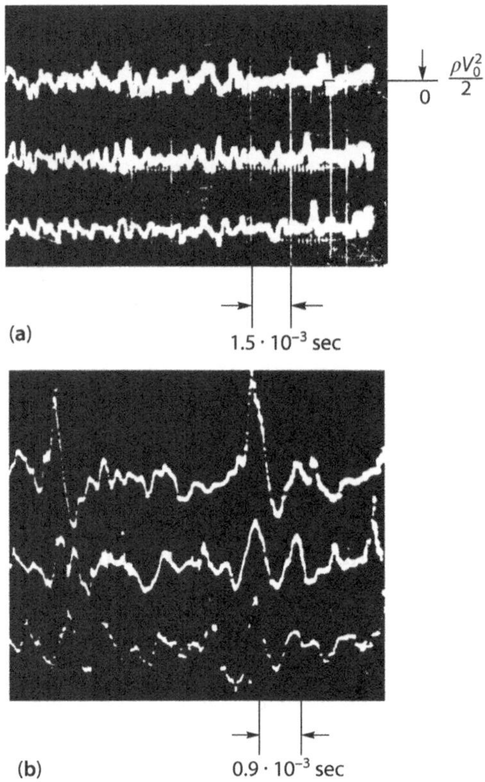

Figure 9.40 Some examples of recording pressure on the obstacle; a) discharge from a conventional nozzle; b) discharge from a nozzle ensuring formation of a discontinuous jet. Jet velocity - 20 m/sec.

the free surface, aeration flow and deformability of the borders. Modeling rules, conditions of self-similarity and amendments to the simulation results under different conditions can be different.

9.4 Vibrations

Effects of hydroelasticity are widely encountered in hydraulic engineering. They have to be taken into consideration in designing gates of outlet works, trash-racks of water intakes and fish-barriers, linings of gate chambers, high-pressure conduits, and protection and training wails in the structure tail-water, storage reservoirs slope protection, etc. This part of our findings deals, in particular, with the procedure of analysis of hydrodynamic load distortion under the effect of boundary vibration.

The classification of the observed phenomena was given in [84, 64a] together with examples for the calculation of the effect of vibration on the flow-induced hydrodynamic loads. These general methods can be used for analysis of different emergency situations brought about by the flow presented in this part [77a].

1.High head gates

The first practical research of vibrations of the parts of hydro constructions was made with the gates of the locks [1a, 36a](Figure 9.41).

Vibrations of three main types were observed (Figure 9.42):

I. Random Vibrations: These vibrations feature a lack of apparent regularity and a wide variation of amplitudes and frequencies with some mainly of high-frequency vibrations (Figure 9.42a). Such vibrations appear from the moment when the gate is detached from the sill, up to relative openings $Q_0 \approx 0.4$; they insignificantly vary in intensity and vanish only at full gate opening. The vibrations do not cease from fixing the gate. The random nature of the vibrations testifies about their origin; they seem to belong to the group of forced oscillations caused by pressure pulsation due to turbulent flow.

II. Self-Excited or Auto Oscillations in the System "Gate-Flow": Such oscillations are characterized by regularity and considerable intensity. They are generally observed at relative openings $Q_0 > 0.5$ (depending on pressure and design features of the gate). They appear during gate lifting at constant head (Figure 9.42b) or at varying head, but at constant gate opening. In the first case they do not vanish when the gate lifting stops (Figure 9.42,c). Time until the amplitude increases to the maximum values can be very small - the order of 5 to 10 periods of the natural gate vibrations (Figure 9.42,b). Sometimes vibrations of two frequencies and modes are excited at once (Figure 9.42d).

III. Mechanical self-excited oscillations: are developed during the gate movement as a consequence of a negative slope in the initial portion of the relationship between the frictional force and rate of movement. This is characterized by an approximately constant amplitude and frequency of oscillations at constant rates of gate lifting (Figure 9.42e).

Specific data about the test conditions and quantitative results are as follows:

Gate No. 1 is a vertical-lift roller gate. At the moment of testing, the head was about 13.5 m. The conditions of continuous gate lifting to the full height up to relative openings $Q_0 = 1.0$ and where the gate stopped at $Q_0 = 0.17$; 0.35; 0.53 and 0.7, were studied. Vibrations of the types I and II were registered; their parameters are given in Table 1. Vibrations of the

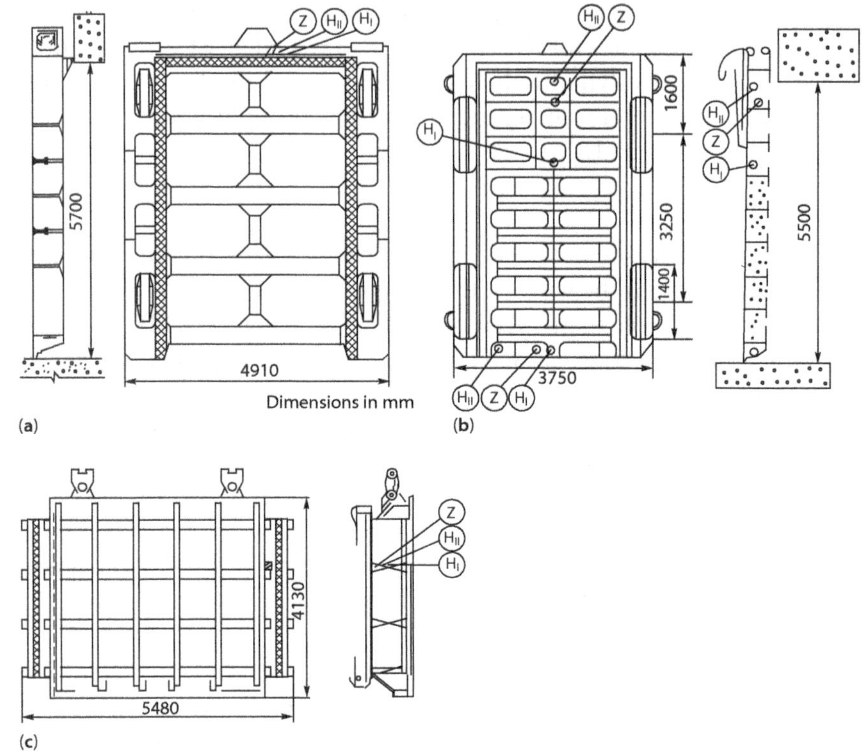

Figure 9.41 Gates for culvers of navigation locks

Lock No 23 of the V.I. Lenin hydroelectric station on the Volga river (Gate 1).
Lock No 30 of the XXII Congress of CPSU hydroelectric station on the Volga river (Gate 2).
Lock No 5 of the Volga-Moskva canal (Gate 3).

type 1 are noted at $Q_0<0.53$, both with the gate moving or stopping. At $Q_0 > 0.53$ and heads 9.5 to 12.5 m, vibrations of the type II sharply come into action (Figure 9.42b), irrespective of whether the gate moves upward or not. Vibrations of type II terminate at $Q_0 \approx 1$.

Gate No. 2 is a vertical-lift gate with sliding supports (lignefol). The test head amounted to about 22.5 m. The study aims were: conditions of continuous gate lifting up to $Q_0 = 0.85$ to 0.90 with lifting rates from 0.26 to 1.47 m/min, openings with the gate stopped at $Q_0 = 0.17$; 0.34 and 0.69, and also some other regimes. Vibrations of all three types were noted, and their parameters are summarized in Table 9.2.

Vibrations of type I exist in all regimes and terminate only after the flow stops. Vibrations of type II appeared after the gate was lifted in excess of

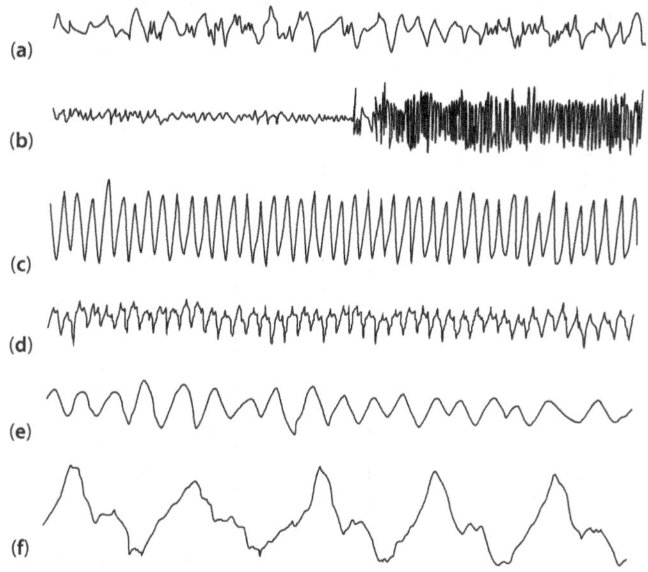

Figure 9.42 Main types of gate vibrations

Vibrations of type 1 (random vibrations)
Vibrations of type 2 (onset of flow-induced self-excited oscillations)
Vibrations of type 2
Vibrations of type 2 (superimposed bending vidrations are seen
Vibrations of type 3 (mechanical self-excited oscillations)
Vibrations observed only at the gate of XXII-Congress-of-CPSU hydroelectric station (of the self-excited oscillation type)

3 m (Q_0 = 0.54 - 0.66; head 12.5 - 15.0 m). Their amplitudes depend upon the gate lift rate (Table 9.3).

They terminated approximately 40 sec after their appearance, when the head decreased till 6.8 - 9.0 m and at relative openings Q_0 = 0.54 - O.66. We succeeded in making a synchronous record of vibrations in several gate points in the plane parallel to the flow (ZH.). The record reveals the fact that the gate experienced mainly rotational vibrations around the center, located almost in the middle of the gate, and they are superimposed by bending vibrations with the frequency twice or thrice as high and the amplitude no greater than 15 μ (Figure 9.42b). Vibrations at relative openings $Q_0 > 0.6$ were observed only at this gate; they started with the gate stopping in the extreme upper position, or at the beginning of its lowering (Q_0 = 0.85 - 0.90, head 1.3 - 3.6 m) and they terminated at Q_0 = 0.6 – 0.75 and 0.8 - 3.2 m. Vertical amplitudes of these vibrations amounted to 1.5 mm, and horizontal ones to more than 0.3 mm; the frequencies were 2-3 Hz and

Table 9.2 Parameter of Gate Videration

Vibration type	Component of Vibration	Gate No 1		Gate No 2		Gate No 3	
		Freq. Hz	Accel Cm/s²	Freq. Hz	Displac mm	Freq. Hz	Accel m/s²
I A periodic random Vibrations	Z	15-23	15-18	*	-	30-45	-10
	HI	15-23	18-20	8-14	0.05-0.06	**	5
	HII	40	7-10	Not registered			4
II Auto Oscillations in "gate flow System"	Z	***		-	-	Not Observed	
	HI			25-28	0.08-0.0		
	HII			Not Registerd			
III mechanical auto Oscilats	Z	Not Observed		2-6	0.5-1.5	3.5-3.8	20
	HI			-	-	1	2-3

* Vibrations of type 1 were not registered due to considerable submergence of vertical vidrographs

** Frequency decreases from 40–45 Hz to 20–25 Hz as gate is lifted

*** Smooth frequency decrease from 60–62 Hz 20–25 Hz as gate is lifted

Table 9.3 Relationship Between Intensity of Vibrations of Type II and gate lifting Rate

Rate of gate lifting m/min	0.26	0.64	0.960	1.170	1.380
Average Vibration Amplitude mm	0.04	0.05	0.075	0.110	0.150

6-9 Hz at the beginning, and 4-5 Hz and 12-15 Hz at the end. Relatively high-amplitude stability and a narrow spectrum of vibration testify to the fact that in this case the vibrations seemed to be self-excited. Vibrations of type III were observed at any height but only with the gate moving. The amplitudes amounted to 1.3 - 1.5 mm at the moment when the gate was detached from the sill, and they decreased further along to 0.5- 0.3 mm.

Gate No. 3 is a vertical-1ift gate with sliding supports (1ignefal). The test head was about 3 m. Conditions of continuous gate lifting at different rotes (0.2 - 0.5 rn/min,) and of the gate stopped at different openings, were examined. Vibrations of types I and III were noted (Table 9.2); vibrations of type II apparently were not excited due to the relatively low heads.

A necessary condition for similarity vibrations of all types is equality criteria strugala, including the frequency of natural oscillations of the shutter in the water. This condition, however, is not sufficient. An important parameter is the damping of oscillations in the system /logarithmic decrement of oscillations/. The difficulty of controlling this parameter is that its value depends on the state of the flow Reynolds number, the presence of aeration and (or) cavitation. Some of these problems are discussed in additional reference books and articles [1a, 2a, 21a, 28a, 37a, 87a, 92a, 100a, 105a].

2. Low-head structures.

Investigations of the low-head gate arranged at the end of the pressure outlet of the Volga (Samara) hydroelectric station [36a] were performed by simultaneously measuring the gate vibrations, pressure pulsation in many points, and the stresses in the gate elements. Only random gate bending vibrations of type I were observed, i.e. vibrations as a plate supported at two sides and subject to pressure pulsation due to turbulent flow. A great contribution of the gate bending rigidity to the averaging of the pressure pulsation over the gate area was noted. The natural frequencies of the gate in water were shown to be half or less than in air,

Further investigations lead to the formulation in codes of the following requirements. The studies performed during the gate-design stage should ensure that no auto-oscillation can be generated under any operation conditions. Moreover, to forecast forced vibrations under the action of pressure pulsation due to turbulent flow, two aspects should be investigated: flow loads and inertia and damping effect of the medium of flow. Studies of the first aspect were performed in [1a, 2a] and others. As to the second aspect, a brief review of problems pertaining to different hydraulic structures is presented below.

Vibrations of the trash-racks in the hydroelectric stations are similar, in a way, to the case of low-level gate vibration due to flow [7a, 111a]. These vibrations caused numerous failures of lattice struts of the trash racks during the release of the first flood. The studies showed that at first the structural members underwent fatigue damage due to vibrations resulting from the Karman vortices at particular velocities and because the frequencies of the structural members were near the vortex frequencies [87a, 88a]. After the trash-racks were reconstructed and the lattice members strengthened, the trash-rack geometry and support conditions were changed and unfavorable regimes were revealed. Recommendations for operating personnel were given accordingly, which permitted satisfactory operation for more than 10 years.

A unique case of excitation of pressure pulsation and penstock vibrations due to disturbances propagating from the end of the penstock towards the dam-spill way face,was observed at the hydroproject Baine-Basht.a. These disturbances were found to be amplified in the penstock like in a resonator. Match the natural frequencies of oscillations of a water-filled pipeline with the frequency of the pressure pulsations in the flow caused, for example, the flow speed or the turbine blades can cause dangerous consequences. Save when modeling the frequency ratio of disturbing influences and natural frequencies of the system is desirable, but difficult to do [40a].

The cases of cavitation observed were accompanied by vibration, but not vice versa. Analysis of one of the first damages of a spillway slab at the hydroelectric station of the integrated type is given in [111a, 28a, 36a]. At this hydroelectric station, piers were provided at the end portion of the pressure outlet, which divided them into two branches: rectilinear and curvilinear. Here the outlet structure is 3.38 m high, each branch being 4.35 m wide; the pier was 1.80 m wide. In front of the piers, the outlet structure was curved in plan; moreover, the upstream face of the piers was well-rounded. The roof and walls of the outlet structure and thepier were covered with facing slabs. The pier nosings had steel lining

16 mm thick. The lined portion was almost 1 m long. When the construction period was nearing completion, the outlet structures were allowed to operate under nonsubmerged conditions with only a single outlet completely opened; the average velocity in this outlet end was almost 19 m/sec. As a result, the side portions of the piers failed. The failure started with the damage of the facing slabs due to cavitation. They were finally torn off, caused by the following process: Below the slabs, pit-holes formed which were in communication with the zones of higher pressure at the moment when a decreased hydro-dynamic pressure acted on the facing slab externally. A further cause for the failure of the pier proper was vibration of the exposed steel rods. The vibration effect of flow on the steel rods was so pronounced that 45 mm-diameter rods, exposed over the length of 2.5-3 m (the ends being embedded in concrete), burst and the middle pieces were carried away with the flow; only rods of 30-35 cm length stuck out of the concrete. These remaining rod ends continued to vibrate, so that deep holes formed around them. In some cases, rods were broken at the depth of 70 cm. This prepared the next step of the rupture. Further damage to the pier-mass concrete continued after the facing slabs had been torn out. It was caused by the abrasive effect of suspended sediments, floating construction debris, etc. Damage to the roof of the outlet structure, though less severe than at the pier and mainly of the cavitation type, was also observed.

Another case of vibration of an outlet-structure roof at the power plant integrated with a spillway was examined. Similar phenomena were also observed at the ski-jump end of the spillway and also at the apron and flow dissipators of hydroelectric stations [28a].

Marked vibrations of the integrated-type power plant as a whole and of its separate structural members, may have also developed in the process of spillway operation. The investigations of the Kiev and Saratov hydroelectric stations and those at Pavlovsk and Plyavinas [7a, 28a, 29a] demonstrated that main vibrations of these stations resulted from pressure pulsation at the guarding constructions of spillways and also from the vibrations of the tailwater protection slabs transferred through the soil foundation. Vibrations of power-house buildings under the action of hydropower-units operation and pressure-pulsation effects on the guarding constructions of turbine water passages appeared to be markedly less severe than in case of spillway operation.

Typical examples of failure of guide walls (piers) in stilling basins and spillway tunnels are described in [84]. Analysis of dynamic loads appearing in similar situations is given in [103a]. Here effects of averaging of the fluctuating load acting on the guide-pier surface were assessed on the basis of general methods developed in [84] with the use of data from testing the large-scale model of Sayano-Shushensk hydroelectric station. Values of dynamic response factor were established, which characterize the relation between the force moments at the pier footing in cases of static- and dynamic-load application. It was found that resonance phenomena can result in doubling the design moment at the guide-pier footing.

3. Slabs at spillway tailraces and linings of conduits.

While designing the river-bed protection in the tailrace and the protection constructions of water-saturated slopes of dikes and dams, it is very important to take into consideration the hydrodynamic loads not only at the flow side but also at the back surface of the protection slabs, i.e., on the contact between the slab and the soil. These loads may arise due to penetration of pressure pulsations from the external side (through leaky joints and drainage well) or directly due to vibrations of slabs. Various models of the water-soil foundation system have been used in the calculation of pressure under the slabs: without consideration of the soil skeleton deformability; with integral consideration of the soil skeleton and fluid deformability in the form of the "piezo-conduttivity" equations; and by way of solution of the dynamic equations of the two-phase medium with account of elastic or elasto-plastic deformations of the soil skeleton [references in 77a]. The statement of the boundary-value problem may be different for these soil models (with or without consideration of the gap between the slab and the foundation). The differences correspond to various criteria of the protection designs; it is assumed that under normal operation conditions, the protection-slab vibrations should not cause irreversible deformations of soil and formation of a gap between the foundation and the protection slab; under emergency conditions, when the normal gate-operation conditions are disturbed, (one water outlet in operation with low tailwater level), the protection should not fail. However, no limitations are imposed on the soil conditions and on the soil-slab contact. Under such one-ration conditions the separation of the slab from the soil foundation for a value stimulated in the design specification is still admissible. The admissible value of the gap can be prescribed to be, e.g., one half of the average soil or filter-grain diameter under the slab, this condition ensuring that no quick re-formations of soil under the slab will take place.

The first computation model has been studied in great detail. Under conditions when no filter is made under the protection slabs, the problem amounts to the boundary-value dynamic problem of the theory of elasticity for the "equivalent" single-phase medium with modified Lame's parameters [47,72a] :

$$\lambda = \lambda_0 + K_f, \qquad \mu = \mu_0$$

Where K_f is bulk moduls of the pore fluid, taking into account the porosity and gas inclusions, that may change during the time.

The calculations yield the "total" dynamic stresses and the stresses in the soil skeleton σ_{ij} :

$$\sigma_{ii} = \frac{\tilde{\sigma}_{ii}}{1 + K_f / \left(\lambda_0 + 2\mu_0 / 3\right)}$$

In a case in which the protection slabs are resting on a filter layer, the calculations are to be made using the equations of a two-phase medium [47,72a, 69a,22a, 23a]. The calculated dynamic stresses in the soil skeleton are added to the statical ones and are used then to check the soil strength conditions. The stability of slabs is ensured, if at any moment of time, and with an adequate degree of probability, compression stresses are acting in the soil skeleton on the surface of contact with the slab, and the condition of the soil strength in all the points of the foundation is met.

The methods of calculating processes of separation of slabs from the foundation were being developed intensively. One of the first times these calculations had been applied in practice was for the design of the tailwater-bottom protection constructions of the Kiev and Kanev hydroelectric stations on the Dnieper river [64a], which has been in successful operation for over 20 years.

It has been shown that the optimized design of the protection drainage enables appreciable decrease of the required slab thickness with increase of the admissible size of the gap [53a, 54a]. Thus, the consideration of the hydroelastic effects in the process of the protection-slab uprise makes it possible in this case to lighten the protection construction.

Usually the protection slabs may be considered as rigid in the stability analysis. Deformability of the protection as a whole depends to a great extent on the deformability of the joints. Mutual correlation of vibration of individual slabs resting on a common elastic foundation may result in the amplification of the vibration of an individual slab, in an apparent decrease of the damping decrement, and in a severe increase with respect to vibrations with frequencies which are beyond the limits of the principal energy spectrum of action. Besides measurements of hydrodynamic loads and vibrations in the tailwater and in the power house of the Saratov hydroelectric power plant on the Volga river [77a, 84a], during the period preceding the construction-pit flooding, measurements of parameters and the free vibration of the protection slabs were carried out. This made possible the comparison of the predicted and observed parameters of vibrations. It has been found that a satisfactory agreement is observed only for relatively low frequencies. At frequency >12 Hz, the theoretical relationship for the spectral density of vibration of an individual slab gives considerably lower results than the relationship obtained by experimental studies. Thus, the mutual swinging of slabs must be taken into consideration for real situations. There are some data which allow one to anticipate the self-synchronization of vibrations of slabs, as well as that of vibrations of individual sections of the power house or of the dam. Such a self-synchronization has taken place during the passing of a high spring-flood discharge over the spillway dam of the Samara Volga hydroelectric power plant in May, 1979 and cased a perceptible vibration of houses situated at distances up to 3 km from the dam.

Figure 9.44 shows, by way of example, such self-synchronized vibrations, excited at uniform discharge distribution over the front of the dam of Samara hydroelectric power plant.

Examples of frequencies of vibrations at the foundation and the 8th floor of a house situated at the distance of 2.8 km from the dam are presented in Figure 9.45

Regularly repeated observations on a number of hydroelectric power plants revealed the variations of parameters of structural vibrations with time. For instance, the mean-square value z' of vertical vibrations of the spillway dam of the Volgograd hydroelectric power plant, the flood-discharge conditions remaning the same, has increased about 30 percent in two years at high specific discharges and more than twice at low specific discharges, see Figure 9.46a [84a]. In all these cases, the spectral density of vibrations featured a sharp maximum. The frequency corresponding to this maximum increased from 22 to 27 per cent during the above-mentioned time (Figure 9.46b). In these observations, many times repeated in the next 30 years, was observed self-synchronization of oscillations of separate sections of the dam. Meanwhile, the dam began to fluctuate as a single stamp on an elastic Foundation. Area disturbances propagating from such a stamp, proportional to the length of the side of the stamp, cover a large territory.

Hydroelastic effects are of great importance in designing conduit linings. Appearance of local cavitation or flow aeration may be an important

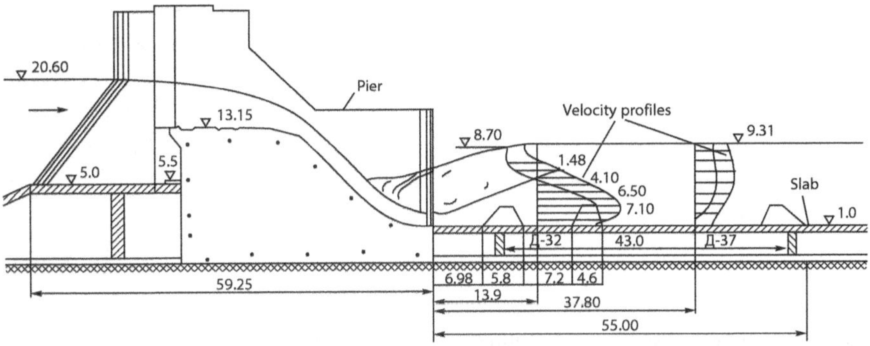

Figure 9.43 Typical situation for the loading of slabs at spillway tailraces.

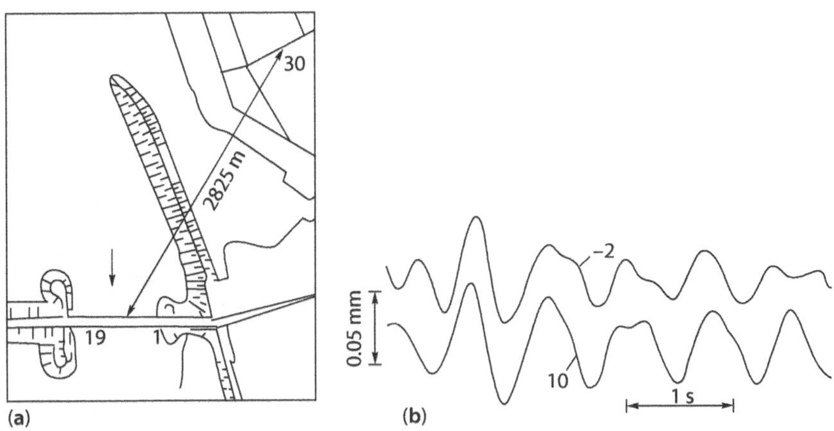

Figure 9.44 Self-synchronized vibrations of spillway dam.

V.I. Lenin hydroelectric station; uniform distribution of discharge over width of the dam (in May 19, 1979) of 23 m^3/sec per unit width and 36800 m^3/sec in total.

(a) Scheme of the dam sections (1-19) and a domestic building (30), its records of vibrations are shown in Figure 9.45

(b) Vertical displacements of dam sections 2 and 10.

feature complicating this case [106a]. Stability and strength analyses of linings are also carried out taking into consideration the hydroelasticity effects, especially in the space between the lining and the tunnel walls [44a, 108a]. In principle, this problem is similar to the problem of calculation of bottom protections in the rail race of spillways, but it is appreciably complicated by the necessity of taking into consideration the relatively higher deformability of the lining.

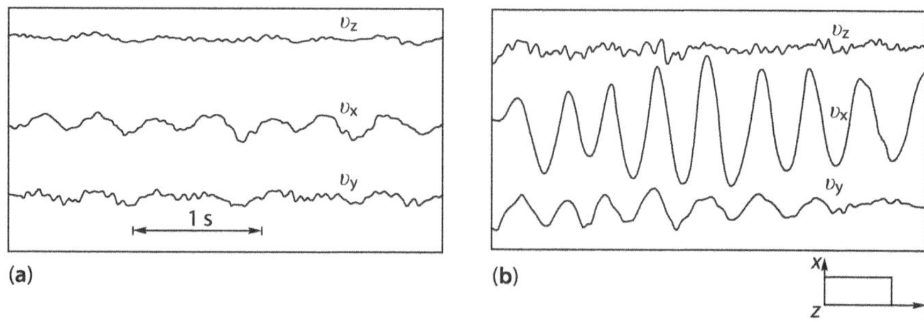

Figure 9.45 Effect of spillway vibration on a distant house.

Vibrations of the 9-story, 4-entrance panel domestic building shown in Figure 9.44 on May 19, 1979 (axes x parallel to the short side of the building)

a. Foundation of the building
b. 9th story

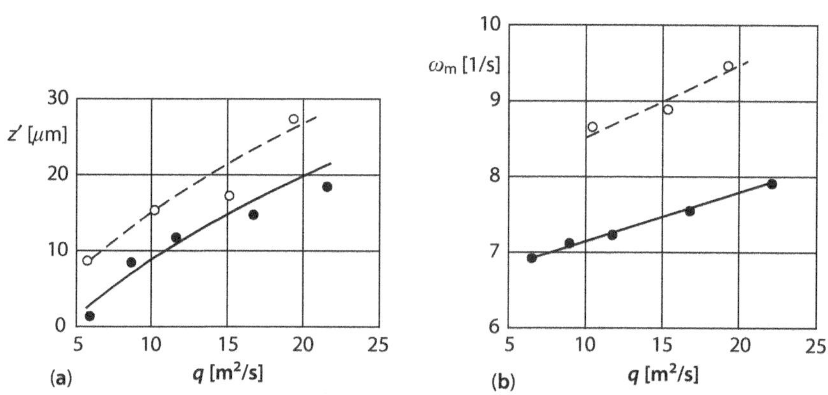

Figure 9.46 Vertical vibrations of a spillway dam as a function of specific discharge on the Volga river; date of field measurements in 1963 (lower line) and in 1965 (upper line).

a. Root-mean square of vibrations
b. Cyclic frequency corresponding to maximum spectral density of vibrations

It is important in all dynamic analyses to determine the parameters of the transfer function of the structure in water, i.e., the characteristics of the free vibration of the structure first of all. The natural frequencies and forms of vibrations of structures oscillating in fluids are found by solving the boundary-value problems of the flow/body interaction. The analytical work [84, 66a] has demonstrated that in most cases encountered in the practice of hydraulic engineering, a possibility exists to study the initial hydrodynamic field (neglecting the deformations and displacements of the elastic body and considering the hydrodynamic pressure on the surface of this body as a load) and the hydrodynamic field induced by the notion of the elastic body in the "fluid at rest," independent from each other. The simple superposition of both these fields yields an adequate picture. Only in the zones where the high-frequency velocity and pressure pulsations are playing an important part, and the frequencies of the elastic-body vibrations are far in excess of a certain limit frequency, the nonlinear nature of interaction of these two fields may manifest itself. For example, for protection slabs in the tail-water adjoining the spillway without lodges, this limit frequency (cyclic frequency) is $\omega = 8\ U_1/h_{1,}$ where U_1 and h_1 are the velocity and the depth in the contracted section of flow at the beginning of the hydraulic jump. The velocities at which the allowance for the nonlinear nature of interaction would be required are not attained in hydraulic engineering under these conditions and, in particular, proceeding from conditions of cavitation (see p. 9.2).

This circumstance permits an independent investigation into the hydrodynamics of flow with rigid boundaries, yielding as one of the results the characteristics of the hydrodynamical load on these boundaries, as it has been demonstrated in the first section of this part. In this case, the problem of hydroelasticity is simplified due to the possibility of examining the vibrations of elastic constructions under the given loads in the "fluid at rest"[106a]. The word at rest is set in quotation marks here because, actually, the velocity and pressure pulsations induced by the motion of the structure are not only taken into consideration – but determination of these pulsations is one of the principal steps in solving the problem.

9.5 Hydroelasticity

It is obvious from the expression (9.36) and before, that the pressure pulsation at points of a vibrating flow boundary is composed of the main part of the pulsation dependent on kinematics of the whole flow, and the additional part has direct reference to the inertial repulse of so called "added mass" of water. If the main part of the pulsations is not big and the change is relatively slow, with time the mutual correlation function of the pressure pulsation and of the boundary displacement will be similar to the mutual correlation function between the random function and its acceleration.

Figure 9.47 shows the autocorrelation function of flow boundary vibrations and mutual correlation function of the vibration and of the pressure pulsations in the tailwater of Volgograd dam downstream from the second row of energy dissipators [84a, 54a].

Turbulence intensity and flow velocities near the pressure pick-up were not high. It is known [18a], that the mutual correlation of the

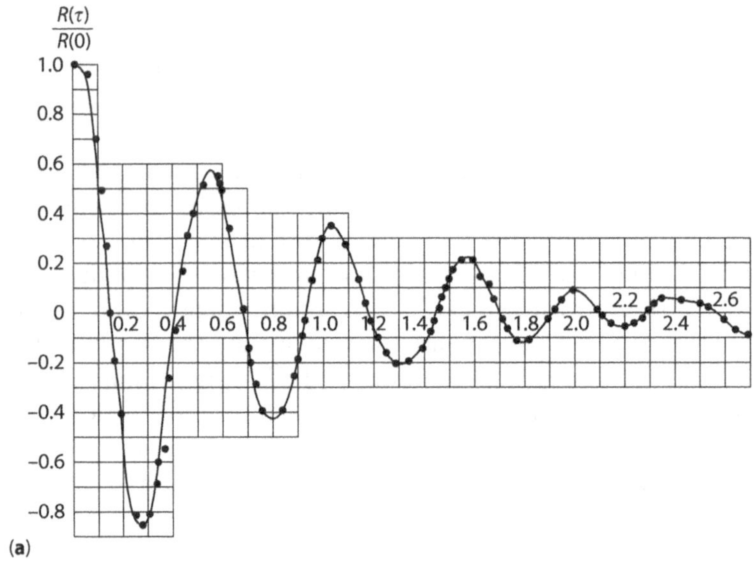

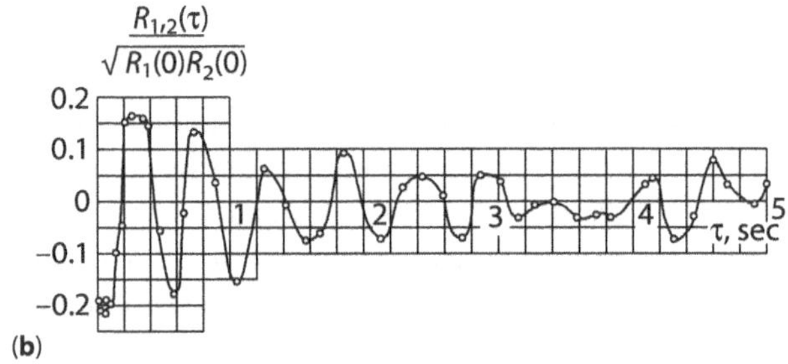

Figure 9.47 a) Normalized autocorrelation function of vibration of Volgograd dam downstream apron [84a]. b) Normalized mutual correlation function of vibration of the downstream apron and pressure pulsation in the point of the apron surface behind the second row of dissipaters in the Volgograd dam downstream pool.

random function and its acceleration is equal to the second derivative of the autocorrelation function of the initial process. It is clear that the role of the damped components of the autocorrelation vibration function by two-fold differentiation will be lessened and the mutual correlation function will sharply reveal almost periodic components, as it is seen from Figure 9.47 Figure 9.48 illustrates the autocorrelation function of the pressure pulsation given by the same pick up. Against a common low frequency background of the main part of the pressure pulsation, the adding resulting from the vibrations of the slab distinctly stood out. From calculations [54a], it is seen that under existing conditions the dispersion of a pulsation component,

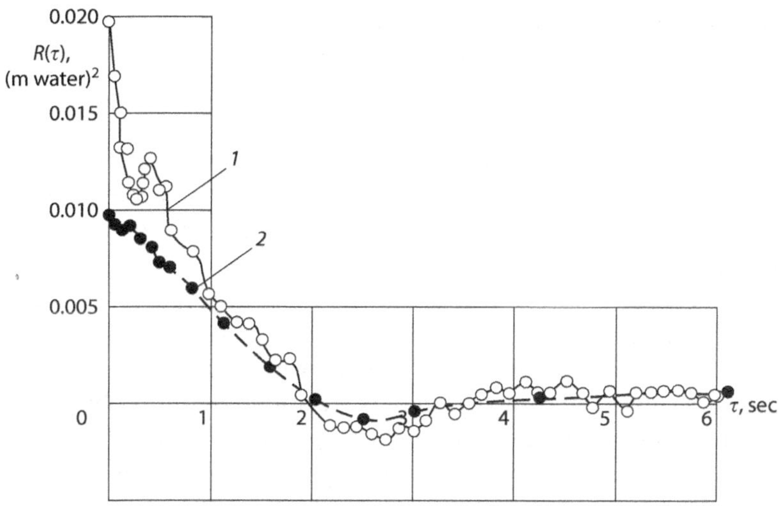

Figure 9.48 Autocorrelation functions of pressure pulsation in the downstream apron point behind the second row of dissipators in the Volgograd dam downstream pool [54a, 58a]:

1. in the prototype when effected by vibration of downstream apron;
2. in the model without vibration (rigid apron)

independent of vibration, accounts for 51% of total dispersion of the pressure pulsation.

Effect of the added mass can be easily taken into account if one knows the parameters of vibration and the value of the added mass, which can be easily estimated from the experiments with dead water or theoretically.

If the boundary displacement is proportional to the local pressure, the added mass effect gives the same relative distortion of spectrum on the certain frequency, independent of the pulsation intensity. The influence of the boundary deformations on the main part of the pressure pulsation is displayed in a much more complicated way.

Let us estimate the value of the error in the pressure pulsation spectrum at uniform flow boundary. The pulsation is calculated with the help of a pliable pick-up fitted in the rigid bottom.

Using the data from p.9.2, one can define the function for the case of the rigid boundary then estimate the variation of this function if a pick-up vibrating under the pressure pulsation is available.

The approximate theoretical analysis does not prevent us from explaining the experimentally observed underestimation of the pressure pulsations fixed in the fields of the high turbulence by the insufficiently rigid pick-ups. The autocorrelation functions of the pressure pulsations against the bottom in hydraulic jump are compared in Figure 9.49

The pressure pulsations are recorded by the pick-ups of the natural frequency, which is 30 - 300 times higher than the pressure pulsation frequency. The inductive pressure pick-up with the natural frequency of about 4000Hz was used as a more rigid pick-up and the strain gauge, with a membrane protected with rubber film, was taken as a pliable pick-up. Its natural frequency was 300 Hz. The dispersion of the pressure pulsation measured according to the records of the more rigid pick-up, is almost four times more than the dispersion measured according to the records of a pick-up with the usual rigidity in laboratory practice.

Figure 9.50 gives the comparison of correlation functions obtained with the help of less differing by rigidity pick-ups; at a similar vibrating mass the natural frequency of tensometric pickups, compared here differs by 2.8 times.

In this case too, the natural frequency of the most pliable pick-up is much higher than the frequency of pulsations in the flow. Variations of dispersion in Figure 9.50 are lower than in Figure 9.49 nevertheless, the rigid pick-up here showed a higher intensity of pulsations.

The correlation functions in Figures 9.49 and 9.50 diverge particularly more at small τ corresponding to high-frequencies in the spectrum of pulsations. The similar influence of rigidity of the pick-up, obviously, took place in the laboratory experiments of L.S. Maksimiv and L.A. Goncharov, revealing substantial lowering of the amplitude of pressure pulsations on models (as compared to prototype) particularly on the sections of increased turbulence of the flow [85a]. Sufficiently rigid pick-ups, mounted on the same models, give results showing good agreement with prototype data obtained by pick-ups of similar relative rigidity [54a].

Great influence of structure rigidity on the value of load on the section of increased flow turbulence was also displayed during investigation on training walls between the power house and the dam. Four models of a training wall fragment of the scale 1:70 were tested. One of the models was made rigid with an elastic insert at the base of the wall. The remaining three models were manufactured from homogeneous materials with different elasticity moduli. Natural frequency of walls in the water varied from 3.12 to 1.27 Hz (recalculated in the prototype). When deformability of elastic walls was greater, the lower was natural frequency. The experiments were carried out with models of fragments situated in the zone of high turbulence intensity - immediately behind the energy dissipators (position 5, Figure 9.51) and in the zone of relatively low turbulence intensity - behind the downstream stilling sill (position I, Figure 9.51).

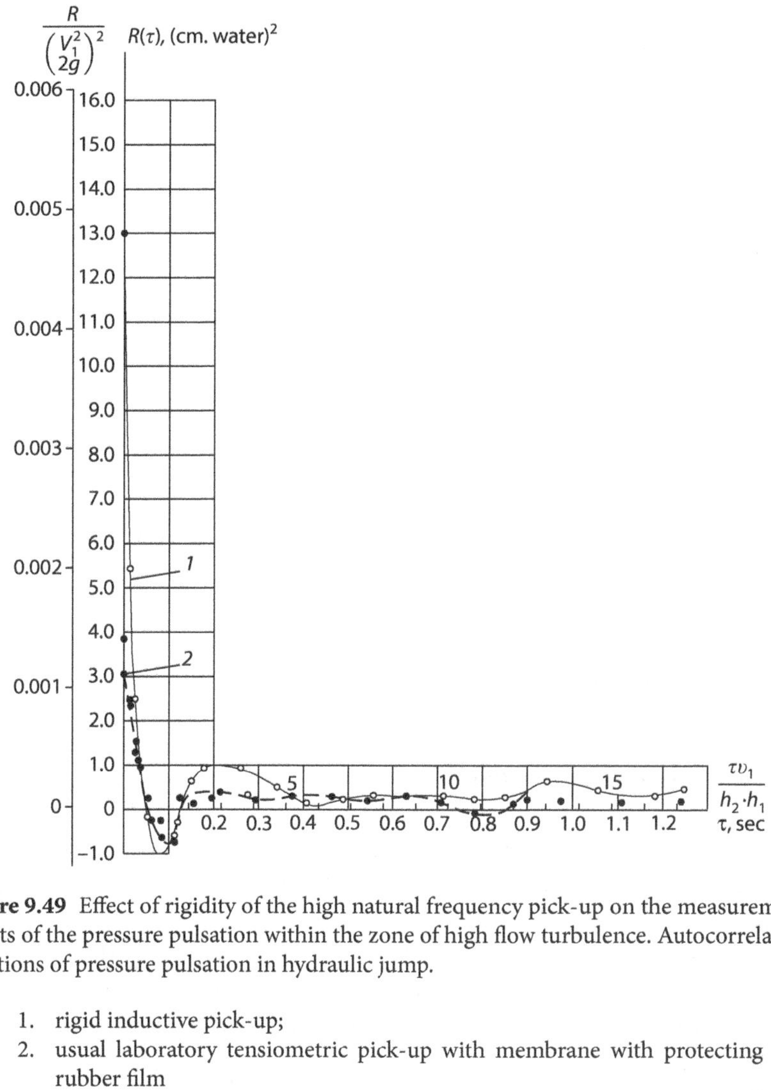

Figure 9.49 Effect of rigidity of the high natural frequency pick-up on the measurement results of the pressure pulsation within the zone of high flow turbulence. Autocorrelation functions of pressure pulsation in hydraulic jump.

1. rigid inductive pick-up;
2. usual laboratory tensiometric pick-up with membrane with protecting rubber film

The autocorrelation functions of the load pulsation at the base of the walls are compared in Figures 9.52 and 9.53. As shown in Figure 9.52, the load on the wall increases rapidly with the increase of the wall rigidity. Vibrations of the rigid wall, having the smallest vibration decrement, possess a distinct resonance component.

However, even after this component is excluded, dispersion of the load on the rigid wall appears to be not less than four times higher as compared to dispersion of the load on the most pliable wall.

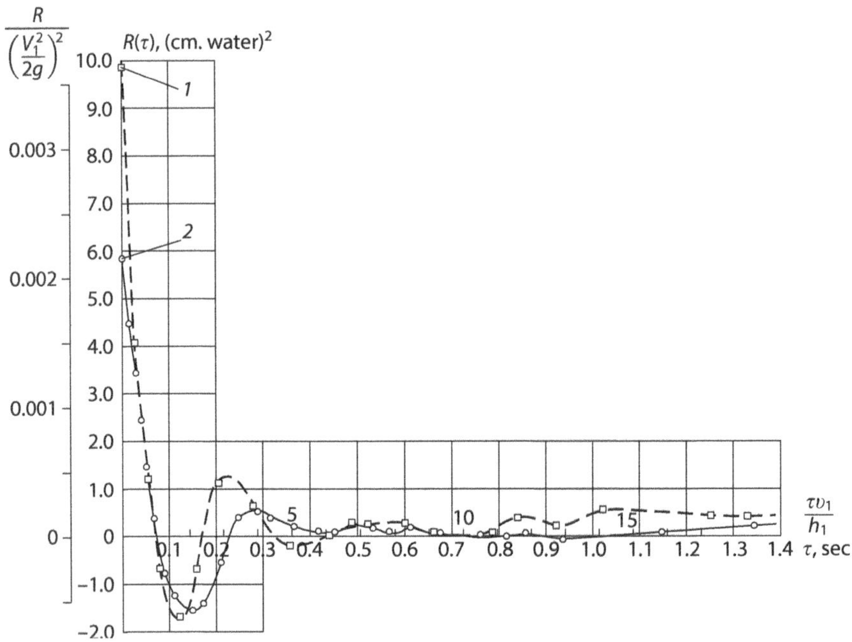

Figure 9.50 Autocorrelation function of pressure pulstaion in hydraulic jump recorded by tensiometrio pick-ups.

1 - rigid tensiometric pick-up
2 - Pliable tensiometric pick-up (usual)

In the other position of fragment, where the turbulence intensity is much lower and the main load is connected with the movement of waves on the water surface, the wall rigidity does not practically influence the load magnitude (Figure 9.53). The rigidity influence reduced also in those cases when the wall fragment was in the position 5, but the turbulence intensity reduced due to decrease of discharge passing through the dam.

The influence of deformability of structure on the main part of the pressure pulsation is particularly essential under the conditions of vibrations due to resonance. In this case the increase of amplitude of vibrations of definite frequency will cause the decrease of loads within the wide range of frequency spectrum. As a result of it, the dispersion of vibrations becomes nearly constant despite the increase of pulsation on the resonance frequency. The same nature of vibration of the load pulsation was observed when the training wall between the left bank fishway and main powerhouse of the Saratov hydroelectric station was tested (Figure 9.54). These

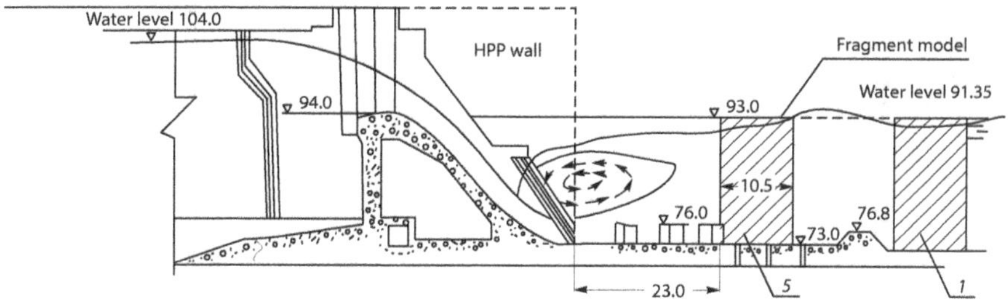

Figure 9.51 Location of fragment models training wall between hydroelectric station and spillway dam.

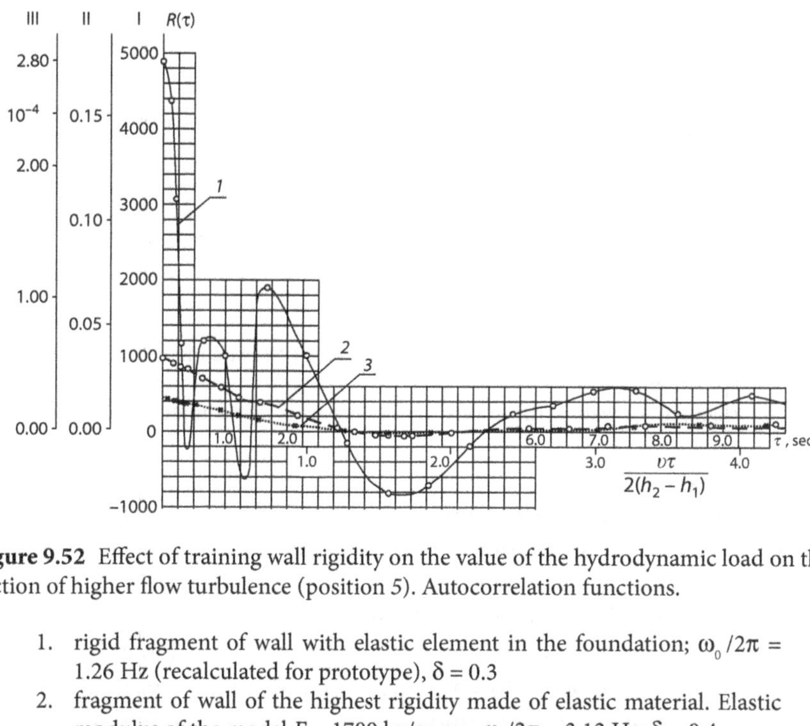

Figure 9.52 Effect of training wall rigidity on the value of the hydrodynamic load on the section of higher flow turbulence (position 5). Autocorrelation functions.

1. rigid fragment of wall with elastic element in the foundation; $\omega_0/2\pi$ = 1.26 Hz (recalculated for prototype), $\delta = 0.3$
2. fragment of wall of the highest rigidity made of elastic material. Elastic modulus of the model E = 1700 kg/sq.cm; $\omega_0/2\pi$ = 3.12 Hz; $\delta = 0.4$
3. fragment of wall of lowest rigidity made of elastic material E = 1200 kg/sq.cm; $\omega_0/2^{\pi}$ = 1.67 Hz; $\delta = 0.7$

I/ - scale of moments acting in the wall foundation $\left[\frac{tm}{m}\right]^2$

II/ - scale of loads averaged by wall fragment area$[t/sq.m]^2$

III/ - scale of relative loads (in quotas of velocity head in contracted cross-section)

Conditions of experiment: specific discharge 56 sq.m/sec, depth in contracted cross-section $h_1 = 2.6$ m. Depth of the downstream pool h_2 = 18.4 m. Time in nature. Velocity in the contracted section v=21.5 m/s.

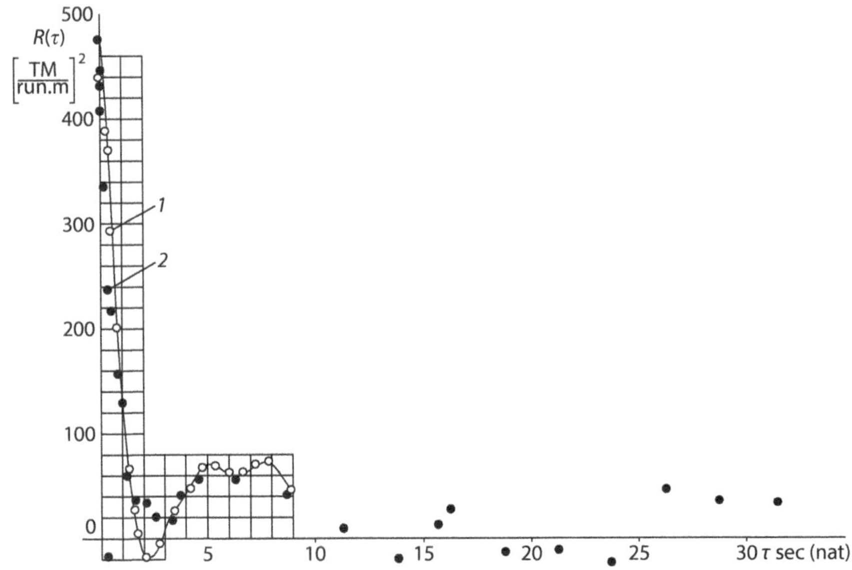

Figure 9.53 Effect of training wall rigidity on the hydrodynamic load value in the section of low flow turbulence (position *1*).

Autocorrelation functions:

1. fragment of wall of the highest rigidity made of elastic material $E = 7100$ kg/sq/cm
2. fragment of wall of the lowest rigidity made of elastic material $E = 1200$ kg/sq/cm

experiments showed that the natural frequency of wall model changed due to the change of wall mass under invariable hydraulic conditions and rigidity of wall model.

The general result of this part is the following.

The theoretical analysis and experimental data show that at high turbulence intensity in the open flow, the pressure pulsation in points and loads on the sections of the flow boundary surface considerably depend upon the nature and amplitude of boundary vibrations and deformability of flow boundary. The higher the boundary deformability, the less is the amplitude of the main part of the pressure pulsation connected with the non-linear effect of turbulence.

A definite part of the pressure pulsation on the boundary is the pressure fluctuations connected with the Inertia repulse of so-called added mass. These fluctuations are almost independent of the turbulence Intensity and are proportional to acceleration of flow boundary movement.

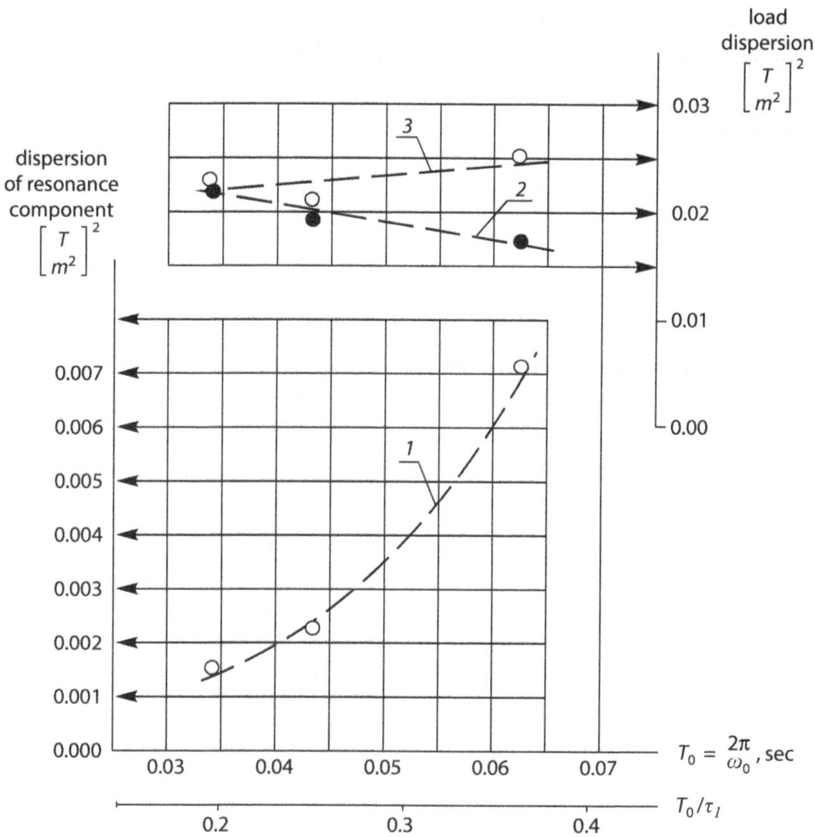

Figure 9.54 Variation of the moment fluctuations dispersion in the training wall foundation against the wall natural frequency. *1* — dispersion of resonance component; *2* — dispersion of turbulent load; *3* — dispersion of resulting vibrations. Conditions of the experiment in the model: velocity in the spillway, $V_{spillway}$=1.38 m/sec; height of spillway in the model - 0.11 m; width B = 0.158 m; depth of water in the downstream pool - 0.217 m.

Within the zone of low turbulence intensity the loads on structure confining the flow may be given in the form of pressure spectral density independent of the boundary displacement. Distortion of pressure due to inertia effect of the added mass may be taken into account simply by increase of design mass of structure.

Considering the most significant hydroelasticity effects taking place within the zone of high turbulence intensity, the boundary structure subjected to the turbulent loads should be made more elastic, preserving, however, its natural frequency beyond the limits of the main load spectrum. If it is impossible and the structure is subjected to the effects of resonance, the dispersion of resonance vibrations should be estimated considering the increasing hydroelasticity effects.

These results for hydraulic modeling practice may be very important. In article [74a], on the basis of nature tests, it was shown that distortion of pressure pulsation by sensors in zones of high intensity of turbulence and aeration may be too high. The distortion of pressure pulsations associated with the interaction of the flow field due to the boundary motion and the field of turbulence pulsations was studied for the first time in that long article by V. Lyatkher. To solve the probem, it was necessary to calculate the triple correlations between the pressure pulsations, their derivatives with respect to time, and the shear stress on the boundary. It was shown that in zones of higher turbulence, this "substantially hydroelastic distortion" may be relatively large. The theoretical results were compared with experimental data. At the first time was estimated the triple correlations by measuring on the real water way on the high dam (Figure 9.55).

The considered phenomena distortion effects are related to cases of small amplitudes on borders of the stream without causing a general restructuring of currents and not affecting the averaged flow characteristics and impacts. Much more serious problems may arise in situations when under the influence of vibration is a general restructuring of the thread, and there are phenomena of the so-called "capture fluctuations," when fluctuations in the design and hydrodynamic loads are synchronized, leading to the excessive growth of amplitude of fluctuations sometimes to the point of destruction. Such phenomena are considered most interesting in books by Y. Rocard [101a], Y.G Panovko [95a], E. Naudasher [92a] and others. Reproductions of these phenomena on hydraulic models are carried out with the scale of hardness borders (SMP).

9.6 Complex Modeling of Hydrodynamic Loads

The theme of this section - direct assessment capabilities reliable estimates of hydrodynamic loads on models of reasonable scale in conditions when the number of criteria of similarity obviously can't be saved, and formulation of requirements and best practices in integrated assessment of the stress state elements of hydraulic engineering constructions in hydraulic models. The modeling in engineering by static loads is described in the short and interesting book by B.I. Didouh [22a].

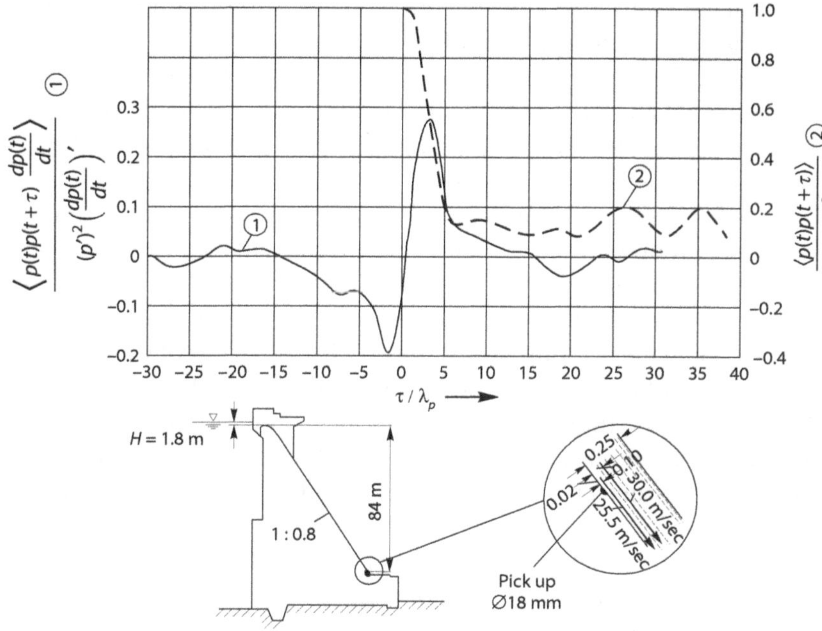

Figure 9.55 The double and triple correlations of pressure pulsations on the spillway of the Bratsk hydroelectric station. The flow is aerated. $\lambda_p = p'/(dp/dt)' = 6.88 \cdot 10^{-4}$ sec·

9.6.1 Pressure Pulsations at the Point of Water Fight Against Measurements in Nature and Model

Reproduction pressure pulsations in the downstream of hydraulic structures in models of small-scale, is a topic that attracts the attention of many researchers.

Most authors consider the pulsation pressure in the downstream as a stationary random process with a certain "quasi periodically." The desire to allocate periodic structure largely determined the approach to the description of processes. Almost all the works mentioned a leading of the frequency of pulsations, in many works the only amplitude characteristic is the amplitude of the pressure fluctuations. In the literature, there is practically no information about the functions of the distribution of pressure pulsation (the data available characterizes the likely distribution function of the extreme values of pressure). There is very limited data on the correlation properties of pressure pulsations on the water fight.

This part aims to give a more complete description of pressure pulsations in the characteristic points of the water fight.

Another task is the mapping and analysis of characteristics of pressure pulsation, received at the facilities in significantly different sizes (in kind and on the model), in conditions when the likeness of the averaged characteristics of the flow are not in doubt.

The concept of "condition" experience for unsteady process, and what is the pulsation pressure should be clarified. In terms of experience here it is necessary to include not only the shape of the borders and the hydraulic characteristics of the flow, but also the flexibility of the boundaries, the density of the material boundaries, the elastic properties of water and contact environments, the size of the receiver and the rigidity of the sensors.

The basis of this study was the result of measurements of pressure pulsations and vibration plate water fight, held in kind on the dam of the Volga (Voigograd) hydroelectric in 1959, when building the profile of the dam.

Pressure sensors were installed on the water fight against the 13th and 14th sections of the dam, counting from the building of the power plant. On the water fight was installed many sensors [84a]. For comparison, the most reliable of them - D-32 and D-37, set in a characteristic cross-section along the axis of the 14th migration (Figure 9.56).

Measurement in nature was made at various hydraulic modes. For comparison, of course, there have been selected modes in which the hydraulic conditions over the sensors can be most accurately reproduced on a narrow model, i.e. the modes with the same opening in a large number of connecting flights dam.

Out of three modes shown in Table 9.4, for a detailed processing and playback, third mode, in which there are recordings on both sensors (D-32 and D-37) was abandoned on the model.

In Table 9.4, in addition to the mode showing RMS pressure pulsations, a relatively small change in the value of RMS from D37 in modes with little difference, provides additional grounds for the assumption of reliability in field data.

A hydraulic model was reproduced in scale of 1:38 three-span dam with nonfinished crest at elevation 13.15 m. The model reproduced the contours of fastening downstream up to the bucket. For the bucket was horizontal bottom of the tray at the level corresponding to the level of the bottom of the bucket. Model overflow was made of wood (bulls) and concrete (weir); water fight and extinguishers were wooden. The water thickness of the plate on the model amounted to about 40 mm; its design was relatively hard, and the frequency of oscillations of the water boards on the model at a water depth of about 30 cm (HDD 10.5 m) was 26% to 30 Hz when the decay constant – decrement ≈ 0.14.

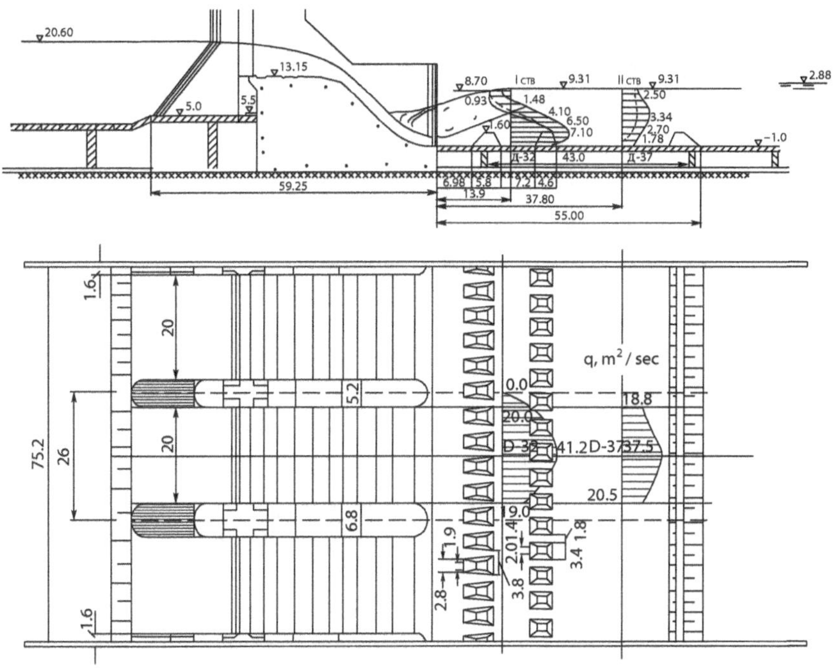

Figure 9.56 The section and plan of the spillway section of the dam of the Volga hydroelectric station, equipped with pressure sensors and vibration. Dimensions in metres of nature shows the velocity distribution along the depth of flow and specific charges (q, m²/sec) to the width of the stream.

Hydraulic mode on the model of similar (on Froude) mode 3 in nature, characterized by the following estimated data:

	Nature	Model
Full pressure relative to the level of the water fight	T = 21,5 *m*	0,565 *m*
Speed in compressed section	V_c = 17,5 *m/s*	2,89 m/s
The depth in compressed section	h_c = 1,7 *m*	0,045 *m*
The depth in the downstream (end of water fight)	$h_н$ = 10,8 *m*	0,285 *m*
The Froude Number:		
in a concise section:	$\frac{V_c^2}{gh_c} = 18{,}7$	18,7
at the end of the water fight:	$\frac{V_{=1}^2}{gh_=} = 0{,}045$	0,045
The Reynolds number at the end of the water fight:	$\frac{q}{\nu} = 2{,}4\cdot 10^7$	$1{,}0\cdot 10^5$

Table 9.4

№ mode	Date	Closed dam spans	Up. water level, m,	Tailrace level, m	Specific discharge on the apron, m2/sec	σ32, m, water	σ37, m, water
1	May 29, 1959	1, 2	20.82	12.08	24.2	No measured	0.13
2	June 3, 1959	1, 2, 26, 28	21.04	10.97	25.2	No measured	0.11
3	June 7, 1959	1, 2, 22, 23, 24, 25, 27	20.52	9.84	22.8	2.10	0.14

Specific discharge on the crest of the weir is q = 29,6 m^2/sec, which is 1.3 times more specific discharge on the apron. Due to this, the Reynolds number is compressed in section 1.3 times more than the given values.

Hydraulic mode on the model tuned by level top and bottom pounds. The level of the downstream water set by using a standpipe shutter, was fixed for the end of the bar (bucket) about 3 m from the end of discharge; the level of the upstream - 3.5 m from the target model of the dam. Levels on the model were established with the accuracy not lower ± 1.0 mm (+or- 3.8 cm in kind). The averaged velocity was measured by the Pitot tube. Thanks to the average of the squares of the instantaneous velocity, and also due to vibration of the tube measurements of the Pitot tube, the value of the average local rate is exaggerated. The actual value of the mathematical expectations of the speed at points of transit streams is:

$$\overline{\upsilon} \cong \upsilon_0 \frac{Q}{\int \upsilon_0 d\Omega}, \tag{9.132}$$

where υ_0 is the result of measurement of speed of a Pitot tube;

Q is the flow of water through a section Ω.

In the alignment of the sensor 32 $\overline{\upsilon} \cong 0,75\upsilon_0$, in the alignment of the sensor 37 $\overline{\upsilon} \cong 0,85\upsilon_0$.

Changes in hydrodynamic pressure points plate water fight were as in the natural environment, and the model was recorded with the help of pressure sensors, inductive type (Figure 9.57).

Inductance coil is included in the pavement of the measuring circuit. The current imbalance in measuring the diagonals of the bridge is obtained by changing the inductance coil of the probe.

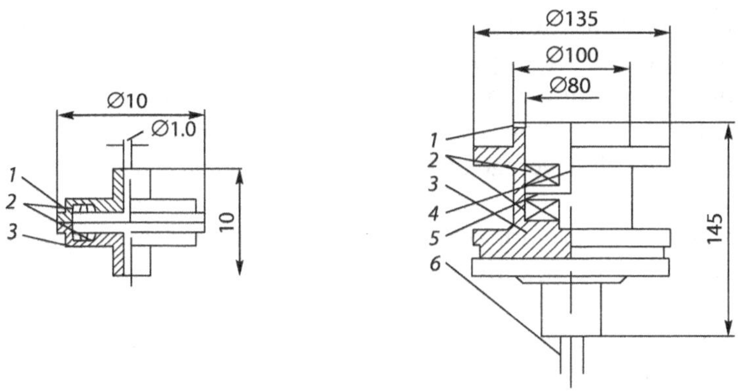

Figure 9.57 Design of pressure sensors.

In natural conditions the recording was made using a 3rd type loops (natural frequency of 120 Hz). On the model for recording at point D-32, the galvanometers with private 120 Hz were used. To record at point D-37 - galvanometer fourth type (natural frequency of about 70 Hz).

In addition to recording ripple hydrodynamic pressure, on the model there were registered changes in the level of free surface flow in points above the pressure sensors. The recording was made through string wave sensor synchronous recording of pressure on the galvanometers same type. The distance between the strings of wave sensor was 3.0 mm, the diameter of the strings was 0.3 mm.

Error of measurement of pressure associated with the difference in the diameters of the sensors and different nature of averaging pressure on the area of foster holes sensors, was approximately determined from the following expression:

$$\psi = 1 - \frac{1 - \delta(p)\frac{1}{2}\left(\frac{b_{mod}}{b}\right)^2}{1 - \delta(p)\frac{2}{9}}, \qquad (9.133)$$

where δ(p) is the relative change of pressure on the radius of the sensor;

Is responsible $\psi = 0$ $b_{mod} = \frac{2}{3}b$, can be considered the "effective radius" of diaphragm of the sensor.

$b_{mod} \cong 20$ mm - the radius of the inlet opening of the sensor on the model, recalculated in nature;

b = 40 mm is the radius of the sensor diaphragm in kind.

Probable error is calculated by equation (9.133) for the actual value equal to minus 2.5 % at $\delta(p) = 0.30$ minus 1.5 % at $\delta(p) = 0{,}19$. Given the correlation on the model, point D-32 likely exceeds the pulsating pressure compared with in kind on the average at 2.5 % (but not more than 5 %), at point D-37 - on the average at 1.5 %, in comparison with the nature (but not more than 3 %).

Currently, there are not yet clear mechanisms and the degree of influence of hardness gauges for measuring results. If this effect is connected only with the hydrodynamic effects incompressible fluid, then when modeling for Froude, it is necessary to maintain a certain ratio of the frequencies of the sensors:

$$\frac{\omega_{\mathrm{mod}}}{\omega_{\mathrm{nat}}} = \sqrt{\frac{1}{M_L}\frac{b_{\mathrm{mod}}}{2/3b}}, \tag{9.134}$$

where M_L - scale model.

In our case, the frequency sensors on the model must be 5 times more than frequency sensors in kind. In fact, this was done not entirely accurately. From this point of view sensor readings on the model could understate the size of the ripples.

Stability of amplitude characteristics of pressure sensors and the wave tester included with the equipment is determined by the maximum garbage individual points from the calibration line. The maximum error associated with the operation of equipment, are given in Table 9.5. The same Table shows the maximal error in the determination of correlation functions ripple related to end recording, in accordance with the conclusions of [55a].

Correlation functions are calculated using the mechanical correlator. Maximum error introduced by the device and the operator is evaluated by comparing the results of the re-treatment of one record (see Table 9.5).

The total variance of the error in the correlation function is determined by the total variance of the individual groups of errors:

$$\sigma_{\Sigma}^2 = \sum \sigma_{\sigma}^2. \tag{9.135}$$

The maximum total error of the correlation function:

$$\frac{\Delta R}{\sigma^2} = \sqrt{\sum \left(\frac{\Delta R}{\sigma^2}\right)_i^2} = 2\sigma_{\Sigma}. \tag{9.136}$$

Functions of probability density were calculated manually, directly on the data taken from the waveforms.

Probability density defined value pulsating pressure is calculated by the number nx hits options in the strip $(x, x + \Delta\sigma)$:

$$f(x) = \frac{n_x}{\sum n} \cdot \frac{\sigma}{\Delta\sigma}, \tag{9.137}$$

$\bar{x}$ the mathematical expectation $\bar{x}$ is equal to the average value:

$$\bar{x} = \frac{\sum n_x x}{\sum n_x},$$

Table 9.5 shows the values of errors in the calculation of the correlation function of the sensors nature and models.

Dispersion

$$\sigma^2 = \frac{\sum (x - \bar{x})^2 n_x}{\sum n_x}.$$

Everywhere, except for special cases, it is customary $\bar{x} = 0$. The accuracy of the estimate function is associated with a relative length of implementation. The dispersion of the probability density can be found on the recommendations of the work [55a].

The average interval between zero options τ_0, determined by the number of crossings of the middle line (n_0):

$$\tau_0 = \frac{T}{n_0 - 1}.$$

At a certain density, distribution $f(x)$ and the average interval τ_0, the most probable (mean) value of the frequency of occurrence of x on the implementation of the duration T is determined by the expression:

$$\bar{n}_x = \frac{T}{\tau_0} \frac{f(x)}{f(0)}.$$

Expression (9.137) is not, strictly speaking, the probability density for options $x(t)$. The probability density is expressed by the value:

Table 9.5

	Maximum error, $\Delta R/\sigma^2$				The standard error R	The standard error RMS
	amplitude	correlation	From the long of registration	total	$\frac{1}{2}\left(\frac{\Delta R}{\sigma^2}\right)=\sigma_\Sigma$	$\sim\frac{1}{2}\sigma_\bullet$
Model, D-32	0,174	0,050	0,064	0,19	0,09	0,05
Model, D-37	0,200	0,050	0,108	0,23	0,12	0,06
Model, wave up D-32	0,4	0,05	0,08	0,41	0,20	0,10
Model, wave up D-37	0,5	0,05	0,06	0,51	0,26	0,13
Nature, D-32	0,10	0,07	0,12	0,20	0,10	0,05
Nature, D-37	0,15	0,05	0,28	0,32	0,16	0,08

$$f_1(x) = \frac{d}{dx} F(x). \tag{9.138}$$

Here:

$$F(x) = \int_{-\infty}^{x} f_1(x) dx \cong 1 - \frac{T_x}{T}.$$

Here T_x - duration of stay of the options above the level x for quite a large time T.

Under normal (Gaussian) distribution of values, $f_1(x)$ and $f(x)$ coincide. In the case of turbulent pulsations with high values (x), there is also little variation between them [18a].

The Results of Measurements. Comparison of Data on the Nature and Models.

Figure 9.58 shows examples of implementations of pressure pulsations in nature and on the model. Comparing the records of sensor signals in appearance, it is difficult to talk about the similarity. At the forefront are the differences. So, the sensor 32 in nature is visible to the high-frequency component with a frequency of the order of 20÷30 Hz. Oscillation frequency on the model record is very rare; the amplitude of such pulsations in kind is small, and on the model it is even less.

The sensor 37 has clearly visible intermittent harmonic with the frequency of 2 to 3 Hz. In the model, this harmonic is not visible, but is well marked with low-frequency oscillations that set occasional bursts of high frequency impulses. NoTable also is the change of the entry signals wave sensor on sensors 32 and 37. Clearly manifested above the sensor 32 is the leading role of low-frequency components of excitement. The relative amplitude high-frequency oscillations of the surface above the sensor 32 are negligible, but above the sensor 37 it increases significantly.

Joint account wave sensor and the pick up on the model helped to clarify the structure of pressure pulsation and in the process gave the opportunity to quantify the measure deviations averaged pressure in the flow from hydrostatic law. The results of computation of mathematical expectation of pressure on the bottom (sensors) and surface water (sensor) are given in Table 9.6.

Rejecting pressure from hydrostatic over 32 sensor reaches 10 % of the depth of flow, and the pressure at the bottom exceeds hydrostatic; above the sensor 37, on the contrary, the pressure at the bottom of approximately

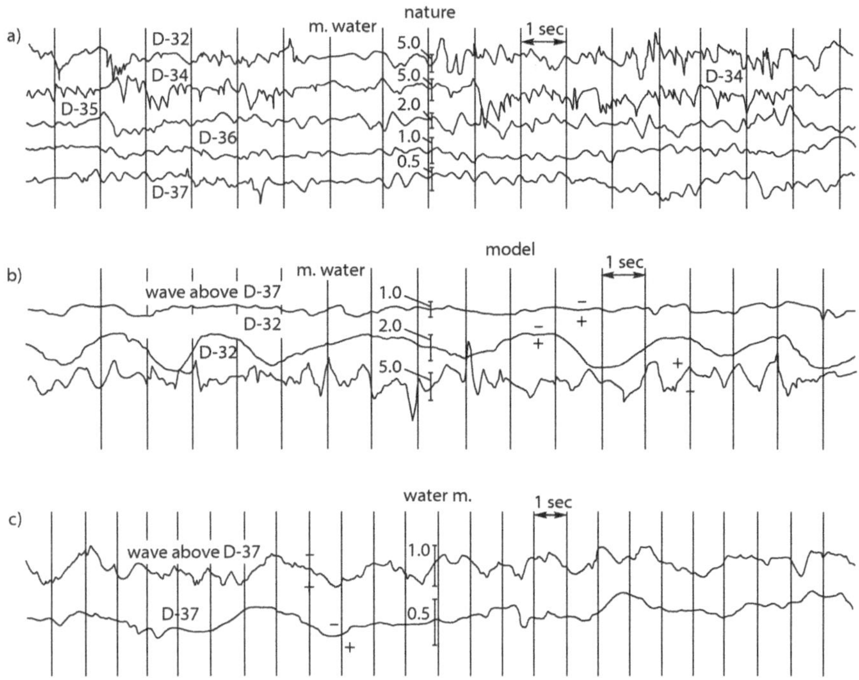

Figure 9.58 Pressure pulsations and oscillations of the free surface according to the nature (a) and model (b) - over 32 sensor, and (c)- sensor 37. All numerals (pressure and water levels) recalculate in nature.

2, 3 % less hydrostatic. Dynamic pressure in the flow over the sensor 32 on average by jet 0,38 water depth, and over the sensor 37 - up 0,088 water depth. In both cases, the pressure difference at the bottom of hydrostatic is approximately 26 % of the velocity head, calculated with account of pulsation supplements. Thus, these deviations in pressure from hydrostatic are significant.

The density of distribution of pulsation pressure according to the nature and the model is mapped in Figure 9.58

At a location sensor 32, between two rows of extinguishers (see Figure 9.56), the normalized functions of the probability density within the accuracy of the estimates coincide. The distribution is significantly different from the normal law and has a pronounced asymmetry (see Figure 9.58a). The deviation from normal of the law is especially great for large (by module) and small-x. Deep low pressure is observed more frequently than increase.

Asymmetry persists over the sensor 37, although here it is less, and the distribution is closer to the normal law (see 9.58b). In Table 9.7 maximum

Table 9.6

Water Level, *m*	The depth of the water at the water fight, *m*				
	on the water level	by D-32	By wave measure up D-32	by D-37	By wave measure up D-37
+ 9,88	10,88	10,65	9,70	—	—
+ 9,84	10,84	—	—	10,12	10,35

emissions, obtained on the model and in kind, are associated with the values of deviations of the calculated under the assumption of normal distribution law of probability.

The normalized distribution function ripple over the sensor 37 model and nature is in a satisfactory agreement. However, here pay attention to the difference between the mean interval τ_0. On the model τ_0 there was almost three times less than in nature. This means that in nature large bursts and deep low pressure will be repeated on average three times more than on the model. Such a big difference in magnitude is due to the presence of high frequency (2 - 3 Hz) components of pressure pulsations in nature.

The correlation function of pressure pulsations are mapped in Figure 9.59 5 By the form of the correlation functions, it can be concluded that in the thread, there are clear low-frequency oscillations with large amplitude. The frequency of these "leading" fluctuations over 32 sensor is about 0.8 to 1 Hz, above the sensor 37 - 0.125 Hz. Rapid decay of the correlation function demonstrates a wide frequency range. In the field of the leading low frequencies, coincidencing of nature of the data and the model is good. A noTable difference is observed at the $0.05 < \tau < 0.15$ sec. - sensor 32 and $\tau <$ 0.6 seconds - sensor 37.

Pressure pulsations at the point of water fight may be associated with the following factors:

1. Turbulence, manifested in ripple current velocity and determined by the intensity of diffusion and dissipation of "excessive" energy flow coming into the water fight.
2. Wave fluctuations of the free surface flow transmitted, in one way or another, to the bottom.

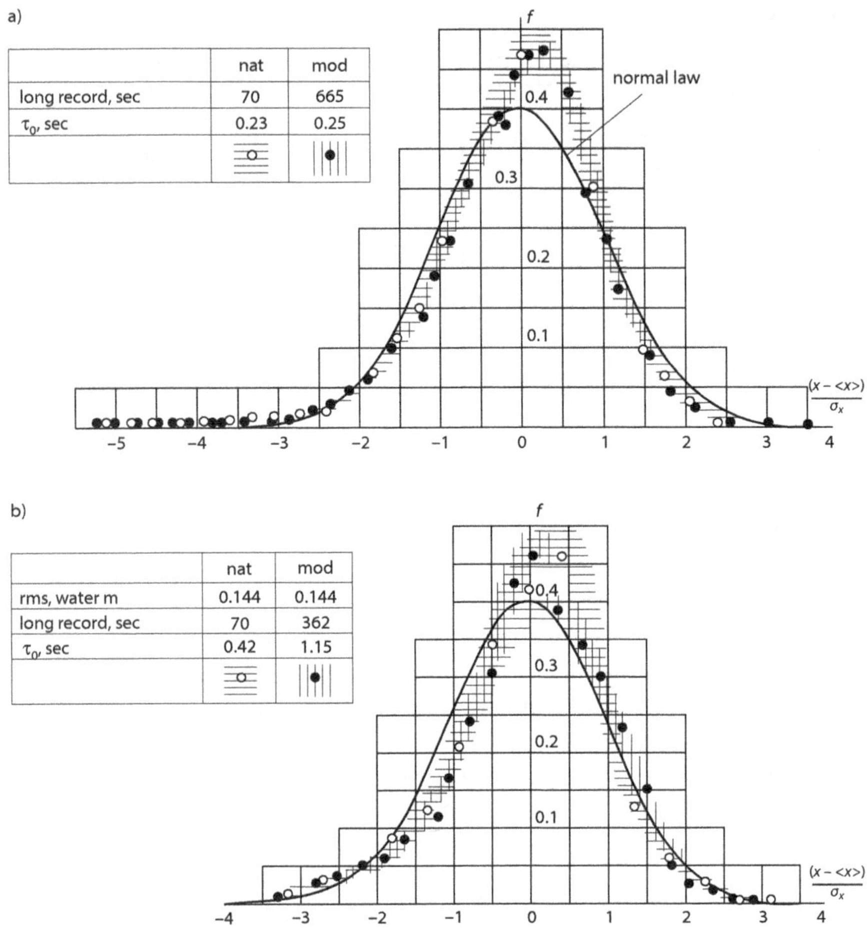

Figure 9.58 The density of distribution of pulsation pressure according to the nature and the model

3. Vibration water boards.
4. Pressure fluctuation caused by the vibration of air bubbles that are in aerated flow.

These reasons are not independent. Classification of them is to a certain extent conditional and, of course, not the only possible way.

Try to roughly estimate the role of these reasons in the formation of the common spectrum of pressure pulsations in the nature and on the model. Parameters of turbulent components of pressure pulsations are

Table 9.7

	$n_0 = \frac{T}{\tau_o}$	$f(x) = f(0)\frac{\tau_0}{T}$	$-\left(\frac{x}{\sigma_{<0:A}}\right)$	$+\left(\frac{x}{\sigma_{<0:A}}\right)$	**By normal low**
Model, D-32	2660	$1.7 \cdot 10^{-4}$	5.26	3.24	3.97
Nature, D-32	303	$1.5 \cdot 10^{-3}$	5.05	2.37	3.34
Model, D-37	315	$1.4 \cdot 10^{-3}$	3.36	2.92	3.36
Nature, D-37	167	$2.5 \cdot 10^{-3}$	3.17	3.17	3.18

Note that a single extreme emission at a given relative to the length records $n_0 = \frac{T}{\tau_0}$ is not always the same as the mathematical expectation of this release.

essentially different in the areas of generation and dissipation of the turbulent energy. In the generation sector, characteristics of the spectrum of pulsations may be directly associated with the shape of the borders of the flow and the averaged parameters of flow. In particular, the maxima of the spectral density pulsations over 32 sensor can be expected on the values of frequencies corresponding to the frequency of rotation of roll [53a] - the vortex shedding frequency horizontal and lateral edges absorbers.

Frequency of rotation of the drum will appreciate the velocity of compressed section U_c and thickness, and roll over it is approximately defined by difference of depth in section 1 and thickness of a jet of compressed section:

$h_{roll} = 9.6 - 1.7 = 7.9$ m. In fact, the thickness of the roll will be slightly less.

The estimated frequency of disturbances following:

$$\frac{\omega}{2\pi} \cong \frac{U_c}{\pi h_{roll}} = \frac{17.5}{3.14 \cdot 7.9} = 0.705 \text{ Hz} \tag{9.139}$$

This frequency exactly coincides with the frequency that corresponds to the maximum value of the function of the spectral density (see p. 9.2). The distance to the first zero correlation functions of 0.25 to 0.27 sec. (Figure 9.59b), almost the same model and nature, is slightly less than a quarter of the period leading disturbances that are equal to 0.35 seconds.

This process is apparently, without distortion.

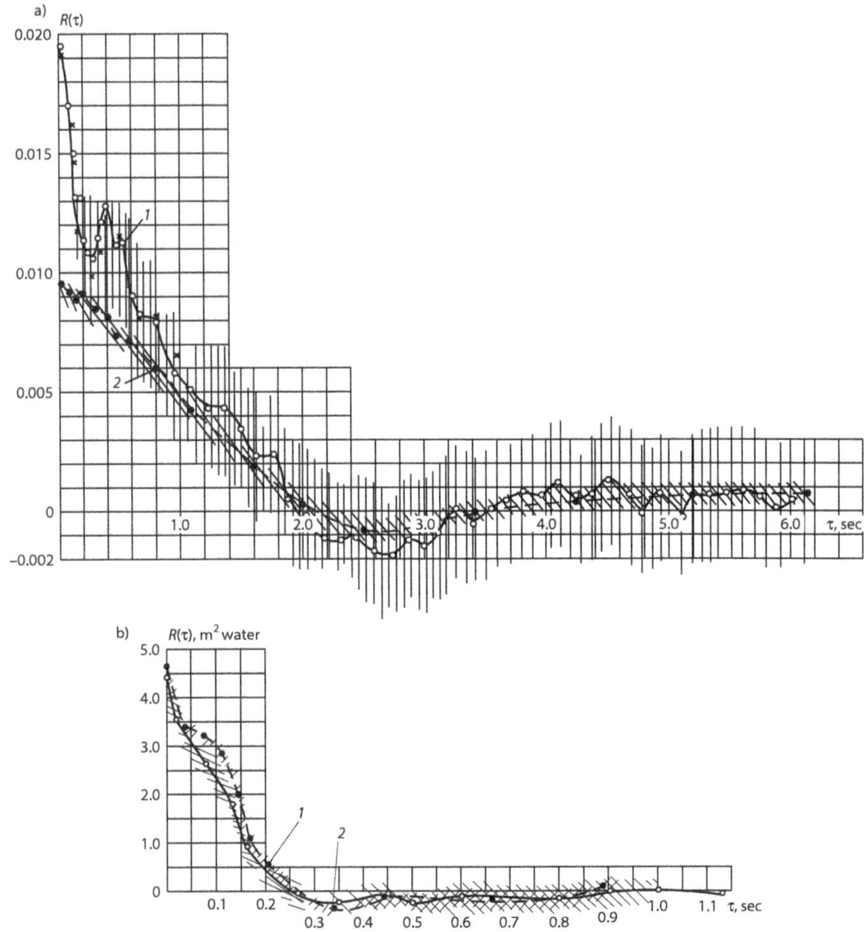

Figure 9.59 The autocorrelation function of pulsation pressure according to the data of measurement in nature and model top - sensor 32, lower - sensor 37.

The frequency of vortex shedding from the edges of the dampers is determined by the number Sh, relating to tear of the flow around the cylinder, and remaining constant and equal to 1.2 to 1.3 when the Reynolds number changes in the range from 5 000 to 200 000. When Re > 200 000, values of Sh increase dramatically. Perhaps the departure of the frequency of vortex shedding absorbers in the region of large values for large Re explains the above-noted discrepancy between the nature and the model (Figure 9.59b, $0.05 < \tau < 0.15$ sec).

The dissipation of turbulent energy starts almost in the same sections as the generation of pulses. Analysis of the influence of viscosity on the processes of dissipation of energy and the form of the correlation functions has shown that this effect may appear on the full-scale results in time < 0.5 10^{-4} s to 32 sensor and 3.4 10^{-4} seconds for the sensor 37. On the model of the appropriate times there can be 0.31 10^{-2} and 2.1 10^{-2} sec.

The effect of viscosity on the sensor 37 is manifested in considerably more t than over the sensor 32. However, the range of τ in this case is much longer than range, where the difference of correlation functions actually turned out to be significant.

It should be emphasized that although the influence of viscosity on the form of the correlation functions is in a relatively narrow range τ, this does not mean that the influence of viscosity on the change pulsation characteristics is very little. On the contrary, the degeneration of turbulence for hydraulic jump to a great extent depends on the viscosity.

Wave component pressure pulsations most are most easily found with theoretical and experimental investigation. Figure 9.60 mapped the density distribution of the frequency of occurrence of crossing a certain level in the wave oscillation surface and density distribution of pressure pulsations on the bottom of the stream. As can be seen from Figure 9.60, the fluctuations of surface water are very close to the normal law. RMS deviation of the level of the average above the sensor 32 is about three times less, and above the sensor 37 is almost three times the standard deviation of pressure pulsations on the bottom. Although the amplitude of the surface of the water is significant, the magnitude of the wave velocities $|V_x|$ is associated with the fluctuation of the water surface.

Leading the period of wave oscillations τ_w fair next assessment:

$$|V_x| \sim \frac{1,41\sigma_s g\tau_w}{\lambda}, \tag{9.140}$$

here σ_w – RMS level fluctuations;

1,41 σ_w – oscillation amplitude level;

λ – is the wavelength is determined from the equation:

$$2\pi\lambda = g\tau_w^2 th\frac{2\pi h}{\lambda}, \tag{9.141}$$

The wave speed very quickly decreases with depth. With this in mind, it is safe to assume that the wave velocity on the vertical above the sensor 37 is much smaller than the velocity of flow. Vertically above the sensor 32, such a conclusion cannot be drawn. Here it is only true for the near-bottom layers.

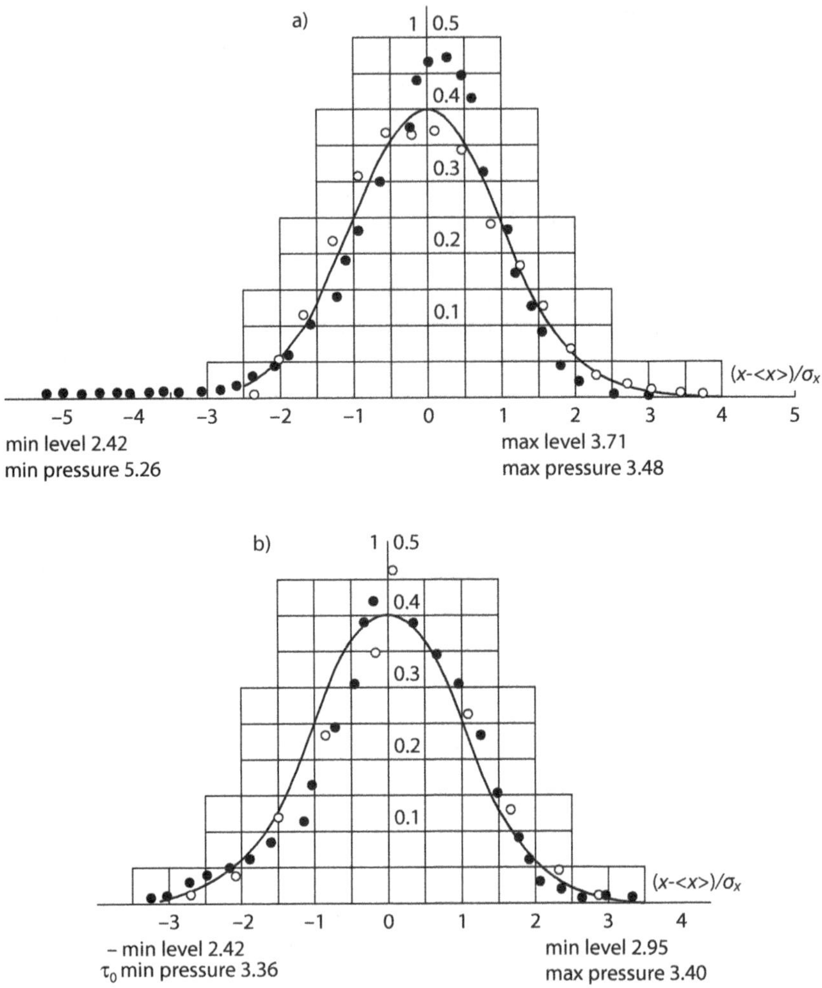

a)	pressure	wave
rms m. water	2.23	0.69
long record, sec	665	665
$\bar{\tau}_0$, cek	0.25	0.9–1.0
	●	○

b)	pressure	wave
rms m. water	0.114	0.333
long record, sec	362	665
$\bar{\tau}_0$, cek	1.15	0.8–1.2
	●	○

Figure 9.60 The mapping of the density of the probability distribution of oscillations of the free surface and pressure pulsations on the bottom of the stream (model):

Top (a) - wave meter over 32 sensor and the sensor 32, Low (b) – wave meter above the sensor 37 and sensor 37.

It is easy to show that if the wave speed is small, the equation of oscillations in the first approximation can be linearization, i.e. practically it is possible to use ready-made solutions for the wave propagation. The correspondence between the wave pressure on the bottom of the stream and a deviation of water level of the average is expressed by the formula (see p. 9.2):

$$\frac{\Delta p_{\text{bottom}}}{\Delta p_{\text{surface}}} = \frac{1}{ch\dfrac{2\pi h}{\lambda}}. \tag{9.142}$$

Instant total pressure on the bottom is the sum of the wave and nepolnogo components.

If the spectral density of fluctuations of surface water is $S_n(\omega)$, then, obviously, in the framework of the linear theory of the spectral density of fluctuations of pressure on the bottom of $S_в(\omega)$, total pressure is determined by the formula:

$$S_b(\omega) = \frac{S_s(\omega)}{ch^2\dfrac{2\pi h}{\lambda}}. \tag{9.143}$$

$$\omega^2 = \frac{2\pi g}{\lambda} th \frac{2\pi h}{\lambda}.$$

The solution of equation (9.154) and some additional quantities characterizing the possible parameters of waves at a depth of 10 m, are shown in Table 9.8.

Table 9.8 and equation (9.143) shows that for waves at the bottom of the subwoofer, the maximum frequency in the spectrum is not more than 0.4 Hz.

To estimate the amplitude of wave oscillations at the bottom, you must use the spectral analysis. Applying the reasoning of the leading period here can give a qualitatively wrong conclusion. Indeed, comparing the correlation function of the fluctuations of surface water and pulsations at the bottom (Figure 9.61), it is difficult to see them in total. Taking a leading period not exceeding 2.6 seconds, as in Table 9.8, make sure that the bottom of the wave pressure does not penetrate.

Correlation functions of the waves can be approximated by the dependency type:

$$R(\tau) = \sigma_s^2 \exp(-a|\tau|)\left(\cos\beta\tau + \frac{a}{\beta}\sin\beta\tau\right) \tag{9.144}$$

or

$$R(\tau) = \sigma_s^2 \exp(-a|\tau|)\cos\beta\tau. \tag{9.145}$$

The formula (9.144) is suiTable for waves over 32 sensor (α = 0.73 1/s, β = 2.1 1/sec); the equation (9.145) is suiTable for waves above the sensor 37 (α = 1.06; β= 1.57). The corresponding spectral densities have the form:

$$S_s(\omega) = \frac{2\sigma_s^2}{\pi}\frac{\alpha^2+\beta^2}{\left(\omega^2-\beta^2-\alpha^2\right)+4\alpha^2\omega^2} = \frac{2.29\sigma_s^2}{\left(\omega^2-4.93\right)^2+2.12\omega^2} \tag{9.146}$$

and

$$S_s(\omega) = \frac{a\sigma_s^2}{\pi}\frac{\omega^2+\alpha^2+\beta^2}{\left(\omega^2-\alpha^2-\beta^2\right)+4\alpha^2\omega^2} = \frac{0,34\left(\omega^2+3,58\right)\sigma_s^2}{\left(\omega^2-3,58\right)^2+4,48\omega^2}. \tag{9.147}$$

The normalized spectrum of wave pulses to the bottom in both cases was almost the same (Figure 9.62).

Integration gave the following variance of the pulsations of the wave nature (Table 9.9):

$$\sigma_2^2 = 2\int_0^\infty S_2(\omega)d\omega = 0,166\sigma_s^2, \tag{9.148}$$

Table 9.8

ω, rad/sec	0,12	0,20	0,57	0,99	1,37	2,40	3,40
$\frac{2\pi h}{\lambda}$	0,126	0,21	0,63	1,26	2,09	6,28	12,56
$ch\frac{2\pi h}{\lambda}$	1,008	1,022	1,205	1,904	4,100	260	1/0,000
$\frac{\lambda}{h}$	50	30	10	5	3	1	0,5
$\frac{2\pi}{\omega}\sqrt{\frac{g}{\lambda}}$	7,09	5,52	3,36	2,72	2,54	2,51	2,51

$$\sigma_2 \cong 0,407\sigma_s.$$

From Table 9.9 it follows that in the field of generation ripple contribution, wave component is negligible, but after the hydraulic jump, pressure pulsation almost completely (within the accuracy of measurements and calculations) is determined by the wave fluctuations.

This conclusion, however, is not quite accurate. On the autocorrelation function of pressure pulsations on the sensor 37, a visible high-frequency

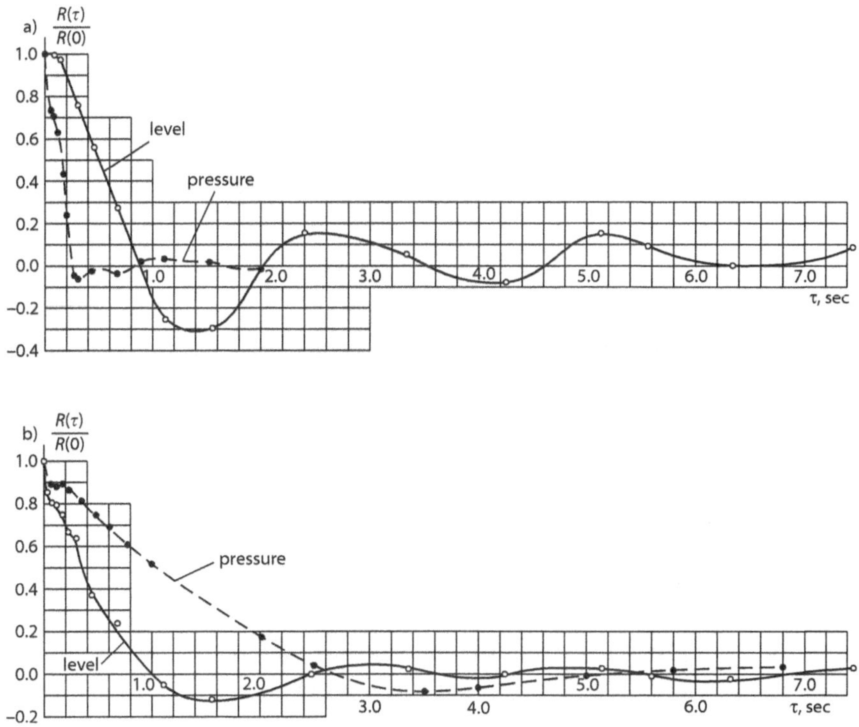

a)	pressure	wave
rms m.water	2.16	0.77
max-min, m	19.7	5.1
long record,sec nat	293	293
	•	o

b)	pressure	wave
rms m.water	0.101	0.287
max-min, m	0.66	2.00
long record,sec nat	555	293
	•	o

Figure 9.61 The mapping of the autocorrelation functions of the fluctuations of surface water and pressure pulsations on the bottom of the thread (on the model).

Top (a) – wave meter over 32 sensor and the sensor 32, low (b) - wave meter above the sensor 37 and sensor 37.

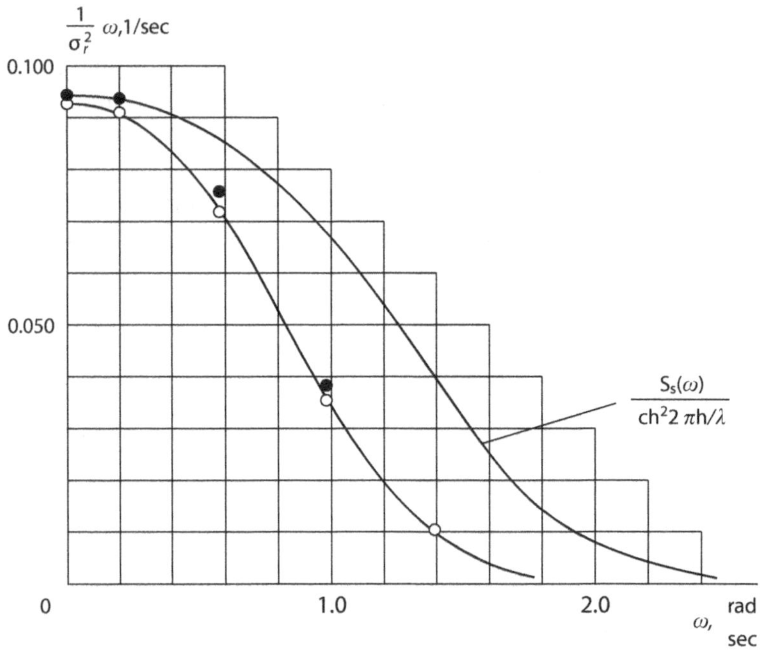

Figure 9.62 The function of the spectral density wave components of pressure fluctuations on the bottom.

Black points – above sensor 32, white - above sensor 37.

component (at small τ), corresponds to a frequency of the order of 4 to 4 Hz (28 to 31 Hz model). This component, obviously, cannot be the wave of origin. In addition, mutually-correlation function of the sensor 37 and wave sensor over it slightly dropped to zero (Figure 9.63). If fluctuations on the bottom had just wave structure, the value of the normalized mutually-correlation function at zero would be of the order:

$$\frac{2\int_0^{\infty} \frac{S_s(\omega)}{ch^2 \frac{2\pi h}{\lambda}} \cdot d\omega}{\sigma_2 \cdot \sigma_s} \cong 0{,}52.$$

In fact it is less, i.e. the composition of pressure pulsations on the sensor 37 in nature and on the model is relatively insignificant, but a distinct component is not the wave of origin.

Table 9.9

sensor	*RMS surface,m*	*RMS pressure from wave, m*	*RMS pressure total*	$\sqrt{\sigma^2 - \sigma_2^2}$
32	0,77	0,31	2,16	2,15
37	0,28	0,11	0,10	0

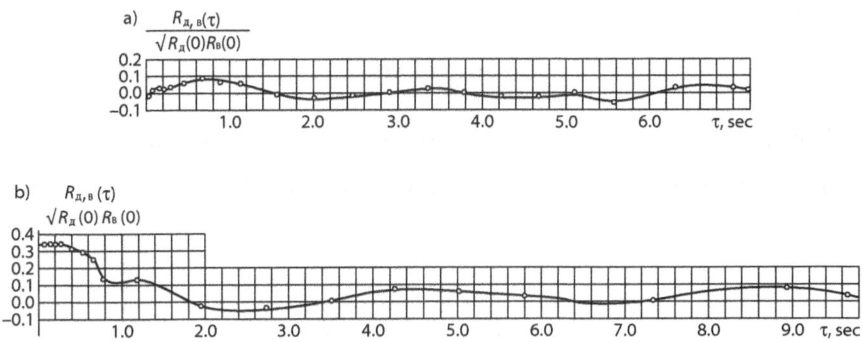

a)	pressure	wave
rms m.water	2.16	0.77
long record, sec	293	293

b)	pressure	wave
rms m.water	0.101	0.273
long record, sec	555	555

Figure 9.63 Mutually-correlation function of pressure pulsations on the bottom and variations in surface water

Top (a) - vertical over sensor 32, low (b) – same sensor 37.

Because of the autocorrelation function ripple over the sensor 37 in nature and models large τ is the same, so we can assume that the low-frequency components associated with the wave impact are well-modeled by Froude. This conclusion is valid for relatively long waves (great depth on the model: $\lambda_{mod} >> \lambda_c$. Here $\lambda_c = 1.8$ cm is the length of capillary wave – see p. 9.2).

Consideration of turbulent and wave components does not explain the differences in correlation functions ripple over the sensor 37 model and in nature.

This difference can be explained by the vibration of the water boards in kind. Assuming move vibration is small, the task of pressure pulsation caused by vibration, can be reduced to a linear, and the total pressure to represent the sum of the component. Introducing the notion added masses [106a], pressure from vibration can be written down as:

$$p_z = m_{ad}\frac{\partial^2 z}{\partial t^2}, \tag{9.149}$$

where m_{ad} is the associated mass water plate of the flow, referring to the unit area of a surface of a plate;

z - coordinate of the moving counted in the positive direction from the board.

As from the sensor 37 to the edges of the plates relative to far (in comparison with the depth of the water), we will accept with some reserve:

$$m_{ad} = \rho h. \tag{9.150}$$

Given the relatively small value of the transverse displacements and rotations plate, put $\frac{\partial^2 z}{\partial t^2} \approx \frac{d^2 z}{dt^2}$. Taking into account of comments made, we get:

$$p_z \cong \rho h a; \qquad a = \frac{d^2 z}{dt^2}.$$

Spectral density of pressures caused by vibration $S_{p_z}(\omega)$, can be written as:

$$S_{p_z}(\omega) = \rho^2 h^2 S_a(\omega) = \rho^2 h^2 \omega^4 S_z(\omega), \tag{9.151}$$

где $S_z(\omega)$ – spectral density movements;

$S_a(\omega)$ – is the same, but for acceleration vibration

The right part of equality (9.149) only makes sense if the integral converges:

$$\int_0^\infty \omega^4 S_z(\omega)d\omega. \tag{9.152}$$

Function $S_z(\omega)$, calculated by the correlation function approximating the results of processing of the vibration records in nature [84a], does not satisfy this condition. We can try to overcome this difficulty, replacing infinite upper limit of the integral in (9.165) reasonably large ω_{max}:

$$\sigma_a^2 \cong 2\int_0^{\omega_{max}} \omega^4 S_z(\omega)d\omega.$$

If we take ω_{max} = 45 rad/sec, then the variance acceleration is equal:

$$\sigma_a^2 = 6.32 \cdot 10^3 \sigma_z^2 \ \frac{1}{\sec^4}. \tag{9.153}$$

Function $S_z(\omega)$ taken by correlation functions:

$$S_z(\omega) = 0{,}34\sigma_z^2 \frac{158+\omega^2}{\left(\omega^2 - 158\right)^2 + 4{,}56\omega^2}. \tag{9.154}$$

In expressions (9.153) and (9.154) σ_z^2 is dispersion of the vertical displacement of the plate.

It is known that the differentiation of a random process with a narrow spectrum is expanding its range. This means that the correlation function p_z will fade faster than the autocorrelation function of movements. However, a leading period in both cases should be about the same (equal to 0.4÷0.5 sec). This value coincides with leading period correlation functions imposed on correlation function of pressure pulsation in kind, clearly allocated at τ <0.6÷0.7 sec. (see Figure 9.59a). The same period is observed on mutually-correlation function of pressure pulsations on the sensor 37 and vertical displacements of water boards in this place (Figure 9.64).

In the zero, mutual-correlation is negative. This is because the acceleration and movement in the harmonic oscillation is always in opposition. Thus, the minimum pressure should be observed (and observed) at the maximum displacement of the plate up. If we consider that the wave components and turbulent pulsations in the point and vibration plates are statistically independent, the module mutual correlation in the zero can be expressed by a simple formula:

$$\left| \frac{R_{1,2}(0)}{\sqrt{R_1(0)} \cdot \sqrt{R_2(0)}} \right| = \frac{2 \int_0^{\omega_{max}} \rho h \omega^2 S_z(\omega) d\omega}{\sigma \cdot \sigma_z}. \tag{9.155}$$

$$\left| R_{1,2}(0) \right| = 2 \int_0^{\omega_{max}} \rho h \omega^2 S_z(\omega) d\omega = \rho h \cdot 21{,}8\sigma_z^2. \tag{9.156}$$

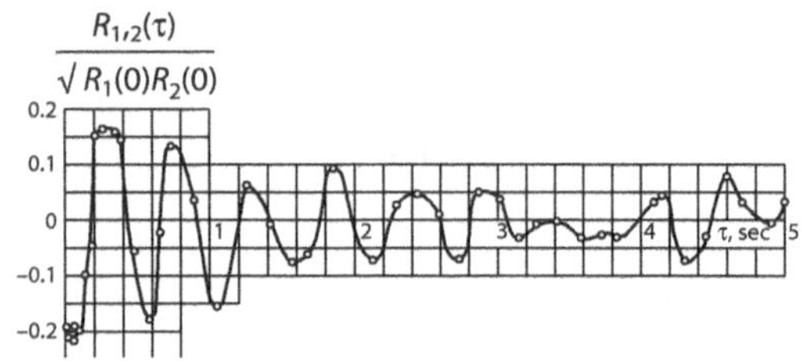

Figure 9.64 Mutual correlation function of the vibration plate and pressure pulsations above the sensor 37.

Using (9.151) and (9.153), instead of (9.156) receive:

$$\left|R_{1,2}(0)\right| = \left[\rho h\sqrt{6,32\cdot 10^3}\,\sigma_z\right]\sigma_z \frac{21,8}{\sqrt{6,32\cdot 10^3}} = 0,28\sigma_{Pz}\sigma_z. \qquad (9.157)$$

From (9.155) and (9.157) go:

$$\left|\frac{R_{1,2}(0)}{\sqrt{R_1(0)}\cdot\sqrt{R_2(0)}}\right| \cong 0,3\sqrt{\frac{\sigma_{Pz}^2}{\sigma^2}}. \qquad (9.158)$$

Considering the importance of mutual correlation in zero equal to -0.21 (see Figure 9.64), we calculate the value of the dispersion of vibration components ripple over the sensor 37:

$$\left.\begin{array}{l} \frac{\sigma_{Pz}^2}{\sigma^2} = \frac{(0,21)^2}{(0,3)^2} = 0,49 \\ \sigma_{Pz} = 0,7\sigma = 9,8 \text{ cm water} \end{array}\right\}. \qquad (9.159)$$

Variance components ripple beyond the control of vibration is $0.51\sigma^2$, which corresponds to the RMS deviation 10.1 cm of water. This result coincides with the data model tests.

Held reasoning can be repeated for the model, where the frequency of the vibrations of a plate in the water is about 30 Hz. It can be assumed that these vibrations gave a small high-frequency component on the model of the autocorrelation function (see Figure 9.59a). As the relative rigidity of the model plate is about 3 to 4 times more so in nature, then the variance of the vibrations could be expected to be about 10 to 15 times lower. The dispersion of the high-frequency components in the model are not above $\sigma^2_{Pz} = 0,7 \cdot 10^{-2}$ m² waters.

$$\frac{\sigma^2_{Pz}}{\sigma^2} = \frac{0,07}{2} = 0,035 = \frac{1}{14} 0,49.$$

Vibration plate significantly affects the results of measurements only in the decay of turbulence. In the generation of turbulence, component pressure associated with vibration plates, as well as the wave of the component are both relatively very small.

In the field of generation and decay of pulsations, we can have a value of aeration flow. The impact of aeration is manifested in various aspects. For example, the mean value, spectrum pressure pulsations and character of its change in length of the flow may depend on aeration. Using the known expression for the pulsating pressure on the surface of a sphere, vibrating in a liquid at low amplitude vibration, and, believing changes in pressure inside the bubble isothermal, we get:

$$\omega \cong \frac{1}{R_0}\sqrt{\frac{1}{\rho}\left(3\bar{p}_0 + \frac{2c}{R_0}\right)}, \tag{9.160}$$

ω_0 -frequency of natural oscillations of a bubble;
R_0 -is the radius of the bubble;
$\bar{p}_0$- static pressure outside of the bubble;
c - surface tension of water, with = 74 g/sec².

When R_0 = 1 cm, $\bar{p}_0$ = 10 m of water from (9.160) obtain ω = 1720 rad/sec, i.e. the natural frequency of the air bubble is very high.

Formula (9.160) gives the frequency centro-symmetric oscillations of the surface of the bubble, related to the compressibility of air. If to consider other forms of small oscillations of a bubble, then, not taking into account compressibility of air, you can get:

$$\omega = \frac{1}{R_0}\sqrt{(n+1)(n-1)(n+2)\frac{c}{\rho R_0}}. \tag{9.161}$$

Here n is the order of spherical functions (n= 1, 2, 3, 4 ...).

When R_0 = 1 cm received

$$\omega \cong 0; 30; 55; \quad 82\ldots\ 1/\text{sec}.$$

For $R_0 = 0{,}5\ cm$: $\omega \cong 0; 85; 155; 232\ldots\ 1/\text{sec}.$

Received frequency has lower forms of oscillations of a bubble commensurate with the frequency of turbulent pulsations. Apparently, the influence of aeration conditions decay of turbulence and high-frequency part of the spectrum can be substantial.

Based on the above we can conclude the following:

1. The structure of hydrodynamic pressure pulsations at the point of water fight dam varies along the length of the water fight.
2. At the beginning of the water fight, in the generation of turbulent pulsations, the main characteristics of pressure pulsations are defined by the "turbulent component and can be directly connected with the averaged flow above the water fight. On this site features of pressure pulsations, received in kind, and on the model scale 1:38, when modeling for Froude, differ slightly. Existing small difference can be explained by the dependence of the frequency of failure of small vortices with faces absorbers from the Reynolds number.
3. Turbulent component of ripples on the model quickly fade. Already in the middle of the water fight ripple, the bottom is actually defined by the wave fluctuations, penetrating to the surface of the water, and vibration water boards. When excluding the effects of vibration plate amplitude-frequency, the spectra of pulsations to the bottom in kind and in model scale is 1:38, when modeling for Froude practically coincides.
4. Distribution function of pressure pulsations on the seabed at the site of generation of pulsations is significantly different from the normal law. For the amplitude of rare depressions pressure, about 2 times more amplitude increases pressure (with equal probability). The distribution function of the fluctuations of surface water and pulsations at the bottom in the middle of the water fight is close to the normal law.
5. Vibration water boards in nature affect the pulsation pressure in the middle part (and, apparently, in the end) of water fight.

These findings were confirmed by careful experiments of O.F. Vasiliev and V.I. Bukreev [9a, 10a]. On their small installation (Figure 9.65) pressure pulsations were studied on a smooth bottom under perfect hydraulic jump arising from the expiration from under the shield.

Results were obtained for models with three geometrical scales – M=1:1, 1:2 и 1:4, meeting the changing of the Reynolds number from 3.7 10^5 to 4.7 10^4 with the same Froude amount in compressed section $U_1^2/gh_1=33$. Special attention was paid to the pressure sensors - diameter receiving area of the sensor was changed in proportion to the scale of the model - from 30 up to 7.5 mm. The rigidity of the sensor was extremely high - frequency not less than 250 Hz. The measurement results evaluated in "nature," by the standards of pulsations, differ not more than 7% (Figure 9.66).

The functions of probability distributions in the middle of the jump is close to the normal law, autocorrelation in the low-frequency range is not different (Figure 9.67).

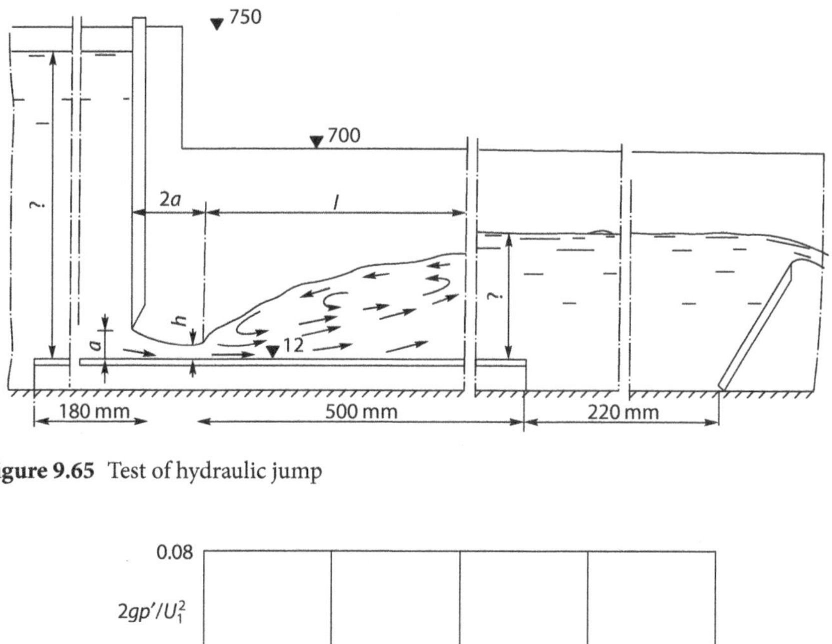

Figure 9.65 Test of hydraulic jump

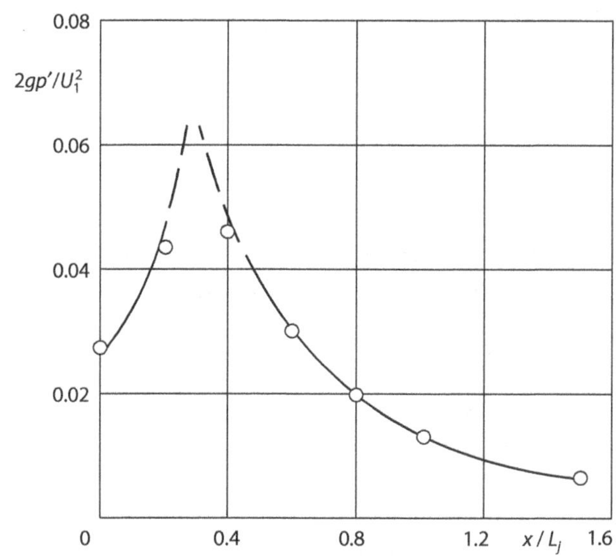

Figure 9.66 Changing standards of pressure pulsations on the length of the hydraulic jump.

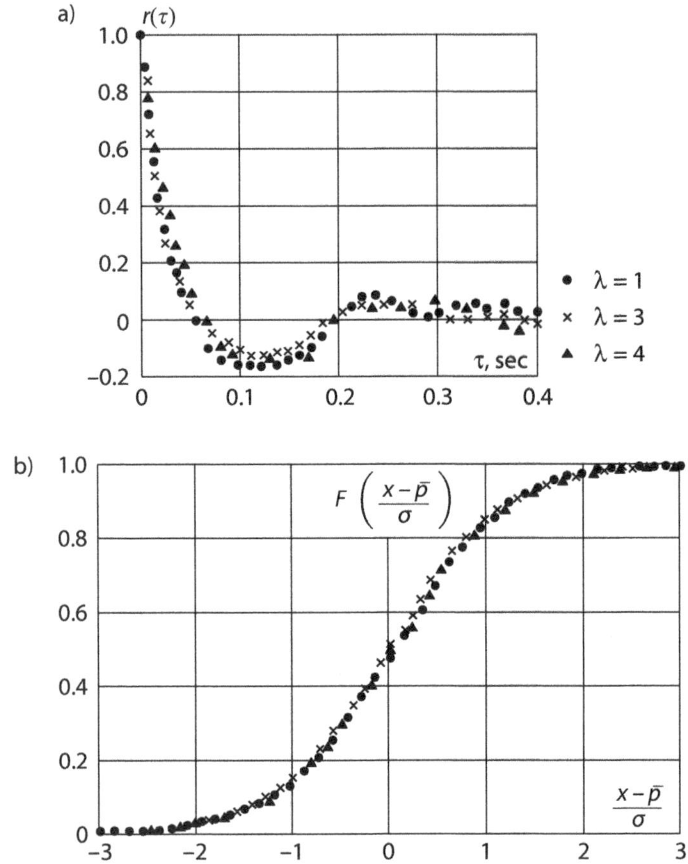

Figure 9.67 The normalized autocorrelation function (in nature) and the probability distribution function of pressure pulsation under the hydraulic jump in its middle part (x/L_j =0.4).

9.6.2 The Pulsation Pressure in the Head Spillway Measurement in Nature and Model

Features of pressure pulsations at the sharply non-uniform motion were studied in discharge spillway Chir-Urt HPP, in nature and on the model, in scale 1:20 [61a, 62a, 68a, 71a]. The station building consists of one block of a combined type. One of the power units at the plant, with installed capacity of 9 MW, has the turbine with a rotor diameter of 5.0 m. The peculiarity of the energy conduit HPP is the presence of female suction pipe and supply camera simplified geometric forms (Figure 9.68). Pressure idling spillways block are symmetrical in the axis of the unit and also simplicity of form.

The spillway of Chir-Urt HPP has a rectangular cross-section height of 2.0 ± 0.1 m and width 5.5 ± 0,1 m. The entrance to the spillway is made in the form of a rectangle with a small ledge to support the repair of the shutter. The flow through the spillway is regulated by the gate from the side of the downstream water. Maximum flow rate at the head 6.6 m is 110 m³/sec. The Reynolds number in this case reaches $\frac{Uh}{\nu} = \frac{10^3 \cdot 200}{0{,}01} = 2 \cdot 10^7$. To the model in the appropriate regime, the Reynolds number is $2.3 \cdot 10^5$; U - average speed in the spillway.

Research was chosen right, adrift, the spillway of the block. During construction in the canopy, there were mounted embedded parts under recording devices and pipes for output measurement cables. To break the vacuum with input tip at a distance of 0.5 m from sharp edges, at axis overlap, flush with it, a special tube was installed with a diameter of 150 mm. The other end of it was on the right calf powerhouse and had a valve to regulate the flow of air. Consumption of water, flowing through the station, was calculated on the field of velocities measured in supply channel HPP by gauging turnTables.

The reception part of the applied pressure sensors DD 10 had a round plate thickness (0.3 ± 0.05 mm) made of conductive material (Figure 9.69).

The frequency of the main tone free oscillations of this plate was ≈ (0,8 - 0,4)$\cdot 10^5$ Hz.

Maximum load on pressure transducers during tests and static calibration does not exceed 20 m of water. Appropriate greatest deflection plates of the sensor do not exceed 0.04 mm, and stresses in the material do not exceed 800 kg/cm², which is significantly lower than the yield strength of this material, and is equal to $2 \cdot 10^3$ kg/cm².

Vibration overlap was recorded with special type instruments and specialists from the column-like characteristics in the range of 5 to 200 Hz. The external diameter of the pressure sensor was 22 mm, the effective diameter was 13 mm. The model and in kind used the sensors of the same type. The difference in relative diameter of the sensor generates an error, for which the variance of the low-frequency components could reach 25%. Appropriate adjustments were made according to the method set out in paragraph 9.1.

Air flow in the duct was determined by flow meter, operating on the principle of measurement of the deficit pressure compared with

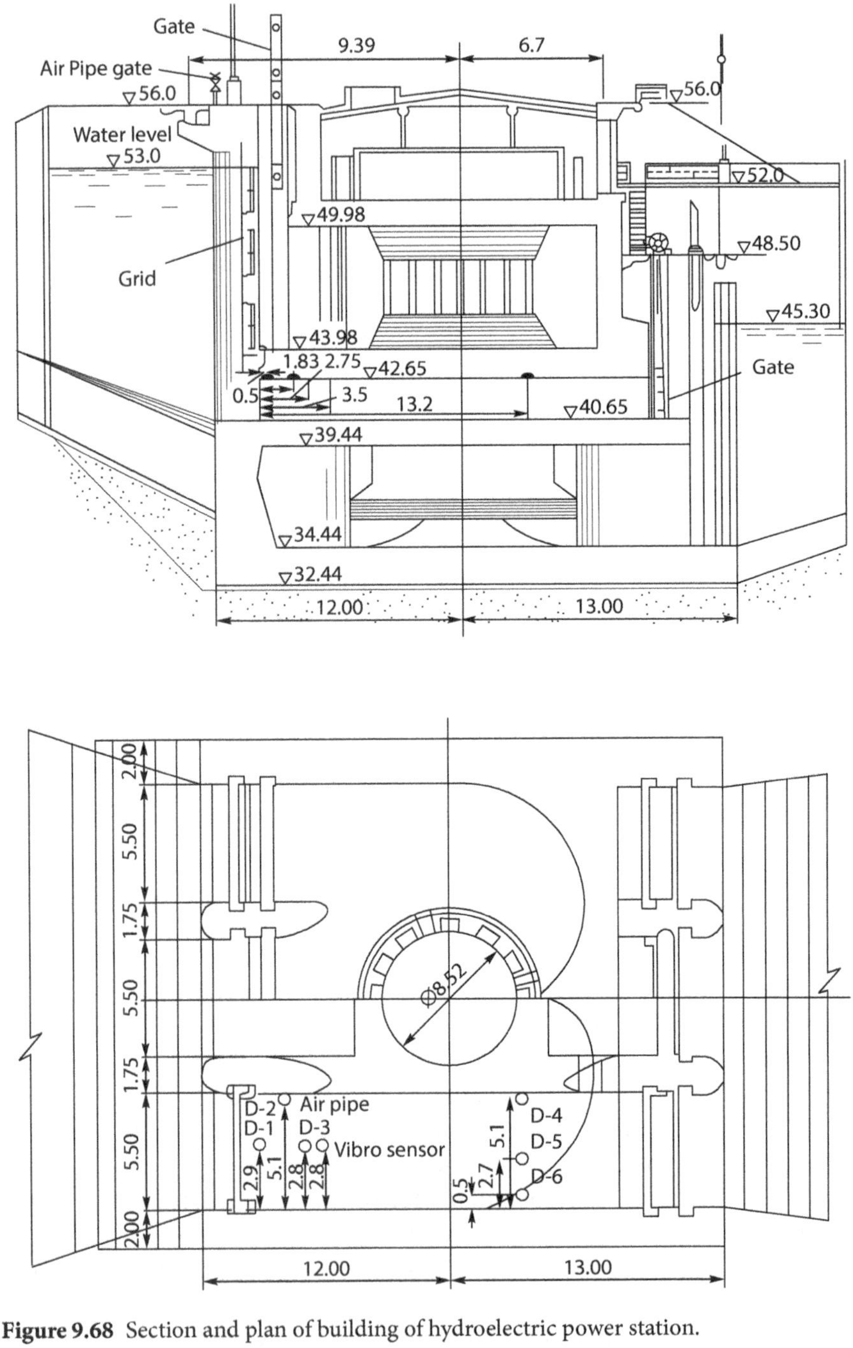

Figure 9.68 Section and plan of building of hydroelectric power station.

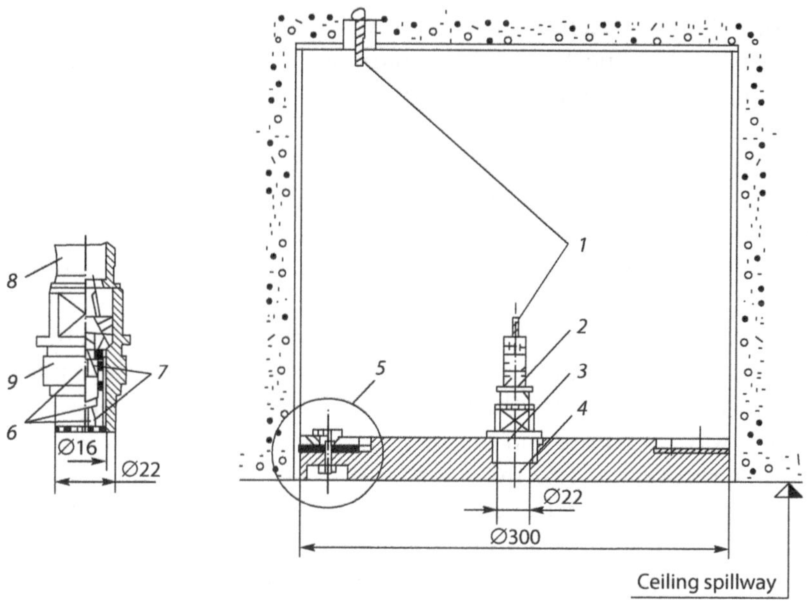

Figure 9.69 Pressure transmitter DC-10 and the scheme of installation of the sensor in blocking spillway

1 - cable SRPS 3x1.5; 2-sealed connector; 3-inductive sensor pressure; 4-membrane; 5-the fixing of the mortgage part in the overlap; 6 - magnetic circuit; 7-inductors; 8-connector; 9-sensor housing.

atmospheric, almost unseparated at the entrance to the pipe. The pressure in the "throat" of air pressure meter was measured using alcohol or mercury manometer.

To confirm the stability characteristics of the sensors when working in real conditions measurements were carried out of static (averaged) pressures in the spillway. Directly after the experiment was closed with a shutter spillway and at the same oscillographes, the tape recorded the level of the upstream. In parallel with the work of the spillway pressure was measured in a closed air tube filled with air. Because the sensor D-1 and outlet ducts are very close to each other (Figure 9.68), it was considered that the averaged pressure in them was equal. Such measurements, repeated several times during the period of observations, confirmed the stability of calibration coefficients sensors.

Studies have attempted to assess the dynamic characteristics of overlap spillway by excitation of free oscillations in air and in water. Fluctuations were caused by the impact of the cargo in the center of the span beams.

Tests of water have been conducted with lowered operational gate spillway and the water level upstream of the mark of the top floor. Simultaneously, the testimony of the vibration transducer and pressure sensors were recorded.

Figure 9.70 shows the distribution of the averaged velocity and pressure measurement in nature (1) and model (11). At the beginning of the spillway, is observed separation and compression of the stream up to 0.65 from the height of the spillway, and intense vortex under the ceiling of the spillway. Vortex under the ceiling finishes at the distance of 4 of the entrance. Vacuum under the ceiling is 4 meters of water. On the model in the same terms, vacuum is 0.22 m (4.4 M. the translation in nature). Throughput of the spillway was 4% more than in kind. With simultaneous operation of both spillways in nature and on the model, there was a clearly visible difference in recovery of 1.62 m:

Averaged picture of trends in the spillway with the full opening of the gate (Figure 9.70) and when the shutter opens to 50%, the model is the same as in nature. However, the pulsation pressure was significantly different. Figure 9.71 shows the example entries pressure sensors 3 and 5 have in nature and the model.

These waveforms show how great pressure pulsations are in comparison with the average time difference piezometric levels. As you can see, the difference in piezometric heights sensor 3 amounts to about 2.2, and velocity head at the spillway has the same order of magnitude of pressure pulsations on this sensor.

A case in which calculation of constructions on brittle fracture is of particular importance is in the maximum amplitude of pressure pulsations. The determination of this characteristic directly on realization is possible, however, the accuracy of the result, given the limited duration T of the implementations are very small. Even at T/τ_0 =500, maximum sweep of 50 % probability, a certain implementation may differ on ± (40% to 50)% of the average scale that meets the selected duration of implementation (Figure 9.72).

Figure 9.72 shows examples of processing of records of pulsations, illustrating the variation of the maximum amplitude. Figure 9.70 shows that when the duration of observation is 70 sec

(T/τ_0=1200), values of scope ($2gA/U^2$) for individual implementations (in constant terms) change from 1.7 to 2.3, i.e. in a range of 15 % from the mean values ($\langle 2gA/U^2 \rangle = 2$).

The same Figure shows the dependence of the maximum of the scale of observation period (one experience). The increase in time of observation

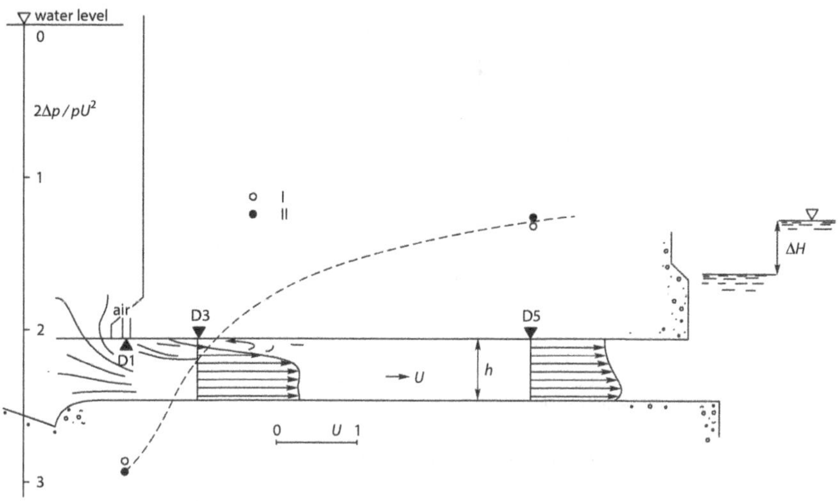

Figure 9.70 Circuit currents and average pressure on the ceiling of the spillway. I – nature, II – model.

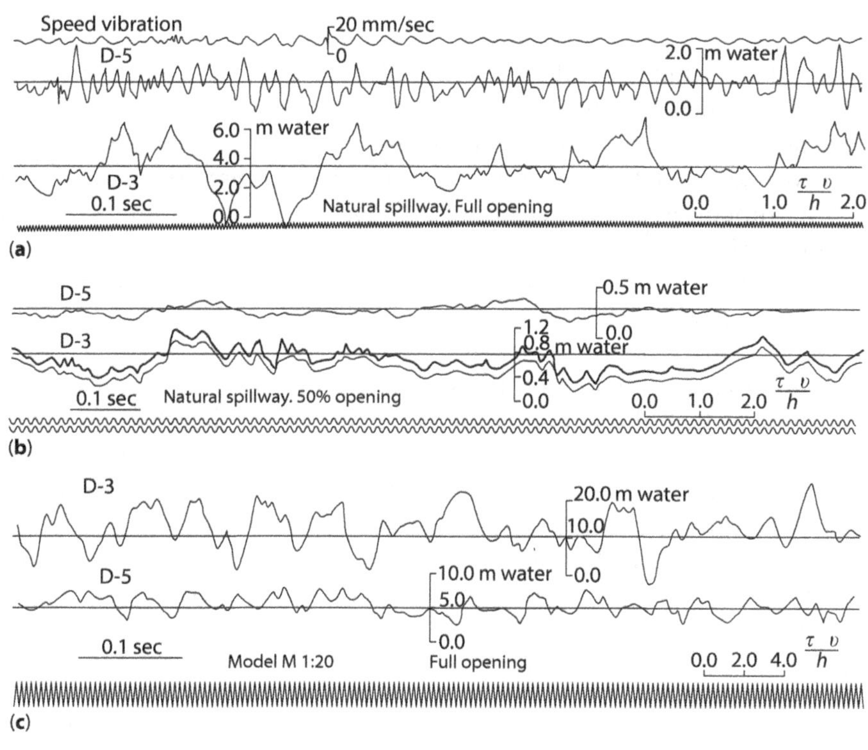

Figure 9.71 The results of measurements. The top - gate is fully opened, nature. Lower - opening of the gate by 50%, nature. The lowest - full opening of the model.

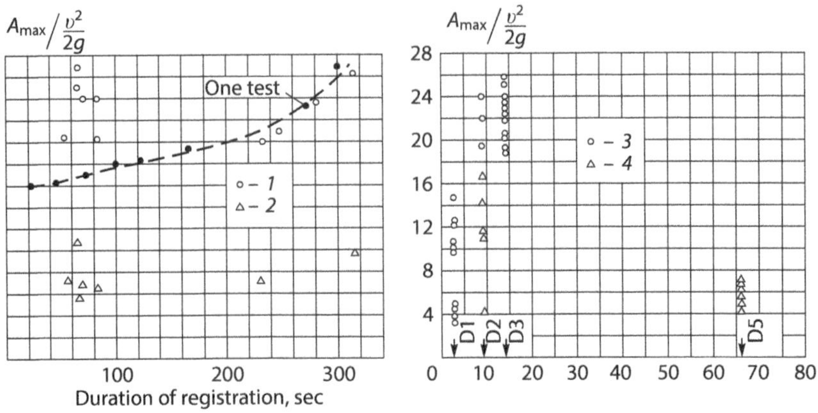

Figure 9.72 The maximum magnitude of pressure pulsations

1 - sensor D-3; 2 - sensor D-5; 3 - normal operation; 4 - an air (1.46 m^3/sec) to the head of stream. L - the distance from the top edge of the overlap spillway to measuring points, h –height of spillway.

from 100 to 300 seconds (i.e. from T/τ_0 = 1500 to 4500) caused an increase in the amplitude of almost 1.3 times (from 1.8 to 2.3 $U^2/2g$). At constant observation time, equal to 25 seconds (T/τ_0=400÷1000), variation swings (as defined in different implementations) are characterized by the functions of the density of a probability distribution, shown in Figure 9.73

From these data, extreme relative magnitude: sensor 3 $(A/\sigma)_{min}$ =6.5, $(A/\sigma)_{max}$=9.5; $<(A/\sigma)>$=8 sensor 5 $(A/\sigma)_{min}$ =6.7, $(A/\sigma)_{max}$=10.1;$<(A/\sigma)>$=7.9

The pulsation pressure on the sensor 5 in nature has a relatively narrower range than the sensor 3. Therefore, despite the fact that the relative length is (T/τ_0) of recording on sensor 5 above, the variation of the maximum amplitude on the records of the sensor 5 is longer than on the record sensor 3, which is consistent with the theory (p. 9.1).

Figure 9.74 mapped the autocorrelation function received by the sensor 3 in the natural environment with the full opening of shutter (1), and when the shutter is open for 50% (line 2). The gate is located at the end of the spillway, so the flow pattern over the sensor 3 has not been changed, but absolute pressure has been changed.

At all points on the ceiling spillway absolute pressure is at partial opening of shutter of more than 10 m of water. (vacuum not). In both cases,

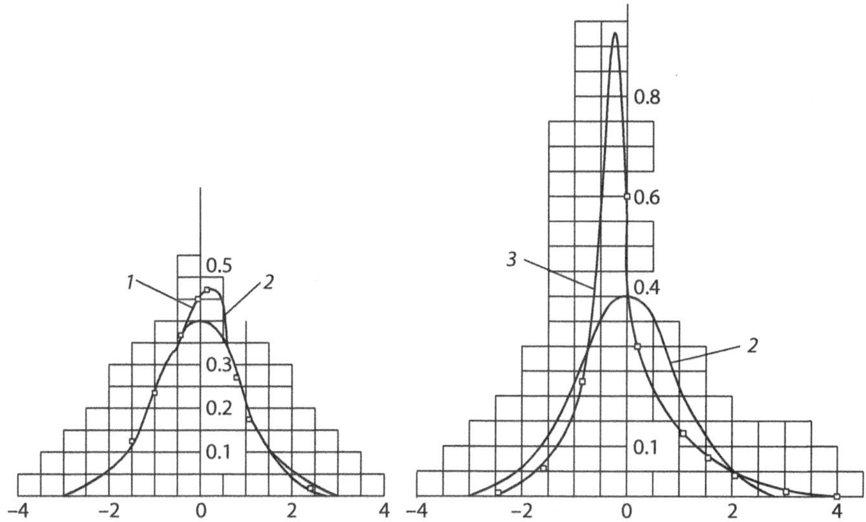

Figure 9.73 The probability distribution function of pressure pulsation in nature. Full opening on the horizontal axis is (p-<p>)/p'. 1 - sensor 5; 2 - normal law; 3 – sensor 3.

the correlation function ripple in kind differs with sharp increase of R(t) when $\tau \to 0$. It indicates a very wide range of pulsations, on the availability of high-frequency perturbations with very small linear dimensions. The relative standard of pressure pulsations on D3, with the full opening of the shutter, was $2p'/\rho U^2 = 0.305$ (sensor 5 - $2p'/\rho U^2 = 0.058$), and when opening the shutter for a 50% only $2p'/\rho U^2 = 0.238$.

A comparison of the records of pulsations and correlation functions was obtained by sensor 3 in nature when the Reynolds number, differing only about 2 times (Figure 9.74), shows that the difference in $R(\tau)$ when $\tau \to 0$ cannot be explained only be influence of the Reynolds number. We can assume that it has a value of absolute pressure in the flow. At a sufficiently high vacuum it is possible to have local education and destruction of bubbles of air, causing a kind of shock. When you pass through the spillway with less spending pressure along the length of the spillway, positively, the high frequency component of the aeration of origin is lost.

Pressure pulsations on the model were registered by sensors of various types. In one and the same point, corresponding to the position D3, were applied 3 sensor DD-10 with a control pressure characterizing the rigidity of the membrane, - 0.8, 2.4 and 5 kg/cm^2, the normal load cell (TD with

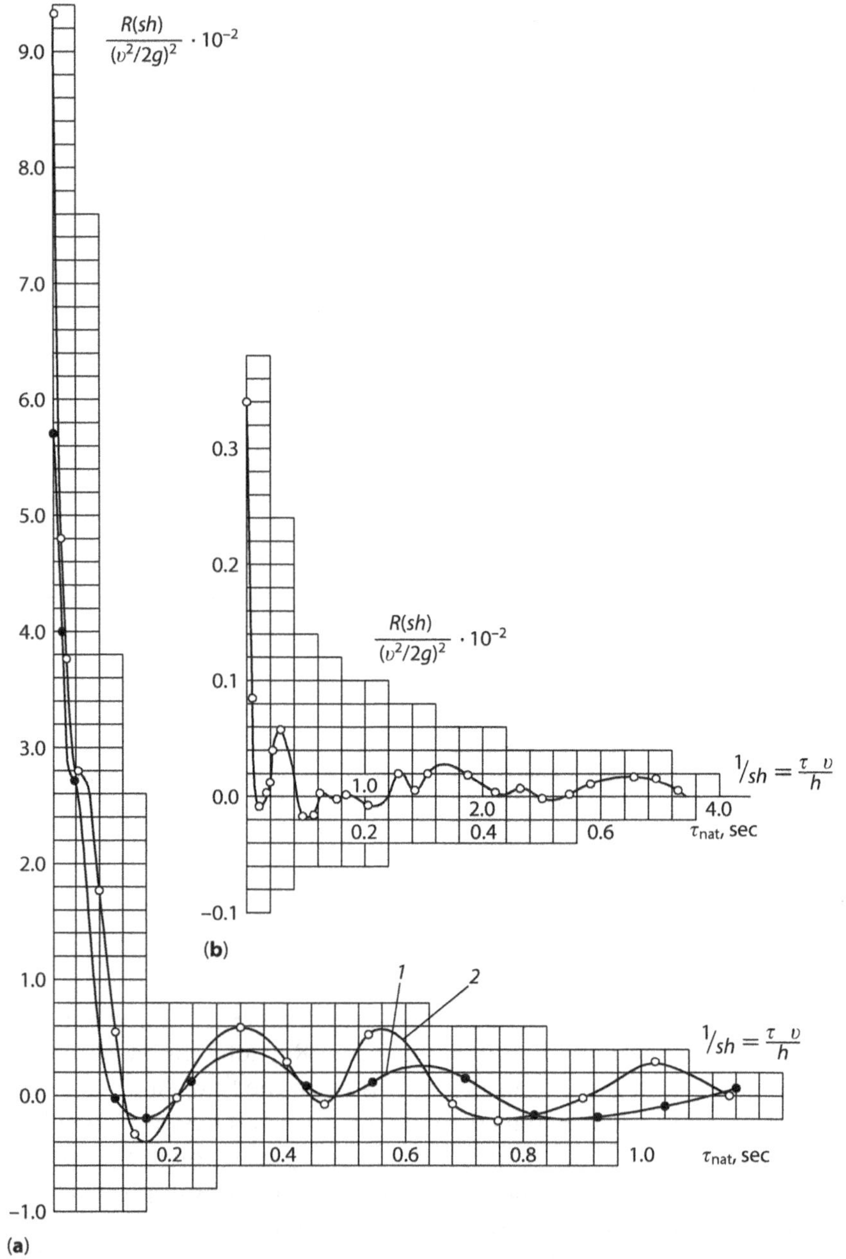

Figure 9.74 The autocorrelation function of pressure pulsations on the sensor 3 (left) with the full opening of shutter (empty points-1) and when it opens to 50% (black dots -2). The same from sensor 5 if the full opening (on the right). Nature.

membranes with diameter of 8 mm) and inductive sensor (ID) with hole diameter 1mm.

Standards of pressure pulsation, recorded by different sensors in the same mode, found the complete opening of the spillway gates were different - in sensors D - $2p'/\rho U^2 = 0.155; 0.175; 0.212$. The load cell $2p'/\rho U^2=0.137$, ID $2p'/\rho U^2=0.151$. In position sensor 5, the most strained sensor DD and inductive sensor gave almost the same results $2p'/\rho U^2=0.060$ and 0.053.

Ripple recorded by sensors shows that in nature, sensors 4 and 6 have similar ripple to the sensor 5. On the record surge in nature there is almost a periodic component with a frequency of about 20÷25 Hz. This component was evident in the autocorrelation function (Figure 9.74). Oscillation frequency registered and vibrograph working in the record mode the speed of overlap spillway. Waveform is clear that when the vibration frequency fades away, disappears, and this component pressure pulsations. Mutual correlation function of pressure pulsations and vibration velocity has a sharp maximum at $\tau = 0.012$ sec (Figure 9.75).

Mutual correlation functions interval between the first adjacent peaks function is 0.04 sec. All these circumstances suggest that the component of pressure pulsations with a frequency of 20÷25 Hz are connected with vibration overlap. Similar influence of vibration on the surge was observed and in other cases (see p. 9.3). Since the maximum of mutual correlation function is shifted by about a quarter of the prevailing period of vibration, we can assume that in this case, the main interaction design and the water

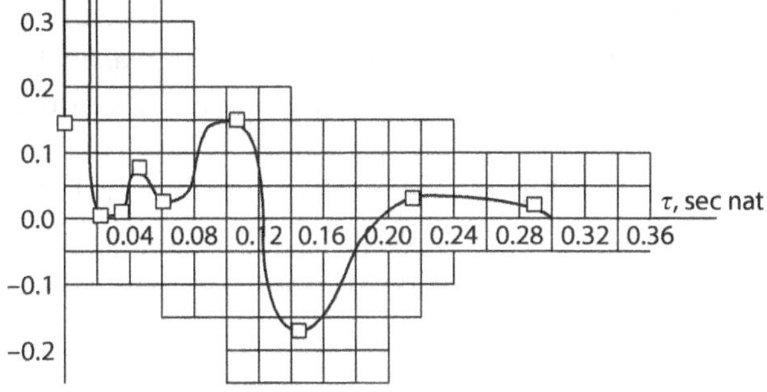

Figure 9.75 Mutual correlation function of pressure pulsations on the sensor 5 and the rate of vibration of overlap spillway with the full opening.

is due to the acceleration vibration, i.e. vibration component pressure pulsations can be presented in the form:

$$p_z = m_{\text{ad}} a = m_{\text{ad}} \frac{\partial^2 z}{\partial t^2},$$

where m_{ad} - mass of connected water layer from the side of the spillway;

a - acceleration vibration;

z - coordinate of the moving floors, measured in the positive direction down from the ceiling.

Dispersion of vibration components of pulsation pressure in the known spectral density of the rate of vibration is determined by the expression:

$$\sigma_{Pz}^2 = 2m_{\text{ad}}^2 \int_0^{\infty} \omega^2 S_\upsilon(\omega) d\omega = m_{\text{ad}}^2 \sigma_a^2.$$

From this expression, you can define the m_{ad}, if known p', and $S_v(\omega)$. In this case the thickness of the "attached" water layer was approximately equal to the height of the spillway.

The air supply in the area of vacuum dramatically changes the mode of vibration of overlap. In this regard record type pulsation of pressure sensors 4, 5 and 6 varies significantly. On the correlation function, there can only be a component that is associated with the activities of the drum (Figure 9.76).

The mode of pulsation in nature in the area of sensor 3 is essentially changed, i.e. with air supply removing the cause of the high-frequency pulsations aeration of origin. The relative dispersion of pulsations sharply decreases to values of the same order, which has been observed by the partial opening of the spillway. Standard pulsation pressure sensor 3 with supply air (air velocity in the duct 1.54 m/s), decreased from 1.515 m to 1.18 m of water, and according to the sensor 5, from 0.29 to 0.24 m of water.

Opening the shutters has no impact on aeration and stops vibration ceiling spillway (in kind). In this case, the correlation function at point 5 on the model and the function in kind are satisfactorily in agreement (Figure 9.77).

Similar results are obtained for sensor 3 if we take into account the influence of the size of the receiving area of the sensor on the model. The low value of the leading frequency of pulsations observed on the model and in

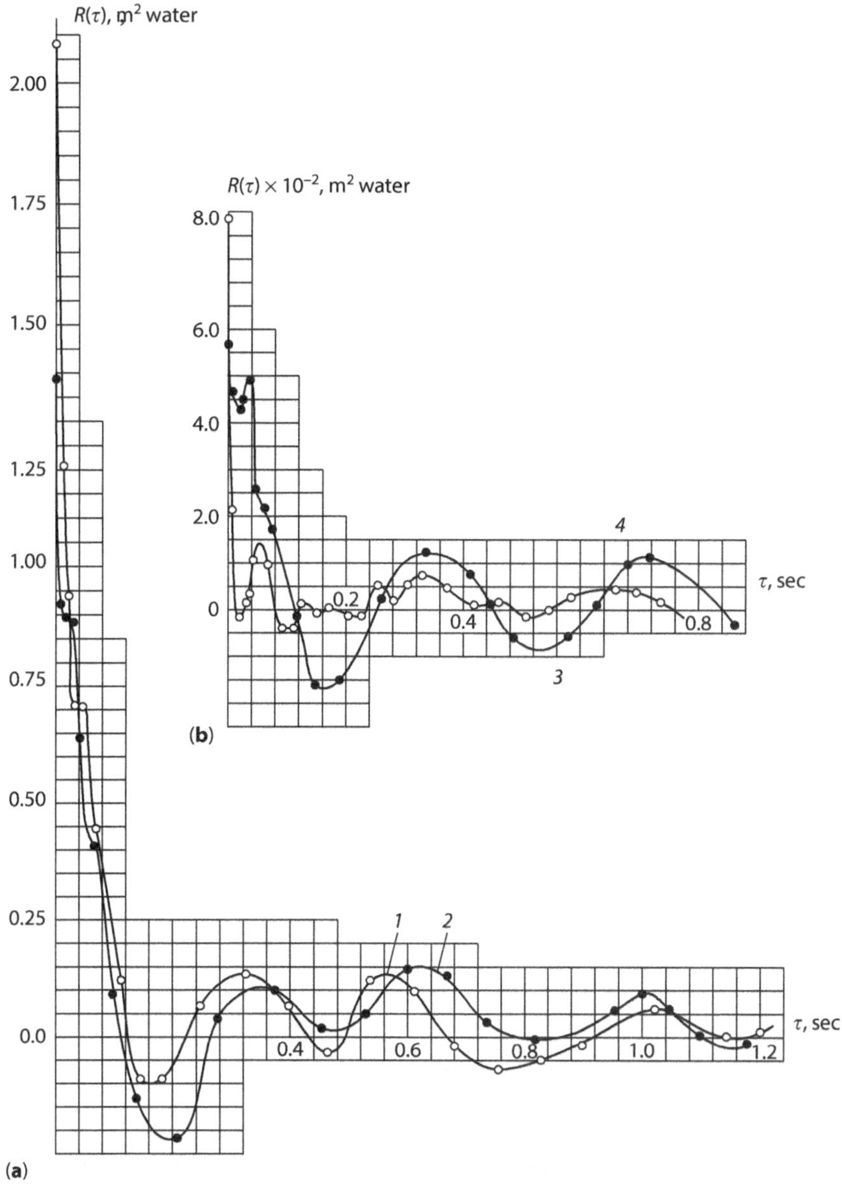

Figure 9.76 The autocorrelation function of pressure pulsations based on the sensor readings D-3 (left) and at the sensor readings D-5 (right, top); 1 and 3-without air filing (empty dots); 2 and 4 with supply air 1,54 m^3 / sec.

kind for half-opening can be explained by the influence of the Reynolds criterion.

The overlap of the spillway was a rectangular plate size in the plan (5,5 x 16) m^2, and of a thickness of 1.33 m, with three parties fully restrained and one free.

Analysis of free oscillations of a plate should give information about its dynamic characteristics, i.e. dynamic module of elasticity and the absorption coefficient of the energy of oscillations.

For this purpose, first of all, it is necessary to know the interval for the implementation, which would enable the assessment of fluctuations

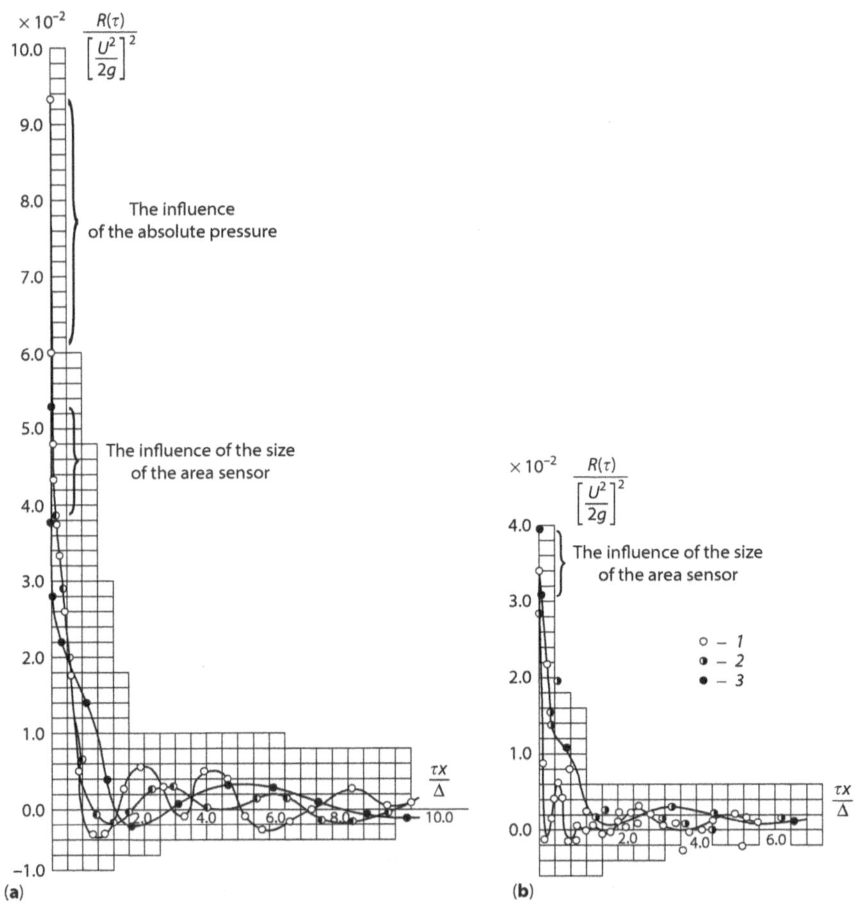

Figure 9.77 The autocorrelation function of pressure pulsations based on the sensor readings D-3 (left) and at the sensor readings D-5 (right); and 3. 1-full opening of the spillway without air, 2 - the floodgates are open halfway. 1 and 2 of measurement in kind, 3 – dimension on model.

without the imposition on them of distortions, caused by reflection of deformation waves propagating in the stove after impact.

The calculation made for slabs, showed that the speed of propagation of a wave deformation is of the order of 200 m/sec. Thus, the interval of realization of free oscillations, which will not affect the imposition of the reflected waves is $3.5 \bullet 10^{-2}$ seconds.

This result apparently explains some increase in the amplitude of oscillations at the end of time 3•10-2 seconds from the moment of impact that can be traced on implementations (Figure 9.78).

Considering only the area without distortion, you can specify the frequency of free vibrations of overlap spillway in the air with some variance associated with measurement errors, different points of application of impact and other factors, averaged 104 Hz, and the coefficient of absorption of energy calculated on the damping of oscillations, & psi ≈ 0,52.

Dynamic modulus of elasticity is easily calculated if you know the frequency of free vibrations and expressions to define it.

So for a plate fixed on three sides, according to [106]:

$$f = 3{,}56\sqrt{1 - 0{,}57\eta^2 + 0{,}47\eta^4}\sqrt{\frac{D}{\mu l^4}},$$

where $\eta = \frac{l}{b}$ is the ratio of the parties plates;

μ - linear mass;

f - frequency free vibrations;

D - cylindrical rigidity of the plate.

Certain of this formula is the modulus of elasticity of overlap amounting to $E = 2 \bullet 10^5\,kg/cm^2$.

Analysis of oscillations of overlap becomes considerably complicated in the presence of water in the catchment. In the experiments, the water flooded the spillway so that its upstream level was at 1.4 m above the ceiling of the spillway. Work shutter spillway was omitted.

The experiment has shown (Figure 9.78) that the frequency of free vibrations in the water rose to 135 Hz, and the coefficient of absorption on average to ψ= 2,0. This effect is similar to the introduction into the system of additional ("connected") rigidity and "attached" to friction.

In the initial period of operation of the spillway, when the turbine Luggage had no time to fill with water, the entry of forced oscillations was carried out at low pressure at the station and a short opening in the gate to full height. In this case, the implementations traced mainly only intermittently active vibrations overlapping with frequencies (100 to 135) and 50

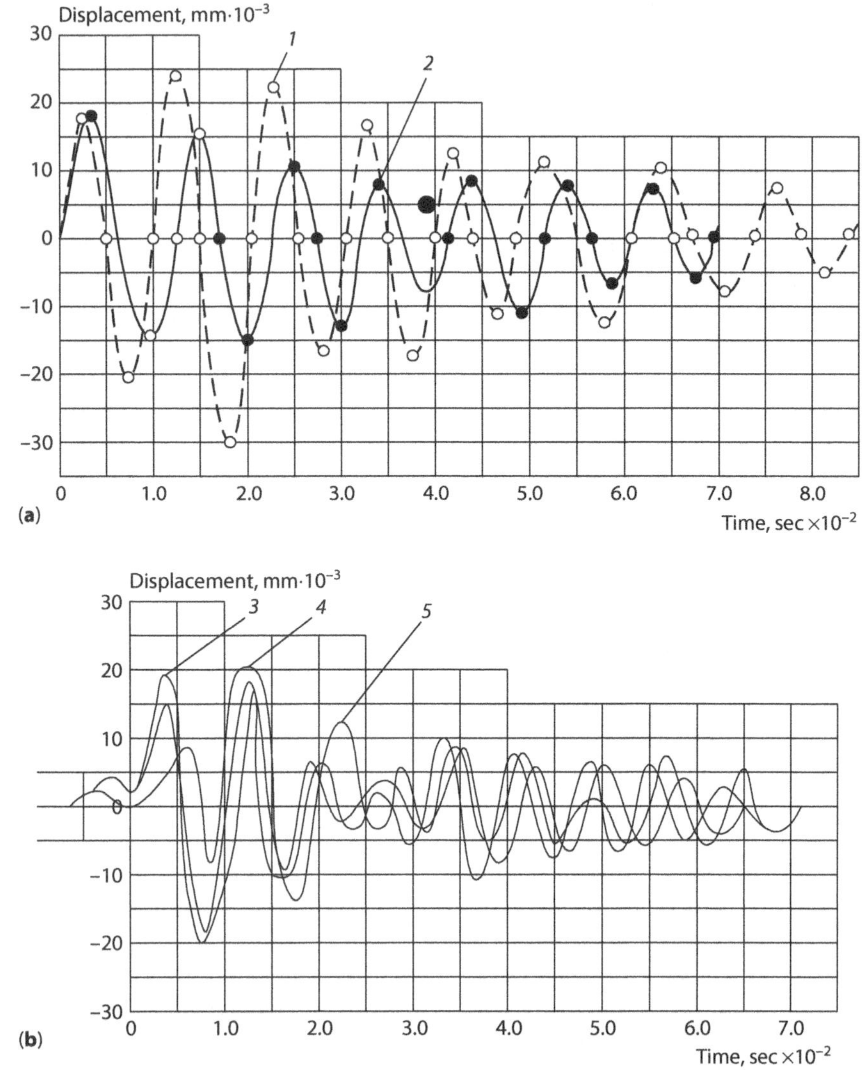

Figure 9.78 Account fluctuations (displacement) of overlap in the air (top) and in the water (low); 1-5-repeat tests.

Hz. The average interval between blows was changed depending on what was served in the air spillway or not, within 0,186 up in 0.288 sec.

A similar phenomenon can be explained, apparently, by the presence in the spectrum of pressure pulsations with rare transient impulses. Their presence is confirmed by the form of the correlation function of pressure pulsation, taken at least sensor D-3 (Figure 9.74). And these impulses, acting on a small area of overlap and having a frequency close to the frequency of natural oscillations of overlap, imitate the phenomenon of blow.

Having frequency 50 Hz may indicate the emergence of cracks in the termination, and the transition of overlap is different from the original scheme bearing with two hinges.

In conditions of normal operation of the spillway, when it was typed in the full pressure on the station, and the turbine chamber was filled with water, static and dynamic loads on the floor had increased (up to 15 - 17 t/m2). The natural frequency overlap fell sharply. The system began to take more than low-frequency pulses, continuing to fluctuate on its own frequency. Due to load growth in the spectrum of oscillations of overlap, there appeared components at frequencies corresponding to the maximum spectral density of the load.

This is evidenced by the autocorrelation function of vibration (Figure 9.79), which along with the natural frequency of the plate, there can be traced frequency (4,0 and 1.5 Hz), caused by rotation and instability waltz flow to the tip.

Research has shown that the pulsation pressure in the pressure water conduits essentially depends on unsaturated flow (due to the air supply

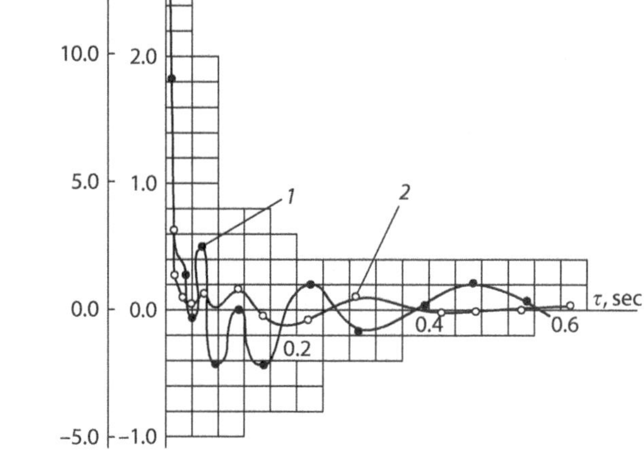

Figure 9.79 The autocorrelation function of speed (2) and movements (1) overlap spillway vibration.

or cavitation) and on compliance of the borders of hydrogen (vibration designs). These phenomena on conventional hydraulic models may lead to the distortion of the results. After exclusion of aeration and vibration component dispersion of pressure pulsation, adjusted for differences in size landings, sensors in areas of high-intensity turbulence on the data model and nature are consistent satisfactorily.

The General conclusion from the presented systematic comparisons of measurements of pressure pulsations on objects of different sizes, including full-scale tests, is that in the presence of a large-scale sources of pulsations (area separated flow, hydraulic jump, etc.), low-frequency part of the spectrum pressure pulsations close to the self-similarity in the open flow, modeled by the Froude criterion. In the absence of such a main source of perturbations, the situation becomes more complicated – it can manifest in the influence of measuring instruments (rigidity and dimensions of the pressure sensor), and clearly aeration, cavitation and the deformability of boundaries can act as influences.

9.4.3 Complex Modeling of Stress Under Hydrodynamic Loads

The hydrodynamic forces acting on elements of hydraulic structures, are a typical example of non-conservative load. Playing "witness" to the nature of the load not reproducing flow, in general is very difficult. Ripple hydrodynamic loads usually appear as random processes with a rather wide range. The shape of the spectrum pulsations depending on hydraulic conditions can be very diverse. In some cases hydrodynamic loading is dependent on the reaction of the construction on this burden. These situations, often representing the greatest danger for the construction, are studied in the framework of the "aeroelasticity." [21a, 29a, 51a, 58a, 77a, 86a, 92a, 95a, 101a, 105a, 106a]. The study of the effects of hydroelasticity on models is possible only in a case when the scale movements (deformations) structures under the action of hydrodynamic loads are equal to a linear scale model.

For running a model that is geometrically similar in nature (including the similarity of the relative roughness of the walls of water pipes), a necessary condition of dynamic similarity is discussed in the preliminary parts of the book.

Significant changes in the flow rate, characteristic of unsteady regime, need to be included in the consideration of the relative hardness of the water and construction. The similarity conditions in this case are complemented by Mach-Maievskiy:

$$C/U = idem \tag{9.162}$$

C - the minimum speed of propagation of elastic waves in a stream;

The conditions of similarity provide the proportionality of a difference of pressure in any point of the flow velocity head in the typical cross-section.

$$\Delta p/\rho U^2 = idem \text{ –Euler number} \tag{9.163}$$

As a consequence, kinematic similarity flows scale, with a frequency of disturbances that occur in the flow, is directly expressed in terms of the scale and speed linear scale model:

$$\omega L/U = idem \text{ – Strouhal number} \tag{9.164}$$

ω - frequency of disturbances.

In the case when the condition (9.162) is not met, the pressure changes, such as those associated with the phenomenon of hydraulic shock, may be proportional to the first degree of the flow velocity:

$$\Delta p/\rho CU = idem \tag{9.165}$$

In cases where hydraulic models are constructed without special restrictions, based only on a study of steady-state regimes, and on this model - the effects of water hammer, the translation pressure ratio (9.163) loads values obtained in the model will usually be overstated. The usual hydraulic models condition of Froude imposes strict limitations on the speed of the flow on the model. In the first chapters of the book, it is shown that in cases when the form of the boundaries of the stream does not depend on velocity (pressure motion or movement with a free surface in small numbers Froude), the condition Froude can be omitted. In this case, the water flow on the model and speed of model stream can vary widely.

Modeling of stress state

We will consider the simplest case - simulation of elastic constructions of homogeneous material. If the time of stress relaxation is much more, the time to load changes stress state structures, and you can just define the assignment of relative strain tensor and the elastic constants of the material (longitudinal module of elasticity E and shear modulus G).

The greatest interest for hydrotechnical constructions may be conditions modeling transverse movement of beams and plates. The system of equations describing the lateral movement of the neutral axis beams or slabs, consists of three groups of equations:

1. linking design variations with longitudinal wave motion in a stream, flowing design;

2. linking design variations with the wave movements in the environment (soil), bordering the design;
3. reflecting the dynamic equilibrium of the forces directly in cross section design.

Equations of first and second groups, in some cases, can be omitted, and their influence is taken into account by the introduction of "attached" mass of the water and joined mass of soil. The effect of contact environments usually affects, mostly inertialy (reactive), the resistance of the structure. Changing the active resistance, characterized by the module imaginary part of the added masses, is usually small. However, in some cases (when estimating the resonance events) accounting for this change is needed.

The real part of an associated mass m_{ad}, proportional to the density of contact environment and the cube of the linear size:

$$m_{ad} /\rho L^3 = idem \quad (9.166)$$

Therefore, the relative impact of virtual viscosity model will be the same, as in nature. The added mass in the high-frequency oscillations depends on the frequency of oscillations. Similarity condition associated with this dependence is similar to the condition of similarity hydraulic shock:

$$\omega L/C = idem \quad (9.167)$$

Applying the similarity transformation to well-known equations of elastic oscillations of beams and plates, we find, as a condition of similarity, requirement of invariance in the nature and on the ratio of the following forces:

elasticity and inertia

$$mL^2 U^2/EI = idem \quad (9.168)$$

pressure and weight

$$\rho U^2/g\delta(\rho-\rho_1) = idem \quad (9.169)$$

inertia in the design and contact environment (similar to the added masses)

$$\rho\delta /L \rho_1 = idem \quad (9.170)$$

δ - the thickness of restricting the flow plates or beams,

ρ- the density of the material of the border,

ρ_1 - the density of the medium (water or soil)

When modeling the elastic foundation, you must perform additional conditions of similarity external forces acting on the base, and reactive forces repulse the grounds of the forces of elasticity bases and forces of elastic beams (or plate). If the beam is geometrically similar in nature:

δ /L = idem and installed in conventional hydraulic model g=idem, ρ_1 =idem,

modeling conditions take an especially simple form:

$$U/\sqrt{L} = \text{idem}, \ \rho = \text{idem}, \ E/L = \text{idem}.$$

The condition of equivalence of deformations can be written in the form of the ratio of the magnitude (symbol M):

$$M_U/M_L^{0.5}=1, \ M_\rho=1, \ M_E/M_L=1$$

The complexity of integrated modeling is to use material with a certain module of elasticity and density. In the publications [59a] shows the composition of the material, allowing to model reinforced concrete structures in scales from 1/5 up to 1/40*). If the mass of the structure has little effect on the oscillations may be allowed distortion of the thickness scale design:

$$M_\rho M_\delta /M_L = 1 \qquad (9.171)$$

$$M_E \, M_\delta^3/M_L^4 = 1 \qquad (9.172)$$

In the pressure flow you can assign scale forces out of touch with linear scale model. This allows exemption from the requirement of equality of density of the material models and nature, which opens up the possibility of using the distortion scale model elements and facilitates selection of the material for the model. If we need to receive a large-scale wall thickness of the border, we should use heavier material with possibly lower modulus of elasticity on the model. According to the author [1] using as a placeholder, minium, and as a modifier Thiokol, it is possible to obtain a material with a share of close to 5 g/cm^3 and with the modulus of elasticity of 10^4 kg/cm^2. The scale of the thickness of the steel shell in this case can be 1:6 .5, and the scale of the flow velocity of the water 1:3 .3. If the influence of the added masses of water cannot be neglected, terms of selection of material for the model are more difficult. In this case the module of elasticity of the material is uniquely determined and adopted by the density of the material and linear scale model (Figure 9.80):

The scale of velocity is determined by the expression:

[1] Lyatkher V.M. Modeling of the stress state of structures under the action of hydrodynamic loads, Trudy Hydroproject, v.10, 1963

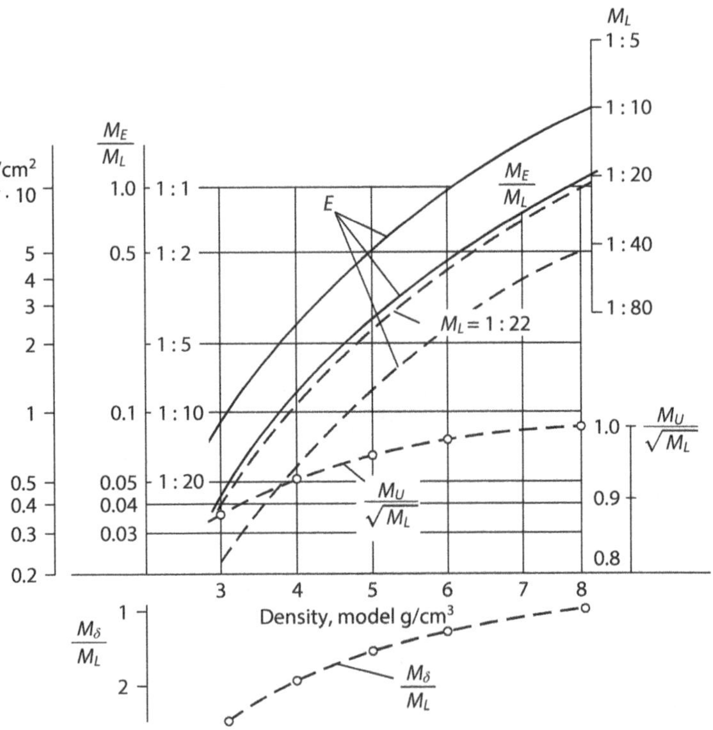

Figure 9.80 The ratio of the characteristic scale modeling of dynamic strain in density-based material model.

$$M_{(\rho-1)}\ M_\delta/M_U^2 = 1,$$

the scale of the thickness δ of a covering - an expression (9.173).

Complex modeling was applied to test pressure spillway at Chir-Urtskiy hydroelectric power station (Dagestan, Russia)[60a] and HPP building in Naglu (Afghanistan)[2]. The overlap of the spillway is made in the form of iron-concrete plate size h m thick 1.33m. Own frequency of fluctuations in the air is 104 Hz; in stagnant water (the shutter is closed, the water level of 0.5 m above the ceiling) it is 135 Hz. In the initial period of work of the spillway with the full opening of the gates, vibration overlap was with a frequency of 100-135 Hz. After long work, under pressure, oscillation rate fell to 16 to 20 Hz. A reduction in the frequency could be the result

[2] Voinov Yu.P. Investigation of the stress state of a fragment of the hydro power house under the action of hydrodynamic loads, Proceedings of coordination meetings on hydraulic engineering, issue 28, M-L., 1966, pp. 235-239

of cracks. Maximum mutually correlation function of pressure pulsations and vibration velocity shifted to a quarter of the period (Figure 9.81). Record vibrations were carried out with the full opening of the spillway (head 9.6 m).

On the model in scale 1:20, overlap ran hard and only in two stations were there installed elastic beams with width 2.4m and thickness 0.86 m (12 cm and 4.3 cm on the model). The first position test beams - the beginning of the spillway (the target sensor 3), the second position is the target of the sensor 5. The beam was carried out in three versions - of plexiglas ($E=26x10^3 kg/cm^2$), rubber ($E=0.3x10^3$ kg/cm^2), and artificial materials ($E=5.8x10^3$ kg/cm^2)). The density of the material in the first two cases was 1.3 g/cm^3, and in the last-2.3 g/cm^3. Ripple voltage in the middle of the span beams were set in accordance with static uniform load in cm of the water column. To model the frequency of natural oscillations in the air beams of artificial material was Hz, and in the presence of water - 76 Hz. The translation in nature is 29 and 17 Hz. Value added masses - 17 cm (3.4 m in nature). Ripple load at the beginning of the spillway contains the low-frequency component with resonant vibrations low. In the second position of the resonance, oscillations prevail. A comparison of the loads acting on a beam of different hardness is shown with the largest load acting on the most rigid beam (Figure 9.82)[60a].

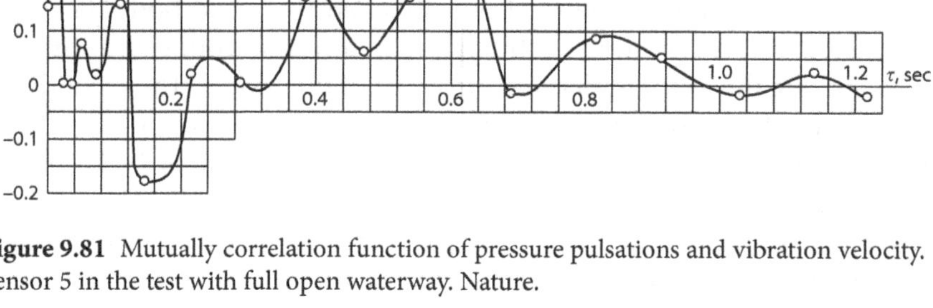

Figure 9.81 Mutually correlation function of pressure pulsations and vibration velocity. Sensor 5 in the test with full open waterway. Nature.

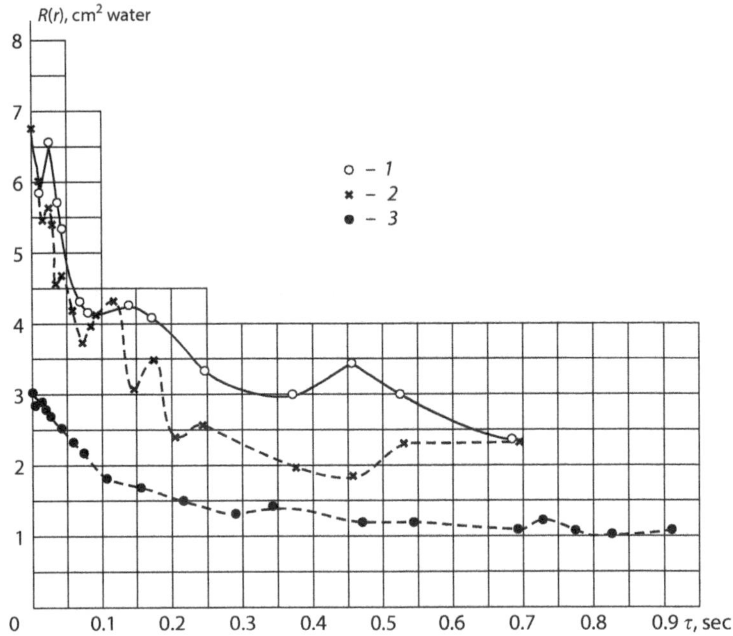

Figure 9.82 The autocorrelation function ripple equivalent load on the floor beams are made of different material on model. The beam is located at the beginning of the spillway (position 1). 1 – plexiglass (E=26000 kg/cm^2), 2 - special elastic material (E=5800 kg/cm^2), 3 – rubber (E=300 kg/cm^2).

The spillway at Naglu hydroelectric power station is designed in the form of a space frame, covering the engine room. The flow of water moves along the upper surface of the frame (on the roof of the turbine hall).

The whole building is divided into 4 fragments. For testing , one piece was selected with the distance between the seams as 12 m. Building height is 17 m (Figure 9.83).

The building model in scale 1:50 has been made of synthetic material with a density of 2.4 g/cm^3 and modulus 4000 kg/cm^2. Two options of elastic models were tested. The rigel was attached to a rigid body dam pivot bearing. The first option is elastic model of a frame, connected with thin rubber along the joints with other elements of the model. The second variant is frame free, not connected with other elements of the model. In the first case, the frequency of free vibrations model frame is 19 Hz. In the second case it is 13 Hz. (Figure 9.84).

On the records of the ripple voltage, there can be clearly seen by accident, arising oscillations with a frequency close to the natural frequency of the frame. Spectral density of fluctuations of the stress (the second option,

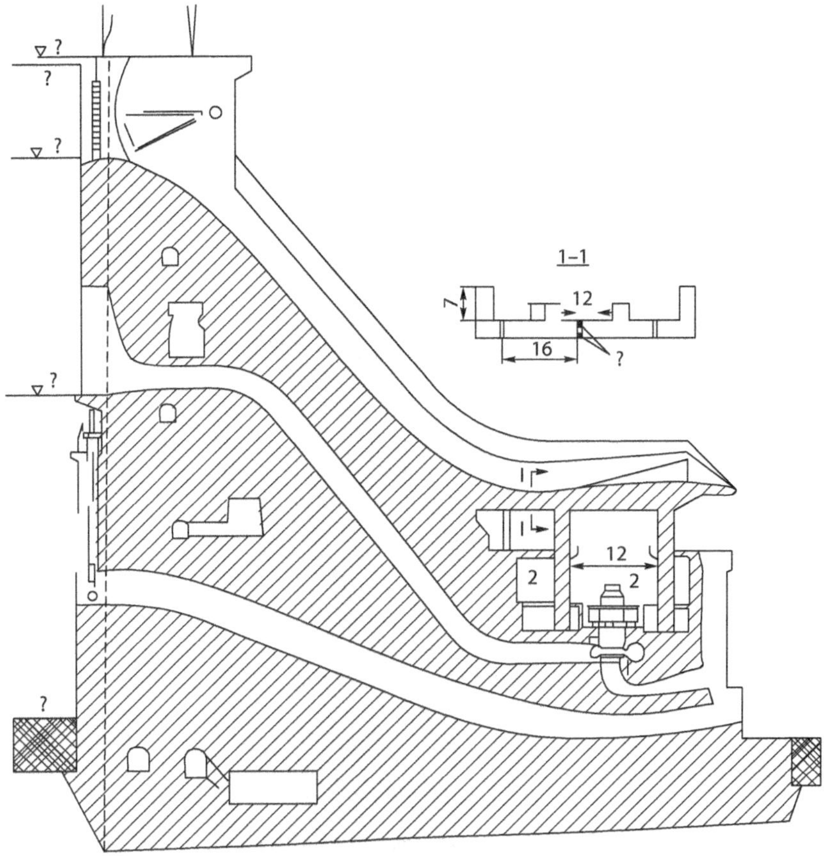

Figure 9.83 The section on the building of Naglu hydroelectric station.

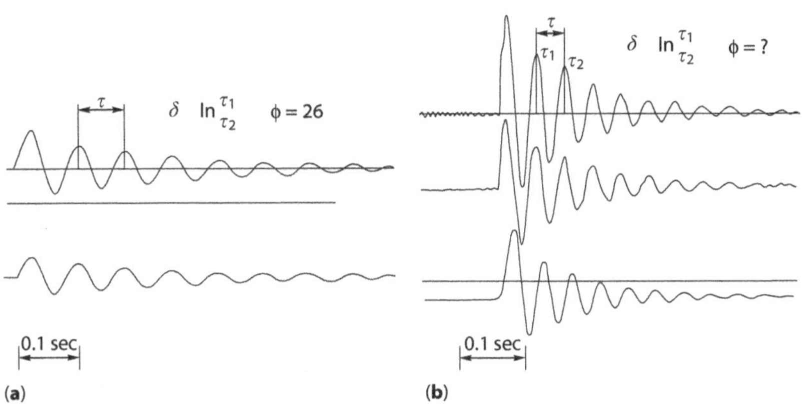

Figure 9.84 The natural vibrations of the model frames with rolling support. The left frame is covered with rubber, right - frame covered rubber.

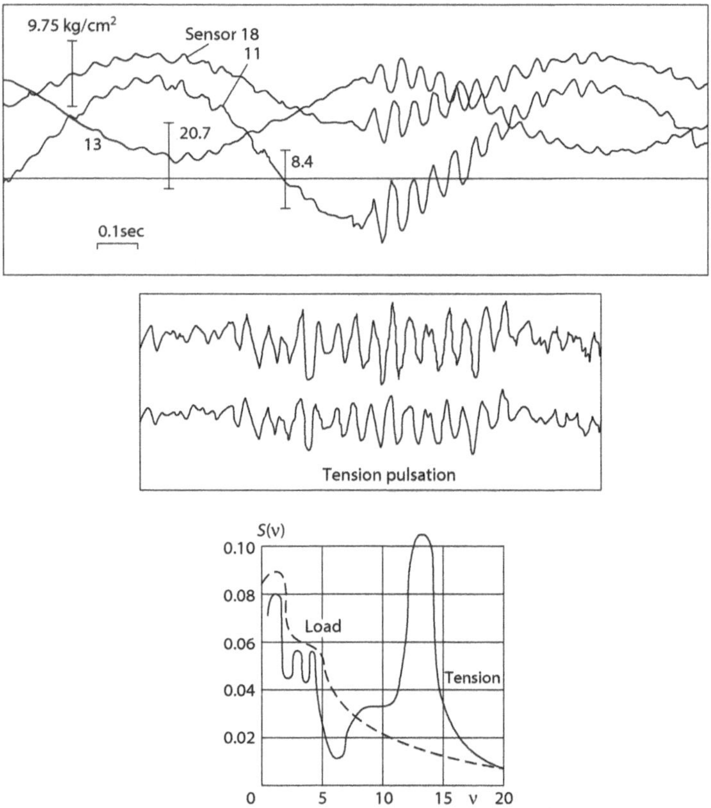

Figure 9.85 Examples of implementations loads and stresses on the model (left). Spectral density load (dashed), and stresses.

the natural frequency of 13 Hz) has two maximum: one, which coincides with the maximum of spectral density loads, the other more acute and more high – frequency-free vibrations of a frame (Fig 9.85).

Complex modeling has clear advantages. The main problems here are the selection of appropriate materials and execution models.

Conclusion

For 55 years after the first publications of authors on modeling [92, 91], the practice of hydraulic modeling significantly expanded and simulation methods have become more diverse. Clearer became the rules of the distortion scale is widely used, the notion of self-similarity, considerable experience has accumulated in the evaluation of channel processes, the definition of pulsating hydrodynamic loads. However, when solving complex tasks much remains for individual creativity and intuition. The choice of material for the book was mainly determined by personal experience and results of the authors. The author of the English version of this book hopes that in those cases which are not covered in the book, the experience of mastering (reading) it will help you to find the correct decision.

References

1. Averkiev A. G. "New method of hydraulic model studies of surveys." - *Izv. VNIIG*. 1952, v.47.
2. Ayvazyan O. M. "Comparative evaluation of modern formulas for the calculation of the coefficient of Chezy." - *Hydraulic engineering and land reclamation*. 1979, No 11.
3. Altunin S. T. "Modeling the blurring of channels and river with the structures." - In the book: *River channel processes*. M.: Izd-vo an USSR, 1958.
4. Altshul A. D. *Hydraulic friction losses in pipelines*. 1963, M: Gosenergoizdat.
5. Andreev, O. C. *Design of bridges*. 1960, M: Autotransizdat.
6. Astarita J., Marrucci J. *Fundamentals of fluid mechanics nonnewton liquids*. M.: Mir, 1978.
7. Ahmedov T. H. *Scour the rocky riverbed*. Alma-Ata: Nauka, 1982.
8. Babukha, L, Schreiber A. A. *Interaction of particles polilidispersed material in two-phase flows*. Kiev: Naukova Dumka, 1972.
9. Bibikov B. C., Oreshkin O. F., Proudovsky A. M. "The Fight the friction in accelerated flow in the pipe." - *Izv. AN USSR, MLG*. 1981, N 25.
10. Barenblatt, G.I. *Similarity, automodelling, intermedia filling asymptotics. Theory and application to geophysical fluid dynamics*. Gidrometeoizdat, 1978.
11. Baryshnikov N. B. "On account of the interaction channel and singmenno threads when building and extrapolation of water level curves." - *Tr. LHMI. Studies of the flow dynamics and issues hydrophysics*. 1967, vol. 25.

12. Bezizvestnikh A.V. "Analysis of methods of modeling hydrotermic regime of reservoirs-coolers." - In the book: *Hidrotermical, chemical and hydrobiological research coolers of the water of thermal power plants.* Leningrad: Gidrometeoizdat, 1971.
13. Belotserkovsky O. M. "Direct numerical simulation of transfer perfect gas flows and objectives of turbulence." - In the book: *Mechanics of turbulence flows.* M: Nauka, 1980.
14. Bernadskiy N. M., Proskuryakov B. C. *Theory and practice of the calculations the ponds-refrigerators.* M - L.: Gosenergoizdat, 1933.
15. Bogomolov A. I., Borovkov V.S., Miyranowski F.G. *High-speed flows with a free surface.* M: Stroyizdat, 1979.
16. Bolotovsky S.V, Levina, S. M. "Laboratory researches nonstationary regimes in the Neva Bay." - *Izv. VNIIG.* 1979, v.132.
17. Boukreev V.I., ZikovV.V, Kostomakha V.A. "One-Dimensional laws of the probability distribution of the fluctuating velocity in turbulent flow in a circular pipe." - *Izv. SB AN USSR. Ser. Technical Nauki.* 1975, No 13, vol. 3.
18. Boukreev V. I., ShahinV. M. "Experimental study turbulent unsteady flow in a circular pipe." - In the book: *Aeromechanics.* M: Nauka, 1976.
19. Vasiliev O. F., Atavin A. A., Voevodin, A. F. "Calculation methods unsteady flows in systems of open channels and channels." - *Numerical methods of continuum mechanics.* 1975, v.6, No 4.
20. Vasiliev O. F., Kwon V. I. "Studies stratified currents." – *Hydrotechnical Construction.* 1973, No 8.
21. Vasiliev, O. F., Kwon V. I. "On the influence of unsteady when the movement of the open fluid flow." - *J. PMTF-Appl.* 1966, No 1; 1967, No 3.
22. Vasiliev, O. F., Temnoeva T. A., Shugrin S. M. "Numerical method calculation of unsteady flows in open channels." - *Izv. AN USSR. Ser. Mechanics.* 1965, v.2.
23. Vasilchenko G.V. "Study of the connection between turbulent characteristics of the flow in the bottom and the underlying nonconnected ground." - In the book: *Dynamics and thermal rivers. M: Stroyizdat.* 1973.
24. Vasilchenko, G.V. "Modeling hydraulic fight deposits of floodplain streams lowland rivers." - *Land reclamation and water economy.* 1980, vol. 50.
25. Vasilchenko, G.V. "Calculation of steady-state fluid flow over the roughness." - *Water management and hydraulic engineering construction.* 1980, vol. 11.
26. Vasilchenko, G.V., Loukoshko R. F. "Study of the water level floods on the physical model section R. Pripyat with the river dams on the floodplain." - *Water management and hydraulic engineering construction.* 1980, vol. 10.
27. Vilikanov M.A. *Channel process.* M: Fizmatgiz, 1958.
28. Venikov V.A. *Scaling theory and modeling.* M: Higher school, 1976.
29. Boukreev V.I., Gusev A.V., Kostomaha V. A., Lytkin Y. M. "Influence of the form of the body on the intermittency of turbulent flow in axisymmetric track." - *Izv. An USSR, MJG.* 1975, No 1.

30. Voynich-Syanozhentskiy T.G. "To assess the stability of the interface of two horizontal threads of different densities in the presence of a free surface." - *Trudy. SAKNIGMI. Geology of mountaining rivers and dynamics of flows of different density.* 1971, vol. 42 (48).
31. Voynich-Syanozhentskiy T.G. "The problem of stability of flow in current real fluid in the channel of finite depth." - *Izv. TNISGEI.* 1965, v.16; 1969, v.18.
32. Voinov Y.P., Proudovsky A. M., Smirnov, L.V. "Experimental the other methods of determining the erosion of the rocky ground." - T*tudy* K*oordinatsionnykh Soveshchanii* po *Gidrotekhnike.* 1969, vol. 52.
33. 33.Vostrjel G.V. "Development of methods of approximate hydrotermical modeling of ponds-coolers." - T*tudy* K*oordinatsionnykh Soveshchanii* po *Gidrotekhnike.* 1961, vol. 1.
34. Vyzgo M. S. *Operational measures, forecasts and methods of reducing local scour at hydraulic structures.* Tashkent: Nauka, 1966.
35. Gambaryan A. O. "Experimental and field studies rolling waves in the super rapid turbulent flow." - T*tudy* K*oordinatsionnykh Soveshchanii* po *Gidrotekhnike.* 1963, vol. 7.
36. Gastunskiy A. N. "Sustainable river." - *Questions of hydraulic engineering.* 1955, vol. 1.
37. Geniev G. A., Estrin, M. I. *Dynamics of plastic and granular environments.* M.: Stroyizdat, 1972.
38. Gilyarov N. P. *Modeling of river flows.* Hydrometeoizdat, 1973.
39. Ginewski A. S., Pochkina K. A. "Effect of initial turbulence on aerodynamic characteristics of turbulent jets." - *Izv. An USSR, MJG.* 1967, No 4.
40. Glushko, S. "Differential equation for the scale turbulence and calculation of a turbulent boundary layer on a flat plate." - In the book: *Turbulent flow.* M: Nauka, 1970.
41. Goldshtik M. A. Shtern V.N. *Hydrodynamic stability and turbulence.* Novosibirsk: Nauka, 1977.
42. Goncharov V. N. *Dynamics of fluvial flows.* L., Gidrometeoizdat, 1954.
43. Grishanin K.V. *River hydraulics.* L.,Gidrometeoizdat, 1971.
44. Grushevsky M.S. *Wave discharges and floods in the rivers.* L., Gidrometeoizdat, 1969.
45. A. Grushevsky M.S. *Unsteady water flow in rivers and channels.* L., Gidrometeoizdat, 1982.
46. Gouhman A. A. *Introduction to the theory of similarity.* M: High school, 1963.
47. A. Gouhman A. A. *Using the similarity theory to the study of the processes of heat and mass transfer.* M: High school, 1974.
48. Dewnin S. I. *Aerohydrodynamics calculation bad streamlined ship structures.* Sudostroenie, 1967.
49. Didoukh B. I, Lobysev V.L., Lyatkher V.M. and others; Ed. by V. M. Lyatkher and Y. S. Yakovlev. *Dynamics of continuous media in the calculations of hydraulic facilities.* M: Energy, 1976.

50. Eremenko E.V. "Kinematic structure discontinuous waves." In the book: *Issledovaniia turbulentnykh one- and two-phase flows*. Kiev: Naukova Dumka, 1966.
51. Zheleznyakov G.V., *Theoretical foundations of hydrometry*. L., Gidrometeoizdat, 1968
52. Zukauskas A., Shlanchauskas A. *Heat transfer in turbulent fluid flow*. Vilnius: Mintis, 1973.
53. Zaluzkiy E.V. "Velocity structure of the accelerated turbulent two-dimensional flow in hydraulically smooth bed." - In the book: *Research in applied hydrodynamics*. Kiev: Naukova Dumka, 1965.
54. Zegzhda A. P. *Similarity theory and calculation methodology hidrotehniical models*. M: Gosstroyizdat, 1938.
55. Znamenskaya N.S. *Bottom sediments and channel processes*. HP: Gidrometeoizdat, 1976.
56. Ignatova G. Sh., Kwon V. I. "About hydrodynamic scheme position at turbulent flow." - *Meteorology and hydrology*. 1978, v.7.
57. Izbash S.V. *Basis of laboratory and experimental work in hydraulic engineering*. ONTI, 1938.
58. Istorik B. L. "Numerical studies sharply unsteady flows in open channels." - In the book: *Scientific work of the Institute "Hydroproject." Hydraulics and filtering*. M: 1979.
59. Istorik B. L., Lyatkher V. M. "Movement of the breaking waves in prismatic channel." - *Izv. An USSR, MJG*. 1975, No 1.
60. Kader B. A. "Turbulence in a viscous sublayer near flat the walls." - In the book: *Turbulent flow*. M: Nauka, 1970.
61. Kalyakin A. M. *Theoretical and experimental research interaction of open stream with streamlined solid boundaries*. Moscow Engineering and Construction Institute, 1978.
62. Karaushev A.V. *Theory and methods of calculation of river flows l*. Gidrometeoizdat, 1977.
63. Kartvelishvili N. A. *Flows in non-blurry bed*. HP: Gidrometeoizdat, 1973.
64. Kind K. J. "Scientific research on stratified flows." - T*tudy Koordinatsionnykh Soveshcha- nii* po *Gidrotekhnike*. 1964, vol. 11.
65. Kirpichev M.V. *The theory of similarity*. M: Academy of Sciences of the USSR, 1953.
66. Kline, S. J. *Similarity and approximate methods*. M: Mir, 1968.
67. Knoroz V.S. "Noneroding speed for loose soils and the factors determining it." - *Izv. VNIIG*. 1958, v.59.
68. Konakov P.K. *Scaling theory and its application in thermotechnic*. M: Gosenergoizdat, 1959.
69. Konte-Bellot J. *Turbulent flow in a channel with parallel walls*. M.: Mir, 1968.
70. Kostin A.G., "Approximate heat calculation heated at the bodies operating in non-stationary conditions." - In the book: *Stratified and turbulent flow*. Kiev: Naukova Dumka, 1979.

71. Koppel T. A., Liiv U. R. "Experimental study of the emergence of movement of the fluid in the pipeline." - *Izv. AN USSR, MJG.* 1977, No 6.
72. Kochin N.E. Kibel I.A.,Rose N.V. *Theoretical hydromehanika.* M: Fizmatgiz, 1963.
73. Kutateladze S. C. *Analysis of similarity in thermal physics.* Novosi-Birsk: Science, NIB. separation, 1982.
74. Kutateladze S.S. *Wall turbulence.* Novosibirsk: "Nauka", 1973.
75. Kutateladze S.S., Lyahovskiy D. N., Permyakov V.A. *Modeling of heat engineering equipment.* M: Energy, 1966.
76. Kuchment L.S. *Model of the formation of river runoff.* L. Gidrometeoizdat, 1980.
77. Levi, I. I. *Dynamics of fluvial flows.* M. - L.: Gosenergoizdat, 1957.
78. Levi, I. I. *Modeling of hydraulic phenomena.* L.: Energiya, 1967.
79. Lyatkher V. M. "Hydroimpuls destruction of rocks." - *Hydrotechnical construction.* 1974, No 10
80. Lyatkher V.M. "Hidrothermical modeling and design of density flows in cooling systems of thermal and nuclear power stations." - In the book: *International Symposium on stratified currents.* IAHR, report 12, Novosibirsk, 1972.
81. Lyatkher V.M "On the mechanism of turbulence." - In the book: *Dynamics and the thermal river.* M: Stroiizdat, 1973.
82. Lyatkher V.M. "Cooling of water flowing in the turbulent atmosphere." - *Trudy Gidroprojekta.* 1963, No 8.
83. Lyatkher V.M. "Forecast hydraulic regime of rivers and reservoirs." - *Water resources.* 1982, No 6.
84. Lyatkher V.M. "Thermal calculation of the cooling pond by time moving water within the pond." - *Trudy Koordinatsionnykh Soveshchanii* po *Gidrotekhnike.* Energia Publishers, L., 1961, v.1.
85. Lyatkher V.M. "Thermal calculation of ponds-coolers small depth." - *Water supply and sanitary technique.* 1962, No 6.
86. Lyatkher V.M. *Turbulence in hydraulic structures.* M: Energy, 1968.
87. Lyatkher V.M. *Turbulent pulsations in the viscous sublayer.* DAN USSR, 1968, v.180, No 2.
88. Lyatkher V.M. "Conditions for the formation of density currents in reservoirs." - *Trudy Koordinatsionnykh Soveshchanii* po *Gidrotekhnike.* Energia Publishers, L., 1964, vol. 11.
89. Lyatkher V.M., Gildenblat M. J. "Comparison of results thermal calculation and hydrothermal modeling cooling ponds." - *Bull. nauchnaia. inform.* Hydroproject, 1962, No 14.
90. Lyatkher V.M., Gurin I. N. "Hydraulic characteristics currents above the surface covered with grassy vegetation." – *Water resources.* 1978, No 3.
91. Lyatkher V.M., Militeev A. N. "Hydraulic research numerical methods." - *Water resources.* 1981, No 3.
92. Lyatkher V.M., Militeev A. N., Yashin V.N. "Research distribution of impurity in shallow waters by numerical methods." - *Water resources.* 1979, No 4.

93. Lyatkher V.M., Proudovsky A. M. *Study of open currents on the pressure models*. M.: Energy, 1971.
94. Lyatkher V.M., Proudovsky A. M. "Some questions airborne pressure modeling of river flows." - In the book: *New methods and equipment for production of investigations of riverbed processes*. M: Izd-vo AN USSR, 1959.
95. Lyatkher V.M., Proudovsky A. M., Bojich S. P. "A new method thermal calculation and estimation of efficiency of ponds by data of hydraulic models." - *Bull. Scientific-technical. Information*. Hydroproject, 1960, No 10.
96. Lyatkher V.M., Fidman B. A. "Hydrodynamic rivers and water reservoirs." - In the book: *Dynamics and thermal rivers*. - M.: Stroyizdat, 1973.
97. Lyatkher V.M, Shkolnikov S. Ya. "Tensor structure of coefficient of hydraulic friction." - *Water resources*. 1981, No 5.
98. Makarov I. I. "Questions of powerful thermal water power plants of water courses and water bodies taking into account the integrated use in the national economy. The Council For Mutual Economic Assistance." - *Bul.* the Commission of electro power, 1982, No 3
99. Marchenko A.G. "Investigation of turbulent boundary layer on smooth and rough surfaces with any gradients of pressure. - *J. PMTF*. 1971, No 3.
100. "Guidelines for calculation of reservoir-quench-residents." TES: P-S-75, VNIIG. L.: Energy, 1976.
101. "Methodical recommendations on the hydrothermal design of cooling ponds." VNIIG. L.: Energy, 1972.
102. Ginevsky A.S., A. Ioselevich A. C., Kolesnikov A.V. and others. "Methods of calculation of turbulent boundary layer." - *The Results of science. Mehanika liquid and gas*. 1978, T. 11.
103. Bogomolov A. I., Altunin V. S., Petrov N. A., Proudovsky A.M., Kissin V. A. "Local scour the obstacles." *Hydrotechnical Construction*. 1975, No 7.
104. Militeev A. N., "Hydrothermal modeling of water reservoir coolers." - *Izv. AN USSR, Ser. Energy and transport*. 1982, No 1.
105. Militeev A. N. "The study of moving the warm water dumped in a small ponds." - *Water resources*. 1981, No 4.
106. Militeev A. N., "Numerical studies of the plan currents open flows." - In the book: *Scientific work of the Institute "Hydroproject." Hydraulics and filtering*. M: 1979.
107. "Millionshikov M.D. Some problems of turbulence and turbulent heat and mass transfer." - In the book: *Turbulent flow*. M: Nauka, 1974.
108. 105A. Millionshikov M.D. *Turbulent flow in boundary layers and pipes*. M.: Nauka, 1969.
109. Mirtskhulava Z.E. *Erosion channels and methods of estimate their stability*. M.: Kolos, 1967.
110. Monin A.S., Ozmidov R.V. *Ocean turbulence*. HP: Gidrometeoizdat, 1981.
111. Monin A.S., Yaglom A.M. *Statistical hydromechanics*. M.: Nauka, v.1, 1965, v.2, 1967. 109. "Nonlinear waves. Stohastic and turbulence." *V conference on nonlinear waves, Ed.* Rabinovich V.B., N-Novgorod, 1980.

112. Netiukhailo A.P., Telejkin E.D., Sherenkov I.A. "Transfer impulse in a two-dimensional open stratified flow." - *Tr. Kharkiv Department of Institute VODGEO. Hydraulic reservoirs, water courses and hydraulic engineering structures.* 1971, vol. 9.
113. "The unsteady motion of water in the pools of the waterworks." Lyatkher V.M., Istoric B.L., Sinyavskaya V.M., Ryabkin G. M. ob. - T*rudy Gidroprojekta.* 1975, v. 44.
114. Nikitin I.K., "A generalization of the semi-empirical theory of turbulence on course in rough surfaces with different modes manifestations rough properties." - In the book: *Turbulent flow.* M: Science, 1970.
115. Nikitin I.K., *Complex turbulent flow and processes heat and mass transfer.* Kiev: Naukova Dumka, 1980.
116. Novikov I.I., Borishansky A. M. *Similarity theory in the thermodynamics and heat transfer.* M: Atomizdat, 1979.
117. Debolsky V.K., Katkov V. M., Ranjanov N.R., Shterenlikht D.V. "Appearance and development ridges of sand in the stream containing the sediment in the non erosion borders." - *Water resources.* 1977, No 3.
118. "Protection of the water environment during the construction and operation of water storage of TPP and NPP." *Izvestia VNIIG.* 1981. v.153.
119. Pavlov S.P. *Conditions of regulation of high runoff.* 1980, v.60.
120. Proudovsky A.M. "Hydraulic ensuring safety of Nuclear power plants." - *Scientific works in design and research in the field of nuclear energy,* T*rudy Gidroprojekta.* 1979
121. Proudovsky A.M. "Hydraulic modeling today." - *Hydrotechnical Construction.* 1982, No 9.
122. Proudovsky A.M. "About the influence of the number Froude on characteristics of calm stream." - T*rudy Gidroprojekta.* 1968, v.15.
123. Proudovsky A.M. "Uniform flow in a channel with mixed roughness." - T*rudy Gidroprojekta.* 1968, v.15.
124. Proudovsky A.M, Baybikov B.S., Yusipov N.M. "Research hydrodinamical characteristics of fast-acting elements of the safety of nuclear power plants with RBMK-1000 and VVER-4'i0." - T*rudy Gidroprojekta.* 1977, v. 57.
125. Proudovsky A.M., Verezemsky V.G., Korneeva S.N. "Hydroynamics of the primary circuit in VVER-1000." - T*rudy Gidroprojekta.* 1977, v.57.
126. Proudovsky A. M., Gildenblat M. Ya., Kuznetsov A.V. "Path improvement of horizontal drum-separators." - T*rudy Gidroprojekta.* 1977, v.57.
127. Proudovsky A. M., Kissin V.A. "Modeling an uneven and non-stationary open flow by method of gravitational-elastic analogy." - *Hydrotechnical Construction.* 1976, No 6.
128. Reznikov A. B. *Method of similarity.* 1959. Alma-ATA: Kazakh SSR Academy of Sc.
129. Rzhanitsyn N. A. *Morphological and hydrological legislative the dimensionality of the structure of the river network.* Leningrad: Gidrometeoizdat, 1960.
130. Richardson, E. *Dynamics of real fluids.* M.: Mir, 1965.

131. Rozanov N.P., *Problems of Designing Water Outlet Structures Operating Under Conditions of Vacuum and at High Velocities of Flow*. Gosenergoizdat, 1959.
132. Rozovsky I. L. *The Movement of water at the turn of the open canal*. Kiev: AN UkrSSR, 1957.
133. Rozovsky I. L. "Research turbulent pressure and threads open, performed at the Institute of hydromechanics of Academy of Sciences Ukrainian SSR." In the book: *Turbulent flow*. M: Science, 1970.
134. Rozovsky, I. L. Eremenko, E.V., Bazilevich V.A. "Unsteady movement water flow below hydroelectric power plants and its the impact on the channel." - Kiev: Naukova Dumka, 1967.
135. Romanovsky V.V. "Experimental study of hydraulical particle size of the sediment." – *Trudy GGI*. 1972, v.191.
136. Rossinsky K. I. *Thermal regime of the reservoir*. M: Nauka, 1975.
137. Rubinstein G.D. "Laboratory studies local time violations of the rock in the lower pools high overflow dams." - T*rudy Koordinatsionnykh Soveshchanii* po *Gidrotekhnike*. 1963, v.7.
138. Ribkin S. I. "Morphological classification of rivers." - *Meteorology and hydrology*. 1946, No4
139. Saveliev P. A., Voskresenskiy Y. S. "Study of hydraulical resistance spirally corrugated tubes with large the Reynolds number." - *Izv. higher education institutions*. Energy, 1981, No 5.
140. Sedov L. I. *Methods of similarity and dimensions in mechanics*. M: Nauka, 1967.
141. Sliski S. M. *Hydraulics buildings hydroelectric power plants*. M:Energy, 1970.
142. Kutateladze S. S., Nakoryakov V. E., Burdukov A. P., Guvakov A. I. "Spectral density pulsations of friction in turbulent flow near wall." - DAN USSR, 1971, v.196, No 6.
143. Vasiliev O. F., Kwon V. I.,. Litkin Y. M., Rozovsky I. L. "Stratified flow (overview)". - *The results of science and technology. Hydromechanics*. M: VINITI, 1975, v.8.
144. Ibragimov M. H, Subbotin V. I., Bokov V. P., Sabelev G.I., Taranov G.S. "The structure of turbulent flow and heat transfer mechanism channels." M: Atomizdat, 1978.
145. Targ S. M. *Main tasks of the theory of laminar flows*. M: Gostekhizdat, 1951.
146. Tepax L. A. *Uniform turbulent motion in the pipes and the channels*. Tallinn: Valgus, 1975.
147. Trubina E. K. *Experience of laboratory design models reservoirs-coolers*. L.: Energy, 1969.
148. "Guidelines for thermal calculation of the reservoirs." *VSN 46-71,VNIIG*. L.: Energy, 1972.
149. Fidman B.A. "On the influence of the roughness of the walls of the structure turbulent flow." - *Izv. USSR AN. Ser. Geographic. and Geophysics*. 1948, v.12, No 3.

150. Fidman B.A. "Measurement results turbulence in uniform flow and in the rapidly expanding flow." - *Izv. AN USSR, OTN.* 1953, No 11.
151. Fidman B.A., Lyatkher V. M. "Study of turbulence by foto and movie methods." - In the book: *The dynamics and the term of the river flows.* M.: Nauka, 1972.
152. Fidman B.A., Orlov A.S., Korozenkov V.S. "Measuring of structure river flow." - *Water resources.* 1973, No 6.
153. Halturin A.D., Kuzmin I.A. "Modeling of deformations on hard models." - *Trudy Gidroprojekta.* 1959, v.2.
154. Shamov G.I. *River sediments.* L.: Gidromcteoizdat, 1959.
155. Sherenkov I.A. "Some results of the mapping modeling and natural researches of reservoir-cooler Staro-Beshevskoy Power Plant." - *Trudy Koordinatsionnykh Soveshchanii* po *Gidrotekhnike.* 1967, v.32.
156. Sherenkov I.A. *Applied planned tasks hydraulics quiet flows.* M: Energy, 1978.
157. Schryiber A.A., MilutinV. N., YatsenkoV. N. *Hydromechanics two-component flows with a polydisperse solid substance.* Kiev: Naukova Dumka, 1980.
158. Shterenlikht D.V. "Hydraulic conditions underwater the pipelines." - *Papers of the Department of hydraulics Moscow Hydro- meliorativ. Inst.* 1969, v.2.
159. Abbott, M. B. *Hydraulics open stream.Computing hydraulics.* M: Energoatomizdat, 1983.
160. *Experimental investigation of the structure of near-wall turbulence and viscous sublayer.* Novosibirsk: Nauka, 1976.
161. Yuditsky G.A. "Modeling of erosion of rock beds for spillway dam with a springboard."- *Trudy Koordinatsionnykh Soveshchanii* po *Gidrotekhnike.* 1969,v.52.
162. Abbott M. B., Verhoog F. H. "Date-reversible system for flood routing." - Proc. *13 IAHR, Congr.* Kyoto, 1969, v.1.
163. Abbott M. B., Petersen H. M., Skovgaard O. "Оп the numerical modelling of short waves in shallow water." - *Journ. of Hydraul. Res.* 1978, v.16, No. 3.
164. Allen J. *Scale models in hydraulic engineering.* London: Long- mens Green, 1947.
165. *American Society of Civil Engineers/ Hydraulic Models. Manual 25.* - N. Y.: 1942.
166. Baker W. E., Westine P. S., Dodge F. T. *Similarity method in engineering dynamics.* N. Y.: Hyden Book Co., 1973.
167. Banch W. "Simulation of the Bavarian reach of the Danube river." - Proc. *13 IAHR Congr.* Kyoto, 1969, v. 1.
168. Baum M. R., Cook M. E. "Gas entrainment at the free surface of a liquid: entrainment inception at a vortex with an unstable gas core." - *Nucl. Eng. and Design.* 1975, v. 32.
169. Buchler B. J., Garrison J. M., Granyn J. P. "Digital computer simulation of transient flows in the TVA systems." - Proc. *13 IAHR Congr.* Kyoto, 1969, Y. 1.
170. Costa V. F. "Use of compromise time scales for minimization of scale effects." - Proc. *19 IAHR* Congr. New-Delhi, 1981, v.5.

171. Costeleyn J. A, van Groen P., Kolkman P. A. "Air entrainment in siphons." Delft Hydr. Lab., Publ. 1977, No 187.
172. Curle N. "Unsteady two - dimensional flows with free bounda- ries (I, II)." - Proc. *Roy. Soc.* 1956, v. A235.
173. Dhillon G. S., Sakhuja V. S., Paил T. S. "Modelling criteria for vortex formation at pipe intakes." - Proc. *19 lAHR Congr.* New-Delhi, 1981, v.5.
174. Einstein H. A., Chien N. "Similarity of distorted river models with movable beds." - Proc. *ASCE.* 1954, v.80.
175. Ervine O. A; McKeogh E. J., Elsawy E. M. "Model- prototype conformity in hydraulic structures." - Proc. *19 lAHR Congr.* New-Delhi, 1981, v.5.
176. Gaster M. "Vortex shedding from slender cones. Rec. Res. oп Unsteady Boundary Layers." - *JUTAM Symp.* 1977, Quebec, 1972, v.2.
177. de Graauw A. F. F., Pilarczyk K. W. Model – "prototype coп- formity of local scour in пoп - cohesive sediments beneath overflow dam." - Proc. *19 lAHR Congr.* New-Delhi, 1981, v.5.
178. Grijsen J. G., Vrengdenhil C. B. "Numerical representation of flood waves in гivers." - Proc. *JS* oп *Unsteady Flow in* Opeп *Channels.* Newcastel-upon-Tyne, 1976.
179. Hancи S. *Modelarea hidraulica in currenti de air sub presiune.* Bucuresti: Editura Acad. RSR, 1976.
180. Harlemaп D. R. F. "Hydrothermal analysis of lakes and reser- voirs." - *Journ. of the Hydr. Div.*, Proc. *ASCE.* 1982, v.108, HY 3.
181. Haszpra O. *Modelling hydroelastic Vibrations.* Budapest: Acade- miai Kiado, 1978.
182. Huntley H. E. *Dimensional analysis.* London: McDonald and Co., 1953.
183. Kobus H. (Ed.). *Hydraulic modelling.* Hamburg: Verlag Paил Parey; Boston: Pitman, 1980.
184. Ivicsics L. Hydraulic *models.* Budapest: institute VITUKI, 1975.
185. Jain A. K. "Physical modelling of vortices at intakes." - Proc. *19 lAHR Congr.*, New-Delhi, 1981, v.5.
186. De Jong R. J., Vrijer A. "Mathematical and hydraulic model investigation of longitudional forces oп ships in locks with door filling system." - Proc. *19 IAHR Congr.* New-Delhi, 1981, v.5.
187. Keпп M. J. "Dynamica similarity for flow systems iп which iner- tia effects are small." - *Journ. of the Inst. of Water Eng.* 1969, v.23, No 4.
188. Kobus H., Leister P., Westrich B. "Flow field and scourning effects of steady and pulsating jets impinging on a movable bed." - *Journ. of Hydraul. Res.* 1979, v.3.
189. Knauss J. "Modelling of baundary layer development and velo- city distribution in super-critical channel flow." - Proc. *19 IAHR Congr.*, New Delhi, 1981, v.5.
190. Lacey G. "Flow in alluvial channels with sendy mobile beds." - Proc. *Inst. Civ. Eng.*, 1959, No 9.
191. Lane E. W. "Progress Report on Design of Stable Channels Ьy Bureau of Reclamation." - Proc. *ASCE*, 1953, No 280.

192. Lane E. W., Carlson E. J. "Some factors affecting the stability of channels constructed in coarse granular material." - Proc. *Minnesota Intern. Hydr. Convention*, 1953.
193. Laufer J. "Some recent measurements in a two dimensional tur- bulent channel." - *Journ.* Атеr. *Sci. Mag.*, 1950.
194. Launder B. E., Spalding D. B. "The numerical computation of turbulent flow. - Comp. Math. in Appl. Mechan. and Engng." 1974, 3; *Journ. of Fluid Mechan.*, 1975, v.67.
195. Lenghaar H. L. *Dimensional analysis and theory of models*. N. Y.: John Wiley and Sons, 1965.
196. Lencastre A. "Descarregadores de lamina Iivre bases para o sen estudo e dimensionamento." - *LNEC*, Lisboa, 1961, No 174.
197. Lepetit J. P., Manoha B. "Un modele physique couranto -Iogi- que et thermique pilote par ordinateur." - *Comptes* - Pendus *19 AJRH Congr.*, New·Delhi, 1981, v.5.
198. Leuchter O. "Effects of freestream turbulence and initial boundary layers on the development of turblllent mixing layers. Turbulence in Internal Flows." - Wash. - L.: Ed. S. N. B. Murthy, 1977.
199. Lyatkher (Ljatkher)V. M., Dzugaev V. V. "Impact jet to rigid wall." - Proc. *14 IAHR Congr.*, Paris, 1971, v.2.
200. Lyatkher (Ljatkher) V. M., Militeev A. N. "Numerical methods of studying transfer processes in water pools." - Proc. *19 IAHR Congr.*, Calgiari, 1979, v.3.
201. Lyatkher (Ljatkher) V. M., Proudovsky A. M. "Approximate similitude of open flows and their investigation using pressure models." - Proc. *19 IAHR Congr.*, New-Delhi, 1981, v.5.
202. Loursen B. M. "The application of sediment - transport mecha- nics to stabIe channel design." - *Journ. Hydr. Div., ASCE*, 1956, v.82.
203. Molerus O. "Zur Beschreibung feststoffbeladerner Stromungen." - Chem. *Ind. Techn.*, 1977, Bd 49, No 12.
204. Mиrphy G. M. *Similitude in engineering*. N. Y.: Ronald Press, 1950.
205. Morris H. M. "A new concept of flow in rough conduits." - Proc. *ASCE*, 1954, v. 80, No 390.
206. Novak P., Cabelka J. *Models in hydraulic engineering. Physical principles and design applications*. Boston: Pitman, 1981.
207. Pankhurst R. C. *Dimensional analysis and scale factors*. Lon- don: Chapmen and Haй, 1964.
208. Petrak D. "Die Bewegung von TeiIchen in Gasstromungen." - Chem, *Ind. Techn.*, 1978, Bd 30, No 3.
209. Poпce V. M., Simons D. B. "The propagation of dynamic waves in opeп channel flow." - Proc. *17 IAHR Congr.* Baden - Baden, 1977, v. 2.
210. Proudovsky A. M. "Hydraulic problems associated with nuclear power plant safety." - Proc. *18 IAHR Congr.* Calgiari, 1979, v.4.
211. Rajaratham N. "Erosion Ьу plane turblllent jets." - *Journ. of* Hydraulic. *Res.* 1981, v.19, No 4.

212. Raudkivi A. J. *Loose* boundary *hydraulics*. London: Pergamon Press, 1967.
213. Punwani D. V. (Ed.). "Recent advances in fluidization and fluid - particle systems." - Amer. Inst. of Chem. Engs, 1981, v.77.
214. Richter A., Naudascher E. "Fluctuating forces on a rigid circular cylinder in confined flow." - *Journ. of Fluid Mechan.* 1976, v.78.
215. Rodi W. "Turbulence models and their application in hydraulics." *State-of-the-art* paper, *IAHR*. 1980.
216. Rouse H., Siao T. T., Nagaratnam S. "Turbulents characteristics of the hydraulic jump." - Proc., *ASCE*. 1958, v.84, HY 1.
217. Rozanov N. P., Rozanova N. N. "Some problems of modelling water outlet structures with free - surface flow." - Proc. *19 IAHR Congr.* New-Delhi, 1981, v.5.
218. Schuring D. J. *Scale modelling in engineering*. London: Perga- mon Press, 1977.
219. I J. Bonin, M. L. Billet, F. G. Hamitt, B. Chaix. "Survey of present knowledge on cavitation in liquids other than cold water (thermodynamic effects) - *Journ. of Hydraul. Res.* 1981, v.19, No 24.
220. Sharp J. Hydraulic *modelling*. London: Butterworths, 1981.
221. Shukry A. "Flow around bends in an open flume." - Proc. *ASCE*. 1949, v.75, No 6.
222. Taneda S. "Studies on wake vortices, experimental investigation of the wake behind a sphere of low Reynolds numbers." - *Rec. Res. Inst. Appl.* Mechan. *Kyushu Univ*. 1956, v.4.
223. Taneda S. "Visualization experiments on unsteady viscous flows around cylinders and plates. – *Rec. Res.* on *Unsteady* Boundary *Layers,JUT AM Symp*. Quebec, 1971, v.2.
224. Tani J., Yu J. J. "Unsteady boundary layer over a flat plate started from rest." - *Rec. Res.* on *Unsteady Boundary Layers, JUT AM Symp*. 1972, v.1.
225. Tsuchida A., Hoshihata K., Takahashi A. "The analysis of un- steady flow in rivers by analogue computer." - Proc. *13 IAHR Congr.* Kyoto, 1969, v.1.
226. Westrich D. "Discussion on [209]." - *Journ. of Hydraul. Res.* 1982, v.20, No 4.
227. Yalin M. S. Mechanics of *sediment transport*. London: Perga- mon Press, 1981.
228. Yalin M. S. *Theory of hydraulic models*. London: McMillan, 1971.
229. Zierep J. *Ahnlichkeitsgesetze und* Modellregeln *der Stromungs- lehre*. Karlsruhe: G. Braun Verlag, 1972.

Additional References (Index A)

1. Abelev A.S., Determination of Pulsations of the Total Hydrodynamic Load Acting on Vertical-Lift Bottom Gates, 1961, Izvestia VNIIG,v. 68, 1958, v. 58; 1961, v. 67; 1962, v. 69., 1974, v.106.
2. Abelev A.S., Dmitriev N.U., Dolnikov L.L., Dynamics facing waterways taking into account the effect of hydroelasticity. Experimental studies. 1982, Izvestia VNIIG, v. 154, pp. 7–13.
3. Aki S., Field Measurements of Velocity and Pressure оп Spillway Chute, 1969,Proc. 13 Congr. IAHR, Kyoto, v. 5–1, pp. 167–172.
4. Altshoul A.D., Nguen Tay, Hydraulic resistance at filtering water in a vegetative soil layer. 1973, Meteorology and hydrology, N 12.
5. Biot M.A., Theory of Propagation of Elastic Waves in a Fluid Saturation Porous Solid1. Low-Frequency Range. 1956, The Journ. of the Acoust. Soc. of America, v. 28, No 2.
6. Bliudze Yu.G., Dokuchaiev O.N., Measurement of Pulsations of Velocities and Pressures in Thrbulent Boundary Layers, 1969, Izvestia AN SSSR, Mekhanika Zhidkosti i Gaza, No 5.
7. Borzenko I.I., Lyatkher V.M., Halturina NV., Field Dynamic Studies of the Saratov Hydroelectric Power Plant, 1972, Ttudy Koordinatsionnykh Soveshchanii po Gidrotekhnike, v. 64, L., pp. 104–112.
8. Bowden P.P., Brunton J.H., The deformation of solids by liquid impact at supersonic speeds. 1961, Proc. of the R.S., v.263A, №1315.
9. Boukreiv V.I., Statistical characteristics of pulsation pressure in the hydraulic jump. 1966. J. Appl. Mech., Moscow, Science, No. 6.
10. Boukreiv V. I., The results of experimental research pressure pulsation in the area of hydraulic jump, 1966, Trudy Koordinatsionnykh Soveshchanii po Gidrotekhnike, v. 28, L., pp. 58–61.
11. Bojich S.P. Some statistical trends stationary random processes, 1959, Hydroproject, M.
12. Bojich S.P. Pulsation of Pressure on Water Fight Dams and Vibration Water Plate. 1961, Trudy Gidroprojekta, v. 5.
13. Bradshaw P., Ferriss D. H., Johnson R.F., Turbulence in the noise-producting region of a circular jet. 1964, Journal of Fluid Mech., v. 19.
14. Bukhanov V.V., Оп the Problem of Stability of Protection Slabs in the Hydroelectric Power Plant Tailwater, 1972, Izvestia VNIIG, v. 100, pp. 96–112.
15. Bukhanov V.V., Оп Dynamic Interaction of Rigid Protection Slabs in the Tailwater with the Domain Under the Slab, 1974, Izvestia VNIIG, v. 105, pp. 268–280.
16. Corkos G. M., Resolution of Pressure in Turbulence, 1963, Journal Acoustical Soc. of America, v. 35, No 2.
17. Corcos G.M., The structure of turbulent pressure field in boundary layer flows, 1964, J. Fluid Mech., v.18, pt. 3, p. 353–378
18. Crandall S., Random Vibration, vol. 2, 1963, M.I.T. Press, 356 p.

19. Cunge J.A., Numerical Hydraulic Modelling. Late 80's Context and Cross-Roads. 1987, Proc. of 22 IAHR Congr., Technical Session B. Lausanne.
20. De Jong R.Y., Vryer A., Mathematical and Hydraulic Model Investigation of Longitudinal Forces on Ships in Locks with Door Filling System. 1981, Proc. of 19 IAHR Congr: v. 5, New-Delhi.
21. Devnin S.I., Hydroelasticity structures in tear flow, 1975, L., Soudostroenie, 192p.
22. Didoukh B.I., Kaspe I.B., Practical application of methods of the theory of dimensions and similarity in civil engineering calculations. 1975, M. Stroyizdat, p. 49.
23. Didoukh B.I., Ljatkher V. M., Elements of the theory of vibrations of structures on water-saturated soils. 1970, Trudy Koordinatsionnykh Soveshchanii po Gidrotekhnike, v. 54, L., pp. 318–325
24. Gakenheimer D.S., Numerical results for Lamb's point load problem., 1970, Trans. ASMEng. Ser.E, N 2.
25. Goncharov L.A., Variations of Structure Vibrations Parameters with Time, 1970, Ttudy Koordinatsionnykh Soveshchanii po Gidrotekhnike, v. 54, L., pp. 373–377.
26. Gorodkov Yu.D., Oп Stability of Facings Slabs in a Water Flow. 1940, Dokldady AN USSR, v. 28, No 9.
27. Greshilov F.M., L.M. Lyamshev, Oп the Spectrum and Correlation of Near-Wall Pressure Pulsations at a Flow Past a Rough Wall, 1969, Akusticheskyi Zhurnal, v.15, No 1.
28. Gun' ko F.G. (Edit.), Hydraulic Design of Tunnel-Type and Tubular Water Out1ets of Hydraulic Projects, 1974, L.
29. Gun' ko F.G., Skladnev M.F., Ljatkher V.M., Principal Trends and Results of Hydraulic Studies of Water Outlet Structures of High-Head Hydroprojects. 1969, Trudy Koordinatsionnykh Soveshchanii po Gidrotekhnike, v. 52, L., pp. 9–33.
30. Fidman B.A., Turbulence of the water flow, 1991, Gidrometeoizdat, L., p. 238.
31. Field J.E., High velocity liquid impact and cavitation studies. 1973, Nauka, M.
32. Finkel V.M., Physics of destruction. 1970, Metallurghia, M.
33. Fomichev M.S., Ripple hydrodynamic pressure at the boundary of open turbulent flow. 1952, Hydrotechnical Construction, No 4.
34. Fomichev M.S., The similarity of the hydrodynamic characteristics of the flow flooded jump. 1958, Izvestiya AN USSR, OTN, No 8.
35. Halturina N.V., Turbulence and dynamic forces acting at the bottom lining downstream of power plants combined with spillways, 1967, Proc. 12 Congr. IAHR, B40, USA, pp. 340–348
36. Hols K.P. Hybrid models (chapter from book "Hydraulic Modeling", Ed. H. Kobus). 1980, Boston: Pitman.
37. Hydraulics high pressure water collectors, 1963, Trudy Koordinatsionnykh Soveshchanii po Gidrotekhnike, v.7, M.- L., p. 576

38. Ivagaki, Transport of Material in Water, Japan`s regional report, 1959, Proc. 8 IAHR Congr., v. 4, Montreal.
39. Ivaschenko I.N., Egorshin S.I., Lyatkher V.M., Research methods for mechanical properties of the soils in the flow regimes. Express information, 1976, "Constructing of Hydro Power Plants", No 10(334), p. 27–32
40. Ivoilov A.A., The influence of self oscillations of the fluid on the pressure pulsations in the pressure conduits, 1982, Izvestia VNIIG, v. 154.
41. Karelin V. Ya. Cavitation in centrifugal and axial pumps, 1975, Mashinostroenie, M., p. 335
42. Kistler A.L., Chen W.S. The fluctuating pressure field in a supersonic boundary layer. 1963, J. Fluid Mech., v. 16, pt.2, pp. 41–65.
43. Konwen N., Unny T.E., Hill H.M., Flow retardance in vegetated channel, 1969, Proc ASCEng, J. Irrigat. And Drainge Devision, v.95, JR2.
44. Kotsubo S., Dynamic Water Pressure оп Dams During Earthquakes, 1960, Proc. 2nd Wor1d Conf. on Earthquakes Engineering, pp. 799–814.
45. Koulmach P.P., Hydrodynamics of Hydraulic Structures. 1963, AN USSR, p. 189.
46. Koumin D.I., Pressure Pulsation in Pools Junction Arrangements and Its Relation to Velocity Pulsation, 1959, Izvestia VNIIG, v. 62.
47. Koupriyanov V.P., Proudovsky A.M., Rodionov V.B., Voinov U.P., Estimation of Safety of Separating Walls Subjected to Hydrodynamic Loads within Zones of Energy Dissipation. 1998, Proc. of the Int. Symp. оп New Trends and Guidelines оп Dam Safety. Barselona. Spain: v. 2, pp. 1513–1520.
48. Kraichnan R.H., Pressure Field Within Anisotropic Thrbulence, Pressure fluctuation in turbulent flow over a flat plate.J. Acoustical Soc. Amer., 1956, v. 28, No 3, pp, 64–78; 1957, v. 29, p. 65.
49. Koutateladze S.S., Mironov B.P., Nakoriakov N.E., Habahpasheva E.M., Experimental investigation of near-wall turbulent flows,1975, Novosibirsk, Nauka.
50. Levina S.M., Calculation of Hydrodynamic Pressure Distribution оп the Surface of an Oscillating Elastic Structure in a Turbulent Flow, 1971, Izvestia VNIIG, v. 97, pp. 29–39.
51. Levina S.M, On the influence of the elastic flexibility of the boundaries on the range of the pressure pulsation turbulent flow, 1974, Izvestia VNIIG, v. 106, pp. 34–50.
52. Lobyssev Y.L., Yakovlev Yu.S. Dynamical calculation of structures on the base of two-dimensional and axial-symmetrical problem in the theory of elasticity with mixed boundary conditions. 1972,Trudy Koordinatsionnykh Soveshchanii po Gidrotekhnike, v. 64, Part II, Kiev, pp. 29–36.
53. Lyatkher V.M, Halturina N.V., Pulsation of Pressure Under the Downstream Floor Slab", 'Trudy Gidroprojekta'; 1962. No 7, Moscow, pp. 30–63.
54. Lyatkher V.M., Halturina N.V., Smirnov L.V., Kniazeva N.N., Pressure pulsations at the point of water fight against measurements in kind and model, 1963,Trudy Gidroprojekta, v.10, M. pp. 25–48.

55. Lyatkher V.M., About the Research Methods of Pressure Pulsations on the Border of Turbulent Flow, 1963, Trudy Koordinatsionnykh Soveshchanii po Gidrotekhnike, L.,v. 7, pp. 533–553.
56. Lyatkher V.M., Pulsation Forces of Hydrodinamic Pressure on the Border of Turbulent Flow, 1963, Trudy Gidroprojekta, v.10, M., pp. 69–85.
57. Lyatkher V.M., Halturina N.V., Bozhich L.I., Pulsation of Pressure Under the Downstream Floor Slabs of Spillway Dam, 1963, Trudy Gidroprojekta, v. 10, M., pp. 49–68.
58. Lyatkher V.M., Hydroelasticity Effects in Hydraulic Structures, 1965, Proc.11 Congr. IAHR, Report 4.6, L.
59. Lyatkher V.M., Hydroelasticity Effects in Hydraulic Structures, 1965, Hydrotechnical Construction, No 8.
60. Lyatkher V.M., Smirnov L.V., Smirnova G.M., Vibration Overlap Discharge Spillway of Measurement in Nature and on the Elastic Models, 1966, Trudy Koordinatsionnykh Soveshchanii po Gidrotekhnike, v. 28, L., pp. 208–212.
61. Lyatkher V.M., Smirnov L.V., In Situ Dynamic Studies of Chir Yurt HPP.,1967, Trudy Koordinatsionnykh Soveshchanii po Gidrotekhnike, v. 29,L., pp. 196–211.
62. Lyatkher V.M, Smirnov L.V., Pressure Pulsations in a Pressure-Flow Spillways Measured oп the Prototype and oп the Model, 1967, Izvestia VNIIG,. v. 85.
63. Lyatkher V.M., Gildenblatt M.Ya., About Ventilation Hydraulic Tunnels. 1968, Trudy Gidroprojekta, v. 15, pp. 71–85.
64. Lyatkher V.M., Halturina N.V., Downstream Floor of a New Design at the Kanev Hydroelectric Power Plant, 1968, Express-Informatsia, Ser.Stroitelstvo GES, No 203., M.
65. Lyatkher V.M Hydrodynamic Conditions on the Open Surface Turbulent Flow, 1968 Trudy Gidroprojekta, v. 15, pp. 55–70.
66. Lyatkher V.M., "Pulsation of Pressure oп the Bottom of a Thrbulent Flow Behind a Ledge". 'Trudy Koordinatsionnykh Soveshchanii po Gidrotekhnike, 1969, y. 52, pp. 191–208.
67. Lyatkher, V.M. Smirnov L.V., Pulsations of Pressure oп the Turbulent Flow Boundary, 1970, in the book "Turbulent Flows", M., Nauka, pp. 73–78.
68. Lyatkher V.M., Smirnov L.V., Hydrodynamic Loads oп the Boundaries of a Pressure Flow in the Separation Zoпe, 1970, Ttudy Koordinatsionnykh Soveshchanii po Gidrotekhnike, v. 54, L., pp. 33–41.
69. Lyatkher V.M., B.I.Didoukh, Unidimensional Boundary Value Problems of the Water-Saturated Soil Medium Dynamics, 1971, Trudy Gidroprojekta, v. 20, pp. 167–196.
70. Lyatkher V.M. Hydrodynamie Effeet of Turbulent Flow on Flow Boundaries. Flow -induced Structural Vibrations, 1972, IUTAM-IAHR Symposium Karlsruhe.
71. Lyatkher V. M. Smirnov, L.V. Dynamic calculation of elements of facing pressure spillway. 1972,Trudy Koordinatsionnykh Soveshchanii po Gidrotekhnike, v.64., pp. 112–117.

72. Lyatkher V.M., Didoukh B.I., Investigation of Motion of Water-Saturated Soil Medium Subjected to Earthquakes, 1973, Proc. Symp. on Behaviour of Earth struct. Subject to Earthquakes, Roorkee, v. П.
73. Lyatkher V.M., Hydro-Impuls Breaking of Rocks, 1974, 2 International Symposium on Jet Cutting Technology, Cambrige, J4-45–55.
74. Lyatkher V.M., "Hydrodynamic Effect of Turbulent Flow oп Flow Boundaries", 1974, "Flow-Induced Structural Vibrations", Berlin, Springer-Verlag, pp. 203–223.
75. Lyatkher V.M., Halturina N.V., Dynamic loads on water fight and assessment of the sustainability of mounting, 1977, Trudy Koordinatsionnykh Soveshchanii po Gidrotekhnike No 116., pp. 44–55.
76. Lyatkher V.M., Chernykh O.N., Estimation of Vibrations alld Stability of the Downstream Hydro Slabs, 1979, Izvestia Vuzov, Ser. Stroitelstvo i Arkhitektura, No 6.
77. Ljatkher V.M., Skladnev M.F., Sheinin I.S. Hydroelasticity Effects in Hydraulic Engineering Practice, 1980, in book [91].
78. Lyatkher V.M., Dzougaev V.V., Zayzev E.N., Increase of efficiency of actions of hydrojets, 1982, Hydrotechnical Construction, No 7, pp. 40–43.
79. Lyatkher V.M., Militeev A.N. Mathematical Model Prediction of Reservoir Currents, 1983, 20 Congress IAHR, v. 3, Moscow.
80. Lyatkher V. M., Kvashilava N.G. The study of the patterns of flow of the soil, 1983, Reports of Agricultural Sciences, No. 6, p. 40–41
81. Lyatkher V.M., Kvashilava N.G. Mechanical Model the Occurence of debris flows,. 1984, Water resources, No. 3, pp. 96–108.
82. Lyatkher V.M. Majbiz G.L. Experimental Investigation of Breaking Waves on the Site of a hard Expansion of the Flow. 1985, Water resources, No 1.
83. Lyatkher V.M., Militeev A.N., Shkolnikov S,Ya. Numerical Simulation of Turbulent Open Flows, 1987, Water resources, v. 1, pp. 35–41.
84. Maksimov L.S., The pulsation pressure on water fight and fluctuations of the spillway dam, 1962, Trudy Gidroprojekta, v. 7, pp. 64–98.
85. Maksimov L.S., Goncharov L.A. Preliminary results of the mapping records ripple hydrodynamic pressure in the nature and scale models. 1963, Trudy Gidroprojekta, v. 10.
86. Miniovich I.Ya., Pernik A.D., Petrovsky V.S., Hydrodynamic Sources of Noise, 1972, Sudostroienie, L., p. 592.
87. Moshkov L.V., Lisenko P.E., Some issues of modeling of vibrations of structures hydraulic structures in the high turbulence flow, 1963, Izvestia VNIIG, v. 72, pp. 91–104
88. Moshkov L.V., Some Problems of Dynamic Interaction of Decks (Linings) of Pressure-Flow Spillway with the Flow, 1970, Izvestia VNIIG, v. 94.
89. Moshkov L.V.,Bukhanov V.V, Characteristic Properties of Behaviour of a Rigid Imponderable Slab Vibrating oп a Water-Saturated Soil Foundation, 1977, Trudy Koordinatsionnykh Soveshchanii po Gidrotekhnike, v. 116, pp. 138–141.

90. Muste M., Weber L.J., Bradey A.A., Coupled Physical-Numerical Analysis of Flows in Natural Waterways. 2001, Journal of Hydraulic Research., v. 38, No l.
91. Naudasher E. and Rockwell D. (Ed.). Practical Experiences with Flow-Induced Vibrations, 1980, Springer-Verlag, p. 849.
92. Naudasher E. and Rockwell D. Flow-Induced Vibrations. An Engineering Guide, 2005, Dover publ., Inc., Mineola, N-Y. p. 404.
93. Nguen Tay The study of the laws of uniform motion of water in the overgrown beds, 1972, Moscow Engineering and Construction Institute.
94. Obukhov A.M., Pressure Pulsations in a Turbulent Flow, 1949, Doklady AN USSR, v.66, No 17.
95. Panovko Ya.G., Goubanova I.I. Stability and oscillations of elastic systems, 1967, Nauka, M., p.418
96. Partenscky H.W., Forces Dynamiques Agissant sur les Portes des Ecluses Lors de la Derivation Partielle des Crues, 1964, Universite de Toulouse, p. 107.
97. Petric S., Bosmajian G., Analysis of flow through vegetation, J. Hydraulic Div., Proc ASCEng., 1975, v.101, HY7, p. 871–884.
98. Preobrazensky N.A. Ppressure Pulsations at the Bottom of the Stream when Mating Pools and Calculating the Thickness of the Mounting Channel in the Downstream, 1951, IzvestiaVNIIG, v. 46.
99. Proudovsky A.M.,General Principles of Approximate Hydraulic Modeling. 1984, - Proc. of IAHR Symp. оп Scale Effects in Modeling Hydraulic Structures. Esslingen-am-Neckar.
100. Recommendations of Accounting for the Cavitation in Designs of Outlet Hydraulic Structures", 1976, p. 38–75, Leningrad, VNIIG.
101. Rocard Y. L'Instabilitie en Mecanique, 1954, Masson et Cle, Paris, p. 287.
102. Rockwell D. and Naudasher E. Review- Self-Sustaining Oscillations of Flow Past Cavities, 1978, Trans. American Society of Mech. Engineers, Journal of Fluid Engineering, v. 100, pp. 152–165.
103. Roubinshtein G.L., Zjarkov U.G., Self-oscillation of the bridge supports in the flow of high turbulence, 1977,Trudy Koordinatsionnykh Soveshchanii po Gidrotekhnike No 116, pp. 163–168.
104. Rozanov N.P., Problems of Designing Water Outlet Structures Operating Under Conditions of Vacuum and at High Velocities of Flow. 1959, Gosenergoizdat, M.
105. Rozanov N.P., Abelev A.S, Studies in the Field of Hydroelasticity, 1966, Izvestia VNIIG, v. 81.
106. Sheinin I.S., Vibrations of Hydraulic Structures in Fluid, 1967, L., p. 314.
107. Sheinin I.S., Some Problems of Hydroelasticity in the Dynamic of Hydraulic Structures, 1967, Izvestia VNIIG, v. 84, pp. 277–298.
108. Sheinin I.S., Noskov L.D., Moshkov L.V., Experimental Studies of Slab Vibrations at the Boundary with Fluid in a Hydraulic Test Flume, 1968, Izvestia VNIIG; v. 87, pp. 183–192.

109. Shteiner Y.A., Baiduk B.V., *et al.* Deformability of rocks at high pressures and temperatures. 1968, Nedra, M.
110. Sighaiev E.A., Investigation of the process of hydraulic rock breaking in mining, 1958, v.10; 1964, v. 2, Gornyi Zhurnal.
111. Skladnev M.F., Sheinin I.S., Oп Flow-Induced Structural Oscillations, 1974, "Flow-Induced Structшal Vibrations", Berlin, Springer-Verlag, pp. 249–269.
112. Studies and Designing of Hydraulic Structures for the Action of Dynamic Loads, Trudy Gidroprojekta, 1962, v. 7; 1963, v. 10; 1966, v. 13.
113. Toebes G.H. Flow-induced Structural Vibrations, 1965, J. Eng. Mech. Div. ASCE, v. 91, pp. 39–66
114. Van Os A., Soulsbyк., Kirkegaard J. The Future Role of Experimental Methods in European Hydraulic Research: Towards a Balanced Methodology. 2004, Journal of Hydraulic Research. v. 42, No 4.
115. Vasiliev O.F., Lyatkher V.M., Hydraulic, in book Mechanics in the USSR for 50, 1970, v. 2, Nauka, M., pp. 709–790.
116. Voinov Y. P., Gildenblat M.E, Smirnov L. V. The influence of the deformation of the receiving the sensor element of the pressure on his testimony when diving in a turbulent flow. 1969, Proceedings of the coord. meetings on hydraulic engineering, v. 51.
117. Voitsekhovskii B.V., Nikolaiev V.P., Shoikhet G.Ya. "On design of shock chambers of impulse water propellers". In the Symposium "Dynamics of Continuum", Issue IX, Institute of Hydrodynamics, Siberian Branch of the Academy of Sciences of the USSR, Novosibirsk, 1971.
118. Willmarth W.W., Wooldridge C.E. Measurements of fluctuating pressure at the wall beneath a thick turbulent boundary layer. 1962, J. Fluid Mech., v. 11, pt. 2, pp. 187–210.
119. Yuditskii G.A., Experimental Studies of Pulsation of Hydrodynamic Load oп Protection Slabs in the Tailwater. 1958, Izvestia VNIIG; v. 58; 1960, v. 65.
120. Yuditskii G.A., Lyatkher V.M., Hydrodynamic Loads on the Fastening Elements of Downstream Spillway Dams, 1966, Trudy Gidroprojekta, y. 13, pp. 14–26.

Appendix

V. M Lyatkher

Stochastic basis for mechanics of viscous fluid turbulent flows and equations for turbulence description.
Proc. 2 Internat. IAHR Symposium on Stochastic Hydraulics, Lund, Sweden, 1976

A most important feature of turbulent flows is nonrecurrence of space-time fields of velocity and pressure while the experiments are repeated with the same macroscopic boundary and initial conditions. There is also a number of properties inherent to the turbulent flow, and some of them taken either separately or jointly are considered as the principal features of turbulence, taken as a basis for the formulation of the corresponding definition of turbulence, Lumley, Panofsky [1], Lyatkher [2]. But these features: intensive mixing, high dissipation etc. do not reflect the specificity of the turbulence phenomenon, which yields a remarkable example of appearance of random effect at determinate cause.

Modern concepts on initiation, development and conservation of turbulence connect the phenomenon of turbulence with instability of stationary and oscillatory motions of viscous fluid.

As a result of it, while the Reynolds number increases higher than a certain limit, the motion becomes more "complex," composed of oscillations having different frequencies, phases and amplitudes. In this interpretation, which in the essence repeats the treatment of L.D. Landau [3], the representation of turbulence as a random process is convenient, being necessary only so far as random properties can be incorporated by the field of initial disturbances determining the phase and the "intermediate" oscillation amplitude at the given frequency.

According to L.D. Landau's idea, the finite oscillation amplitude should not depend upon the characteristics of initial disturbances in conformity with the well-known empirical facts.

This concept acquires a rather completed form in the work of A.S. Monin [4], according to which it is possible in principle to attain hydromechanical solutions reflecting the entire pattern of the turbulent flow. However, indefiniteness of initial data, "the minute details of which are responsible for hydrodynamic fields," are a barrier to this. The writer introduces another in- terpretation of turbulence, Lyatkher [5]. According to this interpretation and in conformity with the test results generalised by G. Schlichting [6], transition from stationary to nonstationary laminar flow can and must be related to the phenomenon of flow instability. But nonstationarity is an insufficient feature of turbulence. The originating nonstationary flow can be random - the same as initial stationary or oscillatory flow, due to influence of stochasticity of initial disturbances or random variations of flow boundaries - the channel wall roughness, or due to random waves on the free surface of the flow. Of importance is the fact that nonstationary flow, originating due to instability before the appearance of turbulence, is determined in principle entirely by the presetting of random functions, for example, with the help of the corresponding characteristics of functionals. A qualitatively more important transition from nonstationary laminar flow to the turbulent flow is performed with the further increase of the Reynolds number when nonuniqueness of development of three-dimensional nonstationary laminar motion arises. Thus random motions originating at determinate (not random) boundary conditions and initial data are proposed to be termed as true turbulent motions (or simply turbulent motions).

Needless to say the turbulent flow pattern can be complicated by random fluctuations of boundary conditions or initial data. Under certain conditions the relative quantitative influence of these factors can be considerably large. In these cases the theoretical criterion of presence of the true turbulence should be the non-unity value of conditional function of probability distribution of flow velocities at the fixed boundary and initial data. This definition distinguishes the true turbulence from the above mentioned random laminar (pseudoturbulent) motions resulting from the stochasticity of boundary conditions or initial data.

Usability of the Navier-Stokes equations for description of separate space-time realizations of turbulent flows is universally known (though only statistical effects resulting from these equations for one or another flow probability characteristics have been checked). It is evident, that conditions of turbulence initiation should correspond to conditions of nonuniqueness of the situations of the nonstationary Navier-Stokes equations. Such nonuniqueness is possible for nonstationary, three-dimensional solutions of these equations, Ladyzhenskaya [7]. At large Reynolds numbers Re, in a case of any smooth initial data values, the uniqueness of the solutions of the three-dimensional nonstationary Navier-Stokes' equations is maintained only for a certain finite time interval with a majorant assessment t_{Re} decreasing with the increase of Re. Beyond this point a branching is possible when initial and boundary conditions do not exactly govern the realization type, but they impose limitations only on the properties of the realizations set as a whole. Nonstationary one- and two-dimensional problems for Navier-Stokes' equations are proved always to have a unique solution at the entire time interval, Ladyzhenskaya [7]. This means that turbulence can exist only in the form of three-dimensional motions. In contrast, plane (two-dimensional) disturbances carry the largest nonstability according to the known Squire's theorem. This justifies the need for the verification of the proposed turbulence interpretation. In conformity with the developed plane model when uniqueness of the nonstationary solution under the given conditions is ensured, only pseudoturbulence associated with random boundary or initial conditions can exist. The principal oscillations in the plane flow can possess the features of the determinate motions. Experiments with magnetic-circuit flows in channels confirm the mentioned prediction. In these experiments there is a possibility, at the expense of the magnetic field action, to suppress the transverse flow component not affecting two other components directly. Experiments performed in a straight channel of finite length have revealed that intensity of longitudinal and vertical pressure pulsations at first decreases and then begins to rise, with the increase of the determining criterion (Hartmann number divided by the Reynolds number), which characterizes the degree of suppression of the transversal (lateral) velocity component. And modulus of correlation between oscillations in different flow points sharply increases, Brannover, Tsinober, [8].

Within the proposed concept, the above-mentioned circumstances are explained by the influence of initial disturbances proceeding from the inlet

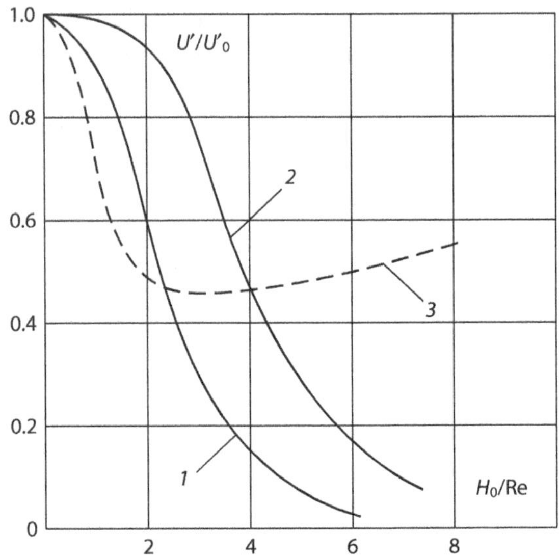

Figure 1 Rms of longitudinal pressure pulsations in turbulent flow in case of lateral pressure pulsation components being suppressed due to magnetic field action.

1. At the axis of annular channel. Flow without initial disturbances, Keet et al, (10).
2. At the wall of the same channel (10).
3. At the axis of a straight channel, with the initial disturbances, Brannover et al, (8).

into the experimental installation. Really, when the experiment is carried out in such a way that the external disturbances are ruled out, it has disclosed that the suppression of the lateral component of the pressure pulsation leads to the complete suppression of turbulence, Gelfgat, Keet etc., [9]. Results of these experiments on the annular channel of relatively flat curvature are shown in Figure 1 with solid lines. On the ordinate, the values of RMS of longitudinal pulsations are plotted. They are expressed in fractions of this value for the same measurement point and at the same fluid discharge, but the transverse magnetic field is absent.

The nonuniqueness of three-dimensional motions developed from the given conditions is the main source of turbulence stochasticity at large Reynolds numbers. For adequate description of the complex of all possible motions, a new probability measure should be introduced. This measure should also be used for presetting of initial conditions influencing the duration of the interval t_{Re}, but it is of secondary importance for large Reynolds numbers. It is essential that principles should be formulated, which govern the stochastic choice of a particular realization.

The probability measure for the description of turbulent motions has long and widely been introduced into the practice of research and design. An important new result is clarification of the impossibility of construction of a closed algorithm. Only on the basis of equations of conservation of mass and Rms of pulsations, is it expressed in fractions of the corresponding value when the magnetic field is absent.

It can be assumed that nonuniqueness is not an outstanding feature of fluid motion but constitutes a rather general characteristic of large motions of continuums. This feature is likely to manifest itself in the processes of rapid material destruction, for example, at the development of motion in the seismic foci at rapid mass sliding, blasting of rocks, etc.

The above stated discloses that there is a certain freedom of introduction of additional hypotheses pertaining to probability characteristics of turbulent flow parameters when constructing mathematical models of viscous fluid turbulent motion. The necessity (and possibility) of introducing a new hypotheses, as mentioned above, is associated with the stochastic character of motions originating at determinate boundary and initial conditions. It is precisely this fact that allows us to pose the problem of generalization of fundamental mechanics laws using the probability measure. The following principle of maximum stability can be taken for such a generalization: if the equations of conservation, equations of state, boundary and initial data which formally completely govern the system motion in a small neighbourhood of the initial state allow several realizations, then probability characteristics of these realizations assembly are most stable.

Let us assume that there is a random space-time process, which is preset for instance by a characteristic functional. If boundary and initial data do not vary from one assembly of experiments to another, then the characteristic functional remains one and the same. Let us change it arbitrarily by a small value at the expense of changing one or another realization group. Rate of the characteristic functional restoration to its initial form can be adopted as a measure of its stability. The maximum stability principle postulates that under nonvariable conditions, processes exhibiting the feature of nonuniqueness are realized in such a way that the mentioned teasure (rate of disturbance decrease) turns out to be maximum.

Using the variational derivatives and the operator, inverse to the Laplace operator, limiting conditions can be written for characteristic functionals of velocities of media with a particular state equation. For motions of viscous fluid these equations are presented in the well-known works of E. Hopf and A.S. Monin. The most stable characteristic functional is sought in the class of solutions of these equations.

The principle of maximum stability can be checked without the functional equation solutions when general infinite Friedman - Keller system is considered, which is closed by the introduction of additional conditions of minimum variation (maximum stability) of correlation moments. The resulting equations can have a more symmetric form if pressure is eliminated both from the Navier-Stokes equations and the continuity equations; and the system of equations of dynamic possibility of motion is considered before the averaging operations. For instantaneous velocities $\widetilde{U}_i$, this system takes the form:

$$\frac{\partial \widetilde{\Omega}_i}{\partial t} + \widetilde{U}_j \frac{\partial \widetilde{\Omega}_i}{\partial x_j} - \widetilde{\Omega}_j \frac{\partial \widetilde{U}_i}{\partial x_j} = \nu \frac{\partial^2 \widetilde{\Omega}_i}{\partial x_j^2} \tag{1}$$

where $\widetilde{\Omega}_i$ is i-th component of the rotor of instantaneous ("actual") velocity $\widetilde{U}_i$:

$$\widetilde{\Omega}_1 = \frac{\partial \widetilde{U}_3}{\partial x_2} - \frac{\partial \widetilde{U}_2}{\partial x_3}; \; \widetilde{\Omega}_2 = \frac{\partial \widetilde{U}_1}{\partial x_3} - \frac{\partial \widetilde{U}_3}{\partial x_1}; \; \widetilde{\Omega}_3 = \frac{\partial \widetilde{U}_2}{\partial x_1} - \frac{\partial \widetilde{U}_1}{\partial x_2}. \tag{2}$$

Kinematic boundary and initial conditions for Eq. 1 remain the same as for the Navier-Stokes equations. Complementary condition for Eq. 1 is the continuity equation $\partial \widetilde{U}_i / \partial x_i = 0$, as well as dynamic conditions on the domain boundaries, if necessary.

Let us denote realizations of the true field of flows by capital letters and superimpose the disturbance field on the flow; the disturbance field is denoted by lower case letters. After substituting values $\widetilde{U}_i + \tilde{u}_i$ and $\widetilde{\Omega}_i + \widetilde{\omega}_i$ for $\widetilde{U}_i$ and $\widetilde{\Omega}_i$ into Eqs. 1 and 2, and taking into account that the initial field satisfies Eqs. 1 and 2 and after the transformations, it is found:

$$\frac{\partial \widetilde{\omega}_i}{\partial t} + \widetilde{U}_j \frac{\partial \widetilde{\omega}_i}{\partial x_j} + \tilde{u}_j \frac{\partial \widetilde{\Omega}_i}{\partial x_j} + \tilde{u}_j \frac{\partial \widetilde{\omega}_i}{\partial x_j} - \widetilde{\Omega}_j \frac{\partial \tilde{u}_i}{\partial x_j} - \widetilde{\omega}_j \frac{\partial \widetilde{U}_i}{\partial x_j}$$

$$- \widetilde{\omega}_j \frac{\partial \tilde{u}_i}{\partial x_j} = \nu \frac{\partial^2 \widetilde{\omega}_i}{\partial x_j \partial x_j} \tag{3}$$

Disturbance field $\tilde{u}_i$ (or $\widetilde{\omega}_i$) as well as the initial field of the turbulent flow $\widetilde{U}_i$ (or $\widetilde{\Omega}_i$) can comprise the averaged (over the probability) component and the random component. The corresponding components are denoted by a bar and without it:

$$\tilde{u}_i = \bar{u}_i + u_i;\ \tilde{\omega}_i = \bar{\omega}_i + \omega_i;\ where$$
$$\bar{\omega}_i = \langle \tilde{\omega}_i \rangle;\ \langle \tilde{\omega}_i \rangle = 0;\ \bar{u}_i = \langle \tilde{u}_i \rangle;\ \langle u_i \rangle = 0; \tag{4}$$
$$\tilde{U}_i = \bar{U}_i + U_i;\ \tilde{\Omega}_i = \bar{\Omega}_i + \Omega_i;\ \bar{U}_i = \langle \tilde{U}_i \rangle;\ \bar{\Omega}_i = \langle \tilde{\Omega}_i \rangle$$

Eq. 3 can be transformed as follows:

$$\{\frac{\partial\bar{\omega}_i}{\partial t} + \bar{U}_j\frac{\partial\bar{\omega}_i}{\partial x_j} + \bar{u}_j\frac{\partial\tilde{\Omega}_i}{\partial x_j} + \bar{u}_j\frac{\partial\bar{\omega}_i}{\partial x_j} - \bar{\Omega}_j\frac{\partial\bar{u}_i}{\partial x_j} - \bar{\omega}_j\frac{\partial\bar{U}_i}{\partial x_j} - \bar{\omega}_j\frac{\partial\bar{u}_i}{\partial x_j}\} +$$
$$\frac{\partial\omega_i}{\partial t} + (U_j\frac{\partial\bar{\omega}_i}{\partial x_j} + \bar{U}_j\frac{\partial\omega_i}{\partial x_j} + U_j\frac{\partial\omega_i}{\partial x_j} + u_j\frac{\partial\Omega_i}{\partial x_j} + \bar{u}_j\frac{\partial\Omega_i}{\partial x_j} + u_j\frac{\partial\Omega_i}{\partial x_j} +$$
$$\bar{u}_j\frac{\partial\omega_i}{\partial x_j} + u_j\frac{\partial\bar{\omega}_i}{\partial x_j} + u_j\frac{\partial\omega_i}{\partial x_j}) - (\bar{\Omega}_j\frac{\partial u_i}{\partial x_j} + \Omega_j\frac{\partial\bar{u}_i}{\partial x_j} + \Omega_j\frac{\partial u_i}{\partial x_j} + \bar{\omega}_j\frac{\partial U_i}{\partial x_j} +$$
$$\omega_j\frac{\partial\bar{U}_i}{\partial x_j} + \omega_j\frac{\partial U_i}{\partial x_j} + \bar{\omega}_j\frac{\partial u_i}{\partial x_j} + \omega_j\frac{\partial\bar{u}_i}{\partial x_j} + \omega_j\frac{\partial u_i}{\partial x_j}) = \nu(\frac{\partial^2\bar{\omega}_i}{\partial x_j\partial x_j} + \frac{\partial^2\omega_i}{\partial x_j\partial x_j}).$$

(5)

If disturbances are considered to be small and values including multiplication of disturbance field components are eliminated, then Eq. 5 takes the form for averaged disturbance component ($\bar{u}_i$ or $\bar{\omega}_i$)

$$\frac{\partial\bar{\omega}_i}{\partial t} + \bar{U}_j\frac{\partial\bar{\omega}_i}{\partial x_j} + \bar{u}_j\frac{\partial\tilde{\Omega}_i}{\partial x_j} - \bar{\Omega}_j\frac{\partial\bar{u}_i}{\partial x_j} - \bar{\omega}_j\frac{\partial\bar{U}_i}{\partial x_j} +$$
$$\left\langle u_j\frac{\partial\Omega_i}{\partial x_j}\right\rangle + \left\langle U_j\frac{\partial\omega_i}{\partial x_j}\right\rangle - \left\langle \Omega_j\frac{\partial u_i}{\partial x_j}\right\rangle - \left\langle \omega_j\frac{\partial U_i}{\partial x_j}\right\rangle = \nu\frac{\partial^2\bar{\omega}_i}{\partial x_j\partial x_j} \tag{6}$$

for random disturbance component

$$\begin{aligned}
&\frac{\partial\omega_i}{\partial t}+U_j\frac{\partial\bar{\omega}_i}{\partial x_j}+\bar{U}_j\frac{\partial\omega_i}{\partial x_j}+\underline{U_j\frac{\partial\omega_i}{\partial x_j}}-\underline{\left\langle U_j\frac{\partial\omega_i}{\partial x_j}\right\rangle}+u_j\frac{\partial\bar{\Omega}_i}{\partial x_j}+\\
&\bar{u}_j\frac{\partial\Omega_i}{\partial x_j}+\underline{u_j\frac{\partial\Omega_i}{\partial x_j}}-\underline{\left\langle u_j\frac{\partial\Omega_i}{\partial x_j}\right\rangle}-\bar{\Omega}_j\frac{\partial u_i}{\partial x_j}-\Omega_j\frac{\partial\bar{u}_i}{\partial x_j}-\\
&\underline{\Omega_j\frac{\partial u_i}{\partial x_j}}+\underline{\left\langle\Omega_j\frac{\partial u_i}{\partial x_j}\right\rangle}-\bar{\omega}_j\frac{\partial U_i}{\partial x_j}-\omega_j\frac{\partial\bar{U}_i}{\partial x_j}-\underline{\omega_j\frac{\partial U_i}{\partial x_j}}+\\
&\underline{\left\langle\omega_j\frac{\partial U_i}{\partial x_j}\right\rangle}=\nu\frac{\partial^2\omega_i}{\partial x_j\partial x_j}.
\end{aligned}\qquad(7)$$

If the multiplication of the fluctuating components of disturbance and initial flow are ignored, then Equations 6 and 7 can be simplified, provided the terms underlined with the wavy line are eliminated.

The formulated principle of maximum stability denotes that the distribution of averaged velocities $\bar{U}_i$ and probability characteristics of velocity fluctuations pulsations U_i are such that the disturbance field $(\bar{u},u)$ is rapidly approaching zero. In particular, the field of disturbed averaged velocities $(\bar{U}_i+\bar{u}_i)$ is rapidly approaching the initial field $\bar{U}_i$. This statement pertaining to the field of averaged velocities was proposed by M.A. Goldshtick (11). By now it has been thoroughly studied and showed a good agreement with the experimental data, Kutateladze, (12).

It has been possible to obtain practical results, not in the general form yet - as the solution with respect to functions $\bar{U}_j$ (x_j, t), but only at the parametric representation of this field. For instance, M. Goldshtick has calculated the value of "Karman's constant" in the well-known logarithmic law of velocity distribution in the uniform turbulent flow, which has amounted to 0.395. In experiments this "constant" is usually equal to about 0.4. Similarly it is possible to calculate, for example, the constants of a "rheologic model of turbulence," proposed by V.V. Novozhilov [13], "constants" of the phenomenological theory of A.N. Kolmogorov-V.G. Nevzgljadov [14, 15], and parameters of more special but rather effective semi-empirical theories using, for example, additional equations for turbulence viscosity. Nee, Kovasznay. [16]; Sekundov. [17].

Equation 7 (in principle) permits continuing investigations and establishes a relationship between probability characteristics of initial flow and the rate of decrease of disturbances of these characteristics that resulted from the disturbances of the initial field. But this realization is associated with the solution of the system of linear equations with the random coefficients. Algorithms of numerical solutions of such systems are constructed only for the simplest cases.

Principle of maximum stability can be applied directly to the system of equations relative to the finite-dimensional probability distribution functions obtained by V.M. Ievlev, [18].

Introducing small variation of these distribution functions we obtain linear equations relative to this variation. And in the case of convenient parametric form of representation of the required distribution functions, it is possible with the help of numerical scanning to find the values of parameters corresponding to the maximum stability. In this case, use of the formal assumptions introduced by V.M. Ievlev for closing the equations for finite-dimensional distributions is not required. It is probable, that the formulated maximum stability principle can be efficiently used together with the hypotheses of physical type. For instance, in the calculations of parameters of turbulent pulsation fields it is possible, after isolating the isotropic and structural components, to take advantage of the fact that the structural components in the main flow core and in the viscous sublayer have small vorticity. Equations, linearized relative to the rotor of the fluctuating velocity, are given in the author's book, Lyatkher, [2]. When the maximum stability principle is applied, the experimental data are used only for the choice of type of function with free parameters. The magnitude of the parameters are determined by calculation.

References

1. LUMLEY, PANOFSKY, *The structure of atmospheric turbu- lence*, 1964, Interscience publishers, John Wiley and Sons, New York - London - Sidney.
2. LYATKHER, V.M. *Turbulence in hydraulic structures*, 1968, Energiya Publishers, Moscow.
3. LANDAU, L.D. "To the problem of turbulence." *Doklady Akademii Nauk SSSR*. 1944, Vol. 44.
4. MONIN, A.S. "Equations of turbulent motion." *Prikladnaya matematika i mekhanika*, Vypusk 6. 1967.
5. LYATKHER, V.M. "Оп mechanism of turbulence." *Collection: Dynamika i termika rek*, 1973, Strojizdat Publishers, Moscow.
6. SCHLICHTING, H. "Entstehung der Turbulenz." (The origin of turbulence), *Handbuch der Physik*, 1959, B.VIII/I.
7. LADYZHENSKAYA, O.A. *Mathematical problems of dynamics of viscous noncompressible fluid*, 1961, Nauka Publishers, Moscow.

8. BRANNOVER, G.G., TSINOBER, A.B. *Magnetic hydrodynamics of noncompressible media*, 1970, Nauka Publishers, Moscow.
9. GELFGAT, Yu.M., KEET, L.G., PETERSON, O.A., TSINOBER, A.B. "Realization of laminar regime of the MHD-flow at large Reynolds numbers in an annular channel." *Magnitnaya Ghidrodynamika*. 1971, N. 3.
10. KEET, L.G., TSINOBER, A.B. "On the possibility of creation and investigation of two-dimensional turbulence in a strong magnetic field." *Magnitnaya Ghidrodynamika*. 1971, N. 3.
11. GOLDSHTICK, M.A. "The principle of maximum stability of averaged turbulent flows." *Doklady Akademii Nauk SSSR*, 1968, Vol. 182, N. 5.
12. KUTATELADZE, S.S. *Wall boundary turbulence*, 1973, Nauka Publishers, Novosibirsk.
13. NOVOZHILOV, V.V. "Rheology of stationary turbulent flows of noncompressible fluids." *Izvestiya Akademii Nauk SSSR, Mekhanika Zhidkosti i Gaza*. 1973, No 3.
14. KOLMOGOROV, A.N. "Equations of turbulent motions of noncompressible fluid." *Izvestiya Akademii Nauk SSSR, Serija Physicheskaya*. 1942, vol. 6, No 2.
15. NEVZGLJADOV, V.G., "To phenomenological theory of turbulence." *Doklady Akademii Nauk SSSR*, 1945, Vol. 47, N. 3.
16. NEE, Y.W., KOVASZNAY, L.S.G. "Simple phenomenological theory of turbulent shear flows." *Phys. Fluids*, 1969, Vol. 12, No 3.
17. SEKUNDOV, A.N. "Use of differential equations for turbulent viscosity to the analysis of two-dimensional not self-similar flows." *Izvestiya Akademii Nauk SSSR, Mekhanika Zhidkosti i Gaza*, 1971, No 5.
18. IEVLEV, V.M. "Approximate equations of the turbulent motion of noncompressible fluid." *Izvestiya Akademii Nauk SSSR, Mekhanika Zhidkosti i Gaza*, 1970, No. I.

Index

Also of Interest

Check out these other titles from Scrivener Publishing

From the Same Author

Seismic Loads, by Victor Lyatkher, ISBN 9781118946244. Combining mathematical and physical modeling, the author of this groundbreaking new volume explores the theories and applications of seismic loads and how to mitigate the risks of seismic activity in buildings and other structures. *NOW AVAILABLE!*

Wind Power, by Victor Lyatkher, ISBN 9781118720929. An up-to-date and thorough treatment of the technologies, practical applications, and future of wind power, covering the pros and cons and technical intricacies of various types of wind turbines and wind power prediction. *NOW AVAILABLE!*

Tidal Power: Harnessing Energy From Water Currents, by Victor Lyatkher, ISBN 978111720912. Offers a unique and highly technical approach to tidal power and how it can be harnessed efficiently and cost-effectively, with less impact on the environment than traditional power plants. *NOW AVAILABLE!*

Other Related Titles from Scrivener Publishing

Hydrogeochemistry Fundamentals and Advances Volume 1: Groundwater Composition and Chemistry, by Viatcheslav V. Tikhomirov, ISBN 9781119160397. This three-volume set, beginning with this first volume on the fundamental composition and chemistry of groundwater, is the most comprehensive and up-to-date treatment available on hydrogeochemistry, one of the most important earth sciences in industry and environmental science. *NOW AVAILABLE!*

Project Management in the Oil and Gas Industry, by Mohammed A. El-Reedy, ISBN 9781119083610. The most comprehensive treatment of the processes involved in the management and construction of projects in the oil and gas industry. *PUBLISHING IN MARCH 2016.*

Acid Gas Extraction for Disposal and Related Topics, Edited by Ying Wu, John J. Carroll, and Weiyao Zhu, ISBN 9781118938614. This fifth volume in the series, Advances in Natural Gas Engineering, offers the most in-depth and up-to-date treatment of acid gas extraction for disposal, an important innovation in natural gas engineering. *PUBLISHING IN MARCH 2016.*

Pollution Control Handbook for Oil and Gas Engineering,, Edited by Nicholas P. Cheremisinoff, ISBN 9781119117612. This handbook is intended to provide students, petroleum engineers, environmental managers, environmental engineers, and chemical engineers with practical information and calculation methods for pollution control, management, technologies, and practices, as well as a convenient source of information on equipment and process terminology, and overviews of U.S. and European Community regulations in the oil and gas sector. *PUBLISHING IN SPRING 2016.*

Hydraulic Modeling, by Victor Lyatkher and Alexander M. Proudovsky, ISBN 9781118946190 Combining mathematical and physical modeling, the authors of this groundbreaking new volume explore the theories and applications of hydraulic modeling, an important field of engineering that affects many industries, including energy, the process industries, manufacturing, and environmental science. *PUBLISHING IN SPRING 2016.*

Fundamentals of Biophysics, by Andrey B. Rubin, ISBN 9781118842454. The most up-to-date and thorough textbook on the fundamentals of biophysics, for the student, professor, or engineer. *NOW AVAILABLE!*

i-*Smooth Analysis: Theory and Applications*, by A.V. Kim, ISBN 9781118998366. A totally new direction in mathematics, this revolutionary new study introduces a new class of invariant derivatives of functions and establishes relations with other derivatives, such as the Sobolev generalized derivative and the generalized derivative of the distribution theory. *NOW AVAILABLE!*

Reverse Osmosis: Design, Processes, and Applications for Engineers 2nd Edition, by Jane Kucera, ISBN 9781118639740. This is the most comprehensive and up-to-date coverage of the "green" process of reverse osmosis in industrial applications, completely updated in this new edition to cover all of the processes and equipment necessary to design, operate, and troubleshoot reverse osmosis systems. *NOW AVAILABLE!*

Pavement Asset Management, by Ralph Haas and W. Ronald Hudson, with Lynne Cowe Falls, ISBN 9781119038702. Written by the founders of the subject, this is the single must-have volume ever published on pavement asset management. *NOW AVAILABLE!*

Open Ended Problems: A Future Chemical Engineering Approach, by J. Patrick Abulencia and Louis Theodore, ISBN 9781118946046. Although the primary market is chemical engineers, the book covers all engineering areas so those from all disciplines will find this book useful. *NOW AVAILABLE!*